Crime and Deviance
in Canada

Crime and Deviance in Canada

· · · · · · · · · · · · · · · · · · · ·

Historical Perspectives

170101

Edited by

Chris McCormick

and

Len Green

Canadian Scholars' Press

Toronto

Crime and Deviance in Canada: Historical Perspectives
Edited by Chris McCormick and Len Green

First published in 2005 by
Canadian Scholars' Press Inc.
180 Bloor Street West, Suite 801
Toronto, Ontario
M5S 2V6

www.cspi.org

Canadian Scholars' Press gratefully acknowledges financial support for our publishing activities from the Government of Canada through the Book Publishing Industry Development Program (BPIDP).

Library and Archives Canada Cataloguing in Publication

　　Crime and deviance in Canada : historical perspectives / edited by Chris McCormick and Len Green.

Includes bibliographical references.
ISBN 1-55130-274-8

　　1. Criminal justice, Administration of--Canada--History. 2. Crime--Canada--History. 3. Punishment--Canada--History. I. McCormick, Christopher Ray, 1956- II. Green, Len

HV6803.C75 2005　　　　364.971'09　　　　C2005-902481-X

Cover design by Aldo Fierro
Cover photo:　Health Canada website and media photo gallery, www.hs-sc.gc.ca. Reproduced with the
　　　　　　permission of the Minister of Public Works and Government Services Canada, 2004.
Page design and layout by Brad Horning

05 06 07 08 09　　　　　　5 4 3 2 1

Printed and bound in Canada by Marquis Book Printing Inc.

Canadä

Table of Contents

● ●

Preface...ix

Introduction...1

PART I: DEVELOPING ISSUES IN CRIME AND PUNISHMENT

Chapter 1: Administering Justice without the State: A Study of the Private Justice
System of the Hudson's Bay Company to 1800
   Russell Smandych and Rick Linden...11

Chapter 2: Criminal Boundaries: The Frontier and the Contours of Upper Canadian
Justice, 1792–1840
   David Murray...27

Chapter 3: The Mounties as Vigilantes: Perceptions of Community and the
Transformation of Law in the Yukon, 1885–1897
   Thomas Stone 37

Chapter 4: Discordant Music: Charivaris and Whitecapping in Nineteenth-Century
North America
   Brian D. Palmer..48

Chapter 5: Railing, Tattling, and General Rumour: Gossip, Gender, and Church
Regulation in Upper Canada
   Lynne Marks...67

PART II: A WORKING CRIMINAL JUSTICE SYSTEM

Chapter 6: Homicide in Nova Scotia, 1749–1815
   Allyson N. May and Jim Phillips...87

Chapter 7: The Shining Sixpence: Women's Worth in Canadian Law at the
End of the Victoria Era
   Constance Backhouse...107

Chapter 8: Gender and Criminal Court Outcomes: An Historical Analysis
  Helen Boritch 124

Chapter 9: The Voluntary Delinquent: Parents, Daughters, and the
Montreal Juvenile Delinquents' Court in 1918
  Tamara Myers 148

Chapter 10: Governing Mentalities: The Deportation of "Insane" and "Feebleminded"
Immigrants out of British Columbia from Confederation to World War II
  Robert Menzies 161

Chapter 11: Crime and the Changing Forms of Class Control: Policing Public Order
in "Toronto the Good," 1859–1955
  Helen Boritch and John Hagan 187

PART III: POLICING ETHNICITY

Chapter 12: Spectacular Justice: The Circus on Trial, and the Trial as Circus, Picton, 1903
  Carolyn Strange and Tina Loo 205

Chapter 13: "Gentlemen, This Is No Ordinary Trial": Sexual Narratives in the
Trial of the Reverend Corbett, Red River, 1863
  Erica Smith 217

Chapter 14: The Relocation Phenomenon and the Africville Study
  Donald H. Clairmont and Dennis William Magill 227

Chapter 15: Criminalizing the Colonized: Ontario Native Women Confront the
Criminal Justice System, 1920–1960
  Joan Sangster 240

Chapter 16: Creating "Slaves of Satan" or "New Canadians"? The Law, Education,
and the Socialization of Doukhobor Children, 1911–1935
  John McLaren 252

PART IV: REGULATING GENDER AND SEXUALITY

Chapter 17: Moral Reform in English Canada, 1885–1925: Introduction
  Mariana Valverde 275

Chapter 18: Defining Sexual Promiscuity: "Race," Gender, and Class in the
Operation of Ontario's Female Refuges Act, 1930–60
  Joan Sangster 286

Chapter 19: "Horrible Temptations": Sex, Men, and Working-Class Male Youth
in Urban Ontario, 1890–1935
  Steven Maynard 299

Chapter 20: Mother Knows Best: The Development of Separate Institutions
for Women
   Kelly Hannah-Moffat 310

Chapter 21: "Character Weaknesses" and "Fruit Machines": Towards an Analysis of the
Anti-Homosexual Security Campaign in the Canadian Civil Service, 1959–1964
   Gary Kinsman 322

PART V: MORAL REGULATION OF PERSONAL BEHAVIOUR

Chapter 22: Chasing the Social Evil: Moral Fervour and the Evolution of Canada's
Prostitution Laws, 1867–1917
   John P.S. McLaren 341

Chapter 23: The First Century: The History of Non-Medical Opiate Use and
Control Policies in Canada, 1870–1970
   Robert R. Solomon and Melvyn Green 353

Chapter 24: Regeneration Rejected: Policing Canada's War on Liquor, 1890–1930
   Greg Marquis 366

Copyright Acknowledgements 385

Preface

. . . .

We began this text with an interest in collecting some of the best research available on the history of crime and criminal justice in Canada because we had been teaching a course of the same name for a couple of years, and had a difficulty in finding the appropriate book. Since this course is a second-year required course in the Criminology Department at St. Thomas University, and forms the foundation for upper-level courses on criminal law, policing, young offenders, and adult courts, we felt the choice of book was important.

First of all, we felt that using American or British sources would submerge key events in Canada's history. It is true that we have inherited a British system of common law in Canada. It is also true that we continue to be influenced by American interests in criminal justice. However, there is something fundamentally different about how crime and criminal justice have developed in our country. Canadian differences are not irrelevant, and we think the readings demonstrate this distinct history.

As editors, we know many of the authors whose writings are collected here, and think that they have produced some of the best work in the field. Collectively, their work will be a substantial corpus of research on the history of crime and criminal justice in Canada.

These articles were selected because of their examination of relations of power in society: relations of gender, social class, ethnicity, and age. Through such topics as prostitution, prohibition, youth courts, and the regulation of sexuality, we can trace these relations of power and how they undergird the definition of crime. An individual is located within power relations in which his or her ethnicity, class, age, or sexuality makes a difference in terms of how the person is treated. These power relations exist apart from the individual, yet affect what crimes the person might be charged with, and how he or she is subsequently treated.

The criminal justice system is always formed in reaction to how crime is defined at any particular point in history. The way behaviour has been defined as criminal in our past might be more strict than how we would define criminality today because of shifts in morality. We have also relaxed as a society in moving away from more punitive treatments for individual offenders.

Through these readings, then, we become richer through a re/collection of our beginnings, and our struggles to define social order and create a criminal justice system. This reader will complement your introduction to crime and criminal justice and, we hope, will enliven your interest in our history. In the introduction, we, with the assistance of one of our colleagues, outline some of our basic theoretical issues.

Chris McCormick and Len Green
Department of Criminology and Criminal Justice
St. Thomas University
Fredericton, New Brunswick

Acknowledgments

We would like to acknowledge the assistance of those who have helped in this project since it began several years ago. It has blossomed into a wonderful book that will serve students of criminal justice history well. We have benefited from the editorial assistance of Vanessa Gallant, Sarah Gilliss, and Juanita Maclean. We would like to especially thank Megan Mueller for her encouragement in this project, and cheerfulness in seeing it to its conclusion.

A Note from the Publisher

Thank you for selecting *Crime and Deviance in Canada: Historical Perspectives*, edited by Chris McCormick and Len Green. The editors and publisher have devoted considerable time and careful development (including meticulous peer reviews) to this book. We appreciate your recognition of this effort and accomplishment.

Teaching Features

This volume distinguishes itself on the market in many ways. One key feature is the book's well-written and comprehensive part openers, which help to make the readings all the more accessible to undergraduate students. The part openers add cohesion to the section and to the whole book. The themes of the book are very clearly presented in these openers.

The general editors, Chris McCormick and Len Green, have also greatly enhanced the book by adding pedagogy to close and complete each section. Each part ends with critical thinking questions pertaining to each reading and detailed annotated further readings.

Introduction

- -

Once the preserve of legal historians and sociologists, the study of crime and punishment in Canada has become more interdisciplinary in content and focus. Issues of crime, criminal justice, law, and society are now critically examined by a broad array of academics, most notably social historians and criminologists. This collection of essays reflects this trend, and begins to show some of the richness of the historical, criminological, and sociological literature on crime and deviance.

This literature combines critical theory and empirical historical evidence to enliven the past and shed new light on how the criminal justice system and Canadian society have responded to the proliferation of crime and deviance. As Smandych and Linden note, through more of this primary scholarship, we can recover a unique aspect of Canadian history and society.

In recollecting Canadian criminal justice history, we are interested in the linkage between economic production, social institutions, and everyday life. People are located in the economic structure of the time, participate in social activities, and through this process shape and are shaped by relations of power. To formulate such an enterprise means recovering those links in the historical evidence, but, more importantly, creating those linkages in the "analytical project." The work of historical analysis crosses over between interpreting the evidence of the past, and interpreting it in such a way as to create an emancipatory understanding of those linkages.[1]

The work of Michel Foucault illustrates our interest in a connection between relations of power in society, forms of knowledge production, and how subjectivity is constituted. The way we come to know ourselves and others is a social construct built through power relations. In this way, human beings are both objects and subjects constructed through certain forms of knowledge and relationships of power.

Central to this proposition is that knowledge and power are inseparable: "there is no power relation without the correlative constitution of a field of knowledge, nor any knowledge that does not presuppose and constitute at the same time power relations."[2]

As social institutions develop, with new legal procedures (technologies), for example, a new knowledge of the subject is constituted that pivots on power relations. Disciplinary technology, which is the work of the criminal justice system, makes individuals subject to the power that runs through the whole social body. The knowledge of the subject involves a documentary record of their offences and disposition and, increasingly, of their background and social characteristics. This documentary record makes makes them more subject to examination and discipline. What we will see in these readings is that the developing Canadian state, with its legal superstructure, revolves around and intensifies existing power relationships.

Social institutions such as schools, churches, and prisons operate through subtle mechanisms or "micro-physics" of power that use, in Foucault's terms, techniques such as "hierarchical observation," "normalising judgements," and "the examination." The state produces a web of control by increasing its specification of individuality.[3]

We are not suggesting that individuals are powerless in the development of these socio-legal relations. In many of the readings we will see resistance and attempts to influence the direction of social change. But as in work on the history of schooling shows, educational practices and techniques of governance attempt to construct and control character habits that are useful in the moral order of capitalism.[4] In this way, relations of power involve practices that are hegemonic.

To develop a non-reductionist approach to the history of criminal justice, Giddens says we need to look at the duality of structure.[5] Through the ongoing dialectic of structure and practice we see the interplay between individual consciousness and the activities of the subject as they are located in relations of power. In this way, social life is recursive, which structure both the medium and the outcome of social life.

As Canada developed, different forms of "doing justice" succeeded and faded from view. Practices that were considered deviant in the past, for example, abortion, are considered quite acceptable today. Similarly, the twentieth century has seen the criminalization of substances that have been used for thousands of years, notably narcotics. This diachronic, or historical, dimension forces us to consider the relative definition of crime, and thus how it has informed changes in criminal justice.

In this way, criminological scholarship today is less concerned with a narrow juridic interest in courts, police, and prisons; we conceive of societal definitions and legal governance in broader ways.

In the late-eighteenth and early-nineteenth centuries the reaction to crime was brutal. The Hudson's Bay's Company and naval courts in Newfoundland often relied upon corporal punishment, including lashings with a cat-o'-nine-tails, to ensure that its workers complied with company regulations.[6] The sheer size of the territory known as Rupert's Land—4 million square kilometres—granted to the Hudson's Bay Company, and its distance from Britain, necessitated the private administration of justice. This patchwork system of private and military justice, combined with an emerging state, moreover, provides insight into the legal plurality that once existed in British North America.

In 1869 Canada bought Rupert's Land, ten times the size of Canada at Confederation, and in 1873 John A. MacDonald commissioned the North West Mounted Police (NWMP) to patrol this new territory.[7] Their mandate was to quell conflict and dissent so as to secure a frontier suitable for Canadian exploration and settlement. The development of east–west trade for Montreal and Toronto was facilitated by the federal police and the construction of a national railway. As Stone comments, the federal police virtually appropriated conflict and the popular ways of dealing with it as they began enforcing the criminal law.

It is interesting that in this interregnum between private and military policing, and the coming era of professional justice, people ordered their lives to principles similar to law. Thousands of men, isolated annually in mining and lumber camps or on the high seas, suppressed and resolved conflicts without recourse to police or courts,[8] and yet we have virtually forgotten this history.

Drawing on the British tradition, the first half of the nineteenth century was an era of public executions. This was a time when legal authorities felt that by publicly displaying the severity of the law, people would refrain from committing criminal acts. The law operated as a repressive instrument, but also as an ideological system, one that combined both force and imagery to sustain the power of the propertied ruling class.[9]

By the dawn of the twentieth century, however, this feeling began to change. Progressive middle-class reformers believed that public executions would have a detrimental impact upon society. As one proponent of conducting hangings within penitentiaries stated in 1925, "such events as these, amid the peaceful and ordered routine of the towns and cities of the country, have a very certain effect upon many classes of people, particularly women and children. They leave in the memory scars that time can never quite remove."[10] Canadians were becoming increasingly uncomfortable with how in the process of maintaining law and order, the criminal justice system, by practising public executions, was in fact disrupting public order.

Certain crimes tended to be specific to the pre-Confederation period of Canada's history. Smuggling, duelling, "machine breaking," and sabotaging a coal mine were acts that not only broke the law, but challenged the social and economic status quo.[11] However, change did not come easy. In the shift to a centralist form of legal governance, the state often conflicted with traditional custom. Smuggling, for example, and its close neighbour, wrecking, were ways of life in a maritime economy. Attempts to enforce the law against popular custom exposed the slippage between policy and practice.

However, as the state developed, class inequality became solidified in the criminal law and traditional economic practices increasingly became defined as contravening capitalist property relations. In this regards, as Alan Hunt has argued, the law became a tool of "ideological domination" within a capitalist society.[12] People learned how to think of crime in capitalism as a violation of property relations, and came to think of justice as something to be administered by the state. While the state has the resources to enforce the law, it also means that popular methods of social control are lost.

In some cases, crimes and how they were dealt with in the community were symbols of a burgeoning working-class consciousness that an informal criminal justice system often struggled to suppress. When oak-cutters rioted in Bytown in 1830, the conflict was as much about class inequality between the Irish, French, and English as it was about public disturbance, drinking, and assault.[13]

Moreover, as Palmer and Marks highlight, the charivari and gossip became informal, community-based methods of rendering justice upon those individuals who had breached an unwritten code of public morality. These were ways for the "lower orders" of society to voice their opposition and hostility toward the social elite and pass judgment upon their family, friends, and neighbours. This was "rough justice," along with social and moral regulation, at its finest. Despite its irregularities, as Murray notes, its practices correspond to what we would fairly call law.

A more formalized system of criminal law and justice emerged as the nineteenth century evolved. Indeed, the onslaught of industrialization and urbanization in late-nineteenth-century Canada and the concomitant population boom necessitated a more concerted response to crime. We begin to see the development of professional policing, for example.

Canada received its own system of codified criminal laws with the introduction in 1892 of the Criminal Code of Canada. These laws were designed to preserve the power of the British Crown and the state in Canada. While it was true that Nova Scotia was the first province to receive a system of judicial procedure in the 1750s,[14] justice was patchy as magistrates were reluctant to travel outside urban centres. Well into the latter part of the 1800s, any justice system that existed was haphazard at best.

The idea of "British justice" that Canada adopted was more than a collection of laws and legal procedures. It was also a means of organizing social relations in modern Canada and of defining, on an official level, the nature of civil society.[15] A society that was meant to be law-abiding and morally righteous did not tolerate crime and deviancy. As Valverde points out, a great period of social and moral regulation at the turn of the twentieth century was responsible for a redefinition of im/morality, especially in Canada's cities.

Justices of the peace were responsible for the administration of justice in most areas outside of capital centres for much of the eighteenth century.[16] Gradually police courts evolved and criminal cases were usually tried without a jury or legal representation for the accused. It was here that the working class and the poor gathered every morning to hear their fate. The Police Court, often housed in city halls across the country, handled over 80 percent of committed offences. Police courts were efficient because they had to be. On an average day at the turn of the twentieth century in Vancouver, Winnipeg, Toronto, Montreal, or Halifax, a stipendiary magistrate would hear between 30 and 40 criminal cases, most of which were summary offences ranging from public intoxication to theft.[17] Often the accused pled guilty because he or she did not have the advice of legal counsel or was intimidated by, or could not comprehend, the proceedings.

The night watch was the forerunner to the police in most towns and cities. This group of concerned citizens served as an informal mechanism for monitoring a community and imposing social order. By the 1860s, organized police forces began to appear in cities such as Saint John, Quebec, and Toronto.[18] As Boritch and Hagan discuss, at the turn of the twentieth century a shift occurred in police operations away from a primitive type of "class-control" to a "crime-control" model. This was in line with a trend toward more rationalization and professionalization of police work in North America. In this sense, the police were a product of the social turmoil wrought by modernity, the need to monitor the activities of new immigrants, and the widening gap between the rich and the poor.

The addition of policewomen represents another important phase in the modernization of police work and the criminal justice system. In the early 1900s, police departments in Vancouver, Calgary, Winnipeg, Toronto, Montreal, and Halifax hired female officers. Policewomen, it was felt, could help to prevent crime through social service intervention and by dealing directly with female suspects. Policewomen often served in departments' "morality squads" where they "looked after the bad girls." They searched the cities' streets for wayward women, especially prostitutes, and tried to persuade them to return home. In various essays, such as Hannah-Moffat, and Myers and Sangster, we see how policewomen played a central role in the criminal justice system's attempts to control vice and regulate social and moral behaviour. At the same time, the development of separate institutions for women, and the creation of family courts, created an extrafamilial arena for dispute resolution that signifies the stress caused by changing relations of production and the evolving roles of women in modern Canadian society.[19]

Law and order, however, often came at the expense of equality before the law. For example, women and girls tended to be arrested for moral offences. Fourteen-year-old Vera was committed to the Industrial Home for Girls in Vancouver in 1929 for "prostituting herself with Hindus." Hilda was charged with being "incorrigible" because "she would not do what her father told her and was too fond of going out to dances."[20] Ironically, these girls were accorded a degree of sexual agency by their parents and by the same criminal justice officials who felt that young women who engaged in illicit sexual encounters were "delinquents" in need of moral guidance and control.

Once captured and sentenced for their crimes, criminals were housed in prisons and asylums. Ontario and Quebec were among the first provinces in the 1850s to construct lunatic asylums.[21] Correctional institutions were makeshift, dark, disease-infested institutions that did little to rehabilitate criminals. Indeed, some housed adult and juvenile criminals together. This practice prompted late-nineteenth-century social reformers, such as the Rev. C.L. Ball of Halifax, to denounce prisons as institutions that "confirm the criminal in crime."[22] Such views precipitated a movement to build reformatories and homes of refuge for juvenile delinquents and "fallen women." Their efforts were part of an attempt to make Canada a more progressive, modern society, a society that had an efficient system of justice that ensured the preservation of social and moral order. Nevertheless, Canada's prisons, at least prior to 1945, usually punished, rather than rehabilitated, men and women who broke the law.

Juvenile delinquents, on the other hand, were seen as representing the country's future, and thus worthy of being reformed. Juvenile courts stood as a testament to a more progressive and modern attitude toward juvenile crime and delinquency. In the minds of some of its supporters, the juvenile court could serve as an instrument of "social betterment," not only for children, but for society as a whole.[23] As Nova Scotia's attorney general, Orlando T. Daniels, argued in 1918, juvenile courts were created in recognition of the fact that "children are children even when they break the law ... and every child has a right to a fair chance to become an honest, useful citizen."[24] This view underscored the belief that the future of the country could be placed in serious jeopardy if children turned to a life of crime when they became adults.

Studying the history of crime and deviance is one way to measure the temperament of a society and the nature of social relations in specific historical periods. Through this study we can see how class relations are reproduced through the law, as are relations of gender, age, and ethnicity. These relations together are relations of power, and the criminal law becomes the pivot around which people's lives are ordered.

The incidence of crime and deviancy, and the efforts to curb their outbreak, also highlights the rise of the state in Canada. Indeed, state formation in Canada produced a strict regime of legal, moral, and social regulation. Regulation that, as McLaren, Solomon, and Green, and Marquis demonstrate, had a direct impact upon people's lives, in particular, the lives of the "other"—Asians, Blacks, First Nations, and "foreigners"—whom the justice system viewed as a threat to the moral and social fibre of Canada. This regulation often assumed the form of laws that targeted these groups, notably the Opium Act and the Pass System for Aboriginals. The implementation of these laws meant that the state was able to exert the power of the criminal justice system over disadvantaged groups, for example, in charging Asian men with possession of opium and purveying White slavery, and confining Natives to their reserves.[25]

Canada also possessed social and criminal deviants whom the criminal justice system, and segments of Canadian society, constructed, feared, and despised. The "other," including homosexuals, were, according to popular beliefs, prone to certain criminal acts, drunkenness and public violence, White slavery, gambling, drug abuse, and "gross indecency." Consequently, their daily activities often came under close supervision by the police. This is where, according to Maynard, Schmidt, and Kinsman, the power of the state to determine who is "normal" and what is acceptable behaviour, and subsequently punish abnormal behaviour, dramatically affected individuals' work and private lives.[26] Moreover, such perceptions fuelled racial and homophobic sentiments, thereby further marginalizing these groups within society.

Class, gender, ethnic, and religious divisions were at times manifested in acts of crime and public disorder. Moral and social order were two of the main principles upon which Canadian civil society was thought to be based. So it was in this context of a fervent belief in the rule of law that crime and deviance posed such a serious threat to social order. Many Canadians believed that crime had to be controlled, criminals should be punished, and law and order must be maintained.

Hence the criminal justice system, despite the underlying principle of equality before the law, failed to treat everyone who appeared in court as equal. The poor, women, ethnic minorities, and social deviants all endured various forms of discrimination from Canada's machinery of law and order. This underscores the fact that in trying to regulate the social and moral behaviour of some Canadians, the criminal justice system both reflected and perpetuated the socio-economic inequalities that characterized much of twentieth-century Canadian society.

We hope you are as excited to learn about the history of crime and criminal justice in Canada as we are to introduce it to you.

Chris McCormick and Len Green
With the assistance of Michael Boudreau

Notes

1. J. Habermas, *Knowledge and Human Interests* (Boston: Beacon, 1971).
2. M. Foucault, *Discipline and Punish: The Birth of the Prison* (London: Penguin, 1977); M. Foucault, "Truth, Power and Sexuality," in *Subjectivity and Social Relations*, edited by V. Beechey and J. Donald (Philadelphia: Open University Press, 1985).
3. P. Rabinow, *The Foucault Reader* (Ringwood: Penguin, 1984).
4. B. Curtis, *Building the Educational State: Canada West 1836–1871* (London: Falmer Press, 1988).
5. A. Giddens, *Central Problems in Social Theory: Action Structure and Contradiction in Social Analysis* (London: Macmillan, 1978).
6. See in particular, E.I. Burley, *Servants of the Honourable Company: Work, Discipline and Conflict in the Hudson's Bay Company, 1770–1879* (Toronto: Oxford University Press, 1997), and J. Bannister, *The Rule of the Admirals: Law, Custom and Naval Government in Newfoundland, 1699–1832* (Toronto: University of Toronto Press, 2003).
7. C. Strange and T. Loo, *Making Good: Law and Moral Regulation in Canada, 1867–1939* (Toronto: University of Toronto Press, 1997), pp. 15–17.
8. D.G. Bell, "A Perspective on Legal Pluralism in 19th-Century New Brunswick," *University of New Brunswick Law Journal* 37 (1988): 86–93.
9. J. Phillips, "The Majesty of the Law: Circuit Courts in Theory and Practice in Early Nova Scotia," unpublished manuscript.
10. *The Halifax Herald*, February 11, 1925.
11. For more on the notion of "rough justice" and violence, see S.W. See, "Nineteenth-Century Collective Violence: Toward a North American Context," *Labour/Le Travail* 39 (1996): 13–38.
12. A. Hunt, *Explorations in Law and Society: Toward a Constitutive Theory of Law* (New York: Routledge, 1993), pp. 17–35.
13. This and similar incidents are discussed in J. Weaver, "Crime, Public Order, and Repression: The Gore District in Upheaval, 1832–1851" and M.S. Cross, "Stony Monday, 1849: The Rebellion Losses Riots in Bytown," in *Lawful Authority: Readings on the History of Criminal Justice in Canada*, edited by R.C. Macleod (Toronto: Copp Clark Pitman, 1988), pp. 22–63.
14. J. Phillips, "The Criminal Trail in Nova Scotia, 1749–1815," in *Essays in the History of Canadian Law*, Vol. VIII, edited by G.B. Baker and J. Phillips (Toronto: University of Toronto Press, 1999), pp. 469–511, and J. Phillips, "Crime and Punishment in the Dominion of the North: Canada from New France to the Present," in *Crime History and Histories of Crime: Studies in the Historiography of Crime and Criminal Justice in Modern History*, edited by C. Emsley and L.A. Knafla (Westport: Greenwood Press, 1996), pp. 163–199.
15. G. Marquis provides an incisive analysis of "British justice" in "Doing Justice to British Justice: Law, Ideology and Canadian Historiography," in *Canadian Perspectives in Law and Society: Issues in Legal History*, edited by W. Wesley Pue and B. Wright (Ottawa: Carleton University Press, 1988), pp. 43–69.
16. D. Murray, *Colonial Justice: Justice, Morality, and Crime in the Niagara District, 1791–1849* (Toronto: University of Toronto Press, 2002).
17. Two excellent accounts of the workings of police courts are P. Girard, "The Rise and Fall of Urban Justice in Halifax, 1815–1886," *Nova Scotia Historical Review* (1988), pp. 57–71, and J. C. Weaver, *Crime, Constables, and Courts: Order and Transgression in a Canadian City, 1816–1970* (Montreal and Kingston: McGill-Queen's University Press, 1995).
18. A. Greer, "The Birth of the Police in Canada," in *Colonial Leviathan: State Formation in Mid-Nineteenth-Century Canada*, edited by A. Greer and I. Radforth (Toronto: University of Toronto Press, 1992), pp. 17–49.

19. These issues are also explored by D.E. Chunn, *From Punishment to Doing Good: Family Courts and Socialized Justice in Ontario, 1880–1940* (Toronto: University of Toronto Press, 1992); A. Glasbeek, "Maternalism Meets the Criminal Law: The Case of the Toronto's Women's Court," *Canadian Journal of Women and the Law* (1998), pp. 480–502; M.A. Poutanen, "The Homeless, the Whore, the Drunkard, and the Disorderly: Contours of Female Vagrancy in the Montreal Courts, 1810–1842," in *Gendered Pasts: Historical Essays in Femininity and Masculinity in Canada*, edited by K. McPherson, C. Morgan, and N.M. Forestell (Toronto: Oxford University Press, 1999), pp. 29–47.

20. I. Matters, "Sinners or Sinned Against?: Historical Aspects of Female Juvenile Delinquency in British Columbia," in *Not Just Pin Money: Selected Essays on the History of Women's Work in British Columbia*, edited by B.K. Latham and R.J. Pazdro (Victoria: Camosun College, 1984), pp. 270–271.

21. For a recent study on the evolution of asylums in Quebec and Ontario, see J.E. Moran, *Committed to the Asylum: Insanity and Society in Nineteenth-Century Quebec and Ontario* (Montreal and Kingston: McGill-Queen's University Press).

22. *The Halifax Herald*, November 29, 1905. For more on the prison reform movement in Canada, see A. Cellard, *Punishment, Imprisonment and Reform in Canada, from New France to the Present* (Ottawa: Canadian Historical Association Booklet, 1905), no. 60.

23. M. Keller, *Regulating a New Society: Public Policy and Social Change in America, 1900–1933* (Cambridge: Harvard University Press).

24. *The Halifax Herald*, February 27, 1918.

25. J. McLaren, "Race and the Criminal Justice System in British Columbia, 1892–1920: Constructing Chinese Crimes," in *Essays in the History of Canadian Law*, Vol. VIII, edited by G.B. Baker and J. Phillips (Toronto: University of Toronto Press, 1999), pp. 398–442; S. Carter, *Aboriginal People and Colonizers of Western Canada to 1900* (Toronto: University of Toronto Press, 1999); S.H. Razack, ed., *Race, Space, and the Law: Unmapping a White Settler Society* (Toronto: Between the Lines, 2002).

26. For more on the construction of "normal" in post-war Canada, see M.L. Adams, *The Trouble with Normal: Postwar Youth and the Making of Heterosexuality* (Toronto: University of Toronto Press, 1997).

PART I

Developing Issues in Crime and Punishment

• •

The majority of readings in this section deal with issues that predate Confederation. We also see glimpses of a criminal justice "system" much different than the one we have today. As such, these readings provide us with a framework with which we can better understand today's system of law and order. In tracing the evolution of a system of crime and punishment that is strongly rooted in a British tradition, we also see a recognition of the French presence in British North America, as well as Aboriginal, American, and Loyalist influences. While these different methods of doing justice are perhaps quite difficult to recognize in our present system, this pluralistic history has nonetheless fed into, and resulted in, the model of justice that we have today.

In the first reading, Smandych and Linden explore the development of the private justice system of the Hudson's Bay Company to 1800. Initially granted a charter to advance trade in what is now western Canada, the company was given authority to enact laws for maintaining order among employees. This form of private policing quickly expanded to controlling relations with local inhabitants, most notably the Aboriginal population that engaged in trade with the company. The purpose of the study is to develop a better understanding of the evolution of forms of governance that exist outside the formal state apparatus.

In the next reading, Murray looks at the role the Canadian–American border played in shaping our criminal justice system in the period before Confederation. Although we might consider problems associated with border control a modern phenomenon, the evidence suggests that a number of issues have a rich history, including policies regarding extradition, banishment, smuggling, and army deserters. In each instance, officials of the day were conscious of the need to maintain good relations with their neighbours to the south, while ensuring that British law was upheld. In deciding whether fugitives should be extradited for crimes allegedly committed on the other side of the border, for example, judges were to decide each case on its own merits. In deciding whether undesirables should be banished to the United States, in contrast, officials appear to have taken a much more relaxed approach.

In the third reading, Stone documents the arrival of the North West Mounted Police on the Yukon in 1894. Prior to their arrival, any disputes had been resolved in the miners' meeting, a relatively informal assembly of all interested miners in the area. The meetings appear to have been quite successful in dealing with most complaints, and were modelled after similar meetings that sprang up during the California gold rush. Thus, with the lack of much criminal activity in the area, the real purpose appears to have been the establishment of a strong Canadian presence in a frontier populated with Americans and American-style justice. As such, the police were dispatched with the duty to not only maintain law and order, but also to control the liquor trade with the Indians and to collect customs duties. More importantly, it shows how the state and its police agents appropriated conflict from people who had already devised ways of dealing with it.

The final two readings look at the regulation of behaviours that were not always strictly within the confines of the law. Early charivaris were organized to demonstrate public awareness of a variety of marital issues, including, for example, suspected cases of cuckolding, adultery, and "May–December" romances; however, the charivari was also used to warn wife-beaters that their conduct would not be tolerated. This was particularly important at a time when such behaviour was considered more of a personal problem than a legal one. Over time, the custom evolved into a less structured way for younger members of the community (usually male) to celebrate the wedding nuptials; the cacophony of noise would usually go on until the noisemakers were invited in for some libation, or given money so they could make their way to the nearest tavern. This form of popular justice also shows how people developed forms of social control in the absence of a formal legal system.

This section ends with Marks's examination of the use of gossip to exert control over members of the church. In an analysis of an underexamined form of social control, churches practised what she calls extralegal justice—that is, a form of administering justice outside the formal justice system. What we say is that for a period of history, church courts were probably more extensive and dealt with far more cases than the formal criminal justice system. It thus constitutes a parallel justice system, again illustrating the pluralistic background that we have inherited in Canada.

CHAPTER 1

Administering Justice without the State: A Study of the Private Justice System of the Hudson's Bay Company to 1800[1]

Russell Smandych and Rick Linden

● ●

*****

This paper undertakes a case study of the development of the private legal system of the Hudson's Bay Company to 1800. The study is based mainly on primary historical data held in the archives of the Hudson's Bay Company.[2] In 1670, a Royal Charter granted by the English monarchy gave the Hudson's Bay Company exclusive control over an area that encompassed most of what is now the western part of Canada. As part of its original charter, the Company was given the power to enact any laws and regulations, not repugnant to the laws of England, that were deemed necessary to govern its relations with its servants and to maintain social order in the territory of Rupertsland. In 1821, the Company was granted a license to extend its trade monopoly and legal authority to encompass the territory referred to as "Indian country," which included all of the land beyond Rupertsland whose rivers drained into the Pacific and Arctic Oceans.[3] In effect, the Charter of 1670, along with later enabling legislation, gave the Board of Governors of the Company the authority to govern a territory that covered approximately 5% of the land surface of the earth.

Elsewhere we have looked at how the private justice system of the Hudson's Bay Company served as a tool of European colonialism in its application to aboriginal peoples in Western Canada.[4] However, this system was also used extensively to control the activities of Company employees. In this paper, we present evidence of the manner in which the private justice system of the Hudson's Bay Company was applied to Company servants in the period before 1800. In addition to drawing on early published correspondence and reports, the study highlights the evidence found in selected Hudson's Bay Company post journals covering the period from 1705 to the beginning of the competitive fur trade era in the 1770s. Specifically, the study is concerned with examining how the orders passed by the Board of Governors of the Hudson's Bay Company concerning the behaviour expected of Company employees were enforced by Bayside governors and other officers of the Company. In addition to offering new historical information about the system of "non-state" governance put into effect by officers of the Hudson's Bay Company, the following study of order and disorder within the ranks of the HBC provides an empirical foundation for broader theorizing about the nature of non-state forms of governance and about the transition from a paternalistic to a contractual system of employee regulation. While traditional historians may feel that it is somewhat misguided and anachronistic to undertake a study that distinguishes between "state" and "non-state" governance in the 17th and 18th centuries, since the role of the "government" (conceived of in the traditional sense of legislatures and lawmakers) was very limited during this period compared to later, this potential criticism of the following study misses the point made by Foucault that the study of the "art of government" can include both the study of the government of populations outside the state, as well as the study of the degree of the role the state itself may have played.[5] In conclusion, we argue that historical case studies of companies like the Hudson's Bay Company offer a more adequate empirical foundation for theoretical work aimed at unraveling the complex and varied ways in which legal ordering and social control occur outside the state.

Hudson's Bay Company Law

The HBC remained a dominant presence in Western Canada until 1870. By the mid 19th century, the Company had established more than 100 fur trading posts in Rupertsland and the "Indian Territories." In the early years following 1670, the Board of Governors of the Company in London (often referred to as the London Committee) produced an elaborate set of laws, policies, rules, and ordinances as a foundation for establishing its own private legal system. For nearly 200 years, the Company exercised the power it was granted by the English monarchy to enact any laws and regulations that were deemed necessary to govern its relations with its servants and to maintain social order throughout the vast territory of Rupertsland, and later the "Indian Territories." Oliver summarizes the law-making powers granted to the Board of Governors of the Hudson's Bay Company in the Charter of 1670:

> The Governor and Company might assemble and make laws and ordinances for the good government of the Company and its colonies and forts, and for the advancement of trade. They might impose penalties and punishments, provided these were reasonable and not

repugnant to the laws of England. None of the Kings' [sic] subjects were permitted to trade within the Company's territories without leave from the Company under penalty of forfeiting their goods, one half to the Company, the other half to the King. The Company was given the right to appoint Governors and other officers, to try civil and criminal cases and to employ an armed force for the protection of its trade and territory.[6]

The legality of the Charter of 1670 and the law-making powers it granted were reaffirmed through the enactment of further enabling legislation by the British Parliament and through legal opinions and judgements that resulted from challenges to the Company. In 1690, the Act for confirming to the Governor and Company trading to Hudson's Bay their Privileges and Trade[7] reaffirmed the legal powers granted to the Board of Governors of the Company in the Charter of 1670.

> [I]t being necessary that such a Company should have sufficient and undoubted powers and authorities privileges and liberties to manage order and carry on the said Trade and to make Bye laws orders rules and constitutions for the due management and regulation as well of the said Company as Trade and for the punishment of offenders and recovering of forfeitures and penalties which cannot be so effectually done as by authority of Parliament.

Although the Act of 1690 also stipulated "this Act shall continue and be in force for the term of seven years and from thence to the end of the next Sessions of Parliament and no longer," for almost 200 years the Hudson's Bay Company continued to claim it had legal jurisdiction over territory of Rupertsland, even when contrary legal opinions declared that the Charter of 1670 was illegal, and should no longer be considered to be in effect.[8]

Until 1803, the London Committee was left on its own to enact laws for maintaining order and for carrying out trade with the Indians. There were a number of challenges to the system during this period, but it was not until after 1812 that the London Committee acknowledged that its power to enact laws in western Canada was limited by its delegation of judicial powers to the Governor and Council of Assiniboia which governed the Red River Settlement.[9]

Merchant Capitalism

Trading companies such as the Hudson's Bay Company and the East India Company exemplified 17th-century British merchant capitalism. They were colonial monopolies operating under the authority of the Crown which were designed to maximize profits for stockholders by harvesting the natural resources of the empire and to "maintain the interests of the crown by carrying out exploration, territorial expansion and law making."[10] The profit motive was clearly stated in the 19th century by Fitzgerald:

> [T]he Hudson's Bay Company enjoys a right of exclusive trade with the Indian population. This right of exclusive trade is, practically and positively, a right of exclusive property in the labour, life and destinies of the Indian race. It is an absolute and unqualified dominion over their bodies and their souls—a dominion irresponsible to any legal authority—a despotism, whose severity no legislative control can mitigate, and no public opinion restrain. It knows but one limit, and obeys but one law,—"Put money in thy purse."[11]

The focus on profit helped determine the labour relations policies of the trading companies, which tried to get the most work from employees at the least cost. Since the motivation of employees was often quite the opposite, the companies had to develop and enforce systems of rules and regulations. The distance from home, along with the harsh physical environment and the dangers of living in Rupertsland, compounded the order maintenance problems faced by the company.

Hudson's Bay Company Labour Relations

*****

In the following sections, evidence is presented which suggests that disobedience and insubordination were also a problem for Company officers in the century prior to 1770. The historical evidence also seems to suggest that the labour relations system of the Hudson's Bay Company was in fact a transitional one between a paternalistic system in which servants were part of the household and treated like part of the family (albeit a poor relative) in exchange for their labour and loyalty, and a capitalist system in which wage labour was a commodity whose value was set by the forces of the market.[12] In several respects, the working conditions of labourers and craftsmen in far-flung trading posts anticipated those of factory workers after the Industrial Revolution. In this respect, Company employees had much in common with those working for the merchant marine.

Parallels between Trading Companies and the Merchant Marine

[...] The situation of employees of the Hudson's Bay Company was very similar. They were working in relatively small groups isolated from friends and family; they were distant from the British legal system; and they were required to work effectively and efficiently in order to ensure profits for their corporate masters. In both cases, the paternalistic system, exemplified by the manorial estate, was breaking down and being replaced by a market-driven system. The strain created by this transition led to conflict and tension between masters and subordinates in both the merchant marine and the trading companies.

Rediker concluded that maritime industries developed a system of "disciplinary paternalism" to work through this transition. Sea captains tried to legitimate their authority symbolically by playing the role of masters, rulers, or even "fathers" who were responsible for ensuring the character of their men as well as for sailing their ships. This degree of authority was upheld by the law through the admiralty courts and through the sailors' contracts. During an earlier time when trade was typically closer to home, ships were run on a more egalitarian basis and all on board often held shares in the goods transported. However, in the late 17th century, voyages became longer, crews became larger, and trade became more important to the empire. Under these new circumstances, the captain's authority became more autocratic. His authority was transmitted through a hierarchical structure with clearly differentiated ranks and roles. Men of all ranks and statuses were clearly subordinate to the captain, who was the representative of an employer far-removed from the direct operation of the deep-sea sailing vessel. The captain had a great deal of authority to define what was right and wrong on his ship. Rediker illustrated this point with a quotation from an 18th-century mariner: "There is no justice or injustice on board ship, my lad. There are only two things: duty and mutiny—mind that. All that you are ordered to do is duty. All that you refuse to do is mutiny."[13]

Rediker has recognized that these sailing ships were total institutions. Like prisons and monasteries, life onboard ship encompassed all aspects of the crews' activities. Goffman[14] has enumerated several characteristics of total institutions. Among these are: all aspects of life are conducted in the same place and under the same authority; all daily activity is carried on in the company of others who are doing the same thing; all activities are scheduled and these schedules are imposed by officials; these regimented activities are part of a plan designed to fulfil the stated aims of the institution; and there are significant barriers between the managed group (inmates, sailors, or workers) and the managers (captains, factors, or officers). The nature of these institutions is such that the manager, in this case the captain, has nearly dictatorial power over all facets of the lives of his subordinates. This power was

often expressed in acts of extreme cruelty, but as with other total institutions, a regime of terror is not an efficient way to manage a ship for an extended period of time and there were many examples of resistance by the sailors even to the point of mutiny. Eventually, order must be negotiated between captain and crew or the work effort will fail.

The parallels between the merchant marine and the Hudson's Bay Company are obvious and are understandable given the similarities we have noted between sailing ships and trading posts. Like the ship, the trading post is a total institution where all residents were supposed to work together under conditions which were at times dangerous, with the goal of making profits for the Company. While there were many paternalistic elements involved in the management of the posts, there were also strains caused by the workers insisting on more freedom than Company officers were prepared to allow.

In the rest of the paper, we will describe the system of employee discipline in the Company with a particular emphasis on one post—Fort Albany. In this analysis, we find that there were many paternalistic elements involved in the management of the posts and discipline was at times highly coercive. However, we also see a transition to a system of discipline that was based on the law rather than on Company order and in which post councils were used as juries and the accused was able to exercise some legal rights. This move away from a strictly paternalistic system of governance illustrates the transitional nature of the disciplinary system within the Company in the 18th century.

Employee Discipline within the Hudson's Bay Company

Although the system of laws, policies, rules, and ordinances that came into being during the period of Hudson's Bay Company control was complex and constantly changing, the London Committee paid particular attention to a number of concerns throughout the period. One of these was the problem of "private trading," while another was regulating the manner in which Company servants were "conversing" with the Indians.

At one of its first recorded meetings, on 17 May 1672, the London Committee passed an order concerning private trade which stated "[t]hat all persons to be imployed Shall enter into articles or otherwise oblige themselves not to trade in beaver upon forfeiture of theyr goods & wages."[15] During the next decade, the London Committee issued several additional orders and policies to prohibit Company servants from siphoning profits from the fur trade that the Committee felt should go to stockholders. It is also noteworthy that, from its earliest years, the Company took steps to ensure the loyalty of its employees. According to the minutes of the meetings of the London Committee, in adherence with an enabling clause of the Charter of 1670, the Company adopted the policy of requiring employees to swear an oath of loyalty to the Company. At the meeting of 22 December 1673, it was ordered "[t]hat the Committee prepare an oath to bee administered to all the members of the Company & others relateing to theyr Service, accordeing as the Charter Shall directe." At the meeting of 29 January 1674, it was ordered that a copy of the Charter be delivered "to Mr. Rastell, accordeing to the direction whereof hee is to prepare an oath to be administered to the members of the Company & to theyr Servantes, & alsoe an affidavit to be drawn up to bee Sworne to by Such as Shall bee deemed needfull."[16] This appeal to loyalty is very similar to symbolic means of order maintenance used on sailing ships. Despite the efforts made to ensure the loyalty of Company servants and to prevent them from engaging in private trade, the London Committee was never able to stop less honest servants from taking some profits from the Company's stockholders.[17]

Company servants were forbidden from engaging in unauthorized fraternizing with the Indians until the late 1700s. This law against "conversing" with the local Indian population was closely tied to the Company

rule prohibiting servants from having sexual relations with Indian women or taking them as "country wives." These policies may have been passed because the English did not trust Indians because of their prior contact with, and potential loyalty to, French fur traders who came to Western Canada overland from Montreal. Limiting contact with the Indians also reduced the likelihood of private trading. [...]

*****

The prohibitions against contact with natives remained in effect until the late 1700s when everyone realized they were impossible to enforce. Almost from the time they began building their posts on the shores of Hudson Bay, the local postmasters (referred to also as Chief Factors and Bayside governors) and other higher-ranking Company servants began marrying "country wives," and sometimes raising sizable families with them. [...]

*****

Although the problems of private trading and fraternizing with the Indians were two concerns that were perennially addressed by the London Committee, [...] it appears that, despite clearly written orders from London disobedience and insubordination were also often the norm in the period before 1770.

Early evidence in support of this argument can be found in the report Governor John Nixon wrote to the London Committee in 1682.[18] In his report, Nixon provides an account of the unruly behaviour of Company servants that he was forced to put up with, along with an account of the steps he claimed he was taking to try and get the servants to obey his orders. Nixon told the London Committee that it was very important to leave a reliable person in charge of the posts that were being set up on the Bay because the men couldn't be trusted to govern themselves. In addition to complaining about the widespread private trading and routine drunkenness he often witnessed among Company servants and the crewmen of HBC ships, Nixon complained that he had to put up with constant verbal abuse and the threat of physical violence, because he did not have the power to force the men to obey his orders. […]

*****

Nixon pointed out that his inability to exert adequate control […] was also due in part to the lack of clear guidelines from the London Committee concerning the type of legal system that should be put into place to deal with disobedient and dishonest employees. Specifically, Nixon noted that he was uncertain about whether either military or civil law was "the law of England" that he should be putting into force. He also offered the London Committee his advice on the system that should be put into place to deal with Company servants who committed acts that were defined as crimes by the Company and the King. Nixon's comments on these matters are worth quoting at length, since they bear directly on the origins of the private legal system of the Hudson's Bay Company that would exist in Western Canada for the next 150 years. Specifically, Nixon told the London Committee:

[M]y commission is to governe efter the lawes of England, but which of them, military or sivill, and if I were capable of both I have not power to put them in practice, all that I can doe at present is only to send them home, and wryt their fact, so that they have the opportuniety of cleering themselves and accusing of me, for it hath been the speach of some all reddy that if they had a minde to goe home, they had no more to doe but to make a mutiny and so they should be sent home, such things is in custome heare for which they would be severely punished in other places, therefore if there be not some lawes put in practice heare, there will unavoydably some notable dissaster befall the country, and I am sure no government at present can stand with the constitution of this country, but military and no law but martiall at present. But if your honors, see that martiall lawe is either too severe or that it can not be granted, I do not desire it in the large latitude thereof, so far as to extend

to lyfe and death, for that is a thing which if I could avoyd I would not pass sentance of death on any man, but the crime being such, as that by a counsell we may prove the fact against a criminall, according to the booke of articles in that casse provyded, and accordingly chastise him with corporall punishment for ane example to others, or else to send him home in irons to receave his punishment in England, as the case may require, these things may bring the country into good order in tyme, and put a great stop to lisentiousness, for without some thing of this nature the country will still lye in danger.[19]

*****

The Role of Post Councils in Maintaining Discipline

From a very early date, the London Committee also appointed a specific number of Company officers and ship captains to serve as members of "Post Councils" (or Councells), that were to assist the governor in making decisions that needed to be made on-the-spot when he was not able to first consult with the London Committee. […]

Post Councils before 1696

Evidence suggests that from as early as the 1680s, post councils played an active role in the operation of the private internal legal system of the Hudson's Bay Company. […]

[…] It is somewhat surprising to find evidence, given that throughout the years from the mid 1680s to 1713, England and France fought over the fur-trade posts in Hudson Bay, and military law was clearly in effect during this period.[20]

It is significant that at the first council meeting recorded by Nixon, which was held at Charleton Island on 28 October 1681, a decision was made bearing on the problem of how social order and discipline were to be maintained at the different locations at which the Company was beginning to set up bayside posts. Specifically, Nixon reported on the decision he and his councillors made when they were faced with potential disciplinary problems that arose from the fact that cold weather and frozen ice had left them stranded on Charleton Island away from the posts on the mainland. In order to prevent the men on the mainland from rising up in mutiny and stirring trouble among the Indians—as Nixon reported usually occurred when they were left without someone to watch over them—the council ordered that:

[f]or the better Saveing of the Companeys Goods, and Keepeing all things In good Order, that the yaucht *Colleton* & her Companey wth the Governor Doe Remaine Att Charleton Island, & there to winter, that she may be the more Safe to serve the Companey the next Spring, & that Mr. Tho. Phypps [Thomas Phipps], whom we have found Abell and Willing be Deputed Deputy Governor & If Wind & weather Shall Searve, with the first Opertunitye himselfe & four hands more will Trye If Possible to Gett to the Maine, In A Boate, & from thence To Travell for Prince Ruperts West River, & there to take Charge of all things, as Deputy Governor ought to doe, Given under our hands this present Instant.[21]

Another indication that the London Committee encouraged collective decision-making, instead of imposing a strict form of military rule in which the governor held absolute power, can be seen in the instructions that were given to James Knight in 1692 when he was commissioned as "Governor & Cheife Commander" of all of the forts and other lands and territories claimed by Hudson's Bay Company in North America.[22] Knight was ordered to sail into Hudson Bay, and begin retaking HBC posts that had been captured previously by the French. [...]

Knight was also told to take into account the advice of councillors in the event that he succeeded in either recapturing or establishing new posts on the bottom of the Hudson Bay: "When you are able & you are possest of a proper place you are to Build & settle a Fort & Factory, but it were much better to take it ready erected & Fortefied from the French

which indeed is our Owne, An as soone as you enter upon Deliberation you shall Constitute a Councell for the better consulting & Concearnes, which we referre to you to Chose out the most discreet & sober persons about you A most faithful to our Intrest.[23]

During the period in which the Hudson's Bay Company was struggling to regain its posts on the bottom of the Bay, James Knight was encouraged to treat the men under his command with a blend of strong military discipline tempered with a system of collective decision-making and benevolent paternalism. The London Committee also hoped that this paternalism would be extended to the Indians who would bring in the furs the Company needed in order to recoup the losses it suffered because of the Anglo-French rivalry over the Bay. This view is clearly reflected in the part of Knight's instructions that spelled out how he was to conduct himself in his role as governor and chief commander. With respect to the treatment of Indians, the London Committee noted:

If you chance to come to a Trade with the Indians Wee need not tell you how you shall treat them, with all humanity Justice & Kindnesse, you being soe well acquainted with their Natures & your owne Experience teaching you. But at this time it is more especially necessary when they have missed us soe long in those parts & wee believe are weary enough of the French, & therefore Wee hope by a smooth Carriage with them you may make them very usefull to your designe or at leat gett good information from them of the strength of the French & (heir Trade wherby to forme your approaches the better.[24]

On the matter of how he was to govern over the men placed under his command. Knight was told that:

Wee have ordered [the ships' captains] with their Crew to attend you all the Winter & as long as they stay there to observe your orders

& Directions, to forward your Buildings &. fortifications, & in fine to Obey & execute what ever Commands you impose upon them in order to [do] Our Service whether of building trading or any other works whatsoever or of attacking the Enemy ... And for the makeing your owne men & the Shipps Companies more useful to you upon any extraordinary occation Wee doe Order you to Muster & Traine them all & to keep them in the exercise & understanding of martiall Discipline, that in Case of an Enemy they may more couragiously stand by you & discharge their Duties either at Sea or Land both to their Matie & us.[25]

The fact that James Knight took this order seriously, and indeed imposed a system of strong military discipline on Company servants in the early years following the retaking of Albany, is revealed in documents relating to the punishment of mutineers at Albany between 1694 and 1696.[26] The miscellaneous files for Albany Fort, dated 2 October 1694, contain two depositions from Company servants who both claimed to have heard Joseph Eglinton threaten to sink the Perry Friggat, because of the way he was being treated by HBC Company officers. […]

Although it is not known how Joseph Eglinton was punished for making these threats, there is evidence that other Company servants who acted in a similar way at Albany Fort in 1696 were severely punished under orders from James Knight and the post council at Albany. In one of these cases, James Knight charged a servant by the name of John Cartwright with "stirring up Mutiny and Rebellion in the Factory (and) endeavouring the utter destruction of the Government and Countrey [by] throwing out lyes and false reports upon my Deputy and his Brother." […]

*****

According to Knight, a further aggravating circumstance in Cartwright's case was that when he was told by another servant that there would

be no ships coining from England, and that as a result they would out of necessity "be forced to eat Succoo's [which] is [the] Indian Name of a Carp," he replied that they should all "[g]o to the Gov:r and demand the ship to go home." The sentence and punishment Cartwright received for his attempt at causing a mutiny were stated as follows:

The Gov:r And Council takeing the above mentioned thinges into serious consideration, well pondering and Considering the Bad Inconveniencie that doth accrue from such factious turbulent follows To prevent the like for the future and that it may be an example to others, hath ordered that you John Cartwright Shall be whipt thirty stripes. Lye in Irons confined close prisoner, and fed upon Succoo's as you call them, till either Our ships arrive here from England to carry you home, or the Ship wee have Now in y:e Countrey Go from their. Dated at Albany fort America y:e 15:th day of August 1696.[27]

*****

Post Councils after 1713

Although it is evident that the London Committee believed that military discipline was needed in order to regain control of the Bay, evidence suggests that, in later years, and certainly after the signing of the *Treaty of Utrecht* in 1713, which ended the French–English rivalry over the Bay, a more civilian- (or English common law-) based legal system, which included the use of post councils as juries and the granting of more legal rights to the accused, was used at certain times to deal with dishonest and disobedient Company servants.

One indication of this can be found in the surviving transcripts of one of the first post council meetings that was held at York Factory after it was reclaimed from the French by James Knight in 1714.[28] On 27 December 1715, a Company servant named Thomas Butler was placed on trial at York Factory for a number of crimes that he was alleged to have committed.

This formal criminal trial was presided over by James Knight and five Company officers "sitting in Councell for Maintaining & keeping the (legal) Rights & Priveleges of (the) Crown of England as by Law Established."[29]

Thomas Butler was arraigned and brought before the Council to be tried for several "high and Misdormeanour" crimes, which included: "Feloniously Stealing at Sundry times," "threatening Mens Lives" using "very Unbecomeing Languages abuseing his worthy Gover:or," and "most Slanderously Scandelizeing his Hon:ble Masters the Company in England (which led) to the Subverting of this Goverm:t by causeing ... Misunderstandings Among the Men" about the wages they were entitled to receive from the Company (Butler was accused of spreading rumors that the Company was broke and that no one would get paid the wages they were owed). Butler was also charged with disobeying the "Expres Orders" of the London Committee which prohibited unauthorized fraternizing with the Indians. Butler was accused specifically of threatening to cause the Indians to rise up against the Company because of his "Abusing the Natives here by lyeing with a Woman of this Country."[30]

*****

In order to ensure him "a fair and Legall hearing," before they proceeded to pass their verdict, the council gave Butler the opportunity to bring forward any person he could who might speak on his behalf or defend his reputation. However, it was recorded that Butler did not do this and that he spoke "but little in his own Defense." Unfortunately, although the surviving transcripts state that "Thomas Butler was found Guilty of the Aforewritten Crimes Unanimously Agreed to by us all the Govern:r & his Councell," there is no record included of the sentence that was imposed on Butler for his crimes. In any event, this trial provides us with a good indication of the role played by early post councils in administering Hudson's Bay Company law.[31] [...]

Order and Disorder on the Shores of the Bay: An Analysis of Albany Post Journals and Correspondence, 1705–1742

In the years following 1714, Albany and York became the largest and most important Hudson's Bay Company posts on the shores of Hudson Bay. During the first half of the 18th century, the size and profits of the Company also grew substantially under the leadership of Sir Bibye Lake,[32] and several other HBC posts were established on and later inland from the Bay. [...]

[...] There is a considerable amount of variation in the manner in which different Bayside governors and other Company officers attempted to enforce the orders and policies written by the London Committee. In addition, evidence suggests that, while some Bayside governors were perceived by Company servants as being cruel and inhumane, others appear to have been much more well-liked and respected (or at least more often listened to) because of the way in which they conducted themselves in dealing with the men who were nominally subjected to their orders. [...]

Crime and Governance at Albany, 1705–1739

With the French occupying York, and with Moose Factory and Rupert House abandoned between 1697 and 1714, Albany was the only permanent post in the Company's possession.[33] From 1693 to 1697, James Knight served as the governor of Albany Fort, and following him, John Fullartine became governor until 1705. When Fullartine decided to resign in 1703, he recommended Anthony Beale to the London Committee as someone who was "a very careful, honest man and knows the affairs of this country as well as most men that ever were in it and deserves encouragement as being an old servant and one that has always been faithful to his masters."[34]

*****

The post journal kept by Beale from September 1705 to July 1706[35] reveals that, during this time, the London Committee was still requiring Bayside governors to enforce British military law. [...]

The post journals Beale kept during his second term from 1711 to 1714 show that he continued to be concerned about keeping his men in a state of military readiness to guard against Indians and the French.[36] However, entries for this period record only one case in which he arguably used "military law" to deal with dishonest Company servants. In his entry for 25 January 1713, Beale reported that he "had the Good fortune" to find out the names of four men who were guilty of stealing food from the "flanker and warehouse By breaking open the flank ports and Leaving y:e [the] factory open to an Enemy." Beale also reported that he put the four men in irons and that he planned to "find outt othars if thare be any" and "punish them" as they deserved. In his journal entry written the next day, Beale reported that although the men would not admit of any other confederates, they did confess that they had stood watch for each other, and that they had frequently stolen extra food [like sugar plums and cheese] from the warehouse since they all arrived together at Albany on the last ship from England. As to their punishment, Beale wrote that he "tied them hand and futt and stript them naked to thar wast and (whipped) them Pretty Souarly in so much (that he promised) Never to be of the Same any Moore."[37]

*****

After Thomas Macklish took over as governor in 1715, he [...] wrote the London Committee on several occasions, outlining the steps he was taking to protect the Company's interests in the Bay.[38] In his letter of 16 July 1716, Macklish noted that, as the London Committee had ordered, after he had taken charge as Governor, he proclaimed King George "as right & Lawfull King of great Britain, & y:e [the] Territories," according to the form perscribed, and he promised that he would "keep good watch both

night and day," remembering how the French had nearly captured the factory in 1709, "had not Governor Fullartine given the first alarm." Macklish also gave the London Committee nearly the same story as Beale about how he promised to watch over the men at Albany, in order to encourage personal discipline and prevent them from spending all of their wages on brandy.

*****

In his letter to the London Committee, written three years later,[39] Macklish reported on how he was continuing to restrict the amount of brandy that the men were allowed to purchase from the Company, warehouse. [...]

Macklish also used this letter to comment on how he would treat the newly hired Company servants who had arrived at Albany in the summer of 1719, noting that "[t]he men sent this year Appears to be lusty able young men And hope will answer expectation, and according as they behave themselves Shall be used with all the Civility Imaginable."

It is no doubt the case that some of the Company's Bayside governors did treat the men under their command with civility and respect, and that the men in turn reciprocated. Evidence of this can be found in letters that the succeeding governors, Joseph Myatt and Richard Staunton, sent back to the London Committee in the early 1720s. On 22 August 1722, Myatt wrote, thanking the London Committee for appointing him as Governor of Albany, and reporting on how he was carrying out the orders that he had received from the Committee.[40] Myatt commented specifically on how he was enforcing the Committee's order against allowing men to borrow against their wages (to buy brandy and pay gambling debts), and he reported that most of the men were now following this order. [...]

*****

However, Myatt was subsequently demoted to deputy governor because the Committee felt he had not exercised sufficient discipline within the post. In addition to allowing Indian women access to the Fort, Myatt let the men drink large quantities of brandy. After writing to the London Committee on 10 August 1726, informing it that four servants had died at Albany in the last year,[41] the Committee wrote back to Myatt, informing him that: "[W]hereas we have to believe the excessive drinking of Brandy hath been the cause of the Death of some of our Servants, to prevent which for the future, we do hereby order you to punish all Persons who are contrivers and promoters of such Wickedness, and to send Us their Names in order to their being sent ... Home, likewise not to suffer them to Collect quantities of Brandy together with a design to make themselves Drunk, which we are inform'd hath often been practis'd, but we are resol'd to remove all such Persons from our Service."[42]

Myatt's experience at Albany in the 1720s highlights the difficulty more than one Bayside governor must have faced in trying to balance, enforcing the orders of the London Committee against the need for getting cooperation from the Company's bayside servants. There is evidence that the chief factors at both Albany and York, as well as at other posts experienced similar difficulties.

Crime and Punishment at Albany under Joseph Isbister

One Bayside governor who acquired a reputation for harsh discipline is Joseph Isbister, the Chief Factor at Albany during the 1740s. Isbister began his career with the Company in 1726 as "servant" on board the Hannah Frigate sailing between England and the Bay, and he worked as a crewman on HBC ships travelling back and forth across the Atlantic until 1835, when he was hired on again as a "Sailor," with orders to proceed to the Bay. On his arrival at Albany in 1735, Isbister was appointed Master of the Eastmain Sloop and in September he sailed for Eastmain where he spent the winter of 1735–1736 and each of the four succeeding winters. In August 1740, Isbister was appointed by the council at Albany to succeed Rowland

Waggoner as the Chief Factor at Albany— who it was commonly believed had died of "immoderate drinking and other debauchery"[43] and this decision was subsequently confirmed by the London Committee. Over the next 16 years, Isbister served several terms as the Chief Factor at Albany and Fort Prince of Wales.[44]

Isbister's career provides a great deal of insight into the "problems of management and discipline" experienced by HBC governors and the London Committee.[45] One reason for this is that, when Isbister's appointment as Chief Factor was confirmed by the London Committee in 1742, he was specifically commanded to stamp out drunkeness and private trade, and "hinder as much as Possible the detestable Sin of Whoring."[46] Following these orders, Isbister instituted a strict military regimen at Albany, and he often resorted to physical force to punish disobedient servants. In addition to antagonizing Company servants by imposing a system of strict military discipline, Isbister raised a great deal of protest because of his attempt to prohibit everyone—except himself—from having contact with Indian women. Mainly because of these reasons, the post journals kept by Isbister at Albany during the 1740s and 1750s, along with coinciding inward and outward correspondence, provide a rich source of primary data on the qualities and problems of governance experienced by servants of the Hudson's Bay Company in the mid-18th century.

The post journal Isbister kept while he was stationed at Eastmain from 1736 to 1740 also contains data on the way in which he tried to impose a strict system of military discipline on Company servants.[47] [...] In the post journal entry he wrote after having served just over a year as the Chief Factor at Albany, Isbister complained to the London Committee about the lazyness of earlier chief factors, and how this resulted in the fact that the fort was in a state of crumbling disrepair. In his journal entry for 16 September 1741, Isbister complained he was forced to make extensive repairs to the fort because the "Masters" that came before him

"Sat att Theire Eas & Cried [they] would Serve There Times Taking no Care for ... Any Part of y:e Factory but y:e Square house That They lived in." Isbister told the London Committee that he could also have sat on his ass like the rest of them, but he wasn't the type to be "Caring for Nothing as Long as they Could but *Get there Mugg and There* boull & Pip of Tobaco to pass The Time away [and] Lete all Go to wreck And rewin."[48]

*****

Despite the boasting he did about his success at restoring order at Albany, the post journals Isbister kept from 1740 to 1742 are full of examples of employee disobedience and insubordination. When he took over as governor in August 1740, Isbister had 17 men under his command at Albany and 9 men at Eastmain. In his very first entry in the Albany post journal, dated 22 August 1740, Isbister reported that, after being appointed as the "Master of Albany Fort" in the afternoon, he ordered some of the men to go out and gather some stones for ballast for the sloop and to cut some wood. Isbister also recorded the fact that, rather than following his commands, a labourer named Ralph Whitte, as he had been doing all winter, "Gave me [an] abundance of ill Language & would Not work" and "he also chalinged me to fight." As he would do so many times in the future, Isbister said that "for his Great incelance [insolence]" he flogged him "Very hartely with my hands."[49]

*****

By the end of March 1742, Isbister felt that he had finally succeeded in restoring order at Albany. To cement his success, he decided both to post a new copy of London Committee's longstanding orders on employee behaviour, and introduce a new set of detailed regulations concerning the officers' and servants' mess. Isbister also wrote a boastful account to the London committee outlining the steps he had taken to put an end to private trading and bootlegging that was still being encouraged by the captains of HBC ships.[50] Reading between

the lines of Isbister's 18th-century English,[51] it is obvious that one of the things he tried to do was to stop Company servants from stealing furs and other goods, which they then bartered for liquor. However, just as we know that other Bayside governors were never able to completely stop private trading, it is unlikely that Isbister actually ever succeeded in putting Albany Fort into a perfect state of order. Indeed, the fact that Isbister resorted to imposing corporal punishment on Indians and Company servants alike throughout the remaining years of his tenure at Albany[52] clearly suggests that he was never able to stamp out resistance and opposition to his rule.

Perhaps, one of the most bothersome obstacles Isbister faced in trying to get men to conform to his style of government was that the men placed under the command of Bayside governors changed significantly every time another ship arrived from England. For example, in the new post journal Isbister began on 11 August 1742, he listed the names of the 14 men under his command. Seven of the men named on the list were new at Albany, having either arrived there by ship from England, or—at least in one case—having been transfered to Albany from another bayside post.[53] As we can see from this example, early HBC fur-trading posts were not entirely the same as Goffman's total institution, and Bayside governors appear as if they were never able to deal effectively with employee insubordination.

Conclusions

*****

While some governors appear to have opted for the practice of showing paternalism and kindness to the men under their command, others, like Joseph Isbister, were undoubtedly cruel and inhuman, even when looked at from 18th-century standards. The evidence presented in this study also suggests that the labour relations system that existed within the Hudson's Bay Company in the 18th century was transitional in nature, resembling a shift from a paternalistic system. [...] In several respects, the experience of labourers and craftsmen in the far-flung HBC trading posts resembled the experience of the labouring poor in 18th- and later, 19th-century Britain.[54] Just as Edith Burley[55] has pointed was the case after 1770, evidence from HBC post journals shows that many of the class divisions and much of the class conflict that existed in Britain before 1770 ended up being reproduced within the ranks of the Hudson's Bay Company. This is not to say, however, that the same conditions of work and social life that existed in Britain for the labouring poor also existed on the shores of Hudson Bay. Rather, as we have seen, the conditions endured by servants who were sent out to work at Albany and other HBC posts on the shores of Hudson Bay in the late 17th and 18th centuries, were more likely similar to those that existed on board British naval ships, and in Goffman-like total institutions. These conditions resulted in different ways of governance, and different problems of governance, for the Company officers who were ordered by the London committee to watch over and protect their economic interests on the shores of Hudson Bay.

*****

Notes

1. An earlier version of this paper was presented at the Law and Society Association Annual Meeting, Toronto, Ontario, June, 1995. We would like to thank the anonymous reviewers and editorial board of the CJLS/RCDS for their constructive reviews and editorial advice, and the Social Sciences and Humanities Research Council of Canada for funding the research undertaken for this paper.

2. The Hudson's Bay Company Archives [hereinafter HBCA] now exist as part of the Provincial Archives of Manitoba in Winnipeg. The HBCA contain a detailed historical record of the operation of the Hudson's Bay Company in western Canada from the 1670s to the end of the 19th century.

3. Hamar Foster, "Long-Distance Justice: The Criminal Jurisdiction of Canadian Courts West of the Canadas, 1763–1859" (1990) 34 *American Journal of Legal History* I.

4. Russell Smandych & Rick Linden, "Co-existing Forms of Aboriginal and Private Justice: An Historical Study of the Canadian West" in K. Hazlehurst, ed., *Legal Pluralism and the Colonial Legacy: Indigenous Experiences of Justice in Canada, Australian, and New Zealand* (Aldershot, Avebury, 1995); Russell Smandych & Gloria Lee, "Resisting Company Law: Aboriginal Peoples and the Transformation of Legal Ordering and Social Control in the Canadian West to 1850" (Paper presented at the meeting of the Western Association of Sociology and Anthropology, Saskatoon, March, 1994) [unpublished]; Russell Smandych & Gloria Lee, "Women, Colonization, and Resistance: Elements of an Amerindian Autohistorical Perspective to the Study of Law and Colonialism" (1995) 10 *Native Studies Review* 21; Russell Smandych & Karina Sacca, "From Private Justice to State Law: The Hudson's Bay Company and the Origin of Criminal Law in the Canadian West to 1870" (1996) *Manitoba Law Annual* [forthcoming].

5. Moreover, during the period considered in this study, the Hudson's Bay Company, and other existing chartered companies—like the English and Dutch East India Companies and the Royal Africa Company—were not companies that acted simply as additional "arms of the state," by supposed virtue of the fact that they catered to the interests of the monarchs who granted them their law-making powers. Rather, other studies have suggested that, far from subservient to the state, these companies likely used the powers they were delegated by the state to pursue their own economic interests. See, for example, Julia Adams, "Principals and Agents, Colonialists and Company Men: The Decay of Colonial Control in the Dutch East Indies" (1996) 61 *American Sociological Review* 12; Robert Brenner, *Merchants and Revolution: Commerical Change, Political Conflict, and London's Overseas Traders, 1550–1653* (Princeton: Princeton University Press, 1993).

6. E.H. Oliver, ed., *The Canadian North-West: Its Early Development and Legislative Records*, vol. 1 (Ottawa: Government Printing Bureau, 1914) at 22.

7. 1690, 2 W. & M. c 23.

8.   Kachryn Bindon, "Hudson's Bay Company Law: Adam Thorn and the Institution of Order in Rupert's Land 1839–54" in D. Flaherty, ed., *Essays in the History of Canadian Law*, vol. I (Toronto: University of Toronto Press, 1981); Arthur Dobbs, *An Account of the Countries Adjoining to Hudson's Bay Company in the Northwest Part of America* (London: Printed for J. Robinson, 1744); Great Britain, Parliament, House of Commons, "Select Committee on the Report from the Select Committee on the Hudson's Bay Company; together with the Proceedings of the Committee, Minutes of Evidence, Appendix and Index" (Chairman: Rt. Hon. Henry Labouchere) (ordered by the House of Commons to be printed, 31 July and 11 August 1857); Joseph Robson, *An Account of Six Years Residence in Hudson's Bay from 1733 to 1736, and 1744 to 1747* (London: J. Payne, 1752). Although they represent an important aspect of the early history of the Company, more detailed discussion of these legal challenges is beyond the scope of this paper.

9.   See, generally, Smandych & Sacca, *supra* note 4; Dale Gibson, "Company Justice: Origins of Legal Institutions in Pre-Confederation Manitoba" (1995) 23 *Man. Law J.* 247; Howard R. Baker II, *Law Transplanted, Justice Invented: Sources of Law for the Hudson's Bay Company in Rupert's Land, 1670–1870* (M.A. Thesis, University of Manitoba, 1996).

10. Glen Makahonuk, "Wage-Labour in the Northwest Fur Trade Economy" (1988) 41 *Saskatchewan History* 1.

11. James E. Fitzgerald, *An Examination of the Charter and Proceedings of the Hudson's Bay Company* (London: 1849) at 135–136, cited in Makahonuk, *supra* note 10 at 1–2.

12. The shift in the nature of HBC labour relations that occurred in the period from the 1690s to the 1790s appears to have occurred more or less simultaneously with the transition to capitalism and corresponding changes in the nature of social class relations that occurred in England during the same period. The shift toward a "free labour" market economy in England, and the manner in which it was linked to both the transformation of master-servant relations and changes in institutions used to control "problem populations" like the poor, the criminal, and the insane, is given detailed attention in the work of revisionist historians like Michael Ignatieff, *A Just Measure of Pain: The Penitentiary and the Industrial Revolution* (New York: Pantheon Books, 1978), and Andrew Scull, *Museums of Madness: The Social Organization*

of Insanity in the Nineteenth Century (London: Allen Lane, 1979). More recently, Peter Linebaugh, *The London Hanged: Crime and Civil Society in the Eighteenth Century* (Cambridge: Cambridge University Press, 1992) has argued similarly that the punishment of the labouring poor for crimes in 18th-century London must be understood within the broader context of structural changes in the economy that affected the labour market and the nature of social class relations.

13. Marcus Rediker, *Between the Devil and the Deep Blue Sea: Merchant Seamen, Pirates, and the Anglo-American Maritime World, 1700–1750* (Cambridge: Cambridge University Press, 1987) at 211.

14. Erving Gottman, "On the Characteristics of Total Institutions: The Inmate World" in Donald R. Cressey, ed., *The Prison: Studies in Institutional and Organizational Change* (New York: Holt, Rinehart & Winston, 1961) at 15.

15. E.E. Rich, ed. *Minutes of the Hudson's Bay Company 1671–1674*, vol. 5 (London: Hudson's Bay Record Society, 1942) at 38.

16. Ibid. at 67, 75.

17. The problem of private trading persisted until at least the mid-19th century. Indicatively, as late as 1834, the London Committee ordered the printing of a new "Deed Poll" respecting the rights and duties of Chief Factors and Chief Traders conducting trade on behalf of the Company in Rupertsland and the Indian territories, which contained an article prohibiting private trading. See Hudson's Bay Company, *Deed Poll, by the Governor and Company of Hudson's Bay. With Respect to their Chief Factors and Chief Traders for Conducting their Trade in Rupert's Land and North America; And for Ascertaining the Rights and Prescribing the Duties of Those Officers* (London: Printed by Henry Kent Causton, 1834). Specifically, Article XIV of the "Deed Poll" of 1834 read that: "The Chief Factors and Chief Traders shall not on their separate account, distinct from the said trade, enter into any trade, business or commerce whatsoever, either directly or indirectly, or be in any wise (sic) concerned or interested therein, neither with Indians nor with any other person whomsoever; and every such Chief Factor or Chief Trader so offending, shall for each such offence, pay the sum of 1,000 (pounds) to the Governor and Company as stated, or liquidated damages."

18. "Report to the Governor and Committee by John Nixon 1682" in E.E. Rich, ed., *Minutes of the Hudson's Bay Company 1679–1682*, vol. 8

(London: Hudson's Bay Record Society, 1946) at 239–304. Jennifer Brown, *Strangers in Blood: Fur Trade Company Families in the Indian Country* (Vancouver: University of British Columbia Press, 1980) at 14, has noted that Nixon's "report" of 1682 is the earliest surviving account of the fur trade sent back to London from Hudson Bay.

19. Ibid. at 272–73.

20. For an overview and documents concerning this Anglo-French rivalry, including a chronology of battles between the French and English over HBC posts, see E.E. Rich, ed., *Hudson's Bay Company Letters Outward, 1679–94*, vol. 11 (London: Hudson's Bay Record Society, 1948) at 39–40, 79–80, 111–112, 149, 179–80, 195, 233, 239 and E.E. Rich, ed., *Hudson's Bay Copy Booke of Letters, Commissions, Instructions Outward, 1668–1696*, vol. 20. (London: Hudson's Bay Record Society, 1957) at 101, 121, 125, 147–149.

21. Rich, ed., *supra* note 18 at 301–02.

22. E.E. Rich, ed., *Hudson's Bay Copy Booke of Letters, Commissions, Instructions Outward, 1668–1696*, vol. 20 (London: Hudson's Bay Record Society, 1957) at 144–48, 164–65.

23. Rich, ed., *supra* note 20 at 147.

24. Ibid.

25. Ibid. at 147–48.

26. Hudson's Bay Company Archives (HBCA), B.3/z/2, fos., 1–3, Albany Fort. Miscellaneous files, 1694–1696. The HBCA miscellaneous files pertaining to Albany Fort are a series of documents that contain depositions of Company servants. Post accounts, Men's accounts, Indian's accounts, lists of Day and Night Watches, and Memoranda. All of these documents appear to have been placed in the Albany Fort miscellaneous files because they were not part of the post journal itself.

27. HBCA, B.3/z/2, fo. 2. It is beyond the scope of this paper to undertake a detailed comparison of the type and severity of punishments administered by officers of the HBC and the captains of merchant ships or officers in the British military. However, a number of studies have been completed that provide a good starting point for such a study. See generally, the data and literature discussed in John Braithwaite, "Shame and Modernity" (1993) 33 *British Journal of Criminology* 1; J.S. Cockburn, "Punishment and Brutalization in the English Enlightenment" (1994) 12 *Law and History Review* 155.

28. HBCA, "York Factory Councils" B.239/a/2, fos. 75–78.

29. The five councillors who participated in the trial were Henry Kelsey (who was then Deputy Governor), Alexander Apthorp, David Vaughan, John Carruthers, and Fotherby Jackson.

30. HBCA, B.239/a/2, fo. 75.

31. Although the recorded post council meetings that were held at York Factory between 1714 and the mid 1720s contain no examples of other criminal trials, it is evident from the council minutes that they were also convened to make collective decisions on how disobedient and dishonest Company servants should be dealt with. For example, at the council held at York Factory on 1 September 1725, presided over by Governor Henry Kelsey, a decision was made to extend the contracts of a number of bayside servants for an additional year because the crew and men who arrived on the "Whalebone Sloop" from England in the summer refused to stay over the winter and take the place of the men who were scheduled to return. The members of Henry Kelsey's council also took steps at the meeting to deal with a case involving the suspected theft of Company furs by a servant by the name of Hall. Specifically, it was reported that the Governor ceased "all M: r Halls papers and Furrs that he Could find in his Cabbbin. Chest or elsewhere, tyed them up on a Bundle and afterwards Open:d them before the S: d Councell (but) found No papers Materiall & of Furrs, (except) one black Beav:r the Gov.r gave him 10 Marins (and) one Red Fox. he Catcht in the Winter." However, the council stated that "we are (still) Senceable he Caught more." HBCA, B.239/b/, fo. 9.

32. Lake became the Governor of the Hudson's Bay Company in 1712 (when he was around 28 years old), and remained the Governor without a break until his death in 1743, a total of 29 years. This was the longest term served by any Governor of the Hudson's Bay Company prior to 1949. Lake was also "a Sub-Governor of the Africa Company." He was also actively involved in buying and selling stocks and annuities, including "East India stocks of various denominations." See E.E. Rich, ed., *Introduction to James Isham's Observations and Notes, 1743–49*, vol. 12 (London: Hudson's Bay Record Society) 1949 at xix. Lake was a key member of the Board of Governors of the Company until his death, and he is said to have exerted a great deal of influence and control over the Company's activities in North America. According to Rich: "During the period of the recovery (following the Treaty of Utrecht and the return of HBC posts to the control of the Company) the dominant personality was undoubtedly the Governor, whose character pervaded not only the London Committee meetings

but also the councils of the remote forts on the Bay; a subtle, reasonable influence, apparently unenterprising except in matters of accountancy but yet keen, shrewd and utterly reliable." Ibid. at 14.

33. Glyndwr Williams, ed., *Hudson's Bay Miscellany 1670-1870* (Winnipeg: Hudson's Bay Record Society, 1975) at 5.

34. "Captain John Fullartine, Governor of Albany Fort in Hudson's Bay, to Governor and Committee of the Hudson's Bay Company, 2 August 1703" in K.G. Davis, ed., *Letters from Hudson Bay 1703– 1740* (London: Hudson's Bay Record Society, 1965) at 5–14. Fullartine returned to Albany in 1708 and successfully defended the post against the French in 1709. Fullartine was not a novice at righting with the French, as he had participated in earlier military campaigns in the Bay in the 1680s and 1690s, and on two of these occasions, he was captured and taken prisoner. Fullartine finally returned to England in 1711, where he became a member of the London Committee until shortly before his death in 1738. Ibid. at 10, note 1.

35. Williams, ibid. at 10–65.

36. HBCA, B.3/a/4, *Albany Post Journals, 4, 15, and 16, May 1713.*

37. HBCA, B.3/a/4, *Albany Post Journal, 26 January 1713.*

38. HBCA, A. 11/2, fos. 26–33, 34–41, *Inward Correspondence, Thomas Macklish, Albany Fort, to the London Committee, 16 July 1716, 12 September 1716, 20 August 1717, 31 August 1719.*

39. HBCA, A.I 1/2, fos. 38–41, *Thomas Macklish, Albany Fort, to the London Committee, 31 August 1719.*

40. HBCA, A. 11/2. fos. 42–45.

41. HBCA, A. 11/2, fos., 56–57, cited in Davis, *supra* note 34 at 113–16.

42. HBCA, A.6/5. fo. 2–2d, *London Committee to Joseph Myatt, 25 May 1727*, cited in Davis, *supra* note 34 at 114.

43. Davis, *supra* note 34 at 323.

44. HBCA, *Search file, Joseph Isbister.*

45. Sylvia Van Kirk, "Joseph Isbister" 6 *Dictionary of Canadian Biography* at 381.

46. HBCA, A.6/7, *Outward Correspondence, London Committee to Mr. Joseph Isbister and Council at Albany Fort, 5 May 1742.* Specifically, the London Committee told Isbister: "We Expect a due Performance of your Promise by your Vertuous example, not only to prevent immoderate drinking and other vices that did occasion M:r Waggoners Death, but that you will take care to hinder as much as Possible the detestable Sin of Whoring w.xh we are informed is practiced in the Factory notwithstanding what we have so often ordered in our former letters to the Contrary."

47. HBCA, B.59/a/1–4, *Eastmain Journals, December 1736 to April 1740.*

48. HBCA, B.3/a/33, *Albany Post Journal, 16 September 1741* [emphasis added].

49. HBCA, B.3/a/3O, *Albany Post Journal, 22 August 1740.*

50. HBCA. B.3/a/33. *Albany Post Journal, 28 March 1742.*

51. Isbister also had awful spelling, even in comparison to his 18th-century peers.

52. HBCA, *Albany Post Journals, 1742–1748, 1753– 1756*; Smandych & Linden, *supra* note 4.

53. HBCA, B.3/a/34, *Albany Post Journal, 11 August 1742.*

54. Ignatieff, *supra* note 12; Scull, *supra* note 12; Linebaugh, *supra* note 12.

55. Edith Barley, *Work, Discipline and Conflict in the Hudson's Bay Company, 1770 to 1870* (Ph.D. Dissertation, University of Manitoba, 1993).

CHAPTER 2

Criminal Boundaries: The Frontier and the Contours of Upper Canadian Justice, 1792–1840

David Murray

· ·

*****

The Frontier

The perception of the boundary between Canada and the United States has changed dramatically over time. In part this has occurred because travel across the border has become so commonplace, creating an easy and automatic sense of familiarity with the other. Even by the 1930s, an estimated thirty million border crossings occurred annually. Today when we cross the border to the United States at Niagara Falls or Fort Erie, or when we enter Canada from the United States, our awareness of passing from one country to another comes primarily from a change in symbols, like flags or our experience with the officious state bureaucracy of customs and immigration, found on both sides of the border. Adam Shortt taught his Queen's University students that at the turn of the twentieth century the boundary line between Canada and the United States was imaginary. One of those students, W. Swanson, after going on to Chicago for further study, wrote to him to acknowledge the truth of Shortt's observations. Swanson added, "really the people of Ontario and New York State have far more in common than the people of Ontario and Quebec," a comment that resonates with much more impact today, in the aftermath of the most recent

Quebec referendum, than it did at the beginning of the twentieth century (correspondence from W. Swanson to Adam Shortt, 13 January 1906, cited in Berger 1972, 34 n. 4).

If the boundary line was believed by some to be imaginary at the beginning of the twentieth century, can we trace this perception back any further? One of the earliest American historians of immigration to North America, Marcus L. Hansen, shrewdly observed that "immigrants viewed the continent as a whole." Hansen went on, "it was not the United States and Canada. It was all of America to them" (1937, 106). Another historian of Canada, J.B. Brebner, carried the idea further still. The immigrants were "eminently capable of allegiance to one country one day and to another the next" (cited in Berger 1972, 47). [...]

We may be much less conscious of fundamental differences between two separate countries than our predecessors were in the early nineteenth century. During the period when Upper Canada was a separate colony, 1791–1840, an era marked by war and rebellion, visitors and inhabitants alike commented knowingly on the contrasts between British America and the United States (Wise 1993, 45–60). [...]

[...] There was a sense of vivid differences between the British colonies and the United States, a vividness born in Upper Canada by a Loyalist culture strongly reinforced by the experience and memories, first of the American Revolution and then of the War of 1812. Underlying it, of course, was a boastful pride of Britons and many colonists in the unquestioned superiority of the monarchy and British institutions, matched no less on the other side of the border by an equally aggressive pride held by Americans in their Republican ideals and institutions, as well as the conviction held by many that the inevitable destiny of the Canadas was to become part of the United States. Even the failure of the 1837 rebellions did not squelch this conviction.

*****

The border between the United States and Upper Canada in the early nineteenth century was much more than a boundary line between republic and empire. The frontier areas on both sides witnessed not only the increased traffic brought by growing trade, population movements, and the tourist magnet of Niagara Falls, but also clashes between rival states and armed incursions during the two periods of war and heightened tension, 1812–14 and 1837–38. What then was the interaction between justice and the frontier?

Apart from periods of war and armed rebellion when restrictions on the usual access to the border were expected, if not always totally accepted, the normal peacetime expectation was that movement across the border was untrammelled and open to anyone. Individuals freely crossed the border, including immigrants, but legal commerce was tied up in the tariffs of the old colonial system until the middle of the century. When anything occurred to interrupt this, the reaction was quick and forceful. The appearance of cholera in the summer of 1832 prompted emergency measures on both sides of the border in an attempt to prevent the rapid spreading of the disease. [...]

*****

Just as there was a growing traffic in legitimate commerce and population flows, so there was also a complicated pattern of illegal movements across the border. Criminals escaping justice or jail regularly fled from one jurisdiction to the other; soldiers deserted or tried to desert by fleeing across the border; African slaves crossed into Upper Canada seeking freedom; and goods were illegally smuggled across the border then as they are now. The illegal movements tended to concentrate in three regions where there was a close proximity between communities on each side of the border; Kingston, the Niagara region, and the area of Amherstberg and Sandwich opposite Detroit.

These activities gave rise to what I will call acts of private or community justice, as well as the ever present efforts of authorities to maintain official justice. [...] A brief survey of the issues of extradition, banishment, desertion, and smuggling, highlighting a few cases, will illustrate the complexity of relationships between the political border and the illegal movements of people and goods across it. For, if borders create regions of interaction and elements of division, the criminal justice system should illuminate both, often in unusual ways.

Extradition

At the local level, by the 1830s, the magistrates on the Upper Canadian side of the border had developed a close and effective working relationship with their counterparts on the American side. When John Fitzgerald, an Irishman suspected of committing a murder in Waterford, Ireland, in the early 1820s, was discovered to be living in Niagara in 1832 and working as a tavern keeper, he quickly slipped across to the United States after learning that he was about to be arrested. Normally, he might have been able to escape, but the Niagara magistrates were able to issue a warrant and persuade the American officials to arrest him within a day. He was brought across the frontier to the Niagara jail and ultimately sent home to Ireland to face trial.[1] Without this prompt action by the Americans, the Canadian authorities would have lost Fitzgerald.

Charles Eliot, an Upper Canadian magistrate at Sandwich opposite Detroit, wanted to act in the same cooperative manner in November 1832, when he received a request from the Michigan authorities to return two men, James Walker and William Bird, suspects in a series of thefts on the Detroit shore. Eliot obligingly had them arrested and jailed, prior to being turned over to the Americans. When he asked the government officials at York to issue the necessary instructions, a wall of legal roadblocks suddenly appeared. Eliot understandably was anxious to facilitate cross-border cooperation in the return of suspected criminals. He pressed his case forcefully with Sir John Colborne, the lieutenant-governor.

> In justice to the Americans I must declare that they have ever evinced extreme eagerness to protect us from the mischief attending the escape of such hardened monsters: they have most readily arrested and resigned, at our request, both murderers and thieves. How merited then, would be the reproach upon us, were we in no one instance to alternate with them.[2]

The governor promptly turned this legal nettle over to his attorney-general, Henry Boulton, who issued an opinion stating that without solid evidence to implicate the accused men in a crime, he could not support the local magistrate.[3] To resolve the impasse, the government arranged for an unusual legal hearing where the attorney-general acted as a private counsel for the prisoners and the solicitor-general acted for the crown before one of the province's King's Bench judges, James Macaulay.[4] The government's purpose was to obtain a definitive judicial ruling on the province's legal obligation to return fugitives to the United States. Mr. Justice Macaulay obliged with a long judgement in which he reviewed all the available legal precedents, including American ones. He found nothing in the warrant of committal of the suspects to verify that they were, indeed, American citizens. He concluded in the absence of such evidence that they were British subjects, entitled to all the protection of British law and specifically the rights of the

Habeas Corpus Act. Macaulay ordered their release from jail under Habeas Corpus, which prevented their being sent to a foreign country for trial, in spite of the general impression of their likely guilt in the cross-border thefts. Walker and Bird were both identified in the court documents as black, but other than this identification, there is no implication that race played any part whatever in the outcome of this case.

The government must have been disappointed in its hope of finding judicial clarification. Macaulay wrote that each case where a request to transfer a fugitive came from the United States "must be decided on its own peculiar features & merits." Cases of murder might be dealt with more expeditiously, but Macaulay stressed that "in each instance the nature of the offence—the degree of proof—the political character of the fugitive—the promptness of the pursuit & application," must all be carefully scrutinized by the Upper Canadian courts before a fugitive could be transferred to the United States.[5] Macaulay also concluded that there was no existing law or treaty governing the transfer of fugitives between territories of the United States and Upper Canada. Jay's Treaty (1794) originally had provided that anyone charged with murder or forgery could be aimed over to the other country, but Article 27 containing this clause had expired in 1803 and had never been renewed (Bemis 1962, 482–83; Burt [1940] 1961, 198). The top legal officials and judges at York, by now all Upper Canadians, were determined to apply British law in each case, even if this meant disrupting the harmonious local networks of cross-border judicial cooperation. Solicitor-General Hagerman summed up the law for the lieutenant-governor, following Mr Justice Macaulay's ruling. "The power to surrender fugitives from a foreign country—*such fugitives being subjects of that Country*—*is Discretionary with the Government,* but that discretion was never exercised in sending away subjects of His Majesty or residents within his dominions."[6]

Charles Eliot, the Sandwich magistrate who originally had raised the question with the government, was dumbfounded by the outcome. When he heard about it in January 1833, he was in the midst of another complicated case involving forgers who were operating on both sides of the border. He pleaded for guidance on what he should do in future and he wrote, plaintively,

What shall I say on this liberation to His Excellency, Governor Porter [of Michigan] after his prompt & effectual exertions to serve us? And how can we now apply to him for Crofts, alias Crawford, who has passed so many forged bills on our side & to so many of our poorer Inhabitants, & against whom I have conclusive testimony?[7]

Not only was Eliot's credibility badly damaged as the story of the release quickly spread on both sides of the border, but he found himself vilified by at least one of his fellow magistrates for arresting suspects at the instigation of the Americans. Eliot's latest dilemma, how to prosecute the suspected forger, Crofts, was made worse by the fact that an American grand jury had not been able to indict Crofts because of a lack of evidence. As Eliot informed the lieutenant-governor, Crofts "has been astute enough never to pass a forged Bill on his own side of the river."[8]

This time, however, the attorney-general was firmly on the side of the magistrate. The Evidence is so strong-and flagrant," that Eliot was ordered to apply immediately to have the suspect, Crofts, transferred to Upper Canada for trial. Should the Michigan laws require a formal request from the lieutenant-governor, Attorney-General Boulton recommended that this be done. Where forgers were concerned, "it is evidently the Interest of both Countries to put down this Nefarious System of fraud which is practised with too much Success by gangs of Villains infecting both sides of the Water."[9] Eliot had not waited for instructions from the Upper Canadian capital. He had visited

the governor of Michigan to lay before him all the evidence he had gathered. Governor Porter ordered Crofts to be imprisoned until a formal application for transfer came from the Upper Canadian government. Eliot strongly believed in reciprocity of treatment across the border and he was immensely relieved to hear that one outcome of the legal imbroglio over fugitive criminals was a new Upper Canadian law, the first one to be passed, outlining the conditions for the return of fugitives to the United States. This would help to reassure the American authorities that the return of criminals would be reciprocated. Eliot asked for extra copies of the law not just for the Upper Canadian magistrates in his area, but some for the Americans as well, "whose ever prompt compliance with our wishes indubitably merits our warmest thanks."[10] The fugitive offenders act came into force early in February 1833, and gave the government all the legal powers it needed to return those "charged with Murder, Forgery, Larceny, or other crime" to the United States upon application through the proper authorities.[11] This act governed all extradition proceedings between Upper Canada and the United States until it was superseded by the Webster-Ashburton Treaty of 1842.

*****

Banishment

Upper Canadian government officials did not view the frontier solely as a source of problems. They were quick to use the proximity of the border when it suited their purposes. Undesirables were banished to the United States. The modification of British criminal law by the Upper Canadian legislature in 1800 to incorporate banishment as a criminal punishment was a conscious recognition of the ease and economy of transferring Upper Canada's criminals to the United States.[12] It was also, as the law itself stated, an acknowledgement that transportation overseas in official Upper Canadian eyes was either "inapplicable" or it could not be implemented without "great and manifest inconvenience."[13] Banishment was the

Upper Canadian version of transportation but, viewed from the perspective of the criminals affected, it was a far less severe punishment and highly preferable to an alternative like execution. Not until 1842 was banishment formally replaced by imprisonment in Canadian law. In practice, however, the opening of the Kingston Penitentiary in 1835 meant that many criminals who earlier might have been banished were now sent instead to Kingston. The following year, the British government opened Van Diemen's land to North American colonies for the transportation of their criminals. A number of Upper Canadian criminals were transported there, including many convicted for their part in the 1837–38 rebellions.

The appearance of cholera in 1832 gave a new twist to the use of banishment by the Upper Canadian government. A number of prisoners confined in local jails and fearing for their own safety in the midst of a cholera epidemic petitioned the lieutenant-governor for pardon. The governor referred these petitions to Chief Justice Robinson for his advice. Robinson's solution for the prisoners convicted of the more serious crimes was to recommend banishment. […] The royal pardon really had become a vehicle for dumping Upper Canada's unwanted prisoners on her neighbour's frontier in the full expectation that they would find a new home somewhere in the United States. Banishment could be controversial in Upper Canada as the Standish affair had proved. A grand jury in the Gore District protested to the lieutenant-governor that the practice had "a most baneful effect ... upon the moral Condition of the people of this District" because several of those banished had returned. They were seen by their neighbours as having escaped the punishment of the law. The grand jury argued that this would "have the effect of encouraging the vicious and unprincipled to go on in Crime with a hope of impunity."[14]

*****

We rarely hear what the criminals themselves felt about being forced to move from one state to another. In one case where an Upper Canadian fugitive sought refuge in the United States to avoid imprisonment on a murder charge, we do have a letter from him, justifying his action. John Ward had escaped to Michigan early in 1830 and wrote a letter home, intended for his family, although it ended up in the hands of the government officials. His explanation does have a certain logic, viewed from his desperate position; "i think it is better for me to keep my liberty untill i Can have my trial. It will make it no better if i Should ly in prison untill then."[15] For Ward, as for the other criminals or criminal suspects who fled across the border seeking sanctuary, the boundary was a minor obstacle easily overcome. […]

*****

Some convicts openly used the United States as a temporary refuge. David Underhill was convicted in the Gore District in 1829 of assault and battery and sentenced to three months' imprisonment and a fine. On the way from court to the jail, he escaped and fled to the United States, where he remained nearly a year. Then he quietly returned to his family, apparently hoping to escape notice. This ploy was unsuccessful. He was recaptured and taken to prison. He was then able to use compassionate circumstances, a likely terminal illness, poverty, and a pregnant wife, to appeal successfully for clemency.[16]

*****

How effective was banishment? Since the Upper Canadian authorities never analyzed it, nor did they even keep statistics of the number banished and those who returned, it is difficult to answer the question. The absence of American complaints suggest the numbers were small enough to escape official notice in the United States. Chief Justice Robinson remained a strong proponent of banishment until feasible alternatives emerged in the middle of the 1830s, principally the Kingston Penitentiary. His continuing support is one indication that in this early period of Upper Canadian history banishment offered a cheap, ad hoc alternative for government officials anxious to avoid either long and costly imprisonments in overcrowded local jails, or a rash of public hangings which might bring unwanted political attention to the colony's largely inherited system of criminal laws. Banishment thus served as a ready safety valve for the Upper Canadian colonial government from 1800 to the mid 1830s.

Deserters

The American border was a powerful magnet for deserters from the British army who were stationed at posts along the frontier from Kingston to Detroit. [...]

*****

The number of British deserters rose rapidly in the years following the end of the War of 1812. Immediately following the end of the war, complaints about British army deserters being seduced by the Americans mounted. [...] Richard Preston, in his study of Kingston before the War of 1812, discovered that "a successful breakaway by one deserter always proved infectious and would be followed by others" (1959, lxxxiv). Their British officers professed to be mystified by the continuous desertions. One wrote in Kingston in 1801, "I have done every thing in my power to find out the cause of this Spirit of Desertion without Effect" (correspondence from Mackenzie to Green, 8 September 1801, cited in Preston 1959, 247). Some deserters were promptly recruited into the United States army, although the Americans insisted that they officially discouraged the practice. John Richardson, writing in the 1840s about his years in the Canadas, claimed that five thousand had deserted for the United States in the years between 1815 and 1838. The main centres for this unofficial emigration movement were Niagara, Kingston, and Amherstberg. [...]

Peter Burroughs has written the most thorough account of British desertion in nineteenth-century British North America. He has tabulated figures for the Canadas of six thousand desertions between 1815 and 1840,

an average annual desertion rate of over five percent of the army establishment (Burroughs 1980, table 1, 30). The highest annual desertion rates occurred in the middle years of the 1830s. Desertions occurred for many different reasons but, as Burroughs stresses, some soldiers had enlisted deliberately to have their fares paid to North America, with a clear intention of staying there by deserting to the United States. British officers especially blamed the Irish. Lieutenant-Governor Arthur wrote to the government in 1838; "They all have relations or friends settled in the States, and what will bind an Irish Soldier if he has the opportunity of seeing his *cousin*" (correspondence from Arthur to Somerset, 24 November 1838, cited in Burroughs 1980, 34–35). The real causes were more mundane and easily understood. British soldiers were no less attracted than civilians to the United States, "where wages were known to be higher than those prevailing in Canada or in Britain itself and where good land was readily available to purchasers of limited means" (Burroughs 1980, 36). For these deserters, crossing the frontier opened the gate to a new life in a new country free from the confines of the military. It was not altogether a one-way movement of soldiers, nor of course were the military authorities on either side content to let it go on unchallenged, even if their efforts to stop it were largely unsuccessful. [...]

*****

The governors of Upper Canada during this period, nearly all of them military officers, along with the colony's judges, regarded the crime of enticing to desert as a most serious one and dealt very harshly with anyone convicted of it. Albert Spear was a young man, aged twenty, when he was convicted of trying to help a soldier to desert to the United States at Amherstberg. Pleading for a pardon after spending fourteen months in the district jail, Spear claimed he had been intoxicated when the offence occurred. The lieutenant-governor referred the petition to Judge L.P. Sherwood, who had presided at the trial. Sherwood replied with an argument he must have known would appeal to Colborne who, in his capacity as governor, was also the Commander-in-chief of the British forces in the colony.

> When it is considered that the facility of passing the frontier of the province from Amherstberg into the United States is a great inducement to desertion, and that the hope of assistance creates confidence in those inclined to desert, the public good seems to require examples to be made of such persons.[17]

Colborne agreed with Judge Sherwood and rejected the petition.

Smuggling

Smuggling was rampant across the border between the United States and Britain's Canadian colonies. The major reason was British insistence on maintaining her mercantilistic system of customs duties, which she applied to her colonies until she finally shifted to free trade in 1846, and then signed the Reciprocity Treaty with the United States in 1854. The Duke de la Rochefoucauld Liancourt observed the impact in the 1790s. "The high duty laid by England upon all the commodities exported from her islands proves a powerful encouragement to a contraband trade with the United States, where, in many articles, the difference of price amounts to two-thirds" (Liancourt 1799, v.1, 247). Key foodstuffs like tea could not be imported directly from the United States without duties because of the monopoly retained by the East India Company. The incentive to smuggling was irresistible. William Lyon Mackenzie wrote of personally witnessing a tea-smuggling operation from Youngstown, New York to Fort George right under the noses of British soldiers who made no effort whatever to intervene. He concluded that smuggling tea and other American goods across the border, especially at Niagara, "must have been nearly universal" (Mackenzie 1833, 81–84).

American treasury officials, perhaps even more than the British, tried their utmost to put a stop to smuggling across the border, but from both sides the officials could only intercept a trickle of the huge stream of smuggled goods regularly crossing the line. [...] Cross border trade, both legal and illegal, steadily increased in the first half of the nineteenth century. The locals, especially those living next to the frontier, refused to equate smuggling with crime, especially since it usually proved so lucrative (Stuart 1988, 106–16).

Smugglers did not always escape the clutches of the magistrates and customs officers. One bizarre episode along the Niagara frontier illustrates the hazards of a smuggling mission gone awry. On 5 December 1825, at about ten o' clock at night, Robert Grant, the Collector of Customs in Queenston, heard that three wagons had just passed through the village. Suspecting smugglers, he took a constable with him and set off immediately in pursuit. They caught up with the suspects at a barn near St. Catharines around midnight. Grant seized the wagons and discovered that they contained metal stoves and boxes of window glass, all manufactured in the United States. There must have been a ready market for American stoves and window glass, but these are not the first objects to come to mind when we think of cross-border contraband in this period. We can, however, infer their value from the subsequent actions of the smugglers. They would not give up their booty without a fight. They attacked the Collector of Customs and his constable with stones, poles, and rails. The constable claimed that "he rather got the better" of one of his assailants, but when another tried "to deprive him of his eyes," he gave in. The smugglers escaped temporarily with all their goods except for a stove, which fell out of the back of one of the wagons as they fled.

Robert Grant petitioned the Quarter Sessions court at Niagara early in January 1826 for a full criminal prosecution, which the court endorsed. A trial occurred at the fall assizes, held in Niagara. The chief culprit, William Terrybery, a forty-two-year-old St. Catharines innkeeper who apparently was well known to the local authorities, was convicted on the charge of rescuing smuggled property and sentenced to three months imprisonment and a twenty-five dollar fine. He was one of the very few of what must have been a steady stream of smugglers along the Niagara frontier in this period to be caught, successfully prosecuted, and imprisoned. Had he not resisted arrest in such a violent manner, he likely would have escaped with only the confiscation of his smuggled goods. Unlike those convicted of enticing soldiers to desert, who regularly appear on the jail returns of the border districts like Niagara, Terryberry stands out as a rare Upper Canadian convict because of the crime for which he was convicted.[18]

Conclusion

*****

However much the notion of a common North American individualism, lying just underneath the surface on both sides of the border, may prove to be a more seductive interpretive framework for early nineteenth-century Canadian–American relations, it should not be given a completely free rein. True borderlanders certainly existed, but even by 1840 they were far from a majority. Cross-border contacts became both broader and deeper, but the border itself never disappeared. In Upper Canada, British law, British institutions, and British concepts of justice had sunk deep roots, giving the border both a political and cultural configuration. Philip Buckner argues that in this period people on both sides of the political border "knew on which side they belonged and, equally importantly, who belonged on the other side" (1989, 157). Like dangerous chemicals, the border regions could

prove to be highly unstable, as in 1837–38, bringing Britain and the United States much closer to possible conflict than either desired. The border remained part of the inescapable and ever present political, social, and economic reality of Upper Canadian existence.

Upper Canada's frontier brought into sharp focus the complex problems thrown up by the criminal justice systems on both sides of the line. Criminals, smugglers, deserters, and others of nineteenth-century society's outcasts moved regularly across the Upper Canadian–U.S. border only to disappear as quickly as water through sand. In their own unique way they were continentalists, operating with a North American individuality, not confined and certainly not shackled by political boundaries. Even Upper Canadian government officials, whose task was to enforce the laws and regulations which made the boundary a very real political frontier, discovered the utility of making it permeable when it came to banishing prisoners. For these officials, the border took on different coloration depending on whether it offered a convenient and cheap solution to the vexing dilemmas of overcrowded local jails, or whether it seemed to be the source of nagging and insoluble problems like smuggling or desertion. Both the criminals and the officials learned quickly how to manipulate the political frontier to their own purposes. Through the criminal justice systems on both sides of the political frontier, we gain a new perspective of the border in this colonial period as well as insights into the different political cultures evolving in the United States and British North America.

Notes

1. Daniel McDougal to Lt. Col. Rowan, 26 December 1832, with enclosed affidavits. NA, R.G. 5. Al, UCS. v. 124:68246–267.

2. Charles Eliot to Lt. Col Rowan, 29 November 1832, N A, R.G. 5, Al, UCS, v. 124:68185–186.

3. Attorney-General Boulton to Lt. Col. Rowan, 10 December 1832, NA, R.G. 5, A1, UCS, v. 124:68187.

4. For a brief biography of Macaulay, see Read (1888, 148–57).

5. Justice Macaulay's "Notes on The King vs. James Bird and William Walker," 29 December 1832, NA, R.G. 5, Al, UCS, v. 124:68614–627.

6. Solicitor-General Hagerman to Lt. Col. Rowan, 1 January 1833, NA, R.G. 5, Al, UCS, v. 125:68817–18. Also see Attorney-General Boulton to Lt. Col.

Rowan, 3 January 1833, NA, R.G. 5, Al, UCS, v. 125:68842–843.

7. Charles Eliot to Lt. Col. Rowan, 14 January 1833, NA- R.G. 5, Al. UCS, v. 125:69014-015.

8. Charles Eliot to Lt. Col. Rowan, 24 January 1833 and enclosed, W.H. Witherell, U.S. District Attorney, to Charles Eliot, 18 January 1833, NA, R.G. 5, Al, UCS, v. 125: 69157–160.

9. Attorney-General Boulton to Lt. Col. Rowan, 19 January 1833, NA, R.G. 5, Al, UCS, v. 125:69110.

10. Charles Eliot to Lt. Col. Rowan, 24 January 1833, NA, R.G. 5, Al, UCS, v. 125:69157–158.

11. William IV, c.vii, "An Act to provide for the Apprehending of Fugitive Offenders from Foreign Countries, and delivering them to Justice."

12. The following argument suggests that banishment was seen as more effective by key members of the Upper Canadian government than John Weaver's

recent conclusion that "it was never a satisfactory form of punishment" (1995, 61).

13. 40 Geo. III c.1, "An Act for the further introduction of the Criminal Law of England into this Province and for the more effectual Punishment of certain Offenders."

14. Grand jury presentment, Gore District, 1 September 1831, NA, R.G. 5. Al, UCS, v. 109:62205.

15. John Ward to Schofleld, 4 April 1830, enclosed in M. Burwell to Z. Mudge, 17 April 1830, NA, R.G. 5, Al, UCS, v. 99s 56093–097.

16. Petition of David Underhill, 18 June 1831, and enclosed John Wilson to Z. Mudge, 13 June 1831, NA. R.G. 5, Al. UCS, v. 107:61178–179.

17. LP. Sherwood to Edward McMahon. 27 September 1831, NA. R.O.5. Al. UCS, v. 109:62053–054.

18. The documents on this case are found in NA, M.G. 24126, v. 49; depositions dated 12 December 1825, and Quarter Sessions decision 11 January 1826.

Works Cited

Baglier, Janet. 1993, "The Niagara Frontier Society and Economy in Western New York and Upper Canada, 1794–1854." Ph.D. dissertation, State University of New York at Buffalo.

Bemis, Samuel Flagg. 1962. *Jay's Treaty: A Study in Commerce and Diplomacy.* 2nd Edition. New Haven: Yale University Press.

Berger, Carl. 1972. "Internationalism, Continentalism, and the Writing of History: Comments on the Carnegie Series on the Relations of Canada and the United States." In *The Influence of the United States on Canadian Development: Eleven Case Studies,* edited by Richard A. Preston. Durham, N.C.: Duke University Press.

_____. 1976. *The Writing of Canadian History, Aspects of English-Canadian Historical Writing, 1900–1970.* Toronto: Oxford University Press.

Bothwell, Robert. 1992. *Canada and the United States: The Politics of Partnership.* Toronto: University of Toronto Press.

Buckner, P.A. 1989. "The Borderlands Concept." In *The Northeastern Borderlands: Four Centuries of Interaction,* edited by Stephen J. Hornsby, Victor A, Konrad, and James J. Herlan. Fredericton, N.B.: Acadiensis Press.

Burroughs, Peter. 1980. "Tackling Army Desertion in British North America," *Canadian Historical Review* 61 (1): 28–68.

Burt, A.L. [1940] 1961. *The United Slates, Great Britain and British North America from the Revolution to*

the Establishment of Peace after the War of 1812. New Haven: Yale University Press.

Callahan, James M. [1937] 1961. *American Foreign Policy in Canadian Relations.* New York: Macmillan.

Canada. National Archives. M.0.24126, Alexander Hamilton Papers, v. 49.

_____. National Archives. R.G. 5, Al, Upper Canada Sundries, v. 9, 82, 99, 101–102, 105, 107–109, 116–117, 122, 123–125.

Cruikshank, E.A. 1931. "The Troubles of a Collector of Customs." In *A Memoir of Colonel the Honourable James Kerby, His Life in Letters.* Welland, Ontario: Welland County Historical Society.

Errington, Jane. 1987. *The Lion, the Eagle, and Upper Canada: A Developing Colonial Ideology.* Montreal and Kingston: McGill-Queen's Press.

Errington, Jane, and George Rawlyk. 1984. "The Loyalist-Federalist Alliance of Upper Canada," *The American Review of Canadian Studies* 14 (2): 157–76.

Fidler, Reverend Isaac. 1833. *Observations on Professions, Literature, Manners, and Emigration in the United States and Canada, Made during a Residence There in 1832.* London: Whittaker, Treacher.

Hall, Basil. [1830] 1974. *Travels in North America in the Years 1827 and 1828.* New York: Arno Press.

Hansen, Marcus L. 1937. "A Resumé of Canadian–American Population Relations." In *Proceedings* [of the Conference on Canadian-American Affairs], edited by R.O. Trotter, A.B. Corey, and W.W. McLaren. Conference held at Queen's University, Kingston, Ontario 14–18 June 1937. New York.

Hansen, Marcus L., and J.B. Brebner. 1940. *The Mingling of Canadian and American Peoples.* New Haven: Yale University Press.

Hillmer, Norman, and Jack Oranatstein. 1991. *For Better or Worse: Canada and the United States to the 1990s.* Toronto: Copp Clark Pitman.

Keenleyside, Hugh. 1929. *Canada and the United States: Some Aspects of the History of the Republic and the Dominion.* New York: A.A. Knopf.

Landon, Fred. 1967. *Western Ontario and the American Frontier.* Ottawa: Carleton University Press.

Mackenzie, W.L. 1833. *Sketches of Canada and the United States.* London: E. Wilson.

Moorman, David. 1996. "Where are the English and Americans in the Historiography of Upper Canada?" *Ontario History* 88 (I): 65–69.

Preston, Richard A., ed. 1959. *Kingston Before the War of 1812.* The Champlain Society: University of Toronto Press.

_____. 1972. *The Influence of the United States on Canadian Development: Eleven Case Studies.* Durham, N.C.: Duke University Press.

Read, D.B. 1888. *The Lives of the Judges of Upper Canada and Ontario from 1791 to the Present Time.* Toronto: Rowsell and Hutchison.

Richardson, John. [1847] 1967. *Eight Years in Canada.* New York: S.R. Publishers.

Shirreff, Patrick. [1835] 1971. *A Tour through North America: Together with a Comprehensive View of the Canadas and the United States.* Reprint edition edited by Benjamin Blom. [1835] Edinburgh: Oliver and Boyd; (1971) New York: B. Blom.

Snell, J.G. 1989. "The International Border as a Factor in Marital Behaviour: A Historical Case Study." *Ontario History* 81 (4): 289–302.

Stevens, Kenneth R. 1989. *Border Diplomacy: The Caroline and McLeod Affairs in Anglo-American-Canadian Relations, 1837–1842.* Tuscaloosa: University of Alabama Press.

Stewart, Gordon T. 1992. *The American Response to Canada since 1776.* East Lansing: Michigan State University Press.

Strum, Harvey. 1988. "A Most Cruel Murder: The Isaac Underhill Affair, 1809," *Ontario History* 80 (4): 293–310.

Stuart, Reginald. 1988. *United States Expansionism and British North America, 1775–1871.* Chapel Hill: University of North Carolina Press.

Thompson, John Herd, and Stephen J. Randall. 1994. *Canada and the United States: Ambivalent Allies.* Athens and London: University of Georgia Press.

Weaver, John. 1995. *Crimes, Constables and Courts: Order and Transgression in a Canadian City, 1816–1970.* Montreal and Kingston: McGill-Queen's University Press.

Wise, S.F. 1993. "Canadians View the United States: Colonial Attitudes from the Era of the War of 1812 to the Rebellions of 1837." In *God's Peculiar Peoples: Essays on Political Culture in Nineteenth-Century Canada,* edited by A.B. McKillop and Paul Romney. Ottawa: Carleton University Press.

Legal Acts

3 William IV, c.vii, "An act to provide for the Apprehending of Fugitive Offenders from Foreign Countries, and delivering them up to Justice."

40 Geo. III ci. "An Act for the further introduction of the Criminal Law of England into this Province and for the effectual Punishment of certain Offenders."

CHAPTER 3

The Mounties as Vigilantes: Perceptions of Community and the Transformation of Law in the Yukon, 1885–1897

Thomas Stone

• •

Introduction

When the North West Mounted Police were dispatched to the Yukon district in the 1890s, they confronted a population of largely American or Americanized miners who were relying on the "miners' meeting"—a fully autonomous, highly democratic, and egalitarian institution—as the basis for law and government in the gold camps.[1] Given the prevailing image of the undisciplined and disorderly American frontiersman,[2] coupled with the distrust of American democratic institutions which characterized Canadian opinion[3] it is hardly surprising that the arrival of the Mounties was widely viewed as posing a confrontation between Canadian law and American frontier lawlessness. In the popular imagination of both Canadians and Americans, the Mounties of the Yukon became a symbol of justice, peace, and order in the district, their presence serving as the only barrier to dangerous and potentially violent anarchy.

The facts of the case, however, appear otherwise. The evidence suggests that before the summer of 1897, when the Klondike rush began in earnest and the character of Yukon society was radically transformed, "lawlessness" was not a problem. There is little indication that people were either in serious danger of having their rights violated or that they lacked an effective

remedy for those grievances that did arise. The presence of the Mounties, which displaced the authority of the miners' meeting in Canadian territory, did little to improve the administration of justice. In certain respects, in fact, it appears only to have incapacitated it. On the other hand the Mounties did effectively symbolize class dominance in a situation where incipient stratification and a perception of threatened class conflict were beginning to emerge. And in this role, ironically, the Mounties stand as the counterpart in the Yukon of the vigilante movements which emerged on the American mining frontier.[4]

The case of the Mounties in the Yukon, however, has even broader relevance. The miners' response to the appearance of the police provides an illustration of the distinction between the symbolic and instrumental functions of law and the role of the former in conditioning public attitudes toward legal institutions. Legal agencies perform an instrumental function through law enforcement and dispute resolution. At the same time they perform the symbolic function of publicly affirming social ideals and dominant norms.[5] While the instrumental and symbolic functions of legal agencies often arise from the same activities, they are analytically separate[6] and often pull in different directions.

In the present case, the appearance of the Mounties failed to improve—and indeed demonstrably weakened—the instrumental functions of law in the Yukon district. Nonetheless, their authority was quickly accepted and hailed as a welcome replacement for the miners' meeting by the established miners and their spokesman. The reason for this, it can be shown, lies in the fact that the authority of the Mounties reliably ensured the public affirmation of established community values and norms at a time when these were perceived as being threatened.

The Miners' Meeting in the Yukon

By 1894, the year the Canadian government first dispatched Charles Constantine of the North West Mounted Police to the territory, the region of the upper Yukon drainage in the vicinity of the Alaska–Canada boundary had drawn a substantial influx of gold miners and prospectors. Their activities were largely centred in two districts on opposite sides of the border. At the junction of Fortymile Creek and the Yukon River, in Canadian territory, there was Fortymile post, a town of some 150 log buildings, mostly cabins, but including saloons, restaurants, a theatre, and a billiard room.[7] Fortymile was the supply centre for the major mining district on the Yukon in 1894. Close to 1000 miners worked in the district in the summer of 1894.[8] Downriver to the Northwest, across the international boundary in Alaska, a new supply post was just being established that same summer to service the newly discovered Birch Creek mining district. A year later, Circle City (as this new post came to be called) and the Birch Creek district not only rivalled but had begun to outstrip Fortymile as a centre of population and mining activity in the region, even though the Fortymile district itself did not substantially decline in population.[9]

Gold prospectors and miners had been drifting into the region in increasing numbers since 1878, but mining activity was scattered and desultory until strikes on the Stewart River in 1885, followed quickly by the Fortymile strike in 1886, concentrated the population first

(briefly) at the Stewart, and then at Fortymile. Fortymile then dominated the upper Yukon, remaining the centre of population and mining activity until the discoveries on Birch Creek. In the early years, a small summer population would typically shrink to an even smaller community of less than one hundred miners and prospectors who would remain during the long winter season, gathered together in winter quarters at the site of a trading post. With the arrival of the relatively short summer season, the men would again disperse to prospecting or mining operations on the creeks, joined by a summer influx of returning and new prospectors entering the district. As time went on, the size of the summer influx and the smaller wintering population grew markedly.

From the beginning of mining operations until the Klondike rush of 1897, other trends in the social development of the region can be noted. Not only did population increase steadily, but noteworthy institutional growth and elaboration took place as Fortymile (and later Circle) acquired the trappings of civilization. The population also became less homogeneous as women began to arrive and occupational diversity increased.

*****

It was this changing Yukon society which provided the context for the operation of the miners' meeting, an institution which had emerged by 1885 to provide for the administration of law and government in the camps and which had its roots in the early system of camp government in California and the American West (reflecting the American origin of many of the Yukon prospectors). The miners' meeting was simply an assembly of all those residents in a particular camp who chose to attend when a meeting was called. This assembly considered with a minimum of formality question which might provide the occasion for its being called. Decisions were rendered by a simple majority vote. In cases where it might be deemed necessary, a committee of the assembled miners was elected to the execution of the meeting's decision. [...]

*****

[...] The jurisdiction assumed by these meetings was wide ranging: they functioned as a forum for the disposition of private disputes; they prosecuted what could be regarded as crimes; they established special mining regulations which might apply in a particular creek or locality; and they established by-laws relating to almost any conceivable matter of public concern within the camp.[10] Decisions and action taken through a miners' meeting might range from seemingly trivial matters, such as the case where a meeting acted to prevent a white saloon-keeper from reneging on a marriage proposal to a half-breed Indian girl,[11] to the potentially dangerous (and, by outside standards, illegal), as in the case of a decision to commandeer a winter supply outfit for each man from a passing riverboat.[12]

During the period of community growth, from 1885 to the Klondike rush in 1897, the setting for these assemblies changed from small camps of a few miners depending on a particular post for supplies, to sizable towns with a substantial population drawn from widely scattered camps and where the meetings in later years were often held in one of the town saloons. [...]

[...] The meetings dispensed a form of justice where character judgments figured prominently and the prevention of possible future trouble was an overriding concern. [...] Decisions regarding the rights which should be accorded and enforced on behalf of any party rested heavily on judgments of individual character derived from participants' knowledge and impressions of a person's behaviour and attitudes.

*****

[...] Evidence for this can be found in the decisions reached in individual cases and in the type of penalties administered for particular offences.

On the Stewart River, for example, in the year before the establishment of Fortymile,

one member of a party of five miners attempted to poison, then shoot the others before he was discovered and apprehended by his partners.[13] The murder attempt was carried out by the man who had originally organized the party, a man referred to simply as "Discoverer." Discoverer claimed to have had first-hand information about a lost mine in the Yukon district. He convinced the others in Seattle of the truth of his information, and headed north with them. After a season of unsuccessful prospecting for this fabulous source of gold, the party was forced to settle in for the winter on the Stewart. One particularly querulous member of the group began to talk of lynching Discoverer for misleading them, and while the others did not appear to take this talk seriously, neither did they openly oppose the idea. Discoverer ultimately concluded that his life was in danger and laced a supper of beans with a generous dose of arsenic. The others in the party became violently ill (and Discoverer feigned illness as well), but not fatally so. The following night when the others appeared to be sleeping, Discoverer was observed preparing to shoot one of the men. He got off his first shot, but fortunately missed, and was quickly restrained before he could fire again. Rather than administering punishment on the spot, it was decided to bring the matter to the whole camp at the mouth of the Stewart, some sixty miles away.

At the Stewart camp, a miners' meeting was called to hear the case, and both Discoverer and the others related their sides of the story. According to Ogilvie's informants, the earnest manner in which Discoverer related his perception of events convinced the miners of the genuineness of his own fear for his life, and some of the others in the party also admitted, quite frankly, that if they had been in Discoverer's position, they would have felt cause for alarm. As a result, according to Ogilvie:

It appeared to the majority that Discoverer acted in self-defence only, nevertheless, he was considered an undesirable citizen, and after much discussion it was decided to banish him, so he was furnished with a sled, provisions enough to get out if he could, and was ordered to move up-river at least one hundred and fifty miles from that camp, and assured that if ever he was seen within that distance of it, any one then present would be justified in shooting him on sight.[14]

In another case on the Stewart recorded by Ogilvie,[15] a seemingly much less serious "crime" which took place in the same winter received virtually the same sentence. Provisions for the camp on the Stewart had run very short by the fall of 1886, and the traders Harper and McQuesten had allotted equal shares of the available provisions to each man known to be working in the district. Later in the winter a miner known as "Missouri Frank" came in from his camp fifteen miles up the river; since he had already received the allotted amount of butter, Harper refused to sell him more. That night, Frank broke into the storehouse and absconded with all the remaining supply of butter, which amounted to the allotment for three or four men who had not yet come in to the post. When the butter was later missed, Missouri Frank was suspected, and a deputation of miners from the Stewart camp travelled up the river to apprehend him. His partner—whom Frank had told that he had purchased the butter at a high price—confessed to the extra supply which Missouri Frank had brought home. Frank was brought down to stand trial at a miners' meeting. In this case the vote was unanimous "that he be exiled from camp at least one hundred and fifty miles, and that he never come near it" again on penalty of death.[16] Ogilvie observes: "This may be considered a severe sentence for such a crime, but the idea appeared to be that he was a bad man, and lest he get the camp into difficulty over a killing, it was deemed best to get rid of him in time."[17] It is perhaps worth noting here that prior to this incident Missouri Frank had (rather unwisely, it would appear) "let it be assumed he was a bad man from somewhere"

and "had notches on his gun, and all the other insignia of the class."[18]

*****

In the case of the mining camps, [...] securing compensation or administering sanctions was, indeed, a function allocated to the community at large through the public institution miners' meeting, and case after case illustrates this. [...] The appeal to public authority and sanction in the institution of the miners' meeting, furthermore, was by no means limited to cases which might be conventionally regarded as involving "criminal" matters. Appeals to secure sanctions or damages or to otherwise adjudicate rights were common enough in disputes stemming from what could be regarded as voluntary and private arrangements.

*****

The Elimination of the Miners' Meeting: Canadian "Law" versus American "Lawlessness"

*****

The circumstances leading to the Canadian decision to establish the Mounted Police in the Yukon district are well documented. The government had dispatched G.M. Dawson, R.G. McConnell, and William Ogilvie to survey the upper Yukon region in 1887–88; this was the first official interest displayed by Canadian authorities in the district.[19] The question of establishing Canadian authority in the Yukon was raised at that point, but Ogilvie recommended against any such action, arguing that an attempt to impose Canadian laws would drive most of the prospectors to the American side of the international boundary[20] and thus militate against development of resources in the district. By 1893, however, the continuing expansion of mining activity and the increasing influx of American miners into the district led Ogilvie to reconsider. In his own words: it was "time we were moving in the matter of establishing authority over the Yukon in the gold fields, as we might, if the work were delayed, have to face annoyances, if not complications, through possession, without protest from us, by American citizens."[21]

Ogilvie's recommendation and the subsequent dispatch of Constantine and Brown the following year reflected a growing concern in Ottawa for the effective establishment and security of Canadian sovereignty in the region. Furthermore, there were private interests which had a stake in the effective imposition of Canadian sovereignty and law. In 1893, the government also received requests for the dispatch of police to the district from two other sources. Bishop William Bompas, an Anglican clergyman who maintained an Indian mission at Fortymile, requested the immediate dispatch of a magistrate and detachment of police to halt what he described as a burgeoning liquor trade with the Indians.[22] And the assistant manager of the North American Trading and Transportation Co., which operated a post adjacent to Fortymile, requested police assistance to regulate the liquor traffic in order to forestall potential trouble between the whites and the Indians, as well as to provide for the collection of customs duties.[23]

*****

Anticipating a hostile reaction from the miners, the Privy Council decision included a recommendation that Constantine proceed cautiously, specifically instructing that he:

Be on the spot to collect customs duties on all importations arriving in the Yukon district during the season of navigation, and that he be authorized to exercise, discretely [sic], but without risk of complications, the powers conferred upon him by his several commissions and towards the end of the season report on all subjects, with suggestions and recommendations, thus placing the government in possession of information upon which further development of a system of government in the Yukon district could be based.[24]

Furthermore, on the recommendation of NWMP Comptroller Frederick White,

Constantine was not to be styled an officer of the police but, rather, an "Agent of the Dominion Government."[25] White doubted "whether a police officer with only five men to enforce his authority would be met in a proper spirit by between three and four hundred miners who hitherto have respected no laws except those of their own making."[26]

In a subsequent letter to the Commissioner, White reiterated the need for circumspection:

With regard to the preservation of law and order. The Yukon District has hitherto been without any form of government, the inhabitants are principally of the mining class, and the mining operation [sic] are reported to be in the vicinity of the International Boundary. These conditions, together with the fact that Inspector Constantine will have to depend on the support of those in the District, will demand most careful judgement and discretion on his part. In the event of his finding a disposition to resist authority, he will abstain from exercising his Magisterial and Police powers until he has reported the condition of affairs for the consideration and instructions of the Government.[27]

Following his first visit to the Yukon camps, Constantine recommended dispatch of a force of more than forty men. "The miners are very jealous of what they consider their rights," Constantine wrote, "and from what I could see and learn, any enforcement of the different laws will have to be backed up with a strong force at least for a time."[28] A force of twenty men was dispatched in 1895, under the command of Constantine, but despite the fears of the police and officials in Ottawa, there was little resistance by the miners to the exercise of police authority and the imposition of Canadian law.

*****

[...] In his annual report for 1895 he noted that "no crime of any seriousness has been committed," and he enumerated only three incidents where the police had become involved: one case where a man was ordered out of the country to prevent trouble after he had taken another man's wife; one case of selling liquor to Indians; and one case of assault following which the accused individual fled Canadian territory.[29] Even the liquor trade appeared to pose no serious problem. In a letter to the Commissioner dated 4 September 1895, he reported that "The arrival of the police in this part of the country has almost finished the moving in of liquor, and in several cases where liquor had been ordered by the saloon men here, was the cause of the orders being cancelled."[30] [...]

*****

The presumption that the police would be faced with the task of imposing order on a chaotic and crime-ridden society was patently false. With or without police control, crime in the Yukon did not pose a problem. At Circle City, where the police exercised no authority whatsoever and where they assumed that the "criminal element" on the Canadian side of the border had retreated in the face of their authority, observers found things every bit as peaceful and crime free as at Fortymile. A.T. Walden, who was working as a dog driver at Circle City in 1896, described that American settlement in the following terms: "Here there was no murder, stealing, or dishonesty and right was right and wrong was wrong as each individual understood it. Here life property and honor were safe, justice was swift and sure, and punishments were made to fit the case."[31] [...]

There was one confrontation between police authority and the miners' meeting. In August 1895, the owner of a claim on Glacier Creek, in the Fortymile District, leased it to a man named Gordon. Gordon hired a number of men to work the claim for him, but failed to pay their wages and "jumped the country," going to Circle City. The workers who had lost their wages called a miners' meeting. Its decision was to order the owner of the claim to pay the wages owed by Gordon—a sum amounting to about $800. If the wages were not paid, the miners' meeting ruled, the claim was to be sold.

The owner protested to Constantine and requested police protection. Constantine then dispatched a notice to the committee of miners which had been appointed to carry out the orders of the meeting, informing it that "there is but one authority in this country, and that is the law as laid down by the Parliament of the Dominion of Canada .... [A]ny action taken by you as to selling the claim for wages due by Gordon is illegal and done at your own peril, and that should you carry out your intention the party buying takes no title and is a trespasser."[33] The incident was quite rightly regarded by the police as a critical test of their authority, and Constantine's response reflected the perceived gravity of the situation.[34]

Constantine's notice was served on the committee three hours after the sale had taken place, on 28 June 1896. Upon reading the notice, the highest bidder refused the claim. Thereupon the committee took possession of the claim and turned it over to the second highest bidder. The owner then notified Constantine of these developments by special messenger in a communication dated 1 July. On 4 July, Constantine responded by dispatching a small force to the creek, with instructions to "remain on the claim until such time as seems to you wise to leave" and "to proceed with greatest caution in dealing with this case. You will, in a quiet manner, be guided by circumstances as they arise, but the law must be upheld."[35] When the purchaser of the claim arrived at Fortymile to register the Bill of Sale given him by the miners' committee, Constantine refused to register it. The purchaser left that night for the creek, in Constantine's words, "breathing defiance, and saying that the miners would see him through."[36]

Strickland, the officer in charge, recounts the events following the arrival of the police contingent on the creek:

We reached Glacier Creek and went to Messrs. Van Wagoner and Westwood claim #19 above discovery, the seat of the trouble. Mr. Westwood informed me that Jerry Barker [the purchaser] had put a man in possession of the claim. I ejected this man and warned Jerry Barker to attempt no further occupation of the place. I saw the chairman of the committee appointed by the miners and gave him a similar warning. I think they saw the force of our argument as one of the committee took to the bush immediately on our arrival at the creek. The better class of miners on the creek are in favor of law and order and seem to be glad that the so-called laws made by the miners meeting are null and void. Several of the miners of the worst class indulged in some big talking and were very anxious that I should call a meeting of the miners—to explain the law to them. I gave a decided refusal to this proposition stating that ... you had sent them a written notice which they had chosen to utterly ignore and that my present business on the creek was not to talk but to act, they had nothing further to say to this.[37]

*****

Once it was evident that the police were opposed to the continuation of the miners' meeting and were ready and willing to take action in response to an appeal front the judgment of such an assembly, the institution was doomed. The attitude of the police meant that the meetings had lost their power of enforcement. [...] By the fall of 1896 they had virtually ceased to function on the Canadian side of the boundary. The fact that the police had undermined and supplanted them was not generally resented. "All in the country," Haskell notes, "were quite ready to join in their [the meetings'] obsequies when the Canadian police instituted a different condition of things."[38] And writing from Fortymile in May 1897, Ogilvie could report that "The cry everywhere is 'let us have law administered by disinterested men who are above influence and reproach' as proof of this sentiment I have only to say no miners' meetings have been held in this District for over six months."[39]

*****

The law as administered by the Mounties failed to serve any significant *instrumental* functions above and beyond those which the

miners' meeting had served prior to 1895. Indeed, in this respect the law of the Mounties proved decidedly more limited than the earlier law of the miners' meeting. However, the law of the Mounties performed certain *symbolic* functions which the miners' meeting could not. The Mounties, unlike the more egalitarian miners' assemblies, were capable of reliably sustaining the public affirmation of a particular set of class norms and values in the face of perceived threat to the supremacy of these norms within the community. [...]

The Consequences of Police Control

*****

The instrumental consequences of police control [...] did not include any radical change in the style of justice as it was being enforced in the community. There was, however, one noteworthy development with respect to the instrumental functions of law in the district. This was the introduction of some significant new limits on the provision of remedies. The miners' meeting, it will be recalled, had exercised wide-ranging jurisdiction: it was bound by no formal distinctions between "civil" and "criminal" matters and could readily be called upon to deal with either as the occasion might arise. On the other hand, even though the Mounties exercised judicial as well as police powers, their jurisdiction was limited to criminal cases. This was a distinction which they scrupulously observed. But since the miners' meeting was discredited and no longer a viable institution, many disputes and issues were left without an appropriate forum for resolution.

*****

[...] As early as 1895, Constantine recognized the need for civil courts. In his report for that year, he wrote: "Civil courts are much required and should be established without delay. Many take advantage of the fact of there being no machinery for the collection of small debts."[40] Again, in his report for 1896, Constantine pleaded:

The necessity for civil courts is daily increasing. They should be established with the least possible delay. The want of them creates a distrust in the administration of government and there is an idea spreading that the country is occupied by the government solely for the purpose of revenue.[41]

The evidence suggests, therefore, that the establishment of police control entailed no profound change in the character of criminal justice from the way it had been administered under the miners' meeting. Elimination of the miners' meeting did create at least a temporary void in the authoritative resolution of civil disputes. [...]

By the time the police arrived in the district, however, the changing character of the mining communities had created an opportunity for the Mounties to assume a significant symbolic role which the miners' meeting was incapable of performing.

*****

[...] The growing population of drifters in the towns began to be viewed as a threat to the peace and good order of Yukon society.

Such perceptions and fears are perhaps reflected in the establishment of the Yukon Order of Pioneers at Fortymile in December 1894. The YOOP was initially limited in its membership to those who had been residents in the Yukon before 1888. The constitution of the organization stated that its purpose "shall be the advancement of the great Yukon Valley, The Mutual Protection and Benefit of its Members" and "to unite the members in the strong tie of Brotherhood and to prove to the outside world that the Yukon Order of Pioneers are men of Truth, Honor and Integrity."[42] The establishment of the YOOP by the earlier miners in the district was an effort to preserve for themselves—through the brotherhood—the kind of community, system of values, and status which they associated with the early camps. [...]

[...] The favourable response of the older miners to the police, as they asserted their control in the district, was a reflection both of this anxiety concerning the miners' meeting and approval of the kinds of norms and values the police themselves represented.

In 1893, Warburton Pike visited the region and expressed the view that the miners' meeting was "an excellent court as long as the better class of men are in the majority, but a dangerous power in the hands of the vile specimens of humanity who sooner or later get the whip hand in most of the mining camps."[43] [...]

*****

The police themselves were decidedly in tune with these sentiments. They were ready to interpret the potential for trouble in general, or perceived abuses of the miners' meeting in particular, largely in class terms. Writing in February 1896, Constantine was moved to comment that "The advent of the police has had a quieting effect ... the greater portion of the tough element have gone to the American territory lower down the river. Being nonproducers have not lessened the wealth or resources of the Country or community."[44] In his annual report of 20 November 1896, his view of the significance of the increasing criminal "element" entering the country surfaced again:

> With such a large number of men coming into the country every spring, of necessity, there is a certain percentage of criminals amongst them. Having no means of learning their past record, it is impossible to pick them out until such a crime is committed. The element is increasing and will increase. It is noticed, however, that through the fear of Canadian law and its enforcement by the small police detachment here many continue their journey a couple of hundred miles down the river to Circle City.[45]

*****

The Mounties as Vigilantes

*****

The symbolic role of police control in the Yukon has a curious parallel in the rise of the vigilante movements, which similarly transformed existing systems of law in the earlier mining communities of the American West. Ironically, the Mounties—that prominent symbol of Canadian "law and order"—may have found support in their effort to eliminate the miners' meeting and assume ultimate authority in the Yukon for some of the same reasons that the vigilantes—that equally prominent symbol of American frontier lawlessness—may have been supported in assuming power and usurping other forms of governance on the American mining frontier. The parallel deserves at least passing notice, not simply because of the irony involved, but because of what it suggests about the broader significance of the symbolic functions of law in the transformation of legal systems.

*****

In the Western mining towns, the newness of settlement, the fact that their inhabitants arrived as relative strangers to one another, and ultimately the increasing differentiation and heterogeneity of the population, all combined to engender uncertainty about community structure and values and about how choices were to be made among opposed normative systems which were recognized as challenging one another for dominance. Under these circumstances, the vigilantes emerged to serve the function of dramatizing and affirming the "behavioral boundaries"[46] of the community, defining and clarifying its structure and supporting establishment values. The fact that the movements were widely applauded, that movement leaders were typically drawn from the upper class, and that upon occasion the movements arose even where uncontrolled crime was not, in fact, an immediate problem attest to the significance of the symbolic function of the vigilantes.[47]

Obvious differences did distinguish the Mounties in the Yukon from the vigilantes in California: the Mounties were a legal rather than extra-legal organization, and their rule was imposed from outside rather than from within the local community. But as to functions and the sources of support in the community, there are noteworthy parallels. The vigilantes, like the Mounties, derived their support from reactions to rapidly increasing community differentiation and increasing lack of certainty with respect to community structure and values. In each case, the new institution for the administration of law symbolized the dominance of a particular normative order. [...]

But the point to be emphasized is that in the mining communities of the American West as well as in the Yukon, we see a significant symbolic function—the capacity to provide a clear public affirmation of the dominance of one particular set of social ideals and norms—supporting a fundamental transformation in the administration of the law. The Yukon case supports the view that increasing differentiation, accompanied by perceptions of increasing conflict of values and interests, may promote the acceptance and institutionalization of specialized, centralized agents of legal control regardless of their relative instrumental effectiveness. From the standpoint of the need for agents or institutions of control which can serve to define clear and consistent "behavioral boundaries" for a community, this is perhaps advantageous, if not necessarily laudable. In a differentiated community, divided by conflicting interests and values, consistency and clarity in the public affirmation and sanctioning of community norms may be best served by the concentration of public sanctioning power in the hands of a specialized body identified with one particular set of such values and interests.

Notes

1. Morris Zaslow, "The Yukon: Northern Development in the Canadian–American Context" in *Regionalism in the Canadian Community, 1867–1967,* ed. Mason Wade (Toronto: University of Toronto Press, 1969), 183–84.

2. John Phillip Reid, "Paying for the Elephant: Property Rights and Civil Order on the Overland Trail," *Huntington Library Quarterly* 41 (1977): 37; Barry M. Gough, "Keeping British Columbia British: The Law-and-Order Question on a Gold-Mining Frontier," *Huntington Library Quarterly* 38 (1975): 278.

3. Robert Craig Brown, "Canadian Opinion after Confederation, 1867–1914" in *Canada Views the United States: Nineteenth-Century Political Attitudes,* ed. S.F. Wise and Robert Craig Brown (Seattle: University of Washington Press, 1967).

4. Richard Maxwell Brown, "The American Vigilante Tradition" in *The History of Violence in America: Historical and Comparative Perspectives*, ed. Hugh Davis Graham and Ted Robert Gurr (New York: Praeger, 1969), 178–90.

5. Joseph R. Gusfield, "Moral Passage: The Symbolic Process in Public Resignations of Deviance," *Social Problems* 15 (1967): 76–77.

6. Ibid.; Joseph R. Gusfield, *Symbolic Crusade* (Urbana: University of Illinois Press, 1963); Murray Edelman, *The Symbolic Uses of Politics* (Urbana: University of Illinois Press, 1964); Kai T. Erikson, *Wayward Puritans: A Study in the Sociology of Deviance* (New York: Wiley, 1966).

7. Charles Constantine, "Report of Inspector Constantine, 10 October 1894," in *Report of the Commissioner of the North-West Mounted Police Force, 1894* (Ottawa: Queen's Printer, 1895); S.A. Archer, *A Heroine of the North: Memoirs of Charlotte Selina Bompas* (New York: Macmillan, 1929), 138.

8. Public Archives of Canada (hereafter PAC), Records of the Royal Canadian Mounted Police (hereafter after RCMP), RG18, vol. 1318, file 212-1894, draft copy of Report of Inspector Charles Constantine.

9. Harold B. Goodrich, "History and Condition of the Yukon Gold District to 1897" in *Geology of the Yukon Gold District, Alaska,* ed. Josiah Edward Spurr (Washington: Government Printing Office, 1897), 119.

10. William Ogilvie, *Early Days on the Yukon* (New York: John Lane, 1913), 245; Zaslow, "The Yukon," 184.

11. Arthur Treadwell Walden, *A Dog Puncher on the Yukon* (Boston: Houghton Mifflin, 1928), 55–56.

12. Ibid., 102.

13. Ogilvie, *Early Days on the Yukon*, 42–51.

14. Ibid., 50.

15. Ibid. 267–71.

16. Ibid., 270.

17. Ibid., 271.

18. Ibid., 268.

19. D.R. Morrison, *The Politics of the Yukon Territory, 1898–1909* (Toronto: University of Toronto Press, 1968), 7; Zaslow, "The Yukon," 183.

20. Ogilvie, *Early Days on the Yukon,* 142–44; Zaslow, "The Yukon," 183–64.

21. Ogilvie, ibid., 144.

22. PAC, Constantine papers, MG 30/E55, vol. 3, file 4, W.C. Bompas to Minister of Interior, 9 Dec. 1893; ibid., W.C. Bompas to Superintendent of Indian Affairs, May 1893.

23. Ibid., CH. Hamilton to Minister of Interior, 16 April 1894.

24. PAC, Constantine papers, MG 30/E55, vol. 3, file 4, certified copy of Report of Committee of Privy Council, approved 26 May 1894.

25. Ibid.

26. Ibid., memo from F. White, comptroller NWMP, 2 May 1894.

27. PAC, Records of the RCMP, RG18, vol. 1318, file 212-1894, Comptroller NWMP to Commissioner, 20 May 1894.

28. Ibid., draft copy of Report of Inspector Charles Constantine.

29. Ibid., Yukon Superintendents' Letterbooks, copy of 1895 report.

30. PAC, Records of the RCMP, RG18, vol. 1345, file 190-1895, Constantine to Commissioner, 4 Sept. 1895.

31. Walden, *Dog Puncher*, 45.

32. PAC, Constantine papers, MG 30/E55, vol. 4, Constantine to Officer Commanding the NWMP, 13 July 1896.

33. PAC, Records of the RCMP, RG18, vol. 123, file 468, Constantine to Oscar Jackson, E.S. Maloney, and Jas. McMahan, the Committee Appointed by Certain Miners of Glacier and Miller Creeks, 19 June 1896.

34. Ogilvie, *Early Days on the Klondike*, 250–52; Hayne, *Pioneers of the Klondike*, 121–24.

35. PAC, Records of the RCMP, RG18, vol. 123, file 468, Constantine to Strickland, 4 July 1896.

36. PAC, Constantine papers, MG 30/E55, vol. 4, Constantine to Officer Commanding the NWMP, 13 July 1896.

37. Ibid., Report of Strickland to Constantine, 14 July 1896.

38. William B. Haskell, *Two Years in the Klondike and Alaska Goldfields* (Hartford: Hartford Publishing Co., 1898), 154.

39. Zaslow, "The Yukon," 187.

40. Ibid., Yukon Superintendents' Letterbooks, copy of 1895 report.

41. Charles Constantine, "Report on the Yukon Detachment 20 November, 1896" in *Report of the Commissioner of the North-West Mounted Police Force, 1896* (Ottawa: Queen's Printer, 1897), 235.

42. Yukon Territorial Archives, Records of the Yukon Order of Pioneers, Minute Book, Dec. 1894 entry.

43. Warburton Pike, *Through the Subarctic Forest* (London: Edward Arnold, 1896), 220–21.

44. PAC, Constantine papers, MG 30/E55, vol. 4, Constantine to T.M. Daly, 11 Feb. 1896.

45. Constantine, "Report on the Yukon Detachment," 234.

46. Erikson, *Wayward Puritans*, 9–11.

47. Richard Maxwell Brown, *Strain of Violence* (New York: Oxford University Press, 1975), 105–12, 124.

CHAPTER 4

Discordant Music:
Charivaris and Whitecapping in
Nineteenth-Century North America

Bryan D. Palmer

• •

> That monster custom, who all sense doth eat,
> Of habits devil, is angel yet in this,
> That to the use of actions fair and good
> He likewise gives a frock or livery,
> That aptly is put on.
> —*Hamlet*, III, 4

> Friend, hast thou hear'd a Strong
>   North Eastern roar,
> Or the harsh discord of Charivari,
>   or Cat's wild scream ere them to
>   love agree?
> —*Quebec Gazette,* 12 January 1786

*****

[…] Charivaris and whitecapping, two prominent forms of extra-legal authority in North America that have received little scholarly attention, reveal important dimensions of the nineteenth-century past.

*****

II

Perhaps one of the most persistent cultural forms known to scholars of popular customs and traditions was the charivari. As a ritualized mechanism of community control, with roots penetrating back to the medieval epoch, the charivari was known throughout the Atlantic world.[1] Although it could be directed against virtually any social offender, the custom was most often used to expose to the collective wrath of the community adulterous relationships, cuckolded husbands, wife and husband beaters, unwed mothers, and partners in unnatural marriage. Many variants were possible, and the phenomenon had a rural as well as an urban presence, but the essential form was generally cut from a similar cloth. The demonstration was most often initiated under the cover of darkness, a party gathering at the house of the offender to beat pans and drums, shoot muskets, and blow the ubiquitous horn, which butchers often rented out for the occasion. Sometimes the guilty party was seized, perhaps to be roughly seated on a donkey, facing backwards, and then paraded through the streets, passers-by loudly informed of his/her transgression. The charivari party was often led by youths, on other occasions by women. In seventeenth-century Lyon and eighteenth-century Paris we know that journeymen and artisans were particularly active, as were rural tradesmen in eighteenth- and nineteenth-century England. As a constant check on misbehaviour, the charivari served an important purpose in many communities and in many different cultural contexts. Its disappearance, usually dated around 1850 at the latest, has been interpreted as an indicator of the potent rise of the nuclear family, which no longer required the collective surveillance of neighbours and townsfolk to assure its stability and continuity.[2] [...]

The English charivari was practised under a multitude of names: rough music, known in East Anglia as tinning, tin panning, or kettling[3]; skimmington, skimmerton, skimmety-riding, or wooseting; [...] riding the stang, apparently most popular in the northern counties and in Scotland[4]; Devon's stag hunt[5]; the occupational variation, the butcher's serenade, artfully employed by London's Clare Market men,[6] or, the American term, shivaree, common among Cornish miners.[7] [...]

Two cases of English charivaris waged against wife-beaters indicate the general contours of the practice.[8] The first instance, recorded in 1860, documented the use of the custom in the Surrey and Sussex region during the 1840s. It was suppressed by the police, who grew irritated with forms of rough music because they frequently rendered the roads impassable. Offending wife-beaters were first warned of the community's wrath, chaff from the threshing-floor strewn on their doorsteps in the dead of night. If the offence continued, the man was subjected to rough music. Under the cover of darkness a procession formed, headed by two men with huge cow-horns, followed by an individual with a large old fish-kettle around his neck, representing the trumpeters and big drum of a serious parade. Then came the orator, leading "a motley assembly with hand-bells,

gongs, cow-horns, whistles, tin kettles, rattles, bones, frying-pans, everything in short from which more and rougher music than ordinary could be extracted." At a given signal, the group halted, and the orator began to recite:

There is a man in this place
Has beat his wife!! (*forte*. A pause)
Has beat his wife!! (*fortissimo*.)
It is a very great shame and disgrace
To all who live in this place.
It is indeed upon my life!!

A bonfire was then lit, and the charivari party danced around it, as if in a frenzy. The noise was heard as far away as two miles. The orator closed with a speech recommending better conduct, and the practitioners of rough music departed, encouraged by the offender's neighbours, who provided beer for "the band."[9]

Another case, this time from Hedon, in the East Riding of Yorkshire, outlines the events of 18–20 February 1889. Jack Nelson had cruelly beaten his wife. An effigy of Nelson was carried by two men through the village, accompanied by a large crowd, wielding the traditional instruments of rough music. The procession eventually came to a halt in front of Nelson's door, and the clatter of pans and horns quickly ceased, the crowd breaking out in voices loud and harsh:

Here we cum, wiv a ran a dan dan;
It's neather fo' man cause nor tha cause
    that Ah ride this stang
Bud it is fo' Jack Nelson, that Roman-nooased man.
Cum all you good people that live i' this raw,
Ah'd he' ya tk wahnin, for this is oor law;
If onny o' you husbans your gud wives do bang
Let em cum to uz, an we'll ride em the stang.
He beat her, he bang'd her, he bang'd her indeed;
He bang'd her afooar sha ivver stood need.
He bang'd her wi neather stick, steean, iron
    nor slower,
But he up wiv a three-legged stool an knockt
    her backwards over.
    Upstairs aback o' bed

Sike a racket there they led.

Doon stairs, aback o' door

He buncht her whahl he meead her sweear.

Noo if this good man dizzant mend his manners,

The skin of his hide sal gan ti the tanner's;

An if the tanner dizzant tan it well,

He sal ride upon a gate spell;

An if the spell sud happen to crack,

He sal ride upon the devil's back;

An if the devil sud happen ti run,

We'll shut him wiv a wahld-goose gun;

An if the gun sud happen ti miss fire,

Ah'll bid y good neet, for Ah's ommast tired.

Upon the conclusion of this serenade, the clamour of rough music was again initiated. Amidst cheering and loud noise, the effigy was carried around the village for three successive nights. The ceremony was terminated on the third evening, when Nelson's likeness was finally burned on the village green.[10]

In France, and indeed on the continent in general, wife-beaters were seldom subjected to the charivari. But the practice was nevertheless quite common, often initiated by the young, resentful of old men who married young women, robbing youth of its rightful access to the marriageable females of the community. Payment was often demanded to appease those who saw themselves wronged by the act of unnatural marriage:

Fork up, old pal

The dough that you owe

We're the boys of the block

And' we want a good show

We're wild as they come

And off on a spree

So out with the cash

Or charivari![11]

Once their palms were greased with coin of the realm, the young men often retired to the nearest tavern, and left the married couple to their wedding-night pleasures. Occasionally, however, the charivari was actually used to punish those who had deprived the local young of potential spouses, and no amount of cash could deflect the final reckoning.[12] [...]

Marital mismatches, while a prominent cause of French charivaris, were rivalled by a series of sexual offences. Married men who impregnated single women, cuckolded husbands, unwed mothers, and those engaged in adulterous relationships were all subjected to the charivari, censured for the threat they posed to community social order.[13] [...]

[...] Natalie Zemon Davis notes that at this early date the ritual could be moved to explicitly political purpose, a mechanism whereby petty proprietors, artisans, and merchants marshalled the urban poor to voice their critique of king and state.[14] Closer to the modern period, charivaris assumed importance in the years of revolutionary upsurge of the 1790s, and in the turbulent political climate of 1824–1848.[15] And yet, even in this context, charivaris are perhaps best seen as a pre-political form of class action, admittedly set firmly against the wall of nineteenth-century authority, but lacking in conscious, political direction. A case in point, perhaps, is provided by the Limoges prostitutes. In 1857 they faced persistent harassment and incarceration in a local hospital. Escaping from the institution, the women resisted efforts to curb their business activities by organizing charivaris that drew the enthusiastic support of the local barracks.[16] This was, to be sure, a political undertaking, and one revealing important social tensions, but it implies no condescension to place it in the category of primitive rebellion.[17]

*****

The charivari, then, was hardly an isolated phenomenon. Bound by neither region nor nation, it was a universally practised custom, an essential component of the "invisible cultures" and "limited identities" of the plebeian world.[18] [...] For the charivari has a North American presence, as well as a European one. Those migrating to the New World brought much of their culture with them: traditions, values, language, and specific forms of ritualized behaviour. Woven into the very fabric of this culture was the charivari, and it would not easily be displaced.

III

Conventional wisdom has it that the charivari was brought to North America by the French, that it was originally prominent in the settlements of Lower Canada, Louisiana, and Alabama, and that it was gradually adopted in English-speaking areas, where the derivative term shivaree was used to denote the custom.[19] And, indeed, the first recorded instances of North American charivaris that have come to my attention occurred in Lower Canada. A Quebec charivari of 28 June 1683 illustrates a common pattern. Francois Vezier dit Laverdure died 7 June 1683, leaving a widow 25 years of age. Three weeks later his mourning spouse took a new husband, Claude Bourget, aged 30. Twenty-one days of widowhood seemed an unreasonably short time for the people of Quebec, and they turned out to charivari the couple. Disorder reigned for more than a week, and the Church authority eventually intervened. [...]

*****

[...] In regions with a sprinkling of French Canadians, the charivari was always present. Ottawa and Peterborough were well known for the practice, and the Smith's Falls and Gatineau regions also witnessed the custom on a number of occasions. Well into the 1870s the ritual remained intact.[20]

Lower Canada, too, was familiar with the charivari. [...] Montreal was the scene of a veritable epidemic of charivaris in the early 1820s. [...]

*****

[...] Common throughout the Cajun districts of the American South, the charivari supposedly gained acceptance out of "an indisposition to allow ladies two chances for husbands, in a society where so few single ladies [found] even one husband! a result, it is to be presumed, of the concubinage system so prevalent [there]."[21]

[...] Alice T. Chase argued that the charivari was common, in the 1860s, in most rural hamlets from Pennsylvania west to Kansas and Nebraska, being particularly prominent in Ohio, Indiana, and Illinois. She saw the ritual coming to America with the Pennsylvania Dutch.[22] Among New Englanders the practice was well established, known as the serenade. In Nebraska in the 1870s belling the bridal couple, giving them a "warming,"[23] was a frequent occurrence.[24] "It was understood," within the Tennessee mining community, "that every bride and groom had to be shivareed."[25] The *sanserassa,* a serenade of tin pans, horns, kettles, and drums, was actively practiced by the Spanish population of St. Augustine, Florida, where the ritual was common in the 1820s.[26] Scandinavian settlements apparently incorporated the practice into their language and their culture.[27] Even in early Upper Canada, or post-Confederation Ontario, where we have seen the French influence to be operative, numerous cities, towns, villages, and rural communities sufficiently removed from the shadow of French culture utilized the charivari, repeatedly directing it against those who flaunted community standards.[28] Across North America, then, the custom had a vital presence, known, according to local and regional taste, as serenade, shivaree, charivari, tin-panning, belling, homing, bull banding, skimmelton, or calathump.[29]

*****

In nineteenth-century Upper Canada, for instance, the charivari was often a force undermining social authority, resolutely opposed by magistrate and police. [...]

*****

Three Kingston, Upper Canada, charivaris of the mid-1830s, all directed against remarriage, forced the hand of the local authorities, one leading to two arrests, another necessitating the calling into operation of the Summary Punishment Act, the third leading to the creation of a special force of constables, 40 strong, to enforce the peace.[30] The latter event, led by one Henry Smith, Jr., illustrates well the deliberate, planned nature of some of these undertakings, revealing the importance, perhaps, of local groups consolidated around a popular figure. Smith was a barrister with a long history of involvement in shady legal entanglements, a man who had himself been in court on charges of assault, perjury, and riot. [...] It could well have been men like Smith who provoked this response from the Hamilton Board of Police, 22 March 1842:

> Whereas the custom of meeting together at night by ill disposed persons disguised by dress, paint, and for the purposes of indulging in what is commonly called a chevari, has been a source of great annoyance to all the peaceable inhabitants of this Town, and whereas such assemblages endanger the peace of the Town, the safety of property and person and are highly disgraceful to all concerned in them ... it is ordered that persons convicted of being a party to any such proceedings shall be fined.[31]

[...] Charivaris directed against domestic impropriety particularly remarriage, could thus raise issues that went well beyond popular distaste for unnatural marriage.[32]

In other cases, too, the charivari extended beyond the purely domestic concerns that so often defined its purpose. Indeed, the custom often reflected essential social tensions. Mrs. Moodie documented the case of Tom Smith, "a runaway nigger from the States" charivaried for his pretentious, and successful, bid to have an Irish woman marry him. Dragged from his bed, ridden on a rail, and beaten, the black died under the hands of the charivari party.[33] [...]

*****

More explicitly, the charivari was often used to show open disapproval for certain forms of behaviour, particularly those judged immoral or illicit.[34] [...] A Bowmanville, Ontario, lawyer, Mr. Loscombe, faced the rough music of his neighbours in 1868, when a crowd gathered at his office to tar-and-feather him, punishment for his unlawful bestowing of affections upon a servant girl. A constable eventually had to escort Loscombe home, but the crowd captured the lawyer, handled him roughly, and threw him over a fence. After an announcement that the man's wife was ill, the crowd discontinued the disturbance. The next morning Loscombe escaped the city, but the group assembled anyway, burning effigies in front of his house.[35] [...] An Ancaster, Upper Canada, lawyer, accused of living adulterously with a woman who had deserted her husband due to ill treatment; a New York City woman thought to be a murderess; and a free-love advocate, cohabiting with his mistress in Utica, New York, in 1860, faced similar forms of rough justice. [...] Prostitutes, too, were likely candidates for the charivari, bearing the brunt of a vicious form of popular justice in the Quebec timberlands and American west well into the twentieth century.[36]

A jealous eye toward property, or resentment of those who attempted to establish themselves as superior elements in a community of equals, also elicited the charivari. [...] Edward Littlejohn, aged 74, was charivaried in 1881 by a group of young men who hoped to drive him off of his Highland Creek, Scarborough Township property so that they could secure access to the land.[37] [...] Social pretensions drew immediate reaction in the timber-lands of western Ontario.[38] Finally, the hostility with which a "ruffian mob" greeted a Saltfleet marriage in 1868, the husband "revoltingly maltreated," and the bride "taken out *en dishabille*, and conveyed some distance in the piercing cold on an ox sleigh, meanwhile being taunted on the felicities of her bridal tour," suggests a strong sense of resentment.[39]

Occasionally, the charivari could be directed, not at domestic impropriety, sexual misbehaviour, or social pretension, but at constituted authority itself, a brazen display of popular contempt for law and order. This appeared to be the case in a series of noisy parades in St. John's, Lower Canada, in August 1841. As the local police seemed incapable of quelling the disturbances, they asked for deployment of troops to the town to aid the civil power in suppressing disorder. Upon official investigation the Magistrates were informed that:

> ... the disturbance, in the first instance, had only amounted to the putting in practice an illegal, but long established custom throughout Canada, called a "chri-vri"—a boyish frolic liable to be treated by the police as a common nuisance or actionable under the more serious charge to extort money .... The indiscreet conduct of the Magistrate, who appeared to have worked himself up into a state of nervous excitement led some idle persons of the Village to direct their petty annoyances against him with too good success.

A small patrol eventually suppressed the charivari, but not before constituted authority had exposed itself "and Her Majesty's troops to the amusement and derision of the mischievous persons who sought to annoy [it]."[40]

[...] Perhaps one of the most striking uses of the charivari to show popular disapproval, in the political realm, occurred in the Placentia, Newfoundland election of 1869, where the ritual was employed to express the inhabitants' hostility to Confederation. Ambrose Shea, the island's delegate to the Quebec conferences, paid a visit to Placentia, where he was greeted by locals carrying pots of hot pitch and bags of feathers, angered at "de shkeemer's" effort to "sell his country." In addition, a crowd of fifty "sounded melancholy insult to the candidate through ... large conchs which the fishermen get upon their 'bull tow' trains in summer, and another band of about thirty, ... blew reproaches and derision through cow horns." Insulted and disgusted by the display, Shea could not even land on the shore.[41]

But this use of the charivari must have been rare. When directed to explicitly political purpose, the charivari was most often a mechanism of popular endorsement, waged to celebrate some notable event, or to support a popular candidate. The Callithumpians, for

instance, were a group of Baltimore "rowdies," patterning themselves after the "Ancient and Honourable Artillery Company" of Boston, who ushered in the fourth of July with grotesque attire and the clamour of tin pans, kettles, bells, and rattles.[42] In New York City the Callathumpians were prominent in the 1830s, when an American story-teller first witnessed them:

> I was in New York, New Years, and all at once I heard the darndest racket you'd ever wish to hear. There was more than ten thousand fellers with whistles, penny trumpets, tin pails, shovels, tongs, spiders, gridirons, warming pans, and all such kind of implements. Why, they made more noise than a concert of cats, or a meeting house full of niggers.[43]

In old Ontario the term Kallithumpian Klan, or "Terribles," often referred to the grotesquely attired processions organized to celebrate the Queen's Birthday or Dominion Day. The term callithumpian band, an American variation of the charivari, seemed appropriately fitted to these parades, always marked by "the sound of discordant 'music'," and outrageous disguise.[44]

*****

Aside from these kinds of festive parades, the charivari was sometimes used to endorse a specific politician. [...] Certainly one of the last recorded cases of this use of the charivari occurred in 1910, after Harry Middleton Hyatt's father was elected to the Quincy, Illinois, City Council. A progressive reformer, the elder Hyatt had fought "the City Hall Gang" for years in his newspaper column. Upon his victory, "the old time charivari bunch" turned out to pay their respects, pounding on drums stamped R.A.R., initials proclaiming them the "Ragged Assed Rounders."[45]

Where the charivari was turned most emphatically to purposes of a political or social nature was when it was used by working men and women to register their discontent. The custom had a long history of this type in the

British Isles.[46] When the English government attempted the enclosure of lands and forests in the western districts in the years 1628–1631, popular resentment flared in the anonymous personage of Lady Skimmington.[47] [...]

In the United States the charivari, or similar forms of ritualistic derision, could also be turned to working-class purpose. As early as 1675 a group of Boston ship carpenters had forcefully ejected another worker from their presence, claiming he had not served his full seven years' apprenticeship. John Roberts and eight other defendants admitted having carried John Langworth, "upon a pole and by violence," from the north end of Boston to the Town dock. A constable eventually rescued the carpenter, and the men were fined five shillings each, payable to the government and the victim. But they justified their action on the grounds that "hee was an interloper and had never served his time to the trade of a ship carpenter and now came to work in theire yard and they understood such things were ususall in England."[48] [...]

In Canada, the use of the charivari in this manner remains obscure. Strikers, of course, often utilized mock processions to denigrate opposing forces. [...] Unskilled labourers at the Chaudière Lumber Mills, engaged in an 1891 battle with their employers, mocked the militia, summoned to preserve order, with a charivari in Hull, Quebec, twenty of their number blackening their faces. Dressed as "Terribles," the men paraded with sticks on their shoulders "and went through military movements in a laughable manner."[49] [...]

The most explicit use of the charivari in this manner, however, occurred in the midst of a weavers' strike in Hamilton, Ontario, in the spring of 1890.[50] On two occasions the striking weavers, blowing fish-horns, shouting, and acting, according to the local newspaper, like a procession of "Grit schoolboys attempted to intimidate women who refuse to join their cause." Mrs. Anne Hale was subjected to similar treatment, charging Moses Furlong, Richard Callan, Henry Dean, and Ann Burke with disorderly conduct. The proceedings ended in $5.00 fines for the "charivaring weavers."[51]

Perhaps this kind of legal suppression took its toll. The charivari certainly continued into the twentieth century, but only the carcass remained, pleasant sport for villagers and small-town North American youth.[52] [...]

*****

[...] It is impossible to date the decline of the ritual, indeed, numerous colleagues have witnessed forms of the charivari in Canadian villages and towns as late as 1963.[53] But the research index cards can tell us something. By the mid 1890s the custom is increasingly rare, and the last nineteenth-century Canadian charivari I have located in the newspapers occurred in 1896, near Brantford, Ontario, on Christmas Eve. Like so many similar affairs, it ended in death, a young farmer succumbing to the shot-gun blast that was meant as a warning.[54] In Adams County, Illinois, the charivari had disappeared in the immediate pre-World War I years.[55] And yet, despite the unmistakable demise of the custom, its function was to be fulfilled by another ritualized method of enforcing community standards and appropriate behaviour. In the years 1888–1905 whitecapping, a distinctively American phenomenon, took up where the charivari had left off.

IV

John S. Farmer, author of *Americanisms—Old and New*, described the White Caps as, "A mysterious organization in Indiana, who take it upon themselves to administer justice to offenders independent of the law. They go out at night disguised, and seizing their victim, gag him and bind him to a tree while they administer a terrible whipping. Who they are is not known, or if known no one dares to make a complaint against them. They are particularly severe," concluded Farmer, "against wife beaters."[56] Other popular dictionaries offered similar definitions of the White Caps stressing their efforts to regulate public morals, and to administer justice to offenders independent of the law.[57] One source concluded that, "The whole White Cap movement was borrowed from English outlawry."[58]

These kinds of assessments, often based on the scantiest of evidence, tell us very little. In some cases they may even lead us into further confusion. For the White Caps owed little to any English predecessor, developing, rather, as a peculiarly North American form of rough justice, one strand in the long history of vigilante activity and popular tribunal that stretched from the tar and feather feats of Comet Joyce, *jun.*, leader of Boston's revolutionary crowd,[59] through the Carolina regulators[60] and into the nineteenth-century associations emerging in San Francisco and Montana to curb the activities of criminals and highwaymen.[61] Lynch-law, and the more individualized acts of cowhiding, rawhiding, and horsewhipping, sustained themselves as part of the same long tradition of American popular justice.[62] These forms, reaching well into the twentieth century, were often used against radical dissidents, as the history of the Industrial Workers of the World and the 1919 Winnipeg General Strike reveal[63] or against oppressed groups, but they could also be employed by those significantly removed from the bastions of social and economic power for their own purposes. Thus, nineteenth-century workers often threatened, and practiced, tarring and feathering, utilizing the ritual against strikebreakers; in the depression decade of the 1930s tarring and gravelling was one popular punishment inflicted on landlords who attempted to exploit hard times, evicting tenants of long residence, drawing out the last penny of rents that, to the suffering victims, seemed highly extortionate.[64] For the student of North American legal and social history, then, the popular tribunal is a realm of vital importance.[65]

Whitecapping drew much of its vigour from this essential continuity in the North American tradition of vigilante activity. But it buttressed this strength, tapping other sources of attachment and commitment. It may, in certain parts of North America, have drawn on the White Cross Movement, a religious crusade of the 1880s raging against prostitution, drink, and lewdness, for moral tone and rigour.[66] The regalia of the White Caps, most commonly masks, hoods, and robes, likely borrowed heavily from the experience of the Ku Klux Klan, and must have attracted many to the ranks of the movement.[67] More important, perhaps, were the elaborate passwords, rituals, and secret oaths that bound members to a fraternity of associates; in many cases the forms were taken directly from organizations like the Knights of Labor or the Masons.[68] [...]

*****

[...] The history of whitecapping was an intensely local affair. Indeed, one early commentator noted the importance of the terrain in southern Indiana in facilitating the growth of the White Caps: the hilly, forested land serving as a haven for those who sought to impose their own brand of rough justice, keeping their distance from the law.[69] Bald knobbing, the Missouri variant of whitecapping, drew its name from the "balds" and "knobs" of the mountains in the southwestern corner of the state, the home of the masked regulators of Taney, Christian, Stone, and Douglas counties.[70] Madelein Noble has argued that this regional context even affected the direction which whitecapping took: in the mid-west and border states the phenomenon was directed against moral improprieties, while the south and far west witnessed the dominance of whitecapping directed against economic ills.[71] She has a point, for this certainly seems to be the case, but the dichotomy is drawn a little too rigidly, and the Canadian material complicates the issue further. But what emerges, in spite of local differences, is the way in which whitecapping was used as an American form of rough music. [...]

Consider, for instance, the home of whitecapping, Indiana, where the movement had precursors in the mid 1850s, attained prominence in the mid and late 1880s, and gained a place in the popular literature of the times with Booth Tarkington's first novel.[72] Of the 80 instances of whitecapping or White Cap warnings, uncovered by Noble in Crawford and Harrison counties in the years 1873–1893, most were directed against those who neglected their family, engaged in wife- or child-beating, exhibited a marked laziness, or stepped outside of the boundaries of appropriate sexual behaviour. Sally Tipton was whipped in July 1884 for giving birth to a child out of wedlock. She claimed to have seen Cornelius Grable in the White Cap party, the man she had previously named in a paternity suit. [...] On 13 December 1888, the *Wooster Republican* warned those citizens who "continually practice adultery" to desist or suffer a visit from the White Caps. [...] Aaron Bitner, John Hilderbrandt, and Fielding Berry were all whitecapped in October 1887, drawing the ire of the White Caps for their ill treatment of wives, daughters, stepchildren, and neighbouring youths.[73]

This kind of community regulation of sexual behaviour and family standards reminds one of forms of the English charivari, and the uses to which they were put in the nineteenth century.[74] If the White Caps lacked the traditional mock processions and instruments of rough music characteristic of the English charivari, they replaced them with appropriate ritual, depositing a bundle of hickory switches containing a threatening letter on the doorstep of the offender. If the warning was not heeded, a whipping followed. And public shame, so crucial in all European forms of the charivari, was also central in the history of whitecapping.[75] From Indiana, whitecapping spread quickly to Ohio, and by 1889 had attained a foothold across North America.[76] [...]

*****

These highly organized forms of whitecapping, prominent in the midwest and border states, were supplemented by activities in the south and far west, where the ritual was directed against economic ills, often complicated by the issue of race.[77] Mississippi's White Caps, active in the years 1902–1906, directed their anger against black tenant farmers, scapegoats in the battle between small dirt farmers and the mercantile elite that controlled credit and dictated land policy.[78] In North Texas, too,

blacks were frequent targets of White Cap gangs.[79] Perhaps the most interesting case of whitecapping emerged in New Mexico, in the mid to late 1880s, led by Juan José Herrera, a migrant from Colorado or Utah. Dominated by small squatters of Mexican-American descent, Las Gorras Blancas fought large cattle ranchers and landowners who began fencing the best pasturing and watering lands. As they burned fences, cut barbed wire, and terrorized the cattle men, the New Mexico White Caps proclaimed their platform: "To Protect the Lives and Property of Our People. Lawyers and judges be fair and just as we are or suffer the consequences."[80]

This kind of structured movement remained rare in Canada, although whitecapping was frequently practiced, often in an organized fashion. White Cap gangs battled other youth groups and police in turn-of-the-century Hamilton, Ontario.[81] But the most impressive documentation comes from Georgetown, Ontario, where the White Caps were led by E. Copeland, "an American desperado, who carried on the same business in the United States, and defies the officers of the law to arrest him." Like their counterparts in Indiana, Georgetown's White Caps drew on the nineteenth-century community's distaste for wife-beaters.[82] Their first victim was a Mr. Crowe, notorious for his acts of cruelty to his wife. In mid February 1889 Crowe was sent a warning. On a Saturday evening, in early March, a dozen armed and masked men attacked Crowe's house, seized the wife-beater, stripped him naked, switched him, and rolled him in the snow. Crowe left town shortly after. From this beginning, the White Caps broadened their activity, sending threatening letters and bundles of hickory switches to a number of persons known for their laziness or social indiscretions. But the Georgetown group took particular delight in tormenting the Salvation Army, penning obscene and threatening letters to the Captain of the religious band and his female officers. Their anger seemed to have been directed against the Salvation Army's tendency to "run on the boys," probably a resentment of the religious body's attacks on irreligious behaviour. Then, too, a letter warned the Captain "to be careful what he says about the Catholics, as we would White-Cap him quick." Tensions finally erupted in an attack on the Salvation Army's barracks: shutters were torn off the building, windows broken, and a meeting loudly disrupted. Three leaders—Copeland, Jack Hume, and Fred Board—were eventually incarcerated, the movement broken. But for days the White Caps had defied the police, pelting them with stones, avoiding arrest, stalking the streets with impunity, accosting innocent women. Like the charivari, whitecapping could reveal vividly the fragile basis of social order in the nineteenth-century community.[83]

These forms of whitecapping, from the highly structured bands of Indiana, Tennessee, Missouri, and New Mexico, to the less cohesive groupings of the southern states and Georgetown, Ontario, were but the most visible peak of the movement. They have survived historical oblivion because they are entrenched in local folklore, because their presence spanned a number of weeks, at least, if not a number of years. But it is entirely likely that the phenomenon of whitecapping was most prominent as a spontaneous, sporadic effort to enforce standards and traditional rights. Like the charivari, it would be used on the spur of the moment, when local outrage exploded at one final transgression.

[...] In Berlin, Ontario, two Germans received three-year prison terms for their role in whitecapping a Mrs. Koehler. On 20 May 1896, Mrs. Koehler, who had recently subjected a stepchild to considerable abuse, was aroused from sleep by cries that a neighbour was ill. As she opened her door she was seized by four men. Then followed the ritualistic enactment of rough justice: her bed-clothes were violently torn from her body; she was ridden on a rail for a certain distance; and, finally, she was tarred and feathered.[84] [...]

White Cap actions against wife-beating, probably the single transgression against social propriety most often punished, were also likely to be spontaneous affairs. [...] In Lambton, Ontario, near London, four or five neighbours whitecapped William Lawson in 1889. On the night of 26 November they rushed up to him, grabbed him, and accused him of mistreating his wife. They then took him to the pump where, according to Lawson, they "half-drowned" him. When Lawson refused to beg his wife's forgiveness, the men forced a large pole between his legs and danced him about the yard. They concluded this version of rough justice by parading the offender up and down the town's streets.[85] [...]

[...] In both its highly structured, organized forms, and in its more spontaneous instances, whitecapping could be turned to distinctly working-class purpose, a threatening tactic employed to enrich the process of class struggle. [...] During the building of the Sante Fe Railroad, whitecappers stopped sectionmen hauling ties, burned the ties, and proclaimed that the railroad was setting wage-rates below an acceptable standard. A blunt note was posted on railroad buildings:

> All section foremen and operators are advised to leave at once or they will not be able to do so.
>
> Signed,
> White Caps[86]

This kind of threat, relying on the fear inspired by the White Cap name, may well have been common in nineteenth-century labour struggles. [...] In Hamilton, Ontario, during an iron moulders' strike in 1892, a non-union moulder, Clendenning, was prosecuted by a constable for carrying firearms. Clendenning attempted to justify possession of the weapon, arguing that whenever he went out, he was followed by union men. He noted that another strikebreaker, a French Canadian named Fleury, had received a threatening letter, headed by a skull and cross-bones, a whip, and a club:

> Scabs, beware! We have formed an association to go and club the life out of scoundrels if you don't cleare this town before Wednesday night.

Ye will a lashing such as white man never got
before what you are looking for badly.

The communication bore the sinister signature,
"WHITE CAPS." Clendenning was bound to
hold the peace for six months, or forfeit $50. But
the strikebreaker's fear was hardly pacified by
the judge's restraining order. "If the union men
get their way," he complained, "I won't be here
for six months.[87]

Whitecapping, then, like the charivari, was
a ritualized form of enforcing community
standards, appropriate behaviour, and traditional
rights. As part of a long tradition of extra-
legal authority, it drew on a rich and complex
heritage. As a force directed against immoral,
illicit, or unjustifiable behaviour, it shared an
essential place, along with North American
forms of rough music, in the history of popular
culture. But what are we to make of these two
ritualized manifestations of rough justice?

V

*****

In the case of the charivari the question as to
who participated is a complex one, although
a pattern does seem to emerge from the data.
The ritual was apparently practised by all social
groupings and classes in the first half of the
nineteenth century, each stratum subjecting its
own members to the discordant sounds of rough
music. Hudson Valley skimetons, for instance,
were utilized by rich and poor alike.[88] While the
weight of the evidence indicates clearly that the
plebeian world was the more appropriate setting
for the charivari, upper-class figures could
also be drawn to the customary wedding-night
celebrations. The involvement of the well-to-do,
perhaps, testifies to the social acceptability of the
practice; a complex web of legitimation seemed
to encase both the participants and the victims.
But this legitimation had its limits. Even in the
opening decades of the century, plebeian crowds
gathered to charivari their social betters seldom,
if ever, received endorsement. The custom was
not meant to cross class lines.

It was in this context that the ritual thrived
in early nineteenth-century North America.
Even when opposed, it was recognized as an
established institution. [...] As late as 1837,
a Kingston editor could defend charivaris,
arguing that magisterial authority had no
place interfering in such popularity sanctioned
assemblies:

Charivari parties may be unlawful, and much
mischief may at times be committed by them,
but the custom is an ancient one and cannot
easily be suppressed. It is the only way in which
the public can shew their distaste of incongruous
or ill-assorted marriages. The interference of
the magistrates on this occasion we fear is
injudicious, since if we know anything of the
spirit of the young gentlemen of Kingston, the
more they endeavour to preserve the fair lady
from annoyance, the more they will subject her
to insult.[89]

*****

[...] Even if the charivari was not exclusively
a patrician affair, [...] a plebeian following could
be led by an upper-class element, Kingston's
Henry Smith, Jr., of the 1830s being a prime
example.[90]

[...] Patrician acquiescence, and even
occasional participation, undoubtedly
legitimized the ritual in plebeian eyes, but it was
a fragile foundation of support. While European
charivaris of the sixteenth and seventeenth
centuries may have been instigated by patrician
elements, willingly sanctioned by constituted
authority, recognized as "according to custom"
and "in some sort necessairie," there is little
indication that North American forms of rough
music were ever given the formal blessings of
the socially superior.[91] [...] As the Montreal
magistrates well knew, as early as 1823,
charivaris had to be suppressed, like all "riots,
bruits, troubles ou réunions tumultueses."[92]

This understanding gradually permeated
the consciousness of patrician elements. From
mid-century on, one must look long and hard to
find an upper-class element involved in some

variant of rough music. And as patrician forces departed, the complex legitimation encasing the custom melted into the background: charivaris were more vigorously suppressed; victims began to respond to the insulting taunts of the crowd with hostility rather than good humour; and violent confrontations often developed. As the charivari became exclusively an affair of the lower orders, men, the ritual came to be associated with the barbarism and savagery of the masses. What had once been defended was to be harshly condemned. It is this process of the proletarianization of a cultural form that marks the charivari as a ritual of particular concern to those interested in an autonomous, working-class culture, and explains the fear and loathing with which bourgeois elements perceived that development.

*****

With the custom linked explicitly to the lower orders, and as any form of legitimation, however mild, collapsed, the charivari drew attack from many quarters. [...] The terrain of the rough, unpolished multitude, the shivaree was, in Alice T. Chase's words, "a Survival of semi-barbaric times; the curious point to note is how nearly this barbarous custom touches our advanced civilization of the present day."[93] And barbarity, of course, was not of the genteel, bourgeois world. Neither, apparently, were the practitioners of rough music, who instead were denigrated, condemned, and persistently held up to the ridicule of the defenders of public virtue: "... lunatics assaulting a man's house after dark and making the night hideous with their howls"; "... a collection of wild, ignorant, howling savages, whatever may be the particular colour of their skins or the depth and variety of their gutturals"; "... the abolition of horning would be very cheaply purchased by the sacrifice of a horner in every community in which the disgusting practice survives."[94]

[...] The large urban centres were apparently the first to succumb, followed by the smaller cities, towns, and villages, trailed by the frontier regions, the outposts of North American civilization. Where bourgeois consciousness matured earliest, the charivari was first attacked; where such consciousness was developing weakly it tended to survive longest. It was in this context that the ritual came to be monopolized by the lower orders. Although certain working-class trades, organized and enamoured of their skilled status, understandably attracted to more respectable, rational forms of protest, may have shied away from the custom as it drew increasing hostility, other members of the plebeian community retained their allegiance: immigrants new to America's shores; agricultural labourers; the urban armies of the unskilled; decimated crafts like shoemaking, weaving, and blacksmithing; small farmers; rural tradesmen; timberworkers, socially, culturally, and geographically on the margins of society; miners in isolated communities; and the underclass town and country. [...]

The practice of whitecapping proves similarly elusive, defying a precise analysis of those involved in the organized and spontaneous manifestations of the movement. Many histories of whitecapping, including Madelein Noble's recent assessment, argue that the White Caps drew upon respectable elements of the community, prominent citizens organizing and leading the crusade against immorality, lewdness, vice, and general social impropriety.[95] And, yet, many of these same sources attribute the decline of whitecapping, especially its legal suppression, to the degeneration of the movement, its take-over by rougher elements, and the increasingly insignificant role of men of position.[96] The transition from patrician to plebeian control, however, is never satisfactorily explained. Moreover, there is more than a hint that historians have been blind to the not inconsequential role that the lower orders played in the beginnings of the local movements of whitecapping. [...] In Hamilton, Ontario, the leaders of the White Cap gang were Robert and George Ollman, the Macklin Street brickmakers.[97] [...] Whitecapping, like the charivari, was never a process totally dominated by men of property and standing. Both forms of enforcing community standards and appropriate behaviour were the terrain of the *menu peuple*.

[...] Charivaris, and their persistent use throughout the nineteenth century thus lend force to an interpretation of culture stressing continuity in the midst of change. [...] Whitecapping, too, drew on cultural continuities: the long tradition of violent enforcement of morality characteristic of American vigilante groups; the southern heritage of resistance to black emancipation ("The people of the 'White Cap' belt [of Indiana] ... ," claimed the *Chicago Record*, "came originally from the South."[98]). But it, also, could be turned to new purpose, continuing in the footsteps of the charivari, moving forcefully against social impropriety, or adapting to the economic needs of the working-class community.

*****

[I]n nineteenth-century North America there were obscure corners of everyday life where the rule of law could or would not intervene, where, by the law's very concerns—in which property always figured centrally[99]—it had little place. Domestic discord, appropriate marital unions, and immoral behaviour were hardly the concern of the law, except in exaggerated cases of gross cruelty or sexual "deviance," as in infanticide, incest, or rape. But these extremes suggest the point. The mundane wife-beater, or the old widower coming to life in the midst of his unnatural marriage, remained outside the rule of law. So, too, was the employer who refused the just demands of "manly" workers, or the strikebreaker imported to break the resistance of working-class forces. Yet, in the plebeian world, such behaviour seemed a serious transgression, a violation of time-honoured conceptions of appropriate behaviour.

In the absence of any recourse to law, the lower orders turned instinctively to custom, posing the discipline of the community against the perceived deficiencies of legal authority. As a force within the plebeian world, custom was obeyed because it was "intimately intertwined with a vast living network of interrelations, arranged in a meticulous manner."[100] "It posed an order, an authority, that was, in contradiction to the law, spontaneous, traditional, personal, commonly known, corporate, and relatively unchanging."[101] [...]

*****

[...] The cultures of the working-class and plebeian worlds clashed with constituted authority: in border, seaside, and river-towns, where smuggling was a way of life; in the settlement of petty scores, where the rule of law was forsaken for the more immediate satisfaction of barn burning, fence destruction, or animal maiming; in urban crowds, purposively directing their anger against perceived threats and recalcitrant employers; in the backwoods and obscure valleys in the shadows of North American civilization, where law always played second fiddle to brute force.

*****

Notes

This is a version of a paper presented to the Canadian Historical Association meetings, London, Ontario, 2 June 1978. I would like to thank the many individuals who directed me to sources, replied to my letters, and shared materials with me. I have acknowledged the aid of a number of friends and scholars who shared specific sources with me in the footnotes. This paper benefitted greatly from a reading by Russell Hann, who suggested a number of revisions. Michael S. Cross graciously shared research with me, and Edward Shorter offered early encouragement at a time when I needed it most. The Canada Council supported the research in its initial stages. Finally, it is a pleasure to acknowledge two other debts. Donald Swainson, whose knowledge of 19th-century Ontario is truly encyclopedic, directed me to many important sources of information. Gregory S. Kealey, who critically assessed a crude first draft, also shared his notes from Toronto's *Globe* with me, allowing me to enrich my presentation.

1. See Eloi-Chrisiophe Bassinet, *Histoire Morale, Civile, Politique et Littiraire du charivari ...* (Paris 1833); Ruth Mellinkoff, "Riding Backwards: Theme of Humiliation and Symbol of Evil," *Viator: Medieval and Renaissance Studies*, 4 (1973), pp. 152–177.

2. As an introduction to the charivari, see Edward Shorter, *The Making of the Modern Family* (New York 1975), pp. 46, 64, 217–228; Roger Pinon, "Qu'est-ce q'un charivari? Essai en vue d'une définition operatorie," in *Kontakete und Frenzen. Probleme der Volks-. Kultur- und Sozialforschung* (Göttingen 1969), pp. 393–405.

3. Robert Chambers, *The Book of Days: A Miscellany of Popular Antiquities* (Edinburgh 1864), II, p. 510; Francis Grose, *A Classical Dictionary of the Vulgar Tongue* (London 1785), p. 291; *Brewer's Dictionary of Phrase and Fable*, revised by Ivor H. Evans (London 1970), p. 937; Frank Hugget, *A Day in the Life of a Victorian Farm Worker* (London 1972), p. 64; Rev. William H. Cope, *A Glossary of Hampshire Words and Phrases* (London 1883), p. 75; Enid Porter, *Cambridgeshire Customs and Folklore* (London 1969), pp. 8–10; Porter, *The Folklore of East Anglia* (London 1974), pp. 27–28; Christina Hole, *English Folklore* (London 1940), p. 23; Joseph Wright, ed., *The English Dialect Dictionary* (New York 1905), V, pp. 156–157.

4. Elizabeth Mary Wright, *Rustic Speech and Folklore* (London 1914), pp. 276–277; Mrs. Gutch, *County Folk-lore: Examples of Printed Folklore Concerning the East Riding of Yorkshire* (London 1912), VI, pp. 130–133; William Henderson, *Notes on the Folklore of the Northern Counties of England and the Borders* (London 1967), pp. 29–30; *Notes and Queries* (London), 5th ser., V (25 March 1876), p. 253; 6th ser., VI (25 November 1882), pp. 425–426.

5. Hole, *English Folklore*, 23; Theo Brown, "The Stag Hunt in Devon," *Folklore*, 63 (December 1952), pp. 104–109.

6. Chambers, *Book of the Days*, I, p. 360; William S. Walsh, *Curiosities of Popular Customs* (Philadelphia 1907), p. 156. The Butcher's Serenade is depicted in Hogarth's "The Industrious 'Prentice Out of His Tune and Married to His Master's Daughter," the sixth print in the *Industry & Idleness* series.

7. A.L. Rowse, *A Cornish Childhood: Autobiography of a Cornishman* (New York 1947), pp. 8–9, where Rowse questions whether the "shivaree" was an old Cornish custom, or whether it was brought to the region by miners returned from America.

8. E.P. Thompson has outlined the English charivari's increasing concern with wife-beating in the 19th century in "Rough Music: Le Charivari anglais," *Annales: E.S.C.*, 27 (1972), esp. p. 297.

9. *Notes and Queries* (London), 2nd ser., X (15 December 1860), pp. 476–477. See also Thompson, "Rough Music," p. 297; Shorter, *Modern Family*, pp. 224–225.

10. Gutch, *County Folk-Lore .... Yorkshire*, VI, 132–133. On other folk-rhymes directed against wife-beaters, see G.F. Northall, *English Folk-Rhymes* (London 1892), pp. 253–257, all of which were recited in the midst of subjecting an offender to "riding the stang."

11. Van Gennep, *Manuel de folklore*, I, p. 626, quoted and translated in Shorter, *Modern Family*, p. 221.

12. Nicole Caston, "La Criminality familiale dans le ressoit du Parlement de Toulouse, 1690–1730," in A. Abbiatecci et al., ed., *Crimes et Criminality en France sous l'Ancien Regime, 17e–18e siecles* (Paris 1971), p. 106.

13. P. Saintyves, "Le charivari de l'Adultere et les courses a corps nus," *L'Ethnographie*, 31, new ser., (1935), pp. 7–36; Shorter, *Modern Family*, pp. 219–220; Eugen Weber, *Peasants into Frenchmen: The Modernization of Rural France, 1870–1914* (Stanford 1976), pp. 400–401.

14. Natalie Zemon Davis, "The Reasons of Misrule," in *Society and Culture in Early Modern France* (Stanford 1975), pp. 97–123.

15. Weber, *Peasants into Frenchmen*, p. 403; Rolande Bonnain-Moerdyk et Donald Moerdyk, "A propos du charivari: discours bourgeois et coutumes populaires," *Annales: E.S.C.*, 32 (1977), pp. 381–398; Yves-Marie Bercé, *Fête et Révolte: Des Mentalités populaires du XVIe au XVIIIe siecle* (Paris 1976), pp. 40–44.

16. Weber, *Peasants into Frenchmen*, p. 404. On similar uprisings by prostitutes in England in the 1860s and 1880s, see Andrew Chier, *Plymouth and Plymouthians: Photographs and Memoirs* (Plymouth 1974), n.p., an account of prostitutes besieging a workhouse, seeking shelter, "beating tin kettles and blowing tin whistles"; and "Report of the House of Commons Select Committee on the Administration, Operation, and Effects of the Contagious Diseases Acts of 1866–1869," *Parliamentary Papers*, 1882, IX, p. 340. A later account, in which prostitutes again use rough music against efforts to suppress their activities, is found in Sarah Robinson, *The Soldier's Friend: A Pioneer's Record* (London 1913), p. 148. I am indebted to Judith R. Walkowitz, whose continuing studies of prostitution and the Contagious Diseases

Acts promise much, for bringing these sources to my attention.

17. See E.J. Hobsbawm, *Primitive Rebels: Studies in Archaic Forms of Social Movements in the 19th and 20th Centuries* (Manchester 1971).

18. Note the discussions in J.M.S. Careless, "Limited Identities in Canada," *Canadian Historical Review*, 50 (March 1969), pp. 1–10; Brian Stock, "English Canada: The Visible and Invisible Cultures," *Canadian Forum*, LII (March 1973), pp 29–33.

19. On the French origins of the term, see William J. Fielding, *Strange Customs of Courtship and Marriage* (Philadelphia 1942), pp. 50–51; Susanna Moodie, *Roughing It in the Bush* (Toronto 1962), p. 145; *The Charivari; or Canadian Poetics: A Tale After the Manner of Beppo* (Montreal 1824), p. 49. [This source has recently been republished in the "Early Canadian Poetry Series," authorship attributed to George Longmore, edited and introduced by Mary Lu Macdonald. See Longmore, *The Charivari or Canadian Poetics* (Ottawa 1977). See, also, Carl F. Klinck, ed., *Literary History of Canada* (Toronto 1976), 1, pp. 140–141, 145, 147.] John S. Farmer, *Americanisms—Old and New* (London 1889); William S. Walsh, *Curiosities of Popular Customs* (Philadelphia 1898), pp. 209–213; Walsh, *Handy-Book of Literary Curiosities* (Philadelphia 1892) p. 149; Sylvia Clapin, *A New Dictionary of Americanisms* (New York n.d.); *American Notes & Queries,* 1 (27 October 1888), pp. 311–312; III (15 June 1889), p. 82. Hereafter *A. N. & Q.*

20. *A. N. & Q.,* I (27 October 1888), pp. 311–312; *Smith's Falls News*, 23 July 1875; 16 August 1875; *Globe*, 2 May 1877; *Pembroke Observer*, cited in *Smith's Falls News*, 4 May 1877.

21. On the practice of the charivari in Louisiana and Alabama see *A. N. A Q.*, I (20 October 1888), pp. 296–297; E. Bagby Atwood, "Shivarees and Charivaris: Variations on a Theme," in Moody C. Boatright, Wilson M. Hudson, and Allen Maxwell, ed., *A Good Tale and a Bonnie Tune* (Dallas 1964), pp. 68–70; Roy V. Hoffpauir, "Acadian Marriage Customs," *Attakapas Gazette*, III (December 1968), pp. 3–19: James Hall, *Tales of the Border* (Philadelphia 1835), pp. 121–124. An excellent discussion is found in the different editions of George W. Cable, *Old Creole Days* (New York 1883), Part ii, pp. 54–55: Cable, *Old Creole Days* (New York 1890), pp. 220–221. The quote is from John F. Watson, "Notilia of Incidents at New Orleans in 1804 and 1805," *American Pioneer*, II (1843), p. 229.

22. Alice T. Chase, "The 'Shivaree,'" *A. N. & Q.*, I (29 September 1888), pp. 263–264, also in Walsh, *Curiosities of Popular Customs*, pp. 209–213.

23. Miles L. Hanley, "Charivaria II: 'Serenade' in New England," *American Speech*, VIII (April 1933), pp. 24–26.

24. *Lincoln Nebraska Daily State Journal*, 22 November 1874;1 January 1878, quoted in Mamie Meredith, "Charivari I: 'Belling the Bridal Couple' in Pioneer Days," *American Speech*, VIII (April 1933), pp. 22–24.

25. Robert S. Thurman, "Twas Only a Joke," *Tennessee Folklore Society Bulletin*, XXXV (September 1969), pp. 86–94.

26. *A. N. & Q.,* I (20 October 1888), pp. 296–297.

27. Nils Flaten, "Notes on American-Norwegian with a Vocabulary," *Dialect Notes*, II (1900), pp. 115–126; V. Stefanson, "English Loan-Nouns Used in the Icelandic Colony of North Dakota," *Dialect Notes*, II (1903), pp. 354–362; George T. Flom, "English Loanwords in American Norwegian, as Spoken in the Koshkonong Settlement (Dane County, Wisconsin)," *American Speech*, I (July 1926), pp. 541–548.

28. See the discussion of the charivari in Bryan D. Palmer, "Most Uncommon Common Men: Craft, Culture, and Conflict in a Canadian Community, 1860–1914," Unpublished Ph.D. dissertation, SUNY at Binghamton, 1977, pp. 184–192.

29. Hans Kurath, *A Word Geography of the Eastern United States* (Ann Arbor 1949), p. 78 and Fig. 184; Gordon R. Wood, *Vocabulary Change: A Study of Variation in Regional Words in Eight of the Southern States* (Carbondale 1971), p. 39; *Time* (Canadian edition), 25 July 1949, p. 41; Walter S. Avis et al., *A Dictionary of Canadianisms: On Historical Principles* (Toronto 1967), pp. 141, 656, 689.

30. *British Whig*, 18 March 1834; 11 March 1837; 31 July 1835. A Kingston charivari of 1877, complete with costumes and effigy is noted in E.Z. Massicotte, "Le Charivari au Canada," *Bulletin des Recherches Historiques*, XXXII (November 1926), p. 717.

31. Hamilton Board of Police, *Minutes*, 1841–1842 (22 March 1842), p. 50.

32. The above account draws on *Montreal Gazette*, 7 June 1823; 14 June 1823; 6 September 1823; *Canadian Courant and Montreal Advertiser*, 4 June 1823; 7 June 1823; 11 June 1823; 30 August 1823; *Quebec Gazette*, 16 June 1823.

33. Moodie, *Roughing It in the Bush*, p. 147.

34. An early eighteenth-century reference is Diary of Simeon Perkins, Liverpool, Nova Scotia, 9 October

1766, reprinted in S.D. Clark, *Social Development of Canada* (Toronto 1942), p. 160.

35. *Globe*, 9 July 1868.

36. Note the discussions in Robert Goulet, *Le Charivari* (Paris 1960), translated as *The Violent Season* (New York 1961), esp. pp. 33, 89, 93, 168–169, 171–174, 314–315, 331–332; Jerome Hart, *A Vigilante Girl* (Chicago 1910), pp. 326–327; *Sarnia Observer*, 24 April 1885.

37. *Globe*, 15 December 1881.

38. *Sarnia Observer*, 31 October 1884; 7 November 1884.

39. *Hamilton Times*, 13 January 1868.

40. Public Archives of Canada, RG8 C 316, Cathcart *et al.*, to the Magistrates, St. John's. Lower Canada, 27 August 1841:24 August 1841; 25 August 1841, 219–223. On the charivari in the Maritimes in the twentieth century, where it was often known as saluting, see Monica Morrison, "Wedding Night Pranks in Western New Brunswick," *Southern Folklore Quarterly*, 38 (December 1974), pp. 285–297; Ernest Buckler, *The Mountain and the Valley* (New York 1952); Avis, *Dictionary of Canadianisms*, p. 656.

41. J.E. Collins, *Life and Times of the Right Honourable Sir John A. Macdonald, Premier of the Dominion of Canada* (Toronto 1883), pp. 311–312. My thanks to James Hiller for providing me with this reference.

42. Farmer, *Americanisms*; John Russell Bartlett, *Dictionary of Americanisms: A Glossary of Words and Phrases* (Boston 1877), p. 93. The Callithumpians were also active in the American west as late as the 1880s. See Mitford M. Mathews, ed., *A Dictionary of Americanisms: On Historical Principles* (Chicago 1951), I, p. 248, citing cases from Glendale, Montana (1879) and Reinbeck, Iowa (1881).

43. *Hill's Yankee Story Teller's Own Book; and Reciter's Pocket Companion* (New York 1836), p. 9.

44. On the American use of the term and its relationship to the charivari, see *New York Times*, 25 May 1904; M. Schele de Vere, *Americanisms: The English of the New World* (New York 1872), p. 589; Craigie and Hurlbert, *A Dictionary of American English: On Historical Principles* (Chicago 1938), I., p. 393; Sylvia Clapin, *New Dictionary of Americanisms; The Century Dictionary* (New York 1897), I, p. 769; Mathews, *Dictionary of Americanisms*, I, p. 248; *Atlantic Monthly*, XV (March 1865), p. 300; *Harper's Magazine* (July 1886), p. 213.

45. Harry Middleton Hyatt, *Folk-Lore from Adams County, Illinois* (Hannibal, Missouri, 1965), pp. 468–469.

46. See Thompson, "Rough Music," pp. 304–308, for a brief introduction.

47. See D.G.C. Allan, "The Rising in the West, 1628–1631," *Economic History Review*, 2nd ser., V (1952–1953), pp. 76–85.

48. Richard B. Morris, *Government and Labour in Early America* (New York 1965), p. 147.

49. Bryan D. Palmer, "'Give Us the Road and We Will Run It': The Social and Cultural Matrix of an Emerging Labour Movement," in Gregory S. Kealey and Peter Warrian, ed., *Essays in Canadian Working Class History* (Toronto, 1976), p. 122; *Ottawa Evening Journal*, 17 September 1891 (my thanks to Russell Hann for directing me to this reference); F.P. Grove, *The Master of the Mill* (Toronto 1967), pp. 155–162. The Chaudière conflict is discussed in more detail, although this incident is ignored, in Edward McKenna, "Unorganized Labour Versus Management: The Strike at the Chaudière Lumber Mills, 1891," *Histoire Sociale/Social History*, V (November 1972), 186–211. See also H. Ferns and B. Ostry, *The Age of Mackenzie King* (Toronto 1976), p. 79.

50. The strike is discussed in Palmer, "Most Uncommon Common Men," pp. 190–192.

51. *Hamilton Spectator*, 4, 5, 9, 10 June 1890.

52. See Harold Wentworth, *American Dialect Dictionary* (New York 1944), pp. 550–551.

53. George Rawlyk, A.R.M. Lower, Donald Swainson, and Peter Goheen all had some personal knowledge of the ritual. My grandmother remembered it practised near Hawkesbury, Ontario. A student tells me that it is still common in Listowel, Ontario. John Weaver witnessed a charivari in Madoc, Ontario, north of Belleville, in 1963, the groom being tied to a rocking chair, and driven around the town in the back of a flat-bed truck. Neil Rosenberg, Director of the Memorial University of Newfoundland Folklore and Language Archive, tells me that the practice is known in Newfoundland, but that the ceremony does not have a standard name. Lawrence Stone, relying on a colleague's recollections, contends that the charivari was still practised in Oregon in the twentieth century. See Lawrence Stone, *The Family, Sex, and Marriage in England, 1500–1800* (New York 1977), fn. on p. 504. As late as 1958 Edmonton passed a law prohibiting charivaris. See *Edmonton Journal*, 30 October 1958.

54. *Windsor Evening Record*, 13, 14 January 1896. Craig Heron has recently informed me that charivaris in St. Catharines, Ontario and Lacrosse, Wisconsin were documented in the *Hamilton*

Spectator, 11 August, 9 June 1904. The St. Catharines event, in which the victim drove off his tormentors with the spray from a garden hose, hints at a changed twentieth century context which makes the violent clashes of the previous century a thing of the past. But note, too, the violent charivari at Bishop's Mills (near Brockville) described in *Hamilton Spectator*, 15 November 1906.

55.   Hyatt, *Folk-Lore from Adams County*, p. 468.

56.   Farmer, *Americanisms*, p. 557.

57.   Clapin, *New Dictionary of Americanisms; Century Dictionary*, VIII, p. 6910.

58.   "White Caps," *The Americana: A Universal Reference Library* (New York 1911), p. XX.

59.   See James Elbert Cutler, *Lynch-Law: An Investigation into the History of Lynching in the United States* (Montclair, N.J., 1969, original 1905), pp. 46–72; R.S. Longley, "Mob Activities in Revolutionary Massachusetts," *New England Quarterly*, VI (March 1933), pp. 112–114; Frank W.C. Hersey, "Tar and Feathers: The Adventures of Captain John Malcolm," Colonial Society of Massachusetts Publications, *Transactions*, XXXIV (1937–1942), pp. 429–473; Richard Maxwell Brown, "Violence and the American Revolution," in Stephen G. Kurt and James H. Hutson, *Essays on the American Revolution* (Chapel Hill 1973), pp. 103–112; Alfred F. Young, "Pope's Day, Tarring and Feathering, and Cornet Joyce, *jun.*: From Ritual to Rebellion in Boston, 1745–1775." Unpublished manuscript prepared for the Anglo-American Conference of Labor Historians, Rutger's University, 1973; Carl Bridenbaugh, *Cities in Revolt: Urban Life in America, 1743–1776* (New York 1955), pp. 121–122. Tarring and feathering, of course, did borrow heavily from the English experience, as many of these sources indicate, and continued well into the nineteenth and twentieth centuries. For the use of tarring and feathering in early Upper Canada, see Josephine Phelan, "The Tar and Feather Case, 1827," *Ontario History*, LXVIH (March 1976), pp. 17–23. Cases of the use of tar and feathers in late nineteenth-century Milan, Monroe County, Michigan, and St. Thomas, Ontario, are outlined in *Ottawa Citizen*, 11 May 1871; *Globe*, 11 November 1886. For popular punishment of sexual offenders in Puritan New England, see Arthur W. Calhoun, *A Social History of the American Family from Colonial Times to the Present* (Cleveland 1917–1919), I, pp. 129–152.

60.   See Richard Maxwell Brown, *The South Carolina Regulators* (Cambridge, Massachusetts, 1963); George R. Adams, "The Carolina Regulators: A Note on Changing Interpretations," *North Carolina*

Historical Review, XLIX (1972), pp. 345–352; James P. Whittenburg, "Planters, Merchants, and Lawyers: Social Change and the Origins of the North Carolina Regulation," *William and Mary Quarterly*, XXXIV (April 1977), pp. 215–238.

61.   Mary Floyd Williams, *History of the San Francisco Committee of Vigilance of 1851: A Study of Social Control on the California Frontier in the Days of the Gold Rush* (New York 1969, original 1921); Hubert Howe Bancroft, *Works: Popular Tribunals, in Two Volumes* (San Francisco 1887); Thomas J. Dimsdale, *The Vigilantes of Montana, or Popular Justice in the Rocky Mountains* (Norman 1953, original 1866). A fascinating account is Josiah Royce, *California from the Conquest in 1846 to the Second Vigilance Committee in San Francisco: A Study of American Character* (Boston 1886), pp. 271–376. See also, Frederick Jackson Turner, *The Frontier in American History* (New York 1920), p. 212; J.D. Hill, "The Early Mining Camp in American Life," *Pacific Historical Review*, I (1932), pp. 303–306; Alexandre Barde, *Histoire des comites de vigilance aux Attakapas* (Saint-Jeane-Baptiste, Louisiana, 1861).

62.   The standard treatment is Cutler, *Lynch-Law*. See also, *Ottawa Citizen*, 3 February 1872; 3, 4 August 1871; 22 February 1872; 27 May 1871; 1 June 1871; 3 May 1871; *Perth Courier*, 18 December 1868; 3 April 1868; *Globe*, 2 September 1868; *Hastings Chronicle* (Belleville), 23 April 1862; John W. Caughey, ed., *Their Majesties the Mob* (Chicago 1960), esp. p. 98.

63.   Melvyn Dubofsky, *We Shall Be All: A History of the Industrial Workers of the World* (Chicago 1969); A. Ross McCormack, *Reformers, Rebels, and Revolutionaries: The Western Canadian Radical Movement, 1899–1919* (Toronto 1977), p. 161.

64.   *Hamilton Spectator*, 3 April 1882; Edward McKenna, "Unorganized Labour Versus Management: The Strike at the Chaudière Lumber Mills, 1891," *Histoire Social/Social History*, V (November 1972), p. 204; Barry Broadfoot, *Ten Lost Years, 1929–1939: Memories of Canadians Who Survived the Depression* (Don Mills 1975), pp. 338–348. John L. Lewis supporters tarred and feathered an insurgent miner in Indiana in 1930. See Melvyn Dubofsky and Warren Van Tine, *John L. Lewis: A Biography* (New York 1977), p. 165.

65.   Note the comment in Theodore Watts-Dunton, "Bret Harte," *Athenaeum* (24 May 1902), p. 659. The best brief, accessible introduction to whitecapping is Hugh Graham and Ted Robert Gurr, eds., *Violence in America: Historical and Comparative Perspectives* (Washington 1969), pp. 70–71, 806.

66. B.F. DeCosta, *The White Cross: Its Origins and Progress* (Chicago 1887); Ellice Hopkins, *The White Cross Army* (London 188?).

67. E.W. Crozier, *The White-Caps: A History of the Organization in Sevier County, Tennessee* (Knoxville 1899), p. 31; Nettie H. Pelham, *The White Caps* (Chicago 1891).

68. Corzier, *White-Caps*, pp. 12–13.

69. Henry Clay Duncan, "White Caps in Southern Indiana," paper presented before the Monroe County Historical Society, 1900, pp. 4–6, cited in Madelein M. Noble, "The White Caps of Harrison and Crawford Counties, Indiana: A Study in the Violent Enforcement of Morality," unpublished Ph.D. dissertation, University of Michigan, 1973, p. 65.

70. Clyde Edwin Tuck, *Bald Knobbers: A Romantic and Historical Novel* (Indianapolis 1910), pp. 7–8.

71. Noble, "While Caps," p. 6.

72. Background on the Indiana White Caps is found in *New York Times*, 12 October 1887; Duncan, "White Caps in Southern Indiana," p. 9; *Journal of the Indiana State Senate*, 38th session of the General Assembly, 4 January 1855, p. 34, quoted in Noble, "White Caps," p. 65. See Booth Tarkington, *The Gentleman from Indiana* (New York 1899); James Woodress, "Popular Taste in 1899: Booth Tarkington's First Novel," in Max F. Schulz, ed., *Essays in American and English Literature Presented to Bruce Robert McElderry, Jr.* (Athens, Ohio 1967), pp. 111–112, 119–120; Woodress, *Booth Tarkington: Gentleman from Indiana* (New York 1955), p. 82; David Graham Phillips, *Old Wives for New: A Novel* (New York 1908), p. 68; Meredith Nicholson, *The Hoosiers* (New York 1916), pp. 43–45, for the impact on literature.

73. Noble, "White Caps," pp. 10, 72–76, 165, and esp. the list on pp. 177–190.

74. Thompson, "Rough Music," pp. 285–312.

75. On the importance of ritual and public shame, see Noble, "White Caps," pp. 70–71, 88; Crozier, *The White Caps,* pp. 10–11.

76. On the emergence of whitecapping in Ohio, see *Biographical and Historical Souvenir for the Counties of Clark, Crawford, Harrison, Floyd, Jefferson, Jennings, Scott and Washington: Indiana* (Chicago 1890), p. 35; *Ohio State Journal*, 26, 29 November 1888, 1, 3, 5, 10, 12, 21 December 1888.

77. In Indiana White Caps occasionally directed their attacks against blacks that had defied their authority. See *Appleton's Annual Cyclopaedia and Register of Important Events of the Year 1888,*

78. new serv., XIII (New York 1889), p. 441; Noble, "White Caps," pp. 177–190; Mathews, *Dictionary of Americanisms*, II, p. 1865.

78. William F. Holmes, "Whitecapping: Agrarian Violence in Mississippi, 1902–1906," *Journal of Southern History*, XXXV (May 1969), pp. 165–185; *New York Evening Post*, 21 December 1904.

79. Noble; "White Caps," pp. 156–158; Samuel L. Evans, "Texas Agriculture, 1880–1930," Unpublished Ph.D. dissertation, University of Texas, 1960, pp. 320–321. See also, C. Vann Woodward, *The Strange Career of Jim Crow* (New York 1966), p. 87; Cultler, *Lynch-Law*, p. 154.

80. C.M. Graham, "Have You Ever Heard of the White Caps?" *New Mexico Genealogist*, 6 (December 1967), pp. 3–8; Robert W. Larson, "The White Caps of New Mexico: A Study of Ethnic Militancy in the Southwest," *Pacific Historical Review*, XLIV (May 1975), pp. 171–185; Andrew Bancroft Schiesinger, "Las Gonras Blancas, 1889–1891," *Journal of Mexican American History*, I (Spring 1971), pp. 87–143. An early instance of fence-cutting is described in *Pembroke Observer and Upper Ottawa Advertiser*, 30 January 1885.

81. *Hamilton Spectator*, 2 May 1900; 19 June 1900.

82. Note the comments on wife-beating in *Hastings Chronicle*, 30 July 1862; *Perth Courier*, 27 October 1871; *Palladium of Labor* (Hamilton), 17 October 1885.

83. This account draws on sketches in the *Globe*, 8, 23, 30 March 1889; 1 April 1889. These sources also document the emergence of White Cap bands in other, nearby towns.

84. *Napanee Star*, 29 May 1896; *Hamilton Spectator*, 10 June 1896.

85. *Globe*, 8, 9 April 1890.

86. See Graham, "Have You Ever Heard of the White Caps?" pp. 3–8; Larson, "White Caps of New Mexico," pp. 171–185; Charles A. Siringo, *Cow-Boy Detective: An Autobiography* (New York 1912), pp. 120–122.

87. *Hamilton Spectator*, 11 April 1892.

88. *A. N. Q.*, I (13 October 1888), p. 288.

89. *British Whig*, 11 March 1837.

90. Smith, the patrician leader of the plebeian crowd, perhaps had a counterpart in Peter Aylen, leader of the Shiners in the Ottawa Valley in the 1830s. See Michael S. Cross, "The Shiners' Wars: Social Violence in the Ottawa Valley in the 1830's" *Canadian Historical Review*, LIV (March 1973), pp. 1–25.

91. See, especially, Bernard Capp, "English Youth Groups and *The Pinder of Wakefield*," *Past &*

Present, 76 (August 1977), pp. 132–133; Davis, "The Reasons of Misrule," pp. 97–123; E.P. Thompson, "Patrician Society, Plebeian Culture," *Journal of Social History*, VII (Summer 1974), pp. 382–405.

92. Jean-Claude Robert, "Montréal, 1821–1871: Aspects de l'urbanisation," Thesis de doctorate en histoire, 3 cycles, Université de Paris, 1977, I, p. 197.

93. *A. N. & Q.*, I (29 September 1888), p. 264.

94. *Globe*, 9 July 1868; 2 May 1877; *A. N. & Q.*, 01 (14 December 1889), p. 81.

95. Noble, "White Caps," pp. 5, 67–68, 83–86; *New York Times*, 28 April 1887; 12 October 1887; Lucille Morris, *Bald Knobbers* (Caldwell, Idaho 1939), pp. 19–20, 52.

96. A.H. Haswell, "The Story of the Bald Knobbers," *The Missouri Historical Review*, 18 (October 1923–July 1924), p. 27; Tuck, *Bald Knobbers*, pp. 8–9. Noble argues that the White Caps of Indiana declined because of an accommodation to the transformation of society and economy that occurred in the 1890s, marking a shift away from the resistance characteristic of the 1880s. The argument is far from persuasive. See Noble, "White Caps," p. 148.

97. *Hamilton Spectator*, 19 June 1900; *Hamilton City Directory* (Hamilton 1902).

98. *Chicago Record*, 13 April 1894, cited in Mathews, *Dictionary of Americanisms II*, p. 1865.

99. In the words of Jeremy Bentham: "Property and law are born together and die together."

100. Paul Radin, *The World of Primitive Man* (New York 1953), p. 233.

101. The best brief treatment of this subject, to my mind, is Stanley Diamond's "The Rule of Law Versus the Order of Custom," in Diamond, *In Search of the Primitive: A Critique of Civilization* (New Brunswick, N.J. 1974), pp. 255–280.

Railing, Tattling, and General Rumour: Gossip, Gender, and Church Regulation in Upper Canada

Lynne Marks

• •

In November 1844 the St. Catharines Baptist Church heard that "there were very evil reports in circulation respecting our Brother William H." The congregation did not ignore the rumours, but appointed "Brethren E. and D. to investigate the matter." In February 1845 "William H.'s case was considered, he was present, confessed himself guilty, the charge being fornication." While William H. expressed contrition, the church members decided that "the honour of the church and the glory of God" required that he be expelled from the church. A few years later Wicklow's Baptist Church also dealt with issues of rumour and sexual misconduct when "Sister Nancy F. charge[d] Sister Matilda G. with having carnal connection with Hiram C. in the same bed that she was in and she had told it before the world and it had become public talk." Church members called both women before them to determine whether Matilda G. was guilty of "fornication" or Nancy F. of slander and falsehood, both serious charges in the context of Upper Canadian evangelical life. The church ultimately acquitted Matilda G., claiming there was no proof of fornication, while condemning Nancy F. for slander.[1]

These cases point to some of the many ways in which speech was part of the church discipline process in Upper Canada. While gossip and rumour were a means of regulating

the behaviour of church members, they could also be the basis for calling sinners to account. "Improper" speech, which included gossiping, spreading false rumours, "tattling," "railing," and lying, were strongly censured by the evangelical churches of Upper Canada. Gossip is perhaps the most difficult form of speech to define. I define it here broadly as talk among people who know each other about the behaviour of other people.[2] The way in which gossip could (and can) be used as a means of social control, and could also be viewed as a socially disruptive force, has been explored by a number of scholars of the subject.[3] Social historians of medieval and early modern Europe and of colonial America have analyzed church use and church regulation of gossip, rumour, and other forms of speech,[4] but this topic has not yet received scholarly attention in the context of Upper Canada.[5] This paper will look at how various forms of speech were both used and regulated by Upper Canadian churches. Such a study not only illuminates the social and moral values and practices of the churches but can also reveal much about the larger society in which these churches were situated, a world about which we still know very little.

This world was quite different from our own. In early Ontario three major denominations, the Methodists, Baptists, and Presbyterians, all regulated spheres of life that we would today consider far beyond the purview of religious control. In addition to regulating "improper" speech, other areas such as family life, leisure activities, business practices, sexuality, and private quarrels could all come under church scrutiny. Only church members were subject to this discipline. By joining an evangelical church and declaring their faith in Jesus, individuals agreed to live according to their denomination's definition of biblically ordained Christian behaviour. If they strayed from such behaviour, they were expected to submit to church discipline. In subjecting each other to "fraternal" correction, church members believed they were adhering to the rules of the early Christian church.[6] The sanctions of church discipline varied. Behaviour that was considered too heinous, or too frequently repeated, could result in either temporary suspension or permanent expulsion from the church. In most cases, however, confession of sin and other evidence of sincere contrition allowed members to be retained in or restored to full membership.[7]

Methodists subjected their members to church discipline, but they did not keep records of such cases. As a result, the Baptists and Presbyterians, who did so, are the focus of this article. The latter two denominations together made up about a quarter of all Upper Canadians in the first half of the nineteenth century.[8] Both Baptists and Presbyterians were divided into various subdenominations, which further divided and reunited over the period. While Baptists were all strongly evangelical, Presbyterians divided along evangelical and non-evangelical lines. Until 1843 both evangelicals and "moderates" could be found within the Presbyterian Church of Scotland, although evangelicals appear to have dominated in Upper Canada.[9] After the division of 1843, evangelicals formed the Free Church, but the nature of discipline does not appear to have differed significantly between this group and "Old Kirk" Presbyterians. The focus of discipline and the structures of regulation did, however, differ considerably between Baptists

and Presbyterians. Among Presbyterians, the behaviour of members was overseen exclusively by the minister and church elders (the Session), who had the power to demand public confession or to excommunicate erring members. Ministers were male, as were the elders. Male Baptist deacons and ministers also had particular power in enforcing discipline, but Baptist discipline cases were discussed, and voted on, at monthly covenant meetings attended by all members, women and men.[10]

This study is based on the church records of forty Presbyterian and twenty-six Baptist churches from various regions of what is now southern Ontario and includes all surviving records available in major church archives.[11] It encompasses churches in large communities, small towns, and rural areas for the period from 1798 to 1860. Surviving records of discipline cases are included among accounts of other church events in church minute books. Depending on the diligence of church clerks and the interest of the local congregations, the recording of these cases ranges from very brief notations to detailed descriptions of the issues involved, the testimony of participants and witnesses, and the outcome of the case. [...]

Most inhabitants of Upper Canada lived in rural communities or in small towns, where people knew their neighbours—and their neighbours' business.[12] The accepted use of gossip and rumour to regulate behaviour points to the face-to-face nature of this society and to the centrality of oral communication within it. It also demonstrates that distinctions we take for granted today—particularly the distinction between public and private—appear to have had little relevance in the colony. Although historians have suggested that a public/private "separate spheres" paradigm was beginning to gain currency among the middle and upper classes of Upper Canadian towns in the 1840s and 1850s,[13] the continued legitimate use of gossip and rumour by the churches to regulate what we would define as private, personal behaviour suggests that this distinction remained blurred for many. I argue that the lines between public and private remained blurred not only because the concept of "the private" was just beginning to emerge in mainstream discourse but also because of the particular relationship between the meanings of public/private and sacred/secular among evangelicals in this period. For evangelicals, the secular world was the world of the unconverted, the "ungodly." The converted renounced the secular world for the sacred, and henceforward for them nothing was truly private. [...]

Once Upper Canadians experienced conversion, they were expected to transform their lives as individuals, and to enter into a community of believers, whose members saw themselves as united with each other in brotherly and sisterly Christian bonds. It was also a community very much separate from the outside, secular world. As American historian Curtis Johnson has put it, such evangelical congregations saw themselves as "islands of holiness" in a surrounding world of sin.[14] Although the majority of Upper Canadian Presbyterians appear to have been evangelical, this ethos of separation from "the world" within a community of "saints" was particularly powerful among Baptists. Historians have noted a contradiction at the heart of such strongly evangelical churches: the preservation of the community was central, but it was cemented primarily by the fragile bonds of faith.[15] Family ties often supplemented ties of faith, but the ethnically diverse Upper Canadian Baptists, who could be of American, English, or Scottish origins, were less likely to share the further tie of a common ethnicity.[16] It is perhaps not surprising, then, that maintaining community cohesion was a central concern of Baptist congregations. Within the churches, considerable attention was paid to the regulation of community harmony, which included the regulation of speech that could rupture such harmony.

Speech was also regulated within the Presbyterian churches, but it was not so central a focus of discipline. The less evangelical nature of the Presbyterian Church, and the legacy of

having been a state church in Scotland, meant that the things of the world, including secular hierarchies and connections, were more visible. Ethnicity was another bond uniting Presbyterian congregations, as most church members were Scottish, with some Irish congregations.

The inequalities of the world—including the inequalities of gender—entered more firmly into Presbyterian congregations than Baptist ones, but gender differences in the regulation of "improper speech" existed within both denominations. At the same time, gender inequalities could be transcended by a concern to preserve community, so that "improper speech," particularly slander, lying, and other speech that was considered a threat to the community, was regulated regardless of the gender of the perpetrator. Although the stereotype of the female gossip and "tattler" is not absent from church records, men within both denominations were more likely to be charged with sins of "improper speech." Men more commonly used such speech to challenge the harmony of the church community.

While the extent to which the churches regulated "improper speech" can be determined in the church records, the nature of the records make it impossible to know just how common it was for the churches to use rumour or gossip as a means of identifying cases of apparent sin. In some cases the church records specifically refer to rumour as the source of information. [...] In other cases Presbyterians simply noted that reports were circulating about an individual or a couple. Among Baptists this was the common way of referring to the use of gossip as a source of information. For example, in March 1828 Boston Baptist Church sent a committee to "labour with" Brother T. "respecting some reports in circulation of his drinking."[17]

[...] Although only a minority of cases were clearly brought forward on the basis of gossip, many more may have been. When the minute books of Brantford's Baptist Church noted tersely in September 1843 that it be "resolved that John L. be excluded from being a member of this Church for the sin of drunkenness," it is impossible to know how the church came to know of his drunkenness.[18] It seems likely that, in small communities, many cases of such behaviour would have come to the attention of church members through some form of gossip or rumour, even when specific information is not provided to this effect.

Among those cases where church records demonstrate definitively that rumour or gossip was the source of information, it is clear that certain sins were more likely to come to the attention of the churches on this basis than others. Drinking "to excess" was often the subject of "general rumour" or "evil reports." However, of all the offences dealt with in the church records, sexual offences and domestic conflicts were the most likely to come to the attention of the churches through rumour or gossip.[19] This is not surprising. Scholars have noted that gossip focuses particularly on more personal issues.[20] Tales of sexual infidelity and family conflicts have been the stuff of gossip for centuries, remaining central within current gossip networks.

Although we still gossip about sex and family conflict, something has changed. Today there is at least some acknowledgment that such topics belong within the personal "private" sphere—even as we violate such privacy through our gossip. The fact that, in Upper Canada, gossipers were assumed to have a relatively accurate knowledge of such activities within particular local communities suggests that there was much less of a sense of a public/private separation in this society. People were assumed to know about the sexual and family lives of their neighbours. These aspects were not part of a hidden, private world. The fact that the churches made use of such gossip in an official capacity reflects not only the blurring of any public/private division in the larger "worldly" society but also the nature of evangelical communities, where no sin was "private" and all aspects of life were to bear witness to "the power of the Spirit."[21]

The use of gossip and rumour as legitimate sources of information also reinforces the extent to which Upper Canadian society, and particularly local communities, were still very much face-to-face communities, in which oral communication was of central importance. Not all Upper Canadians could read, but existing evidence suggests that, by the 1830s, most Upper Canadians had attained at least a basic literacy, and newspapers certainly provided a textual medium for spreading information throughout the colony.[22] The written church records themselves point to the value placed on text-based discourse at this time. Nonetheless, it is clear that among the majority of the population, and indeed within institutions of authority such as the churches, an alternative form of discourse—the spread of information through oral communication, or "word of mouth"—retained considerable importance, as well as legitimacy, particularly at the local level.[23]

Today we see gossip and rumour as informal, almost irrational, sources of information.[24] This assessment is based partly on the greater legitimacy we accord to text-based, as compared with word-of-mouth, communication. More broadly, in making judgments about the churches' use of rumour in regulating behaviour, we are comparing such approaches to what we see as the more rational, formalized, bureaucratic approaches to social control of the modern state.[25] During this period, however, institutions of the state—such as the secular legal system—were only gradually gaining legitimacy within the colony.[26] More informal, extra-legal forms of regulation and social control still existed. Church discipline was one such form, but others, such as charivaris and duelling, also retained a certain legitimacy in this period, like the churches, both of the latter also relied on gossip—community talk or rumour about a situation—as the basis for regulatory action.

Charivaris allowed local inhabitants to express their disapproval of certain behaviour, particularly behaviour within what we now define as the private sphere of the family. For example, an old widower who married a much younger woman could expect to be "charivaried" by members of the community, who would surround the house of the unlucky couple after the wedding, making a huge din until they received some payment. [...] Information about local wife beaters or unacceptable sexual relationships was spread through the medium of rumour or "public talk" While charivaris were popular largely among the "common people" of Upper Canada, duelling was practised by the men of the colonial elite—or those aspiring to that status. Many challenges to a duel were issued in reaction to deliberate insult, but others occurred in response to gossip that circulated within Upper Canadian high society—gossip that was seen to damage the reputation of the challenger or a female relative.[27]

The reason for such challenges was the assertion that the circulating tale was in fact not true. This uncertainty was the chief danger in using gossip and rumour as a means of regulation and the churches were well aware of the problem. They used "general rumour" or "evil reports" as the basis for calling sinners before them, but once the case was heard by the session or church meeting, they tried to determine the facts of the case—though in a less formal manner than was true of the secular legal system. If those charged failed to confess their guilt, the churches often summoned witnesses to shed more light on the case. If it was decided that the suspect was innocent and that the charges were based on lies or slander, then the slanderers could, in turn, find themselves subject to disciplinary proceedings.

The desire to avoid false accusations helps to explain the churches' vigilance in calling church members before them on a range of speech-related offences. In both denominations, slander and lying were the most common speech-related offences.[28] The desire to regulate the means of regulation was certainly part of the churches' motivation in seeking to control speech, but other issues are also involved. [...]

Although members of Presbyterian churches saw themselves as part of Christian communities of faith, their sense of separation from the world was weaker than was the case among Baptists. The Baptists' strong evangelicalism drew them apart from the world into a separate community of believers. At the same time that the notion of community was important to Baptists, it was also fragile—in part because such communities were held together primarily by belief. Unlike the Presbyterian congregations, Baptists had no previous state tradition to buttress them and were linked less firmly by ethnicity.[29] As well, the evangelical focus of the Baptists, with their emphasis on individual conversion experiences and the direct relationship between an individual and God, left more space for distinctive interpretations of God's word and could result in conflict within the community of "saints."[30]

Specific entries within Baptist Church records point to the emphasis these churches placed on attempting to maintain harmony within the church community. For example, in November 1844 the Port Burwell Baptist Church voted that "a standing committee of three persons be appointed in each Church whose duty it shall be to promote peace and harmony. If any member ... shall be found stirring up strife they shall be dealt with as offenders."[31] Any conflict between members was seen as damaging to the larger church community. The church records of Woodstock's Baptist Church note, for example, that in September 1825 the entire church was harmonious "except for Brother P. and Sister H. who were somewhat at variance, Sister H. having reported some unfavourable stories respecting Brother P. which are not so." The records note that the church members "humbly trust and pray that matters may be arranged so as not to wound the feelings of the body of the Church." Matters in this case were brought to a satisfactory conclusion when "Sister H. ... confessed to Brother P. and acknowledged her faults publicly."[32]

A quantitative analysis of the nature of offences brought before the Baptist churches makes it clear that the primary focus of church discipline was to preserve community harmony. Over 42 per cent of offences involved family quarrels, personal or business quarrels, or church-related quarrels. Church-related quarrels, such as disputes over doctrine, or challenges to ministers or deacons, alone made up almost a quarter of all offences dealt with by the Baptist churches. In contrast, only 17 per cent of Presbyterian offences focused on any form of quarrelling or community disharmony. Less than 6 per cent of offences among the more hierarchical and less evangelical Presbyterians involved quarrels over doctrine or challenges to the minister or elders.[33] Most Presbyterians were charged with "sins of the flesh" such as sexuality and drinking.

The Baptists' particular focus on preserving community harmony helps to explain why they were much more likely to regulate speech than were Presbyterians. Speech itself can be a potent means of stirring up community disharmony. As the eighteenth-century New England Baptists studied by Susan Juster noted, "It is the rash using of the Tongue that greatly enflames our differences. Surely the Tongue is an unruly Member."[34] The concern of the Upper Canadian Baptists with speech-related offences is reflected in the fact that they made up a higher proportion of the church discipline case-load than was true among Presbyterians, and also in the fact that more types of speech-related charges can be found within the Baptist records. For example, "tattling" and "railing" were both offences among Baptists, but were not found in Presbyterian records. Tattling is certainly a speech-related offence that would be likely to undermine community peace and harmony, and thus would be of concern to the Baptists. Railing—speaking out against or insulting someone—was also a concern. Some Baptist accusations of railing focused on quarrels between members, which in themselves would have undermined church harmony. A number of other cases focused on railing in the context of church quarrels, which would have been even more disruptive. For example, in May 1836 Port Burwell Baptist Church excluded William E. from church membership. He had accused the local minister of preaching false doctrine, and was "excluded for railing against the Church and refusing to obey the voice of the said Church."[35]

The more hierarchical and less evangelical Presbyterians appear to have faced fewer such disruptions, or certainly focused less regulatory attention upon them. Nonetheless, the 17 per cent of charges in the Presbyterian Church discipline records which involved personal, family, or church quarrels, and the 13 per cent of charges focusing on speech-related offences, point to the fact that maintaining community harmony was not irrelevant to these churches. While maintaining harmony within the church community was important, the Presbyterians were also concerned with upholding the image of the church community in the larger community context. Here again gossip, rumour, and "public talk" were important—but in this case it was the public talk of non-Presbyterians that worried the elders. In some of the more serious cases of wrongdoing that came before the Presbyterian churches, the session noted that the wrongdoing here was not just the particular sin involved but also the damage done to the church's reputation in the larger community. For example, when the Picton Presbyterian Church charged John D. with forging a signature on a contract and a bank note, the church decided that "whereas it would bring scandal on the cause of religion and on the standards and discipline of this church in particular were the said John D. to remain in communion ... we do now declare the said John O. to be no longer a member of this church." In a case brought against an elder of Dundas Presbyterian Church, the concern was clearly not just with his public drinking, but with the fact that such drinking brought "scandal upon the congregation and upon the character and discipline of the Church." In Smith's Falls, when rumours circulated that an elder was guilty of "fornication" and procuring an abortion for the woman involved, the session was not only concerned with the sins themselves but with the fact that "the report was generally believed, and was thus calculated to cause serious detriment to the interests of religion in this place."[36] The Presbyterian elders were very well aware of the potentially damaging impact of gossip and rumour on the public reputation of the church.

The fact that the majority of cases of session discipline focused on "sins of the flesh" such as drinking and sexual matters may reflect a particular Presbyterian approach not only to sin but also a particular Presbyterian concern with broader public opinion, since these kinds of transgressions would be the ones most likely to bring the church into disrepute within the larger community.

*****

The Upper Canadian experience points to the danger of over-generalizing about the relationship between women and "improper" speech. The gender breakdown of speech-related charges reveals that, among both Baptists and Presbyterians, almost three-quarters of all charges involved men, while only a quarter involved women. This apparent reversal of gendered assumptions is not quite what it seems: the gender breakdown differed significantly depending on the category of speech-related offence. Male predominance in certain categories actually reinforces certain traditional gendered norms. Women's failure to predominate in most other categories points less to gender equality within the churches, and more to the significance that congregations placed on speech, and the dangers of its misuse, regardless of the gender of the speaker.

In some cases the gendered breakdown of particular speech-related offences seems readily explicable. For example, in the case of swearing, twenty-eight out of thirty of those charged with this sin were male. The newer ideals of pure, virtuous, pious womanhood which were gradually gaining currency in Upper Canada in this period certainly had no place for female swearing.[37] [...]

Lying and slander were other significant categories of speech-related offences. "Bearing false witness" is obviously a sin in the Christian context. As well, given the stress that the churches placed on the use of rumour in regulating behaviour, it is not surprising that they placed considerable emphasis on censuring those who lied or spread false rumours. Over three-quarters of Presbyterian speech-related charges fall into this category, as do half of Baptist ones. What is perhaps more surprising here is the predominance of male offenders—with 82 per cent of Presbyterian cases of lying and slander involving men, as do 69 per cent of Baptist cases. Although the stereotype of the female rumour-monger does not fit with such figures, the reality of men's greater involvement in the public sphere helps to explain the churches' focus on male slander and falsehood. Many of these cases involved quarrels about business—and most business matters occurred among men, outside the household. In the small face-to-face communities of Upper Canada, a person's business reputation could be readily made or lost through "public talk."[38] Those who felt their reputations had been unfairly besmirched readily turned to the churches for remedy. [...]

While men were generally overrepresented in cases of slander and lying, they were particularly likely to be charged with such sins in church-related cases—cases that involved quarrels with deacons, elders, or ministers, or disagreements about doctrine or church practices. In church-related cases, Baptist men were also overrepresented in another speech-related offence—railing—though in non-church-related cases both men and women were equally likely to be accused of railing. The Baptist records include a number of lengthy reports, such as the case of Brother C. of St Catharines Baptist Church, who, among other things, was charged with "interrupting and breaking up a covenant meeting" and "slandering the Church among members and others." [...] As we know, the Baptist Church, in particular, sought to retain harmony among members and placed considerable emphasis on regulating speech that could undermine church harmony. [...]

Why might women be less likely to use their legendary "wicked tongues" against the churches? For Baptist women, the days when the denomination's radical evangelical focus on the power of the Spirit within each individual, a gift that had even justified female challenges to church doctrine and leadership, was largely past.[39] In fact, within Presbyterian and many Baptist congregations, women were not allowed to speak in church.[40] Although this restriction did not prevent women from expressing their concerns informally outside church walls, many women may have internalized the newly emerging ideas about women's particular piety, passivity, and morality.[41] Or perhaps older ideas about womanly obedience remained powerful. Women may also have been less likely to challenge the churches for their own reasons. The Baptist and Presbyterian churches closely regulated and constrained women's behaviour, as they did that of men, but they offered something to women beyond the power and solace of faith they also offered to men. Churches provided women with one of their only options for community. If expelled from their church, men had other options for fellowship within the larger world and were also more mobile, able to leave behind disapproving neighbours.[42] Women, particularly mothers, were much less mobile. For poor women, or those facing the possibility of destitution in old age and widowhood, the churches also offered some minimal financial protection. In an era when state welfare was almost non-existent, and private charity grudging and demeaning at best, many churches provided some assistance to poorer members, usually widows.[43] As well as the possibility of material aid, the churches, particularly the Baptist Church, provided women with some protection from wife abuse. The churches also advocated a code of appropriate sexual behaviour that at least attempted to hold men to the same standard of sexual purity as women, and was thus less hostile to women's interests than were the sexual norms of the larger society.[44]

We should not, however, overstate the extent of female passivity and piety within the churches. Although men were overrepresented among those who spoke out against the church, or were accused of circulating reports against it, women were not absent from such cases. Some of women's speech-related offences against the church suggest an active open defiance, again countering stereotypes of feminine behind-the-scenes rumour-mongering. [...]

While women who railed against the church or slandered it were a small minority, a larger minority of those slandering other church members were female, particularly among Baptists. Women were accused of slandering each other, and male church members, on a number of issues. Some cases of women slandering other women involved sexual reputations, as in the case that began this article, where Nancy F. accused Matilda G. of "having carnal connection with Hiram C. ... and it had become public talk." Other cases in which a woman's sexual reputation was challenged involved a married couple, or a man. For example, in February 1812 Sister Polly A. of Boston Baptist Church complained to the church that Joseph B. had made "a request to her to the violation of her chastity against her husband." When she refused his advances, he apparently circulated reports that she was guilty of adultery.[45]

The stereotypical gossiping woman is not entirely absent from these records. The Baptist and Presbyterian records each include two charges of gossiping—all four of which were levelled at women. Of the seven charges of "tattling" in the Baptist records, six involve women. Three of the charges are found in one entry in Brantford's Baptist Church records. In July 1840 it was resolved that "Brother M. and Brother N. shall visit Sister T., Sister R. and Sister C. and inform them that tattling shall not exist amongst us that we expect them to bury it and bring it up no more amongst us."[46] Although the image of mischief-making female tongues was not entirely absent from church concerns, cases of gossip made up 4 per cent of Presbyterian speech-related cases, and gossip and tattling, 6 per cent of Baptist ones. Gossip appears to have been defined fairly narrowly here. Charges that we might see as related to gossip, such as lying and slander, were of far greater concern to the churches, and were more likely to focus on male offenders. In an era when speech really mattered—when the business reputation of an individual, or the reputation of a church could be destroyed by "public talk," and when the harmony of church communities relied on the absence of strife and disharmony that could be created by "unruly" tongues—the regulation of all such speech was essential. The fact that men's speech was much more likely to be regulated than women's may reflect men's more active role in the public world, or it may suggest that male words were considered more powerful and dangerous, and thus in need of regulation. Or it may simply point to the fact that in communities that took all forms of improper speech very seriously, men's tongues were in fact more unruly than those of women.

By the middle of the nineteenth century, the churches gradually moved away from efforts to constrain either male or female speech. In most Baptist and Presbyterian churches, efforts to oversee all aspects of what we would define as private life declined significantly after mid century. By the 1880s, references to such cases almost disappeared from church records.[47] The reasons for this decline in church discipline are complex and not yet fully understood. Social forces such as urbanization, class-stratification, and industrialization, which fostered a growing public/private division, particularly among the middle classes, may have had significant implications for the practice of church discipline. [...] Businessmen, who in earlier years readily turned to the churches to mediate disputes or restore reputations, came to resent religious interference in an increasingly large scale and complex capitalist workplace.[48] These broader social forces also affected the evangelical discourse of sacred and secular which had legitimized church discipline practices. Historians have found that over the second half of the nineteenth century, a range of more secular, materialistic values and hierarchies became integrated into the world view of most evangelicals.[49] As the firm distinction between "islands of holiness" and the secular world gave

way to greater accommodation to things of the world, Christians became less concerned with the cohesion of separate church communities, and thus had less need to police the speech of those who might fracture it. Also, with the boundaries between the churches and the secular world becoming more permeable, middle-class Christians could adopt mainstream "separate spheres" discourse and the increasingly powerful discourse of individualism to insist that some facets of their lives were indeed private and personal and so should be left to individual conscience, rather than being subject to the "fraternal oversight" and community gossip of fellow Christians.[50]

While a range of social forces and accompanying shifts in discourses of public/private and sacred/secular played a significant role in the decline of church discipline, the growing power and legitimacy of the secular legal system may provide the most potent reason for its demise. The legal system provided an alternative model of regulation to that of the churches, a model that was formalized, "rational," and text-based. Indeed, this system was associated with the rational masculine virtues of the Victorian age, providing a potent challenge to the legitimacy of older church traditions with their emphasis on more informal—even feminine—verbal forms of regulation.

We should not, however, create too firm a distinction between an old-fashioned informal church system of regulation, which accepted the legitimacy of gossip, and a formal, rational state, which did not. Gossip appears to have remained a resource—albeit an unofficial one—particularly for social welfare branches of the state in the twentieth century. The popularity of welfare "snitch lines," which encourage people to inform on neighbours who they believe are "cheating" on welfare, is the most recent manifestation.[51] However, a significant difference between state-sponsored snitch lines and earlier church regulation is that it is now only the powerless—the poor, the young—who are subject to such regulation. Today, a dominant discourse of liberal individualism, with its clear separation of public and private, protects those with resources from official regulation through neighbourhood gossip. While most in our society would not wish to return to the prying eyes of early nineteenth-century church communities, it is illuminating to recognize that the current use of gossip to control the poor does not include earlier community-based understandings that if gossip is to be taken seriously as a means of regulation, there must be means of controlling the "incorrect speech" of all.

Notes

1. Canadian Baptist Archives (CBA), St Catharines Baptist Church, Church Minutes, 30 Nov. 1844 and 1 Feb. 1845; Wicklow Baptist Church, Church Minutes, 22 July and 20 Sept 1849. Full names have not been used in order to preserve anonymity.

2. For definitions of gossip, see Karen V. Hansen, "The Power of Talk in Antebellum New England," *Agricultural History* 67, 2 (1993): 43–64; Melanie Tebbutt, *Women's Talk? A Social History of "Gossip" in Working-Class Neighbourhoods, 1880–1960* (Aldershot, England: Scolar Press 1995).

3. See Hansen, "The Power of Talk"; Tebbutt, *Women's Talk?*; Mary Beth North, "Gender and Defamation in Seventeenth-Century Maryland," *William and Mary Quarterly* (1987): 3–39; Robert F. Goodman and Aaron Ben Ze'ev, *Good Gossip* (Lawrence: University Press of Kansas 1994); Steve Hindle, "The Shaming of Margaret Knowsley: Gossip, Gender and the Experience of Authority in Early Modern England," *Continuity and Change* 9, 3 (1994): 391–419.

4. See, for example, L.R. Poos, "Sex, Lies, and the Church Courts of Pre-Reformation England," *Journal of Interdisciplinary History* 25, 4 (1995): 585–608; Laura K. Deal, "Widows and Reputation in the Diocese of Chester, England, 1560–1650," *Journal of Family History* 23. 4 (1998): 382–93; Susan Juster, *Disorderly Women: Sexual Politics and Evangelicalism in Revolutionary New England* (Ithaca and London: Cornell University Press 1994); Jane Kamensky, *Governing the Tongue: The Politics of Speech to Early New England* (New York and Oxford: Oxford University Press 1997); Mary Beth Norton, *Founding Mothers and Fathers: Gendered Power and the Forming of American Society* (New York: Vintage Books 1996).

5. The few existing examinations of Upper Canadian church discipline have focused on it in the context of church history. See, for example, Duff Willis

Crerar, "Church and Community: The Presbyterian Writ-Session in the District of Bathurst, Upper Canada" (MA thesis, University of Western Ontario 1979), and Crerar, "'Crackling Sounds from the Burning Bush': The Evangelical Impulse in Canadian Presbyterianism before 1875," in G.A. Rawlyk, ed., *Aspects of the Canadian Evangelical Experience* (Montreal and Kingston: McGill-Queen's University Press 1997), 123–36.

6. Jean E. Friedman, *The Enclosed Garden: Women and Community in the Evangelical South, 1830–1900* (Chapel Hill and London: University of North Carolina Press 1985), II.

7. Among Presbyterians, church members could be excommunicated only by the higher level of church court, the Presbytery. See Crerar, "Church and Community," 25.

8. The Presbyterians were far more numerous, at about 20 per cent of the population, while the Baptists always made up less than 5 per cent of the total population in this period. See John Webster Grant, *A Profusion of Spires* (Toronto: University of Toronto Press 1988), 224.

9. Crerar, "Crackling Sounds from the Burning Bush," 127. Some Presbyterian evangelicals (the United Presbyterians) had left the church before to 1843. See Grant, *A Profusion of Spires*, 123–4.

10. Female participation may not have been the norm in all churches, but it was certainly the case in most smaller communities. See Judith Colwell, "The Role of Women in the Nineteenth-Century Church of Ontario" (unpublished paper, 1985, CBA), 8–9. See also Gregory A. Wills, *Democratic Religion: Freedom. Authority and Church Discipline in the Baptist South, 1785–1900* (New York: Oxford University Press 1997).

11. Among Baptists, church discipline cases are to be found in the congregational minutes. Presbyterian discipline cases are found in the minutes of the Kirk sessions. The church records examined include surviving church records for the 1798–1860 period from Presbyterian and Baptist churches found

in the United Church Archives, the Canadian Presbyterian Archives, the Canadian Baptist Archives, the National Archives of Canada, and the Family History Archives of the Church of the Latter Day Saints. All records found in these archives that began before 1850 were examined for all years up to 1860, while some records that existed for only the 1850s and later years were not included. As well, this study includes records generously given to me by Duff Crerar, based on his research on eastern Ontario Presbyterian churches.

12. For recent work on Upper Canadian social and gender history, see Cecilia Morgan, *Public Men and Virtuous Women: The Gendered Languages of Religion and Politics in Upper Canada, 1791–1850* (Toronto: University of Toronto Press 1996); Jane Errington, *Wives and Mothers, Schoolmistresses and Scullery Maids: Working Women in Upper Canada, 1790–1840* (Montreal: McGill-Queen's University Press 1995); Katherine McKenna, *A Life of Propriety: Anne Murray Powell and Her Family, 1755–1849* (Montreal: McGill-Queen's University Press 1994); and Janice Potter-MacKinnon, *While the Women Only Wept: Loyalist Refugee Women in Eastern Ontario* (Montreal: McGill-Queen's University Press 1993).

13. See Morgan, *Public Men and Virtuous Women*, and Errington, *Wives and Mothers*. For an excellent discussion of the concept of separate spheres, see Leonore Davidoff and Catherine Hall, *Family Fortunes: Men and Women of the English Middle Class, 1789–1850* (Chicago: University of Chicago Press 1987). Certain feminist scholars have begun to challenge the concept of "separate spheres." See Linda Kerber, "Separate Spheres, Female Worlds, Woman's Place: The Rhetoric of Women's History," *Journal of American History* 75, I (1988): 9–39. This critique is useful in reminding us that these spheres were not inviolable and that both men and women moved between public and private worlds. However, the emergence of the concept of a private sphere that was somehow "personal" and less open to community gaze and intervention remains worthy of further historical study.

14. Curtis O. Johnson, *Islands of Holiness: Rural Religion in Upstate New York, 1790–1860* (Ithaca and London: Cornell University Press 1989). See also Randolph A. Roth, *The Democratic Dilemma: Religion, Reform and the Social Order in the Connecticut River Valley of Vermont, 1791–1850* (Cambridge: Cambridge University Press 1987), and, in the Upper Canadian context, William Westfall, *Two Worlds: The Protestant

Culture of Nineteenth-Century Ontario (Montreal and Kingston: McGill-Queen's University Press 1989).

15. See Juster, *Disorderly Women*, chap. 3.

16. Daniel C Goodwin, "'The Footprints of Zion's King': Baptists in Canada to 1880," in Rawlyk, ed., *Aspects of the Canadian Evangelical Experience*, 197. Many Baptist congregations were originally based around one or another of the American, English, or Scottish ethnic groups, but such patterns changed over time. Particularly in the case of Americans, who made up the majority of Upper Canadian Baptists, ethnicity did not appear to provide the same basis for tightly knit communities as was true of Scottish and Irish Presbyterians.

17. CBA, Boston Baptist Church, Church Minutes, 8 March 1828, Murray Meldrum notes.

18. CBA, Brantford Baptist Church, Church Minutes, 16 Sept 1843. Also see, for example, PCA, Stamford Presbyterian Church, Niagara Falls, Session Minutes, 22 June 1837.

19. Among Presbyterians 12 per cent of drink cases were clearly reported through gossip (n. 77), and among Baptists, 5 per cent were reported this way (n. 62). Among Presbyterians, 11 per cent of speech-related offences were reported through gossip (n. 47), while among Baptists, 5 per cent were reported in this way. Among Presbyterians 33 per cent of cases of family conflict were reported through gossip (n. 12), while among Baptists, 7 per cent (n. 27) were reported this way. Among Presbyterians, 13 per cent of sexual misdemeanours were reported through gossip (n. 166), while among Baptists, 14 per cent of such cases were reported this way (n. 21).

20. See, for example, Hansen, "The Power of Talk."

21. Juster, *Disorderly Women*, 82.

22. Regarding literacy, see Susan Houston and Alison Prentice, *Schooling and Scholars in Nineteenth-Century Ontario* (Toronto: University of Toronto Press 1988), 84–5.

23. Also see Kamensky, *Governing the Tongue*, and Mary Beth Norton, *Founding Mothers and Fathers*, for discussions of American colonial cultures where face-to-face communities were the norm and oral communication was central.

24. See, for example, Lorraine Code, "Gossip, or in Praise of Chaos," in Goodman and Ben-Ze'ev, eds., *Good Gossip*.

25. Of course, we should not set up firm dichotomies here. Gossip and rumour have been, and are still, used informally by agents of the state—such as social workers. Nonetheless, gossip and rumour are not used in the same official way within state

institutions, such as the legal system, as they were within church courts.

26. See Susan Lewthwaite, "Violence, Law, and Community in Rural Upper Canada," in Jim Phillips, Tina Loo, and Susan Lewthwaite, eds., *Essays in the History of Canadian Law,* vol. 5: *Crime and Criminal Justice* (Toronto: University of Toronto Press 1994), 353–86. Also see Allan Greer and Ian Radforth, eds., *Colonial Leviathan: State Formation in Mid Nineteenth-Century Canada* (Toronto: University of Toronto Press 1992).

27. Cecilia Morgan, "'In Search of the Phantom Misnamed Honour': Duelling in Upper Canada," *Canadian Historical Review* 76, 4 (1995): 536, 543.

28. Among Presbyterians, such charges made up 72 per cent of all speech-related offences (n. 72), while among Baptists they made up 49 per cent of all such offences (n. 165). In both denominations they were the largest category of such offences. [...]

29. See note 16.

30. See Juster, *Disorderly Women,* and George Rawlyk, *The Canada Fire: Radical Evangelicalism in British North America, 1775–1812* (Kingston and Montreal: McGill-Queen's University Press 1994).

31. CBA, Port Burwell Baptist Church, Church Minutes, 1 Nov. 1844.

32. CBA, Woodstock Baptist Church, Church Minutes, 24 Sept. 1825.

33. However, these numbers do not include the serious charge of heresy, which was generally referred to the higher-level court of the Presbytery. See Crerar, "Church and Community," 25. It is also possible that more quarrels were mediated privately by minister or elders among Presbyterians than among Baptists, and thus did not find their way into the church records.

34. Cited in Juster, *Disorderly Women,* 88.

35. CBA, Port Burwell Baptist Church, Church Minutes, May 1836.

36. PCA, Picton Presbyterian Church, Session Minutes, 28 Dec. 1845; Dundas Presbyterian Church, Session Minutes, 20 Jan. 1846; National Archives of Canada (NA), Smiths Falls Westminister Presbyterian Church, 2 April 1858. Such concerns about public opinion occasionally appear in Baptist records, but are much more common in Presbyterian session minutes.

37. See Morgan, *Public Men and Virtuous Women,* and Davidoff and Hall, *Family Fortunes.*

38. See also Kamensky, *Governing the Tongue,* and Norton, *Founding Mothers and Fathers.*

39. See Rawlyk, *The Canada Fire,* and Juster, *Disorderly Women,* for a discussion of women's roles within radical evangelical communities.

40. Women spoke and voted at many Baptist covenant meetings. See Colwell, "The Role of Women." Women's right to speak in church was more contested, with congregations clearly having different perspectives on this issue. See, for example, CBA, Woodstock Baptist Church, Church Minutes, 28 Dec. 1844, and Wicklow Baptist Church, Church Minutes, Sept. 1811.

41. In this period, women were rarely allowed to speak on public platforms, even beyond church walls. However, there would have been many more informal public and private spaces where women could make their views of church members and church practices known.

42. For a discussion of men's alternative options in a slightly later period, see Lynne Marks, *Revivals and Roller Rinks: Religion, Leisure, and Identity in Late Nineteenth-Century Small-Town Ontario* (Toronto: University of Toronto Press 1996).

43. Crerar, "Church and Community," 113. For poor relief to widows among Baptists, see Colwell, "The Role of Women," 4. Also see CBA, Oxford Baptist Church, Church Minutes, 1808, and Brantford Baptist Church, Church Minutes, 1 April 1855. For a discussion of the limitations of secular social welfare in this period, see David R. Murray, "The Cold Hand of Charity: The Court of Quarter Sessions and Poor Relief in the Niagara District, 1828–1841," in W. Wesley Pue and Barry Wright eds., *Canadian Perspectives on Law and Society: Issues in Legal History* (Ottawa: Carleton University Press 1988), 179–206.

44. See Lynne Marks, "Christian Harmony: Family, Neighbours, and Community in Upper Canadian Church Discipline Records," in Franca Iacovetta and Wendy Mitchinson, eds., *On the Case: Explorations in Social History* (Toronto: University of Toronto Press 1998), and Lynne Marks, "No Double Standard? Leisure, Sex, and Sin in Upper Canadian Church Discipline Records, 1800–1860," in Kathryn Macpherson, Cecilia Morgan, and Nancy Forestell, eds., *Gendered Pasts: Essays in Masculinity and Femininity* (Toronto and Oxford: Oxford University Press 1999), 48–64.

45. CBA, Boston Baptist Church, Church Minutes, 1 Feb. 1812, Murray Meldrum notes. Also see FHL, Iona Station Baptist Church, Church Minutes, 2 Dec. 1847.

46. CBA, Brantford Baptist Church, Church Minutes, July 1840.

47. Duff Crerar argues that the Free Church Presbyterians retained church discipline practices into the 1860s, after they had been largely abandoned among other Presbyterians, but that even within the Free Church these practices declined by the 1870s. See Crerar, "'Crackling Sounds from the Burning Bush,'" 134. Neil Semple argues that Methodists also largely abandoned church discipline practices after mid-century. See Semple, *The Lord's Dominion: the History of Canadian Methodism* (Kingston and Montreal: McGill-Queen's University Press 1996), 228–30. By the 1880s the occasional reference to cases of excessive drinking can be found in some Presbyterian and Baptist records, but other sins are not recorded.

48. See, for example, Semple, *The Lord's Dominion*, 218–19. Also see Goodwin, "'The Footprints of Zion's King,'" 202, and Johnson, *Islands of Holiness*, 169.

49. See Semple, *The Lord's Dominion*, chap. 13; S.D. Clark, *Church and Sect in Canada* (Toronto: University of Toronto Press 1948), chap. 7; and Marks, *Revivals and Roller Rinks*, chap. 3.

50. This respect for the private sphere does not mean that evangelicals abandoned the moral concerns of Christianity. Personal piety remained important See, for example, Van Die, "The Marks of a Genuine Revival." As well, evangelicals increasingly focused attention on the sins of those outside their church communities—on the poor and the immigrants—who became the focus of evangelical reform movements for temperance and sexual purity.

51. See Margaret Little, "He Said, She Said: The Role of Gossip in Ontario Mothers' Allowance Administration," paper presented at the Canadian Historical Association meeting, St. Catharines, Ontario, June 1996. Also see Franca Iacovetta, "Gossip, Contest, and Power in the Making of Suburban Bad Girls Toronto, 1945–1960," *Canadian Historical Review* 80, 4 (1999): 585–623.

Critical Thinking Questions

Chapter 1: Administering Justice without the State: A Study of the Private Justice System of the Hudson's Bay Company to 1800, *Russell Smandych and Rick Linden*

1. The authors outline the private system of justice the Hudson's Bay Company enjoyed. How did this private system develop? What are the advantages and disadvantages of this system compared to a public system?
2. The private system of justice applied to employees of the company, those who traded with the Company, and individuals who lived in the area. What problems did company officials experience in attempting to control such a disparate group of individuals? What authority did the company possess to ensure compliance?
3. The Hudson's Bay Company received their authority to carry out trade from the English monarchy, but they were ultimately responsible to stockholders in the company. How did this dual responsibility affect decisions that were made in the territory? Did governors feel they owed a greater allegiance to one group more than the other?

Chapter 2: Criminal Boundaries: The Frontier and the Contours of Upper Canadian Justice, 1792–1840, *David Murray*

1. Prior to the development of the criminal justice system we know today, our forefathers had to resort to different methods to control crime. What were some of these methods? How do they compare to modern responses to crime?
2. How did proximity to the border affect frontier justice? Consider the role the border played in decisions about whether or not to extradite "problem" citizens.
3. Murray uses the term "banishment" to refer to sentences where the offender was required to leave the country—with the assumption that she or he would relocate to the United States. How does this use of the idea compare to the English use of banishment? Why does Murray suggest that our neighbours to the south did not appear to have a problem with such sentences?

Chapter 3: The Mounties as Vigilantes: Perceptions of Community and the Transformation of Law in the Yukon, 1885–1897, *Thomas Stone*

1. Who participated in the miners' meeting, and how did the organization deal with problems prior to the arrival of the Mounties? How did the Mounties undermine the authority of the miners' meeting? Did the majority of miners appear to support or oppose the role of the Mounties?
2. The author presents evidence that suggests that crime was not a significant problem in the Yukon. If this is the case, why did the Canadian government dispatch the North West Mounted Police to the Yukon in the summer of 1897? What was the real purpose for the presence of the Mounties?
3. Why does Stone compare the Mounties to vigilantes? How did the Mounties act like vigilantes? How were they different? What factor, if any, did the distance between the Yukon and Ottawa affected how the Mounties were able to respond to less serious problems?

Chapter 4: Discordant Music: Charivaris and Whitecapping in Nineteenth-Century North America, *Brian D. Palmer*

1. What are the differences between charivaris and whitecapping? What role did charivaris and whitecapping play in community cohesion? Were charivaris always detrimental? In what instances might they be beneficial?
2. Why did local residents sometimes resort to the charivari rather than the law to resolve a problem in the community? Over time, the charivari appears to have fallen out of favour. Why did this occur, and why might rural communities be slower to abandon the tradition of the charivari? How did the nature of the charivari change over time?
3. According to Palmer, most historians who have studied the ritual of the charivari have tended to ignore the reality that most participants came from the working class. How might such an examination help us to better understand the phenomenon of the charivari? Does such a perspective present an unrealistic ideal of the culture of the working class?

Chapter 5: Railing, Tattling, and General Rumour: Gossip, Gender, and Church Regulation in Upper Canada, *Lynne Marks*

1. How did churches of the day use gossip to control improper conduct? What are some of the problems the author cites in attempting to determine whether the gossip was actually true? How did authorities within the church deal with this dilemma?
2. How was gossip gender-specific? Were women more or less likely to repeat unfounded rumours than men? Was this the case in the different denominations?
3. Marks indicates that gossip, as a mechanism to control church conduct, fell out of favour by the mid nineteenth-century. Why did this happen? What other recourse was available to the church to censure inappropriate behaviour?

Further Readings

● ●

Pioneer Policing in Southern Alberta: Deane of the Mounties, 1880–1914 by William M. Baker (Calgary: Historical Society of Alberta, 1993).

This book is about Richard Burton Deane, and is a collection of reports written during his years as a Mounted police officer from 1883 to 1914. This was a significant period prior to the establishment of the RCMP and in the opening of the West. Deane was instrumental in supervisory positions in quelling unrest by insurgents, and the portrait drawn here gives an insight into the past. With stories ranging from booze to murder, the book provides revealing insights into social history and administration of justice in pioneer Alberta.

The North West Mounted Police and Law Enforcement, 1873–1905 by R.C. McLeod (Toronto: University of Toronto Press, 1976).

The book makes for good stories, such as how in 1877, 11 months after Custer's disaster, NWMP Major James M. Walsh, a sergeant, and three troopers followed an Indian trail that led to Sitting Bull, who had fled persecution in the U.S. They were able to convince the Sioux that peace could be had if they obeyed the law.

Canadian State Trials, Volume Two: Rebellion and Invasion in the Canadas, 1837–1839, edited by F. Murray Greenwood and Barry Wright (Toronto: Osgoode Society for Canadian Legal History, University of Toronto Press, 2002).

The late F. Murray Greenwood was associate professor emeritus of history at the University of British Columbia, and Barry Wright is a professor of legal studies and director of criminology at Carleton University. This second volume of the Canadian State Trials series focuses on the largest state security crisis in nineteenth-century Canada: the rebellions of 1837–1838 and patriot invasions in Upper and Lower Canada (Ontario and Quebec). Over 350 men were tried for treason in connection with the rebellions. The essays, written by historians, legal scholars, and archivists, examine trials and court martial proceedings in their political, social, and comparative contexts; the passage of emergency legislation; the treatment of women; and the plight of political convicts transported to the Australian penal colonies.

Essays in the History of Canadian Law: Volume Five—Crime and Criminal Justice, edited by Jim Phillips, Tina Loo, and Susan Lewthwaite (Toronto: University of Toronto Press and Osgoode Society for Canadian Legal History, 1994).

Jim Phillips is the director of the Centre of Criminology and professor in the Faculty of Law at the University of Toronto; Tina Loo is a professor of history at

Simon Fraser University; Susan Lewthwaite is with the Law Society of Upper Canada Archives Department. This stellar collection is a tribute to R.C.B. (Dick) Risk, who has been writing about Canadian legal history since the 1960s. His articles on law and the economy, and legal-historical studies stand as a model for others. The articles gathered here point to how legal history is situated in place and time, and how the law is indigenous, both influencing and influenced by its environment. Some of the articles include the "Racially Motivated Murder of Gus Ninham, Ontario, 1902" by Constance Backhouse; "Ontario Water Quality, Public Health, and the Law, 1880–1930" by Jamie Benidickson; "Taking Litigation Seriously: The Market Wharf Controversy at Halifax, 1785–1820" by Philip Girard; "'Our Arctic Breathren': Canadian Law and Lawyers as Portrayed in American Legal Periodicals, 1829–1911" by Bernard J. Hibbitts; "Race and the Criminal Justice System in British Columbia, 1892–1920: Constructing Chinese Crimes" by John McLaren; "Power, Politics, and the Law: The Place of Judiciary in the Historiography of Upper Canada" by Peter Oliver; "The Criminal Trial in Nova Scotia, 1749–1815" by Jim Phillips; and "'The Disquisitions of Learned Judges': Making Manitoba Lawyers, 1855–1931" by W. Wesley Pue.

A Few Acres of Snow: Documents in Post-Confederation Canadian History and *A Country Nourished on Self-Doubt: Documents in Post-Confederation Canadian History*, both by Thomas Thomer (Peterborough: Broadview Press, 2003).

Thomas Thomer is a member of the Department of History at Kwantlen University College. These books amalgamate many documentary sources on pre- and post-Confederation Canadian history. Each chapter offers source materials on significant themes and events, such as the trial of Louis Riel, residential schools, the FLQ, and the Royal Commission on the Status of Women. Writings by Nellie McClung, Grey Owl, René Lévesque, and David Suzuki are among the many contributions that look at the history of Canada's various regions, the experiences of women, Native peoples, immigrants, and the working class.

PART II

A Working Criminal Justice System

• •

With the move toward nationhood, the criminal justice system that we know today began to take shape. This section presents an overview of some of the issues that confronted Canada throughout the nineteenth and early twentieth centuries as it struggled with urbanization, immigration, and the development of a modern criminal justice system. While there were serious offences to deal with, such as rape and homicide, authorities began to concern themselves increasingly with more mundane matters, including vagrancy and drunkenness. Homicide, although serious, was relatively rare. More troublesome was the question of how to control a strong working class given the temptations city life had to offer. It is no accident then that youth courts and police develop to control the growing juvenile underclass.

Dispelling the notion that murder and mayhem are modern phenomena, May and Phillips examine homicide rates in Nova Scotia between the mid-eighteenth and early nineteenth century. From the extant records of the Supreme Court, they uncovered evidence of 133 people prosecuted for 89 murders. The findings indicate that homicides were both quantitatively and qualitatively different in and around the port of Halifax compared to the rest of the colony. In Halifax, a strong military and marine presence meant a continuous influx of young, unattached men who lacked any real social bonds in the community. Both soldiers and civilians could be victims, but the offenders were more likely to be military men; during this period, there were only two known cases in which civilians killed military men. In both instances, the civilians were pardoned on the grounds that they had acted in self-defence. In contrast, there were only 17 documented homicides outside Halifax, generally involving victims who knew their assailants—either kin or neighbours.

The next reading examines "women's worth at the end of the Victorian era." This chapter provides an insight into how the law reflects and resists the changing role of women. Backhouse pulls together pieces of legislation to illustrate the relative lack of power for women, from laws on infanticide, abortion, divorce, and whether they could control their own property. Using a story of infanticide, the author weaves together a panoramic picture of how criminal law reflected societal prejudice against single women, especially when they were confronted with an unwanted pregnancy. For these women, condemned to poverty and servitude, infanticide must have often seemed the only option, unenviable as it was. Remarkably, defendants were treated with much more understanding than they were in the timeframe of the previous chapter when, 100 years earlier, proof of murder was not even required in such cases.

In the next reading, we see how research on gender differences in criminal sanctions generally finds a pattern of more lenient outcomes for female offenders, while noting that the effect of gender varies in relation to a number of contextual influences. As yet, however, little attention has been paid to how the relationship of gender to court outcomes varies across different historical periods. This paper examines the issue, using data from female and male offenders committed to Middlesex County Jail, Ontario, during the Urban Reform era (1871–1920). The findings reveal an overall pattern of more severe dispositions for female offenders in the past. At the same time, there is considerable variability in the impact of gender across different measures of sanction severity, various offender and offence attributes, and for the late nineteenth to early twentieth century. The study highlights the need for research in this area to be sensitive to the historically specific nature of the relations among gender roles, formal and informal control mechanisms, and criminal sanctions.

The following two readings deal with the systemic regulation of girls and young women. Through a review of the Juvenile Delinquents' Court in Montreal in 1918, Myers underscores the participatory process parents, particularly mothers, played in the social, moral, and sexual control of their recalcitrant daughters. While the majority of cases came from the working class, the active role the parents played in the process demonstrates that this was no mere passive acceptance of the power of the state in the lives of the less privileged. The family courts served as an extra-familial arena for conflict resolution. The institutionalization of maternal guidance was also evident in prisons for women as well. In this case, rehabilitation meant encouraging chastity before marriage and developing domesticity afterwards. Ironically, this was achieved through the hiring practices in women's prisons, whereby female officers were hired to achieve the broader goal of encouraging maternal, nurturing instincts in women prisoners.

In his article, Menzies discusses how more than 5,000 immigrants were deported from British Columbia between Confederation and World War II on the basis of being "insane" and "feebleminded." This paper examines the role of the British Columbian government in immigration and the subsequent deportation of the individuals they felt to be unfit for residence within Canada. It also examines how the federal government's legislation, the Immigration Act, helped support this deportation. The process of screening individuals immigrating to British Columbia evolved from a poorly organized system that allowed many unsuitable immigrants into the country who then had to be placed in asylums, to a hybrid medicalized screening process that attempted to block unsuitable immigrants at their home ports. At the height of deportation in British Columbia, the eugenics movement helped support deportation, and the era was dubbed the "golden age" of deportation.

The final reading analyzes the policing of morality and public order. Utilizing a data set from the Police Department's Annual Reports for the period 1859–1955, Boritch and Hagan note a similar trend in Toronto. Moving from a "class-control" model of policing to a more modern "crime-control" system, findings suggest tensions between controlling vice and developing a more modern police force.

CHAPTER 6

Homicide in Nova Scotia, 1749–1815

Allyson N. May and Jim Phillips

• • • • • • • • • • • • • • • • • • • •

On the last day of August 1749, a few weeks after Edward Cornwallis arrived with some 2500 settlers, the first criminal trial was held in the newly established settlement of Halifax. Peter Cartcel, a settler of Swiss origin, was tried and convicted for the murder of Abraham Goodsides, mate of the *Beaufort* transport, and hanged two days later.[1] Cartcel was the first of at least 133 men and women, mostly men, who were brought to court in mainland Nova Scotia between 1749 and 1815 because they allegedly killed, or assisted in the killing of, another human being.[2] This does not mean that there were 133 victims of homicide, for some cases involved multiple defendants and a small number had multiple victims; the 133 homicide prosecutions represented eighty-nine "incidents" of homicide and at least ninety-three victims.[3] As we will demonstrate, the profile of homicide in the second half of the eighteenth and the early nineteenth centuries was markedly different between Halifax and the rest of the colony. In the capital, prosecutions for homicide were frequent occurrences, with homicides often the result of spontaneous acts of violence directed against strangers. [...] Elsewhere in the colony, homicide occurred much less frequently and was much more likely to involve violence within the family or community.

The Law of Homicide

*****

[...] The English criminal law, both common law and statute, was received in Nova Scotia after 1749. [...] Many of the principal aspects of English statutory law were enacted as local law by the colony's first assembly in 1758, including a variety of homicide provisions. Although statutory law played an important role, the fundamental precepts were those of the common law.[4]

At common law, "homicide" included suicide, murder, and manslaughter.[5] By English and local law, murder was always punishable by death, whereas a person convicted of manslaughter could claim "benefit of clergy" for a first offence.[6] The essential distinction between murder and manslaughter [...] was that the former was a killing committed "with malice aforethought." This definition did not mean that premeditation was required, but, rather, that the killing was deliberate.[7] [...] Murder included deliberate homicides that could be justified or excused. A person who committed homicide while acting lawfully—for example, in making an arrest or in preventing a person from escaping prison—was "in no kind of fault whatsoever." [...] Excusable homicide included acts of self-defence or accidents; the latter meant that a death resulted from a lawful act, including the act of punishment of a servant or child.[8] Nova Scotia's Treasons and Felonies Act placed justifiable and excusable homicide together in a general exempting provision.[9] It should be stressed, however, that the exemption was from punishment; the common law theoretically required all justifiable or excusable homicide cases to be prosecuted as murder. This was hardly ever done in accident cases, but it was the common practice in self-defence cases.[10]

Manslaughter, while still culpable homicide, was […] a killing "without malice," […] one that "resulted from a spontaneous outburst."[11] When […] John Bruff was indicted for manslaughter in Halifax in 1791, he was accused of killing "in the fury of his mind." […] Murder might be reduced to manslaughter when there had been sufficient provocation. […]

The statute law of both England and Nova Scotia also contained a special provision to deal with the deaths of children born to unmarried women. A married woman, or a man, who killed a new-born child would be charged with murder in the regular way and found guilty only if the prosecution could bring evidence to show that the child had been killed. But if an unmarried woman gave birth secretly and then sought to conceal the death of the child, she would "suffer death as in case of murder" unless she could prove by the testimony of at least one witness that the child had in fact been born dead.[12] While the theory of the presumption of innocence was rarely voiced until the late eighteenth century, the prosecution was required to present a case to the court, and it was notoriously difficult to do that in these kinds of cases.[13] The English Infanticide Act of 1624, a statute intended to

prevent "immorality," obviated the need to provide evidence of a murder. In Nova Scotia the provision remained in force until 1813, when it was repealed and replaced with legislation modelled on an English statute of 1803, which provided that infanticide had to be proved in the same way as any other murder. Because it was very difficult to find evidence that a child had been born alive, this change was accompanied by a measure making concealment of the birth a separate offence punishable by imprisonment.[14]

The Nova Scotia Data

The figures of 133 homicide prosecutions and 89 incidents of homicide cited above are derived from court records and represent only those cases brought to court.[15] The lack of consistent coroners' inquest records means that suspicious deaths that did not lead to prosecution have not been included. Of the 133 prosecutions, 124 involved indictments for murder, two were manslaughter charges, and seven came under the special infanticide provision discussed above. One hundred and nine of the persons charged (82 per cent), and 72 of the incidents (81 per cent), derived from Halifax, with the remainder emanating from elsewhere in the colony. […]

It is most unlikely that the data presented in Table 1 includes all incidents of homicide in Nova Scotia between 1749 and 1815, for the surviving records are incomplete. […] Three volumes of court proceedings have survived, recording between them almost every serious criminal case brought between 1749 and the 1804 Hilary (January) Term in the General Court (until 1754) and the Supreme Court of Nova Scotia (after 1754) sitting in Halifax.[16]

Table 1: Homicide Prosecutions and Incidents, Nova Scotia, 1749–1815

Place of Offence/Period	Persons Prosecuted	Incidents
Halifax, 1749–1805	83	63
Halifax, 1811–1815	26	9
Other communities, 1754–1815	24	17
Total	133	89

[…] The cases listed under "other communities" in Table 1 are mentioned in a variety of disparate sources. […]

Homicide in Halifax

Incidents of homicide in Halifax occurred at the rate of 1.16 per annum, with persons being charged at the rate of 175 per annum. Using an average population figure of 9000, this number works out to rates of 12.9 and 19.4 per 100,000 per annum (the standard measure used in historical and contemporary studies of homicide).[17] […]

[…] In England, the American colonies/states, and British North American jurisdictions, in the years between approximately 1700 and 1850, it is rare to find rates of more than 2 per 100,000 per annum, and many places had rates lower than that.[18] […]

Across the Atlantic, the eighteenth- and nineteenth-century eastern seaboard colonies and states saw rates rather higher than in England as well as significant regional variation. Rates ranged from 0.90 in later eighteenth-century New Hampshire and Vermont to 74 in the Philadelphia of the 1760s.[19] On the whole the New England states had the lowest rates, with the South somewhat higher but still generally below Halifax levels; a notable exception was Louisiana, which in the second half of the nineteenth century had a rate much higher than that of Halifax.[20] For Canada, historians have posited a rate of 3.9 prosecutions per 100,000 per annum in New France,[21] 1.9 in Upper Canada/Canada West between 1806 and 1848,[22] and between 1.7 and as high as 7.5 for Quebec/Lower Canada.[23] […]

Nonetheless, conclusions about social behaviour based on court records are always open to two related critiques: that too many cases go unreported or unprosecuted to make the figures reliable indicators, and that the figures tend to represent prosecutorial practices at least as much as homicidal behaviour. There were certainly plenty of unprosecuted homicides in eighteenth-century Halifax,[24] but two points should be made here. First, while it is undoubtedly true that many offences—assault, drug offences, prostitution, and the like—are subject to dramatic changes in criminal definitions, in individual willingness to report, and in societal interest in prosecution, homicide, at least in the modern period, is not. Indeed, it is generally accepted by historians and by contemporary criminologists that homicide statistics provide the most reliable correlation between prosecution and actual behaviour.[25] Second, we are less concerned with establishing a "correct" rate for homicide occurrences than with offering a comparison between Nova Scotia and other societies. It is highly unlikely that the gap between unlawful killings and reported and prosecuted unlawful killings was notably different from one place to another.

There is a third reason for accepting these comparative homicide figures as a reasonably reliable indicator that Halifax was a violent city: Halifax experienced unusually high levels of prosecution for other violent offences. Between 1791 and 1815, the period for which reliable figures are available for most years, the assault prosecution rate in Halifax was 148 charges per annum per 100,000, much higher than in eighteenth-century England or mid nineteenth-century Massachusetts.[26] […]

*****

Explaining the high rate of homicidal violence in Halifax requires a closer examination of the circumstances in which killings took place, set against the background of the nature of this eighteenth-century city. Established in 1749 primarily for strategic reasons, Halifax's fortunes for its first half century or more were inextricably linked to the ebb and flow of continental warfare. It prospered or fell on hard times according to the levels of British government spending, its population fluctuated dramatically as large numbers of soldiers and sailors moved in and out (see the appendix), and the military involvement and dependence gave the city a particular character.[27] It was […] an authoritarian society. […] The military

Table 2: Temporal Distribution of Homicide Prosecutions, Halifax, 1749–1815

Period	Charges	Incidents	Annual Incident Rate, per 100,000
1749–65	29	21	19.7
1766–84	34	23	13.1
1785–1805	20	19	10.2
1811–15	26	9	14.4

presence made its impact in a host of small ways on a daily basis. Its naval yard dominated the waterfront, the fortifications on Citadel Hill overlooked the streets below running down to the harbour, and the area around the Citadel Hill/barracks region was full of taverns, brothels, and cheap boarding houses. "The business of one half of the town is to sell rum, and the other half to drink it," ran one oft-quoted quip from 1760.[28] [...]

Having delineated the setting, we turn to an analysis of the nature of homicide in Halifax. [...]

[...] The most notable feature [...] was the extent to which men in the armed forces were involved as perpetrators. Thirty-six of the fifty-nine males accused of murder or manslaughter who can be identified as either civilian or military were soldiers or sailors (61 per cent). Thus, as in the garrison town of Quebec, soldiers were responsible for a disproportionate amount of criminal activity.[29] Most of the military defendants were, as one might expect, from the lower ranks. The total of thirty-six comprised twenty-seven private soldiers or NCOS, six naval personnel, and only three officers. These figures are probably slightly misleading; officers likely caused the deaths of others through duelling, which was not prosecuted. They may also have caused death by excessive punishment and/or restraint, but in only one case did such conduct lead to a prosecution in the civilian courts.[30]

The link between military presence and homicide is also demonstrated through a closer examination of the temporal distribution

of homicide. Table 3 shows that there was substantial fluctuation in that distribution, which can in a number of cases be linked to periods of war and thus to an enhanced military presence. For example, the sixteen incidents in the decade after 1756 correlate largely with the Seven Years' War, during which large numbers of soldiers and sailors visited the city for weeks and months at a time. Following a decade which saw just two incidents, the revolutionary war period, one of substantial immigration and expanded military activity, witnessed a tenfold increase. Similarly, after a few years of no prosecutions, there were a number of homicides in the 1790s, a decade marked by wars with revolutionary France.

The correlation between military presence and a high homicide rate was the result of a number of factors. First, the military presence meant large numbers of young, unattached males in the city, men prone to drink heavily and who belonged to a "manly" culture in which honour was defended and insults refuted through violence. Military misconduct was a frequent source of concern in the eighteenth- and nineteenth-century Anglo-American world.[31] [...] The army itself supplied some of the drink, issuing daily rations of spirits or wine to troops stationed abroad. Drunkenness often led to violent behaviour, and military practice with respect to discipline—flogging was the punishment of choice into the nineteenth century[32]—contributed to a culture of violence, perhaps ultimately serving to encourage rather than curtail violent behaviour among enlisted men.

Table 3: Fluctuations in Incidents of Homicide Prosecutions, Halifax, 1749–1815

Period	Charges	Incidents	Annual Incident Rate, Per 100,000
1749–52	6	5	19.5
1753–5	0	0	—
1756–65	23	16	26
1766–75	2	2	2.6
1776–84	31	21	26.4
1785–8	0	0	—
1789–1803	21	19	14
1811–15	26	9	14.4

[…] It is also evident that violent disputes that might not otherwise have led to homicide often did so because military men had ready access to weapons. When Royal Fencible American corporal John Boyar got into an argument with marine corporal John Corns in a drunken fight over money in 1760, death might not have been the result had Boyar not had his bayonet with him and chosen to use it to make his point. Two years later Thomas Evans met his end from a three-inch-deep stab wound inflicted by private William Reach. Owen Kervan was shot by Cornelius Driscoll or David Lawlor in 1765, and, when three soldiers set out to burgle a farm in 1776, they took with them the musket that killed farmer Christopher Schlegal. The soldiers who attacked and killed wharf labourer Henry Publicover were likewise armed, with bayonets.[33]

We are not suggesting that it was the military presence alone that accounted for the deadly violence in Halifax, given that some 40 per cent of male homicides and all the female homicides were committed by civilians. Indeed, the civilian rate by itself was high, approximately 6.6 incidents per annum per 100,000, similar to the figures for Philadelphia, New Orleans, Quebec, and Montreal cited above.[34] This pattern suggests that the urban environment was partially responsible for Halifax's rate. Presumably such factors as the relative anonymity of the city, the generally greater potential for people living close together to become involved in deadly disputes, and the tensions caused by periods of immigration all contributed to an enhanced rate, although it is hard to test such an hypothesis.[35] But while urbanism played a role, it was the military presence that gave Halifax its particular character and raised the rate to almost thirteen, far above that of other contemporary communities, even urban ones. […]

The unruly soldiery was a factor in at least some of the homicides committed by civilians, a point illustrated by the case of William Andrews. On the night of 16 October 1756 half-a-dozen grenadiers tried to gain access to the house of Andrews, a mason and one of the first settlers of Halifax. Believing that they could obtain drink there, the soldiers noisily demanded entry and were refused more than once. Eventually two of them, Jonathan Montgomery and John Connor, forced their way in the back door. Andrews pointed his gun at them and ordered them to leave. According to a boarder in the house, Charles Parkinson, Montgomery told Connor that the gun was not loaded and suggested he rush Andrews. Montgomery was wrong, and Connor paid the price for that mistake.[36]

*****

Generally the victims of soldiers' and sailors' violence were civilians. […] George Osborne, a sailor from HMS *Assistance,* was charged with the 1797 murder of Bridget Eacott. With her husband, Eacott had tried to expel a group of sailors who entered the house demanding "grogg"; in the ensuing melee she received a blow from Osborne, lingered a couple of days, and died.[37] Henry Publicover was also a victim of military violence. He was one of a group of wharf labourers attacked, on very slight provocation, by some soldiers on the night of 25 January 1813, and he died from stab wounds three days later. Of three soldiers tried for the murder, only Richard Hart was found guilty, and he was later pardoned in a highly unpopular act of executive clemency.[38]

A few prosecutions involved homicides in connection with robberies or burglaries. Marines James Goff, John Ward, and John Scarr left barracks on 20 October 1776 and went into the country to steal some poultry. They broke into a barn and, when surprised by Christopher Schlegal and his son, Goff shot the farmer. The three escaped with nothing more than a few potatoes. While the evidence of the Halifax courts is that homicides committed during robberies and burglaries were uncommon, it does seem that they were viewed with special foreboding. When Goff and his colleagues were apprehended, the Supreme Court had adjourned. The authorities elected not to wait until the Easter Term to deal with the offence, but issued a special commission of "oyer and terminer" (to hear and determine) to try them and also "to prevent as far as may be possible the Commission of such horrid offences."[39] [...] Military men were killed by civilians in only two known cases—the shootings of John Connor by William Andrews (discussed above) and of John Collins by Thomas Leathum— and in both the accused was convicted and pardoned on the grounds that he had killed in self-defence.[40] Otherwise military victims were slain by other members of the forces. Examples included Thomas Evans, a sailor off HMS *Intrepid*, who was murdered by William Reach of the Highland Regiment in 1762, and sailor George Hackett, killed by four soldiers in 1782.[41] [...]

[...] Most of the civilian perpetrators were men. In Halifax, of the twenty-three non-military men charged with homicide, six were unskilled labourers and seven are best described as artisans. A further three had slightly higher social status; James Connor was clerk to a navy captain; James Leonard was a shopkeeper; and Thomas Bambridge was a small farmer.[42] Three of the civilians charged were "gentlemen." Interestingly, none of these three was convicted of murder. John Neal's indictment was returned ignoramus; Nicholas Olding, JP and the coroner for Halifax County, was acquitted; and Abraham Van Buskirk, a Loyalist from New Jersey who had served as an officer in the British Army, was found guilty of "manslaughter in his own defence" and sentenced to give a recognizance for good behaviour for a year.[43] [...]

[...] Soldiers and civilian men killed women in what were probably sexual assaults or the result of male-female sexual and power relations. [...] Where homicide was committed by women, the offender and the victim were likewise generally well known to each other. [...]

[...] Although the sources do not often give precise locations, taverns, lodging houses, and brothels feature frequently in the cases reviewed above, with the area around the wharfs also a common site of deadly violence. [...]

Homicide outside Halifax

Homicide in the other communities scattered throughout mainland Nova Scotia in many respects presented a mirror image of homicide in the capital. [...] We know of seventeen incidents between 1754 and 1815 which involved the prosecution of twenty-four individuals. Four of these incidents (seven people) were prosecuted in Halifax, and thirteen (seventeen people) in the communities in which they occurred. Five incidents led to trials in Liverpool, Queen's County, and three to proceedings at Annapolis. Two occurred in King's County, one of which was tried at Halifax. Otherwise no other community appears more than once in the database. Sixteen of the seventeen incidents involved murder charges, and one was an infanticide case.

[…] The database is thus partial, based only on cases that appear in sources other than systematic court records, which have not survived for any community other than Halifax.[44]

*****

[…] Two general observations about homicide can be made. First, it was much less prevalent outside the capital than within it, the rate being something in the region of 1.09 (incidents) and 1.37 (persons charged) per annum per 100,000 population.[45] […]

*****

Another feature of homicide outside Halifax was its domination by the killing of people at least reasonably well known to the accused—family members, neighbours, or other acquaintances […] [such as] John and Amy Pomp, who were tried at Annapolis in 1813 for the death of their young boy, and of Frances Shannon, a nine-year-old girl from Windsor, who was tried in Halifax for killing her four-year-old sister.[46] The latter group includes the case of Walter Lee, whose dispute with a neighbour and business customer turned ugly enough for Lee to fire a gun at Nicholas Wright. He apparently intended only to frighten Wright, but ended up fatally shooting him.[47] Patrick Holland similarly killed his near neighbour Samuel Allen in the course of an argument, and Peter Manning of Falmouth killed his neighbour Malachi Caigin, who had successfully sued Manning for £16.[48] Alexander McIntosh's victim had stood bail for McIntosh's court appearance in a civil case; Dougall MacDonald was one of three men who went to McIntosh's house to try to force him to appear in court, presumably because he was concerned about forfeiting the bail money.[49]

Not all the non-Halifax cases were neighbourly disputes or family killings. Two which attracted substantial public attention, both locally and in Halifax, were murders committed for gain in the course of robberies. John and James Woodrow and Lauchlin Gallagher were tried for the murder of Thomas Gordon at Liverpool

in 1765, and John and George Boutelier for the triple murder of Frederick Eminaud, his wife, and niece at Lunenburg in 1791. Both cases represented the type of homicide most feared by contemporaries—deliberate killing for money. John Woodrow and Gallagher were convicted and hanged, and the publicity surrounding the case stressed the heinous nature of the crime.[50] The other robbery/murder, the case of John and George Boutelier, was perhaps the most notorious and well-publicized case of the period, and produced the only published trial account. […] The fact that […] the murderers tried to hide the evidence of their crime by burning the house and the bodies […] riveted public attention on what Chief Justice Strange told the Halifax County grand jury was a "dreadful crime" and a "horrid murder." The legal system also gave the defendants its full attention, with Strange and Supreme Court judge James Brenton sailing to Lunenburg to preside over the trial.[51] […]

Women and Homicide

Women's involvement in homicide is considered separately here for two reasons. First, many of the women charged were subject to the special infanticide provision. Second, women as victims are of special interest, for the evidence suggests that lower-class women were especially vulnerable in Halifax to deadly violence from men.

Women constituted a distinct minority of offenders. There were only three females among the twenty-four people charged in non-Halifax cases. […] Halifax had approximately the same representation of women (Table 4),[52] although, if the infanticide cases are extracted from the count to give a sense of women's involvement in the killing of someone other than a newborn, the figure is much smaller: 87 per cent of incidents and 6.8 per cent of charges. Very low rates of female involvement in both non-violent and violent serious crime are a staple of both historical and contemporary studies.[53] […] Excluding infanticide, there were six incidents over sixty-six years.

Table 4: Homicide Incidents and (Charges), by Gender, Halifax, 1749–1815

Offence	Men—Incidents (Charges)	Women—Incidents (Charges)	Total	Percentage of Women
Murder and manslaughter	63 (96)	6(7)	69 (103)	8.7 (6.8)
Infanticide	0	6(6)	6(6)	100
Total	63 (96)	12(13)	75 (109)	16.0 (12.0)

Biological explanations for the gender gap in prosecuted crime have long given way to arguments that emphasize social structure. In the patriarchal world of the eighteenth century, women were expected to cultivate the female virtue of selflessness, to defer to male authority, and to eschew confrontational behaviour. Social conditioning functioned to limit female participation in crime, especially violent crime.[54] The informal social controls exercised by patriarchy, however, were less effective in urban areas;[55] patriarchal controls were also weaker among the marginalized population, loosened by economic necessity.

Attempts to explain female criminality [...] are hampered by our lack of knowledge about the history of women in the province. We know that some women lived independently in Halifax: as midwives, storekeepers, teachers, even undertakers.[56] But these women appear to have been exceptional. Lower down the social scale the employment opportunities were doubtless more limited, given the lack of nascent manufacturing, with domestic service and/or prostitution prominent among the alternatives. [...] Women, like men, generally stole what they could easily lay their hands on and carry away, and these goods fell by and large into the "basic food and clothing" category. [...] Women were rarely charged with breaking and entering, and, when they were, the premises in question were private homes rather than warehouses, whereas men routinely targeted various government depots.[57]

The record of female participation in homicide in eighteenth-century Nova Scotia is likewise consistent with that of other jurisdictions, within

the norm, one might say, of a patriarchal society. Excluding the infanticide cases, in two of the homicides documented here the women charged were acting not alone, but in the company of their husbands.[58] Again excluding infanticide cases, where women killed on their own, their victims were another woman, and a child.[59] In only one case did a woman alone kill an adult male, John Murphy. Murphy was probably an innkeeper; unfortunately, no record remains of the circumstances of the case.[60] Of the seven women charged with homicide who did not kill a new-born infant, we can identify four as being of humble social origin. Judy Philpot was the madame of a brothel; Margaret Murphy was a domestic servant and part-time prostitute; Martha Orpin was the wife of a small trader; and Mary Collins was the wife of a dock labourer. Murphy was Irish; the ethnic identity of the other women remains unknown.[61]

The remaining six female offender cases in Halifax, and the Nancy O'Neal case from Liverpool, all involved the killing of new-born children. Five of these women were tried under the special infanticide law, two after it had been repealed in 1813. A number of studies have shown a consistent pattern in infanticide cases: the offenders were young, often in domestic service, and ran the risk of losing both employment and future marriage prospects if their pregnancies were discovered. They concealed first the pregnancy, then the birth, and destroyed the evidence.[62] Nancy O'Neal's case fits this characterization in many respects. She was a young, unmarried woman whose employer, James Barss, apparently suspected she was pregnant very shortly after she had taken up a position in his household. O'Neal denied it, but when a body was discovered in the privy by a workman in September, six local JPs questioned her. She confessed to giving birth, but claimed the baby was stillborn. O'Neal benefited from the recent change in the law and was convicted of concealment only; a year before she could well have been convicted of murder.[63] [...]

[...] While female victims were clearly a minority, their presence is significant for two reasons. First, because of the military presence in the city, women constituted no more than one-third of its population. Second, half of the twenty-two known adult male victims were soldiers or sailors: women therefore represented nine of twenty adult civilian victims.[64]

The victims of a number of the military murderers were women resisting soldiers' sexual advances. Mary Pinfold was assaulted so violently by three soldiers in 1760 that she died shortly afterwards. Mary Burt, a lodger in the house of William Peters, met her end in March 1761. Sergeant John Taylor had been invited to eat supper at the house. [...] At some point [he] complained that water had fallen on him from above. He was told that it might have come from Burt's room and went upstairs to investigate. He came down again a few minutes later complaining of being attacked simply because he had asked Burt for a kiss. But Burt was seen later that evening with her mouth bleeding, and the following morning she complained that Taylor had been "very rude to her and "used her very ill" when she refused him, She later complained of pain in her side and died within a few days. Taylor was acquitted, presumably because there was no direct evidence.[65] [...]

Of the ten female homicide victims, four appear to have been prostitutes or "camp followers, perhaps looking for temporary liaisons, while another was a single woman of slender means living in a lodging house, beyond the protection of family and friends.[66] [...] Another woman's body was discovered in December 1796, "in a very indecent posture, on her back, her clothes thrown up over her breasts,

her lower parts entirely naked." According to the person who found her, "there was a great number of footsteps of men leading to the place the body lay, and ... the snow was much trodden down as though many persons had been with the deceased." Suspicion fell on private Charles Collins, [...] but he was never indicted.[67] [...]

In two cases the victims were killed by intimate partners.[68] The precise circumstances in which shoemaker Gotlieb Seidler killed his wife, Catherine, in their Dartmouth house in 1771 are unknown, although there is some indication that he was exercising his "right" to chastise her and overstepped the bounds.[69] The court records speak in greater detail of the circumstances of Thomas Bambridge's murder of Mary Russell. Bambridge, a young Dartmouth farmer, had been rejected as a suitor. Presumably enraged by this rejection, he burst into the Russell house on the night of 27 September 1798 demanding to speak to Mary; when permission was refused, he stabbed her in the chest with a butcher's knife, killing her more or less immediately.[70]

Outside Halifax, only four victims can be identified as female. Two were killed in the robbery perpetrated by the Boutelier brothers; two were wives killed by their husbands. The circumstances in which Michael Hayes of Liverpool killed his wife in 1786 cannot be determined from the records.[71] The records speak fulsomely, however, with respect to Gad Sanders's murder of his wife, Jude. Again male jealousy and possessiveness—as well as alcohol—were involved. Sanders was a black man from Yarmouth. After a day out, from which they both returned "much intoxicated," the Sanders spent the evening at home with their twenty-year-old daughter and one John Williams, a man of whom Gad Sanders was, according to his daughter, "jealous." At some point Gad went to sleep; shortly afterwards so did Jude, but with her head resting on Williams's knee having, according to her daughter's account, "fallen accidentally there." The furious attack that followed shortly afterwards is best reproduced as it was described in the trial report's summary of Sanders's daughter's testimony:

being apprehensive her father might be angry if he saw it she went to her mother and lifted her head up. Soon after ... her father asked her where John was. She answered there he is on the floor, on which her father arose and going to Williams said "go you home John" .... Williams immediately got up and went out of the house, her father following him to the door and fastening it after him. Her father then said to her mother "you damn bitch do you want to steal more things and give to John" ... and immediately taking an ... axe from the corner of the room gave ... three or four blows on her back as she sat on the floor with the blunt end or eye of the axe, holding the handle with both his hands .... [T]he blows were so hard that she heard the bones crack as he struck. As the prisoner was going to strike the deceased the witness called out "Mammie, Daddy will kill you," to which the deceased answered "let him kill me if he will." The witness ran to her father and endeavoured to take the axe from him on which he said to her, if you are not quiet I will serve you so. She was frightened and desisted. There was a good fire .... Her mother lay along the hearth after she had received the blows and the prisoner took coals of fire and burned her face and hands. The witness said to him "Daddy pray don't do so." He replied "Damn her I will burn her up." He dragged her legs to the fire to burn them and the witness endeavoured to prevent him. He then desisted and went to bed.

Sanders was not hanged. Although convicted, his contrition and a belief that he had acted "under derangement of mind" made him appear, to the male presiding judge and governor, fit for mercy, and a pardon was duly issued for him. Given this description of the crime, it is difficult to imagine a more obvious case of a deliberate attempt to kill, and one suspects that only the killing of a wife in such circumstances could evince such judicial sympathy. In this period a charge of murder could be reduced to manslaughter if the accused was provoked by the infidelity of his wife. Although this partial defence was usually employed only in cases

where the husband killed the other man, not the wife, Sanders was perhaps able to invoke in the authorities some sense that the circumstances had provoked him and that he should be spared as a result.[72]

Conclusion

Homicide rates in eighteenth- and early nineteenth-century Nova Scotia reveal distinct patterns. Outside Halifax homicide occurred infrequently and, when it did occur, the victim and the perpetrator were generally known to each other. [...] Deadly violence was much more prevalent in Halifax, and the city's comparatively high homicide rate can be explained partly by the urban environment and partly by demographics. The circumstances of some Halifax homicides mirror those that occurred elsewhere in mainland Nova Scotia: instances involving murder in the course of a robbery or the murder of a wife by her husband. In other cases, however, the circumstances in which a killing took place reflected the unique character of the capital; the level of lethal violence in Halifax owed substantially, although certainly not entirely, to the nature of its population. A significant portion of the inhabitants of this military base and naval town were young, single men belonging to the forces. Such men lacked the family ties that function to constrain violence and antisocial behaviour—or, in the worst-case scenario, to keep violence within the family. Moreover, armed forces create a "super masculine" culture in which violence and aggression are deliberately cultivated to promote the interests of the state: violent and disorderly behaviour among off-duty soldiers is an unwanted side effect of this culture. [...] The fact that these men tended to be armed meant that such altercations could easily result in a death. The military presence rendered Halifax, compared with the rest of eighteenth-century Nova Scotia, a dangerous place in which to live.

Appendix: Population Figures

Population data for eighteenth-century Nova Scotia is not plentiful, nor is it always reliable.

It is better for Halifax than for the colony as a whole. Halifax grew slowly from about 2500 in 1749 to around 5000 by the early 1770s to 8000 or 9000 at the end of the eighteenth century to perhaps 10,000 in 1815.[73] But its population could also fluctuate substantially, so growth was by no means consistent. This article uses an estimate of the average civilian population for the entire 1749–1815 period, excluding the 1806–10 period for which prosecution figures are not available. It was arrived at by using the figures available for a variety of years, assigning estimates to missing years, totalling the whole, and dividing by the number of years. Rounded up to err on the side of conservatism in calculating the homicide rate, the figure came to 6000. This figure is not, of course, the right one for most of the years, for it combines years when the population was lower and years when it was much higher, and, overall, it is almost

certainly too high. To this 6000 we have added 3000 to represent the military/naval population of the city, which fluctuated much more wildly than the civilian population. This estimate is probably over-generous, but, again, we want to err on the side of caution.[74]

Population information is even less plentiful and reliable for the rest of the colony. The non-Acadian and non-Native population of mainland Nova Scotia outside Halifax grew from practically nil at the beginning of our period to perhaps 12,000 in 1776 to 50,000 in 1800 to around 65,000 in 1815.[75] We have used the same technique as for Halifax—mixing a few known estimates with our own estimates for missing years, and then totalling and averaging the whole. We began in 1760, with the beginnings of planter settlement. The average for the 1760–1815 period was 25,929, rounded up to 26,000.

Notes

1. For Cartcel's trial, see the report in Nova Scotia Archives and Records Management (NSARM), Colonial Office Series (CO) 217, vol. 9, Cornwallis to Board of Trade, 11 Sept. 1749, 97–101. A draft of the report is at NSARM, Supreme Court Records, Record Group [hereafter RG] 39, Series C, vol. 1, no. 2, 6, and a brief account is at RG 39, Series J, vol. 117. Other documents are at RG 1, vol. 342, nos. 1–4. The Cartcel trial is discussed in J. Chisholm, "Our First Trial for Murder: The King v. Peter Cartcel," *Canadian Bar Review* 18 (1940): 385–9; C. Townshend, "Historical Account of the Courts of Judicature in Nova Scotia," *Canadian Law Times* 19 (1899): 32–4; and J. Phillips, "The Criminal Trial in Nova Scotia, 1749–1815," in G.B. Baker and J. Phillips, eds., *Essays in the History of Canadian Law*, vol. 8: *In Honour of R.C.B. Risk* (Toronto: University of Toronto Press and The Osgoode Society for Canadian Legal History 1999), 471–2.

2. This article is derived from a larger study of crime and criminal justice in Nova Scotia from the founding of Halifax in 1749 to the end of the Napoleonic Wars. That study, and this article, exclude Cape Breton Island—a Nova Scotia county from 1763 to 1784, but a separate colony until

reannexation in 1820—and Prince Edward Island, also part of Nova Scotia from 1763 to 1769.

3. The number of victims is given tentatively because there are many cases for which it is not known whether there was one or more than one victim. For only three cases is it certain that there were two or more victims; two had two victims, one had three.

4. For the reception of English criminal law from 1749 and consequent debates and developments, see J. Phillips, "'Securing Obedience to Necessary Laws': The Criminal Law in Eighteenth-Century Nova Scotia," *Nova Scotia Historical Review* 12 (1992): 87–124. English criminal law was partially in effect in the colony during the pre-1749 Annapolis period: see T.G. Barnes, "'The Dayly Cry for Justice': The Juridical Failure of the Annapolis Royal Regime, 1713–1749," in P. Girard and J. Phillips, eds., *Essays in the History of Canadian Law*, Vol. 3: *Nova Scotia* (Toronto: University of Toronto Press and The Osgoode Society for Canadian Legal History 1991). The local legislation was the Treasons and Felonies Act, *Statutes of Nova Scotia* (SNS) 1758, c. 13.

5. This discussion of the common law of homicide is based largely on W. Blackstone, *Commentaries on*

the Laws of England, 4 vols. (1765–69) (Chicago: University of Chicago Press 1979, facsimile ed.) vol. 4, chap. 14, and on J.M. Beattie, *Crime and the Courts in England, 1660–1800* (Princeton: Princeton University Press 1986), 77–81. Also useful are J.M. Kaye, "The Early History of Murder and Manslaughter," *Law Quarterly Review* 83 (1967): 365–95 and 569–601, and T. Green, "The Jury and the English Law of Homicide, 1200–1600," *Michigan Law Review* 74 (1976): 413–99. Suicide is not discussed in this article.

6. The local murder provision is found in the Treasons and Felonies Act, s. 2. "Clergy" originated in the medieval period and was initially available only to the ordained. Personal eligibility for it was widened in piecemeal fashion over the centuries, a process that culminated in its becoming available to everyone in 1706. A person convicted of an offence within clergy was branded in court, usually on the thumb, to show that he or she had received clergy, and then discharged. Clergy was not finally abolished in Nova Scotia until 1841: Administration of Criminal Justice Act, SNS 1841, c. 4.

7. Blackstone, *Commentaries*, vol. 4, 198–201. Blackstone offered the examples of a master who intended only to correct a servant, but did so with an iron bar, or a person who "intends to do another felony, and undesignedly kills." In the first example given, "the correction being excessive ... it was equivalent to a deliberate act of slaughter."

8. Ibid., 178–88; quotations at 182.

9. Section 4 stated that "this act," by which it meant the prior sections making those convicted of murder "felons without benefit of clergy," did not "extend to any persons, who shall kill any person in his own defence, or by misfortune, or in any other manner than as aforesaid [with malice]." It also did not "extend to any persons who in keeping the peace, shall chance to commit manslaughter, so as the said manslaughter be not committed willingly and of purpose, under pretext and colour of keeping the peace," or to "any person who, in chastising or correcting his child or servant, shall besides his purpose, chance to commit manslaughter."

10. Although, by the eighteenth century, accidental deaths resulting from lawful activity were rarely prosecuted as murders in England, there was at least one such prosecution in the Nova Scotia courts in this period, See the case of Ezekiel Hooper, prosecuted for murder at Annapolis in 1783 when the horse he was racing hit a young boy: Bench Book of Judge James Brenton, 1782–1783, Acadia University Archives, 58 (microfilm at NSARM). For England, see the discussion of both accident and self-defence cases in Beattie, *Crime and the Courts*, 86–7.

11. Quotations from Blackstone, *Commentaries*, vol. 4, 191, and Beattie, *Crime and the Courts*, 91.

12. Treasons and Felonies Act, s. 5. This is a copy of an English statute of 1624–21 Jas. 1, c. 27. It is discussed in Beattie, *Crime and the Courts*, 113–14, and a detailed account of the origins is in P.C. Hoffer and N.E.H. Hull, *Murdering Mothers: Infanticide in England and New England, 1558–1803* (New York: New York University Press 1981), chap. 3. For a sustained analysis of its operation, see M. Jackson, *New-Born Child Murder: Women, Illegitimacy and the Courts in Eighteenth-Century England* (Manchester and New York: Manchester University Press 1996). The 1624 statute was received into Nova Scotia as part of the whole of English criminal law in 1749, and one woman was likely convicted under it. See the case of Mary Webb, tried and convicted in May 1758: RG 39, Series J, vol. 117; CO 217, vol. 18, Belcher to Board of Trade, 12 Dec. 1760, 85.

13. On the presumption of innocence and the standard needed for a criminal conviction, see Phillips, "The Criminal Trial," 491–5.

14. Treasons and Felonies Amendment Act, SNS 1813, c. 11. The English legislation was 43 Geo. III, c. 58 (1803). The infanticide provision was also introduced into the laws of Prince Edward Island (by specific provincial statute, see *Statutes of Prince Edward Island*, 1792, c. 1, s. 5) and Upper Canada (by the general reception statute, see *Statutes of Upper Canada* 1800, c. 1, s. 1). It was "standard in early American colonies": M.D. Smith, "Unnatural Mothers: Infanticide, Motherhood, and Class in the Mid-Atlantic City, 1730–1830," in C. Daniels and M. Kennedy, eds., *Over the Threshold: Intimate Violence in Early America, 1650–1856* (London and New York: Routledge 1999), 173.

15. By "brought to court" we mean that a defendant was brought before a grand jury at the beginning of a court term for a determination of whether there was a case to go to trial. The grand jury heard only the evidence for the prosecution and, if satisfied that there was sufficient evidence to proceed to trial, marked the indictment as a "true bill." If there was not enough evidence, the indictment was marked "ignoramus" and the prisoner was discharged. For a full account of the criminal trial process, see Phillips, "The Criminal Trial." An incident has been included in the database whether or not the grand jury found a true bill, and the data

therefore cover more than cases tried. We have not included incidents where it is clear that a homicide occurred or where an investigation would have been conducted by a justice of the peace, but where nobody was arrested and then brought to a grand jury.

16. For the 1749–1804 period, see the proceedings books at RG 39, Series J, vols. 1, 2, and 117. They record in summary form all cases prosecuted in these courts in the years noted, although 1761–63 are missing as are the other three terms for 1804. As a result, the total of eighty-three prosecutions for homicide might be low by one or two. Note, however, that the database does include two cases from the missing years, those of John Taylor (1761) and William Reach (1762), which we know about from other sources. We have added to the cases derived from these sources one from 1805, which is known about from other sources. Note also that eight prosecutions (five incidents) were tried in Halifax, although the offences occurred elsewhere in Nova Scotia. One of them, the prosecution of Robert Bacon, a soldier who allegedly killed a comrade while stationed at Louisbourg, is omitted from the database because it occurred in Cape Breton: RG 39, Series J, vol. 1, 23; RG 39, Series C, vol. 4, no. 47. The other seven prosecutions (four incidents) are included in the count for "other communities" in Table 1. For the 1811–15 period we rely on a listing of all criminal cases tried in the Supreme Court sitting at Halifax from Michaelmas Term (October/November) 1811 to the end of 1815. It was compiled by James W. Nutting and included in his 1829 petition to the Assembly for payment for his services as clerk of the crown: see NSARM, Assembly Records, RG 5, Series P, vol. 41, no. 102. The list is also in the Supreme Court records at RG 39, Series C, box A, no. 3.

17. For the Halifax and Nova Scotia population figures used in this article, see the appendix. In calculating the Halifax rate we used just sixty-two years—1749–1805 and 1811–15—eliminating the 1806–10 period because there is no consistent information on prosecutions during those years.

18. Beattie, *Crime and the Courts*, 108. The rate was 1.4 per annum between 1760 and 1779 and 0.9 per annum between 1780 and 1802. See also the same author's "The Pattern of Crime in England, 1660–1800," *Past and Present* 62 (1974): 47–95, which shows that the eighteenth-century decline affected both rural and urban areas.

19. For the former, see R.A. Roth, "Spousal Murder in Northern New England, 1776–1865," in Daniels and Kennedy, eds., *Over the Threshold*, 66. The

rate dropped to 0.58 between 1794 and 1827. For the latter, see G.S. Rowe and J.D. Marietta, "Personal Violence in a 'Peaceable Kingdom,'" ibid., 23 and 24.

20. New Orleans's annual homicide rate was 23 per 100,000 during Reconstruction, and dropped but remained comparatively high thereafter. Gilles Vandal attributes these high rates to politics and racial conflict: see G. Vandal, *Rethinking Southern Violence: Homicides in Post-War Louisiana, 1866–1884* (Columbus: Ohio State University Press 2000). The other work on which the comparisons drawn in this paragraph are based includes D. Spindel, *Crime and Society in North Carolina, 1663–1776* (Baton Rouge: Louisiana State University Press 1989), 59 and 65 (a rate of 6–7 in the 1750s), Richmond County, Virginia, which saw twenty-two persons accused of homicide between 1714 and 1749, in an area that enjoyed a population around 2500, may provide another example of a rate higher than Halifax; see P.C. Hoffer and W. Scott, eds., *Criminal Proceedings in Colonial Virginia* (Athena, Ga.: University of Georgia Press 1984), xii–xiv and lxiv. There are no studies computing rates for New England, other than Roth's cited above, but David Flaherty's unpublished study of Massachusetts shows just twenty-one prosecutions for murder in Boston in seventy-seven years, and only 128 homicide prosecutions in Massachusetts as a whole in fifty-seven years. He does not provide rates, but the Boston rate in particular must have been infinitesimal compared with Halifax's: see D. Flaherty, "A Well-Ordered Society: Crime and the Courts in Massachusetts, 1692–1780," unpublished manuscript, chap. 9. For similarly low absolute numbers in Massachusetts and Maryland, and for somewhat higher rates in the southern colony of South Carolina, see M. Hindus, *Prison and Plantation: Crime, Justice and Authority in Massachusetts and South Carolina, 1767–1878* (Chapel Hill: University of North Carolina Press 1981), 64, and R. Semmes, *Crime and Punishment in Early Maryland* (Montclair, NJ: Patterson Smith 1970), 119.

21. A. Lachance, "Women and Crime in Canada, 1712–1759," in L. Knafla, ed., *Crime and Criminal Justice in Europe and Canada* (Waterloo: Wilfrid Laurier University Press 1981). The rate has been calculated by us, using Lachance's homicide count and population figures. This should be compared to the higher Halifax rate, that for persons charged, of 19.4. Elsewhere Lachance shows that there were only six cases of homicide brought before the

district of Quebec courts between 1670 and 1759: "La criminalité à Québec sous le regime francais: étude statistique," *Revue d'histoire de l'Amerique française* 20 (1966): 411–12.

22. P. Oliver, *"Terror to Evil-Doers": Prisons and Punishment in Nineteenth-Century Ontario* (Toronto: University of Toronto Press and The Osgoode Society for Canadian Legal History 1998), 31. While the rate varied between 0.4 and 47 in different years, the average of the annual rates, 1.9, was a tenth of the equivalent Halifax rate. For Upper Canada/Canada West, see also J. Weaver, *Crimes, Constables and Courts: Order and Transgression in a Canadian City, 1816–1970* (Montreal and Kingston: McGill-Queen's University Press 1995), 55, to the effect that there were "few homicides in the immediate Hamilton area" in the first half of the nineteenth century. Elsewhere he suggests that the rate for Hamilton was generally between 2 and 4 per 100,000 per annum in the later nineteenth and early twentieth centuries: 217–18.

23. D. Fyson, "Blows and Scratches, Swords and Guns: Violence between Men as Material Reality and Lived Experience in early Nineteenth-Century Lower Canada," unpublished paper, 1999, gives 1.7 and 2 for the districts of Quebec and Montreal, respectively. However, the two cities had substantially higher rates in the 1765–93 period—7.5 in Quebec City and 5.6 in Montreal. We are indebted to Professor Fyson for these as yet unpublished figures. Regrettably there is no study of homicide in the other Maritime provinces, although we do know that only one person was hanged for murder in pre-Confederation Prince Edward Island: see J. Hornby, *In the Shadow of the Gallows: Criminal Law and Capital Punishment in Prince Edward Island, 1769–1941* (Charlottetown: Institute of Island Studies 1998), 2. Canada had a rate of 2.2 between 1951 and 1984: R. Gartner, "Homicide in Canada," in J. Ross, ed., *Violence in Canada: Sociopolitical Perspectives* (Don Mills: Oxford University Press 1995).

24. There is plenty of evidence in a variety of sources of other likely homicides for which no one was apprehended. See, for example, *Nova Scotia Gazette and Weekly Chronicle*, 23 July 1782 (reward for the murderers of Ann Dunbrack); RG 39, Series C, vol. 3, nos. 121 and 132 (coroners' inquests on the bodies of Mrs Bennett and Isaac Letherby); and *Boston Weekly Newsletter,* 8 March 1756 (body of Pegg How found stripped and with extensive wounds and bruises). See also, for various references to unattributed murders,

Boston Gazette, 3 July 1750 and 5 Feb. 1754; *Boston Weekly Newsletter,* 19 Jan. 1765; Wilmot to Board of Trade, 29 Aug. 1768, RG 1, vol. 37; Proclamations by Belcher, 1 Sept. 1761 and 3 May 1762, RG 1, vol. 165, 178–9 and 223; A.E. Marble, *Deaths, Burials, and Probate of Nova Scotians, 1749–1799, from Primary Sources,* 2 vols. (Halifax: Genealogical Association of Nova Scotia 1990), 1: 72 and 146, and 2: 46 and 141; and, generally, NSARM, Coroners' Records, RG 41, vols. 1 and 2, passim. In addition, there were doubtless many other homicides that have left no trace at all in the historical record.

25. See, for example, Gurr's assertion that while "the reported incidence of many kinds of offenses can be affected by changing degrees of public concern and by changes in the level and foci of police activity," such problems are much reduced when one examines "the most serious offenses." Thus, he argues, "murder is the most accurately recorded violent crime": T.R. Gurr, "Historical Trends in Violent Crime: A Critical Review of the Evidence," in M. Tonry and N. Morris, eds., *Crime and Justice: An Annual Review of Research* (Chicago: University of Chicago Press 1981), 298. See also Monkkonen's assertion that homicide is "the least definitionally ambiguous" of crimes, and the one "most likely to be reported": E. Monkkonen, "Diverging Homicide Rates: England and the United States, 1850–1875," in T.R. Gurr, ed., *Violence in America,* vol. I: *The History of Crime* (Newbury Park, Cal.: Sage 1980), 82.

26. The calculation of the Halifax assault rate is based on the records of the Court of Quarter Sessions, where the vast majority of assaults were prosecuted for the 1791–1806 and 1810–15 periods, using a population figure of 10,400 to reflect the larger population in these later years of our period. The Quarter Sessions records are at NSARM, RG 34-312, Series P. We have calculated the English and Massachusetts rates using the figures in Beattie, *Crime and the Courts,* 402, and Hindus, *Prison and Plantation,* 65 and 77.

27. This is very much the traditional picture of the city's history, best exemplified by older studies such as T. Raddall, *Halifax: Warden of the North,* rev. ed. (Toronto: McClelland & Stewart 1971), and T.B. Akins, *History of Halifax City* (1894; Belleville, Ont.: Mika Reprint 1984). The recent city history by J. Fingard, J. Guildford, and D. Sutherland, *Halifax: The First 250 Years* (Halifax: Formac 1999), takes issue with the Raddall thesis as a paradigm for the general history of the city, but its chapters on this period do not paint a different picture.

28. Alexander Grant to Ezra Stiles, May 1760, cited in Fingard et al., *Halifax*, 17.

29. For Quebec before and after the conquest, see D. Hay, "The Meanings of the Criminal Law in Quebec, 1764–1774," in Knafla, ed., *Crime and Criminal Justice*, 84–5.

30. This was the 1751 prosecution of Captain William Clapham and Private Samuel Iles for causing the death of a drunken prisoner by gagging him too tightly: see RG 39, Series C, vol. 1, nos. 33, 43, 44, and 56. Note that the presence of this case, and of others that involved military personnel as offenders and victims, suggests that, as a routine matter, such interservices killings were dealt with in the civilian court. This impression is reinforced by an examination of the army and navy collections at NSARM, which do not show such cases being dealt with internally. Deaths that resulted from floggings for military offences were not prosecuted as homicides.

31. S. Conway, "The Great Mischief Complain'd of: Reflections on the Misconduct of British Soldiers in the Revolutionary War," *William and Mary Quarterly* 47 (1990): 370–90, quotation at 382. See also P. Burroughs, "Crime and Punishment in the British Army, 1815–1870," *English Historical Review* 100 (1985): 545–71.

32. See G. Steppler, "British Military Law, Discipline, and the Conduct of Regimental Courts Martial," *English Historical Review* 102 (1987): 867–77, and A. Gilbert, "Military and Civilian Justice in Eighteenth-Century England: An Assessment," *Journal of British Studies* 17 (1978): 41–65, especially 50–5.

33. For these cases, see, respectively, RG 39, Series C vol. 3, no. 75, and *Diary of Elijah Estabrooks, 1758–1760* (Halifax: Privately published, nd), 27; Belcher to Board of Trade, 31 March 1762, CO 217, vol. 19, 1; RG 39, Series J, vol. 117, and Arbuthnot to Germain, 20 Nov. 1776, CO 217, vol. 52, 256; Sherbrooke to Bathurst, 29 July 1813, CO 217, vol. 91, 157–60. There is an interesting current parallel here. The United States has a much higher homicide rate than Canada, not because it has noticeably more interpersonal violence—it does not—but because the availability of guns means that much more of that violence translates into death for one or more of the participants: see F. Zimring and G. Hawkins, *Crime Is not the Problem: Lethal Violence in America* (New York: Oxford University Press 1997).

34. This figure is calculated in the same way as the overall homicide rate given above. We have attributed thirty-seven homicides to civilians, the twelve for which women were responsible and twenty-five of the sixty-three male homicides. The twenty-five is an extrapolation from the percentages of male homicide incidents known to have been committed by civilians. We are grateful to Don Fyson for suggesting this point.

35. Indeed, the high urban rates seem to be a North American rather than an English phenomenon. Beattie shows that while there were earlier periods in which the urban rate substantially outstripped that of rural areas, by the second half of the eighteenth century the rates were very similar, although always slightly higher in urban areas: see *Crime and the Courts*, 108.

36. This account is from the various depositions at RG 39, Series C, vol. 2, no. 18. See also from the same file the certificate from Dr Arthur Price attesting that Connor died from the gunshot chest wound. Andrews arrived in 1749 and was described at that time as a bricklayer. By the time a pardon was issued to him for the offence described here, he had risen to the appellation of mason: see E.C. Wright, *Planters and Pioneers* (Hantsport, NS: Lancelot Press 1982), 34; RG 1, vol. 163 [3], 98–9.

37. RG 39, Series J, vol. 2, 170, and Series C, vol. 77. Osborne was acquitted, according to presiding Judge Blowers, because "it was doubtful whether the blow she received caused her death": Blowers to Strange, 25 Oct. 1797, CO 217, vol. 69, 277.

38. RG 39, Series C, box A, no. 3; *Acadian Recorder*, 17 April 1813; Sherbrooke to Bathurst, 29 July 1813, CO 217, vol. 91, 157–62; Akins, *History of Halifax*, 161.

39. Special Commission, 1 Nov. 1776, RG 1, vol. 168, 482. For this case generally, see RG 39, Series J, vol. 1, 265–8; Arbuthnot to Germain, 20 Nov. 1776, CO 217, vol. 52, 256. Execution Warrant for Goff, 12 Nov. 1776, RG 1, vol. 170, 227, Scarr turned King's Evidence and was pardoned, while Ward also escaped with a pardon, partly because he received the intercession of his officers and partly because he had not fired the fatal shot: see Pardon for Scarr, 12 Nov. 1776, RG 1, vol. 170, 223–5; Respite for Ward, 14 Nov. 1776, RG 1, vol. 170, 228; Germain to Arbuthnot, 14 Jan. 1777, CO 217, vol. 53, 1. The sixty-four-year-old Schlegal had arrived in the colony in 1752 and settled first at Lunenburg: Bell's Register, Lunenburg County Records, NSARM, M[anuscript] G[roup] 1, vol. no. 194.

40. Leathum's case was very similar to Andrews's, discussed above. Lieutenant John Collins of HMS *Prince of Orange* and a group of sailors were out drinking very freely and, after some hours,

their minds turned to "going for a Girl." They went to a house, knocked loudly, and demanded to see "Polly." The householder denied that any Polly lived there. Leathum, who occupied the neighbouring house, came out of his door and, after some questions, ended up arguing with and shooting Collins. Like Andrews, he "was by the jury found guilty of homicide in his own defence" and, at the next sitting of the court: Quotation and other facts from evidence at the coroner's inquest, RG 39, Series C, vol. 3, no. 20; see also RG 39, Series J, vol. 117; RG I, vol. 165, 23.

41. Belcher to Board of Trade, 31 March 1762, CO 217, vol. 19, 1–11; RG 39, Series J, vol. 1, 407; Parr to Townshend, 26 Oct. 1782, CO 217, vol. 56, p. 3; Release Warrant, 7 July 1783, RG 1, vol. 170, 342, See also the cases of John Boyar, discussed above, and of Artilleryman Benjamin Brown, who killed Sergeant Scott, also of the Royal Artillery, in 1803: RG 39, Series J, vol. 2, 253, and Wentworth to Wilkins, Oct. 1803, RG 1, vol. 171. Ensign John Fleming killed Sergeant John Taylor in 1752: RG 39, Series J, vol. 117; Marble, *Deaths*, vol. 2, 107.

42. Bambridge's case is discussed below, in the section on women and homicide. For Connor, see RG 39, Series C, vol. 1, no. 83; for Leonard, see RG 39, Series J, vol. 1, 277, and Poll Tax Records, RG 1, vol. 444.

43. For these three individuals, see RG 39, Series J, vol. 1, 345; Marble, *Deaths*, vol. 2, 116 (Van Buskirk); RG 39, Series J, vol. I, 367, and vol. 98, 312 (Neal); RG 39, Series J, vol. 1, 421, and Petition of Nicholas Olding, 21 July 1789, RG 39, Series C, vol. 56, no. 65 (Olding).

44. There are Court of Sessions records for some places (see below), but homicides were not tried at Quarter Sessions, since such serious crimes were within the jurisdiction of the Supreme Court. The Supreme Court tried these cases either as part of its regular circuit, after circuits were established in 1774, or, both before and after 1774, on special commissions of oyer and terminer. For the system of administering justice in the out-settlements, see J. Phillips, "'The Majesty of the Law': Circuit Courts in Theory and Practice in Eighteenth-Century Nova Scotia," paper presented to the Conference on Canadian Legal History, University of Toronto Law School, 1998.

45. For the population estimate for Nova Scotia as a whole, see the appendix. This rate has been calculated using the sixteen incidents and twenty persons charged over the fifty-six years from 1760, the beginnings of planter settlement. It therefore

excludes a 1754 case that occurred in the Bay of Fundy and involved sailors from a Boston-based merchantman killing two navy men when the naval ship tried to apprehend the vessel. The case is discussed in Phillips, "The Criminal Law," 87–90.

46. For the Pomps, see Report on the Trial of John Pomp and Amy Pomp, 1813, RG 1, vol. 226, no. 114. For Shannon, see RG 39, Series J, vol. I, 79; *Boston Weekly Newsletter,* 30 March and 4 May 1769.

47. See Lee Trial Report, RG I, vol. 226, no. 16. The case is extensively discussed in Phillips, "The Criminal Trial," 472–4.

48. For Holland, see Report of the Trial of Patrick Holland, CO 217, vol. 87, 56–9. Manning was the father of the well-known New Light preacher James Manning, and, ironically, Caigin was the stepfather of James Payzant, another leading New Light Baptist and the man who converted James Manning: see D.G. Bell, ed., *The New Light Baptist Journals of James Manning and James Innis* (Hantsport, NS: Lancelot Press 1984), 359. For Manning's case, see Chipman Papers, MG 1, vol. 183, nos. 7 and 18, and Petition of Widow Caigin, Probate Records, Windsor, vol. 2A.

49. Report on the Trial of Alexander McIntosh, 1811, RG 1, vol. 225, no. 107.

50. See the report of the execution in *Boston Weekly Newsletter*, 6 Oct. 1768. For other details of this case, see ibid., 15 Aug. 1768; RG 39, Series J, vol. 1, 61–5; *Nova Scotia Gazette*, 28 July and 15 Sept. 1768. James Woodrow was found guilty of manslaughter only, given benefit of clergy, and branded.

51. See, variously, J. Stewart, *The Trials of George Frederick Boutelier and John Boutelier* (Halifax: Stewart 1792); Strange's Charge to the Grand Jury, 4 April 1791, CO 217, vol. 63, 301; *Gazette*, 3 May 1791.

52. Table 4 comes to a total of seventy-five incidents, three more than the seventy-two incidents in Halifax given in Table 1, because in three cases (Benjamin and Mary Lewis, 1760; John, James, and Mary Collins and George Heywood, 1783; and Judy Philpott, Patrick Power, and Margaret Murphy, 1791) men and women were charged together. Those cases have been recorded as an incident on both the male and female sides of the table. The number of persons charged was 109, the same as the figure given in Table 1.

53. Women constituted about 10 per cent of those accused of murder and manslaughter (that is, homicide excluding infanticide) in eighteenth-

century England; Beattie, *Crime and the Courts*, 83 and 97. For similar findings, see J.M. Beattie, "The Criminality of Women in Eighteenth-Century England," *Journal of Social History* 8 (1975): 85 (13 per cent); Lachance, "Women and Crime in Canada," 171 (9 per cent); P. Lawson, "Patriarchy, Crime and the Courts: The Criminality of Women in Late Tudor and Early Stuart England," in S. Devereaux, A. May, and G. Smith, eds., *Criminal Justice in the Old World and the New: Essays in Honour of J.M. Beattie* (Toronto: University of Toronto Centre of Criminology 1998), 22 (11.5 per cent); J. Sharpe, *Crime in Seventeenth-Century England: A County Study* (Cambridge: Cambridge University Press 1983), 124 (15 per cent); M. Hindus, "The Contours of Crime and Justice in Massachusetts and South Carolina, 1767–1878," *American Journal of Legal History* 21 (1977): 234 (11–12 per cent); Monkkonen, "Diverging Homicide Rates" 92 (9 per cent); D. Spindel and S. Thomas, "Crime and Society in North Carolina, 1663–1740," *Journal of Southern History* 49 (1983): 238 (13.5 per cent). See also, generally, N.E.H. Hull, *Female Felons: Women and Serious Crime in Colonial Massachusetts* (Champaign: University of Illinois Press 1987). Note also that women comprised just 57 of the 1512 (3.8 per cent) people condemned to death for murder in Canada between Confederation and 1962: C. Strange, "The Lottery of Death: Capital Punishment 1867–1976," *Manitoba Law Journal* 23 (1996): 607. This is, of course, a percentage of convictions, not accusations, and it is likely that the former was higher—but it could not have been much higher.

54. An extensive literature makes this argument for a variety of periods and places. A representative sample includes Beattie, "Criminality of Women"; Lawson, "Patriarchy, Crime and the Courts," especially at 43–52; Hull, *Female Felons*; B. Hanawalt, "Women before the Law: Females as Felons and Prey in Fourteenth Century England," in D.K. Weisberg, ed., *Women and the Law: A Social Historical Perspective* (Cambridge, Mass.: Schenkman 1982); C.J. Weiner, "Sex Roles and Crime in Late Elizabethan Hertfordshire," *Journal of Social History* 8 (1975): 38–60; L. Zedner, *Women, Crime and Custody in Victorian England* (Oxford: Clarendon 1991). The literature is more extensively reviewed in J. Phillips and A. May, "Women and Crime in Eighteenth-Century Halifax," unpublished, under review, 2001. There is no secondary literature providing evidence of the ideology of female roles in Halifax, but we

can glean something of it from contemporary newspapers and other sources. One extolled the need for women to submit to their husbands and devote themselves to home and children: see "Advice to the Fair Sex," *Halifax Gazette*, 9 Feb. 1754. For similar sentiments, see ibid., 29 Aug. 1752, and *Nova Scotia Chronicle*, 4–11 April 1769 and 13–20 Feb. 1770.

55. See J.M. Beattie, "Crime and Inequality in Eighteenth-Century London," in J. Hagan and R. Peterson, eds., *Crime and Inequality* (Stanford: Stanford University Press 1995); J.M. Beattie, "'Hard-Pressed to Make Ends Meet': Women and Crime in Augustan London," in V. Frith, ed., *Women and History: Voices of Early Modern England* (Toronto: Coach House Press 1995); M. Feeley and D. Little, "The Vanishing Female: The Decline of Women in the Criminal Process, 1687–1912," *Law and Society Review* 25 (1991): 719–51; M. Feeley, "The Decline of Women in the Criminal Process: A Comparative History," *Criminal Justice History* 15 (1994): 235–73.

56. The presence of women in the occupations noted has been gleaned from a few secondary sources and from a survey of Halifax newspapers. See, in particular, J. Gwynn, "Female Litigants in the Civil Courts of Nova Scotia, 1749–1783," paper presented to the Toronto Legal History Group, 1994; Akins, *History of Halifax*, 84 and 98; C.B. Fergusson, ed., *The Life of Jonathan Scott* (Halifax: Public Archives of Nova Scotia 1960), 41; G. Davies, "Literary Women in Pre-Confederation Nova Scotia," in Davies, *Studies in Maritime Literary History, 1760–1930* (Fredericton: Acadiensis Press 1991), 73–4; *Halifax Gazette*, 23 March 1752; *Nova Scotia Gazette and Weekly Chronicle*, 8 Nov. 1774, 2 May 1780, 6 Sept. 1785, 5 Dec. 1786, 9 Dec. 1788; *Nova Scotia Chronicle*, 7–14 Nov. 1769.

57. See Phillips and May, "Women and Crime in Eighteenth-Century Halifax," 21–8, and Table 6: Nature of Goods Stolen—Male and Female Property Offenders, 1749–1803.

58. Mary Lewis was charged with her husband, Benjamin, in 1760 and, while the grand jury found a true bill against her, the result of her case is not known: RG 39, Series C, vol. 3, no. 77. Mary Collins was tried and convicted along with John and James Collins and George Heywood in 1783; John was likely her husband, a John Collins, labourer in the dockyard, having married a Mary Fitzgerald in 1782. James and Mary were executed: RG 39, Series J, vol. 1, 427–30; Parr to North, 13 Dec. 1783, CO 217, vol. 56, 17; Marriage Bonds, 10 Oct. 1782, RG 32.

59. Mary Orpin killed a neighbour's eight- or nine-year-old boy and was the first woman to be hanged in the colony: see RG 39, Series J, vol. 117, and Series C, vol. 3, no. 77; Lawrence to Board of Trade, 16 June 1760, CO 217, vol. 18, 1; Lawrence to Foy, 16 May 1760, RG 1, vol. 165, 62; *Diary of Elijah Estabrooks*, 27. Margaret Murphy, whose case is discussed above, likely killed a fellow prostitute in a brothel: RG 39, Series C, vol. 63, no. 40.

60. RG 39, Series J, vol. 1, 366 and 376; *Gazette*, 4 April 1780.

61. For Orpin and Collins, see above. For Philpott and Murphy, charged along with Patrick Power in 1791, see RG 39, Series J, vol. 2, 120, and Series C, vol. 63, no. 40; *Nova Scotia Gazette*, 18 and 25 Oct. 1791; *Nova Scotia Magazine*, Oct. 1791, 633.

62. For studies of infanticide in the early modern period, see, especially, R.W. Malcolmson, "Infanticide in the Eighteenth Century," in J.S. Cockburn, ed., *Crime in England 1550–1800* (Princeton: Princeton University Press 1977); K. Wrightson, "Infanticide in European History," *Criminal Justice History* 3 (1982): 1–20; Beattie, *Crime and the Courts*, 113 ff; Jackson, *New-born Child Murder;* Smith, "Unnatural Mothers"; and Hoffer and Hull, *Murdering Mothers*. The principal Canadian study, which argues that the killing of new-borns was a device by which Canadian women frequently avoided having to bring up an unwanted child, remains C. Backhouse, "Desperate Women and Compassionate Courts: Infanticide in Nineteenth-Century Canada," *University of Toronto Law Journal* 34 (1984): 447–78. For the preponderance of domestic servants among those charged, see Beattie, *Crime and the Courts*, 114, who calculates that as many as two-thirds of the women prosecuted for infanticide in Surrey in the eighteenth century were domestic servants, and Malcolmson, "Infanticide in the Eighteenth Century," 202. For the same trend in nineteenth-century Ontario, see Backhouse, "Desperate Women," 457.

63. Report of the Trial of Nancy O'Neal, RG 1, vol. 343.

64. This argument is made at greater length in J. Phillips, "Women, Crime and Criminal Justice in Early Halifax, 1750–1800," in J. Phillips, T. Loo, and S. Lewthwaite, eds., *Essays in the History of Canadian Law*, vol. 5: *Crime and Criminal Justice* (Toronto: University of Toronto Press and The Osgoode Society for Canadian Legal History 1994).

65. RG 39, Series C, vol. 3, no. 99.

66. See the case of James Richardson, accused of killing Catherine McIntosh in 1758 by beating her as she lay in bed: RG 39, Series C, vol. 2, no. 57; RG 1, vol. 342, no. 50.

67. Quotation from the Deposition of John Anderson, 7 Jan. 1797, RG 39, Series C, vol. 78. For other stories of the finding of women's dead bodies in such suspicious circumstances, see Proclamation, 3 May 1762, RG 1, vol. 165, 223, and *Nova Scotia Gazette and Weekly Chronicle*, 23 July 1782. See also the prosecution of Charles Dayley, Daniel Dayley, John Connelly, and Patrick Oram (1764), whose indictment for the murder of Elizabeth or Rebecca Young was returned ignoramus. The depositions suggest there was no evidence linking the four soldiers to Young, but she was with them for a period of time during the evening she died and she was very drunk: RG 39, Series J, vol. 117, and Series C, vol. 4, no. 33.

68. For contemporary studies of what has been termed "intimate femicide," see R. Gartner and M. Crawford, *Woman Killing: Intimate Femicide in Ontario, 1974–1990* (Toronto: Women We Honour Action Committee 1992). The historical evidence is inconsistent. One study suggests that the most common victims of male murderers in mid nineteenth-century London were their wives, at 32 per cent; R. Anderson, "Criminal Violence in London, 1856–1875" (PhD thesis, University of Toronto 1990), 172. Lower numbers have been found for earlier centuries: see Sharpe, "Domestic Homicide," *Historical Journal* 24 (1981): 29–48, and Roth, "Spousal Murder." The latter suggests that the rate of wife murder increased substantially in the nineteenth century, an assertion supported by Dodge's finding that half the female victims in his sample were wives of the perpetrators; T. Dodge, *Crime and Punishment in New Hampshire, 1812–1914* (New York: Lang 1995), 113. Beattie's study of eighteenth-century England does not single out partner killings, but suggests that perhaps a third of all indictments for murder in the 1678–1774 period involved murders committed within the family: *Crime and the Courts*, 105.

69. RG 39, Series J, vol. 1, 105; *Boston Weekly Newsletter*, 16 May 1771. For Seidler, see Wright, *Planters and Pioneers*, 249.

70. RG 39, Series J, vol. 2, 191, and Series C, vol. 79; *Nova Scotia Gazette*, 2 Oct. 1798. An inventory of Bambridge's effects gave his property as 125 acres of land in Dartmouth on the Cole Harbour Road with a small house, a very few cows and pigs, and other farm-related equipment and goods. For Russell, see A. Marble, *Surgeons, Smallpox*

and the Poor: A History of Medicine and Social Conditions in Nova Scotia, 1749–1799 (Montreal and Kingston: McGill-Queen's University Press 1993), 226. Bambridge fits a pattern familiar to students of the contemporary killing of women by their partners or other intimates: rejection leads to deadly violence as the only remaining recourse of the male who wishes to possess and control, and keep from any other man, the object of his pursuit.

71. *The Diary of Simeon Perkins*, 3 vols. (Toronto: Champlain Society 1948–1967), 1: 301, 304, 315–16, 322–3; RG 1, vol. 170, 390.

72. For this case, see RG 39, Series J, vol. 2, 219; Portland to Wentworth, 6 June 1801, CO 218, vol. 27, 180. Report of S.S. Blowers on the Trial of Gad Sanders, 2 Feb. 1801, CO 217, vol. 75, 7. For Chief Justice Blowers's and Governor Wentworth's opinions, see Blowers to Wentworth, 2 Feb. 1801, and Wentworth to Portland, 25 April 1801, CO 217, vol. 75, 6 and 8–9. Blowers also gave as reasons for recommending mercy the fact that public sympathy was with Sanders, that the trial took place in Halifax and the offence in Yarmouth, that no coroner's jury had met to consider "the apparent effects on the body of the deceased of the blow she received," and that there was only one witness to the events, Sanders's daughter. While there may indeed have been some public sympathy for Sanders, it is difficult to see the relevance of the other factors offered. There was a coroner's inquest (see RG 41, Series C, vol. 1), and in any event there could hardly be any dispute about the cause of death. Moreover, Sanders "called no witnesses in his defence but addressed the jury and without denying the facts testified against him, endeavoured to excuse himself on account of his intoxication and jealousy": Blowers Trial Report, 2 Feb. 1801, CO 217, vol. 75, 8. There are very few historical studies on intimate femicide and attitudes to it; the best include Roth, "Spousal Murder," and C. Strange, "Masculinities, Intimate Femicide and the Death Penalty in Australia, 1890–1920," paper presented to the Toronto Legal History Group, October 2000. For the rules on provocation, and for cases applying them, see Beattie, *Crime and the Courts*, 95.

73. The principal sources for the calculation were *Censuses of Canada, 1665–1871* (Ottawa: Queen's Printer 1876), xxiv and 69–70; "Early Descriptions of Nova Scotia," *Report of the Public Archives of Nova Scotia for 1933* (Halifax: Public Archives of Nova Scotia 1934), 21–51; Akins, *History of Halifax*, passim; Fingard et al., *Halifax*; J. Gwynn,

Excessive Expectations: Maritime Commerce and the Economic Development of Nova Scotia, 1740–1870 (Montreal and Kingston: McGill-Queen's University Press 1998), chap. 1.

74. The military population figure is more approximate than that given for civilians, and represents an attempt to reconcile the fact that while the permanent establishment was perhaps between 2000 and 2500, at various times there were many fewer or many more than that. As with the civilian population, information on military numbers is scattered through a variety of sources. The principal ones used here include R.A. Evans, "The Army and Navy at Halifax, 1783–1793" (MA thesis, Dalhousie University 1970), chap. 1 and 148; C.P. Stacey, "Halifax as an International Strategic Factor, 1749–1949," *Canadian Historical Association Report* (1949): 46–48; "Journal of Benigne Charles de Saint Mesmin, 1793," *Report of the Public Archives of Canada* (Ottawa: Public Archives 1946), xxv; Marble, *Surgeons, Smallpox and the Poor*, passim. Troop numbers at various times, and movement in and out, are also reproduced in many issues of the *Halifax Gazette* (which went by various titles in this period) as well as the *Boston Gazette* and the *Boston Weekly Newsletter*. Examples of substantial fluctuations in troop numbers include the fact that several thousand troops spent time in the city in the 1750s before the assault on Louisbourg. Conversely, in 1775 just thirty-six men were left in Halifax when the army was ordered to Boston: see Akins, *History of Halifax*, 49 and 53–4; *Boston Gazette*, 19 June 1758; J.B. Brebner, *The Neutral Yankees of Nova Scotia* (Toronto: McClelland & Stewart 1969), 300.

75. Acadians are excluded from our calculations because we effectively start in 1760, after the expulsion began; also, there is no evidence that any who remained were effectively governed by the English courts. The same is true for the Native peoples; not a single Native person was tried in the Supreme Court, in Halifax or elsewhere, in this period. The population figures used here are culled in particular from *Censuses of Canada*, xxxviii, xliv, and 69; G. Rawlyk and G. Stewart, *A People Highly Favoured of God: The Nova Scotia Yankees and the American Revolution* (Toronto: Macmillan 1972), xii; Wright, *Planters and Pioneers*, passim; T.F. McHwraith, "British North America, 1763–1867," in P. Graves and R. Mitchell, eds., *North America: The Historical Geography of a Changing Continent* (Totowa, N.J.: Rowan and Littlefield 1987), 221; J. Martell,

Immigration to and Emigration from Nova Scotia, 1815–1838 (Halifax: Public Archives of Nova Scotia 1942), 8; and Gwynn, *Excessive Expectations*. An early draft of this article was presented to a joint meeting of the Toronto Legal History and Early Canada groups. We thank the participants for their helpful suggestions and would like to thank as well Rosemary Gartner, Keith Wrightson, and the anonymous CHR reviewers for their comments on later versions.

CHAPTER 7

The Shining Sixpence:
Women's Worth in Canadian Law
at the End of the Victorian Era

Constance Backhouse

• • • • • • • • • • • • • • • • • • • •

On Tuesday evening, 7 April 1896, the body of a new-born infant girl, wrapped in a rough potato sack, washed up on the shores of the Nanaimo Harbour Beach, on the east coast of Vancouver Island. A group of startled children playing on the beach stumbled over it, and dumped the contents from the sack. As the *Nanaimo Free Press* would report the next day, the dead infant's body was "stark naked," with the exception of "a bright English six-pence," which was "loosely attached to the child's neck by a piece of string."[1]

Infanticide was an unsavoury but surprisingly common feature of daily life in nineteenth-century Canada. It was one of the tragic, but historically inevitable responses to the overwhelming problems posed by unwanted pregnancies. Despite the absence of modern contraceptive knowledge, many nineteenth-century heterosexual women endeavoured to limit the number of their offspring, using other methods such as abstinence from sexual intercourse, prolonged nursing, coitus interruptus, sheaths, pessaries, douches, and abortion where all else had failed.[2] But the law did not encourage such reproductive control. Indeed, as the century progressed criminal legislation against abortion, first enacted in New Brunswick in 1810, expanded nation-wide to prohibit the artificial termination of pregnancy at

any stage of gestation, by whatever means.[3] By 1892, parliament banned the sale, distribution, and advertising of all contraceptives. That same year feminists demanding the right to "voluntary motherhood" inside marriage suffered the ultimate outside intervention, when parliament enacted an express exemption for husbands from charges of wife-rape.[4]

Infanticide had become, for many, a device of last resort. Bodies of newborn infants were frequently discovered in ditches, in privies, in stove pipes, in pails of water, inside hollow trees, buried in the snow, floating in rivers, at the bottom of wells, under floor-boards, and under the platforms of railway stations. Fifty or more such bodies were found by the coroner in the 1860s in each of Toronto and Quebec City alone. Not all of the bodies would have been found, of course, and even when they were, it was often impossible to determine who was responsible.[5]

News of the gruesome discovery in Nanaimo spread quickly through the bustling resource town. The finger of suspicion settled upon Anna Balo, a woman known to have been pregnant, who had abruptly taken flight from the city upon discovery of the infant's body. A 44-year-old, married Finnish immigrant, the mother of six children, Anna Balo was an unusual suspect. Most women charged with infanticide in the nineteenth century were young, unmarried, domestic servants. Frequently they attempted to hide their pregnancy and childbirth, no doubt motivated by fear. Giving birth to an illegitimate child resulted in disgrace, termination of employment, and severely diminished job prospects for the single parent. For most of these women, harsh economic and social realities left virtually no options.

Most attempted to carry out concealment plans with courage and extraordinary determination. They had to keep normal appearances in front of employers and acquaintances despite pregnancy-related illnesses, disguising their growing bulk with layers of clothing and excuses. They would have to secure some degree of privacy in which to give birth unobserved, serve as their own midwife and do away with the child and its body before discovery. Afterwards, many tried to continue daily routines as if nothing had happened. Those who fell before any of these hurdles were caught and swept into the criminal justice system.[6]

It was unusual for married women to find themselves charged with infanticide. This may have reflected the fact that they were less likely to be involved in child-murder. Unlike single women they did not face life-altering shame at pregnancy. Furthermore, bearing and raising a child within a heterosexual marital unit was economically much more feasible than trying to do so alone. On the other hand the relative absence of accusations against married females may simply have reflected the greater difficulties of proof. Married women would rarely need to conceal their full pregnancy, could give birth openly, kill the child, and later declare that it had died of natural causes. With the collusion of their husbands, it would have been virtually impossible to obtain a conviction. The newspapers not infrequently reported incidents of "laying over," where infants were smothered or suffocated while sleeping in their parents' beds. Such situations were typically acclaimed "accidental" and criminal charges would not be pressed.[7]

Anna Balo's marital status did not protect her. The press duly recounted, "her husband [was] said to have deserted her three years ago."[8] Legal prospects for a woman abandoned by her husband in nineteenth-century Canada were stark. In part, marital laws created a distinctly gender-skewed family unit. The English common law "doctrine of marital unity" transported to all Canadian jurisdictions except Quebec, held that the legal personality of the wife was absorbed by her husband. "By marriage, the husband and wife are one person in law," wrote eighteenth-century English jurist Sir William Blackstone, leaving no doubt that the "one person" was the husband. Upon marriage, a woman forfeited the right to manage all of her real estate, although she did not actually lose ownership in the property. All rents and profits from the land flowed by right to her husband during the marriage. Married women were legally incapable of contracting, suing, or of being sued in their own names. Indeed, women were only permitted to carry on business separately from their husbands if they had their spouses' consent. Furthermore, all personal property belonging to the wife, including her wages, transferred absolutely to her husband.[9] A few wealthy women were able to protect their property through recourse to highly technical "equitable" exceptions to the common law, but for the bulk of women there was no recourse.[10]

In Quebec, the rules for property and status derived from the Coutume de Paris and, after 1866, from the Civil Code of Lower Canada. Quebec women experienced the same legal incapacity upon marriage as women in the rest of Canada. They could not contract, take legal action, or start a business without their husbands' authorization. But they were not subject to the English "doctrine of marital unity." French marriage built on the legal concept of "community of property." All property that the two spouses obtained after the marriage became "jointly" owned. The catch was that the husband alone had the lawful right to administer and dispose of it. Couples could opt out of this system, but only in advance, by signing special marriage contracts permitting a wife to retain control over her own property. The extent to which women and their families managed to bargain such exemptions remains unclear.[11]

Although Quebec law did not change significantly throughout the nineteenth century, after 1851 the law of married women's property began to experience incremental reform in the common law provinces. Prodded by women's rights activists, provincial legislatures slowly enacted a cross-section of new statutes increasing the ability of married women to control their own property. It would take British Columbia women until 1873 to obtain control over their property and their wages. Restrictions such as requirements for written spousal consent and court orders for protection continued to plague women in Nova Scotia and Prince Edward Island into the twentieth century.[12] Canadian judges displayed widespread uneasiness over these statutory reforms, repeatedly dispensing rulings which watered down the new rights and freedoms.[13]

It was difficult enough for some women to manage in the face of discriminatory property laws, even within a stable marital unit; but for deserted women such as Anna Balo, the situation was intolerable. Consigned to legal non-existence through patriarchal doctrines, they were left in the unenviable position of trying to enforce dependence upon a man who had balked his moral and economic obligations by abandoning his child. Responding to the desperate situation of deserted women, several colonial legislatures had passed reform statutes permitting such women to obtain limited rights over marital property after abandonment. The legislature of Vancouver Island had enacted one such statute in 1862, in response to a wave of desertions in the wake of the Fraser River and Cariboo gold rush.[14] But Anna Balo would have required a court order to give her control over her own wages and property under this legislation, and few poor immigrants made any practical use of the provisions.

Nor was Anna Balo, deserted for three years, offered much by way of access to divorce. Canadian divorce law differed greatly depending upon the province of one's residence, but for most nineteenth-century heterosexual couples, marriage was a tie for life. English tradition derived ultimately from ecclesiastical canon law and forbade divorce, although the English parliament allowed private bills to pass granting divorces to named individuals, almost always members of the aristocracy. The English position, first adopted in Upper Canada in 1839, typically provided divorce only to men whose wives had committed adultery. Utilising a blatant double standard, the English rules forced a woman seeking divorce to prove not only that her husband had committed adultery but that he had been guilty of some other serious crime, such as incest or bigamy.[15] In neighbouring Lower Canada, the environment was even less hospitable for those seeking divorce. French law transported to Quebec simply never recognised the concept of divorce. The Civil Code of Lower Canada, enacted in 1866, stated: "Marriage can only be dissolved by the natural death of one of the parties; while both live it is indissoluble."[16]

The Maritime provinces had traditionally been somewhat more tolerant of divorce. Legislation enacted in Nova Scotia in 1758, in New Brunswick in 1791, and in Prince Edward Island in 1833, permitted divorce to either spouse on grounds such as adultery, impotence, frigidity, and cruelty. Nova Scotia briefly recognised an additional ground of "wilful desertion while withholding necessary maintenance for three years" from 1758 to 1761, at which point this ground was deleted from the statutory list.[17] The Maritimes led the rest of the country in divorce rates, but even so the numbers remained small. The 1881 census revealed the ratio of divorced to married people in Nova Scotia and New Brunswick (the two provinces with the highest divorce rates) as 1:2608 and 1:2350 respectively.[18]

Although Confederation turned matters of divorce over to the federal government in 1867, parliament did not manage to pass a general divorce statute until well into the twentieth century. In the vacuum after 1867, the Maritime provinces continued to follow their own laws.[19] The federal government began haltingly to exercise its original jurisdiction, adopting the English policy of passing private statutes of divorce in individual cases. Citizens of Ontario, Manitoba, and the North West Territories who availed themselves of this option found that parliament continued to follow the sexual double standard in most cases.[20] The year 1888 marked the first time that a woman procured a parliamentary divorce on grounds of her husband's adultery alone.[21]

In British Columbia, the law which governed Anna Balo was explicitly biased with respect to gender. Courts of that province chose to adopt the discriminatory English law, permitting men to obtain divorce upon proving simple adultery. By contrast, women were required to prove "incestuous adultery, or bigamy with adultery, or rape, or sodomy, or bestiality, or adultery coupled with cruelty ..., or adultery coupled with desertion without reasonable excuse for two years or upwards."[22] Lacking proof of adultery, rape, sodomy, or bestiality on the part of her husband, the law irrevocably tied the deserted, pregnant Anna Balo to her missing husband for life.

Anna Balo's abrupt departure from Nanaimo, upon discovery of the dead infant's body on April 7th, triggered the suspicion of authorities. Frantic with fear, she had abandoned her six children and fled north on foot. Before police caught up with her a day and a half later, Anna Balo had walked thirty miles to Qualicum.[23] Arrested on April 10th, she was back in Nanaimo for arraignment in police court the next morning. Dr. Robert S.B. O'Brian entered the county gaol to examine the prisoner that afternoon. "I asked her a few questions and examined her breasts and they had the appearance of a woman that had lately been confined," he would later testify. Almost immediately thereafter, Anna Balo broke down and confessed to being the mother of the dead infant.[24]

Speaking through a Finnish interpreter, whose services had been requisitioned because Anna Balo was unable to understand English, the distraught woman told Police Chief Crossan that the child was indeed hers. Of how she had come to be pregnant, she said not a word. Gossip and rumours had been circulating within the Finnish community of Nanaimo, but whether Anna Balo's pregnancy was the result of a consensual heterosexual relationship or a forcible seduction or rape will never be known.[25] Anna Balo's admission was that she had given birth at home one week previously on April 4th. The child had died almost immediately after its birth, she stressed. Trying to dispose of its body, she had wrapped it in an empty potato sack and deposited it upon the beach of the Nanaimo Harbour.[26]

This confession catapulted Anna Balo immediately into a full-scale coroner's inquest and subsequent trial at the Spring Assizes of the Supreme Court of British Columbia in May. Throughout these proceedings, she was unrepresented by legal counsel. There was no indication from court records that anyone advised the accused woman that she would do well to retain a lawyer. Indeed it was not until 1836 in England that persons accused of a crime were unequivocally granted the right to defence counsel at all. There was no institutionalised legal aid available; many nineteenth-century accused without funds were simply out of luck.[27]

For Anna Balo, finding the financial resources to retain legal assistance was out of the question. A deserted wife trying to cope with six children, she was the victim of acute financial distress. Even for single women without child-care responsibilities, employment opportunities were limited. Customarily relegated to the fields of domestic service, seamstressing, nursing, shop clerking, factory work and teaching, women found working conditions strenuously difficult and their efforts poorly paid.[28] Occasionally legal intervention barred women's access to certain jobs entirely. Statutes passed in British Columbia in 1877 and Ontario in 1890 rendered mining off-limits to women.[29] Manitoba prohibited women from serving liquor in bars in 1886.[30] Prostitution, a traditional female occupation, came increasingly within the reach of the criminal law throughout the nineteenth century, as social purity reformers sought to eradicate the gender-imbalanced trade in sexual services.[31]

Finnish immigrant women typically found jobs as domestic servants, but Anna Balo's large family would have obliterated most job prospects.[32] One of her sons was apparently helping to support the family by working in the Dunsmuir coal mine, but his earnings were simply not enough for seven mouths. The tightly knit Finnish community of Nanaimo was unable or unwilling to extend sufficient support to relieve the Balos. The family's financial situation became so precarious that the City of Nanaimo had been forced to provide a small welfare pension of $5 a week.[33] This level of impoverishment meant that legal representation was beyond hope.

The coroner's inquest opened on April 9th, before the Nanaimo Coroner, Lewis Thomas Davis, and seven jurymen.[34] The all-male composition of the tribunal was unremarkable for an era in which women were almost universally denied formal participation within legal and political structures. Throughout the century women had been forbidden the vote in provincial and federal elections, and could not sit as elected representatives for provincial legislatures or the Dominion parliament.[35] Not one woman sat as coroner, justice of the peace, police magistrate, or judge for the entire century. Coroner's juries and trial juries were composed solely of men.[36] Clara Brett Martin, the first white woman admitted to the profession of law in the British Commonwealth, called to the bar in Toronto on 2 February 1897, was the only nineteenth-century Canadian woman to challenge the all-male legal system from within.[37]

Dr. O'Brian, who conducted the post-mortem examination on the infant's body, testified at length to the coroner's inquest. Noting that the child had been dead some time before it was immersed in water, the doctor concluded that death had occurred during delivery, possibly before full legal birth or immediately thereafter. The infant had been slightly premature, had apparently drawn breath and then died, although from what cause the doctor could not ascertain.[38]

Mrs. Anna Sharp, the Finnish woman who lived on Pine Street, opposite the Balos, was called next. She stated that she had known Anna Balo for the past five years, but that she had "never been on very good terms" with her. Anna Balo had become quite reclusive since the fall, and although many of the neighbours were curious, no one knew for sure if she was indeed pregnant. Mrs. Sharp was just one of the local Finnish women who made a point of visiting Anna Balo to learn more. It was early in March, she told the inquest, and "I went to see Mrs. Balo but she put me out of the house for talking about her, and I never went back again ...." Nevertheless, she was able to assure the jurors: "I then saw it with my own eyes that she was pregnant." Unable to write or sign her name, Anna Sharp completed her deposition by placing an "X" beside her name.[39]

The next witness was none other than Alexandra Balo, Anna's twelve-year-old daughter. How she felt about testifying is not clear, but it was obvious that she was quite ignorant about her mother's status. In fact, she told the inquest, she did not even know when her mother had been arrested. Under close questioning, Alexandra admitted that her mother had been sick about two weeks ago. "My mother was awfully white," she admitted, and she "told me that I couldn't go to school because she was sick." Instead, Anna Balo sent Alexandra off downtown to purchase 50 cents worth of alcohol for medicinal purposes. When Alexandra returned Anna Balo mixed the alcohol with some warm water and sugar and drank it. Young Alexandra was terribly anxious to get back to school. This time her mother was too weak to argue. "Go if you want to, I can't do anything because I am sick," she yielded from her bed.[40]

What Alexandra discovered when she returned from school made her decide to stay home for the next week. There was blood on the floor in her mother's bedroom, blood on the bedspread, and blood on some of her mother's dresses. Anna told Alexandra to wipe up the blood on the floor, but she got up herself and washed the bedclothes and dresses. Although Alexandra could not be certain, she told the inquest that she thought her mother had left the house for a few hours several days later. "I did not see her take anything with her when she went away," she added. Rather plaintively she tried to excuse her inability to answer all of the questions: "I am twelve years of age. Mother didn't tell me anything more," she repeated.[41]

Perhaps the most damning piece of evidence concerned that shiny English sixpence. Alexandra was asked about it at some length and her reply was devastating. "There was a sixpence in the house which my mother and myself thought was no good," she admitted. "It was kept in the cupboard, and the morning my mother went away I went to look for the sixpence and could not find it." The sixpence coin that had been found on the infant's body was then produced, and Alexandra identified it as the same one.[42]

It is hard to know how Alexandra could have been so certain of the identity of the sixpence coin. Perhaps it was damaged in some way that left it both unusable and easily identifiable. In any event, its identification clearly traced the infant's body to the Balo home. With that, the evidence drew to a close. Anna Balo was asked whether she wished to have the testimony re-read to her and, through her interpreter, she responded "no." Asked whether she wished to give a formal statement herself, she replied, again through the interpreter, "Nothing to say."[43]

The coroner's jury retired to consider their findings. Despite the damaging revelations of Anna Sharp and Alexandra Balo, the complexity and contradictions inherent in the medical evidence seemed to have been the predominant concern. The verdict reflected the jurors' uncertainty over the cause of death. "We the Jury find that the child found on the Beach on

the 7th of April died during Child Birth," they inscribed on the formal "Inquisition" document. And with that, they adjourned, having neither condemned nor exonerated Anna Balo.[44]

That same day, Police Magistrate J.H. Simpson committed Anna Balo for full trial at the Spring Assizes. Given the inability of the medical experts to ascertain the cause of death, she was not charged with either murder or manslaughter. Instead the charge was "concealment of a birth," a Criminal Code offence which read as follows:

s. 240. Every one is guilty of an indictable offence, and liable to two years' imprisonment, who disposes of the dead body of any child in any, manner, with intent to conceal the fact that its mother was delivered of it, whether the child died before, or during, or after birth.[45]

This offence, originally punishable by death, had first appeared in New France in 1722, spreading in the early nineteenth century to the colonial jurisdictions of Lower Canada, Nova Scotia, New Brunswick, Prince Edward Island, Newfoundland, and Upper Canada.[46] In its original form, the offence of concealment was an attempt by all-male legislators to address the difficulties of obtaining murder convictions against women who committed infanticide. Authorities claimed that such women eluded conviction because there were few witnesses to these sorts of births. If caught, the terrified mothers would claim that the child was stillborn or that it died right after birth. Since so many babies died at birth from natural causes anyway, prosecutors were sorely pressed to dispute this.[47]

In response, the early concealment statutes set forth some rather extraordinary rules. There was to be a presumption of guilt, rather than innocence, in such cases. Prosecutors were relieved from having to prove that the mother had actually murdered her illegitimate infant. The mere fact that an infant had died where the mother had been trying to conceal the childbirth was henceforth to merit capital punishment. Courts were instructed to convict unless the accused woman could provide some other person as a witness to her innocence. This witness would have to testify that he or she had seen the mother give birth and that the child had been stillborn. Since the purpose of concealment would have been undone by inviting a witness to attend the birth, it must have been clear to legislators that few women accused of the crime would be able to meet this high burden of proof.[48]

The severity of concealment laws was apparent not only to the women concerned, but also to large sectors of the community.[49] Even many of the legal officials who were charged with administering the law balked. They strained for evidence which would permit them to evade the draconian implications of a guilty verdict under the capital concealment offence.[50] Beginning with New Brunswick in 1810, and culminating with Prince Edward Island in 1836, Canadian legislators slowly began to amend the concealment law. They reinstituted traditional rules of proof for women charged with murdering their infants, relegating the concealment crime to the status of a lesser and included offence, subject to a maximum of two years' imprisonment.[51] It was this law, swept into the consolidation process mounted by the federal government when it obtained jurisdiction over criminal law, which ultimately found its way into the Criminal Code (1892) as section 240.[52]

The deputy attorney-general of British Columbia, who acted as the crown attorney in this case, was a thorough, careful prosecutor. His handwritten notes on the back of the coroner's deposition documents reveal that he was worried about his ability to secure Anna Balo's conviction, even on the two-year concealment charge. "We should have some better evidence of the birth," he scrawled. His next entry read: "Can the sack be identified?" He must have thought that Alexandra's identification of the silver sixpence was insufficient to tie the body to Anna Balo. He also wanted to locate a new witness, a Mrs. Mattison. Alexandra had

revealed at the inquest that Mrs. Mattison, a neighbour, had dropped by the Balo home the week after her mother took sick, while she was still bedridden. The deputy attorney-general must have thought that Mrs. Mattison would be able to offer some first-hand account of Anna Balo's condition.[53]

The notes also reveal the deputy attorney-general's serious reservations about Anna Balo's confession to Chief Crossan. This he described as her "supposed confession."[54] Was he worried that a court would decide it had not been made voluntarily? Coming so quickly on the heels of that intrusive physical examination that Dr. O'Brian had carried out on Anna Balo in jail, it just might have struck a jury that the confession was tainted by the events that had preceded it. There were long-standing rules of evidence concerning the acceptability of confessions. Customarily, confessions were treated as inadmissible in court if obtained under coercive circumstances. According to S.R. Clarke's 1872 Treatise on Criminal Law as Applicable to the Dominion of Canada, these were important, time-honoured principles of law:

> It is a general and well-established principle that the confession of a prisoner, in order to be admissible, must be free and voluntary. Any inducement to confess held out to the prisoner by a person in authority, or any undue compulsion upon him, will be sufficient to exclude the confession.[55]

The crown attorney anticipated some difficulty in getting Anna Balo's confession into court around such rules.

The Spring Assizes opened on 5 May 1896. Montague William Tyrwhitt Drake, a judge with a dour reputation, strict and to the point, presided.[56] Anna Balo, without funds and clearly unfamiliar with legal proceedings, appeared without defence counsel. Judge Drake apparently saw no reason to order a court-appointed lawyer for a non-capital offence.[57] Without legal advice Anna Balo must have had no inkling that the crown perceived its case as weak. After arraignment, the prisoner announced that she intended to plead "guilty" to the charge.[58] No one contested the identification of the dead infant as Anna Balo's child. No one took issue with the crown's position that Anna Balo had flung the child into the Nanaimo Harbour with the intention of concealing her pregnancy and birth from the community. The perceived inadequacies of Anna Balo's confession suddenly became irrelevant with her decision to plead guilty.

But Anna Balo's big break came at the time of sentencing the next day. His Lordship, Judge Drake, pronounced as follows:

> He considered that a nominal punishment would be sufficient under the circumstances, as beyond the mere concealment of birth there was no suggestion of impropriety. The sentence of the Court was 24 hours' imprisonment, and as this dated from the first day of the Assizes, the prisoner was now discharged.[59]

This was truly a "nominal" punishment, a mere slap on the wrist compared with the maximum penalty allowing two years' imprisonment. Anna Balo's immediate discharge provided a clear signal that legal officials were prepared to tolerate, if not exactly condone, the secret disposal of the bodies of dead infants, and potentially even outright infanticide.

With this decision, Judge Drake followed in the footsteps of a long line of male judges and jurors exhibiting similar sentiments in other nineteenth-century infanticide cases. In some areas of the country, up to two-thirds of the courts were issuing outright acquittals of women charged with murder or manslaughter, despite often overwhelming and gruesome evidence of maternal guilt. On the lesser charge of concealment, up to nearly half of the women charged were being discharged and released.[60] If Anna Balo had been legally represented and pleaded not guilty, the chances were good that she would have been acquitted. Lenience in verdicts and sentencing indicated a pervasive sense of tolerance, even compassion, within

the legal system toward women accused of infanticide.[61] It also indicated widespread judicial and popular male rejection of the law itself.

Why were legal authorities so "soft" on these women? First, they seem very sympathetic to the motives which drove women to take the lives of their own offspring. According to the legal authors of an *Upper Canada Law Journal* article in 1862, women frequently destroyed their own flesh and blood out of a "sense of shame," to prevent the "loss of reputation." "The loss of character is the loss of earthly prospects," emphasised the lawyers. "The consequence at times is a life of prostitution, loathsome disease—in a word, a living death."[62]

It was almost as if the male lawyers believed that these women acted from a sense of honour, to preserve reputation and avoid descent into unimaginably harsh circumstances. If anything, they seemed to have been impressed by the courage and resourcefulness that the women exhibited as they struggled to hold their lives together. There was virtually no discussion of mental illness or insanity. Instead these acts were seen as deliberate and rational steps that women alone took to reassert order upon a situation tragically altered by an illegitimate pregnancy.

Second, the infant victims occupied a position of little status in the nineteenth century. Infant mortality rates were relatively high well into the twentieth century, frequently above 100 deaths for every 1000 live births. Infant death was everywhere and everyday, leaving a certain sense of inevitability, even complacency, over its commonness. Many individuals responded to infant death with what would seem to us today to be visibly callous behaviour. One remarkable example of this surfaced at a coroner's inquest in Halifax in 1861. Evidence revealed that when the body of an infant was found in an alley behind a rum shop on Water Street, people laughed and joked about the discovery, referring to the body as the "prize in the alleyway."[63]

Prominent medical authorities frequently referred to infants as somewhat less than human. For example, in his *Crime and Insanity*, published in England in 1911, Dr. Charles Arthur Mercier stated:

> In comparison with other cases of murder, a minimum of harm is done by [infanticide]. The victim's mind is not sufficiently developed to enable it to suffer from the contemplation of approaching suffering or death. It is incapable of feeling fear or terror. Nor is its consciousness sufficiently developed to enable it to suffer pain in appreciable degrees. Its loss leaves no gap in any family circle, deprives no children of their breadwinner or their mother, no human being of a friend, helper, or companion. The crime diffuses no sense of insecurity.[64]

Victims of infanticide went virtually unnoticed in societies which often treated infants as less than human. Their mothers could not care for them, their fathers would not acknowledge or support them. Nineteenth-century children assumed importance in the eyes of the law when disputes between grown adults arose over custody. Issues regarding the proper descent of male blood lines and the orderly conveyance of family property to future generations brought children's legal status to the fore. In that context, children were traditionally viewed as the property of their fathers, and nineteenth-century courts tended to opt for paternal custody, except in rare cases where the father had serious defects of character considered socially intolerable. Mothers of these children were granted custody only in situations where they lived under the protection of some other male, usually their fathers or brothers, and only if they had not disqualified themselves by an adulterous relationship or some other conduct that judges considered unseemly.[65] But the women who committed infanticide were primarily poor, working-class, and unmarried, seduced and abandoned by men. There were no blood lines to protect and certainly no estates to be concerned about transferring. In Anna Balo's case, that the child was the offspring of a "foreigner" would have consigned the infant to even greater social margins. These were infants whose interests the courts could afford to ignore almost completely.

Finally, the lenience of the courts was at least in part a response to the desperate plight of most women charged with child-murder or abandonment. There were simply no options. Child-welfare agencies, which might have provided facilities for unwanted children, barely existed. In the meantime, a woman who could not care for her own infant faced painfully few, mainly unpalatable alternatives. In some areas, neighbourhood women took unwanted infants into their own homes. They did this as a business and charged a lump sum or regular fees. Occasionally they would also place these infants for private adoption. Vituperatively described as "baby farms," these homes came under increasing criticism by the turn of the century for their high infant death rates. Accusations were regularly voiced that the infants in these homes were deliberately murdered through neglect or drug overdose. But in Anna Balo's case, she would no doubt have been unable to afford the required fees, even if she had been able to find a willing home.[66]

In some larger cities, charitable organisations and religious institutions had begun to establish "Infants' Homes" to look after deserted children. Operating on "voluntary contributions," religious donations, and in some cases small government grants, these homes also had infant death rates that were shockingly high. La Creche D'Youville, managed in Montreal by the Grey Nuns, accommodated over 15,000 abandoned children between 1801 and 1870. Between 80 and 90% died while under institutional care.[67]

There were no such institutionalised resources whatsoever in Nanaimo. In the whole province of British Columbia by the end of the nineteenth century there were only three. The closest "Infants' Home" Anna Balo could have found would have been in Victoria, where the Roman Catholic Orphanage and the Protestant Orphan Home competed for "clients." There were considerable tensions between the Finnish Lutheran churches and the more established religions in Canada, and a Finnish immigrant would have been unlikely to feel comfortable seeking assistance from either. Even if she had wished to try, and been able to secure transportation with the child to Victoria, it is by no means clear that the child's future would have been significantly different. Women for whom child-rearing created impossible demands often chose infanticide out of necessity, and the courts by and large respected their decisions.[68]

Notes

1. *Nanaimo Free Press*, 8 April 1896. This case is also discussed in C. Backhouse, *Petticoats and Prejudice: Women and Law in Nineteenth-Century Canada* (Toronto: The Osgoode Society, 1991), chapter 4. Accounts were taken from the British Columbia Archives and Records Services [hereafter BCARS], GR 1327, No. 37/1896, Coroner's Inquest, Nanaimo, 16 April 1896; GR 419, Box 63, file 2/1896 Depositions, Brief for Crown R. v. Balo. See also, *Nanaimo Free Press*: 9 April 1896, 11 April 1896, 16 April 1896, 6 May 1896. I am indebted to Indiana Matters, then of BCARS, for bringing this to my attention.

2. For a discussion of the methods of reproductive control used in the nineteenth century, see Angus McLaren and Arlene Tigar McLaren, *The Bedroom and the State: Changing Practices and Politics of Contraception and Abortion in Canada 1880–1980* (Toronto: McClelland & Stewart, 1986); Angus McLaren, "Birth Control and Abortion in Canada 1870–1920" (1978) 59 *Canadian Historical Review* 319; Constance Backhouse, "Involuntary Motherhood: Abortion, Birth Control and the Law in Nineteenth-Century Canada" (1983) 3 *Windsor Yearbook of Access to Justice* 61; Linda Gordon, *Woman's Body, Woman's Right: A Social History of Birth Control in America* (New York: Grossman, 1977); James C. Mohr, *Abortion in America* (Oxford: Oxford University Press, 1978).

3. For a detailed discussion of the common law and statutory positions on abortion in nineteenth-century Canada, see Backhouse, *supra* note 2; Shelley Gavigan, "The Criminal Sanction as it Relates to Human Reproduction" (1984) 5 *Journal of Legal History* 20; An Act ... for the further prevention of the malicious using of means to procure the miscarriage of women, 50 George III (1810), c. 2 (N.B.); as amended 9–10 George IV (1829) c. 21 (N.B.); An Act to Provide for the Punishment of Offences against the Person, 6 William IV (1836), c. 22 (P.E.I.); An Act for Consolidating ... Offences against the Person 4–5 Victoria (1841), c. 27 (U.C.); An Act Respecting Offences against the Person, 32–33 Victoria

(1869) c. 20, s. 59, 60 (D.C.); The Criminal Code, 1892, 55–56 Victoria (1892) c. 29, ss. 219, 271–4 (D.C.).

4. For legislation banning birth control, see The Criminal Code, 1892, 55–56 Victoria (11892) c. 29, s. 179 (D.C.). For discussion of the women's drive to obtain sexual control within marriage and the Criminal Code's exemption of husbands from rape convictions in 1892, see Constance Backhouse, "Nineteenth-Century Canadian Rape Law 1800–92" in David H. Flaherty, ed., *Essays in the History of Canadian Law*, vol. II (Toronto: The Osgoode Society, 1983) 200.

5. For general discussion of nineteenth-century infanticide in Canada, see Constance B. Backhouse, "Desperate Women and Compassionate Courts: Infanticide in Nineteenth-Century Canada" (1984) 34 *University of Toronto Law Journal* 447; Marie-Aimée Cliche, "L'Infanticide dans La Région de Quebec 1660–1969" (1990) *Revue d'Histoire de l'Amérique Française* 31; W. Peter Ward, "Unwed Motherhood in Nineteenth-Century English Canada" *CHA Historical Papers* (Halifax, 1981) 34; Mary Ellen Wright, "Unnatural Mothers: Infanticide in Halifax 1850–1875" (1987) *Nova Scotia Historical Review* 13. For a comparative perspective, see Keith Wrightson, "Infanticide in European History" (1982) 3 *Criminal Justice History* 1; Peter C. Hoffer and N.E.H. Hull, *Murdering Mothers: Infanticide in England and New England 1558–1803* (New York: New York University Press, 1981); W.L. Langer, "Infanticide: An Historical Survey" (1974) 1 *The History of Childhood Quarterly* 353; R.W. Malcolmson, "Infanticide in the Eighteenth-Century" in J.S. Cockburn, ed., *Crime in England 1550–1800* (London: Methuen, 1977) 198; J.M. Beattie, *Crime and the Courts in England 1660–1800* (Princeton: Princeton University Press, 1986), 113–24. For details concerning the number of infants' bodies examined by the Toronto coroners, see Eric Jarvis, "Mid-Victorian Toronto: Panic, Policy and Public Response 1856–73" (Ph.D. Thesis, University of Western Ontario, 1978) at 134–35. With respect to

Quebec City, see Cliche, *supra* note 5, Tableau 1 at 35.

6. For details of the typical infanticide prosecutions, see Backhouse, *supra* note 2.

7. See, for example, the *Toronto Weekly Leader*, 15 December 1858, where it was reported that Mrs. Meutto of Yorkville awoke one morning to find her twelve-week-old infant lying dead in her arms. The coroner's inquest delved mainly into the reputation of the parents. As the paper recounted, "the evidence elicited at this inquest was sufficient to satisfy the jury that the parents were respectable and strictly sober persons, and a verdict was therefore returned that the child was accidentally suffocated."

8. *Nanaimo Free Press*, 1 April 1896.

9. In return for these legal privileges over marital property, husbands were legally liable for their wives' debts, torts, and contracts. For a full discussion of the English common law rules of married women's property and their reception into English-Canadian jurisdictions, see Constance Backhouse, "Married Women's Property Law in Nineteenth-Century Canada" (1988) 6 *Law and History Review* 211. See also William Blackstone, *Commentaries on the Laws of England* vol. I (London 1765); Lee Holcombe, *Wives and Property: Reform of the Married Women's Property Law in Nineteenth-Century England* (Toronto: University of Toronto Press 1983) 30–1.

10. The injustice of the common law rules had become apparent as early as the late sixteenth century in England where the courts of chance developed a body of equitable precedents that undermined the doctrine of coverture and permitted women to retain their property separately through devices such as ante-nuptial and post-nuptial contracts, marriage settlements, and trusts: Maria Cioni, *Women and Law in Elizabethan England, with Particular Reference to the Court of Chancery* (New York: Garland, 1985). In Canada the courts of chancery were by no means as well established and access to lawyers experienced in equity was at a premium. The sheer expense of tying up estates in trust settlements was another major impediment; George Smith Holmested, writing at the turn of the century, concluded that for Canadians, marriage settlements were "as a rule enjoyed by the few only who could indulge in [this] luxury ...; to the ordinary run of married women they were a dead letter": *The Married Women's Property Act of Ontario* (Toronto, 1905) 1–6. For a more detailed description of common law rules and equitable precedents, and the various exceptions to them, see

Backhouse, *supra* note 9. For a full discussion of the English provisions, see Holcombe, *supra* note 9.

11. The wife retained property received as an inheritance or gift from her parents, although the husband had access to any profits made on these assets. For a more detailed description of the Quebec married women's property law, see Marie Gérin Lajoie, "Legal Status of Women in the Province of Quebec" in *Women of Canada: Their Life and Work* (Ottawa: National Council of Women of Canada, 1990) at 41–50; Micheline Dumont et al., *Quebec Women: A History* (Toronto: Women's Press, 1987) 68–128, 254–55; André Morel, "La libération de la femme au Canada: Deux itinéraires" (1970) 5 *La Revue Juridique Thémis* 399–411; Michelle Boivin, "L'évolution des droits de la femme au Québec: un survol historique" (1986) 2 *Canadian Journal of Women and the Law* 53.

12. An Act to Extend the Rights of Property of Married Women, 36 Victoria (1873), c. 29. See Backhouse, *supra* note 9, for details of the reform legislation throughout the nineteenth century. The reasons for statutory reform were varied, ranging from a desire to preserve married women's property from seizure for husbands' debts during time of economic downturn, through an egalitarian concern to improve the legal status of married women.

13. See Backhouse, *supra* note 9, for a detailed analysis of the nineteenth-century judicial rulings regarding married women's property. Scornful of the legislative goals and palpably concerned about the dangers such reform measures posed for the Canadian family, the majority of nineteenth-century judges embarked upon a campaign of statutory nullification. They consistently refused to grant women the right to dispose of their property, they restricted married women's right to contract, they refused to recognise domestic labour as work done for separate wages, and they narrowly construed what constituted "separate property" and what constituted a "separate" business undertaking, giving married men control over the vast bulk of family assets and business ventures.

14. An Act to Protect the Property of a Wife Deserted by Her Husband, 1862, Public Statutes of the Colony of Vancouver Island 1859–1863, c. 51 at 20. For a discussion of the other "marriage breakdown" statutes, passed in New Brunswick in 1851 (as amended in 1869 and 1874), Prince Edward Island in 1860, and Nova Scotia in 1866; see Backhouse, *supra* note 9. In other geographic areas, there was no relief at all. The grave injustices

this could cause were starkly evidenced by the case of Whibby v. Walbank (1869), 5 Nfld. R. 286 (S.C.). James Whibby had abandoned his wife, Mary, and four children sixteen years earlier, but returned upon his wife's death to lay claim to the wages she had managed to put together from years of labouring as a washerwoman. Newfoundland Chief Justice Sir H.W. Hoyles ruled categorically that James Whibby was fully entitled to Mary's earnings.

15. For discussion of divorce law generally, see Constance Backhouse, "Pure Patriarchy: Nineteenth-Century Canadian Marriage" (1986) 31 *McGill Law Journal* 265; Constance Backhouse, *supra* note 1, chapter 6. By the time of Confederation, only seven ad hoc petitions had been presented to the Legislature of Upper Canada (and later to the Legislature of the United Province of Canada). Two were abandoned, four were granted, and one was granted but later disallowed; see Backhouse, ibid. at 270. See Mary Lyndon Shanley, *Feminism, Marriage, and the Law in Victorian England 1850–1895* (Princeton: Princeton University Press, 1989) 36, for a discussion of the English situation.

16. The French law was stated by Judge René-Edouard Caron, President of the Commission responsible for drafting the Quebec Civil Code: "Le divorce n'a jamais existé pour nous comme faisant partie des lois françaises": see John E.C. Brierley "Quebec's Civil Law Codification" (1968) 14 *McGill Law Journal* 521 at 560. See also Civil Code of Lower Canada (1865) 29 Victoria c. 41, art. 185. In Quebec, couples could obtain *séparation de corps* (separation from bed and board), which was in the nature of a legal separation. Discriminatory standards affected this remedy as well: a husband could obtain *séparation de corps* with proof of his wife's adultery; a wife had to prove that her husband was keeping his concubine in their common habitation: see arts. 187, 188.

17. The grounds, which also included kinship within the prohibited degrees, varied over the years and between jurisdictions. For more detailed discussion of the grounds, see Backhouse, *supra* note 9. An Act Concerning Marriages, and Divorce, and for Punishing Incest and Adultery, and Declaring Polygamy to Be Felony 32 George II (1758), c. 17 (N.S.); as amended 1 George III (1761), c. 7 (N.S.); 56 George III (1816), c. 7 (N.S.); 29 Victoria (1866), c. 13 (N.S.). An Act for Regulating Marriage and Divorce, and for Preventing and Punishing Incest, Adultery and Fornication 31 George III (1791), c. 5 (N.B.); 48 George III (1808), c. 3 (N.B.); 4

William IV (1834), c. 30 (N.B.); 6 William IV (1836), c. 34 (N.B.); 10 Victoria (1847) c. 2 (N.B.); 23 Victoria (1860) c. 37 (N.B.). See also An Act for Regulating Marriage and Divorce, and for Prohibiting and Punishing Polygamy, Incest, and Adultery, Provincial Archives of New Brunswick R.S. 24 S1-B6 (1786 New Brunswick); and P.A.N.B. R.S. 24 S2-B5 (1787 New Brunswick) for earlier drafts which were not formally enacted. An Act for Establishing a Court of Divorce and for Preventing and Punishing Incest, Adultery and Fornication 3 William IV (1833), c. 22 (PEI), as amended 5 William IV (1835), c. 10 (PEI).

18. For statistical details of the operations of the Nova Scotia and New Brunswick courts, see Kimberley Smith Maynard, "Divorce in Nova Scotia 1750–1890" in Philip Girard and Jim Phillips, eds., *Essays in the History of Canadian Law: Vol. III, Nova Scotia* (Toronto: The Osgoode Society, 1990) and Angela Crandall, "Divorce in 19th Century New Brunswick: A Social Dilemma" [unpublished, 1988]. By 1890 the Nova Scotia matrimonial court had dealt with between 150 and 200 divorce applications. Maynard noted that of the 44 petitions in which cause and outcome were recorded, 34 received divorces: "Table Two: Divorces by Cause." By 1900 the New Brunswick court had dealt with approximately 130. Crandall found that approximately half of the New Brunswick applications were granted. There has been some difficulty determining the number of divorce applications in Prince Edward Island prior to 1900. In an earlier article I erroneously suggested that there had been none: see Backhouse, *supra* note 15 at 270. Maynard cited only one application in her "Divorce in Nova Scotia." Jack Bumsted and Wendy Owen uncovered three applications in their "Divorce in a Small Province: A History of Divorce on Prince Edward Island from 1833" in (1991) 20 *Acadiensis* 20 at 86: Peter Fisher's petition in 1833 spawned the passage of the 1835 legislation, although there are no further records on whether he carried through with his application after the new statute was passed. Two other divorce applications achieved success: Collings v. Collings 1840–31, Public Archives of Prince Edward Island 2810/141–2 and Capel v. Capel, 1864, referred to in an assault decision, Public Archives of Prince Edward Island, Supreme Court Reports, Case Papers, 1864 (no divorce records apparently survive in this case.) For census details, see R. Pike, "Legal Access and the Incidence of Divorce in Canada: A Sociohistorical Analysis" 12 (1975) *Canadian Review of Sociology and Anthropology*

115. Quebec had the lowest divorce ratio, at 1:62, 334.

19. The British North America Act, (1867) 30–31 Victoria, c. 3, s. 91(26). England gave jurisdiction over divorce to parliament, but s. 129 laid the foundation for provincial divorce courts to continue when it provided that the laws then in force, and all the courts of civil and criminal jurisdiction, should continue in Ontario, Quebec, Nova Scotia, and New Brunswick.

20. Between 1867 and 1900, only sixty-nine such divorces were granted by parliament. See Backhouse, *supra* note 15, for a list of the parliamentary divorces (at 276), and fuller legal analysis of why individuals from these provinces adopted the practice of applying to parliament (at 271–79). For Ontarians, there were simply no other options; for citizens from Manitoba and the North West Territories (then including Saskatchewan and Alberta), it was more a matter of custom.

21. The Canadian parliament theoretically was not bound to impose a sexual double standard and the senators insisted that there were no arbitrary rules respecting divorce, each case being considered on its own merits. John Gemmill proudly proclaimed that parliament had generally abolished the sexual double standard in his 1859 treatise, but An Act for the Relief of Eleanora Elizabeth Tudor, 51 Victoria (1888), c. 11 (D.C.) was the first such decision. The case spawned an intense legal confrontation over the pros and cons of the sexual double standard. While some argued that the 1888 case had abolished the inequality of treatment, by the turn of the century only three other women had fared as well: Gemmill, Bills of Divorce 22; Backhouse, *supra* note 14 at 284–91.

22. The law of reception in British Columbia provided that the province should apply the law of England as of 19 November 1858: "Proclamation" by His Excellency James Douglas, Governor, Colony of British Columbia, 19 November 1858; English Law Ordinance, 1867 Cons. S.B.C. 30 Victoria (1877), c. 103; see also R.S.B.C. 1897, c. 62. In M. falsely called S. v. S. (1877), 1 B.C.R. 25, the British Columbia Supreme Court ruled that it had jurisdiction to apply the English divorce law. Noting that Nova Scotia and New Brunswick had been granting divorces for over a century, Judge John Hamilton Gray pronounced them "England's more practical Colonies." Manitoba and the North West Territories were in similar legal situations, but their courts did not follow the British Columbia lead in the nineteenth century; see Backhouse, *supra* note 15 at 278–79. The English divorce law

so received was An Act to Amend the Law Relating to Divorce and Matrimonial Causes in England, 20–21 Victoria (1857), c. 85 (Eng.).

23. *Nanaimo Free Press*, 11 April 1896.

24. Ibid., 11 April 1896; and BCARS GR 419, Box 63, File 2/1896, Deposition.

25. For a reference concerning the community rumours, see BCARS, Deposition; Coroner's Inquest. An abundance of legal records of rape trials and seduction lawsuits suggests that coercive male sexuality was a serious and continuing threat to many nineteenth-century Canadian women. See Backhouse, *supra* note 14; Constance Backhouse "The Tort of Seduction: Fathers and Daughters in Nineteenth-Century Canada" (1986) 10 *Dalhousie Law Journal* 45; Backhouse, *supra* note 1, chapters 2 and 3.

26. *Nanaimo Free Press*, 11 April 1896.

27. For a discussion of the development of the right to counsel, see P. Romney, *Mr. Attorney: The Attorney-General For Ontario in Count, Cabinet and Legislature 1791–1899* (Toronto: The Osgoode Society, 1986) at 208. John Beattie has explained the historical reluctance to permit defence lawyers into the criminal justice process by quoting William Hawkins, whose *Pleas of the Crown* was published in England between 1716 and 1721. Hawkins wrote that "It requires no manner of skill to make a plain and honest defence, which in cases of this kind is always the best." Beattie, *supra* note 5 at 356.

28. For a discussion of nineteenth-century protective labour legislation affecting women, see Backhouse, *supra* note 1, chapter 9. Ramsay Cook and Wendy Mitchinson, eds., *The Proper Sphere: Woman's Place in Canadian Society* (Toronto: Oxford University Press, 1976) 166, noted that in 1901 the largest percentage of women were still employed either as domestic servants, dressmakers, or seamstresses. As the new century dawned, however, jobs for women were slowly beginning to expand. Nursing and teaching were most frequently mentioned, and by 1900 the National Council of Women of Canada listed the following occupational pursuits as open to women: musicians, actresses, artists, authors, journalists, printers, masseuses, midwives, stenographers, secretaries, factory inspectors, librarians, civil servants, farmers, horticulturists. A small number of women were acknowledged to have entered medicine, dentistry, and pharmacy. Lajoie, *supra* note 11 at 47, 63.

29. An Act to Make Regulations with Respect to Coal Mines, 40 Victoria (1877), c. 122 (B. s. 3, 7, 10, 55), abolished women's labour underground in the coal mines. See also 46 Victoria (1883), c. 2 (B.C.)

and C.S.B.C. 1888, c. 84. For no apparent reason, all of these restrictions were repealed in 1892: An Act to Amend the "Coal Mines Act," 55 Victoria (1892), c. 31 (B.C.), s. 1. Without explanation, they were enacted again in 1897: An Act to Make Regulations with Respect to Coal Mines, R.S.B.C. 1897, c. 138. An Act to Amend the "Coal Mines Regulation Act," 53 Victoria (1890), c. 33, s. 1 (B.C.), added the words "and no Chinaman" to the prohibited groups. An Act to Amend the "Coal Mine Regulation Act," 62 Victoria (199), c. 46, s. 1 and 2 (B.C.) added the words "or Japanese." The wording of the latter amendment was peculiar since it was not restricted to Japanese men. Women were already excluded, but presumably the legislators did not think Japanese women fit within the generic term. See also, An Act for Securing the Safety and Good Health of Workmen Engaged in or about the Metalliferous Mines in the Province of British Columbia by the Appointment of an Inspector of Metalliferous Mines, R.S.B.C. 1897, c. 134, s. 12, which extended these provisions to metalliferous mines. An Act Respecting Mining Regulations, 53 Victoria (1890), c. 10, s. 2, 4, 8 and 18 (Ont.) barred women from underground and surface work at mines. See also, An Act Respecting Mines, R.S.O. 1897, c. 36.

30.   An Act Respecting the Sale of Intoxicating Liquors, and the Issue of Licenses There, 49 Victoria (1886), c. 21, s. 27 (Man.). Maximum fines of $100, or four months in default thereof, were set out in s. 91. Exception was made for service in the dining room and for family members of the owner. See also, 52 Victoria (1889), c. 15 (Man.); R.S.M. 1891, Vol. I, c. 90.

31.   For a detailed discussion, see Constance Backhouse, "Nineteenth-Century Canadian Prostitution Law: Reflection of a Discriminatory Society" (1985) 18 *Social History* 387; Backhouse, *supra* note 1, chapter 8. [...]

32.   For details about the experience of Finnish women who immigrated to Canada, see Varpu Lindstrom-Best, *Defiant Sisters: A Social History of Finnish Immigrant Women in Canada* (Toronto: Multicultural History Society of Ontario, 1988) 22, 23, 26, 84–5, 140 and Varpu Lindstrom-Best, "I Won't Be a Slave!—Finnish Domestics in Canada 1911–30" in Jean Burnet, ed., *Looking into My Sister's Eyes* (Toronto: Multicultural Society of Ontario, 1986) 33.

33.   *Nanaimo Free Press*, 11 April 1896. For details of the Finnish community, see E. Blache Norcross, *Nanaimo Retrospective: The First Century* (Nanaimo: 1979); Lindstrom-Best, ibid., "Defiant

Sisters" 23, 140. The newspaper revealed that an unnamed male Finn had been the first to tip off the authorities regarding his suspicion of Anna Balo. This, combined with the evidence against Anna Balo produced by other Finnish neighbours, suggested that the deserted woman was an outcast even within her own ethnic community. Anna Balo had violated several important social maxims that were firmly entrenched within the Finnish community. First, she had become pregnant and borne a child as a single parent. There was no great stigma attached to being single within the Finnish immigrant community, and common-law marriages were widespread. However, sexual activity outside of a stable family unit was still viewed as a serious transgression. Second, infanticide was relatively uncommon among the Finnish population, many of whom had acquired comparatively more sophistication regarding birth control and abortion practices than the general population. Third, Anna Balo had abandoned her other children in her acute distress following childbirth. The Finns were widely admired for their child-rearing skills, and generations of public officials would attest that they were model immigrants in their abilities to rear healthy, well-scrubbed, educated children. It is likely that Anna Balo's flight to Qualicum, leaving behind her impoverished children to fend as best they could, shocked the Finnish community as much as the discovery of the infant's body. For descriptions of the Finnish immigrant community's perspectives regarding marriage, sexual relationships, and child-rearing, see Lindstrom-Best, ibid. at 59–78, 111–14.

34.   The inquest opened before Anna Balo's arrest in order to examine the body of the dead infant. After the jurymen viewed the body, they turned it over to Dr. O'Brian for a post-mortem examination. His report was filed when the inquest resumed on April 16th.

35.   See Catherine Cleverdon, *The Woman Suffrage Movement in Canada* (Toronto: University of Toronto Press, 1974); Carol Bacchi, *Liberation Deferred? The Ideas of the English-Canadian Suffragists 1877–1918* (Toronto: University of Toronto Press, 1983). In contrast, the nineteenth century witnessed a marked broadening of the franchise for white men, although racial minority groups such as Chinese and Aboriginal men were not included in the widening electoral process. There was some evidence that certain propertied white women exercised the vote despite their theoretical exclusion. For example, some women in Lower Canada voted between 1792 and 1834, and

were allowed to do so by the returning officers. But specific legislative exclusions were enacted against female voting in New Brunswick in 1791, Prince Edward Island in 1836, the United Province of Canada in 1849, and Nova Scotia in 1851. Electoral politics on local matters was more inclusive of women; unmarried women could be elected to school boards and could vote in municipal elections in many jurisdictions. See Alison Prentice et al., *Canadian Women: A History* (Toronto: Harcourt Brace Jovonavitch, 1988) 98–100, 174–88; Cleverdon, ibid. at 5.

36. Cleverdon, ibid., 67, 73–4, 102 noted that Emily Murphy, appointed a police magistrate in Edmonton, Alberta on 13 June 1916, was the first woman in the British empire to hold such a post. Alice Jamieson, appointed in December 1916 in Calgary, was the second. British Columbia first permitted women to serve as jurors in 1922.

37. For a more detailed discussion of Clara Brett Martin's admission and career, see [...] Constance Backhouse, "To Open the Way for Others of My Sex: Clara Brett Martin's Career as Canada's First Woman Lawyer" (1985) 1 *Canadian Journal of Women and the Law* 1; Theresa Roth, "Clara Brett Martin—Canada's Pioneer Woman Lawyer" (1984) 18 *Law Society of Upper Canada Gazette* 323.

38. BCARS, Deposition; Coroner's Inquest.

39. BCARS, Coroner's Inquest.

40. BCARS, Coroner's Inquest; Deposition.

41. BCARS, Deposition; Coroner's Inquest.

42. BCARS, Coroner's Inquest; Deposition.

43. BCARS, Deposition.

44. BCARS, Coroner's Inquest.

45. Criminal Code, 1892, 55–56 Victoria (1892), c. 29, s. 240 (Dominion of Canada).

46. First enacted in France in the mid-sixteenth century, the law spread to England in 1623 and entered colonial jurisprudence in New France in 1722. For reference to the early French provisions, see *Recueil Général des Anciennes Lois Françaises* (Paris: 1822–33), vol. XIII at 471–73; P.G. Roy, *Inventaire des Ordonnances des Intendants de la Nouvelle-France* (Beaceville, 1919) 1 at 216–17; Ward, *supra* note 5 at 43. See also, An Act to Prevent the Destroying and Murdering of Bastard Children, 21 James 1 (1623), c. 27 (Eng.); An Act Relating to Treasons and Felonies, 32 George 11 (1758), c. 13 (N.S.); An Act Relating to Treasons and Felonies, 33 George III (1792), c. 1 (P.E.I.). The other jurisdictions adopted the statute by way of general legislation receiving English law into the colonies.

47. For a discussion of the motivation behind the early legislation, see Backhouse, *supra* note 5.

48. The wording of a typical statute was as follows: "[I]f any woman be delivered of any issue of her body, male or female, which being born alive, should by the laws of the realm of England be a bastard, and that she endeavour privately, either by drowning or secret burying thereof, or in any other way, either by herself, or the procuring of others, so to conceal the death thereof, as that it may not come to light whether it were born alive or not, but be concealed, the mother so offending shall suffer death as in the case of murder, except such mother can make proof by one witness, that the child whose death was by her so intended to be concealed, was born dead." [English Act (as received into Upper Canada), s. 2; Nova Scotia Act, s. 5.]

49. See, for example, the public outcry which attended the trial of Angelique Pilotte, whose sentence of death was commuted in 1818 in Niagara, Upper Canada, as recorded in Backhouse, *supra* note 5 and Backhouse, *supra* note 1, chapter 4.

50. The early reported cases reveal the courts' preoccupation with the technically irrelevant evidence concerning the cause of the child's death, seemingly reluctant to convict without information which would warrant a finding of murder or manslaughter: see Backhouse, *supra* note 5.

51. An Act for Making Further Provisions to Prevent the Destroying and Murdering of Bastard Children, 50 George III (1810), c. 2 (N.B.); An Act to Repeal "An Act to Prevent the Destroying and Murdering of Bastard Children," 52 George III (1812), c. 3 (Lower Canada); An Act for Repealing ... "An Act Relating to Treasons and Felonies," 53 George III (1813), c. 11 (N.S.); An Act to Prevent the Operation of "An Act to Prevent the Destroying and Murdering of Bastard Children," 2 William IV (1831), c. 1 (Upper Canada); An Act to Provide for the Punishment of Offences against the Person, 6 William IV (1836), c. 22 (P.E.I.).

52. Additional amendments also made it possible to charge married women with concealment. For full details of the statutory amendments in the various jurisdictions prior to Confederation, see Backhouse, *supra* note 5. The first statute unequivocally to include married women within the scope of the concealment offence was passed in New Brunswick: Offences against the Person Act, 1 William IV (1831), c. 17 (N.B.). The first federal legislation was found in An Act Respecting Offences against the Person, 32–33 Victoria (1869), c. 20 (D.C.). The statute which extended

this package of criminal law to British Columbia was An Act to Extend to the Province of British Columbia Certain of the Criminal Laws, 37 Victoria (1874), c. 42 (D.C.).

53. BCARS, Deposition.

54. BCARS, Ibid.

55. S.R. Clarke, *A Treatise on Criminal Law as Applicable to the Dominion of Canada* (Toronto: 1872) 467. See Beattie, *supra* note 5 at 364–366, for discussion about English rules concerning the reception of confession evidence.

56. For details about Justice Drake, see Alfred Watts, Q.C., "The Honourable Mr. Justice Montague W. Tyrwhitt-Drake" (1967) 26 *The Advocate* 225 at 226.

57. It was customary for the judge to appoint legal counsel where an impoverished accused person was on trial for a capital offence. Any barrister so appointed would, of course, have the right to decide whether or not to work for free: see Backhouse, *supra* note 1 chapter 4.

58. *Nanaimo Free Press*, 5 May 1896; BCARS GR 1727, vol. 589, Bench Book Entries. R. v. Balo, 4 May 1896, by M.W.T. Drake.

59. *Nanaimo Free Press*, 6 May 1896.

60. An examination of the surviving archival court records for Ontario between 1840 and 1900, showed 66.7% verdicts of "not guilty" in charges of murder and manslaughter, and 46.7% verdicts of "not guilty" in charges of concealment. (See Tables 1, 2, and 3 in Backhouse, *supra* note 1 at 462, 465, and 468.) Analysis of the court decisions in the judicial district of Quebec between 1812–1891 showed 60% verdicts of "not guilty" in charges of murder and manslaughter, and 38.8% findings other than "guilty" in charges of concealment. (See Tableau 3 in Cliche, *supra* note 5 at 49.)

61. Similar lenience was not expressed toward those accused of procuring abortions in the nineteenth century. Abortion trials were a rarity then, usually surfacing only when major medical complications or death resulted from an abortion. But in contrast to infanticide verdicts, approximately half of the abortion-related charges in some provinces resulted in guilty verdicts. During abortion trials, in contrast to infanticide cases, courts appeared to be using loose standards of factual proof and legal analysis, convicting despite evidence that would clearly have permitted acquittals if judges and juries had been so inclined: see Backhouse, *supra* note 2. Part of the explanation may have related to who was on trial. Abortion trials typically focused on the abortionist, who was symbolically removed from the immediate desperation of an unwillingly pregnant woman. Distinctions between the sort of women who committed infanticide and those who obtained abortion may also have been relevant. Unlike the impoverished, single women charged with infanticide, women who sought abortions were more representative of the population at large. Many, particularly those who paid relatively high sums of money to professional abortionists, came from the married, middle and upper classes. The medical profession, which lobbied strenuously for stricter criminal prohibition of abortion, made specific reference to class concerns, as well as religious, racial, and ethnic biases, leading them to denounce the efforts of Protestant, English-Canadian women of the "respectable classes" to control their fertility: see, for example, (1867) 3 *Canadian Medical Journal* 225 at 226; (1889) 18 *Canadian Medical Record* 18 at 142. For reference to "race suicide" discussions, see McLaren and McLaren, *supra* note 2 at 17.

62. (1862) 8 *Upper Canada Law Journal* December at 309.

63. For details on Ontario infant mortality rates, see "Ontario Registrar-General Report Relating to the Registration of Births, Marriages and Deaths 1880–1979" cited in Joan Oppenheimer, "Childbirth in Ontario: The Transition from Home to Hospital in the Early Twentieth Century" (1983) 75 *Ontario History* 36 at 38. See also, Public Archives of Nova Scotia, RG 41, Coroner's Inquest, 25 April 1861, as described in Wright, *supra* note 5 at 24–5.

64. Charles Arthur Mercier, *Crime and Insanity* (London: Williams and Norgate, 1911) at 212–13.

65. For a more detailed discussion, see Constance Backhouse, "Shifting Patterns in Nineteenth-Century Canadian Custody Law" in David H. Flaherty, ed., *supra* note 4, vol. I at 212; Backhouse, *supra* note 1, chapter 7; Rebecca Veinott, "Child Custody and Divorce: A Nova Scotia Study 1866–1910" in Girard and Phillips, *supra* note 18. Provincial legislation passed first in Canada West in 1855, New Brunswick in 1890, Nova Scotia in 1893, and British Columbia in 1897 eroded the dominance of paternal custody rights to some extent, but Canadian judges tended to apply the new rules reluctantly, greatly diminishing the force of the reforms. For an American comparison, see Michael Grossberg, *Governing the Hearth: Law and the Family in Nineteenth-Century America* (Chapel Hill: University of North Carolina Press, 1985).

66. For a brief discussion of baby-farming, see Backhouse, *supra* note 5. There was a series of prominent cases in the late nineteenth century

where the owners of "baby farms" were charged with child-murder, and legislation soon sprang up to regulate these organisations. Further research would be necessary to determine whether the accusations made against "baby farmers" were fair, or whether social reformers were motivated primarily by the taint of sexual license that surrounded illegitimate births, and a dislike of the class of women who ran such establishments.

67. For details, see Peter Gossage, "Les Enfants Abandonnés à Montréal au 19e Siècle: La Crèche D'Youville Des Soeurs Grises 1820–1871" (1986–87) 40 *Revue d'histoire de L'Amérique Française* 537. For a description of all of the institutionalised infants' homes operated in Canada in 1900, see Lajoie, *supra* note 11 at 324–40.

68. Lajoie, *supra* note 11 at 340. The Protestant Methodist, Congregationalist, and Presbyterian churches were actively seeking to convert "foreigners" in Canada during this period, and the Finnish Lutherans were often targets (Lindstrom-Best, *supra* note 32 at 130).

CHAPTER 8

Gender and Criminal Court Outcomes: An Historical Analysis[*]

Helen Boritch

* *

*****

Research examining the relation of gender to criminal court outcomes tends to find an overall pattern of leniency toward female offenders. In the context of this general set of findings, the most recent work in this area has attempted to specify more precisely the nature and extent of this gender-based leniency. For example, some of the less severe treatment of women is attributable to the fact that women usually are less serious offenders than men. As a result, studies that control for legally relevant variables, such as case seriousness and prior record, tend to find less evidence of differential leniency in sanction severity. As well, gender-based leniency does not appear to be constant across all stages of decision making, for all types of offenses, nor for all categories of female offenders. So, for example, leniency toward women is more often found in sentencing and pretrial release decisions rather than in those for case dismissal or conviction; for women charged with less serious offenses; and for women who are economically dependent, married, or have children (Daly, 1987; Nagel and Hagan, 1983; A. Edwards, 1989; S. Edwards, 1984; Kruttschnitt, 1981, 1982; Kruttschnitt and Green, 1984).

The variability in the relation of gender to case outcomes is seen to reflect different dimensions of gender role attitudes, reproduced at the level of judicial sanctioning decisions. As yet, however, little is known about the factors related to changes in judicial attitudes and how they are reflected in gender-based sanctioning patterns. Almost a decade ago, Nagel and Hagan (1983:136), in their review of the existing literature, underscored the need for future research to "systematically vary the social context in which sanctioning occurs [if it is] to yield results that are informative and generalizable." In the interim, only a few studies have followed up on this suggestion by examining gender-based disparities in criminal court outcomes across different jurisdictions and in relation to changes in the involvement of women in crime over the past few decades (e.g., Johnson and Scheuble, 1991; Kruttschnitt and Green, 1984).

One way to extend this work and to introduce greater variation in the data sets used to examine sentencing issues generally, and the impact of gender in particular, is to observe the operation of the law in a variety of historical contexts. An historical perspective makes it possible to discern more clearly the structural factors underlying patterns of continuity in the differential treatment of male and female offenders, as well as important shifts in sanctioning patterns over time. This study addresses these issues through a quantitative analysis of gender differences in criminal court outcomes using data from the prison registers of Middlesex County, Ontario, between 1871 and 1920.

Historical Context

Although it is possible to examine the relation of gender to criminal court outcomes in a variety of historical contexts, it seems logical to focus on time periods characterized by significant changes in gender roles, gender-based social control policies, and levels of official female criminality. The decades spanning the late nineteenth and early twentieth centuries in North America represent one such important epoch. This period, generally referred to as the Urban Reform Era in Canada and the Progressive Era in the United States, witnessed an urban reform movement common to all industrializing nations. Beginning in the mid nineteenth century, the steady movement of populations toward the cities generated a growing concern and fear over the social problems that industrialization had brought in its wake. In particular, early Canadian reformers saw the highly visible and concentrated spread of crime, disease, and poverty as having reached crisis proportions, and they launched major reform efforts to eradicate those problems (Allen, 1968; Artibise, 1975; Decarie, 1974; Rutherford, 1971, 1974). Although urban reform ultimately came to encompass varied and diverse phenomena, the vice-ridden world of the lower classes was viewed as one of the most serious threats facing the modern city. Moral reform, then, was at the center of the progressive tradition in Canada and clearly reflected the class bias of its major advocates. In this regard, "moral reform was an experiment in social engineering, an attempt to force the city dweller to conform to the public mores of the church-going middle class" (Rutherford, 1971:206).

It is also during this era that traditional definitions of gender, viewed as central to an understanding of contemporary sanctioning patterns, first arose in response to the changing social and economic role of women (Klein and Roberts, 1974; Morrison, 1976; Roberts, 1976). The importance of these new images of femininity and women's familial role to the administration of criminal justice is evident in numerous events during this period, including the establishment of separate female correctional institutions (Feinman, 1983; Rafter, 1990; Strange, 1986); moral crusades against prostitution (Backhouse, 1983; Daly and Chesney-Lind, 1988; Holmes, 1972); and the development of new informal social controls created to augment formal legal controls in dealing with deviance and crime among working-class women (Boritch and Hagan, 1990; L. Kealey, 1979; Miller, 1987).

By drawing attention to the way in which these social changes made women subject to an ever-increasing set of controls to enforce middle-class standards of femininity, social historians have sought to dispel the commonly held assumption of chivalry toward female offenders in the past. Equally important, it is presumed that these gender stereotypes continue to be major determinants of gender-based disparities in court outcomes in the contemporary context. For the most part, however, conclusions with respect to the harsh treatment of women who deviated from prescribed standards of appropriate behavior and with respect to overall patterns of gender-related differences in sanction severity in the past are not based on systematic quantitative analyses of case outcomes. In the absence of such empirical studies, the nature of the historically conditioned and potentially variable relation among gender stereotypes, formal and informal control structures, and sanctioning patterns has yet to be determined. In order to provide such an historical analysis, this study examines the relation of gender to court outcomes in Middlesex County, Ontario, during the Urban Reform Era. Toward this end, it is first necessary to examine more closely the most important features of this era and the existing historical research as they pertain to the analysis of gender-based disparities in criminal sanctions.

Gender, Social Control, and Crime during the Urban Reform Era

The advent of industrial capitalism and the sexual stratification of the labor process led to major shifts in the social status of women and the social control mechanisms governing the lives of men and women (Currie, 1986; Hagan et al., 1979, 1987; Tilly and Scott, 1978). Men's participation in the paid labor force and public visibility made them the principal objects of formal legal regulation, while women's exclusion from wage labor confined them to the domestic sphere and informal social controls operating through the family. The distinctly domestic sphere was characterized by women's increased economic dependency on men and by intensified regulation of their reproductive roles. According to the prevailing middle-class ideology of "separate spheres," women were expected to conform to the ideals of the "cult of true womanhood" and "maternal feminism," which emphasized their moral purity and only appropriate vocation as motherhood (Cott, 1987; Morrison, 1976; Roberts, 1976).

The sexual stratification of the labor process, and its links to gender-based forms of social control, however, "was tied tightly to that of social class" (Hahn, 1980:20). The exclusion of women from wage labor did not apply to working-class women, whose cheap labor as domestic servants and in mills, factories, and restaurants was an integral feature of the larger industrialization process (Barber, 1980; G. Kealey, 1973; Klein and Roberts, 1974). For example, by 1891 in Ontario, women constituted 12.5% of the entire wage labor force and 19% of those employed specifically in manufacturing and industrial occupations (Palmer, 1983:116; Trofimenkoff, 1986:84). As young women moved into the cities to take advantage of these new employment opportunities, they also were freed from traditional familial constraints and began to lead social lives that conflicted sharply with middle-class definitions of womanhood. In turn, middle-class women saw their roles as defenders of domesticity and rigid standards of

female sexual propriety increasingly threatened by working-class women who took such roles more lightly. This proved a powerful impetus for middle-class women to become involved in a variety of causes dedicated to preserving and reinforcing prevailing gender definitions. In response to the perceived absence of strong informal social controls in the lives of many working-class women, much of the early focus of these "first wave feminists" was directed at bringing pressure to bear on the police and courts to enforce more vigorously a particular moral order (Boritch and Hagan, 1990; Cott, 1987; Rafter, 1985; Valverde, 1991).

One result was that, in Canada as elsewhere, the preeminent focus of urban police forces during the nineteenth century centered on the regulation of working-class recreations, morality, and life-styles that violated conventional middle-class notions of respectability and urban order. To this extent, because of their participation in the labor force, working-class women were subjected to formal legal regulation in the same way as their male counterparts. In view of the dominant ideology, which saw drunkenness and immorality as self-evident causes of poverty and criminality, the majority of male and female arrests consisted of various public order offenses, especially drunkenness, disorderly conduct, and vagrancy (Boritch and Hagan, 1990; Friedman and Percival, 1981; Giordano et al., 1981; Monkkonen, 1981). In the case of women, vagrancy statutes were also the primary means used to criminalize prostitutes who plied their trade on the streets. Taken together, these offenses, which occur in public and have high visibility, were viewed by early reformers as indicative of the moral decay of cities and the working class alike.

The issue of gender added another dimension to the class bias inherent in the criminalization of various public order offenses during the nineteenth century. The corollary of the prevailing gender stereotyping that imbued women with higher moral sensibilities than men was that female offenders who breached these moral standards were regarded as more depraved than male offenders (Rafter, 1990). As a result, while drunken or disorderly behavior on the part of working-class men was somewhat expected if not condoned, the police and courts seemed to take an especially dim view of women who engaged in the same behaviors. Because by definition, these offenses represented the very antithesis of the prevailing ideology of "maternal feminism" and "moral purity," female offenders were viewed as not only fallen, but as symbolic of "why the lower classes were low" (Hahn, 1980:21). Consequently, in Ontario, the limited available evidence from the mid nineteenth century indicates that women charged with various public order offenses, especially recidivists, were dealt with particularly harshly by the courts (Graff, 1977; Katz et al., 1982; Weaver, 1988).

By the late nineteenth century, anxiety over changing gender roles crystallized in a preoccupation with the potential corruption of young, working-class women who came from surrounding rural areas and abroad to seek employment. Insofar as a single issue came to symbolize and unify the diverse components of the moral reform movement, it was prostitution, or the "social evil." Because prostitution makes sex public, it challenged the very essence of gender roles based on the notion of separate spheres for men and women by drawing attention to women's active economic role in the public sphere. The perceived need to regulate female sexuality and to reinforce the conventional female role in marriage and the family led to concerted efforts on the part of reformers to intensify further the controls on women's personal and social lives (Cott, 1987; L. Kealey, 1979; Miller, 1987; Morrison, 1976). Moreover, the propensity of reformers to define the problem as a moral failing of working-class women proved an ideal focus for it allowed them to direct their efforts at suppressing prostitution without altering the patriarchal and class relations that were the root causes of women's economic and sexual exploitation (Messerschmidt, 1987; Rotenberg, 1974; Valverde, 1991).

Over the course of the next several decades, moral reformers in Ontario directed much of their effort to restructuring the legal processing of female offenders as reflected in the increase in the maximum penalty for vagrancy from two months to two years (Backhouse, 1985; McLaren, 1986), the establishment of separate Courts for female offenders (Homel, 1981), and the building of a female prison, the Andrew Mercer Reformatory and Refuge for young girls in Toronto in 1879 (Splane, 1965; Strange, 1986).

It is, however, important to recognize that in their quest to uplift working-class women and to purify city life, first-wave feminists did not confine themselves solely to reshaping the formal criminal justice system. Gradually, beginning in the 1880s, these efforts were augmented by the development of a wide array of informal social controls intended to compensate for the perceived breakdown of traditional familial controls and to socialize women to conform to their appropriate role. By the turn of the century, women reformers were largely responsible for overseeing a broad network of community-based programs and social services, usually created under the auspices of organizations such as the National Council of Women, Women's Christian Temperance Union, and the Young Women's Christian Association. Through their work in these organizations, active throughout Ontario, women hoped to guide the temporal, moral, and religious welfare of young, single women, to rescue and rehabilitate "wayward women," and generally, to prevent the behaviors that made women subject to formal legal controls (Klein and Roberts, 1974; Mitchinson, 1979; Morrison, 1976; Pederson, 1986; Roberts, 1976; Splane, 1965; Valverde, 1991). As such, these developments marked a significant change in the locus of social control of women from an earlier exclusive reliance on the criminal justice system to a growing dependence on informal social controls wherein women were both the primary instruments and objects of regulation.

Most of the existing historical research on the treatment of women offenders during the

Urban Reform Era has tended to focus on the gender discrimination that characterized the incarceration of women in female correctional institutions. As has been well documented, women reformers' success in establishing female reformatories, however well intended, served to give formal recognition to a double standard and to justify incarcerating large numbers of young women for immorality and minor sexual misbehaviors that had no corollary in men's prisons (Daly and Chesney-Lind, 1988; Feinman, 1983; Freedman, 1974; Rafter, 1983, 1985, 1990). Nevertheless, to study the operation of the law only in its most visible form leaves unexplored the issue of how the parallel development of new, informal controls (firmly established by the beginning of the twentieth century) might have affected female criminality and the judicial treatment of female offenders.

Equally important, however, findings based on inmates of women's prisons cannot be generalized to all female offenders because women sentenced to these prisons represented only a small proportion of all female offenders during this era—generally those sentenced to terms of at least six months. In this regard, despite the widespread establishment of female reformatories, in Ontario as elsewhere in North America, most women (and men) were sentenced to relatively short periods of incarceration and continued to serve their time in local jails. This was especially true of the majority of female offenders sentenced to prison for various public order offenses, which generally carried relatively short jail terms of several weeks to months. By way of illustration, the Mercer Reformatory, which served all of the province of Ontario, had an average inmate population of only 100 women a year throughout the nineteenth century (Splane, 1965:181). In contrast, during the same period, the number of female committals to Ontario's county jails averaged approximately 1,700 a year (Carrigan, 1991:259).

Moreover, it is significant that, contrary to the impression fostered by reformers and reinforced by the establishment of separate female prisons that female crime was on the rise, the available

evidence suggests that female criminality, as measured by arrests and committals to county jails, actually declined steadily during this period. For example, in Toronto, male and female arrest rates decreased for all offenses during the Urban Reform Era, and the most noticeable decline was in female crime rates and, in particular, the relative proportion of women arrested for various public order offenses. Whereas in the 1860s females accounted for 40% of all arrests for drunk and disorderly behavior and vagrancy, by the Depression of the 1930s, their relative share had dropped to only 6% (Boritch and Hagan, 1990:587). This decline in female criminality was reflected further in a corresponding drop in the relative proportion of women committed to all the common jails of Ontario during the late nineteenth century. While the ratio of male to female committals was approximately 3:1 in 1869, it increased to 10:1 by 1889 (Carrigan, 1991:259).

The research setting for this paper is no exception to this trend: there is a very clear pattern of decline in the percentage of women in the inmate population of Middlesex County Jail over the course of the Urban Reform Era. Based on data from the jail registers (discussed in more detail below) on the number of men and women committed in each year from 1868 to 1920, Figure 1 shows that the proportion of female prisoners dropped from a high of 38% of all committals in 1871 to a low of 6% in 1901. Thereafter, despite an abrupt increase in the proportion of female prisoners in 1902 (due to a steep drop in the number of men rather than an increase in the number of women), the percentage of female inmates rose only slightly in the early twentieth century and reached approximately 10% by 1920.

Several factors may have combined to reduce the criminalization of women, if not actual levels of female criminality. Part of the decline may be attributable to changing police priorities, especially with respect to the enforcement of public order offenses. Urbanization and its attendant increasing privatization of life, decline in the intensity of street life, and separation of

Figure 1: Percent Female Commitals, to Middlesex County Jail, 1868–1920

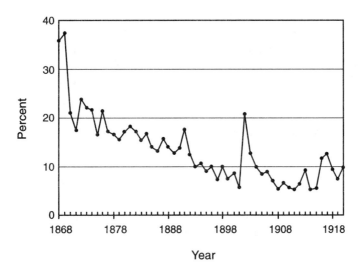

middle- and working-class residential areas may all have contributed to reducing the visibility of public disorder and, therefore, pressure on the police to make arrests (Carrigan, 1991; Monkkonen, 1981; Schneider, 1980). The drop in official female criminality also may be linked to an increasingly discriminating use of formal and informal controls on different categories of women (Boritch and Hagan, 1990). Over time, meting out longer sentences to recidivists may have lessened female criminality among that group of offenders through simple incapacitation. At the same time, the increasing use of informal controls directed at younger and "pre-delinquent" women may have prevented many of those women from incurring criminal sanctions in the first place. Thus, various incremental changes in social control policies during this era may help to account for the apparent decline in female criminality.

Gender and Sanction Severity: The Historical Legacy

Combining the insights from contemporary research with those gleaned from the foregoing historical review, this study examines gender differences in case outcomes during the Urban

Reform Era in terms of continuity and change. First, it seeks to determine the extent to which contemporary findings with respect to the alternatively harsher or more lenient treatment of female offenders represent a continuation of historically conditioned patterns. Insofar as attempts to account for these patterns have emphasized the pervasive influence of traditional gender stereotypes, it is reasonable to expect that similar patterns will be observed in the past, when standards of femininity and respectability were considerably more rigid. Second, this study seeks to identify the broad structural factors related to changes in judicial attitudes and sanctioning patterns over time. In particular, the major changes in gender-based forms of social control and levels of female criminality that occurred during the Urban Reform Era suggest the possibility of a shift in gender-related sanctioning patterns from the nineteenth to the twentieth century.

Research in contemporary settings has shown that males and females are treated differently across different offense types, consistent with a double standard of acceptable behavior. In particular, evidence of the more severe treatment of female offenders tends to be found most often for offenses that involve sexuality, however remotely. In this regard, the greater likelihood of females coming to the attention of law enforcement personnel and being treated more punitively than males is not limited to prostitution-related offenses, but is also a feature of the treatment of girls for various "status" offenses. Moreover, the harsher treatment of female offenders for these offenses is evident even after controlling for various legally relevant factors, such as prior criminal record and case seriousness. In contrast, in the realm of conventional types of criminal activity (typically property offenses), much of the allegedly more lenient treatment of female offenders is reduced when these same factors are taken into account (for reviews of this research, see Chesney-Lind, 1986; A. Edwards, 1989; Nagel and Hagan, 1983).

The historical counterpart of modern-day status offenses are the public order offenses of drunk and disorderly conduct and vagrancy. And, unlike today, when property crimes predominate in court cases, public order offenses made up the bulk of male and female cases in the past. In the case of women, vagrancy statutes were a primary means of criminalizing prostitutes who worked on the streets, but as well, men and women were subject to prostitution charges stemming from being a keeper, inmate, or client of a house of ill fame. Taken together, these behaviors were seen by reformers as symbolic of the forces eroding traditional values and family stability and as much more serious lapses in morality for society's future mothers and moral guardians. More generally, because any form of criminality breached the prevailing notion of women's moral purity, women who came before the courts experienced a greater loss of respectability than men.

It is expected first, then, that the influence of gender stereotypes should be manifested in decision makers' differential assessment of the seriousness of various offenses when committed by men as opposed to women. That is, among male offenders, it is predicted that public order offenses would be regarded and treated as less

serious than property or violent crimes. In contrast, among female offenders, it is expected that judges would tend to view and sanction offenders charged with public order offenses similarly to those charged with crimes against persons or property.

Second, in terms of differences between men and women, it is hypothesized that women charged with various public order offenses received more severe dispositions than men charged with the same offenses. Third, because vagrancy statutes were used to criminalize prostitutes, the harsher treatment of women should be most pronounced for this offense. Fourth, and in contrast, there is less reason to expect that men and women charged with more conventional crimes (e.g., larceny) would be treated markedly differently. Fifth, it is expected, that even after controlling for offense type, women with more serious case factors and criminal records were treated more severely than men with similar attributes.

Research in contemporary settings also suggests that much of the current leniency toward women is accounted for by gender-related differences in informal controls operating in offenders' personal lives. In particular, various studies indicate that women already under constraints imposed by economic dependency, marriage, and family responsibilities are treated more leniently than women not subject to these informal controls in their daily lives. Further, married women are treated more leniently than married men (Daly, 1987; Kruttschnitt, 1982, 1984). The greater reluctance of judges to incarcerate married women and thereby separate them from their families is seen to reflect the ongoing influence of traditional gender stereotypes and the view that women's "care-taking labor is more indispensible to maintain the family unit than is [men's] economic support" (Daly, 1987:156). One might, therefore, expect to observe the same pattern of differential leniency toward married women during the Urban Reform Era, when gender divisions in work and family life first arose.

Finally, an important concern of this research

is to examine the impact of societal-level changes in gender-based forms of social control and levels of female criminality on criminal court outcomes. In this regard, gender-based differences in informal controls, at the level of individual offenders, reflect a more fundamental gender-based differentiation of formal and informal social controls in society (Hagan et al., 1979, 1987). Moreover, as the Urban Reform Era demonstrates, the particular form of these social control processes, and their relation to gender, is subject to change. The development of alternative control strategies and the effect of such changes on crime rates and the criminal processing of cases are likely to be incremental and thus can only be assessed over a considerable period of time. In the case of the Urban Reform Era, the development of new, informal social controls was a gradual process, beginning in the late nineteenth century and reaching a peak of intensity by the turn of the century. Consequently, the impact of those changes on judicial sanctioning patterns is likely to be observed most clearly in the early decades of the twentieth century.

Data and Methods

Sample
In order to examine gender differences in court outcomes during the Urban Reform Era, this study uses data constructed from the original, handwritten records of the Middlesex County Jail. Situated in southwestern Ontario, Middlesex County, and its administrative center, London, exemplifies the processes of growth, urbanization, and industrialization during this era and, hence, is an ideal setting for this study (Bertram, 1963; Bloomfield, 1986). In addition, given the problems of availability and inadequateness of data that plague historical analyses, Middlesex County is relatively unique in having preserved its prison records for the years 1868 to 1920. As the lowest level of the prison structure in Ontario, the common (county) jails held not only convicted offenders serving sentences of two months or less, but also those arrested and awaiting the disposition of

their cases and convicted offenders held pending transfer to another institution. In Middlesex County as elsewhere, then, virtually all prisoners first passed through this jail, regardless of final case outcome or place of incarceration.[1] Compared, then, with historical data drawn from any one particular stage of the criminal justice system (e.g., police, courts), data from these local jail registers have the singular advantage of providing the most complete information on offenders and court outcomes.

Data on a sample of male and female offenders were compiled by coding all pertinent information on every committal in each of the six census years—1871, 1881, 1891, 1901, 1911, and 1920. Although there are some missing data, the registers provide fairly complete information on various demographic characteristics of offenders, the offense charge, number of arrest charges, prior criminal record, and the ultimate disposition of the case.[2] Specifically, the sample included all men and women committed for the following most frequently occurring offenses: common assault, larceny, drunkenness (which included disorderly conduct), vagrancy, and the specific prostitution offense of being a keeper or inmate of a house of ill fame. The relative infrequency of other offense types (e.g., robbery, murder, fraud), especially among female offenders, precluded their inclusion. It is important to note that because an offender could be committed more than once in any year, the unit of analysis is case dispositions, not individuals. The included offenses, which represented 83% of female committals and 75% of male committals, resulted in a final sample size of 2,280 dispositions, of which 14% (317) involved females and 86% (1963) involved males. Table 1 presents the operationalization, coding, and distribution within gender categories of the variables used in the analysis.

Control Variables

Marital Status
Marital status is included in the analysis to explore the possible interactive effects of

Table 1: Distribution and Coding of Control (X) and Dependent (Y) Variables

	Coding	Males (%) N = 1,963	Females (%) N = 317
Gender (X$_1$)			
Female	(0)		14.0
Male	(1)	86.0	
Marital Status (X$_2$)			
Single (includes widowed)	(0)	69.9	53.8
Married	(1)	30.1	46.2
Age (X$_3$)			
Under 19 (reference category)	(0)	16.0	17.6
20–29	(1)	26.6	34.8
30–39	(1)	24.3	16.4
40–49	(1)	16.0	18.6
50 & over	(1)	17.1	12.6
Offense Type (X$_4$)			
Larceny (reference category)	(0)	23.6	14.8
Assault	(1)	11.0	4.1
Drunkenness	(1)	49.0	31.7
Vagrancy	(1)	15.4	39.3
Keeper/Inmate House of Ill Fame	(1)	1.0	10.1
Number of Arrest Charges (X$_5$)			
One Only	(0)	90.9	91.2
Two or More	(1)	9.1	8.8
Prior Committals to Prison (X$_6$)			
None	(0)	45.0	44.7
One or More	(1)	55.0	55.3
Time Period (X$_7$)			
1871–1891	(0)	48.2	78.0
1901–1920	(1)	51.8	22.0
Type of Disposition (Y$_1$)			
Discharged	(0)	39.7	36.5
Acquitted	(0)	1.3	.9
Remanded	(0)	1.4	1.9
Bailed	(0)	3.3	.3
Fined	(0)	.5	.3
Suspended Sentence	(0)	1.2	1.3
Other	(0)	1.0	1.3
Fine: Default Prison	(1)	30.3	21.7
Prison	(1)	21.3	35.8
Sentence Severity (Y$_2$)			
0 days	(0)	48.4	42.5
1–1,825 days	(days)	51.6	57.5
Mean		116.3	138.5
S.D.		270.0	241.1

gender and marital status on case outcome. Unfortunately, because the jail registers contained no information on whether the offender had children, it is not possible to provide a more in-depth analysis of the effect of a defendant's familial situation.

Age

Prior research suggests that age coexists with a variety of social characteristics that are predictive of overall differences in the severity of sanctions meted out to offenders generally, and women in particular (Kruttschnitt, 1981). In this analysis the effect of age is controlled for through a set of dummy variables that allows for more detailed comparisons across age categories than would be possible with a continuous measure. Offenders aged 19 years and under are the reference category to which all other age groups are compared.

Offense Type

Controls for the offense for which men and women were charged are also in the form of dummy variables. Larceny is the reference category throughout the analysis.[3]

Case Seriousness and Prior Record

The analysis also controls for two other variables relevant to case outcome. The first is a measure of case seriousness based on whether the offender had one or more arrest charges pending. The second variable controls for prior record, measured by whether the offender had been committed previously to prison.[4]

Time Period

To control for the possibility of changes in the relation between gender and criminal sanctions over time, the data were dichotomized into two time periods reflecting the earlier and later decades of the Urban Reform Era: 1871 to 1891 and 1901 to 1920.

Dependent Variables

In comparison to current court proceedings, which are characterized by several stages of decision making, different sets of criteria in determining successive outcomes, and a wide variety of sentencing options, "justice" during the Urban Reform Era generally was swift, unencumbered by legal "technicalities," and limited in the types of dispositions meted out. In the vast majority of cases, involving the less serious offenses considered here, case outcomes generally were decided in daily police court sessions, during which it was not unusual for the police magistrate to process a case and impose a sentence in a matter of minutes (Homel, 1981). Despite the fact that conviction and sentencing decisions generally occurred at the same time, it would be a serious omission to examine gender differences in court outcomes solely in terms of the sentences imposed on offenders. Failing to first take into account the influence of gender on the decision to impose a prison sentence might well lead to biased estimates and conclusions with respect to the impact of gender on sentence length (Kruttschnitt and Green, 1984; Wilbanks, 1986). For this reason, in this study, two measures of case outcome were constructed.

The first dependent variable dichotomizes case outcome in simple terms of whether or not the offender received a prison sentence (with or without the option of paying a fine) versus all nonprison dispositions, which included discharge, acquittal, remand, bail, fine, suspended sentence, and other miscellaneous outcomes.[5] The decision to combine the two dispositions of straight prison sentences and prison sentences that included the option of paying a fine was made in light of the fact that few offenders during this period were able to avoid a prison term by paying their fines. For the second dependent variable an interval measure of sentence length (days) is used. In this analysis, sentences ranged from 1 to 1,825 days for those offenders receiving a prison sentence.[6]

Method of Analysis

Because little prior research exists that systematically examines gender differences in case outcomes during this era, an exploratory analysis involving several models for each of the dependent variables was carried out. First, to assess variations in case outcomes within gender categories, separate equations were estimated for males and females. Supplemental main-effect equations (not reported in the tables) were also carried out to assess the effect of gender after controlling for all other variables.[7] Second, to examine differences in case outcomes between men and women, a model containing all two-way interaction terms between gender and the control variables was estimated. In the final model, interactions that were not significant (p. 10) were excluded, and the model was reestimated to maximize parsimony and to produce more consistent parameter estimates.

The first dependent variable is dichotomous (prison sentence versus all other dispositions) and, accordingly, logistic regression is used to estimate the relative importance of the independent variables (Hosmer and Lemeshow, 1989). In the case of the second dependent variable, because sentence length is contingent on the offender's first receiving a prison sentence, the two processes are not independent. Excluding cases not receiving a prison sentence and then using ordinary least squares (OLS) regression to estimate the model raises the problem of censorship of cases because of the nonrandom way in which cases are selected (Kennedy, 1985; Maddala, 1986). Using OLS regression with a censored dependent variable amounts to estimating a mis-specified version of the equation, in this case, one that will tend to confound the effect of an exogenous variable on sentence length with its impact on the likelihood of receiving a prison sentence.

To overcome this problem, a tobit model is used that "corrects" for the problem of censorship by estimating a regression line using all observations, those at the zero prison days limit and those above it (see Amemiya, 1984; Kennedy, 1985; Maddala, 1986). The tobit coefficient thus measures effects on the probability of being above the limit and effects

conditional on being above zero. Importantly, the relative magnitudes of these two quantities can be determined by decomposing the tobit coefficient, thus making it possible to assess changes in sentence length, weighted by the probability of receiving a prison sentence (see Greene, 1991; McDonald and Moffitt, 1980).

Results

Distributions of Offender Attributes, Offences, and Case Outcomes

Table 1 reveals significant differences in the various attributes of male and female offenders during the Urban Reform Era. Interestingly, married offenders made up a larger proportion of women (46.2%) than men (30.1%) committed to prison. As well, female offenders tended to be younger than their male counterparts; the majority of women were under age 29 (52.4% compared with 42.6% of men). As expected, the offense of vagrancy constituted the largest proportion of female cases (39.3%), while men were most likely to be committed for drunkenness (49.0%). Taken together, the three public order offenses of drunkenness, vagrancy, and being a keeper or inmate of a house of ill fame made up a larger proportion of female (81.1%) than male (45.4%) cases. There were few differences between men and women in the relative seriousness of their cases or criminal careers—roughly equal proportions of men and women had more than one arrest charge (9.1% and 8.8%, respectively) and were recidivists (55.0% and 53.3%, respectively). In addition, there was a dramatic decline in female committals to prison from the late nineteenth to the early twentieth century. While the proportion of men committed in the two time periods was roughly equal, the vast majority of women (78%) in the sample were committed to prison in the early period (1871–1891).

In terms of case outcomes, the majority of male and female cases were disposed of either through discharge (39.7% of men and 36.5% of women) or the imposition of a prison sentence with or without a fine option (51.6% of men and

57.5% of women). Of those offenders receiving a prison sentence, males averaged 116 days and women 139 days. Overall, Table 1 reveals few differences between men and women in the likelihood of being sentenced to prison, but some indication of longer sentences being meted out to female offenders. It remains to be seen whether these findings are sustained when control variables for offender attributes, offense type, and time period are introduced.

Gender and Case Outcomes: Prison Sentence versus No Prison Sentence

Table 2 presents the results of the logistic regression analysis in which the outcome variable is a binary measure of whether or not the offender received a prison sentence. Examination of the coefficients and associated odds ratios in the separate equations for males and females (Equations 1 and 2) reveals some similarities but also clear differences in the determinants of case dispositions within gender categories.[8] Being married reduced the odds of receiving a prison sentence among male offenders ($b = -.69, p$ .001) and female offenders ($b = -.87, p$ .01). As well, for men and women, being older increased the odds of receiving a jail sentence. However, whereas for men the odds of receiving a jail sentence increased in a linear fashion from the younger to older age categories (1.38 to 1.95), the effect of age for women was most pronounced for those 40 to 50 years old. Compared with the youngest group of women, the odds of the older women incurring a prison sentence increased by a factor of 9.49.

Examination of the effect of offense type on case disposition also reveals significant differences within gender categories, which generally are consistent with initial expectations. For men, the odds of receiving a jail sentence were greatest for larceny (the reference category), followed by drunkenness (.87), vagrancy (.76), being a keeper or inmate of a house of ill fame (.68), and assault (.39). In contrast, among women, there were no statistically significant differences in the odds of receiving a prison sentence between larceny

and each of the other offense types. At the same time, the effect on case outcome is not the same for all offenses. Ranking the offenses, the odds of a woman being sentenced to prison were greatest for larceny and vagrancy (.14); and reduced and roughly equal for assault (.63), drunkenness (.56), and being a keeper or inmate of a house of ill fame (.58).

For men and women, having multiple charges ($b = 2.12, p$ .001 and $b = 4.00, p$ .001, respectively) or being a recidivist ($b = .58, ^$ .001) and ($b = 1.21, p$ .001, respectively) were strong predictors of a prison disposition. The negative impact of both these case factors is especially pronounced among female offenders. Women with more than one arrest charge increased their odds of being sentenced to prison by a factor of 54.6 compared with women with only one arrest charge. Further, the odds of a female recidivist being sentenced to prison increased by a factor of 3.35 over first-time female offenders.

For males, the probabilities of receiving or not receiving a prison sentence were unaffected by time. In contrast, time period was a strong predictor of female court dispositions ($b = -1.23, p$ .01). More specifically, by the early twentieth century, the odds of a woman being sentenced to jail had decreased by .29 compared with a woman in the late nineteenth century.

Within gender categories, then, there are striking differences in the factors related to receiving a prison sentence. But it has yet to be determined whether these differences among male and female offenders translate into marked differences between men and women. Examination of the gender coefficient in the main-effect model (not shown in Table 2) reveals that gender is a significant determinant of a prison sentence: overall, women were more likely than men to be sentenced to prison ($b = -.39, p$ .01). Specifically, holding all other variables constant, the odds of a male being sentenced to prison are decreased by a factor of .67.

In order to specify more precisely the influence of gender on the decision to impose

Table 2: Logit Coefficients, Standard Errors, and Odds Ratios for Case Outcome (Prison/No Prison)

Variables	Equation 1 (Males)			Equation 2 (Females)			Equation 3 (All)		
	Coefficient	S.E.	Odds Ratio	Coefficient	S.E.	Odds Ratio	Coefficient	S.E.	Odds Ratio
Marital Status	-.69****	(.11)	.50	-.87***	(.31)	.42	-.71****	(.10)	2.03
Age[a]									
20-29	.32**	(.16)	1.38	.41	(.42)	1.51	.20	(.40)	1.22
30-39	.53****	(.17)	1.70	.49	(.54)	1.63	.17	(.49)	1.18
40-49	.44***	(.19)	1.55	2.25****	(.57)	9.49	1.81****	(.49)	6.11
50 & Over	.67****	(.19)	1.95	.87	(.54)	2.39	.53	(.50)	1.70
Offense[b]									
Assault	-.95****	(.19)	.39	-.46	(.82)	.63	-.92****	(.18)	.40
Drunkenness	-.14	(.13)	.87	-.58	(.50)	.56	-.17	(.13)	.84
Vagrancy	-.28*	(.16)	.76	.14	(.48)	1.15	-.19	(.15)	.83
House of Ill Fame	-.38	(.49)	.68	-.55	(.60)	.58	-.51	(.35)	.60
No. of Arrest Charges	2.12****	(.23)	8.33	4.00****	(1.11)	54.60	4.08****	(1.03)	59.15
Prior Committals	.58****	(.10)	1.79	1.21****	(.30)	3.35	1.24****	(.28)	3.46
Time Period	.07	(.09)	1.07	-1.23***	(.35)	.29	-1.40****	(.34)	.25
Gender							-.26	(.37)	.77
Gender X Time Period							1.49****	(.36)	4.44
Gender X Age									
20-29							.13	(.43)	1.14
30-39							.39	(.51)	1.48
40-49							-1.33***	(.51)	.26
50 & Over							.16	(.53)	1.17
Gender X No. of Arrest Charges							-1.96*	(1.11)	.14
Gender X Prior Committals to Prison							-.64***	(.30)	.53
Constant	-.42			-.39			-.19		
-2 Log Likelihood	-1235.2			-162.9			-1401.5		
N[c]	1,946			316			2,262		

a Reference category: under 19.
b Reference category: larceny.
c Differences in sample sizes from Table 1 are due to missing observations.

* $p < .10$
** $p < .05$
*** $p < .01$
**** $p < .001$

a prison sentence, an equation including two-way interaction terms was carried out. The results from this model, after eliminating those interaction terms that were not significant and reestimating the model, are shown in Equation 3 of Table 2. Only the interaction terms of gender by marital status and gender by offense type were not significant. So, in a statistical sense at least, the mitigating effect of being married in reducing the likelihood of receiving a prison disposition was the same for men and women. Similarly, although there were marked differences in the effect of offense type within gender categories on case outcome, they did not translate into marked differences between men and women.

With the inclusion of the remaining interaction terms in the model, the main effect of gender is insignificant, and one is able to assess more precisely the nature of the relationship between gender and case outcome. First, age differentiated the treatment of men and women only among offenders aged 40 to 50 years ($b = -1.33, p$ .01).[9] Compared with women in this age group, elder men were substantially less likely to receive a prison sentence. Second, having more than one arrest charge pending was related more strongly to a prison sentence for women than men ($b = -1.96, p$ .10). Similarly, being a recidivist was a stronger predictor of a prison sentence for women than men ($b = -.64, p$ .01). Third, controlling for all other variables, there were no differences between men and women in the likelihood of receiving a prison sentence in the late nineteenth century. However, in the early twentieth century, men were substantially more likely than women to receive a prison disposition ($b = 1.49, p$ .001).

Put more succinctly, for the period as a whole, the findings indicate an overall pattern of women being more likely than men to be sentenced to prison. Differences between men and women in the factors associated with this decision are largely accounted for by, on the one hand, the greater probability that women who were older, had multiple charges, or were recidivists would receive the harsher outcome

compared with men with these same attributes and, on the other hand, the reduced likelihood of women receiving a prison sentence in the early twentieth century compared with the late nineteenth century. On this measure of case outcome, while the findings indicate that judges made differential assessments of the seriousness of different offenses when committed by men as opposed to women, they do not support the expectation that women charged with public order offenses were treated more severely than men. Nor do the findings provide evidence of greater leniency toward married women in comparison with married men. In contrast, the findings do reveal significant changes in the treatment of female offenders over time. However, since this part of the analysis is concerned only with the decision to impose a prison sentence and not the actual length of sentence meted out to offenders, it represents only the first step in assessing gender-related differences in sanction severity. Thus, the next part of the analysis assesses gender differences on this second measure of case outcome.

Gender and Sentence Severity

Table 3 reports the results from the tobit regression models of sentence severity, which include all observations (both those at or above the zero prison days threshold). For each of the equations (males, females, and interaction models), two sets of results are reported. The first column gives the unadjusted tobit coefficients. The second column reports the "adjusted effect" coefficients, which represent estimates of sentence length for those sentences above the zero limit, weighted by the probability of being above the limit. These "adjusted effects" were obtained by first calculating the fraction of the total effect of the independent variables due to being above the limit and then multiplying the tobit coefficients by that fraction (see McDonald and Moffitt, 1980, for a description of the equations used to obtain these decomposition effects).

The valuable information provided by this disaggregation of the tobit coefficients is readily illustrated. In the case of males, roughly half (51.6%) of all offenders received a prison sentence. Among men, the fraction of the total effect of an independent variable due to changes in sentence length is .32. Evaluating the data at this point, it is now possible to say that 32% of the total change in overall sentence severity resulting from a change in the independent variables is generated by changes in sentence length. However, importantly, this means that 68% of the change is generated by changes in the probability of receiving a prison sentence at all. The results of the decomposition for females are almost identical and have similar substantive implications. Among female offenders, 57.5% of the cases were disposed of with a prison sentence, and the fraction of the total effect conditional on receiving a prison sentence is .34. This means that 66% of the change in sentence severity is due to changes in the probability of receiving a prison sentence in the first place, whereas 34% is due to changes in actual sentence length for those receiving a prison disposition. Among males and females, then, most of the effect of the control variables on case outcome is due to their effect on the decision to impose a prison sentence. Having previously analyzed gender-related differences on this measure of case outcome, I focus now on the adjusted-effect coefficients in column 2, which estimate changes in sentence length conditional on receiving a prison sentence.

Among male offenders, married offenders received shorter sentences than single offenders ($b = -18.83$). In addition, offenders under 19 years of age received the longest sentences. These results suggest that while the youngest group of offenders was less likely than older offenders to receive a prison sentence, those who did received the longest sentences. Judges also made clear distinctions among male offenders on the basis of offense type. Rank ordering offenses, the longest sentences were meted out for larceny (the reference category), followed by vagrancy ($b = -37.59$), being a keeper or inmate of a house of ill fame ($b = -43.74$), drunkenness ($b = -51.56$), and lastly,

assault ($b = -66.32$). Males with more than one arrest charge pending received substantially longer sentences ($b = 101.40$), as did those with a prior record ($b = 21.49$). In addition, there is a trend toward longer sentences in the early twentieth century compared with the late nineteenth century ($b = 16.19$).

In the case of females, only the number of arrest charges, recidivism, and time period are strongly related to sentence length. Interestingly then, and in contrast to men, marital status was not related to sentence length among women. So, it would appear that while being married reduced the likelihood of being incarcerated, this mitigating effect was effectively counteracted by the long sentences meted out to married women. Also in contrast to their treatment of male offenders, judges did not appear to consider the nature of the offense as an important differentiating factor in the sentences they imposed on women. There are no statistically significant differences in sentence length between larceny and each of the other offense types, and differences across all offense types are also fairly minimal. Rank ordering offenses by sentence length shows the longest sentences were given to women charged with vagrancy ($b = 19.85$), followed by larceny, being in a house of ill fame ($b = -9.99$), assault ($b = -26.53$), and drunkenness ($b = 29.28$).

However, as with male offenders, females who had more than one arrest charge or who were recidivists received longer sentences ($b = 77.15$ and $b = 26.32$, respectively) than female offenders with only one charge and no prior criminal record. Time period also was a significant determinant of sentence severity for women. In particular, because a smaller proportion of women were sentenced to prison in the twentieth century compared with the nineteenth century, this latter period is associated with an overall reduction in sentence severity for women offenders ($b = -34.00$).

The next issue to be considered is the findings with respect to differences between men and women in sentence length. Examination of the gender coefficient in the main-effect model

Table 3: Tobit Estimates, Standard Errors, and Adjusted Effects for Sentence Severity

Variables	Males		Females		All	
	(1)	(2)	(1)	(2)	(1)	(2)
	ML Tobit Coefficient (S.E.)	Adjusted Effect[a]	ML Tobit Coefficient S.E.	Adjusted Effect	ML Tobit Coefficient S.E.	Adjusted Effect
Marital Status	−59.98**** (16.75)	−18.83	−59.35 (39.58)	−20.18	−58.69**** (15.39)	−18.60
Age[b]						
20–29	−37.25* (22.36)	−11.70	−83.22 (52.87)	−28.29	−43.93** (20.58)	−13.93
30–39	−17.90 (24.47)	−5.62	−61.36 (64.58)	−20.86	−23.92 (22.84)	−7.58
40–49	−32.35 (27.12)	−10.16	36.85 (65.67)	12.52	−20.74 (25.00)	−6.57
50 & Over	−7.04 (16.83)	−2.21	−29.58 (67.94)	−10.06	−10.74 (24.95)	−3.40
Offense[c]						
Assault	−211.20**** (27.80)	−66.32	−78.02 (97.29)	−26.53	−42.95 (95.73)	−13.62
Drunkenness	−164.21**** (19.19)	−51.56	−86.14 (63.64)	−29.28	−20.05 (54.13)	−6.36
Vagrancy	−119.74**** (23.67)	−37.59	58.39 (61.47)	19.85	113.03** (52.06)	35.83
House of Ill Fame	−139.31* (75.14)	−43.74	−29.39 (74.26)	−9.99	−.06 (71.01)	−.02
No. of Arrest Charges	322.94**** (23.94)	101.40	226.93**** (64.11)	77.15	313.58**** (21.63)	99.40
Prior Committals	68.43**** (14.59)	21.49	77.40** (38.46)	26.32	68.75**** (13.64)	21.79
Time Period	51.56**** (14.11)	16.19	−99.99** (44.79)	−34.00	−103.27** (44.47)	−32.74
Gender					65.39 (47.65)	20.73
Gender X Time Period					154.88**** (46.67)	49.10
Gender X Offense						
Assault					−168.90* (99.36)	−53.54
Drunkenness					−147.02*** (55.69)	−46.61
Vagrancy					−234.59**** (55.91)	−74.37
House of Ill Fame					−142.31 (102.98)	−45.11
Constant	4.24		3.80		−56.90	
Log Likelihood	−7534.2		−1334.5		−8872.4	
N[d]	1,946		316		2,262	

[a] Effect conditional on being above limit (0).
[b] Reference category: under 19.
[c] Reference category: larceny.
[d] Differences in sample sizes from Table 1 are due to missing observations.
* $p < .10$
** $p < .05$
*** $p < .01$
**** $p < .001$

(not shown in table) reveals that gender is a significant influence on overall sentence severity ($b = 51.02$, p .01), with women receiving harsher outcomes than men. Disaggregating the tobit coefficient, most of the influence of gender is due to its effect on the decision to impose a prison sentence (68%) and substantially less to its effect on sentence length (32%) for those offenders receiving a prison sentence. Still, after taking this differential effect of gender into account, women received, on average, sentences that were 16 days longer than those men received. Examination of the interaction model makes it possible to account more fully for the influence of gender on sentence length. Excluding the interaction terms that were not significant reveals that, once the relative proportions of married and unmarried male and female offenders are controlled for, marital status does not figure as a significant gender-related difference in sentence length. As well, there are no significant differences between men and women in the effect on sentence length of having multiple charges or being a recidivist.

In terms of differences between men and women, the most significant factors are offense type and time period, which have opposite effects on sentence length. Controlling for all other variables, the interaction terms for gender by offense type reveal an overall pattern of longer sentences being meted out to females compared with males. More specifically, there are no significant differences in the sentences imposed on men and women for larceny. At the same time, males received substantially shorter sentences than females for vagrancy ($b = -74.37$) and drunkenness ($b = -46.61$). As well, the negative coefficient for assault ($b = -53.54$) and the negative (but not significant) coefficient for being a keeper or inmate of a house of ill fame give some indication that women received somewhat longer sentences for these offenses as well. However, the small number of women charged with assault and the small number of men charged with prostitution-related offenses caution against drawing broad generalizations with respect to these particular offenses.

The effect of time period is determined primarily by gender differences in the probability of receiving a prison sentence in the early twentieth century compared with the late nineteenth century. Because sentence length is weighted by the probability of receiving a prison sentence, and because women were less likely than men to receive a prison sentence over time, the adjusted gender-time period interaction term shows an overall increase in sentence length for men compared with women ($b = 49.10$).

Discussion and Conclusions

The preceding analysis reveals considerable complexity in the nature and extent of gender-related differences in court outcomes during the Urban Reform Era. While much of the contemporary sentencing research has sought to explain (and sometimes, qualify) the predominant pattern of leniency toward female offenders, the historical evidence suggests that the opposite pattern of gender discrimination prevailed in the past. Looking at the period as a whole and controlling for all other variables, women were more likely to receive prison dispositions and to incur longer sentences than men. At the same time, the results show that gender-related differences in sanction severity varied substantially across the two measures of case outcome in relation to various offender and offense attributes, and across time. These findings are reviewed in the context of the hypotheses stated at the outset and in terms of their implications for future research in this area.

First, gender stereotyping on the part of decision makers is evidenced in the dissimilar assessment of the seriousness of different offenses when committed by men as opposed to women. Among males, prison terms and the longest sentences were reserved for larceny, and public order offenses were treated considerably more leniently. Although it was expected that men also would incur harsher outcomes for violent offenses, this proved not to be the case. It is likely that this is due to the inclusion of only common assault in the analysis. During the period considered, most instances of common assault brought before the police court consisted of relatively minor disputes between family members and friends (Friedman and Percival, 1981; Katz et al., E982). Clearly, by the standards of the times, judges did not regard these offenses as particularly serious expressions of male criminality. In contrast, the nature of the offense was a less important determinant of case outcome and, especially, sentence length among female offenders. By and large, judges appeared to adopt the attitude that the form a woman's criminality took was secondary to the fact that a woman appeared before the court on any charge.

Second, as the most general pattern, it was expected that women charged with public order offenses during the Urban Reform Era would be dealt with more harshly than men. While there were no significant gender differences by offense type in the probability of receiving a prison sentence, women did receive longer sentences for vagrancy, drunkenness, and, to a lesser extent, assault. Third, although women were given longer sentences for most offenses, gender differences in sentence length were, as predicted, most pronounced for the offense of vagrancy. Undoubtedly, some (unknown) part of the more punitive reaction to women charged with vagrancy is due to the use of this statute to criminalize street prostitutes. At the same time, there were no differences between men and women in case outcome for the specific prostitution offense of being a keeper or inmate of a house of ill fame. This finding suggests that judges made some distinctions among different types of prostitutes on the basis of their social status and public visibility. The comparatively more lenient treatment of prostitutes who worked in brothels, compared with those women who worked on the streets, implies that judges reserved their harshest responses for the most socially and economically marginal of women—those whose crimes occurred in public and, therefore, represented the most flagrant affront to prevailing constructions of femininity and sexuality. Fourth, consistent with

expectations, men and women charged with the more conventional offense of larceny were treated similarly, being both equally likely to receive a prison disposition and similarly long sentences.

Fifth, although there were no gender differences in sentence length for offenders with more than one arrest charge or a prior record, compared with men with these attributes, women were more likely to receive a prison sentence. Gender discrimination, the tendency to view female offenders as more immoral than male offenders, and the attendant greater loss of respectability experienced by women who came before the courts during this era are, perhaps, exemplified in the harsh treatment of older women, who were more likely than younger women or older men to incur prison dispositions. Lacking the employment opportunities available to younger women, frequently widowed or abandoned by their husbands, having lost their capacity to reproduce and, consequently, much of their social value, and viewed as too old or entrenched in their criminal tendencies to be reformed, these older women were victimized by society and the criminal justice system alike.

The findings with respect to differences in the treatment of male and female offenders for the period as a whole contribute to a greater understanding of the impact of gender-based stereotypes on judicial attitudes and court outcomes in the present as well as the past. Not only do the findings provide further evidence to dispel the myth of chivalry toward female offenders in the past, but the historical legacy of these sanctioning patterns is seen in the continued harsh treatment of women who deviate from accepted standards of feminine behavior. In addition, several other findings from this analysis merit further comment.

One of the more interesting findings is that most of the influence of gender on court outcomes is accounted for by the decision to impose a prison disposition and comparatively less is due to decisions with respect to actual sentence length. At the most general level, and consistent with research in contemporary contexts, this finding underscores the importance of controlling for the potentially variable influence of gender across different decision-making contexts before drawing generalizations about the nature and extent of gender-related disparities in sanction severity (Daly, 1987; Kruttschnitt and Green, 1984; Nagel and Hagan, 1983; Wilbanks, 1986).

At the same time, the results of this historical analysis stand in marked contrast to research in contemporary contexts, which generally finds an overall pattern of more lenient outcomes for women, especially in sentencing decisions. Recent explanatory frameworks have focused on gender-based differences in familial relations and informal social controls to account for this gender-based leniency in court outcomes. This study highlights the historically specific nature of those relations, thus broadening our understanding of the structural factors that mediate sanctioning patterns over time.

Daly (1987), for example, argues that contemporary gender differences in court outcomes reflect the influence of traditional gender divisions in work and family life, a concern with maintaining the family unit, and the higher priority accorded to women's care-taking role than men's economic support in maintaining family life. Because the state can compensate more easily for men's economic role than women's parental role, judges are more reluctant to incarcerate married women than married men. Daly (1987:170), however, notes that this pattern of gender-based leniency is subject to change, persisting only so long as women retain primary responsibility for child care and existing "asymmetries remain in state supports for father and mother surrogates."

The Urban Reform Era provides a concrete example of such historical variability in the differential treatment of males and females on the basis of marital status. Although gender-based divisions in work and family first arose as a result of urbanization and industrialization, the analysis revealed no evidence that married women were treated more leniently than married

men as might be expected. In fact, a larger proportion of married women than married men were committed to prison, and being married was more strongly associated with less severe outcomes among male offenders than among female offenders. The marked absence of leniency toward women implies that whether married women are treated more leniently than married men by the courts is crucially influenced by prevailing considerations of social class, economic conditions, and levels of state supports for families.

It is perhaps not surprising to find that the middle-class ideology of "maternal feminism," which idealized women's role as mothers, did not extend equally to the predominantly working-class women who found themselves before the courts.[10] To a large extent, the realities of their working lives stood in marked contradiction to the ideology of domesticity, which portrayed women's place as in the home. The acceptance of these new definitions of gender by working-class women, and the fusion of middle-class and working-class notions of familial life, occurred only gradually (Tilly, 1978; Tomes, 1978). And, it would seem, commensurate changes in judicial attitudes and sanctioning patterns also were slow to develop. During the Urban Reform Era, judges appeared to view women's criminality as prima facie evidence of their inadequacy as mothers and showed little hesitancy in removing them from their child-care roles.

In addition, judges' differential treatment of married women and married men must be seen in light of the overall economic precariousness of the working class during this era. In the absence of state supports to compensate families for the loss of a male wage earner, incarcerating married men frequently had dire consequences for the family. Men's economic role in maintaining the family unit would be seen as more indispensable than it is today, when such state supports exist. In the past, unlike the present, women's primary responsibility for child care did not confer the same special advantage in court over men's financial responsibility to the family. So, for all the disadvantages associated with traditional stereotypes, contemporary female offenders have benefitted from them in ways their counterparts during the Urban Reform Era did not.

Finally, one of the most important findings from this analysis concerns the impact of broad changes in gender-based forms of control on male and female court outcomes over time. Within a social control framework, gender-based variations in social control have been used to explain lower levels of female criminality, court responses to different types of female offenders, and the differential treatment of male and female offenders (Hagan et al., 1979, 1987; Kruttschnitt, 1981, 1982, 1984). This historical analysis suggests that, in addition to this level of analysis focusing on individual attributes, equal consideration might be given to the impact of societal-level changes in gender-based forms of social control to account for broad shifts in sanctioning patterns.

As previously suggested (Boritch and Hagan, 1990), the rise and intensification of informal community controls regulating the lives of working-class women during the late nineteenth century likely contributed to both a decline in levels of female criminality and a change in the judicial treatment of different types of female offenders. On the one hand, an increasing reliance on informal controls likely prevented many women from being subject to criminal sanctions in the first place. As well, community-based organizations provided judges with alternatives to imposing prison sentences on first-time offenders. On the other hand, long sentences for repeat offenders may have further reduced levels of female criminality through simple incapacitation of these women.

Certainly, the findings with respect to the harsh treatment of female recidivists are indicative of such a pattern. The "success" of such sentencing practices may account for the drop in female recidivism over time. While, among men, roughly 50% of offenders were recidivists in both the late nineteenth and early twentieth century, the proportion of female recidivists declined from 56 to 44% over the same period.

The findings also suggest that changes in gender-based forms of social control and declining levels of female criminality over the course of the Urban Reform Era contributed to a long-term reduction in gender-related differences in case outcomes. Viewing the period as a whole, there is a predominant pattern of more severe sanctions being meted out to female offenders. However, it is also fairly evident that the more severe treatment of female offenders is primarily a feature of the late nineteenth century since the majority of female offenders were committed to prison in those decades. By the early twentieth century, there is a noticeable change in sanctioning patterns with women being less likely than men to receive a prison disposition. And while women continued to receive longer sentences than men for various offenses, men now also received substantially longer sentences than they had in the nineteenth century. Over time, then, there is a trend toward women being subjected to higher levels of informal control and men being subjected to more intensified formal controls. Taken together, these changes contributed to a long-term reduction in the level of female criminality and the magnitude of gender-related disparities in sentence severity.

Notes

*   An earlier version of this paper was presented at the annual meeting of the American Society of Criminology, San Francisco, November 1991. The research was supported by grants from the University of Alberta's Central Research Fund and Contributions Grant of the Solicitor General of Canada to the Centre of Criminology. I would like to thank Douglas Baer for his assistance with the data analysis and Leslie Kennedy, William Johnston, John Hagan, and the anonymous reviewers for their helpful comments and suggestions.

1. By the late 1870s, the prison system in Ontario consisted of three tiers, distinguished by the length of sentence imposed on offenders. At the lowest level were the local county jails, which held those awaiting disposition of their case, as well as the majority of offenders sentenced to two months or less. At the next level, men sentenced to periods of two months to two years were transferred to Central Prison, and women receiving such sentences were sent to the Andrew Mercer Reformatory, both in Toronto. Finally, those offenders sentenced to terms of two years or more were sent to the Federal Penitentiary at Kingston, Ontario (Splane, 1965; Wetherell, 1979). In practice, however, many prisoners whose sentences made them eligible to be sent to Central Prison or the Mercer Reformatory served their time in the local county jails. In the case of men this was usually the result of overcrowding at Central Prison, while for women it usually stemmed from local judges simply failing to take advantage of this alternative facility (Province of Ontario, 1891).

2. Several pages in the 1881 register are missing, which resulted in the loss of 75 cases. As well, it should be noted that the data for 1920 do not span the entire year but conclude with the end of the institution's fiscal year, September 30.

3. While a prominent concern was to control for the effect of offense type on case outcome, it is recognized that the offense categories included in the analysis contain charges that vary in behavioral content and, therefore, seriousness. The offense of vagrancy is also somewhat unique in its gender specificity since it included women charged with prostitution. Unfortunately, there is no way of precisely determining the proportion of women charged with vagrancy who actually were arrested for prostitution as opposed to all of the other behaviors and status attributes that made both men and women subject to this charge. It is, in part for this reason, that the less frequent offense of being a keeper or inmate of a house of ill fame is included as it represents the only "pure" prostitution charge involving both men and women during this era.

4. There were too few cases of offenders with more than two arrest charges pending to construct an interval scale for this variable. For different reasons, an interval scale could not be constructed for prior committals to prison because prison officials were not consistent in the way they recorded this information over time. In particular, in some of the sample years, multiple arrest charges were recorded as separate committals. Therefore, as a first step, it was necessary to distinguish among multiple arrest charges and prior committals in any

given year. It was then possible to separate first-time offenders from recidivists and, by matching offender information, to determine the correct number of prior committals for a given offender for any year in the study. However, it was not possible to reconstruct accurately the number of prior committals an offender may have accumulated in the intervening years not included in the sample.

5. Because the vast majority of male (92.6%) and female (94.9%) cases were disposed of either by discharge/acquittal or conviction and a prison sentence, the operationalization of case outcome in terms of prison sentence versus all other dispositions most accurately reflects the bivariate nature of judicial sanctioning patterns during this era. It is rendered an only slightly imperfect measure of conviction versus nonconviction by the inclusion of a small proportion of offenders (1.7% of men and 1.6% of women) who were convicted but received a nonprison sentence (i.e., a fine or suspended sentence). The other types of dispositions in the nonprison category include a number of infrequent outcomes in which the offender was neither convicted nor received a criminal sanction. A small proportion of offenders (1.4% of men and 1.9% of women) were remanded. This disposition was recorded only in 1871, and, since those cases never reappear in the register, it is assumed that no further proceedings were taken and they were, in effect, discharged. A few offenders (3.3% of men and .3% of women) were bailed. Those offenders also never reappear in the register, and it is assumed they forfeited their bail in lieu of appearing in court and were not pursued by the authorities. The remaining offenders (1.0% of men and 1.3% of women) received a variety of other dispositions. These included being sent to a hospital, the insane asylum, or some other noncriminal facility.

6. Of the offenders sentenced to prison, a small minority (1.6%) were sentenced to indeterminate terms of either up to two years, or up to five years (34 men and 4 women). As the upper limits of these sentences were not atypical for the offenses involved (primarily larceny), it was decided to code these cases at the maximum penalty.

7. Since the primary concern in this analysis is the effect of gender on case outcome, only the gender coefficient is reported in the discussion and these main-effect equations are not presented in the accompanying tables for either dependent variable. The full equations are available from the author.

8. The odds, ratio, or Exp(B), is the antilogarithm of the difference between the logit coefficient of any category of a variable and its reference category,

calculated as $1/1 + e^{-z}$. An odds ratio of 1 means that the odds of receiving or not receiving a prison sentence are roughly equal. An odds ratio greater than 1 means that the odds are increased, whereas an odds ratio of less than 1 means that the odds are decreased. Technically speaking, the odds ratio refers to the ratio of offenders receiving a prison disposition to offenders not receiving a prison disposition, and not to the probability of receiving a prison disposition.

9. Since the interaction coefficients (and odds ratios) refer to the difference of a difference—that is, the difference between men and women in one category of the independent variable compared with the difference between men and women in the other category—these terms are not readily meaningful. Therefore, the interpretation of each interaction coefficient in the analysis of both dependent variables was supplemented by specifying and comparing different cells of the interaction.

10. There was virtually no variation in the social class of the female offenders in the sample, as measured by their occupation. Of those women (86.4%) recording an occupation, fully 86.5% were employed in domestic service. Of the remainder, 4.5% were factory workers, 4.6% were dressmakers, and 4.4% had various other occupations (e.g., peddler, photographer). Male offenders also were overwhelmingly from the working class. Of the men (96.2%) listing an occupation, 65.4% were common laborers, 24.8% were tradesmen (e.g., carpenter, tinsmith), 3.7% were fanners, 5.7% were lower white-collar workers (e.g., clerk, store proprietor), and only .4% were professionals (e.g., doctor).

References

Allen, Richard
1968 The social gospel and the reform tradition in Canada, 1890–1928. *Canadian Historical Review* 49(4):381–399.

Amemiya, Takeshi
1984 Tobit models: A survey. *Journal of Econometrics* 24:3–61.

Anderson, Etta A.
1976 The "chivalrous" treatment of the female offender in the arms of the criminal justice system: A review of the literature. *Social Problems* 23:350–357.

Artibise, Alan F.J.
1975 *Winnipeg: A Social History of Urban Growth, 1874–1914*. Montreal: McGill-Queen's University Press.

Backhouse, Constance B.
1985 Nineteenth-century Canadian prostitution law, reflection of a discriminatory society. *Social History* 18(36):387–423.

Barber, Marilyn
1980 The women Ontario welcomed: Immigrant domestics for Ontario homes, 1870–1930. *Ontario History* 62:148–172.

Bertram, Gordon W.
1963 Economic growth in Canadian industry, 1870–1915: The staple model and take-off hypothesis. *Canadian Journal of Economics and Politics* 29(2): 159–184.

Bloomfield, Elizabeth
1986 Urban-industrial growth processes in southern Ontario, 1870–1930. Institute of Urban Studies,

Research and Working Paper, No. 24, University of Guelph.

Boritch, Helen, and John Hagan
1990 A century of crime in Toronto: Gender, class, and patterns of social control, 1859 to 1955. *Criminology* 28(4):567–599.

Carrigan, D. Owen
1991 *Crime and Punishment in Canada: A History*. Toronto: McClelland & Stewart.

Chesney-Lind, Meda
1986 Women and crime: The female offender. *Signs* 12:78–96.

Cott, Nancy F.
1987 *The Grounding of Modern Feminism*. New Haven: Yale University Press.

Currie, Dawn
1987 Female criminality: A crisis in feminist theory. In Brian D. MacLean (ed.), *The Political Economy of Crime*. Scarborough: Prentice-Hall Canada.

Daly, Kathleen
1988 Discrimination in the criminal courts: Family, gender, and the problem of equal treatment. *Social Forces* 66(1):152–175.

Daly, Kathleen, and Meda Chesney-Lind
1988 Feminism and criminology. *Justice Quarterly* 5(4):101–141.

DeCarie, M.G.
1974 Paved with good intentions: The Prohibitionists' road to racism in Ontario. *Ontario History* 66(1):15–22.

Edwards, Anne R.

1989 Sex/gender, sexism and criminal justice: Some theoretical considerations. *International Journal of the Sociology of Law* 17:165–184.

Edwards, Susan S.M.

1984 *Women on Trial: A Study of the Female Suspect, Defendant and Offender in the Criminal Law and Criminal Justice System*. Manchester: Manchester University Press.

Feinman, Clarice

1983 An historical overview of the treatment of incarcerated women: Myths and realities of rehabilitation. *Prison Journal* 63:12–26.

Freedman, Estelle B.

1974 Their sisters' keepers: An historical perspective on female correctional institutions in the United States: 1870–1900. *Feminist Studies* 2:77–95.

Friedman, Lawrence M., and Robert V. Percival

1981 *The Roots of Justice: Crime and Punishment in Alameda County, California 1870–1910*. Chapel Hill: The University of North Carolina Press.

Giordano, Peggy C., Sandra Kerbel, and Sandra Dudley

1981 The economics of female criminality: An analysis of police blotters, 1890–1975. In Lee H. Bowker (ed.), *Women and Crime in America*. New York: Macmillan.

Graff, Harvey

1976 "Pauperism, misery, and vice": Illiteracy and criminality in the nineteenth century. *Journal of Social History* 11(2):245–268.

Greene, William H.

1990 *Limdep, User's Manual and Reference Guide*, Version 6.0. Bellport, NY.: Econometric Software.

Hagan, John, John H. Simpson, and A.R. Gillis

1979 The sexual stratification of social control: A gender-based perspective on crime and delinquency. *British Journal of Sociology* 30(1):25–38.

1987 Class in the household: A power-control theory of gender and delinquency. *American Journal of Sociology* 92:788–816.

Hahn, Nicholas F.

1980 Too dumb to know better. *Criminology* 18(1):3–25.

Holmes, Kay A.

1972 Reflections by gaslight: Prostitution in another age. *Issues in Criminology* (1):83–101.

Homel, Gene H.

1981 Denison's law. Criminal justice and the police court in Toronto, 1877–1921. *Ontario History* 73:171–186.

Hosmer, David W., Jr., and Stanley Lemeshow

1989 *Applied Logistic Regression*. New York: John Wiley & Sons.

Johnson, David R., and Laurie K. Scheuble

1991 Gender bias in the disposition of juvenile court referrals: The effects of time and location. *Criminology* 29(4):677–699.

Katz, Michael B., Michael J. Doucet, and Mark J. Stern

1982 *The Social Organization of Early Industrial Capitalism*. Cambridge, Mass.: Harvard University Press.

Kealey, Greg

1973 *Working-Class Toronto at the Turn of the Century*. Toronto: New Hogtown Press.

Kealey, Linda (ed.)

1979 *A Not Unreasonable Claim, Women and Reform in Canada, 1880's to 1920's*. Toronto: Women's Educational Press.

Kennedy, Peter

1985 *A Guide to Econometrics*. Cambridge, Mass.: MIT Press.

Klein, Alice, and Wayne Roberts

1974 Besieged innocence: The "problem" and the problems of working women—Toronto 1896–1914. In Janice Acton, Penny Goldsmith, and Bonnie Shepphard (eds.), *Women at Work: Ontario 1850–1930*. Toronto: Women's Educational Press.

Kruttschnitt, Candace

1981 Social status and sentences of female offenders. *Law and Society Review* 15(2):247–265.

1982 Women, crime and dependency. *Criminology* 19(4):495–513.

1984 Sex and criminal court dispositions: The unresolved controversy. *Research in Crime and Delinquency* 21(3):213–232.

Kruttschnitt, Candace, and Donald E. Green

1983 The sex-sanctioning issue: Is it history? *American Sociological Review* 49(4):541–551.

Maddala, G.S.

1985 *Limited-dependent and Qualitative Variables in Econometrics*. New York: Cambridge University Press.

McClaren, John P.S.

1986 Chasing the social evil: Moral fervour and the evolution of Canada's prostitution laws, 1867–1917. *Canadian Journal of Law and Society* 1:125–166.

McDonald, John F., and Robert A. Moffitt

1980 The uses of tobit analysis. *The Review of Economics and Statistics* 62(2)318–321.

Messerschmidt, James

1987 Feminism, criminology and the rise of the female "sex delinquent," 1880–1930. *Contemporary Crises* 11:243–263.

Miller, Leslie J.
1988 Uneasy alliance: Women as agents of social control. *Canadian Journal of Sociology* 12(4):345–361.

Mitchinson, Wendy
1979 The WCTU: "For God, home and native land": A study in nineteenth-century feminism. In Linda Kealey (ed.), *A Not Unreasonable Claim, Women and Reform in Canada, 1880's to 1920's*. Toronto: Women's Educational Press.

Monkkonen, Eric
1981 *Police in Urban America, 1860–1920*. New York: Cambridge University Press.

Morrison, T.R.
1975 "Their proper sphere": Feminism, the family and child-centered reform in Ontario, 1875–1900. *Ontario History* 63:45–74.

Nagel, Ilene H., and John Hagan
1984 Gender and crime: Offense patterns and criminal court sanctions. In Michael Tonry and Norval Morris (eds.), *Crime and Justice: An Annual Review of Research*. Chicago: University of Chicago Press.

Palmer, Bryan D.
1982 *Working-Class Experience: The Rise and Reconstitution of Labour, 1800–1920*. Toronto: Butterworth & Co.

Pederson, Diana
1986 "Keeping our good girls good": The YWCA and the "Girl Problem," 1870–1930. *Canadian Woman Studies* 7:20–24.

Province of Ontario
1891 *Report of the Commissioners Appointed to Enquire into the Prison and Reformatory System of Ontario*.

Rafter, Nicole Hahn
1983 Chastising the unchaste: Social control functions of a woman's reformatory, 1894–1931. In Stanley Cohen and Andrew Scull (eds.), *Social Control and the State, Historical and Comparative Essays*. Oxford: Martin Robinson.
1985 Gender, prisons and prison history. *Social Science History* 9(3):233–247.
1990 *Partial Justice*, 2nd ed. New Brunswick: Northeastern University Press.

Roberts, Wayne
1976 *Honest Womanhood: Feminism, Feminity and Class Consciousness among Toronto Working Women, 1893 to 1914*. Toronto: New Hogtown Press.

Rotenberg, Lori
1974 The wayward worker: Toronto's prostitute at the turn of the century. In Janice Acton, Penny Goldsmith, and Bonnie Shepphard (eds.), *Women at Work, Ontario 1850–1930*. Toronto: Women's Educational Press.

Rutherford, Paul
1971 Tomorrow's metropolis: The urban reform movement in Canada. *Historical Papers*: 203–224.

Rutherford, Paul (ed.)
1974 *Saving the Canadian City: The First Phase, 1880–1920*. Toronto: University of Toronto Press.

Schneider, John C.
1980 *Detroit and the Problem of Order, 1830–1880: A Geography of Crime, Riot, and Policing*. Lincoln: University of Nebraska Press.

Splane, Richard B.
1965 *Social Welfare in Ontario 1791–1893: A Study of Public Welfare Administration*. Toronto: University of Toronto Press.

Strange, Carolyn
1985 Unlocking the doors on women's prisons. *Resources for Feminist Research* 14(4):13–15.

Tilly, Louise A., and Joan W. Scott
1978 *Women, Work, and Family*. New York: Holt, Rinehart & Winston.

Tomes, Nancy
1977 A "torrent of abuse": Crimes of violence between working-class men and women in London, 1840–1875. *Journal of Social History* 11(3):328–345.

Trofimenkoff, Susan Mann
1986 One hundred and two muffled voices: Canada's industrial women in the 1880's. In V. Strong-Boag and A.C. Fellman (eds.), *Rethinking Canada: The Promise of Women's History*. Toronto: Copp Clark Pitman.

Valverde, Mariana
1991 *The Age of Light, Soap, and Water: Moral Reform in English Canada, 1885–1925*. Toronto: McClelland & Stewart.

Weaver, John
1987 Crime, public order and repression: The Gore District in upheaval, 1832–1851. In R.C. Macleod (ed.), *Lawful Authority: Readings on the History of Criminal Justice in Canada*. Toronto: Copp Clark Pitman.

Wetherell, Donald G.
1979 To discipline and train: Adult rehabilitation programmes in Ontario prisons, 1874–1900. *Histoire Sociale/Social History* 12(23):145–165.

Wilbanks, William
1986 Are female felons treated more leniently by the criminal justice system? *Justice Quarterly* 3(4):517–529.

CHAPTER 9

The Voluntary Delinquent: Parents, Daughters, and the Montreal Juvenile Delinquents' Court in 1918

Tamara Myers

● ●

For many working-class girls living in Montreal in the early twentieth century, adolescence was marked by the end of schooling, a series of low-paying jobs, an increase in independence, and sexual experimentation. Traditional family arrangements, which normally bound adolescent girls, strained under the impact of rapid social change. Parents reacted to their daughters' growing desires for autonomy with alarm, outrage, and fear, and often sought means to bolster waning familial authority. As a result, hundreds of delinquent daughters were brought before Montreal's Juvenile Delinquents' Court, which opened in 1912. Their "crimes" consisted primarily of defying parental authority over contributions to the family economy and housework, and their seemingly precocious attitude toward sexuality.

The first generation of girls processed by a distinct court for youthful offenders were introduced to probation officers, who systematically investigated their work histories, social and sexual behaviour, and family relations. The intrusive nature of the juvenile court's activities has led historians interested in the rise of "socialized" justice to emphasize the coercive relationship between court officials acting for the state and working-class families.[1] Central to juvenile justice historiography is the notion that juvenile court officials and their social

reform contemporaries aimed to regulate the social, moral, and sexual lives of the working class. Absent in this historiography is the role of parents within this new system of justice. The longstanding focus on the child-saving rhetoric of the new juvenile court has meant historians have relegated parents to a passive role in the system, ignoring how juvenile justice functioned in practice.[2]

As this article documents, parents were at the core of this new juvenile justice system: they exercised significant influence over the definition of delinquent conduct, brought to court a surprising number of cases (especially adolescent girls), and insisted on their right to have the state discipline their children. Indeed, a history of early juvenile justice must account for, and integrate, family decisions to engage the new juvenile court.

This study analyzes how juvenile justice functioned through an examination of the roles of parents, adolescent girls, and court officials in the Montreal juvenile court system that emerged in the wake of the 1908 Juvenile Delinquents Act (JDA). It focuses on female delinquents who came before Judge François-Xavier Choquet at the Montreal Juvenile Delinquents' court in 1918, by which time court officials had acquired considerable experience and had created a discernible pattern of juvenile justice. This year marks an important moment in Montreal history, especially for gender and moral regulation: it was the year that the social and sexual behaviour of young women elicited dramatic attention from the newly formed anti-vice organization, the Committee of Sixteen, and the city's first policewomen.[3] Although social commentators, mental hygiene experts, and women's organizations had decried the unchecked growth of female delinquency during the First World War, they had little impact on developing trends[4]: the number of adolescents appearing before the court increased steadily each year [...], with female cases representing 20 per cent of the total through the 1920s.[5] In terms of numbers or gender composition of cases appearing before the court, 1918 was a year characterized by continuity, not spiraling female delinquency.

The court depended on parents to provide it with "clients," but the reporting of delinquent children by parents often exposed contradictory notions regarding familial responsibility and the role of the state in brokering family relations. An examination of the records of the Montreal Juvenile Delinquents' Court exposes a dichotomy between parents, who often supported a traditional penal style of punishment (incarceration), and the judges and court personnel, who favoured probation. [...] Faced with state resistance to imprisoning their children, parents used their prerogative to institutionalized them, particularly daughters, as "voluntary" cases.

Some historians have argued that juvenile courts did not adhere to the child-saving principles that the architects of the JDA had advocated; others have suggested that the effect of the new courts—intended or not—was an oppressive regime targeting the working class.[6] This study joins the growing literature on social welfare reform that portrays the relationship between agencies and clients not simply as one of social control but as an interactive process in which clients and their families were not entirely passive.[7] Historians' discovery of the complicity of parents has tempered the assertion

that the court was strictly an instrument of bourgeois oppression even though the majority of the court's "clientele" was generated from the working class. Historian Mary Odem prefers to see the juvenile court as a "triangulated network of struggles and negotiations among working-class parents, their teenage daughters, and the court officials."[8] Feminist scholars also point to the immigrant and working-class families' use of state institutions to illustrate how power was less hegemonic and more diffuse than earlier social control theories had allowed.[9] While power in this scenario was not evenly distributed, the case can be made that parents were not rendered passive by the system. [...]

The federal Juvenile Delinquents Act of 1908, which set the twentieth-century legal and social agenda for Canadian juvenile justice, was the culmination of intense lobbying and activism on the part of the so-called child savers. Representing a new generation of social reformers, they were determined to systematize and professionalize the response to child welfare.[10] Toronto's J.J. Kelso, probably Canada's best-known child saver, and W.L. Scott, president of the Ottawa Children's Aid Society, who is attributed with the successful passage of the JDA, were typical in their promotion of the bourgeois family ideal through the growth of agencies of the "interventionist state," such as the juvenile courts.[11]

Designed to encourage the most modern child-saving practices, the [...] legislation introduced the possibility of decriminalizing the youthful offender by radically altering his or her experience of the criminal justice system: the new juvenile court was to substitute enlightened treatment for punishment.[12] W.L. Scott explained that "the child's offence [is] regarded before the law, as essentially a behaviour problem, with which the State will deal, not as an offence committed against its precepts and canons, but as the manifestation of a child's unadjusted reactions to new, uncomprehended, or overwhelming experiences."[13] The most important tenets of this new court were that trials were to be held *in camera* (the family and accused protected from public knowledge of their ordeal), and that the criminal justice principle of determining guilt was put aside as the trial focused on the circumstances that led to the delinquency.[14] One of the means employed to achieve child-saving aims was what Vancouver juvenile court judge Helen Gregory MacGill called "constructive probation." Favouring probation over incarceration, the new legislation took cognizance of current child welfare theory, which promoted the family as the ideal institution for reform of problem adolescents.

Following the passage of the federal Juvenile Delinquents Act, provincial statutes gave municipalities the right to open juvenile tribunals.[15] The devolution of power over the courts to municipalities created the potential for local particularities to prevail. In Montreal the highly paternalistic F.X. Choquet intended to foster a brand of justice that was significantly "plus clémente."[16] A graduate of the Seminary of Montreal and McGill University Law School, former police magistrate and judge of sessions of the peace, Choquet had been active in establishing the Montreal chapter of the Children's Aid Society and was its first president.[17] Fancying himself as a father figure to juvenile delinquents, he claimed: "there will be nothing to suggest a criminal court [in the new tribunal] ... no dock, no raised platform or bench, but the child will be brought into the room exactly as a father would bring his child into his parlour to talk with him and try to gain his confidence."[18] Located in a converted house on Champ de Mars Street adjacent to city hall, Choquet's juvenile court was set to embrace the new form of justice influenced by child-saving principles.

While the judge maintained ultimate authority in sentencing, the outcome of a trial was based on the input of new court officials whose job it was to investigate the family, work, and school lives of all adolescents appearing in the court. Many jurisdictions saw "the extension of maternal rule into the larger life of the community" through the juvenile court.[19] This was achieved by appointing women as juvenile court judges,

probation officers, and police officers, thereby asserting the propriety of women's domain over children and family life.[20] When Montreal's juvenile court opened in 1912, two women and one man were appointed probation officers and voluntary court committees were struck. Female juvenile delinquents were dealt with exclusively by female probation officers; all probation officers were required to discuss their cases with the Juvenile Court Committee.[21] Parallel to a confessional school arrangement, the probation officers' caseloads were organized by religion, essentially divided between Catholics and non-Catholics,[22] until the 1920s, when the Federation of Jewish Philanthropies created a Juvenile Aid Department and appointed a probation officer.[23]

[...] Rejecting the atmosphere of the criminal courts, Choquet promised to create an ambiance suitable for rehabilitating people. Rose Henderson, one of the court's first probation officers, remarked that "the cold letter of the law has but little place in solving the problems of mothers and children and only a man of great practical experience and one who understands human nature as does Choquet could ever in a great complex cosmopolitan city like Montreal make the success which he has done of the Juvenile Court."[24] However, Choquet's *modus operandi* would collide with the determination of reform schools to stay open in the face of increased use of probation and with parental goals of maintaining control over their recalcitrant children.

Montreal's juvenile court opened at a time when the problem of female delinquency became a topic of public concern. In the 1910s social reformers intent on eradicating prostitution and exposing the white slave trade shifted blame for fallen womanhood from male procurers to the loosening of sexual mores among young, single, working-class women.[25] Explanations for increasing female sexual autonomy varied from environmentalism (bad homes) to genetics (feeblemindedness), but the conclusion remained the same: bad girls were on the rise and it was imperative to control them.

The First World War exacerbated this situation, especially in cities like Montreal, where soldiers were allegedly enticing adolescent girls into sexual encounters, where venereal disease had become a major public health concern, where fathers were absent and mothers worked outside the home, and where dance halls, restaurants, moving pictures houses, and brothels proliferated. Reformers and working-class parents in Montreal, as elsewhere, often agreed that the social and sexual habits of their daughters demanded close attention, even to the extent that female police officers or caseworkers were employed to scour commercial amusement venues for young, unchaperoned women. For many people, the new court designed to control wayward youth was long overdue.

Of the 1105 new cases heard by the Montreal juvenile court, almost one-fifth, 181, involved girls.[26] I have examined all these cases, as well as every tenth case involving male juveniles. Juvenile delinquents were defined by law as being more than twelve and less than sixteen years. Seventy-six per cent, or 137 female delinquents brought to court, were French Canadian, Catholic, and born in the province of Quebec. Protestant girls, described simply as "Canadian," represented 6 per cent, Irish Catholics 2 per cent, and Canadian-born Jews 1 per cent. Seven per cent were Catholics of British origin. Recent immigrants from outside the United Kingdom made up a sizable minority of female delinquents: Italian Catholics 3 per cent; Russian and Austrian Jews 2 per cent; Belgian, Russian, Portuguese, and Lithuanian Catholics combined just over 2 per cent of cases. While these ratios correlate generally with Montreal's population at the time, French Canadians were slightly overrepresented: in the early twentieth century Montrealers of French origin made up approximately 63 per cent of the population.[27] According to the income of parents and the description and geographic location of households, the majority of families involved in the court system were from a broadly defined working class.

*****

Certain common female juvenile offences—especially desertion and incorrigibility—were hidden from the usual policed public domain and were therefore contingent on family members or guardians to bring cases forward. Even in cases where young women had stayed out all night or were habitually frequenting dance halls, there were simply not enough policewomen or caseworkers to keep up with "delinquent" girls. Effectively, parents assumed a policing role for the courts, initiating a process in which they would also stand as key witnesses and offer recommendations as to punishment.[28] [...] Of the seventy girls who came before the court in its first year, thirty-nine (55.7%) were the result of complaints lodged by relatives.[29] In 1918, 101 (56%) of the 181 cases of delinquency concerning girls were initiated by family members. [...]

The provincial statutes regarding delinquents facilitated this result. When the Quebec legislature amended the provincial statutes to take into account the new juvenile court, it expanded rights of guardians.[30] [...]

This provincial legislation had specific implications for the legal processing of children in the Montreal Juvenile Delinquents' Court. In the words of one of the administrators of the court, broadening the definition of juvenile delinquency in the provincial statutes meant that the court "greatly increased its jurisdiction."[31] Its impact was felt immediately in the dramatic rise in number of children coming to the court.[32] Moreover, it was up to parents and guardians to make the first judgment about what were "unmanageability," "incorrigibility," and "reasonable orders." In 1918 mothers lodged forty-six complaints and fathers thirty-nine, representing over 87 per cent of the cases brought before the court. Although the Quebec Civil Code stipulated that a married woman did not have the right to correct her children,[33] this did not prevent mothers from demanding that the juvenile court step in to do so. Of course, a substantial number of these women parented alone; more than one-third of the mothers who made complaints against their daughters were widowed, deserted, or estranged from husbands.[34]

*****

Gendered definitions of juvenile delinquency were most clearly exposed when family members brought a daughter to court. In 1918 the majority of girls (as many as three-quarters) were charged with incorrigibility, desertion, or vagrancy; in most cases these were offences that related directly to a daughter's failure to comply with rules at home, often because she transgressed the boundaries of normative femininity, meaning any threat to modesty and chastity.[35] For girls at this time, living outside parental discipline was widely defined in terms of "precocious sexuality."[36] [...] Boys were more commonly charged with theft (41.5%), breaking and entering, damaging property, and a wide range of public order offences. [...]

While boys' social proclivities (swearing, smoking cigarettes, attending the cinema) concerned probation officers, their sexual histories were never interrogated. Girls, in contrast, were examined by a court-appointed doctor to verify that their hymens were intact; they were also tested for venereal disease. In 1918 the girls—regardless of religion or ethnicity—were typically taken to a convent, the Provincial House of the Soeurs du Bon-Pasteur on Sherbrooke Street, for examination by a male doctor. The interrogation of delinquent girls' sexual histories by female probation officers and an intrusive pelvic examination by a male doctor were in keeping with up-to-date "progressive" juvenile corrections. [...]

[...] The results of the examinations were held as scientific evidence of delinquency to the point where a girl's words of protest or explanation were ignored or, worse, deemed lies. After examining fourteen-year-old Alice Viau in March 1918, Dr. Lebel wrote that her hymen was not intact, "bien que la jeune fille nie tous coit and toute habitude de masturbation." She denied having sexual intercourse and explained that "cet accident est arrivé par un homme qui l'a touchée de force avec sa main." Probation officer Marie Mignault did not find her denial of sexual intercourse credible and recommended to the judge that she be placed at the École de réforme.[37]

[...] Probation officers [...] were instructed to assemble personal histories for the judge. [...] [Their] reports during the First World War tell intriguing stories of adolescents engaged in all varieties of Montreal nightlife; many young women frequented the city's dance halls, moving picture theatres, skating rinks, restaurants, and even brothels. The court's standardized questionnaire, which asked for information about smoking, drinking, and attendance at dance halls and moving picture houses, suggests what indicators were evidence of juvenile delinquency. Probation officers often commented on the poor education of female delinquents. [...] Where truancy appears to have been the major preoccupation of juvenile courts elsewhere in Canada,[38] it was not central in the Montreal court at this time, in part because Quebec's compulsory schooling laws were not introduced until the 1940s. [...]

Because adolescents [...] were commonly expected to work for wages, those who rebuffed parental demands over this issue found little mercy in the court. Along with parents, probation officers defined well-behaved girls as those who worked consistently and brought home their wages. [...]

Young women working for pay proved to be a source of both income and intergenerational tension within families. Although factory work did not provide sufficient wages to permit adolescents to live on their own, it did enable them to indulge [...] in the growing commercial amusements that filled the city's downtown core. [...]

The two most common issues in female delinquency cases—precocious sexuality and refusal to contribute to the family economy—often dovetailed, as the example of Bernadette Bertrand, who failed to meet parental expectations regarding work, illustrates.[39] The Bertrand family had recently migrated from rural Quebec to working-class St. Henri. At fourteen, Bernadette worked for four months for Sweet Caporal, earning $6 weekly. Her wages were most likely important to the family economy, since her father was periodically unemployed. At the time of her court appearance she had not worked for two months and was refusing to do housework. Her father claimed that she threatened to leave Montreal to find employment in Ontario. Before she could leave the city, Bernadette's father had her charged with desertion. Judge Choquet placed her on probation and she went back to work, first at a cotton factory and then as a domestic. One year later her father again brought her to court, this time for incorrigibility. She still refused to help her mother in the home, and she was caught spending evenings at dance halls in the red-light district. Apparently willing to give up the potential wages she might have earned for the family, her father recommended that she be placed in "the convent"—a euphemistic term for the reform school run by the religious order, the Soeurs du Bon-Pasteur. The judge agreed and sentenced her to two years at the École de réforme. Although these parents depended on their daughters' incomes and expressed genuine concern when the girls took advantage of the independence that paid labour afforded them, their parental concern was often mitigated with a desire to punish daughters' errant ways.

[...] Adolescents faced harsher outcomes in parent-initiated cases.[40] In Montreal in 1918 almost 39 per cent of girls faced sentences in reform schools if their parents filed complaints against them, compared with only 17.5 per cent of cases in which parents were not responsible for bringing them to court. A juvenile court complaint lodged by parents often served as a successful warning to adolescents. In as many as 12 per cent of cases lodged by family members against girls the warrants were not executed, which many have meant the threat was enough to correct wayward behaviour, though it may have meant that the adolescent was not found. [...]

*****

[...] Ultimately, many parents wanted the juvenile court's intervention to bolster their own authority within the home, though they diverged with Judge Choquet over the disposition of cases.

*****

Choquet believed in the potential and promise of probation, boasting that of the 2000 cases he saw in 1913, only 6.5 per cent were placed in reformatory. The rest remained with their families under the "potent" influence of parents and probation officers.[41] But parental wishes often contradicted Choquet's reform position. While parents asked that their child be incarcerated in a reform or industrial school, there is no evidence from the dossiers of the Montreal Juvenile Delinquents' Court of parents asking for probation. Sometimes the parents turned to another option: admitting their daughters to the reform school "classes des volontaires" and paying for their incarceration.

*****

[...] In 1918 twenty-one girls (more than 10 per cent of 181 female delinquency cases) were committed as voluntary cases. In Montreal reform schools at the turn of the century there were two categories of incarcerees: those known as court cases and others known as "voluntary" cases. The latter category suggests a partnership in the decision-making process between judges and delinquents, or at the very least a willingness on the part of the accused to accept institutionalization. Rarely, however, did girls and boys appearing before the juvenile court volunteer to be rehabilitated at reform school; the power of volunteering rested firmly with the guardians, most often the parents, of the children in question. Often probation officers recommended voluntary status in cases where parents were able to pay or where parents were seen to be shirking their responsibilities in raising their children. Most families, though, would have found the costs prohibitive and looked to the court to absolve them of pecuniary responsibility.

The reasons parents advocated incarceration for their children defy easy categorization. Individual families chose to institutionalize adolescent girls for many reasons, among them education, supervision, and discipline. These choices reflect the continued belief in religious institutional care. [...]

Certain cases reveal that problems with a single parent or a step-parent could accentuate the delinquent acts of young women.[42] Annette Dumas, the daughter of a widowed electrician, was brought before the court in June 1918 because she stayed out until the late hours of the night.[43] When she attended school she was considered a problem, learning little; at the time of her interview with the probation officer, she was able to sign her name, "but little else." For her incorrigibility she was placed as a voluntary case at the Bon-Pasteur, and her father paid to keep her there for one year. Eighteen months later she was back in court at the behest of her father, again for incorrigibility. While she could give a long list of jobs she had held over several months, she still refused to help out at home, which put her in direct conflict with her new stepmother. She claimed that her father's wife hit her and the other children in the family. She also said she had been seduced many times by her older brother, thereby explaining the physical evidence that she had been sexually active.[44] For her behaviour, for shaming the family with claims of incest, and for accusing her stepmother of being a bad parent, her father again asked the court to send her to "the convent." This time the court sentenced her to three years.

[...] In rare cases adolescents asked probation officers if they could live with the nuns. Marianne Bienvenu, for example, told the probation officer that she wanted to stay with the Soeurs du Bon-Pasteur. Marianne's mother had died when she was thirteen months old and her father had initially put her up for adoption. In 1914, at the age of ten, Marianne's father retrieved her from the adoptive parents. In 1917 he placed her at Parc Laval (Ste-Domitille) with the Soeurs du Bon-Pasteur, where she stayed for one year. On returning to her father's home, Marianne came into conflict with her stepmother, prompting her father to bring her to court for incorrigibility. Rather than live with her father's new family, she asked the court if she could return to the Soeurs du Bon-Pasteur. The nuns accepted her into the voluntary class.[45] Such cases did not predominate, however, as the dossiers of the court illustrate the multiple strategies girls used to avoid being incarcerated.

Montreal reform and industrial schools were permitted to accept voluntary cases—those brought by parents or guardians—under the original 1869 provincial legislation that established these institutions.[46] Most reform school administrations promoted the use of the voluntary category. [...] Recruited to Montreal from France in the 1840s, the Soeurs du Bon-Pasteur created a niche for themselves in community service work involving the protection of girls and women. [...]

The smaller, less financially stable Protestant reform schools, the Boys' Farm and Training School and the Girls' Cottage Industrial School (GCIS), recruited voluntary cases to augment meager provincial subsidies that were based on the number of court cases.[47] [...] For each voluntary case the GCIS could charge as much as $10 per month, though no girl was refused on the basis of inability to pay; the directors accepted as little as 50 cents per month.[48] Towards the end of the First World War the directors of the GCIS, like those at the Boys' Farm, promoted the conception of their institution as a social agency working to prevent and correct "predelinquency." [...] Resenting the fact that the institution was being considered a last resort by the juvenile court and preferring to do more "preventive" work with predelinquents, the directors encouraged the promotion of the category of voluntary delinquent. [...] The directors were able to depend on the fact that, while Judge Choquet was reluctant to mandate incarceration, parents were not.

In the 1910s more than half the population at the Girls' Cottage Industrial School were voluntary cases.[49] Between 1913 and 1919, sixty-three girls were incarcerated: thirty-eight were voluntary cases and twenty-five were court cases. The "voluntary" girls averaged much longer sentences than did the court cases; half the voluntary cases (nineteen) waited out sentences of more than one year, some as long as four, five, or six years. Another sixteen were incarcerated for one to ten months. A much smaller percentage of the girls sentenced by the juvenile court stayed for more than one year. More than half the girls in this category were confined for less than three weeks.[50]

*****

[…] Superintendents at the school attempted to implement a one-year minimum rule for voluntary cases, but parents' authority sometimes clashed with the directors' desire to uphold the one-year rule. In 1917 the superintendent of the GCIS reported an incident involving a voluntary case that had been admitted in the autumn. At first the inmate wanted to escape and resisted her "placement" at the reform school, but within a short time had "settled down for a proper training."[51] According to the administration of the institution, the girl's mother sabotaged the school's progress with her by removing the daughter before year end. This parent had found her daughter a job at a rubber factory and apparently preferred that her daughter work rather than stay at the industrial school. […]

The solution to social problems such as delinquency became a subject of debate in industrializing Montreal. In 1912, the year the juvenile court opened, more than 300,000 people visited Montreal's Child Welfare Exhibit to witness the most up-to-date plan for healthy, disciplined, and educated children. The organizers, Anna Louise Strong and Rufus D. Smith, gave space to Catholic, Protestant, and Jewish organizations, but later warned of the propensity of the Catholic community to continue interning children.[52] They cautioned:

Montreal seems not to know that she is threatening to turn herself into that Frankenstein of mismanaged charity, an "institutionalized"

city …. So it was that in the [Child Welfare] exhibition sections on philanthropy, law and industry, a strong stand was made for the integrity of the home against the easy and insidious encroachment of the institution. The extension of careful case work in order to stop the breaking up the family and the building up of a more accurate, substantial body of facts in regard to the actual conditions surrounding home life were urged.[53]

On the surface the debate over the role of the family in industrial society appears to have revolved around Catholic-Protestant differences in approach to, and construction of, social problems, but the reality was more complex.

Internment must be placed within the context of prevailing ideas about the child in Quebec culture and traditions among the predominantly Catholic working class. The Catholic Church played a major role in the education and socialization of children well into the twentieth century. […] Childhood in general was to be spent most appropriately in religious institutions cloistered from the outside world, including the child's family.[54] [P]arents' right to intern children was bolstered by the fact that the child's identity in law was submerged within the family under the male patriarch.[55] According to the Civil Code of 1866, the child was considered the property of the parents, tutor/guardian, or custodians of religious institutions.

[…] Single parents, especially mothers, made frequent use of institutions. The latest ideas governing child welfare were simply not practicable to the families who relied on institutional care for their children, as the case of Aline Guingras illustrates. When Aline's widowed mother went out to work, she placed most of her children in institutions. Of four children, one daughter was married, one son and another daughter were placed in the convent of the Sisters of Providence, and Aline was sent to work for the same order of nuns at their Maison des Sourdes et Muettes. When the Sisters of Providence brought Aline forward for theft and it became clear there was no supervision at home, they put her in the classe des volontaires at the Maison de Lorette under the Soeurs du Bon-Pasteur.[56] […]

In the rest of Canada, ideas supporting internment of dependent, neglected, and delinquent children were beginning to change. While the nineteenth century was "one of institutions," the twentieth saw an invigorated commitment to the "natural" family setting as the optimal environment for children in their formative years.[57] Fundamental to the advancement of probation was the rejection of the reform and industrial schools experiment.[58] […] Sutherland and others suggest that the shift to probation and away from institutionalization in English Canada happened in the early twentieth century owing to shifts in social science thinking, particularly in child psychology. The child was no longer considered property, but a person in need of protection.[59] In Quebec the turn away from internment was evident by the mid twentieth century, peaking after 1960 in the Quiet Revolution, when religious institutions were increasingly replaced by secular solutions and facilities.[60]

While detractors of the network of religious institutions appeared to be Anglophone Protestants, as with the case of the organizers of the Child Welfare Exhibition, the move away from internment of children also came from within the Catholic community.[61] Ethnicity and tradition played major roles here, but it would not be entirely correct to state that the issue split Quebecers along religious and ethnic lines. Indeed, François-Xavier Choquet, the first judge of the juvenile court and president of the Children's Aid Society, favoured secular solutions to juvenile delinquency such as probation, while still supporting reform school sentences for extreme cases. Protestant reform

school boards[,] for their part [,] encouraged parents to incarcerate their children, especially children of poor families, even when evidence of delinquency was slim. The disposition of delinquent daughters in the Montreal Juvenile Delinquents' Court, then, was determined by the tension between the secular solution of probation and the long-standing tradition of interning children, especially with religious orders among the working class.

When the new juvenile court opened in 1912, it required the participation of working-class parents to generate a clientele. With a vague definition of delinquency, parents brought their daughters to court for a wide variety of social-sexual activities that displeased their parents. Court officials often concurred with parents in condemning the behaviour of their daughters, promoting the new probation system to correct that wayward behaviour. Many parents, however, often preferred to see daughters placed in reform institutions, especially those run by religious orders. If Judge Choquet would not mandate incarceration, parents asked that the delinquent be admitted to the reform schools' voluntary classes. In this early history of the court, the rights of children were subordinated to the state's broad definition of delinquency, and its attempt to be an arbiter of family relations. Children's rights also fell victim to the reform school administrators' determination to preserve their social function, as well as to the prerogative of parents to intern their children. Judge Choquet's court was infused with "progressive" juvenile justice thinking, but this new system had to be grafted onto a society in which internment as a solution to familial problems persisted well into the twentieth century.

Notes

1.   Anthony M. Platt, *The Child Savers: The Invention of Delinquency* (Chicago: University of Chicago Press 1969); Steven L. Schlossman, *Love and the American Delinquent* (Chicago: University of Chicago Press 1977); Ellen Ryerson, *The Best-Laid Plans: America's Juvenile Court Experiment* (New York: Hill and Wang 1978); Jacques Donzelot, *The Policing of Families* (New York: Pantheon 1979); Neil Sutherland, *Children in English-Canadian Society: Framing the Twentieth-Century*

Consensus (Toronto: University of Toronto Press 1976).

2. Mary E. Odem, *Delinquent Daughters: Protecting and Policing Adolescent Female Sexuality in the United States, 1885–1920* (Chapel Hill: University of North Carolina Press 1995), chap. 6; Dorothy M. Chunn, "Boys Will Be Men, Girls Will Be Mothers: The Legal Regulation of Childhood in Toronto and Vancouver," *Sociological Studies in Child Development 3* (1990): 107.

3. Andrée Lévesque, "Eteindre le 'Red Light': Les réformateurs et la prostitution à Montréal, 1865–1925," *Urban History Review* 17, 3 (1989): 191–201; Tamara Myers, "Women Policing Women: A Patrol of Women in Montreal in the 1910s," *Journal of the Canadian Historical Association* 4 (1993): 229–45; Andrée Lévesque, *Making and Breaking the Rules: Women in Quebec, 1919–1939,* trans. Yvonne M. Klein (Toronto: McClelland & Stewart 1994), 53.

4. Carolyn Strange, *Toronto's Girl Problem: The Perils and Pleasures of the City, 1880–1930* (Toronto: University of Toronto Press 1995); Jennifer Stephen, "The 'Incorrigible,' the 'Bad,' and the 'Immoral': Toronto's 'Factory Girls' and the Work of the Toronto Psychiatric Clinic," in Louis A. Knafla and Susan W.S. Binnie, eds., *Law, Society, and the State: Essays in Modern Legal History* (Toronto: University of Toronto Press 1995), 413.

5. Based on an examination of plumatifs and dossiers of the Montreal Juvenile Delinquents' Court held by the Ministère de la Justice du Québec at the Centre de Pré-Archivage.

6. In addition to the works by Platt, Schlossman, Ryerson, Donzelot, and Sutherland cited above, see Alison J. Hatch and Curt T. Griffiths, "Child Saving Postponed: The Impact of the Juvenile Delinquents Act on the Processing of Young Offenders in Vancouver," in Russell Smandych, Gordon Dodds, and Alvin Esau, eds., *Dimensions of Childhood: Essays on the History of Children and Youth in Canada* (Winnipeg: Legal Research Institute 1991), 233–266.

7. See, for example, Linda Gordon, "Family Violence, Feminism and Social Control," in Ellen Carol Dubois and Vicki L. Ruiz, eds., *Unequal Sisters: A Multicultural Reader in U.S. Women's History* (New York: Routledge 1990), 141–56; Eileen Boris, "Restructuring the 'Family': Women, Progressive Reform, and the Problem of Social Control," in Noralee Frankel and Nancy S. Dye, eds., *Gender, Class, Race and Reform in the Progressive Era* (Lexington: University of Kentucky Press 1991),

110–26; Elizabeth J. Clapp, "Welfare and the Role of Women: The Juvenile Court Movement," *Journal of American Studies* 28 (1994): 359–83.

8. Odem, *Delinquent Daughters*, 158.

9. Linda Gordon, "Feminism and Social Control: The Case of Child Abuse and Neglect," in Juliet Mitchell and Ann Oakley, eds., *What Is Feminism? A Reexamination* (New York: Pantheon Books 1986), 63–84; and her *Heroes of Their Own Lives: The Politics and History of Family Violence* (New York: Penguin Books 1988).

10. See Sutherland, *Children in English-Canadian Society*, chap. 8; John Bullen, "J.J. Kelso and the 'New' Child-Savers: the Genesis of the Children's Aid Movement in Ontario," in Smandych, Dodds, and Esau, *Dimensions of Childhood*, 135–58; Andrew Jones and Leonard Rutman, *In the Children's Aid: J.J. Kelso and Child Welfare in Ontario* (Toronto: University of Toronto Press 1981); Patricia T. Rooke and R.L. Schnell, *Discarding the Asylum: From Child Rescue to the Welfare State in English Canada* (New York: University Press of America 1983).

11. Dorothy E. Chunn, *From Punishment to Doing Good: Family Courts and Socialized Justice in Ontario, 1880–1940* (Toronto: University of Toronto Press 1992), 25.

12. Until the early twentieth century, the process of segregating youths in the criminal justice system was mainly restricted to the incarceration experience; in Canadian courts and local jails, youths were still often exposed to accused adults. Starting at the mid nineteenth century, youths under sixteen years of age had been conferred a "special legal status" through legislation pertaining to trials and punishment.

The Criminal Code of 1892 and An Act Respecting Arrest, Trial and Imprisonment of Youthful Offenders (SC 1894, c. 58) also provided for the possibility of trying juveniles separately from adults. With child protection legislation in place, the door was opened for the possibility of courts that dealt exclusively with minor children. Jean Trépanier, "Origins of the Juvenile Delinquents Act of 1908: Controlling Delinquency through Seeking Its Causes and through Youth Protection," in Smandych, Dodds, and Esau, *Dimensions of Childhood*, 206.

13. W.L. Scott, *The Juvenile Court in Law and the Juvenile Court in Action* (Ottawa: Canadian Council on Child Welfare 1930), 50. The JDA defined the juvenile delinquent as "any child who violates any provision of *The Criminal Code* ... or of any Dominion or provincial statute, or of any

by-law or ordinance of any municipality … or, who is liable by reason of any other act to be committed to an industrial school or juvenile reformatory. …" Canada, An Act respecting Juvenile Delinquents, 7–8 Ed. VII, c. 40.

14. Lucien A. Beaulieu, "A Comparison of Judicial Roles under the JDA and YOA," in Alan W. Leschied, Peter G. Jaffe, and Wayne Willis, eds., *The Young Offenders Act: A Resolution in Canadian Juvenile Justice* (Toronto: University of Toronto Press 1991), 131. Situating the juvenile court in the realm of the therapeutic state, Andrew J. Polsky argues that the "institution took its distinctive shape from tutelary doctrine rather than juridical or penal forerunners." See "The Odyssey of the Juvenile Court: Policy Failure and Institutional Persistence," *Studies in American Political Development* 3 (1989): 161.

15. The provinces proceeded slowly. Twenty years after the JDA, only eighteen cities had juvenile courts. Hatch and Griffiths, "Child Saving Postponed," 234. See also Canadian Welfare Council, *Juvenile Courts in Canada*, Publication No. 121 (Ottawa 1942).

16. Quebec, *Débats* de l'assemblé législative, 6 mai 1910, 493.

17. *Montreal, 1535–1914: Biographical*, vol. 3 (Montreal: S.J. Clarke Publishing Company 1914), 594–5.

18. Montreal *Gazette*, 3 Jan. 1912, 3.

19. Rose Henderson, "The Juvenile Court," *Canadian Municipal Journal* (March 1916): 84.

20. Juvenile courts were one justice arena where women were successful in attaining the position of judge. Ethel MacLaughlin of the Juvenile Court of Regina and Helen Gregory MacGill of Vancouver are two examples. See Elsie Gregory MacGill, *My Mother the Judge* (Toronto: Ryerson Press 1955).

21. This committee consisted of religious and lay leaders of three communities, as reported by the Montreal *Gazette*, 3 Jan. 1912, 3.

22. Unlike the confessionality of Quebec's education and hospital systems but in keeping with the province's judicial practice of non-confessional courts, the Quebec government established one juvenile court in Montreal in 1910 to serve all religions (Quebec, An Act respecting juvenile delinquents, 1910, I Geo. V, c. 26; section VI of the act established the Juvenile Delinquents' Court in Montreal). The court's non-confessionality aroused the ire first of the Roman Catholics and later of Anglophones. In 1915 *Le Devoir*, suspicious of the court's Protestant and American tendencies, called for confessional juvenile courts. While a court system constructed along religious lines was never created, the importance of Catholicism in the court system was emphasized in the newspaper: "Assurer le respect des consciences des enfants, et des consciences catholiques plus exigeantes, pousser ce respect jusqu'au scrupule, ce doit être votre première préoccupation dans l'organisation d'une Cour Juvénile"; *Le Devoir*, 17 avril 1915, I. In the early 1930s the Anglophone press similarly argued for a separate court for the (predominantly non-Catholic) English-speaking community. Lillian E. Mendelsohn and Sharon Ronald, "History of the Montreal Juvenile Court" (MSW thesis, McGill University 1969), 49.

23. See the Federation of Jewish Philanthropies, *Annual Reports* (1920s), and the Canadian Jewish Congress National Archives, MB I, series B, Box I, file "Juvenile Aid Department."

24. Henderson, "The Juvenile Court," 84.

25. Strange, *Toronto's Girl Problem*, chaps. 4 and 5; Chunn, "Boys Will Be Men," 92–3; Stephen, "The Incorrigible," 413–15.

26. Some 213 female cases originated in 1918. For purposes of this research I eliminated the 33 cases that concerned neglected and abandoned girls. The new dossiers generated in 1918 numbered 1105. (This number is probably a low estimate as, occasionally, if more than one adolescent was arrested, only one file number was assigned. As well, cases dealt with informally were not given file numbers. The juvenile court officials claimed they dealt with 2000 plus cases annually during the First World War, including recidivists, and neglected and abandoned children.) Male cases numbered 892; my sample consisted of 92 boys.

27. Paul André Linteau, *Histoire des Montréal depuis le Confédération* (Montreal: Boréal 1992), 162, 317–18.

28. Relationship of complainant in 101 cases of female adolescents before the Juvenile Delinquents' Court in 1918: 49 (48.5%) mother; 39 (38.6%) father, 8 (8%) aunt/uncle; 1 (1%) of each—brother, guardian, step-parent, cousin, brother-in-law (percentages are rounded off and therefore add up to 100.1%).

29. In 1912, the year the court opened, it heard 771 cases. Girls were involved in just over 9 per cent of cases. Montreal Juvenile Delinquents' court, plumatifs and dossiers, 1912.

30. Revised Statutes of Quebec, 1999, Article 4036.

31. Dr. I.J. Lemieux, "Report of the Administrator of the Detention House for Young Delinquents of the City of Montreal," in Quebec, *Sessional Papers* (1914). Judge Choquet fully supported

the widening of the description of delinquency. Choquet to Lomer Gouin, 28 Nov. 1912, Quebec, *Documents de la Session* (1912).

32. The number of adolescents appearing before the court increased in 1913.

33. Clio Collective, *Quebec Women: A History*, 255 (Article 245).

34. Of the 101 female cases initiated by parents, it was possible to determine the status of the parents' marriages in 69. Of the forty-nine mothers who filed complaints, nineteen were clearly widowed or not living with their husbands (twelve separated, seven widowed). Eight of the fathers who complained were similarly on their own.

35. This interpretation would be made explicit in an amendment to the JDA in 1924, which specified that anyone "who is guilty of sexual immorality or any other form of vice" would be considered a delinquent. Bruno Théorêt, "Régulation juridique pénale des mineures et discrimination à l'égard des filles: La clause de 1924 amendant la Loi sur les jeunes délinquents," *Canadian Journal of Women and the Law* 4 (1990–1): 541.

36. This term was first employed by Steven Schlossman and Stephanie Wallach in "The Crime of Precocious Sexuality: Female Juvenile Delinquency in the Progressive Era," *Harvard Educational Review* 48, I (1978): 65–95.

37. Choquet rejected this advice and returned Alice to her parents on her promise to be good. Within a year, however, the judge had changed his mind as she continued, according to her parents, to lie and steal money to attend the theatre and threatened to spend nights out. MJDC, no. 4689, 26 Feb. 1918.

38. Chunn, "Boys Will Be Men," 97.

39. MJDC, no. 4650, 5 Feb. 1918 (follow-up, 26 March 1919).

40. This was also the case in some American jurisdictions. See Dale Dannefer, "Who Signs the Complaint? Relational Distance and the Juvenile Justice Process," *Law and Society Review* 18, 2 (1984): 249–70.

41. Choquet, "The Juvenile Court," *Canadian Municipal Journal* (June 1914): 232.

42. See Peter Gossage, "La marâtre: Marie-Anne Houde and the Myth of the Wicked Stepmother in Quebec," *Canadian Historical Review* 76, 4 (1995): 563–97, and "Tangled Webs: Remarriage and Family Conflict in 19th-Century Quebec," in Tamara Myers et al., eds., *Power, Place and Identity: Historical Studies of Social and Legal Regulation in Quebec* (Montreal: Montreal History Group 1998).

43. MJDC, no. 5007, 11 June 1918.

44. On incest cases in this court, see T. Myers, "Qui t'a débauchée?: Female Adolescent Sexuality and the Juvenile Delinquents' Court in Early Twentieth-Century Montreal," in Ed Montigny and Lori Chambers, eds., *Family Matters: Papers in Post-Confederation Canadian Family History* (Toronto: Canadian Scholars' Press 1998), 377–94.

45. MJDC, no. 4726, 11 March 1918.

46. Statutes of Quebec, An Act respecting Industrial Schools/Reform Schools, 32 Vict., c. 17, 1869.

47. The aggressive recruiting of voluntary cases at the Boys Farm and Training School is discussed in Prue Rains and Eli Teram, *Normal Bad Boys: Public Policies, Institutions, and the Politics of Client Recruitment* (Montreal and Kingston: McGill-Queen's University Press 1992), chap. 2.

48. Underfunding problems were chronic at the GCIS, especially in its first decade. The annual reports from the period illustrate their indebtedness to benefactors.

49. National Archives of Canada, Girls' Cottage School, MG 28, I 404, vol. I, file 34. "The Girls' Cottage School: Historical Report. Summary of Cases [1919]."

50. If the voluntary girls' committal depended on their parents or guardians, so, too, did their release. Almost half were released after months and years in the institution on the request of parents. Another quarter of these girls were placed by the GCIS into domestic service.

51. Girls' Cottage Industrial School, *Annual Report*, 1917, 14.

52. Anna Louise Strong and Rufus D. Smith, "Beneath the Surface in Montreal," *Canadian Municipal Journal*, Jan. 1913; The Child Welfare Exhibit, *Souvenir Pamphlet*, 1912.

53. Strong and Smith, "Beneath the Surface in Montreal."

54. See Philippe Ariès, *Centuries of Childhood*, trans. Robert Baldick (New York: Alfred A. Knopf 1962); John Gillis, *Youth and History: Tradition and Change in European Age Relations, 1770–Present* (New York: Academic Press 1974).

55. For a discussion of the origins of "la puissance paternelle" in French law, see Pierre Petot, *Histoire du droit privé français: La Famille* (Paris: Éditions Loysel 1992), 365–83.

56. MJDC, no. 5137, 17 July 1918.

57. Trépanier, "Origins of the Juvenile Delinquents Act of 1908," 216; Sutherland, *Children in English-Canadian Society*, 100; Rooke and Schnell, *Discarding the Asylum*.

58. Andrew Jones, "Closing Penetanguishene Reformatory: An Attempt to Deinstitutionalize Treatment of Juvenile Offenders in Early Twentieth-Century Ontario," *Ontario History* 70 (1978): 227.

59. John Alan Lee, "Three Paradigms of Childhood," *Canadian Review of Sociology and Anthropology* 19, 4 (1982): 591–608.

60. A good example of this process is the women's prison being taken over by the state in 1964.

See Danielle Lacasse, *La prostitution féminine à Montréal, 1945–1970* (Montreal: Boréal 1994).

61. One historian has argued that the impact of social sciences on Quebec education and social welfare institutions beginning in the 1930s eventually led to a rejection of institutionalization. Marie-Paule Malouin, *L'univers des enfants en difficulté au Québec entre 1940 et 1960* (Montreal: Bellarmin 1996), 59.

CHAPTER 10

Governing Mentalities: The Deportation of "Insane" and "Feebleminded" Immigrants out of British Columbia from Confederation to World War II

Robert Menzies[*]

● ● ● ● ● ● ● ● ● ● ● ● ● ● ● ● ● ●

*****

Introduction

From Confederation through to 1939, more than 5,000 people were deported from Canada as "insane" or "feebleminded" under the provisions of the federal Immigration Act. In the province of British Columbia, 750 mental hospital patients were officially removed or informally repatriated to their countries of origin through the 1920s and 1930s alone.[1] In late 19th- and early 20th-century Canada, banishment was an increasingly popular strategy for the regulation of mentally disordered populations. Burdened by hospital overcrowding and underfunding, and seeking to expand their influence and exercise control over the quality of patients admitted to their institutions, medical superintendents forged alliances with provincial bureaucrats, federal immigration authorities, and a variety of nativist and restrictionist groups to assemble a powerful and efficient system for jettisoning those new Canadians who failed to meet the mental standards for Canadian citizenship. Bolstered by theories of eugenics and race betterment, and drawing on public fears about unregulated immigration and the spectre of insanity, psychiatric officials turned to deportation as an opportune and generally permanent device for ridding hospitals of their

least-wanted inmates. Like other dependent, delinquent, redundant, and politically dangerous populations,[2] the mentally disordered and cognitively disabled represented a convenient target for the practitioners of deportation.[3] Despite resistances from foreign governments, transportation companies, and pro-immigration groups, and in individual cases from deports themselves and their allies, the practice of medical banishment proved to be an immensely successful enterprise. Over the first four decades of this century alone, during which more than 80,000 people were removed or rejected at our ocean ports,[4] about a tenth of all deportations and half of medical exiles were ordered out of Canada on the grounds of imputed insanity or feeblemindedness.[5]

This paper chronicles the role of British Columbian provincial authorities and medical practitioners in securing the removal of those immigrants deemed unworthy of citizenship by virtue of their disordered and deficient mentalities. Enlisting provincial and federal government records and correspondence, hospital documents, media reports, and clinical files, I explore the official and professional discourses and strategies that were invoked for the purpose of identifying and expelling such mentally inadequate aliens. I argue more generally that the deportation of "insane" and other "undesirable" immigrants was nourished by the flood of nativist, rac(ial)ist, exclusionist, eugenist, and mental hygienist thinking that dominated British Columbian and Canadian politics and public culture throughout this "golden age" of deportation.

In the context of the time, it is scarcely surprising that deportation should have presented such an attractive safety valve for the guardians of British Columbia's segregative institutions, or that the mentally disordered were considered such prime candidates for expulsion. Through the turn of century and beyond, as progressivist ideas flourished and an incipient welfare state began to germinate, radically new ideas emerged about the quality and scope of citizenship and governmentality.[6] The province and country were experiencing convulsive transitions towards an industrialized economy, an urbanized workforce, a public system of regulation and care, innovative technologies of communication and transportation, and a rapidly diversifying population amid the mammoth immigration boom of the pre-World War I period. Tumultuous cycles of economic expansion and depression; intensifying labour-capital conflict; and the continuing contradictions of class, race, and gender combined to destabilize the conventions of liberal laissez-faire politics and to explode the notions of autonomous free citizenship and non-interventionist state minimalism that they had embodied. They occasioned the apprehensions of the nation's elites who were desirous of preserving their affluence and influence, and of white male workers and agriculturalists who were struggling to retain what few advantages they had wrested from their 19th-century world.[7]

With these staggering social transformations came efforts from the country's political and organizational leadership, and from their allies in intellectual and cultural contexts, to fundamentally rethink the relationship between the individual and the state. The myriad benefits of citizenship in Laurier's new century of Canada—the promises of prosperity, sociality, security, and freedom it embraced—were seen to demand reciprocal contributions from those who sought membership. As a *Toronto Globe* editorialist wrote in 1910:

[t]he problem of citizenship is quite the most serious on Canada's program to-day .... Immigrants of to-day will be the voters of tomorrow .... It is of the very essence of Canadian democracy that every citizen .... shall take his part in the country's government. If a people has no aptitude for self-government, that people has not the first qualification for citizenship in Canada.[8]

Coupled with such citizen duties were the economic obligations to the community and the nation that befell all individuals. In the words of Henry Esson Young, British Columbia's Provincial Health Officer and former Provincial Secretary, "[t]he human being is beginning to be looked on not as an individual altogether independent from other individuals and from the community, but as an economic unit of the community who has a very definite productive value."[9]

But not all prospective entrants to the British Columbian and Canadian way of life were deemed worthy. The racialist debarment of Chinese, Japanese, Sikh, Doukhobor, and First Nations peoples has been long documented.[10] For their part, the vast majority of women were consigned to a subordinated subjecthood forged from ideologies of domesticity, fertility, and motherhood, and were sequestered far from the seductive realms of public life, congregate labour, and the franchise.[11] The quintessential Canadian citizen was white, male, productive, responsible, and compliant. In "exercising its prerogative to select suitable future citizens,"[12] the state invoked powerful images of social order, and of well-regulated minds and bodies. These ideas, and the laws and practices they spawned, permitted authorities both to discipline those who had inherited or achieved citizenship and to disqualify others whose attributes or conduct fell short of apprehended standards.

One further criterion for citizenship eligibility was the candidate's ascribed aptitude for reasoned, rational, and intelligent participation in public and private affairs. The new citizen was conceived as an enlightened and stable being who could absorb the lessons of this progressive social order and contribute both culturally and genetically to the nation's betterment. In contrast, those disordered and defective souls who carried the millstones of madness or imbecility were "indigestible lumps"[13] who gravitated to the lowest social echelons, bloated the rolls of asylums and penitentiaries, polluted the national gene pool, and were incapable of assimilation into the good life of rectitude, hygiene, and (re)productive labour. British Columbia and Canada were already burdened with the care of disordered and deficient charges who had unavoidably been born into citizenship. But it was beyond tolerance that they should be expected further to assume responsibility for the human detritus of other countries. Deportation, along with medical examination and rejection prior to entry, were adopted as the preferred strategies for defending the mental frontiers of province and nation. Moreover, as the 20th century progressed, psychiatrists and immigration authorities assembled a litany of theories and methods for scientifically screening out insane and feebleminded immigrants. The result was a convoluted legal and administrative apparatus that traversed provincial, federal, and international spheres, and that in its operation revealed much about the values, preoccupations, and fears of citizenry and state during this volatile period in British Columbian and Canadian history.

Historical Patterns of Rejection and Removal

Prior to 1902, there were no systematic data published on the exclusion or expulsion of Canadian immigrants, insane, feebleminded, or otherwise. Thereafter, according to statistics compiled by the Immigration Branch of the federal government[14] (see Table 1), among the 59,734 official deportations effected from Canada between fiscal years 1902–1903 and 1938–1939, 10,840 were for medical causes.

For the years in which medical cases were disaggregated by category in the official reports (29 of 37 years across the period in question),[15] "insanity" and "mental defect" accounted respectively for 40 percent and nine percent of all such removals. Extrapolating these proportions through the eight missing years results in an estimated total of 4,344 deportations for reasons of insanity, and another 947 based on "deficiency" or "feeblemindedness." Therefore, nearly a tenth of all those deported from the country through to World War II were ousted on the basis of their purported psychiatric condition. Moreover, of 22,142 persons refused admission to Canada at the country's ocean ports of entry, 5,961 were rejected for medical reasons. While separate statistics were assembled only through the 1918–1919 fiscal year, up to that point 153 aspiring immigrants had been rejected as insane, and another 280 as mentally defective.

In British Columbia, the statistical summaries of patient movements contained in the psychiatric hospital annual reports[16] throughout the inter-war period permit an aggregate look at deportation practices in the province's mental health system (see Table 2). Between fiscal years 1921–1922 and 1937–1938, 553 inpatients resident in British Columbia's three main psychiatric institutions[17] were officially deported, and from 1926–1927 to 1936–1937 (the only years for which such records were kept) another 197 were informally repatriated (ostensibly with their consent and/or the cooperation of family or friends). For the years reported, deportations represented 5.8 percent of all discharges from the province's hospitals, and informal returns contributed another 3.0 percent. The annual tally of deportations peaked in 1931–1932 at 60 (11.2 percent of all discharges for that year). Shortly thereafter, however, emulating the sharp decline by mid-Depression of overall immigration and deportation statistics across the country, the number of insanity deportations from British Columbia plummeted. By fiscal years 1936–1937 and 1937–1938, only two and eight patients respectively were subjected to deportation, and thereafter the psychiatric authorities ceased publishing deportation statistics altogether.

British Columbia's medical authorities also amassed systematic data on the origin, gender, and length of time hospitalized and in Canada for all persons deported over the 15-year period between 1921–1922 and 1935–1936. As depicted in Table 3, 5,099 of 8,201 psychiatric admissions for whom information was available (62.2 percent) were foreign-born, with England (36.1 percent), Scotland (12.5 percent), and the United States (11.5 percent) being the most frequent points of origin. While these three countries were again prominent in the enumeration of patients actually deported, overall there were striking variations in the proportionate representation of different nations in the admission and deportation statistics. For example, only 5.8 percent of Scots, 6.7 of English, and 9.9 percent of U.S.-American patients were returned to their homeland. In contrast, the 15 deportations of Czechoslovaks represented a full 65 percent of admissions from that country. Other groups with remarkably high deportation-to-admission ratios included Hungarians (40 percent) and those from Jugoslavia/Serbia/Montenegro (38 percent), Switzerland (36 percent), and Finland (35 percent). Just a single patient originating in the Soviet Union was deported in these years, owing largely to the prevailing Soviet practice of revoking the citizenship of its émigrés.[18]

When it came to gender (see Table 4), there were measurable differences in the susceptibility of men and women mental patients to deportation. Of 543 B.C. psychiatric patients jettisoned from the country, 453 (83.4 percent) were male. These represented 8.9 percent of all men certified to the province's psychiatric hospitals during the time period, while in comparison the 90 deported women comprised only 3 percent of female admissions. These gender differences were no doubt at least partially attributable to the higher proportions among the men of unmarried migratory workers with little social support in their adopted country and relatively few impediments to removal.

In the lower part of Table 4, the number of years spent by patients in Canada prior to hospitalization, and time in hospital before deportation, are enumerated. The average tenure in the country was 2.69 years, with a range from less than one through to 23 years. Worthy of note is the finding that 40 of the 541 individuals (7.4 percent) had been in the country for at least the minimum five years necessary to establish domicile under the federal Immigration Act—a status which under normal circumstances should have shielded them from the invocation of deportation proceedings.[19] Lastly, the majority of patients (456, or 84.0 percent) were deported within the first year of hospitalization (with an overall mean of 1.04 years), although in a few isolated cases long-term inmates were also subjected to expulsion. In most instances, the medical superintendents of British Columbia's hospitals, as subsequent sections will reveal, were determined to expel foreign patients at the earliest opportunity with a view to conserving resources and opening up beds.

Desultory Beginnings

The formal legal machinery for the exclusion and deportation of insane persons and other "prohibited classes" evolved in stages from the passage of the first federal Immigration Act in 1869.[20] This legislation provided, among other things, for the appointment of immigration officers at Canadian ports of entry, and with some exceptions barred entry into the country of "every lunatic, idiot, deaf, dumb, blind or infirm person."[21] With amendments to the Act in 1887[22] came the authority to repatriate ineligible migrants to "the port whence they came." Prior to the turn of century, however, there were no formally entrenched procedures for the deportation of those who had already entered the country.

During these first few post-Confederation decades, medical professionals in the province of British Columbia had already begun to focus their attention on the insane immigrant as a potent source of social perils. The burgeoning asylum system in B.C., as elsewhere, provided a highly fertile context for the fostering of ideas about dangerously insane foreigners, and an ideal institutional site for the identification, containment, and removal of these populations. From the very inauguration of the Victoria Lunatic Asylum in 1872, the state psychiatric apparatus in B.C. rapidly developed into the province's predominant site of segregative confinement.[23] In the process, a succession of medical superintendents, along with their political mentors in the Provincial Secretariat and Cabinet, soon joined and ultimately came to conduct the chorus of voices decrying the influx of undesirables and unfits into the newly confederated Western province.

During the earliest years of the British Columbian asylum establishment, the trepidations of medical authorities were couched in the discourse of moral economy, and were targeted mainly on the parasitic waifs and strays of the British homeland who were allegedly being foisted on the province and country through the invigilant policies and practices of immigration authorities, while scattered informal removals of "lunatics" had occurred as early as the 1850s, the first officially recorded repatriations of mental patients from B.C. were recounted in 1896 by Medical Superintendent G.F. Bodington (1894–1900). Bodington, a recent immigrant himself, had presided over an asylum in the English Midland Counties for 17 years before relocating to Western Canada. Bodington noted in his Annual Report for 1896 that one woman and four men had been shipped back to friends in Liverpool, "two of them at their own cost, and three ... partly at the cost of the Provincial Government." He stressed that these patients were all linked by the obvious constitutional underpinnings of their disorders: "... in one the patient was of feeble intellect, and the insanity strongly hereditary, in another the patient was obviously weak-minded originally, and a third was a pronounced epileptic with consequent mania, while the brother and sister suffered from strong family taint." In his case summary, Bodington was moved to wax indignant about

"the practice too much in vogue in Great Britain, of shipping off to the colonies weak-minded young persons who are unmanageable at home, and unable to make a career for themselves, or earn a livelihood here." According to the good doctor, "the struggles and difficulties of Colonial life" were too great a burden for such an "undesirable class of immigrants" who, once "sent out to get rid of, ... naturally gravitate to the Asylum and swell the ranks of the already too numerous lunatics [thereby] adding to the pecuniary burden of the province."[24]

Throughout his tenure as medical superintendent and as the asylum rolls inflated, Bodington continued to agitate for the removal of defective interlopers. The moral pragmatism of his rhetoric, and his social darwinistic explanations for the crisis of insanity that was breaking out around him, contained the seeds from which the more overtly nativist and racialist thinking among his successors would germinate for a generation to come. As he wrote in 1897, addressing the remarks to both provincial authorities and his "brethren" in Britain:

I cannot too strongly urge the inexpediency [*sic*] of shipping off either from the East or from Europe the wastrels of society. Useless and unmanageable as they may be at home, they become still more useless and unmanageable in the remote West, where the difficulties of life to be encountered are greater and the resources at command for their relief are less than those to be met within old and more settled communities. It seems to be forgotten that life in the colonies is not easier than it is at home. It requires for success men not only stalwart in body, but healthy in mind .... [P]atients who are the subjects of incipient or borderland insanity, or of inveterate moral depravity, or any form of mental deviation or twist ... arrive at the west coast, and being confronted by the Pacific Ocean, can wander no further. [T]heir condition becomes aggravated many-fold. They throw discredit upon the old countries whence they sprang .... [T]hey gravitate to our Asylum and tend to swell unfairly the percentages of lunatics to population. They are not wanted in the Province, where they are looked down upon as undesirable vagrants .... Any medical practitioner having to deal with a case of this kind should remember before "shipping the patient off to the colonies," that he is not likely by so doing to drive the unclean spirit out of the man. He may truly be sending him where he will walk through dry places seeking rest but finding none, but in the end, too frequently "the last state of that man is worse than the first."[25]

True to his hyperbole, and despite the fact that formal legal authority via the Immigration Act was still several years away, Bodington managed to jettison numerous patients to their homeland during the years of his superintendency. Most of these were conveyed individually in the company of family or friends, although on occasion group returns were also engineered. One such example was chronicled by Bodington in 1899, when, spurred by "an accumulation of similar cases in the Asylum over-crowding the building and creating a serious drain upon the resources of the Institution and the revenues of the Province," the Provincial Secretariat arranged for the mass expulsion of 22 patients, "of whom 13 went to the United Kingdom, 7 to Eastern Canada, and 2 to the United States." The costs were borne by the Province.[26]

Subsequent ranks of psychiatric and state authorities in British Columbia continued to pursue the extraction of unfit outsiders as the new century unfolded. New Westminster Medical Superintendent G.H. Manchester (1900–1905) had prior experience with foreign patients during his three years as a physician at the Verdun Protestant Hospital in Montreal. Like his forerunner, Manchester endeavoured to usher immigrant patients out of the province whenever the opportunity arose. Manchester expressed special alarm about what he considered the laxity of assessment procedures for screening out mentally unsound candidates for citizenship. Advocating heightened vigilance, Manchester protested the state's enlistment of the asylum as

a dumping ground for cases gone awry while, at the same time, authorities were failing to address the more pernicious folly of a promiscuous federal immigration program. Some officials, he allowed, "do not seem to understand that it is not the wish of the Government to permanently support all the foreign insane, who may be either accidentally or intentionally brought to our provincial doors, and they may gather them in with never a thought as to where they came from, so long as they know an easy way of getting rid of them for the time being." The inundation of such defective souls from afar was not merely a mental health problem, but presented an inherent social risk that demanded more forceful measures. The province's police, for example, "ought to be instructed that it is their business to help protect the country from this kind of imposition and to make inquiry into the origin of every wandering lunatic, with a view to repatriating him if possible."[27]

Authorities viewed the 1901 case of "The Honourable" F.J.L.[28] to be emblematic of this alleged inundation of "weak-minded" British and Continental immigrants into the Canadian hinterland. The son of an English Earl and described as "a wealthy and highly respected rancher of the Columbia valley,"[29] F.J.L. had migrated to British Columbia in the 1890s and purchased land near Canal Flats. In May of 1901, with little warning, F.J.L., then 29 years of age, shot and killed his Chinese cook with a 45-90 Winchester rifle. While violence against Chinese immigrants was scarcely an exceptional occurrence in frontier B.C., the abrupt and purportedly motiveless nature of this particular incident implied a pathological origin. At his subsequent arraignment, F.J.L. was bundled off to the Public Hospital for the Insane under Manchester's care. The latter diagnosed him to be suffering from "acute hallucinatory paranoia"[30] and detained him in hospital custody until the Fall Assizes in Golden, where a jury found him not guilty by reason of insanity. Following his return to the PHI in October 1901 under a Lieutenant-Governor's Warrant, [31] F.J.L.'s family hired a local firm of attorneys who lobbied provincial officials for his release and transportation back to England. However attractive such a prominent and prosperous inmate might have appeared to asylum officials, the overriding impulse to evict apparently eclipsed any such parochial motives of organizational or economic bearing. With the full compliance of doctors, the Executive Council produced an Order-in-Council on 29 November authorizing his removal "into the care of his relatives" in England, to be accompanied en route by a member of his lawyers' firm and by hospital attendant Granby Farrant. As a condition of his release, F.J.L. was barred from returning to Canada. He left on 6 December 1901. A mere six months had elapsed between the shooting and the young blueblood's unceremonious dispatch whence he came.

An Expanding Exile Apparatus

Such cases as that of F.J.L. undoubtedly stoked the apprehensions of asylum keepers as they watched the populations of their asylums spectacularly soar, and as Canadian immigration statistics began to escalate in a wave that swelled upwards from turn of the century through to the outbreak of World War I.[32] It was at this juncture that federal lawmakers began to respond. In 1902, revisions to the Immigration Act signalled the official foray of medical authorities into the realm of Canadian immigration. Procedures were established for the screening of prospective entrants at the nation's admission centres. And for the first time, on the basis of medical assessments, some classes of already-landed immigrants became subject to return.[33] The 1906 version of the Act, ushered in under the new Liberal Minister of the Interior Frank Oliver (who described the legislation as "a brake upon the wheel"[34]), was the first to spell out general provisions for the deportation of unfit landed aliens. Inspired by the 1903 exclusionary legislation passed by the United States Congress, this law formalized the 1902 regulations prohibiting anyone deemed "feebleminded, idiotic, epileptic

[or] insane." Municipal officials were charged with the duty of reporting suspected ineligibles, and municipalities were to bear the costs of deportation where immigrants were judged to be indigent.[35] Moreover, this legislation, in concert with further revisions enacted the following year, stipulated that an immigrant was eligible for deportation where, within two years of landing in Canada, (s)he "committed a crime involving moral turpitude, or bec[a]me an inmate of a jail or hospital or other charitable institution."[36]

Not all were impressed with the new law. During the first decade of the new century, public health reformers and physician activists in central Canada like Helen MacMurchy,[37] Peter H. Bryce,[38] and C.K. Clarke,[39] along with organizations like the National Council of Women,[40] were pressuring the government to further expand its powers to debar and segregate "feebleminded," insane, and other medically and morally undesirable populations. Clarke in particular was a formidable and pugnacious proponent of radical restrictionism. He alienated federal immigration authorities with his contentions that the laws and practices did not go far enough,[41] and he tirelessly proselytized and wrote innumerable articles condemning the escalating influx of damaged foreigners.[42] Farther afield, powerful currents of eugenist thinking and anti-immigration protest were sweeping the medical establishment south of the 49th parallel,[43] leading to the formation of the Immigration Exclusion League in 1894 and to the rise of influential restrictionists like G. Adler Blumer, Thomas Salmon, and William A. White.[44] The widely disseminated views of Canadian and U.S.-American eugenicists, nativists, social darwinists, and mental hygienists on such topics as immigration, racial purity, sterilization, insanity, feeblemindedness, sexual immorality, venereal disease, and white slavery, among others, flooded across borders and merged to comprise a powerful force in the campaign for more prohibitive legislation.

British Columbia, with its well-earned reputation for incendiary politics and xenophobic public values,[45] provided fertile soil for these spreading ideas. As the preeminent British Columbian psychiatric authority of his generation, Charles E. Doherty (1905–1920) in many respects personified medical attitudes regarding the mental health implications of the "immigration question" during this era. Doherty's views also represented the transition toward a more hardened exclusionary impulse, as medical, legal, and public discourses became increasingly saturated with the vocabularies and values of hereditarianism, public health, and social hygiene. As he wrote with typical alarmist flourish in 1908, the problem of defective aliens represented

> one of the most vital questions of the day. Canada posing as a refuge for people of other lands, dissatisfied with their own country, is all very well, but when an attempt is made to make it also a refuge for those with whom their native countries are dissatisfied, it is time that the closest inspection be given each landing immigrant. For the past four or five years the degenerate "Flotsam and Jetsam" of other countries have been entering Canada in a continuous stream. Paupers, inebriates, insane and even known criminals have been deposited on our shores, and already have begun to fill our public institutions at an alarming rate .... [N]o expense should be spared in the matter of sieving at the ports of entry, if our institutions are to be prevented from becoming filled with the sweepings of other countries.[46]

The representations of medical superintendents from across the country were at least partially responsible for expediting the next incarnation of the federal Immigration Act, authored by Ontario-born lawyer T.R.E. MacInnes.[47] In the wake of the devastating 1908–1909 Depression, which had further incited antipathy to immigration, the 1910 Act added "prostitutes, pimps, professional beggars or vagrants, and charity-aided immigrants" to the ranks of the deportable. Further, according to section 3(1) of the Act, "idiots, imbeciles, feeble-

minded persons, epileptics, insane persons, and persons who have been insane at any time previously" were the first-listed among 20 classes of barred people.[48] All persons so designated were subject to refusal on entry. Those who had not established domicile (the term of which was raised from two to three years and further extended to five in 1919) faced deportation following an administrative hearing.[49] Everyone entering Canada was to be inspected by a designated medical officer.[50] Once inside the country, an immigrant was to be reported by municipal officials under section 40 should (s)he, *inter alia*, "become an inmate of a penitentiary, gaol, reformatory, prison, asylum or hospital for the insane or the mentally deficient." Lastly, section 42 granted the Governor in Council the license to order the deportation of anyone found by an examining officer or Board of Inquiry to be a member of any prohibited group enumerated in section 3— the insane, feebleminded, and mental hospital inmates being among their number.

These were formidable powers. They would be further bolstered at the height of the post-War Red Scare in 1919 when, in addition to mandating a new literacy test for newcomers,[51] protracting the domicile term from three to five years and expanding the inventory of prohibited classes, a revised Immigration Act inaugurated the infamous section 41, which was targeted specifically at political dissidents.[52]

As legislative authority was being consolidated, provincial mental health and federal immigration authorities collaborated to forge a routine system for the ejection of patients from abroad who had yet to establish domicile, or whose insanity or imbecility was seen to predate their entry to Canada. It appeared that British Columbia's psychiatric institutions received steadfast cooperation from the Immigration Branch, and the medical superintendents corresponded regularly and harmoniously with the local Vancouver Immigration Branch office (which from the first to fourth decades of this century was presided over in turn by A.L. Jolliffe, A.E. Skinner, and F.W. Taylor). As early as 1907, Superintendent of Immigration William Duncan (Big Bill) Scott was providing reassurances to British Columbia's Provincial Secretary Henry Esson Young that "... when cases are brought to my attention I will have them investigated immediately and if they are found to come within the provisions of the Immigration Act there will be no undue delay in having matters attended to and thus relieve the Province of any unnecessary expense in maintaining aliens for any length of time."[53]

Procedures for undertaking these removals were relatively straightforward in theory. If physicians suspected newly admitted patients of being potential deports,[54] they notified the local Branch authorities who conducted an investigation to determine the individual's country of origin, date and point of entry, her or his financial and social circumstances, the shipping company involved,[55] whether family or friends were available to defray the transportation costs and receive the patient at the far side, and other particulars. If the person's prohibited status was confirmed, authorities convened a (typically perfunctory[56]) hearing under the terms of the Immigration Act. For those ordered out of the country, the formal deportation order was completed and signed, officials informed the transportation company and consul for the country of origin, and travel arrangements were finalized. The Winnipeg offices of the Immigration Branch coordinated deportations from Vancouver to Europe. Deports generally travelled under escort[57] via Canadian Pacific Railway trains to Montreal,[58] after which they were handed over to the designated shipping company for the final stage of their repatriation.

In practice, however, various predicaments plagued the operations of this human assembly line. Itineraries were often poorly coordinated, with the result that severely disordered and sometimes violent patients were stranded for days and weeks in Montreal under the care of disgruntled ship medical officers. And when deports disembarked at the other end, often no arrangements had been worked out for their shelter and care.[59] The personal and psychiatric information accompanying banished patients across the continent and ocean was often threadbare, and sometimes non-existent. Transportation companies were constantly carping for more extensive and precise details about the medical condition of their charges.

The implications of these assorted shortcomings were painfully driven home as early as August of 1908 with the suicide of a homeward-bound deport aboard the H. & A. Allan Lines steamship *SS Hesperian*. T.M., a 22-year-old Scot, had arrived in Canada only three months earlier. Landing at the port of Quebec in May, he soon made his way to British Columbia. There, destitute and alone, he attempted to throw himself in front of the Great Northern Seattle Express train in Cloverdale. Onlookers pulled him away and engineered his commitment to the Public Hospital for the Insane. A deportation order soon followed and T.M. was summarily dispatched east for return to the custody of his father in Scotland.

But he was never to arrive. PHI Medical Superintendent Doherty's medical propensity slip, marking T.M. as suicidal, failed to reach the hands of the Allan Lines physicians. On the evening of 29 August T.M. broke away from his "keeper" while being escorted to the toilet, and proceeded to jump overboard and disappear "in the most dangerous part of the channel below Quebec." The suicide precipitated a three-year-long correspondence in which, through an agent, T.M.'s father demanded an accounting for his son's death, and federal authorities scrambled to absolve themselves of responsibility. Although there is no record that any formal legal action ensued, Allan Lines officials demanded that the Immigration Branch reform its methods for conveying psychiatric and other medical information to company doctors.[60] In turn, Superintendent W.D. Scott distributed a general memorandum in January 1911 to the medical superintendents of mental institutions from coast to coast, requesting that they henceforth provide "a more exact history of the mental condition of such persons, ... more especially bearing upon their liability to become violent."[61]

Meanwhile, at the receiving end of the system—where the federal Branch was busy assembling a burgeoning apparatus for the screening out of unfit immigrants before they could infiltrate the country—a similar litany of conflicts and contradictions surfaced. When it came to the evaluation of new arrivals, in the wake of the 1902 legislation, medical officers were first hired at the ports of Halifax, Quebec, and Montreal in 1903. By the following year, detention facilities were opening at these sites, and the officers and their staff soon found themselves overwhelmed by an indiscriminate avalanche of medical and other rejection and deportation cases. These hybrid hospital-reception-detention centres were under siege almost from the outset.[62] In W.D. Scott, they were overseen by a Superintendent of Immigration who was steadfastly opposed to expending public funds on the medical or psychiatric treatment of unwanted foreigners. The guardians of provincial institutions from coast to coast, along with organizational and public opponents of "promiscuous" immigration (and in some cases other federally appointed physicians such as the disputatious J.D. Page of Quebec City[63]) were quick to vilify the detention hospitals for their alleged lax procedures and inability to measurably stem the tide of degenerate aliens. Doctors and other officials worked under appalling conditions, particularly at the Montreal centre, which assumed an increasing proportion of the workload. By the end of World War I, the mandate of Immigration Branch authorities at ports of entry had shifted dramatically away from medical care to assessment and pre-deportation confinement, and medical officers had been rendered subservient to lay bureaucrats who were more willing to fulfil such a purely prophylactic and custodial role. As Roberts writes, physicians ultimately became "merely quality-control technicians on an assembly line, examining the products passing in front of them for a specific set of defects."[64] The transfer of physicians to the newly formed federal Department of Health under the 1919 Immigration Act, while perhaps welcomed by beleaguered immigration doctors hungry for some measure of autonomy, virtually completed the demedicalization of the Immigration Branch admission process.

Deportation's Golden Age

As the inter-war period began to unfold, the attention of deportation advocates shifted away from the law itself toward procedural resolutions, and especially toward the tightening of inspection standards at the ports of entry. Authorities were divided, both along provincial-federal lines and between immigration managers and line staff, regarding the apprehended quality of inspections and the factors underlying any perceived failings. From the standpoint of provincial hospital administrators and physicians—who viewed their institutions as the embattled receptacles for an ever-growing human tide of defective and incurable outsiders—the blame lay squarely at the feet of politicians and civil servants who were in conspiratorial league with transportation companies, corporate interests, and the immigration lobby to expand the nation's labouring population at any price. While central Canadian psychiatrists like C.K. Clarke and his Quebec counterpart, Thomas Burgess, might have attained the highest profile amongst the medical lobby, in many respects the mental hospital officials of Western Canadian provinces like British Columbia were even more grievously weighed down by the influx of disordered and otherwise afflicted patients. Far removed from the federal corridors of influence over immigration policy,[65] British Columbia's psychiatrists nevertheless became effective crusaders in their own right. They allied themselves with provincial politicians and anti-immigration organizations, and established connections with forces in other parts of the country, in a decades-long campaign aimed at reforming the medical assessment of immigrants and closing the gates to potential asylum inmates. For the province's institutional psychiatrists, as for their colleagues elsewhere, this issue was an integral component of their struggle to uplift the conditions of their professional existence and to augment their influence beyond the hospital walls.

Upon his return from wartime service and until his death in 1920, Charles Doherty once again turned his attention to the disproportionate representation of foreign-born patients in the province's mental hospitals. Amid the post-war immigration boom, Doherty gave voice to the widely circulating apprehension that the powers conferred by immigration legislation were not being adequately harnessed. "In our British Columbian institutions," he intoned in 1919, "not quite 8 per cent, are British Columbia born, and not over 20 per cent Canadian born ... I go into this matter ... in order to show you just how very important the matter of promiscuous immigration is to one Province, in only one branch of incapables, and to give you some idea of what a tremendous burden it will eventually become if allowed to go on." Aiming his remarks at his provincial superiors, and decrying the marginalization of physicians from the immigration selection process, Doherty stressed "the necessity for some method of more adequate supervision and intelligent inspection, not by laymen, but by medical men with the proper experience as psychiatrists."[66]

Doherty's successor as British Columbia's chief medical superintendent, Harold Chapman Steeves (1920–1926), soon found himself presiding over an explosion in the province's mental patient population. But it was as much the content as the quantity of his clientele that evoked apprehensions. As he observed with alarm in 1925, "only one-third of our admissions were Canadians by birth. These figures indicate to me the necessity of a more searching examination of immigrants coming into the country before citizenship is allowed them." Interestingly, Steeves cited with approbation the cooperative efforts of Immigration Branch officials in engineering the removal of prohibited persons who had already landed in hospital. The problem resided rather at the point of ingress, where better facilities were needed "to more effectively cull out the unfitted before they are admitted to the country."[67]

Like many of his peers, Steeves decried the purging of medical inspectors from the Immigration Branch. His rhetoric was also representative of general medical discourse about immigration during the inter-war period, in its unresolved tension between a growing fiscal pragmatism, and an enduring residue of eugenical extremism. In his hospital annual report of 1923, addressed to the provincial secretary and cabinet, he stressed the economics of investigative efficiency: "In the great majority of cases careful psychiatric examination would have detected these cases and they would have been returned to their own countries before becoming a financial burden to the taxpayer .... These facts should appeal to the business-man and enlist his active support for the expenditure necessary to provide the proper examinations and inquiries at the ports of entry and thus prevent the subsequent much longer outlay."[68] Writing in a local medical journal, on the other hand, Steeves's more nativist tendencies were plainly in view: "I feel that every effort should be made to add to the population, but, at the same time, the people so added must be strong and healthy in mind as well as body, in order that a virile, intelligent race of Canadians may result."[69]

The importunings of Doherty, Sleeves, and their confederates were partially responsible for the 30 December 1925 appointment of the B.C. Royal Commission on Mental Hygiene. This Commission was a watershed event in the provincial campaign for racial and mental purity. Chaired by provincial M.L.A. Edwin James Rothwell and comprising a membership of four other legislative representatives (V.W. Odium, W.A. McKenzie, R. Hayward, and P.P. Harrison), the Commission was charged with inquiring into, inter alia, the reasons for the increase in mental hospital populations, the causes and prevention of lunacy, and the entry into the province of "insane, mentally deficient and subnormal persons."[70]

Largely through the efforts of journalist J.A. Macdonald,[71] who was hired as Assistant Secretary, the Commission undertook correspondences with politicians, physicians, and other interest groups throughout Canada, the United States, and Britain. Macdonald assembled a formidable body of statistics, reports, and scholarly literature on insanity, eugenics, immigration, venereal disease, sterilization, and other pressing social issues. The Commissioners convened consultations and public hearings on both the mainland and Vancouver Island. Helen Davidson of Stanford University was recruited to conduct a survey of immigrant representation in the province's mental hospitals.[72] Based on his accumulated research, Macdonald became fervently convinced that Canada had become a "dumping ground" for unscrupulous European governments. Writing to Harrison, the Commissioner responsible for immigration, Macdonald reported in September 1926: "For everything I have been able to learn, you would be perfectly justified in reaching the conclusion that Canada has admitted an even greater proportion of unfit aliens than the U.S. and that the danger to be avoided in the immediate future is very great indeed."[73]

In his report on immigration released on 8 January 1927, Harrison took pains to reinforce these assertions. "I have no hesitation in coming to the conclusion that the proportion of Foreign-born far exceeds that of the Canadian-born, and that immigrants have contributed far too greatly to the increase of the insane in Canada."[74] He recommended a tri-level system of medical inspection of immigrants (before embarkation, on board steamer, and upon landing in Canada). In its final report, the Commission laid the blame squarely at the feet of federal officials who were insufficiently vigilant in enforcing the restrictionist legislation:

The conclusion that too many mentally unfit immigrants have been allowed to enter Canada is an almost superfluous statement of fact if viewed from the incontestible assumption that we have the moral and legal right to refuse them entrance. If the intent of our immigration laws and regulations could be carried out entirely, then none of this class could enter the

country .... [W]e are convinced that increased population by immigration is bought at too great a price if it entails the admission of any considerable number of individuals who will add to the burden of the nation caused by mental abnormality.[75]

The Royal Commission was already close to completing its mandate when Arthur L. Crease ascended to the Medical Superintendency of British Columbia's mental hospitals in 1926. Crease, like his predecessors, was a staunch restrictionist and deportationist who endeavoured to keep the issue alive through to the outbreak of World War II. Both Crease's exclusionist objectives and the recommendations of the Commission appeared to receive further ammunition with the descent of the Depression and its mounting pressures on British Columbia's care and control institutions commencing in 1929. During the fiscal crisis of the 1930s, Crease periodically raised the question of insane and feebleminded immigrants in communications with Deputy Provincial Secretary P.D. Walker, suggesting, for example, that hospitalization should be reserved for only those newcomers who had already established domicile,[76] and that relief agencies should be more exacting when inquiring into the mental and citizenship backgrounds of their charges.[77] But significantly, there was little evidence that such overtures had much impact.

For on the national stage, other events were beginning to dampen the anti-immigration momentum. By the late 1920s, the eugenics movement in Canada had already crested. With the 1924 death of C.K. Clarke, and his succession as Medical Director of the Canadian National Committee For Mental Hygiene (CNCMH) by the pragmatic C.M. Hincks,[78] immigration came to be supplanted by education and sterilization as the CNCMH's preferred strategies for regulating the public's mental health. At a theoretical level, the influence of Freud, Watson, and their contemporaries was being reflected in trends away from somatic psychiatry and toward psychodynamism and behaviourism.[79] Moreover, as noted below, with the resulting demise of Canadian immigration's second great wave, the Depression ultimately tolled the politico-economic knell for psychiatric campaigns against unfit aliens, as it did for the mainstream eugenics movement more generally.

The rejectionist enthusiasm was further blunted by reforms in the medical and psychiatric evaluation of prospective immigrants. Over the span of a quarter-century, among various interested authorities, the only consistent apologists for prevailing screening practices at the nation's ports of entry were federal bureaucrats like Immigration Branch Chief Medical Officer Peter H. Bryce,[80] Superintendent Scott,[81] Commissioner A.L. Jolliffe,[82] and Deputy Minister of Health John A. Amyot.[83] But even those responsible for these operations were alert to their limitations. Despite efforts to validate inspections with standardized forms[84] and to train Immigration officers through the good offices of the CNCMH,[85] pessimism generally reigned. Amyot's presentation to the 1925 meeting of the Dominion Council of Health illustrated some of the more dire obstacles:

> [O]ur doctors' opportunity for picking out these individuals is a limited one. The train is going to leave in an hour, and another one is going to leave in two hours, and the railroad company is in a hurry and everybody is in a hurry. We have arranged that our medical officers will stand at the head of the lines. We make the individuals walk a "maze" and during that time one of our medical officers picks them out. That is the one opportunity they have .... The great bulk of immigrants ... come over here and take their chances at the ship's sideband if their defect is not very obvious, they very frequently get through.[86]

Others such as C.K. Clarke and J.D. Page were even more blunt in their condemnation of these practices.[87] A litany of impediments was recurrently cited by these and other commentators, including the clandestine tactics of disreputable transportation companies, the sheer numbers of inspections involved, the craftiness of immigrant subjects contriving to escape detection, and the impenetrable character of some forms of mental defect.[88]

Whatever their estimation of disembarkation inspection procedures, everyone seemed to agree that evaluations needed to be instituted at the point of departure for all prospective citizens. Indeed, arguments for medical appraisals had been advanced since the turn of century, and advocates had included even social gospel reformer J.S. Woodsworth.[89] Following World War I, Professor W.G. Smith of the University Toronto published his influential book *A Study in Canadian Immigration*, which was commissioned by the CNCMH and excerpted in the Committee's *Mental Hygiene Bulletin*. In it, Smith recommended a centralized system of inspection fashioned after the U.S.-American Ellis Island model, to be supplemented by medical evaluations conducted prior to embarkation: "There must be two examinations at least, and that means double staffs of examiners, and consequent expense. But it is manifestly better to spend money that way than to allow persons suffering from a contagious disease, insanity, mental deficiency, to add to their misery by the trying experiences of a long voyage and then to be rejected, or deported."[90] A multitude of proponents, like the British Columbia Royal Commission as noted above, echoed Smith's claim that such measures would simultaneously serve the national interest and spare unnecessary hardship for defective foreigners.[91]

By the mid 1920s, federal authorities had issued concrete proposals that Canada emulate the United States in establishing a roster of physicians overseas to assess people on the far shores of the Atlantic. In 1927, the plans were finally implemented, with the result that every aspiring entrant was henceforth, at least in theory, subjected to three echelons of medical and mental filtering: first on application, second on board ship by company physicians, and finally at the port of entry.[92] While the effect was not immediately discernible in the Immigration and Colonization statistics,[93] by 1933 the numbers of medical deportations did begin to decline measurably, and along with them the intensity of criticism subsided. As Godler notes, "This change, long demanded by the Canadian medical profession, promised to eliminate the need for most deportations from Canadian ports on medical grounds. By the same stroke it saved Canadian taxpayers the cost of ministering to the sick as they awaited their deportation."[94] By adding another prophylactic layer to the nation's shield against unsound strangers, federal officials had effectively taken the wind from the sails of their most bellicose critics.

But before British Columbia's campaign to eject mental misfits collapsed totally in the wake of these reforms, and under the cumulative weight of the Depression and World War II, there was one final coup. On 9 February 1935, the province effected the mass deportation of 65 Chinese male patients who were rounded up from the province's three mental hospitals and repatriated to the Honam Mental Asylum in Canton aboard the Canadian Pacific liner *Empress of Russia*.[95] This collective banishment capped more than two decades of manoeuvring among mental health and immigration authorities, along with protracted negotiations with a succession of less-than-receptive Chinese consular officials. When at last the 65 men were dispatched, with the provision that they be permitted never to return, Provincial Secretary G.M. Weir trumpeted their departure to the local press. "[T]he full saving," he claimed, "would run about $20,000 to $25,000 a year .... Furthermore, the removal of these patients will allow room for other cases with which the institutions are overcrowded."[96] While Weir, his Deputy P.D. Walker, and Provincial Psychiatrist A.L. Crease were careful to couch their claims in the discourse of institutional economy and fiscal restraint, the racialist undercurrents were at times scarcely submerged. Further, reports circulated regarding the prospects for similar purges of Japanese, "Hindoo," Italian, and Jewish patients.[97] These latter projects, however, never came to fruition. The entire sorry episode was, in effect, the last hurrah for those who sought to transport away the province's mental health problem.

Aftermath

From the mid 1930s onward, the campaign to rid the country of unfit immigrants waned appreciably among government and professional elites, and in public culture more generally. With the rise of Nazism in Europe, the eugenics movement came to be associated with the most virulent streams of racist ideology, hastening its decline in popularity throughout North America.[98] State officials and medical professionals concentrated decreasingly on the polluting effects of degenerated populations, and more on the administrative prophylactics needed to ensure that neither province nor country should bear more than its fair share of the responsibility for managing the mentally unwell.[99] The main problem of the immigrant insane became less their liabilities for the nation's genetic pool, and more the simple fact that they "are taking up the beds which should be for our own citizens."[100]

Moreover, global tensions in the pre-war era impeded international population movements. Rates of immigration to Canada plummeted in the decade leading to World War II, with a consequent shrinkage in the pool of potential deports. In Britain and on the continent, fiscally burdened and strife-ridden governments were decreasingly disposed to cooperate in the repatriation of Canada's rejects. On the domestic front, as the Depression tightened its grip on Canadians, the material preoccupations of individual and collective survival took precedence over the longer-term and more arcane aspirations of race betterment. With a diminishing target population, mounting administrative encumbrances, and an exploded scientific foundation, deportation's "golden age" had come to a decisive, if impermanent, close. From 1935 through to war's end, expulsion rates declined both in general terms and for insanity and deficiency cases specifically. As noted in Table 2, British Columbia's mental hospitals reported only ten deportations in fiscal years 1936–1937 and 1937–1938, and thereafter its Annual Reports ceased publishing deportation statistics altogether.

World War II, however, by no means spelled the end of psychiatric deportations from British Columbia and Canada. The rejection and removal of mentally disordered and cognitively disabled immigrants continued as in-migration rates once again achieved pre-Depression levels through the late 1940s and into the 1950s. But with the decline of hereditarian thinking in public and official arenas, and with shifts toward cultural and psychogenetic understandings about the causes and consequences of mental disorder, the "insane" and "retarded" came to be seen less as dangerous carriers of dysgenic materials and more prosaically as economic inconveniences and potential burdens on the social welfare system. Commencing in the 1950s, the Department of Citizenship and Immigration began to consider abolishing Immigration Act provisions which mandated the automatic prohibition of immigrants with histories of mental disorder.[101] In 1964, the Immigration Medical Service instructed its physicians to adopt a discretionary approach to findings of prior insanity where the illness was unlikely to relapse or "interfere significantly with the person's occupation or activities or require prolonged institutional care."[102] Finally, in the wake of sweeping amendments to the Immigration Act in 1976,[103] statutory reference to psychiatric or cognitive disability as a discrete grounds for rejection or deportation disappeared altogether.

Still, to the present day, the Immigration Act provides that everyone seeking admission to Canada must undergo a medical assessment,[104] including a mental examination.[105] More than two million of these occur annually.[106]

Moreover, persons desiring to enter the country may be detained under s. 91(l) for compulsory treatment or observation "where a medical officer is of the opinion that ... [they are] ... suffering from sickness or mental or physical disability."[107] Among the 12 categories of prohibited persons enumerated in Part 3 of the present version of the Act are those who are "likely to be a danger to public health or to public safety," or "whose admission would cause or might reasonably be expected to cause excessive demands ... on health or prescribed social services."[108]

While the mentally and cognitively afflicted are no longer explicitly singled out for prohibition in Canadian law, the codewords of dependency and risk have become convenient discursive substitutes for lunacy and feeblemindedness. And whereas the Department has ceased publishing deportation statistics disaggregated by individual category of exclusion, the staggering volume of ejections from this country[109] is almost certain to include an abundance of persons deemed psychiatrically ill. The controversial 1997 case of Michael Holmes—a diagnosed schizophrenic from Scotland whom immigration officials had ordered deported from Edmonton as a "public danger" until the Federal Court of Canada later quashed the order—offers graphic evidence that the Canadian state's preoccupation with mentally disordered foreigners has not entirely abated.[110] For Michael Holmes and others like him, the prejudicial policies of a restrictionist immigration bureaucracy, and the pseudo-scientific theories of therapeutic professionals, are not merely a regrettable historical remnant. To the contrary, despite the contemporary flow of rhetoric about mental patient rights, and about open international borders in the new age of global citizenship, there is much to suggest that the national frontiers remain firmly closed to those prospective Canadians who carry the stigma of psychiatric illness.

Notes

*   A version of this paper was originally presented at the 1998 Meetings of the Western Association of Sociology and Anthropology in Vancouver, B.C. Funding support was furnished in part by the Social Sciences and Humanities Research Council of Canada. For their various and indispensable contributions, my thanks go to Robert Adamoski, Dorothy E. Chunn, John McLaren, Jeffie Roberts, Anna Tremere, Marie-Andree Bertrand, and the two anonymous reviewers of the *Canadian Journal of Law and Society*, and the professionals and staff of the British Columbia Archives and Records Service, the National Archives of Canada, the Archives on the History of Canadian Psychiatry and Mental Health Services, and Riverview Hospital. Inquiries should be addressed to the School of Criminology, Simon Fraser University, 8888 University Drive, Burnaby, B.C. V5A 1S6, Canada (email: menzies@sfu.ca).

1.   On the sources and historical patterns of federal and provincial deportation statistics, see tables 10.1 and 10.2.

2.   On the general history of deportation in Canada, see D. Avery, *Dangerous Foreigners: European Immigrant Workers and Labour Radicalism in Canada, 1896–1932* (Toronto: McClelland & Stewart, 1979); H.F. Drystek, "'The Simplest and Cheapest Mode of Dealing with Them': Deportation from Canada before World War II" (1982) 15:30 *Social History* 407; D. Galloway, *Immigration Law* (Toronto: Irwin, 1997), c. 1; S. Imai, "Deportation in the Depression" (1981) 7:1 *Queen's Law Journal* 66; V. Knowles, *Strangers at Our Gates: Canadian Immigration and Immigration Policy, 1540–1997,* 2nd ed. (Toronto: Dundurn, 1997); B. Roberts, "Shovelling Out the 'Mutinous': Political Deportation from Canada before 1936" (1986) 18 *Labour* 77 [hereinafter "Shovelling Out the 'Mutinous'"; B. Roberts, *Whence They Came: Deportation from Canada 1900–1935* (Ottawa: University of Ottawa Press, 1988) [hereinafter *Whence They Came*].

3.   On Canadian physicians and the rejection and removal of unfit immigrants, see I. Dowbiggin, "'Keeping This Young Country Sane': C.K. Clarke, Immigration Restriction, and Canadian Psychiatry, 1890–1925" (1995) 76:4 *Canadian Historical Review* 598 [hereinafter "'Keeping This Young Country Sane'"]; I.R. Dowbiggin, *Keeping America Sane: Psychiatry and Eugenics in the United States and Canada 1880–1940* (Ithaca: Cornell University Press, 1997) c. 1, 3 [hereinafter

Keeping America Sane]; Z. Godler, "Doctors and the New Immigrants" (1977) 9 *Canadian Ethnic Studies* 6; A. McLaren, *Our Own Master Race: Eugenics in Canada, 1885–1945* (Toronto: McClelland & Stewart, 1990), c. 3 [hereinafter *Our Own Master Race*]; B. Roberts, "Doctors and Deports: The Role of the Medical Profession in Canadian Deportation, 1900–20" (1987) 18:3 *Canadian Ethnic Studies* 17 [hereinafter "Doctors and Deports"].

4.   Canada, House of Commons, "Annual Reports of the Immigration Branch," in *Sessional Papers* (Ottawa: Queen's Printer, 1902–1903 to 1938–1939). See Table 1.

5.   A federal government study conducted in the early 1950s reported that, between 1930–31 and 1944–45, there were 2,724 deportations for medical reasons, 1,596 of these (58%) being attributed to mental diseases. The study concluded that "from 50% to 60% of deportations for medical reasons are occasioned by mental disease. This means that from 1902 to 1944, there have been from 5,400 to 6,500 persons deported as a result of mental disease." Department of Citizenship and Immigration, "Immigration Studies with Special Reference to Mental Disease," National Archives of Canada [hereinafter NAC] RG 29, vol. 3091, file 854-4-300, pt. 1-A.

6.   The literature on citizenship and governmentality has exploded in recent years. Illustrations include J.M. Barbalet, ed., *Citizenship: Rights, Struggle and Class Inequality* (Milton Keynes, UK: Open University Press, 1988); L. Becker & W. Kymlicka, eds., "Symposium on Citizenship, Democracy, and Education" (1995) 105 *Ethics* 465; C. Mouffe, ed., *Dimensions of Radical Democracy: Pluralism, Citizenship, Community* (London: Verso, 1992); M. Roche, *Rethinking Citizenship: Welfare, Ideology and Change in Modern Society* (Cambridge, UK: Polity, 1992); G. Shafir, ed., *The Citizenship Debates: A Reader* (Minneapolis, MN: University of Minnesota Press, 1998); B. van Steenbergen, ed., *The Condition of Citizenship* (Thousand Oaks, CA: Sage, 1994); B.S. Turner, ed., *Citizenship and Social Theory* (London: Sage, 1993).

7.   Some classic works on the transition in Canada from the 19th-century liberal state to 20th-century progressivism are: A. Armitage, *Social Welfare in Canada: Ideals and Realities* (Toronto: McClelland & Stewart, 1975); D. Guest, *The Emergence of Social Security in Canada* (Vancouver: University of British Columbia Press, 1980); F. Iacovetta,

P. Draper, & R. Ventresca, eds., *A Nation of Immigrants: Women, Workers, and Communities in Canadian History, 1840s–1960s* (Toronto: University of Toronto Press, 1998); A. Moscovitch & J. Alberts, eds., *The Benevolent State: The Growth of Welfare in Canada* (Toronto: Garamond, 1987); J. Struthers, *No Fault of Their Own: Unemployment and the Canadian Welfare State 1914–1941* (Toronto: University of Toronto Press, 1983).

8. "Canada's Most Serious Problem," *Toronto Globe* (2 July 1910) NAC. RG 76, vol. 474, file 729921.

9. Henry Esson Young, "Presidential Lecture to Canadian Public Health Association, Vancouver," *Victoria Daily Colonist* (22 June 1920) 5; British Columbia Archives and Records Service [hereinafter BCARS] GR 144, vol. 3, book 1.

10. D. Cole & I. Chaikin, *An Iron Hand upon the People: The Law against the Potlatch on the Northwest Coast* (Vancouver: Douglas & McIntyre, 1990); R. Fisher, *Contact and Conflict: Indian-European Relations in British Columbia, 1774–1890* (Vancouver: University of British Columbia Press, 1979); H. Johnston, *The Voyage of the Komagata Maru: The Sikh Challenge to Canada's Colour Bar*, 2nd ed. (Vancouver: University of British Columbia Press, 1995); P.E. Roy, *A White Man's Province: British Columbia Politicians and Chinese and Japanese Immigrants, 1858–1914* (Vancouver: University of British Columbia Press, 1989); P. Tennant, *Aboriginal Peoples and Politics: The Indian Land Question in British Columbia, 1849–1989* (Vancouver: University of British Columbia Press, 1990); W.P, Ward, *White Canada Forever: Popular Attitudes toward Orientals in British Columbia* (Montreal: McGill-Queen's University Press, 1990); G. Woodcock & I. Avakumovic, *The Doukhobors* (Toronto: Oxford University Press, 1968).

11. G. Creese & V. Strong-Boag, eds., *British Columbia Reconsidered: Essays on Women* (Vancouver: Press Gang, 1992); M. Jolly & M. MacIntyre, eds., *Family and Gender in the Pacific: Domestic Contradictions and the Colonial Impact* (Cambridge: Cambridge University Press, 1989); L. Kealey, ed., *A Not Unreasonable Claim: Women and Reform in Canada, 1880s–1920s* (Toronto: Women's Press, 1979); B.K. Latham & C. Kess, eds., *In Her Own Right: Selected Essays on Women's History in B.C.* (Victoria: Camosun College, 1980); B.K. Latham & R. Pazdro, eds., *Not Just Pin Money: Selected Essays on the History of Women's Work in British Columbia* (Victoria:

Camosun College, 1984); A. Perry, "'Fair Ones of a Purer Caste': White Women and Colonialism in Nineteenth-Century British Columbia" (1997) 23 *Feminist Studies* 501.

12. Imai, *supra* note 2 at 93.

13. William Byron, "The Menace of the Alien" (1919) 32 *Maclean's Magazine* 19 at 19.

14. The federal ministries responsible for immigration and deportation through the period of this study were: the Department of Agriculture at Confederation, the Department of the Interior commencing in 1892, the Immigration Branch of the DI as of 1893, the Department of Immigration and Colonization from 1917, and finally the Department of Mines and Resources starting in 1936. Immigration Branch, *Finding Aid,* NAC. RG 76.

15. Separate statistics on deportations based on insanity and defect were published in Immigration Branch Annual Reports from 1902–1903 to 1915–1916, and again from 1933–1934 to 1938–1939 (excepting the 1936–1937 fiscal year). The numbers for ten additional years (1916–1917 through 1925–1926) were prepared separated by Dominion Statistician R.H. Coats for the B.C. Royal Commission on Mental Hygiene. Letter from J. Macdonald to R.H. Coats (28 June 1926) BCARS. GR 865, box 1, file 2.

16. *Annual Reports of the Medical Superintendent* [hereafter *ARMS*] Public Hospital for the Insane (to 1923–1924) and Provincial Mental Hospital, Essondale (from 1924–1925) B.C. Sessional Papers, 1921–1922 to 1937–1938.

17. Following the closure of the Victoria Lunatic Asylum in 1872, the Public Hospital for the Insane (PHI) in New Westminster was inaugurated in 1878. Subsequently, the Essondale Mental Hospital opened in 1913 on a 1,000-acre tract of land in Port Coquitlam; and the Colquitz Mental Home, an institution for male "criminally insane" inmates, operated between 1919 and 1964. See generally V. Adolph, *In the Context of Its Time: A History of Woodlands* (Richmond, B.C.: Ministry of Social Services, Government of British Columbia, 1996); M.J. Davies, "The Patients' World: British Columbia's Mental Health Facilities, 1910–1935" (M.A. Thesis, Department of History, University of Waterloo, 1989); R. Foulkes, "British Columbia's Mental Health Services: Historical Perspectives to 1961" (1961) 20 *The Leader* 25; R. Menzies, "The Making of Criminal Insanity in British Columbia: Granby Farrant and the Provincial Mental Home, Colquitz, 1919–1933" in H. Foster & J. McLaren, eds., *Essays in the History of Canadian Law: Vol.*

VI: British Columbia and the Yukon (Toronto: Osgoode Society and University of Toronto Press, 1995), 274.

18. *Whence They Came, supra* note 2, c. 7.

19. As noted below, the length of time in Canada required to establish domicile under the Immigration Act was set at two years in 1906, then raised to three years in 1910, and five years in 1919. See also ibid., c. 2.

20. Immigration Act. 1869. 32, 33 Vic. c. 10.

21. Drystek, *supra* note 2 at 408.

22. Immigration Act. 1887. 50, 51 Vic. c. 34.

23. *Supra* note 17.

24. G.F. Bodington, *ARMS.* Provincial Asylum for the Insane. 1896. 60 Vic at 845.

25. Ibid. 1897. 61 Vic. at 830.

26. Ibid. 1899. 63 Vic. at 896.

27. G.H. Manchester, *ARMS.* Provincial Asylum for the Insane. 1902. 3 Ed. VII at E7.

28. Case files for British Columbia mental hospital patients discharged prior to 1942 are contained in the GR 2880 records collection of the BCARS. Patient names are initialized in this paper to safeguard confidentiality.

29. The newspaper source is withheld to protect the individual's identity.

30. BCARS. GR 419, box 89, file 1900/80; GR 1754, box 6, vol. 10.

31. These warrants, abolished by Parliament in 1992, mandated the indeterminate confinement "at the pleasure of the Lieutenant-Governor" of persons found not guilty by reason of insanity or unfit to stand trial.

32. Through the period 1903–1913, in only two years (1907 and 1909) did the annual federal immigration numbers decrease from the prior 12-month figures. See Table 1, and *Whence They Came, supra* note 2 at 38.

33. Immigration Act, 1902, 2 Ed. VII, c.14. As Drystek reports (*supra* note 2 at 410), "regulations were made for the proper inspection of all immigrants by medical officers. Immigrants who were criminals, insane, epileptics, idiots, blind, deaf and dumb, 'defectives,' advanced consumptives, or suffering from chronic venereal disease were to be refused admission. Those who were deformed, crippled, suffered dangerous, contagious or loathsome diseases not dangerous to life were to be prohibited 'if they are likely to become a public charge.'" See also E. Cashmore, "The Social Organization of Canadian Immigration Law" (1978) 3:4 *Canadian Journal of Sociology* 409 at 417.

34. House of Commons Debates (1906) at 5249.

35. Immigration Act. 1906. 6 Ed. VII, c.19. See Drystek, *supra* note 2 at 414; Imai, *supra* note 2 at 91.

36. Immigration Act, ibid. See also R. Cameron, "The Wheat from the Chaff: Canadian Restrictive Immigration Policy, 1905–1911" (M.A. Thesis, Department of History, Concordia University, 1976) at 78 [unpublished].

37. See C.R. Comacchio, *"Nations Are Made of Babies": Saving Ontario's Mothers and Children, 1900–1940* (Montreal: McGill-Queen's University Press, 1993); *Keeping America Sane, supra* note 3 at 162; H. MacMurchy, *Sterilization? Birth Control? A Book for Family Welfare and Safety* (Toronto: Macmillan, 1934); K.J. McConnachie, "Methodology in the Study of Women in History: A Case Study of Helen MacMurchy" (1983) 75 *Ontario History* 61; *Our Own Master Race, supra* note 3 at 28.

38. Bryce began his career as secretary of the Ontario Board of Health before serving as chief medical officer of the federal Immigration Branch from 1904 to 1921. On the details of his career, see especially *Keeping American Sane*, ibid., at 144; "Doctors and Deports," *supra* note 3.

39. The quintessential works on Clarke's career are: "Keeping the Young Country Sane," *supra* note 3; *Keeping America Sane, supra* note 3; C. Greenland, *Charles Kirk Clarke: A Pioneer of Canadian Psychiatry* (Toronto: Clarke Institute of Psychiatry, 1966); K.J. McConnachie, "Science and Ideology: The Mental Hygiene and Eugenics Movements in the Inter-War Years, 1919–1939" (Ph.D. Dissertation, Department of History, University of Toronto, 1987) [unpublished].

40. On the work of the National Council of Women, see generally C. Bacchi, "Race Regeneration and Social Purity: A Study of the Social Attitudes of Canada's English-Speaking Suffragettes" (1978) 11 *Social History* 460; N. Griffiths, *The Splendid Vision: Centennial History of the National Council of Women* (Ottawa: Carleton University Press, 1993); *Our Own Master Race, supra* note 3; C. Strange, *Toronto's Girl Problem: The Perils and Pleasures of the City, 1880–1930* (Toronto: University of Toronto Press, 1995); V. Strong-Boag, *The Parliament of Women: The National Council of Women of Canada, 1893–1929* (Ottawa: National Museum of Man, 1976); M. Valverde, *The Age of Light, Soap and Water: Moral Reform in English Canada, 1885–1925* (Toronto: McClelland & Stewart, 1991).

41. *Keeping America Sane, supra* note 3 at 152.

42. Examples of his prodigious writings on immigration include: "The Defective and Insane Immigrant," *Bulletin of the Ontario Hospitals for the Insane* (1908) 2 3; "Canada and Defective Immigration" (1908) 65 *American Journal of Insanity* 186; "Why Is the Immigration Act Not Enforced?" (1909) 25 *Canadian Journal of Medicine and Surgery* 251; and "The Defective Immigrant" (1916) 7 *Public Health Journal* 462.

43. D.J. Kevles, *In the Name of Eugenics: Genetics and the Uses of Human Heredity* (New York: Knopf, 1985); E.J. Larson, *Sex, Race, and Science: Eugenics in the Deep South* (Baltimore: Johns Hopkins, 1995); K.M. Ludmerer, *Genetics and American Society: A Historical Appraisal* (Baltimore: Johns Hopkins, 1972); S.B. Thielman, "Psychiatry and Social Values: The American Psychiatric Association and Immigration Restriction, 1880–1930" (1985) 48 *Psychiatry* 299.

44. See generally *Keeping America Sane, supra* note 3, c. 1, 2, 4.

45. *Supra* note 10.

46. C.E. Doherty, *ARMS,* Public Hospital for the Insane. New Westminster (1908) D5.

47. Cameron, *supra* note 36 at 89. In later years MacInnes relocated to British Columbia and became a journalist, author, and notorious campaigner against Asian immigration. See Tom MacInnes, *Oriental Occupation of British Columbia* (Vancouver: Sun, 1927).

48. *Immigration Act*. S.C. 1910, 9–10 Ed. VII, c. 27, s 3(a). Purloined from the U.S. legislation, s. 3(k) added to the list "persons of constitutional psychopathic inferiority" (a term concocted by U.S.-American physician William Healy: see N.H. Rafter, *Creating Born Criminals* (Urbana: University of Illinois Press, 1997), at 177). There is little evidence that this concept was much invoked in Canada. Indeed, the law's draftsperson, Tom MacInnes, was later to describe this amendment, along with another excluding "persons with chronic alcoholism," as "sheer quack-psychology verbiage, by virtue of which any immigration officer with a grouch can put anyone except a Canadian citizen out of Canada." MacInnes, ibid., at 120. In retrospect, however, it is difficult to discern how categories such as constitutional psychopathic inferiority and chronic alcoholism were any less nebulous than many of the other reigning psychiatric concepts of the day such as "feeblemindedness" and "imbecility." See, for example, J. Stephen, "The 'Incorrigible,' the 'Bad,' and the 'Immoral': Toronto's 'Factory Girls' and

the Work of the Toronto Psychiatric Clinic" in L.A. Knafla & S.W.S. Binnie, eds., *Law, Society and the State: Essays in Modern Legal History* (Toronto: University of Toronto Press, 1995), 405. For example, one is led to speculate, as did one of the reviewers of this article, whether the consuming practices of politicians and medical practitioners might have lain behind this tendency to affirm the pathologies of mental disorder while so readily dismissing the disease model of alcoholism.

49. Section 23 of the Act, which empowered immigration officers to order the deportation of any prohibited person without recourse to judicial review, was generally known as the "skidoo section." MacInnes retrospectively referred to this section as "about the worst thing in which I ever took a hand." Ibid., at 122.

50. Immigration Act, *supra* note 48, s. 25–30.

51. Ibid., at s. 40. See *Keeping America Sane, supra* note 3 at 174.

52. An Act to Amend the Immigration Act, S.C. 1919, c. 25. See Avery, *supra* note 2; "Shovelling Out the Mutinous," *supra* note 2.

53. Letter from W.D. Scott to H.E. Young (9 July 1907) BCARS. GR 542, box 12, file 4.

54. According to B.C. Provincial Secretary J.D. MacLean, in an address to the Kiwanis Club of Victoria, the identification of deportable patients had become a top priority by the 1920s: "The Hospital staff are constantly alert for the citizen of another country who has not been in Canada the five years required by the Dominion Immigration law, and application is made at once for the return of all such cases to the care of his (or her) own country." "Insane Mostly Foreign Born," *Victoria Colonist* (2 August 1922) BCARS. GR 645, file 4.

55. Immigration Act provisions held the shipping companies responsible for returning those prohibited individuals whom they had transported to Canada. In 1914 the Department of the Interior (then responsible for the Immigration Branch) contributed $50 to the transportation companies if the three-year domicile limit had expired or if the deport was being conveyed by a different shipping line from the original. The Department paid $15 if the deportation was ordered after one year, and made no defrayment at all if repatriation occurred within the first year. Letter from W.D. Scott to P.V.G. Mitchell, White Star-Dominion Line (14 July 1914) NAC. RG 76, vol. 530, file 803572, pt. 2.

56. From September 1926 onward, the Immigration Branch began to retain a record of every deportation

effected from mental hospitals across the country by obtaining a copy of the medical reports addressed to Assistant Deputy Health Minister Dr. D.A. Clark. These reports occasionally contained verbatims from the inquiry board hearings, which typically covered at most two or three pages of text. Letter from A.L. Jolliffe to Mr. J.S. Fraser (26 September 1926) NAC. RG 76, vol. 530, file 803572, pt. 2.

57. Escorts comprised one or more immigration officers or designated police officers. Letter from F.C. Blair, Secretary, Immigration Branch to F.E. Lawler, Medical Superintendent, Nova Scotia Hospital, Dartmouth (26 November 1920) NAC. RG 76, vol. 530, file 803572, pt. l.

58. Immigration Branch files contain an ongoing correspondence between federal officials and CPR management and agents, in which the latter recurrently expressed their discontent with their compulsory role in transporting insane persons across the country. They were especially frustrated with lack of communication and the occasional failure to provide advanced notice of pending deportations; with the requirement that some aggressive or floridly ill patients be given special treatment or assigned to private compartments; and with the potential for disruption to paying passengers. See generally NAC. RG 76, vol. 530, file 803572.

59. Patients deported to Newfoundland, for example, were routinely dumped without escort at the Port-aux-Basques steamship terminus, some 500 miles from the mental hospital in St. John's. Letter from A. Reid, Deputy Colonial Secretary, Newfoundland to F.C. Blair (31 March 1922); Letter from R. Thews to A.L. Jolliffe (25 April 1925); Letter from A.L. Jolliffe to R. Thews (18 May 1925) NAC. RG 76, vol. 530, file 803572, pt. l.

60. George Hannah of the Allan Lines addressed the following to W.D. Scott in August 1909: "This letter is to ask that in future ... [a letter] should be sent to Mr. [John] Hoolahan [Dominion Immigration Agent in Montreal] to be delivered with the passenger on board the steamer .... we fear we will be found at fault because we were not aware that M. had been deported until after he had sailed, and hence the doctor was not advised that the passenger had suicidal inclinations and to guard him accordingly." Letter from Hannah to Scott (14 August 1909) NAC. RG 76, vol. 530, file 803572, pt. l.

61. W.D. Scott Memorandum (27 January 1911) NAC. RG 76, vol. 530, file 803572, pt. l.

62. "Doctors and Deports," *supra* note 3.

63. J.D. Page, "Inspection Too Fast, Feeble-Minded Enter; Steamship Arrivals Examined at Four-a-Minute; Not One Specialist Employed" (Speech to Provincial Association for the Care of the Feeble-minded) *Toronto Star* (1 July 1917) NACRG 76, vol. 530, file. 803572, pt. l.

64. Ibid., at 31.

65. Vancouver was assigned a single local Commissioner of Immigration (A.L. Jolliffe, who was succeeded in turn by A.E. Skinner and F.W. Taylor).

66. C.E. Doherty, *ARMS,* Public Hospital for the Insane (1918) at V7, 8.

67. *ARMS,* Provincial Mental Hospital (1924–1925) at R9.

68. *ARMS,* Provincial Mental Hospital (1922–1923) at V9.

69. H.C. Steeves, "Community Mental Health Problems" (March 1926) *Vancouver Medical Association Bulletin* 12 BCARS. GR 865, Box 2, File 15.

70. Order-in-Council: For Edwin James Rothwell (New Westminster), Brigadier-General Victor Wentworth Odium (Vancouver), William Alexander McKenzie (Penticton), Reginald Hayward (Victoria), Paul Phillips Harrison (Cumberland). Signed by William Sloan, Provincial Secretary (30 December 1925) BCARS. GR 865, box 1, file 4. See also "Mental Commission Will Sit Here" *Vancouver Sun* (31 March 1926) at 11.

71. Macdonald had been a reporter for the *Vancouver Sun*, as well as Publicity Commissioner for Parliament in Ottawa. Letter from J.A. Macdonald to J.S. Woodsworth (17 June 1926) BCARS. GR 865, box 1, file 2.

72. H.P. Davidson, "A Report on the Heredity and Place of Origin of the Patients Admitted to the Provincial Mental Hospitals of British Columbia" (November 1926). BCARS. GR 865, box 2, file 6.

73. Letter from J.A. Macdonald to P.P. Harrison (28 September 1926) BCARS. GR 865, box 1, file 2.

74. P.P. Harrison, "Immigration and Its Effects on the Increase of Insanity" (8 January 1927) Report to the B.C. Legislature. Royal Commission on Mental Hygiene GR 865, box 1, file 2.

75. British Columba, Legislative Assembly, "Royal Commission on Mental Hygiene Report," *Sessional Papers* (1927) at CC30.

76. Letter from A.L. Crease to P.D. Walker (15 February 1932). In response, Deputy Attorney-General O.C. Bass ruled that no such residential prerequisite existed in law. Letter from Bass to Walker (2 April 1932) BCARS. GR 542, box 16, file 7.

77. BCARS. GR 542, box 17, file 1.

78. On the history of the CNCMH and the career of Hincks, see, e.g., *Keeping America Sane*, *supra* note 3; J.D. Griffin, *In Search of Sanity: A Chronicle of the Canadian Mental Health Association* (London: Third Eye, 1989); McConnachie, *supra* note 39; D. MacLennan, "Beyond the Asylum: Professionalism and the Mental Hygiene Movement in Canada, 1914–1928" (1987) 4 *Canadian Bulletin of Medical History* 7; T.R. Richardson, *The Century of the Child: The Mental Hygiene Movement and Social Policy in the United States and Canada* (Albany: State University of New York Press, 1989); C.G. Roland, *Clarence Hincks: Mental Health Crusader* (Toronto: Dundurn, 1990).

79. Environmental theories, however, could also be mobilized to support arguments in favour of deportation. Witness, for example, Crease's efforts to persuade federal Immigration and Colonization Minister W.A. Gordon that banishment could operate in the best medical interests of his patients: "It is especially noted with mental patients that a change of environment, in other words, their returning home, is a great aid in their compensation. Even though they may have to go to a Mental Hospital for a time, they are so improved by the change that often their stay is only for a short time, and so what appears to be a hardship is in reality a very definite compensation." Letter from A.L. Crease to W.A. Gordon (20 May 1931) BCARS. GR 542, box 16, file 4.

80. *Supra* note 38.

81. Writing to Parliamentary Under-Secretary for External Affairs Hugh Clark, Scott averred: "I have no doubt that a number of feeble-minded or insane people have got into Canada without detection, or, at least, a number have been found in Canada within 3 years of arrival ... [but] ... [i]n every case where these have been reported to me we have endeavoured to bring about their deportation ...." Letter from W.D. Scott to Hugh Clark (11 November 1916) NAC. RG 76, vol. 530, file 803572, pt. 1.

82. According to Jolliffe, while "the department does not, of course, claim that the medical inspection is 100 per cent perfect and results in every physical or mental case being discovered at the port of entry, but it is claimed that every reasonable precaution is taken to prevent the admission of persons prohibited on account of physical and mental condition." *Vancouver Sun* (1 June 1926) BCARS. GR 865, box 2, file 14.

83. In his report to the Dominion Council of Health in December 1925, Amyot asserted: "[W]e have a staff developed for the examination of immigrants that we think is a very efficient one .... They are skilled and we have been looking for nothing else but defects for the last three or four years, particularly defects coming under the medical sections of the Immigration Act." BCARS. GR 865, box 1, file 2.

84. Form 30A was the assessment instrument employed by immigration officers. Letter from J.D. Page to A.L. Jolliffe (13 November 1926) NAC. RG 76, vol. 530, file 803572, pt. 2.

85. "Training of Immigration Inspectors in Psychiatry" (October 1920) *Mental Hygiene Bulletin* at 14. See Godler, *supra* note 3 at 14.

86. J.A. Amyot, *Presentation to the 13th Meeting of the Dominion Council of Health* (Ottawa: 8–10 December 1925). BCARS. GR 865, box 1, file 2.

87. *Keeping America Sane*, *supra* note 3 at 156.

88. Page, who was by this time Chief of the Division of Quarantine and Immigration Medical Inspection for the Department of Health, offered the following logic to the 21st Meeting of the DCH in 1930: "You will, I think at once agree that if there is one class of immigrant against which this country must be guarded it is the mentally defective, not only for its own sake but because of its effect on future generations, through propagation. On the other hand, it must be realized that no class presents so much difficulty in the application of medical knowledge .... You have, for instance, dementia praecox cases which during their lucid intervals often appear mentally brighter than the average normal individual. In the majority of cases this type would in fact escape the attention of the experienced psychiatrist under similar conditions as our medical officers have to work." J.D. Page, *Memorandum to Dominion Council of Health* (10–12 December 1930) BCARS. GR 2826, box 1, file 4.

89. J.S. Woodsworth, *Strangers within Our Gates* (Toronto: University of Toronto Press, 1972 [1909]), at 229. See T. Chapman, "Early Eugenics Movement in Western Canada" (1977) 25 *Alberta History* 200 at 203.

90. W.G. Smith, *A Study in Canadian Immigration* (Toronto: Ryerson, 1919), at 323. See also (October 1920) 1:2 *Mental Hygiene Bulletin* BCARS. GR 865, box 2, file 1.

91. In the intemperate flourish of Dr. John A. MacGregor, in his outgoing presidential address to the Ontario Medical Association in London on 26 May 1925: "Immigration is a crying need in this country. Our expansive fertile fields invite the coming of hundreds of men and women into this

land of promise, but we must be very particular regarding the types that we admit. Unfortunately, no small percentage of those finding their way here at the present time, and for some time past, have been of a definitely inferior type .... The medical profession can perform a lasting public service by bringing the matter to the attention of the Immigration Department, and impressing on them the necessity of more carefully investigating particularly the assisted immigrant, as to his mental status before he leaves his native country." BCARS. GR 865, box 1, file 2.

92. Godler, *supra* note 3 at 14.

93. See Table 1.

94. Godler, *supra* note 3 at 15.

95. See R. Menzies, "Race, Reason and Regulation: British Columbia's Mass Exile of Chinese 'Lunatics' Aboard the CPSS *Empress of Russia*, 9 February 1935" [unpublished manuscript in submission].

96. *Victoria Daily Times* (11 February 1935) BCARS. GR 144, book 4.

97. BCARS. GR 542, Box 21, File 5 and GR 1665, Box 8, File 3; NAC. RG 625, vol. 1803, file 1936-729.

98. *Our Own Master Race, supra* note 3 at 66, 165.

99. Typical of this preoccupation was a flurry of activity in 1935 that involved W.A. Gordon and the provincial premiers and ministers responsible for health. Following years of ambiguity and bickering among the provinces, the Canadian Department of Immigration and Colonization reached an agreement with the United States Immigration Service to the effect that mental cases apprehended in the U.S. would be returned to their province of birth rather than last residence whenever the two differed. Letter from T. Magladery, Deputy Minister of Immigration and Colonization to Premier T.D. Pattullo (23 January 1935) BCARS. GR 542, box 17, file 5.

100. Letter from Walker to Crease (5 February 1934) BCARS. GR 542, box 17, file 3.

101. NAC. RG 29, vol. 3091, file 854-4-300.

102. Department of Citizenship and Immigration, *Operations Memorandum* (28 July 1964); *ibid.*

103. Immigration Act, SC 1976, c. 52.

104. On medical provisions contained in the Immigration Act, see generally D. Galloway, *Immigration Law* (Toronto: Irwin, 1997), at 129; F.N. Marrocco & H.M. Goslett, *The Annotated Immigration Act of Canada* (Toronto: Carswell, 1994), at 86, 97, 380.

105. *Supra* note 103, s. 11(l)(3).

106. In one sample year (1987–1988), there were 2,270,648 examinations of persons seeking entry to Canada, and 41,498 reports on those suspected of being inadmissible. *Annual Report: Canadian Department of Employment and Immigration, 1987–88* (Ottawa: Queen's Printer, 1989) [hereinafter ARCDEI].

107. *Supra* note 103, s. 91(1).

108. Immigration Act, 1992, c. 49, s. 19.

109. In the nine-year period from 1980–1981 through 1988–1989, for example, 36,794 individuals were the subjects of deportation orders, departure notices, or exclusion orders. *Supra* ARCDEI, 1980–1981 to 1988–1989, *supra* note 106.

110. "Outlook Called Grim for Schizophrenic Man Deported to Scotland," *Vancouver Sun* (31 May 1997) A7; Ed Struzik, "Schizophrenic Man Faces Battle to Stay in Canada," *Vancouver Sun* (16 February 1998), A7.

Table 1: Canadian Immigration, Deportation, and Rejection Statistics, 1902–1903 to 1938–1939

Year	Total Immigration	Deportations Total	Medical	Insanity	Defect	Rejections at Ocean Ports Total	Medical	Insanity	Defect
1902–1903	128,364	67	49	1	8	273	257	0	1
1903–1904	130,331	85	61	5	9	274	225	5	0
1904–1905	146,266	86	58	5	7	611	529	3	4
1905–1906	189,064	137	110	12	18	524	404	11	11
1906–1907	124,667	201	126	53	22	440	264	8	5
1907–1908	262,469	825	392	110	45	1,172	513	19	12
1908–1909	146,908	1,748	467	113	36	509	216	13	28
1909–1910	208,794	734	212	95	12	1,515	585	15	31
1910–1911	311,084	784	222	121	17	2,210	585	6	27
1911–1912	354,237	959	229	133	9	972	256	17	27
1912–1913	402,432	1,281	370	221	10	756	328	24	25
1913–1914	384,878	1,834	570	210	15	1,827	398	18	45
1914–1915	144,789	1,734	379	144	10	998	319	6	54
1915–1916	48,537	1,243	206	62	6	163	34	6	5
1916–1917	75,374	605	98	49	12	174	30	0	4
1917–1918	79,074	527	39	32	0	71	12	3	1
1918–1919	57,702	454	70	49	3	70	19	0	0
1919–1920	117,336	655	123	89	9	662	21		
1920–1921	148,477	1,044	133	82	6	953	99		
1921–1922	89,999	2,046	313	132	37	1,083	60		
1922–1923	72,887	1,632	282	154	49	632	37		
1923–1924	148,560	2,106	649	122	50	992	130		
1924–1925	111,362	1,686	420	126	69	1,031	83		
1925–1926	96,064	1,716	410	160	61	266	40		
1926–1927	143,991	1,585	470			689	95		
1927–1928	151,597	1,866	519			319	104		
1928–1929	167,722	1,964	650			360	94		
1929–1930	163,288	3,963	600			321	78		
1930–1931	88,223	4,376	789			483	39		
1931–1932	25,752	7,025	697			324	26		
1932–1933	19,782	7,131	476			229	16		
1933–1934	13,903	4,474	301	166	14	194	17		
1934–1935	12,136	1,128	144	98	4	215	9		
1935–1936	11,103	610	81	52	7	196	13		
1936–1937	12,023	576	47			247	11		
1937–1938	15,645	413	42	30	8	210	8		
1938–1939	17,128	434	36	19	12	177	7		
TOTAL	4,821,948	59,734	10,840			22,142	5,961		

Table 2: British Columbia Mental Hospitals: Admissions, Discharges and Deportations, 1921–1938

Year	1921–1922	1922–1923	1923–1924	1924–1925	1925–1926	1926–1927	1927–1928	1928–1929	1929–1930	1930–1931	1931–1932	1932–1933	1933–1934	1934–1935	1935–1936	1936–1937	1937–1938	Total
Total Admissions	478	438	447	461	475	494	542	543	602	632	562	635	610	653	679	783	834	9868
Total Discharges	488	483	450	443	439	440	474	567	652	597	538	566	570	641	658	766	768	9540
Total Deportations	32	36	17	37	35	39	28	48	55	53	60	45	34	13	11	2	8	553
Informal Repatriations						11	14	11	12	13	24	26	20	28	17	21		197
Deportations as % of Discharges	6.6	7.5	3.8	8.4	8	8.9	5.9	8.5	8.4	8.9	11.2	8	6	2	1.7	0.3	1	5.8%
Informal Repatriations as % of Discharges*						2.5	3	1.9	1.8	2.2	4.5	4.6	3.5	4.4	2.6	2.7		3.0%

* Statistics on informal repatriations reported for years 1926–27 through 1936–37 only

Table 3: Country of Origin for British Columbia Mental Hospital Admissions and Deportations, 1921–1922 to 1935–1936

Where Originated[a]	Admissions			Deportations		
	N	%	% Foreign Born	N	%	As % of Admissions
British Columbia	1,143	13.9				
Canada-Other	1,959	23.9				
England	1,840		36.1	124	22.9	6.7
United States	586		11.5	58	10.7	9.9
Finland	145		2.8	50	9.2	34.5
Scotland	636		12.5	37	6.8	5.8
Sweden	198		3.9	34	6.3	17.2
Norway	157		3.1	31	5.7	19.7
Ireland	285		5.6	29	5.4	10.2
Germany	89		1.7	21	3.9	23.6
Jugoslavia/Serbia/Montenegro	53		1.0	20	3.7	37.7
China	177		3.5	15	2.8	8.5
Poland	65		1.3	15	2.8	23.1
Czechoslovakia	23		0.5	15	2.8	65.2
Switzerland	31		0.6	11	2.0	35.5
Denmark	35		0.7	9	1.7	25.7
Wales	71		1.4	8	1.5	11.3
Italy	92		1.8	7	1.3	7.6
Japan	83		1.6	7	1.3	8.4
Austria	71		1.4	6	1.1	8.5
Holland	25		0.5	6	1.1	24.0
Hungary	15		0.3	6	1.1	40.0
Newfoundland	38		0.7	5	0.9	13.2
France	44		0.9	4	0.7	9.1
Greece	20		0.4	4	0.7	20.0
Australia	29		0.6	3	0.6	10.3
Europe-Other[b]	27		0.5	3	0.6	11.1
South Africa	12		0.2	3	0.6	25.0
New Zealand	11		0.2	3	0.6	27.3
Belgium	16		0.3	2	0.4	12.5
Russia	103		2.0	1	0.2	1.0
India	45		0.9	1	0.2	2.2
Americas - Other[c]	13		0.3	1	0.2	7.1
Galicia-Ukrainia	20		0.4	0	0	0
Roumania	17		0.3	0	0	0
Iceland	11		0.2	0	0	0
West Indies	11		0.2	0	0	0
Other[d]	3		0.1	0	0	0
Asia - Other[e]	2		0	0	0	0
Unknown	50			1		
TOTAL	8,251			543		

a   Countries are arranged in descending order by total number of deportations. All countries with 10 or more admissions are listed.
b   The Channel Islands (8), Gibralter (4), Lithuania (4), Spain (3), Latvia (3), Bulgaria (2), Malta (1), Luxembourg (1), and Estonia (1).
c   Alaska (3), Chile (3), Mexico (2), British Guiana (2), Brazil (1), Argentina (1), and Salvador (1).
d   The Hawaiian Islands (1), the British East Indies (1), and Egypt (1).
e   Korea (1) and Syria (1).

Table 4: Attributes of Deported British Columbian Mental Patients, 1921–1922 to 1935–1936

	Women		Men	
	N	%	N	%
Total Admissions	2,962	35.9	5,289	64.1
Total Discharges	2,898	36.2	5,108	63.8
Total Deportations	90	16.6	453	83.4
Deportations as % of Discharges		3.1		8.9

	Time in Canada Prior to Hospitalization		Time in Hospital Prior to Deportation	
	N	%	N	%
LT 1 Year	137	25.3	456	84.0
1–2 Years	116	21.4	47	8.7
2–3 Years	89	16.5	11	2.0
3–4 Years	77	14.2	10	1.8
4–5 Years	82	15.2	1	0.2
5–6 Years	8	1.5	1	0.2
6–7 Years	10	1.8	0	0
7–8 Years	5	0.9	3	0.6
8–9 Years	1	0.2	3	0.6
9–10 Years	4	0.7	1	0.2
10–11 Years	5	0.9	3	0.6
11–12 Years	2	0.4	3	0.6
12–13 Years	1	0.2	0	0
13–14 Years	1	0.2	1	0.2
14–15 Years	0	0	0	0
15–16 Years	1	0.2	0	0
16–17 Years	0	0	1	0.2
17–18 Years	0	0	1	0.2
18–19 Years	0	0	0	0
19–20 Years	0	0	0	0
20–21 Years	0	0	0	0
21–22 Years	1	0.2	1	0.2
22–23 Years	1	0.2	0	0
Total	541		543	
Mean	2.69 Years		1.04 Years	

CHAPTER 11

Crime and the Changing Forms of Class Control: Policing Public Order in "Toronto the Good," 1859–1955

Helen Boritch and John Hagan

* * * * * * * * * * * * * * * * * * *

*****

It is now rather commonplace to depict the creation of modern police forces in the mid–nineteenth century as a response to rising levels of riots, disorder, and crime. The concern on the part of the middle and upper classes with the presumed deleterious effects of rapid urbanization and industrialization on social order put pressure on civic authorities to provide an effective means of controlling the "dangerous classes" and led to the widespread introduction of centralized, uniformed municipal police forces in North America and Western Europe (Johnson 1976; Lane 1980a; Miller 1977; Parks 1974; Silver 1967). As a result, nineteenth-century policing has been characterized as involving an aggressive enforcement policy toward various public order offenses that was designed primarily to curb the activities of the lower classes. In addition, in the absence of specialized civic agencies, the police also became responsible for administering and overseeing a plethora of social welfare and public services. Among other things, this included regulating health standards, providing an ambulance service, taking censuses, and giving overnight shelter to tramps in police stations. The consequence was that policing rapidly evolved into a multifaceted institution with broad and amorphous powers to intervene

in the lives of city dwellers. The control of crime was but one aspect of this social role.

These features of nineteenth-century urban policing are the central components of a style of police organization, enforcement practices, and nonarrest activities which have been variously described as "class control" (Monkkonen 1981), "social control" (Watts 1983), and "service" (Ferdinand 1976). Although there are important differences in the usage of these terms to characterize policing in the last century, there is a general consensus that the objective consequence of policing was disproportionately high arrest rates for and police involvement with, the working classes, immigrants, transients, the chronically unemployed, and other problem populations.[1] [...]

[...] The gradual shift in policing to a more legalistic, "crime-control" model is attributed to several interrelated factors. The first involves technological innovations in police work. The advent of the patrol wagon and signal system, together with advanced communication and information systems in the late nineteenth century, served to significantly reduce the response time of the police and to increase the possibility of arrests for more serious crimes. In addition, the development of various crime-detection and identification techniques such as the Bertillon system of physical measurements, photography, fingerprinting, and international information systems, increased the prominence of police detectives and the image of the police as crime specialists. Following the American lead, these new developments were incorporated in the Toronto force, as evidenced in the growth of the proportion of detectives from approximately 4 percent in the nineteenth century, to 12 percent in the period after 1920 (see Boritch 1985).

The second major change in police organization and ideology came as a result of the larger movement to restructure city governments along more centralized, bureaucratic, and specialized lines. Numerous reforms were instituted which were designed to further professionalize the police, improve efficiency in administrative tasks, and increase specialization in police work. The personal style of policing associated with the constable on the beat was increasingly replaced with a style of policing consciously modeled on business principles and practices. In 1935, the Chief Constable of the Toronto Department argued that,

In this modern and constantly changing age, the administration of any public service, must, in an ever-increasing degree, be conducted along sound business lines. This in the first instance means that sound business principles must be applied in the same way that they are made to function in any successful Industrial or General Business Organization (Toronto Police Department Annual Report 1935, p. 7).

Third, the creation and expansion of various government welfare and service bureaucracies beginning in the reform era eliminated many of the social service functions performed by the police. As police responsibility for noncriminal problem populations (and, therefore, an important means of control) declined, the police had the opportunity to orient themselves more exclusively to crime prevention and control. [...] During this era, Toronto police authorities repeatedly stressed the *idea* that the police role consisted, first and foremost, in the control and

prevention of crime, and that "[n]o other form of service demanded from the police by the public can justify any sacrifice being made at the expense of this one" (Toronto Police Department Annual Report 1935, p. 7). Although there is some difference of opinion as to the timing of this shift, it is generally argued that, by the mid twentieth century, the ideology of policing changed from a focus on controlling *a class of people*, to a focus on preventing and controlling *certain classes of criminality* (Ferdinand 1976; Monkkonen 1981; Watts 1983).

*****

[...] As conceived by Monkkonen, the shift from class control to crime control represents a fundamental change quite similar to the distinction drawn between proactive and reactive policing by Black (1970) and Reiss (1971). Black describes proactive policing as "a social welfare model of law, with the legal good of the citizenry being defined and then imposed by government administration .... A proactive system does not merely make law available, it imposes law" (1980, p. 53). Accordingly, a proactive style of policing is most evident when social problems are defined in relation to the bottom of the class structure, and is characteristic of nineteenth-century policing (Black, 1980). In contrast, contemporary police forces are based primarily on a reactive style of policing organizing around citizen calls for service. Reactive policing reflects an "entrepreneurial" model of law in which the public plays a determinant role in the nature and scope of arrest practices.[2]

******

On the surface, policing in Toronto outwardly conforms to the model of a historical transition from class control to crime control. However, a closer examination of policing during the reform era reveals that, in fact, the class-control model of policing was not diminished. The major change in police ideology and enforcement practices was not from class control to crime control, but rather to different types of public order offenses. [...] For example, although the police maintained their vigilant attitude toward drunkenness and vagrancy, they increasingly came to express concern about other problem populations and behaviors such as prostitution, gambling, liquor law violations, Lord's day violations, and narcotic law violations. These offenses fit within a class-control model of policing, as arrests for these behaviors rest fundamentally on police initiative and a proactive style of policing (see also Watts 1983). Moreover, these "victimless" offenses disproportionately criminalize lower-class populations.

Beyond this, there is another substantial category of offenses which fit within a proactive, class-control model of policing. During the urban reform era the enforcement of social order generally, and public morality in particular, also was accomplished through the enactment and enforcement of city bylaws. Like the other public order offenses discussed, city bylaws concern largely victimless, minor offenses in which arrests rest principally on police, aggressiveness, and deliberate enforcement policies. The essential similarity of bylaw enforcement to other public order offenses during this period was expressed in 1912 when the Toronto Board of Police Commissioners instructed the police "that a refusal on the part of a citizen to give his or her name for a breach of a bylaw might be regarded as disorderly conduct and treated accordingly by arrest if necessary" (Board of Police Commissioners Minutes, June 18, 1912, p. 234).

Moreover, the content of bylaws enacted during the reform era clearly reflected middle-class interests and extended the capacity of the police to regulate working-class morality, recreations, and economic activities. For example, in response to the anxiousness of middle-class reformers to eradicate vice, bylaws were enacted to strengthen prostitution and blue laws, to regulate the location and hours of dance halls, theatres, movie houses, and billiard halls, and to give the police the authority to act as censors.[3] Further, this control extended to a direct control over working-class economic activities when the duties of the License Department came under police control in 1896. As a result, unlike larger business interests, which were regulated through provincial legislation, small working-class enterprises, from rag pedlars to tradesmen to small businesses, were under police jurisdiction.

A further feature of city bylaws which makes them especially worthy of attention is the direct role the police played in their creation. In Toronto, under the Municipal Act of 1858 (and various amendments throughout the years), Boards of Police Commissioners were empowered to enact bylaws with respect to a wide variety of concerns. As a result, bylaws represent a category of public order offenses where the police not only defined the "law in action" through discretionary enforcement policies, but actually legislated a significant proportion of the "law in the books." Responding directly to the concerns of various middle-class groups during the reform era, the police enacted a multitude of bylaws which served to further expand the presence and pervasiveness of the police in previously unregulated public and private domains.[4] [...] During the urban reform era, from 1891 to 1920, the proportion of bylaws arrests to total arrests more than doubled from approximately 15 to 35 percent. A contemporary court reporter observed that Toronto had become a city of "shall nots" where it was more important for citizens to memorize 6,000 bylaws than the Ten Commandments (Wodson 1917).

*****

[...] Throughout the entire time period from 1859 to 1955, public order arrests comprise the largest proportion of arrests, indicating a continuation of a "class-control," proactive model of policing. Although from 1921 to 1955 the arrest rate for all public order offenses declined [...] and the arrest rate for crime began to increase [...], suggesting a move toward a greater emphasis on crime control, the most important finding is the consistently higher arrest rate for public order offenses.[5] Even when the public order arrest rate dropped to its lowest point of 2,208 in 1933, this was still almost twice the crime rate of 1,211.

Second, whereas the arrest rate for crime traces a steady decline from the mid nineteenth century to the 1920s, the public order arrest rate fluctuates dramatically and, in some instances, varies by over 1,000 arrests in the space of a year. This difference underscores the preeminent role of police initiative and departmental policy in the production of public order arrests. Nevertheless, despite the large variations in the public order arrest rate, these arrests constituted 60 to 85 percent of all arrests from 1859 to 1955 and averaged approximately 70 percent. Therefore, while the total arrest rate declined, the proportion of proactive to reactive policing remained much more stable.

*****

For example, the average annual rate of change among arrest rates for drunkenness, disorderly conduct, and vagrancy, other public morality offenses ("vice"), and bylaws provide further evidence that the Toronto police varied their focus from one type of public order offense to another during different periods. In "the formative period" of Toronto policing, from 1859 to 1890, arrests for drunkenness, disorderly conduct, and vagrancy decreased dramatically. [...] During the same period, the arrest rate for vice displays no discernible trend [...] while the rate for bylaw arrest shows a significant increase. [...]

However, the most interesting change in police activity occurs during "the urban reform era," from 1891 to 1920. During this period, arrests for drunkenness, disorderly conduct, and vagrancy actually increased to about 1912, but then decreased suddenly with the enactment of the Ontario Temperance Act in 1916. [...] Yet even during this period these arrests continue to be about twice those for "crime." At the same time, however, arrests for vice [...] and bylaws [...] noticeably increased. Finally, from 1921 to

1955, after the repeal of the Ontario Temperance Act in 1927, the arrest rate for drunkenness and disorderly conduct increased, [...] while arrests for both vice [...] and bylaws [...] declined from the previous era.

[...] While the police in Toronto did, in fact, adopt the organizational reforms and public image of a crime-control model, especially after 1920, these changes did not translate into notably different arrest practices; instead, it appears that the police expanded their attention from drunkenness and vagrancy to encompass other forms of vice in accordance with a changing spatial development of the city, and the urban reform movement. As middle-class citizens increasingly moved to outlying areas of the city in the late nineteenth century, the core of the city became a predominantly lower-class, immigrant area with demarcated disreputable sections (Lemon 1984). On the one hand, this served to reduce the exposure of middle-class citizens to public drunkenness, but at the same time it increased perceptions and concerns with the ghettoization and open proliferation of vice in the "Ward" area, making it a prominent target of reformers' efforts. The establishment of a morality department in 1886 with a sweeping mandate to control immorality is evidence that far from reflecting a distinctive change in police priorities, the urban reform era was characterized by an intensification of proactive and class-control arrest policies.

Nevertheless, these results do not discount the possibility that important structural changes did occur in policing in terms of the relative influence of a variety of factors on arrest rates for public order offenses, taken as a whole, as well as individually. For example, despite the preponderance of public order arrests relative to arrests for more serious crimes, the arrest rate for these offenses did decline from 1859 to 1955, and the decline in public order arrests from 1921 to 1955 coincided with an increase in crime arrests. Therefore, while it is apparent that even by the 1950s the Toronto police had not given up their predominant attention to public order offenses, it is still plausible that police responses were closer to a class-control model in the two eras of 1859 to 1890 and 1891 to 1920, and somewhat closer to a crime-control model after 1921. [...]

*****

The Formative Years (1859–1890)

The mid-nineteenth century was a period of increasing labor militancy, political unrest, and economic recession in Toronto, as elsewhere in North America. From 1852 to 1854 there were at least 14 strikes, and in the period from 1839 to 1866, 29 riots erupted (Kealey 1984). It was within this mid nineteenth-century context that Toronto set about the task of reorganizing its police department. The new distribution of personnel, duties, and regulations of the force was determined after careful consideration of information received from a number of American cities, especially New York, Albany, Portland, and Boston. The Board of Commissioners concluded after this review that the "Boston system seems the most applicable to the city of Toronto ...." (Toronto City Council Minutes 1859, Appendix 14, p. 83).

In all of this, class concerns were manifest, and linked particularly to problems of drunkenness, both among officers and the citizenry. The number of police who were disciplined each year, mostly for alcohol-related offenses, was seldom less than 25 percent of the force and in 1890 this figure reached 66 percent (Toronto Police Department Annual Reports). It seems that clear class boundaries were to be drawn, and then exemplified as well as enforced by the police. The Toronto police officer was to be in all possible ways "a man above the class of labourers" (Toronto City Council Minutes 1859; Appendix 4, p. 7). [...]

[...] The advent of the patrol wagon and the signal system in the 1880s illustrates the ways in which the control of violence and drunkenness were linked. The signal system allowed officers to be dispatched in response to reports of violence, and the wagons allowed drunk and disorderly offenders to be more easily returned to the station houses. This system, together with the newly created mounted squad, were attractive new tools for the control of collective as well as more isolated threats of violence. These points were quickly incorporated into the arguments of the Toronto Police for adopting tike patrol wagon and signal system. Indeed, after what was widely regarded as an effective response by the Department to the Toronto Street Railway Company strike of 1886, the Chief Constable added to his usual list of supporting arguments the system's capacity "for rapid concentration of men at any particular point when needed" (Toronto Police Department Annual Report 1887, p. 110).

*****

The Urban Reform Era (1891–1920)

The Toronto Department of 1891 was barely recognizable from its humble beginnings: from 3 stations and 60 men in 1859, the force had grown to 7 stations and 285 men serving a population of 185,000. By 1920, there were 11 stations and 683 men serving a population of over half a million. Note, however, that the latter figures represent a proportionate reduction in the ratio of police to population during the urban reform era. The population was expanding while police strength was declining. The population growth was in large part a result of the role of the railways in Canada's development and the emergence of Toronto as "the hub of a railway network" (Careless 1978, p. 16). The simultaneous decline in police strength was a result of the depression of the 1890s.

One consequence of the drop in police strength was a continuation in the decline in drunkenness, disorderly conduct, and vagrancy arrests. [...] However, while the latter offenses continued their long-term decline, other offenses were taking their place. [...] To understand this change, we must first say more about the urban reform era in Toronto.

Notwithstanding an influx of immigrants, Toronto at the turn of the century retained a predominant Anglo-Saxon, Protestant character, and puritanical moral code (Glazebrook 1971; Goheen 1970). A fear that urban squalor would soon contaminate the lives of the respectable classes led clergymen, temperance societies, women's groups, and self-styled moral crusaders on a mission to purify the city and rebuild the existing welfare system. In the late 1880s the newly elected reform Mayor, William Howland, established a Morality Department under the equally zealous Staff Inspector Archibald. The Inspector's new jurisdiction included prostitution, gambling, liquor laws, Sabbath-breaking, censorship, sports, pool rooms, dance halls, and any new forms of "immorality" which came to police attention.[6] Subsequently, and notwithstanding these efforts, the meetings of the Board of Police Commissioners were opened to a continual stream of delegations which appeared to criticize the police for laxity in the enforcement of public morality. [...] The police responded to this pressure by enforcing existing morality laws more vigorously and by using their authority to create new bylaws.

*****

Several further points should be made about the new prominence of bylaws. Harring has observed that the "criminologists definition of 'public order crimes' comes perilously close to the historian's description of 'working class leisure time activity'" (1983, p. 198). This is particularly true of bylaw enforcement that went so far, for example, as attempting to control such behaviors as ball-playing in the streets, swimming at public beaches, tobogganing in parks, and spitting in public places.[7] However, in addition to regulating working-class morality and recreations, bylaws were also a principal means by which the police regulated the economic activities of the working class. Taken together, this widespread authority gave the police far-reaching control over public order and the working and nonworking poor.

Police enforcement of existing and new public morality offenses served several related purposes. First, prosecuting offenders for minor

offences was a relatively easy and successful means of bolstering the city's revenues through fines, thus promoting the legitimacy of the entire police department to the municipal government. Second, it enhanced the capacity of the police to increase arrests within the class that already constituted the bulk of arrest statistics. Third, the belief that vice was at the root of more serious forms of crime, including much violence, justified a heavy-handed enforcement policy and promoted the image of the police as effective crime fighters. This belief held sway well into the twentieth century.

Most of the individuals charged with the various public order offenses were discharged or fined. As an example, of 21,553 offenders arrested in 1909, 9,247 were arrested for drunkenness and 5,935 for breaches of city bylaws and other minor offenses, totalling 15,182. Of those cases, 8,295 of the charges were withdrawn or dismissed by the police court magistrate. Nonetheless, when confronted with this information the police responded with a strong defense of their arrest and detainment policies.

... it would be decidedly incorrect and unwise to assert that any of those dealt with as above described should not have been arrested ... the drunkard must be protected not only for the sake of himself, his wife and his children, but also for the sake of society in general. So it becomes necessary to place him under restraint until he is sufficiently sober to be allowed his liberty again. A similar procedure is followed in dealing with all minor offenses, including breach of City By Laws (Report, signed by Chief Constable Grasett and Chief Inspector Archibald, n.d., Toronto Police Museum Archives).

The legacy of the urban reform era in Toronto was to further entrench and intensify the class-control nature of policing and its heavy emphasis on public order offenses. While this aspect of police work was evident within the first few decades of the reformed police force, it was given its fullest expression during this era.

The middle-class eye may have been blind to its own hypocrisy, but it maintained an unblinking stare on the sins of the lower classes.

Centralization and Specialization (1921–1955)

With a population of over a half million by 1920, the city once called "Hogtown" had taken its place among North America's growing urban centers. However, the city's growth slowed over the next several decades, and in 1955 its population was approximately 682,000. The police force grew from 743 members in 1920 to 1,132 members in 1955. For the police and municipal government more generally, this was a period of increasing bureaucratization. In seeking ways to respond to the problems accompanying urban industrial growth, a system of municipal government and policing emerged that was modelled on the principles of professionalism, centralization, and specialization.

Numerous examples of these changes are apparent in the record of the Department. In 1934, a centralized system of licensing persons and premises was implemented at Police Headquarters and in 1936, the summons system also was centralized at Headquarters. A new emphasis on professionalization was formalized with the establishment of the Ontario Provincial and Municipal Training School at Headquarters in 1935. At the same time, noncriminal functions were reduced. In 1919, the employment of police as truant officers was discontinued. In 1931, the duties of dog-catching were transferred to the Toronto Humane Society. In 1933, the ambulance service was moved to the Medical Health Department. The Department had secured its position in municipal government, and it no longer needed noncrime-related services for public legitimation. Finally, specialization was also evident within the Department with, for example, the creation of the arson squad in 1932 and the increase in different ranks above the level of constable. The number of these positions grew from 9 in 1889 to 11 by 1920,

and jumped to 16 by 1955 (Toronto Police Department Annual Reports).

The emphasis now was one of dispassionate, professional crime fighting. [...]

However, simultaneous developments cast doubt on the assumption that the new crime-fighting image promoted by police authorities signified a major change in police practices. In particular, the Morality Department established in the urban reform era did not recede into the background of policing in the era of centralization and specialization. To the contrary, the control and regulation of vice was still regarded as indispensable to the effectiveness of the police in combatting serious crime. In the police view, the control of vice was crime control. Using the example of gambling, the Chief Constable articulated the fundamental connection between vice and more serious crime in the following uncompromising way:

> Professional gambling dives are, for the most part, operated by foreigners, who, if they are not vicious criminals, can be classified as racketeers whose unlawful activities promote crime in the community. There is no place for these highly organized professional gambling houses in Canada .... (Toronto Police Department Annual Report 1940, p. 10).

This view was to harden and become more encompassing as the era progressed. In 1947 the Chief Constable responded vociferously to supporters of a less repressive enforcement policy, arguing that the connection between vice and more serious crime was indisputable.

> There have been indications in the past of a tendency on the part of some Police officials and others charged with law enforcement and the administration of justice to lean toward the theory that the thief, burglar, and hold-up man are the arch-criminals of the community and that offenders of a much lesser degree are the brothel keeper, the boot-legger and the professional gambler; and that operations of the latter groups are to be suffered on the principle that their

presence in all communities is inevitable ... operators of speak easies, houses of prostitution and gambling "dives," perhaps not individually, but as a collectivity are a more degrading and more permanent bad influence ....

Let us beware of any attempts to draw a line of demarcation in the underworld. Police officers of experience realize that often in the brothel, speak-easy and gambling "joint" stolen property is handled, sometimes narcotic drug deals framed, criminal enterprises hatched and planned, criminals and fugitives harboured and alibis concocted for later false testimony (Toronto Police Department Annual Report 1947, pp. 10–11).

These quotations underscore the persistent priority accorded by the police to the regulation of public morality well into the twentieth century. The drunks, tramps, and unemployed who had constituted the nineteenth-century police identification of the dangerous classes were increasingly supplemented by new targets of enforcement policies drawn from the same classes, perhaps often even including the same persons. This continued emphasis on morality enforcement substantially modifies assumptions about the extent of changes in police organization and activities from the nineteenth to the twentieth centuries. We have seen that many organizational and administrative changes did occur in the mid twentieth century. Many of the social services of the police were eliminated, major campaigns to promote a new image of the police were launched, and significant changes in police administration took place. At the same time, however, the longstanding role of the police in suppressing vice continued to be regarded as an essential part of the police mandate. In this regard, our findings are consistent with Skolnick's (1966) analysis of the prominent role of vice law enforcement in his classic observational study of an American police department in the 1960s.

The historical development of policing in Toronto, therefore, appears to undermine any strict interpretation of the evolution of municipal policing as one of clear-cut change from a proactive class-control to a reactive crime-control model. Both elements coexisted in mid twentieth century police work in Toronto. Perhaps this explains more generally why the works of Black and Reiss and of Skolnick have become such classic pieces in the literature on modern policing. Each may represent one facet of an emerging and ongoing historical synthesis of class and crime control in contemporary police work.

Conclusions

This analysis of policing and crime in Toronto has produced results that both qualify and extend our understanding of the evolution of modern policing. On the one hand, the Toronto police embraced the organizational reforms, prevailing rhetoric, and ideology of a crime-control model after 1920. However, at the level of arrest practices, it is evident that the mid twentieth-century police image as crime fighters was only partially realized. Incorporating vice and bylaws as categories of public order arrests shows that policing in Toronto retained a strong class-control focus from 1859 to 1955. The historical analysis of policing in Toronto reflects both change and continuity.

More specifically, the evidence of nineteenth-century policing in Toronto reinforces the findings of much previous research, while the findings for the twentieth century reveal some important discrepancies. [...] Our most important finding is that the focus of the police varied across different kinds of public order offenses depending on the specific historical context. As one type of problem behavior and one part of the "dangerous classes" receded from police attention, another type of public order offense replaced it. Examination of arrest rates for public order offenses, collectively and individually, showed that the urban reform era did not witness a dramatic change in police priorities but rather an intensification of proactive, class-control policing. [...]

Based on such findings, two sets of conclusions are suggested. At the broadest level, the essential role of the police as agents of class control, focused on the less powerful segments of society, was the predominant feature of policing in both the nineteenth and twentieth century. While the substantive content of public order offenses and enforcement policies changed, the proactive, class-control form of policing persisted. Contemporary critical analyses of class and crime, which view the role of the modern police in these terms (e.g., Balbus 1977; Harring 1983; Spitzer 1975), are thereby encouraged and given an added historical dimension.

However, this conclusion must also be tempered by the findings, which point to changes in the determinants of public order

arrests from the nineteenth to the twentieth century. The nature of these variations indicate that, to a limited degree after 1921, the ideology of crime control influenced arrest practices. Albeit to a lesser extent than previously asserted, the changing relation between proactive and reactive policing over time indicates that policing in Toronto did evolve into a *relatively* more reactive, crime-fighting enterprise by the mid twentieth century. Our analysis suggests that the shift from class to crime control is both less certain and complete than is widely assumed. Indeed, there is less evidence of a shift than of an ongoing historical synthesis in the class and crime-control functions of the police.

Notes

1. Beyond this general consensus, the usage of the terms "class" and "class control" in studies of policing varies considerably. So, for example, Harring's (1983) Marxist analysis emphasizes the creation and control of nineteenth-century police forces by an industrial elite for the preeminent purpose of controlling the working classes. In contrast, Monkkonen (1981) employs a broader meaning of class to encompass the notion of a "dangerous class" composed of a variety of marginal groups which may be differentiated on political, religious, and social dimensions but which, nevertheless, constitute an identifiable subordinate class. This latter usage raises the possibility that police attention varied from one segment of the urban poor to another over time and, moreover, that social-control efforts were not necessarily characterized by repressiveness or a sole concern with the working class. So, while policing is probably best viewed as involving a complexity of purposes, the overall consequence was a concerted control over the urban poor. This more broadly defined concept of class control appears most applicable to policing in nineteenth-century Toronto. As Rogers (1984) notes, it was the marginal poor (casual laborers, prostitutes, and vagrants) and, especially, Irish Catholic immigrants who bore the brunt of police vigilance in the mid nineteenth century. So throughout this period, the percentage of Irish Catholic men and women prosecuted was roughly twice as high as

the percentage of their numbers within the total population. As well, data from the Annual Reports of the Police Department on the occupation of arrested persons from 1870–1873 (the only period in which they were available) reveal that casual laborers, the unemployed, and prostitutes comprised over 60 percent of all arrests. The rest consisted primarily of various tradespeople with less than 1 percent listed as professional men in each year.

2. Classifying policing as proactive or reactive rather than as "class control" or "crime control" may also be preferable in that it avoids the implicit and arguable assumption that police control of more serious crime does not also exhibit a class bias. Our adoption of Monkkonen's terminology is meant as a conceptual convenience to underscore the differences in police organization from the nineteenth to the twentieth century and styles of police enforcement practices with respect to public order offences versus more serious crimes. Our analysis does not pursue the further question or imply as a corollary that the population of arrestees was substantially different across these categories of offenses.

3. Thus, for example, bylaws were enacted in 1890 to prohibit female children from selling newspapers as this was seen to inevitably lead to their demoralization and prostitution (Board of Police Commissioners Minutes Jan. 25, 1890, p. 173). For the same reasons, bylaws were enacted

in 1912 and 1915 to prohibit females from working as organ grinders and to license massage parlours (Toronto Police Department Annual Report 1912; Board of Police Commissioners Minutes Dec. 14, 1915). More generally, bylaws were used to geographically segregate and regulate working-class leisure activities so they could be effectively supervised and not offensive to middle-class sensibilities. Responding to concerns about the "moral atmosphere" of billiard halls in 1907, the Chief Constable recommended a continuation of the "policy of confining these places as much as possible to the business districts of the City ... as their presence in residential districts would be objectionable" (Toronto Police Department, Annual Report 1907, p. 8).

4. A partial list of the many different interest groups that routinely appeared before the Board to either request the enactment of a new bylaw or greater enforcement of existing laws includes the Residents of Centre Street, Law and Order League, Women's Christian Temperance Union, St. Paul's Methodist Church, Lord's Day Alliance, Toronto Humane Society, Local Council of Women (Board of Police Commissioners Minutes Dec. 27, 1889, p. 162; June 14, 1890, pp. 199–200; June 30, 1903; May 3, 1899, p. 232; Sept. 16, 1897, p. 131; June 13, 1899, pp. 242–43; July 2, 1901, pp. 242–43; Jan. 25, 1890, p. 173; Feb. 18, 1913, p. 292; Apr. 19, 1904.

5. Standardized correlation coefficients are used for the purposes of illustrating the effect of the independent variable (year) on the dependent variables (arrest rates) where comparisons are within the same time period. Comparisons of the relations among arrest rates across different time periods are reported as unstandardized regression coefficients.

6. Upon his appointment, Staff Inspector Archibald of the Morality Department (or Staff Inspector's Department as it was euphemistically titled) visited the principal and particularly well-known houses of ill fame in an effort to reduce prostitution. "I gave them distinctly to understand that unless the business was discontinued the law would be strictly enforced, that the authorities desired information rather than prosecution and ... if they wanted to do better that they would be taken charge of by Christian ladies ... or if they wanted to go home passes would be furnished them if necessary .... I found that on a second visit a considerable number had gone to the United States." According to Archibald, this policy resulted in a reduction in the number of houses of ill fame from 49 to 25 in one year (City Council Minutes 1886, Appendix 185, pp. 1011–1012). Archibald's exploits are discussed further in Hagan and Leon (1977).

7. According to Harring, the anti-spitting bylaw, which was enacted as a public health measure, also was a "significant weapon against working class enjoyment of leisure hours. Such a measure served both as a weapon to harass crowds of working-class young people congregated on street corners and as a publicity tool for a police department beleaguered by reformers" (1983, p. 199). Similarly, although Monkkonen (1981) argues against a Marxist analysis of policing, he nonetheless suggests that whatever positive immediate benefits may have accrued to the urban poor as a result of various police activities, these functions had the consequence of enhancing the social- and class-control role of the police.

8. An interesting exception to this trend is the continuation of the police regulation of the tramp population. Although Monkkonen (1981) finds that most major American cities ceased to provide overnight shelter to tramps in the late nineteenth or early twentieth century, the Toronto police continued this practice until the end of the period under study.

References

Balbus, Isaac D. 1977. "Commodity Form and Legal Form: An Essay on the 'Relative Autonomy' of the Law." Pp. 73–90 in *The Sociology of Law: A Conflict Perspective*, edited by Charles Reasons and Robert Rich. Butterworths.

Black, Donald. 1970. "Production of Crime Rates." *American Sociological Review* 35:733–48.

——. 1980. *The Manners and Customs of the Police*. Academic Press.

Boritch, Helen. 1985. "The Making of Toronto the Good: The Organization of Policing and Production of Arrests, 1859 to 1955." Unpublished Ph.D. dissertation, University of Toronto.

Careless, James M.S. 1978. *The Rise of Cities in Canada before 1914*. Canadian Historical Association, Booklet No. 32. Love Printing.

Ferdinand, Theodore N. 1976. "From a Service to a Legalistic Style Police Department: A Case Study."

Journal of Police Science and Administration 4:302–19.

Glazebrook, G.P. 1971. *The Story of Toronto.* University of Toronto Press.

Goheen, Peter G. 1970. "Victorian Toronto, 1850 to 1900: Pattern and Process of Growth." Research Paper No. 127, Department of Geography, University of Chicago.

Hagan, John, and Jeff Leon. 1977. "Rediscovering Delinquency: Social History, Political Ideology and the Sociology of Law." *American Sociological Review* 42:587–97.

Harring, Sidney L. 1983. *Policing a Class Society: The Experience of American Cities, 1865–1915.* Rutgers University Press.

Johnson, Bruce C. 1976. "Taking Care of Labor: The Police in American Politics." *Theory and Society* 3:89–117.

Kealey, Gregory S. 1984. "Orangeman and the Corporation." Pp. 48–86 in *Forging a Consensus: Historical Essays on Toronto*, edited by Victor Russell. University of Toronto Press.

Kitsuse, John I., and Aaron V. Cicourel. 1963. "A Note on the Uses of Official Statistics." *Social Problems* 2:131–39.

Lane, Roger. 1980a. "Urban Police and Crime in Nineteenth-Century America." Pp. 1–43 in *Crime and Justice: An Annual Review of Research*, Vol. 1, edited by Norval Morris and Michael Tonry. University of Chicago Press.

_____. 1980b. "Urban Homicide in the Nineteenth Century: Some Lessons for the Twentieth." Pp. 91–109 in *History and Crime: Implications for Criminal Justice Policy*, edited by James A. Inciardi and C.E. Faupel. Sage.

Lemon, James. 1984. "Toronto among North American Cities." Pp. 323–54 in *Forging a Consensus: Historical Essays on Toronto*, edited by Victor Russell. University of Toronto Press.

Miller, Wilbur R. 1977. *Cops and Bobbies: Police Authority in New York and London 1830–1870.* University of Chicago Press.

Monkkonen, Eric H. 1981. *Police in Urban America, 1860–1920.* Cambridge University Press.

Parks, Evelyn L. 1974. "From Constabulary to Police Society: Implications for Social Control." Pp. 271–89 in *The Criminologist: Crime and the Criminal*, edited by Charles E. Reasons. Goodyear.

Reiss, Albert J. 1971. *The Police and the Public.* Yale University Press.

Rogers, Nicholas. 1984. "Serving Toronto the Good: The Development of the City Police Force 1834–1880." Pp. 116–40 in *Forging a Consensus: Historical Essays on Toronto*, edited by Victor Russell. University of Toronto Press.

Silver, Allan. 1967. "The Demand for Order in Civil Society: A Review of Some Themes in the History of Urban Crime, Police and Riot." Pp. 1–24 in *The Police: Six Sociological Essays*, edited by David Bordua. Wiley.

Skolnick, Jerome H. 1966. *Justice without Trial: Law Enforcement in Democratic Society.* Wiley.

Spitzer, Steven. 1975. "Toward a Marxian Theory of Deviance." *Social Problems* 22:638–51.

Watts, Eugene J. 1983. "Police Response to Crime and Disorder in Twentieth-Century St. Louis." *Journal of American History* 70:340–58.

Wodson, Harry M. 1917. *The Whirlpool: Scenes from Toronto Police Court.* University of Toronto Press.

Critical Thinking Questions

• • • • • • • • • • • • • • • • • • •

Chapter 6: Homicide in Nova Scotia, 1749–1815, *Allyson N. May and Jim Phillips*

1. How do homicides in Halifax compare to those that occurred in the rest of the province? Who was more likely to be the victim of a homicide in Halifax? What differences are there in the rate of executions for those convicted of homicide between the two locations? What might explain this apparent discrepancy?
2. Does violence appear to be more prevalent at this time than today? What problems are there in attempting to draw such a conclusion? Does the author think that the extant records are an accurate reflection of the rate of murder in the colony? Why or why not?
3. What are the differences in deciding whether a suspicious death was a murder or a case of manslaughter? How did common law define "homicide" during this period? What distinctions did the law make between deliberate, justifiable, and excusable homicide? Does the threat of execution appear to have been a sufficient deterrent to homicide?

Chapter 7: The Shining Sixpence: Women's Worth in Canadian Law at the End of the Victoria Era, *Constance Backhouse*

1. How did attitudes about women influence Canadian legislation about infanticide in the late nineteenth century?
2. Various changes were made to laws affecting women in this period. What are some of these changes, and how do they represent the social and moral regulation of gender?
3. At the end of the infanticide case, the author asks why these defendants were treated so leniently. What do such cases say about the relative worth of infants at this time?

Chapter 8: Gender and Criminal Court Outcomes: An Historical Analysis, *Helen Boritch*

1. During the mid-nineteenth century, industrializing nations were experiencing an urban reform movement. What social problems accompanied industrialization?

And how did Canadian reformers respond to these social problems? Who did reforms perceive to be the "most serious threat facing the modern city?"

2. Contrary to popular belief, female criminality, according to the female incarceration rates in the Middlesex County jails, was on the decline during the Urban Reform era. What factors may have contributed to this decline?

3. Current research on gender differences in criminal court outcomes generally finds a pattern of lenient sentences toward female offenders. Based on Boritch's study, did a similar pattern exist in the Urban Reform era? What five findings, in relation to gender differences, did this study reveal?

Chapter 9: The Voluntary Delinquent: Parents, Daughters, and the Montreal Juvenile Delinquents' Court in 1918, *Tamara Myers*

1. Myers's research focuses on the ways parents controlled their errant daughters. Implicit within the author's thesis, however, is the notion that parental expectations were different for daughters than they were for their sons. Why did this idea appear to exist? How did parents control unruly daughters?

2. What role did parents play in assisting the court system? Why did parents appear to prefer incarceration rather than probation? How did parents overcome the problem of a court system apparently reluctant to incarcerate their daughters?

3. A lack of clients forced some institutions to look for alternatives to increase their numbers. What were some of these ways? What problems did institutions encounter when they focused on "voluntary delinquents" to fill their beds?

Chapter 10: Governing Mentalities: The Deportation of "Insane" and "Feebleminded" Immigrants out of British Columbia from Confederation to World War II, *Robert Menzies*

1. How could the notion of an individual of the state as an "economic unit" have fuelled the deportation of "feebleminded" immigrants before World War II?

2. Prior to 1902 there were no medical authorities involved in the immigration or deportation process in Canada. How was the deportation of the "insane" and "feebleminded" affected when the deportation process became medicalized?

3. Deportation on the basis of mental deficiency declined during World War II when eugenics was becoming a popular theory in Canada and throughout the rest of the world. Why, then, did this decline in deportation of the mentally unfit occur in Canada during the war?

Chapter 11: Crime and the Changing Forms of Class Control: Policing Public Order in "Toronto the Good," 1859–1955, *Helen Boritch and John Hagan*

1. According to the authors, Toronto experienced a shift in policing styles that was not directly related to the level of crime. Where did this shift in policing come from? Who was involved in deciding what the police should focus their energy and time on?

2. What are the major characteristics of "class-control" and "crime-control" styles of policing? Did the level of crime, or the types of crime that occurred, change throughout this period? In what way did this shift in focus affect those being policed?

3. Many historical studies tend to focus on homicide as a barometer of the level of violence. However, Boritch and Hagan suggest such an emphasis may not present an accurate picture of the level of violence within a community. What are the benefits of using homicide statistics to gauge the level of violence within a community? What are the problems with such an approach? What other types of crimes do the authors suggest might be more helpful?

Further Readings

. . . .

Crimes, Constables and Courts: Order and Transgression in a Canadian City, 1816–1970 by John C. Weaver (Montreal: McGill-Queen's University Press, 1995).

This book, written by a professor of history at McMaster, was short-listed for the Harold Adam Innis prize. It looks at the evolution of urban policing, and has made a mark in criminal justice history. The author is able to use narrative to bring his description of the evolution of the Canadian criminal justice system to life. He uses newspaper accounts and police, court, and jail records to trace the evolution of courts, juries, police, and punishments. He shows how the increased centralization and professionalization of the criminal justice system and policing deprived communities of input, continued to be male dominated, and biased against newcomers, strangers, and marginalized social groups.

The Supreme Court of Nova Scotia, 1754–2004: From Imperial Bastion to Provincial Oracle, edited by Philip Girard, Jim Phillips, and Barry Cahill (Toronto: Osgoode Society for Canadian Legal History and University of Toronto Press, 2004).

Coinciding with the 250th anniversary of Nova Scotia's Supreme Court, this volume provides a comprehensive history of Canada's oldest common law court. The essays include an account of the first meeting in 1754, surveys of jurisprudence, and the various courthouses it has occupied. This is the first complete history of any Canadian provincial superior court. All of the essays are original, and many offer new interpretations of familiar themes in Canadian legal history.

From Punishment to Doing Good: Family Courts and Socialized Justice in Ontario, 1880–1940 by Dorothy E. Chunn (Toronto: University of Toronto Press, 1992).

Dorothy Chunn is co-director of the Feminist Institute for Studies in Law and Society, and a member of the Criminology Department at Simon Fraser University. This book reflects her research interests in feminism, law and the state; ideology and the family; and the historical sociology of crime, law, and social welfare. The family court system was an important development in policing young women in a quickly industrializing state.

Colonial Justice Justice, Morality, and Crime in the Niagara District, 1791–1849
by David Murray (Toronto: Osgoode Society for Canadian Legal History, and University
of Toronto Press, 2002).

David Murray is a professor in the Department of History at the University of
Guelph. In 1791, with the creation of a legislative assembly in Upper Canada, a
criminal justice system was adopted from England. Using the rich court records from
the Niagara District, Murray analyzes the criminal justice system during the first half
of the nineteenth century. He looks at how local characteristics affected the operation
of a criminal justice system, and also how legal processes affected Upper Canadian
morality. He looks at the treatment of the insane, welfare cases, crimes committed in
the district, and an examination of the roles of the Niagara magistrates, constables,
and juries. Despite the principles of British justice, justice was unequal for women
and visible minorities.

Making Law, Order, and Authority in British Columbia, 1821–1871 by Tina Loo
(Toronto: University of Toronto Press, 1994).

In the early nineteenth century, British Columbia was occupied by the Native
population and the Hudson's Bay Company. The history of pre-Confederation British
Columbia is heavily influenced by the fur trade, conflict between settlers and the
Hudson's Bay Company, and the gold rush. Loo details these incidents and puts
them in a wider historical background. She relates the disciplinary practices of the
Hudson's Bay Company, the establishment of courts in the gold fields, and conflicts
over the role of juries.

PART III

Policing Ethnicity

• •

One of the more troubling problems most societies have to deal with is the historical treatment of ethnic populations, and Canada is no exception. As the readings in this section demonstrate, the policing of ethnicity was not limited to the use of the criminal law to achieve homogeneity. Instead, control was diffuse, spilling over from criminal justice to expand into the fields of health, social welfare, and education. While those facing assimilation rarely proved passive in their acceptance of the role the state was playing in their lives, the state was a powerful adversary. Surveillance in the criminal justice system was aided by professionals in many diverse fields.

The first two readings demonstrate the difficulties of attempting to understand verdicts in jury trials. In both cases, trial transcripts have been lost to history. As a result, the trials are recreated through newspaper accounts of the day. One problem with this approach is that newspapers do not provide an accurate legal record of the proceedings. However, newspapers also provide a cultural record, giving us an inside look into the sensibilities of the day. While reporters may have lacked a legal insight into trial proceedings, or simply not have the space necessary for presenting a full accounting of the circumstances behind the verdicts, this would be little different than today. More important, as Smith finds, the news media may have other motivations at work than simply reporting the news. For example, after the trial of the Reverend Corbett, convicted for attempting to procure an abortion for a household servant, the defendant's counsel, James Ross, serialized the outcome for publication in his newspaper.

In their article, in which the defendant was found not guilty of murder, Strange and Loo suggest that the verdict may not have been the result of any underlying sense of fairness, but the fact that both the victim and the defendant were "outsiders" to the community. As such, an acquittal would not send a message that local residents could get away with murder. In addition, the acquittal of a Black man, in an overwhelmingly White community, helped to reinforce the notion that the rule of law could fairly apply to all. In both cases, the trials are seen as an attempt to carefully balance justice with interests in economic development, through tourism, in the case of Picton, Ontario, and immigration, in Red River. The rule of law went a long way to informing colonial identity, and the trial and its outcome, although predictable in retrospect, shows how criminal justice both reflects and reinforces prevailing social ideology.

In their classic study on Africville, Clairmount and Magill discuss the consequences of Canada's experiment with urban renewal in the 1950s as a way to improve major cities. Halifax was also touched by this phenomenon, and the community of Africville was selected for renewal in 1964. Africville was a small black community of 80 families within Halifax city. The community had gone into disrepair as it had no electricity, running water, or sewage and was seen as a black mark on Halifax that had to be abolished. The city chose to relocate the residents of Africville to other areas of the city and to destroy the community. The model of relocation was liberal welfare in that the city claimed that the residents required assistance such as employment and education, which was to be met through this relocation. However, subsequent studies have shown that the residents were not satisfied with their relocation, and that they never received what the city had promised them. This paper chronicles the disparities between the city and the relocated. While the city of Halifax viewed the relocation as a progressive and successful move, the Africville residents felt as though they were forced into relocation and never received adequate support.

Using case files from the Mercer Reformatory for Women, Sangster explores the incarceration of Native women in Ontario during the period 1920–1960. The records are problematic because they record all Native and Métis nations under the single heading "Native" and they present evidence about the cases from the perspective of the recorder rather than the women themselves. However biased, they do create a picture of Aboriginal communities controlled by the criminal justice system, but also manipulating that same system to respond to pressing social problems. The majority of Native women incarcerated at the Mercer during this period were there for moral or public order infractions, such as prostitution and vagrancy. The latter was a relatively loose designation for a wide array of offences from drunkenness and child endangerment to wandering the streets. However, these categories of offences reflect what outsiders considered to be crimes and how they should be policed, not what the Native communities considered to be the problems facing them.

The final reading in this section looks at how the education system could be used, in concert with the law, to assimilate immigrant populations. The Doukhobors lived a communal way of life, and saw the formal education system as a threat to their existence. Previous attempts to convince them to register their children in local schools had met with little success. Beginning in the 1920s, therefore, the government took a different approach. Rather than enforcing compliance within the Doukhobor community, local school boards were penalized if school attendance fell below an acceptable level. This threat only increased friction between the Doukhobors and their neighbours, and had only a minimal effect on school attendance. Because short-term solutions had not achieved the desired result, the decision was eventually made to entirely remove the children from their families and educate them in a special facility, where they would stay for a period of years, rather than a few months.

The selections in this section, in particular, show how *social and moral regulation* needs to be understood in broad terms as embodying the work of the criminal justice collectively in everyday practices that encompass many different areas of surveillance and control.

CHAPTER 12

Spectacular Justice:
The Circus on Trial, and the Trial as Circus, Picton, 1903

Carolyn Strange and Tina Loo

• • • • • • • • • • • • • • • • • • • •

The "Negro Murder"

Twelve hours after elephants, lions, tigers, and "an army of circus talent" transformed Picton's Main Street into a "grand street pageant," the quiet Ontario town was once again thrown into tumult. But now, cries of "Murder!" rather than the blare of calliopes broke the stillness of the night. Provincial detective Joseph Rogers, sent on routine assignment by Deputy Attorney General Cartwright to keep an eye on the circus, suddenly found himself with matters on his hands more serious than short-change artists or lewd sideshow dancers. The Pan-American Circus's afternoon and evening shows had gone off without a hitch on their Picton stop on 22 July 1903, but later, when the roustabouts were packing up the tents and herding the animals back into the train cars, a fatal stabbing occurred. One of the Black tent workers, Edward "Yellow" Johnson, lay beside the grandstand of the fair grounds, bleeding to death from a wound to the heart. His fellow circus workers suspected another Black labourer—Edward Clarke, a.k.a. "Side Show Shorty"—and the hunt was on to find the murderer.

Rogers rushed towards the train station, but found the wanted man on Main Street, standing with a pocket knife in his possession and circled by a crowd of men. An eyewitness who had been on the circus grounds claimed to have seen the man kill Johnson. Several other local men reported overhearing the suspect complain that the Pan-American was "a fake" and that he was going to "jump the job" after killing yet another man. Shorty made no attempt to resist arrest as Rogers placed him in custody for the murder, the first the town had witnessed in years.[1] The following day the Pan-American packed up and rolled on towards Trenton as scheduled. However, a spectacle every measure as sensational as the circus began to unfold.

Side Show Shorty's court appearances not only involved the trial of a circus man, but they exposed surprising resemblances between the trial and the circus—parallels flagged by spectators' irreverence and noted by disgruntled lawmen. But capital murder trials, in which jury members perform their roles as the triers of fact, are, ironically, less orderly than circuses. Unlike daring but well-rehearsed circus acts, jury trials are open ended: verdicts may be anticipated, but they are rarely predetermined. Whereas circuses are artificial intrusions into daily life, cleverly designed to divert attention temporarily from the routine, trials expose local culture and raise uncomfortable questions about the limits of behaviour. In particular, jury trials draw upon and help to define community values and identity. In this sense, even unexpected verdicts, like Shorty's acquittal, can be understood as the expression of local identity through the formality of the law.

To develop a richer sense of *R.* v. *Clarke*'s outcome, we first need to consider Picton's history and its tenor at the turn of the century. As a settlement proud of its loyalist past, and eager to invest its future in tourism, the town was consciously constructed in this period as a haven from urban industrialization. Yellow Johnson's murder was evidently not a crime that could be connected to this conservative, law-abiding community, as grand jurymen later stated. Both men were quintessential "others": they were foreign, they were Black (in an overwhelmingly white county), and, to top it off, they were circus men. Even among circus folk, men like Johnson and Clarke were the most ruthlessly exploited, both as workers and as "wild savages" placed on display for white audiences to gawk at. Finding Clarke innocent replicated such distancing practices by allowing the town to forget that a man had been murdered in town. Once Clarke was acquitted, the case was closed and virtually erased from local memory.[2]

In our treatment of Side Show Shorty's story, we are less prepared to accept the false certainty of the legal verdict than we are to speculate about the extralegal factors that underpinned the spectacular trial and acquittal of a circus man in small-town Ontario. It is to these elements of culture, history, and identity that we turn, less for answers than for meanings.[3]

David and Goliath

The first "chapter in the murderous drama," as the Picton *Gazette* announced, was the inquest that took place on 24 July 1903. The adjournment of the proceedings from the Council Chambers to the more commodious Opera House was prompted by the throngs of people who pressed to hear the tale of two "negros": one dead and the other soon to stand trial for his life. Without a lawyer to cross-examine witnesses at the inquest or at the police court hearing several days later, the circus man's chances seemed slim. The two local newspapers, the *Gazette* and the *Times*, entertained no doubts in their

reports on the "Negro Murder" that Side Show Shorty was guilty.[4]

If an acquittal seemed unlikely at the time of his committal on 29 July, it appeared even less likely when the case was tried in October. Without the funds to hire his own lawyer, Clarke depended on a local member of the bar to take on the hopeless case. Although he was neither a criminal law specialist nor a trial lawyer, E.M. Young, the county clerk for Prince Edward and its solicitor, volunteered.[5] His adversary would normally have been the local crown attorney, J. Roland Brown, but Cartwright felt that a man more experienced in capital trials would ensure a thorough prosecution. Cartwright found his man in Roger C. Clute, QC. Not only was Clute an experienced trial lawyer and a leading member of the Ontario bar, but he had been the last prosecutor to convince a Picton jury to render a guilty verdict in a capital case.[6] Convicting two murderers, who were later hanged in the jail behind the Prince Edward Country courthouse in 1884, had been a feather in the young lawyer's cap, and his earlier success suggested that he might be just the man to secure another conviction.

In October 1903 Pictonians finally witnessed the David and Goliath court battle. Before them stood a penniless Black man, a citizen of a foreign country, who found himself in a white man's court before an all-white jury. Furthermore, as the self-consciously humble Young conceded, the defence faced "one of the ablest and most eloquent criminal lawyers in the High Court." As expected, Clute presented the crown's case forcefully, marshalling the testimony of eye witnesses and townsfolk who identified Shorty as the man they had seen brandishing a knife and shouting his intent to murder. The tables began to turn, however, when the rookie Young proved to have done his homework. Since the only plausible defence was mistaken identity, he managed to find townsfolk, most of whom had rarely seen Blacks outside minstrel shows, who challenged the crown's certainty about the murderer's identity. [...] For every crown witness who claimed to have seen Shorty, the defence countered with another who stated that the murderer was taller, or shorter, or stouter, or darker-skinned than the defendant. Several claimed that a man who looked like the defendant had spent the evening at Main Street's Quinte Hotel, singing and dancing for coins. In spite of Clute's impressive closing address, strongly supported by Judge James Teetzel's damning charge, Young had managed to introduce a measure of doubt in the jury's mind. After two hours' deliberation, the good citizens of Picton returned a verdict of not guilty.[7]

Unlike the courthouse crowd, who greeted the verdict with "a good deal of excitement," the judge, the crown attorney, and the provincial detective were not amused.[8] The prosecution team was convinced that a guilty man had been set free, not because it had botched the case but because the jury had been overanxious to acquit. [...]

The Trial as Circus

To the crown agents, the parallels between the trial and the circus were unsettling. Spectators raised a cheer at the verdict, and the judge and the crown attorneys were disgusted at their apparent levity. It was almost as if the trial had turned out to be the ultimate death-defying act: the jury had irresponsibly set a murderer free. Roger Clute, the supposed star, had been upstaged by a comparative amateur who had stolen the show. Just as escape artists and magicians seemed to defy the laws of physics in their acts, so a small-town lawyer had miraculously freed his client.

Although it has become a cliché for solemn legal actors to liken trials to "circuses" whenever they appear to have run off the rails of decorum, we suggest the opposite: that trials are most circus-like when they are most orderly. In this sense, Shorty's trial exposed parallels between criminal trials and circuses that the judge and the prosecution were loathe to admit. Both forms of drama are public spectacles that juxtapose the high and the low, the powerful and the vulnerable: they foreshadow outcomes, building in the possibility of surprise endings. Management techniques, the organization of the performance space, and the structure of rules suggest further affinities.[9] Assize court judges, like the travelling shows that rumbled through North America on road and rail, moved from town to town according to pre-established circuits. Although the arrival of the judge and his retinue did not occasion the pomp and ceremony that their forebears had commanded a century earlier (or the excitement that the unloading of circus trains afforded in local yards), the coming of the circuit judge was a notable event, particularly in small towns like Picton that rarely provided the High Court with sufficient business to warrant a stop. Visiting judges had a keen sense of the impact of their sittings on the locals. For Teetzel, the fall assizes of 1903 marked his first appearance on the bench, and he used his new position to pronounce on the virtues of Picton, much as travelling showmen traditionally ingratiated themselves with their hosts.[10] The arrival of the court may not have been preceded by roaring lions and sequined maidens, but it rivalled the Pan-American's stop for thrills, because a man was on trial for his life.

The criminal trial, like the circus, is largely an orchestrated event, complete with advertisements and free previews to whet spectators' appetites for the headliner act. The inquest and the grand jury hearing raised expectations of a dramatic conclusion to Shorty's story, and hundreds of Pictonians pressed for admission to catch the last act in this public performance of justice. Although the trial, unlike the circus, could have been conducted without any witnesses, the presence of the community conveyed a sense of legitimacy to the proceedings. Twelve men, most of them farmers and small-scale businessmen, were the official representatives, but hundreds of other Pictonians added their presence.

Where circuses deployed frenetic music, boldly coloured advertisements, and exotic costumes to boost the lustre of performances, the trial court chose sober props to achieve similar effects. In the centre ring of the courtroom, each player occupied appointed positions: spectators at the rear; counsel in the centre; jurymen to the judge's left; and the judge himself on a raised dais, flanked by a reporter and a constable. The defendant, like a caged lion, was penned in a wooden enclosure and sandwiched between the public and the court officers. Costumes helped observers to decode the status and the roles of the various players. In this case, Young wore the stuff gown of the barrister, Clute his QC's silk, and Teetzel his judicial robe. A further adornment—a black cap—was at the ready, in case the judge had to pass a sentence of death. Architecture and costume were visual cues to the coded sets of meaning in the spectacle of justice.[11]

A further resemblance between circuses and trials lies in their calculated manipulation of risk. Observing the trial of a person who faces a capital charge is not unlike watching a high-wire artist perform without a net: the possibility of death electrifies the air and heightens the drama.[12] Exercising oratorical skills worthy of ring masters, the main players in death penalty trials try to sway the odds of execution one way or another, with the crown calling for death, and the defence urging a miraculous escape. Viewed this way, the announcement of the verdict in the Clarke case can be seen as the crowning act of a show which promised the risk of death but which, astoundingly, delivered life. Not surprisingly, the courtroom audience burst into applause.

In circuses, the potential for unforeseen outcomes in performances is minimized through careful planning and the skilful execution of difficult manoeuvres. The boisterous disruptions of mischievous clowns are, in fact, practised digressions in the principal acts. The contorted acrobat may look topsy-turvy, but she always knows which way is up. Similarly, in a courtroom, the rules of evidence and procedure reduce arguments, testimony, and exhibits into information that lawyers, the judge, and the jury try to mould into a coherent narrative. Already in nineteenth-century England the

system of largely private prosecution had been transformed to one based on crown prosecution; defence lawyers assumed greater rights, and restrictions on hearsay evidence were tightened, leading to an increasingly professional image of justice. In Canada, as in England, there were ever more legal controls over trial proceedings, along with a firmer sense of solemnity. In the late eighteenth century, trial judges would have thought nothing of Pictonians' shouts and cheers at the announcement of the acquittal; by the turn of the century, men like Teetzel, Clute, and Brown found such exuberance embarrassing.

Yet lawmen could not orchestrate jury trials as craftily as ringmasters directed circus acts; they could not determine the outcome. Over the nineteenth century, statutory change and evolving trial procedures had whittled away at British subjects' much heralded right to trial by jury. In fact, the Criminal Code of 1892 had defined capital defendants as among the few who still enjoyed that right. As the critical impediment to streamlined, predictable justice, the jury was a group of legal actors who, unlike lawyers and judges, had not spent years learning the rules and culture of the law. Rules of evidence and procedure determined the evidence that jurors were allowed to hear, but they did not ensure the trial's predictable closure. And the jury certainly had no counterpart in the context of the circus. Audiences may have booed and heckled inferior shows, and selected members may have been invited on stage to be made fun of, but they were never granted the power of life and death over circus performers.

Herein lies the most significant distinction between circuses and trials. The modern circus, unlike the medieval or early modern carnival, is a series of staged events that modulates transgressive energy into entertainment.[13] In contrast, democratic legal procedures do not impose similar constraints over the outcome of criminal jury trials, and lawyers, working at cross purposes, can do little more than fight to earn the jury's confidence. The more powerfully positioned judge may prevent a weak case from going to the jury, or, conversely, deliver a strongly worded charge that directs a jury to convict. Ultimately, though, jury trials, through their inherent unpredictability, maintain the potential for unexpected endings to otherwise carefully controlled performances.

In the case of *R. v. Clarke*, although the verdict was surprising, it was not perverse or "circus-like." The jury deliberated for more than two hours (longer than many capital trial juries in the period), and the mistaken identity defence was plausible, since the defendant was a stranger. More important, the acquittal of a poor Black man powerfully affirmed the myth of equality before the law. The legal technicality that had prevented the admissibility of absent circus witnesses' testimony was just that: legal. No matter how irksome the trial's outcome to the losers, everyone had behaved according to the rules, and the jury had discharged its duty to weigh the evidence. In the end, authorities were snubbed, but authority was upheld.

*****

Pictonians' recollections of an earlier capital trial, the town's emerging identity as a tourist retreat, and the status of the victim and the offender in the circus murder each contributed to Clarke's acquittal. Picton juries were renowned for their reluctance to convict in capital trials after at least one possibly innocent man was hanged in 1884, thanks to a young crown attorney's skills. In Picton, Clute's name was clouded by his association with this infamous case of injustice. For peaceable Pictonians, the circus murder was shocking, not so much because a man had died, but because they prided themselves on their law-abiding reputation. In the twenty-five-year period preceding Shorty's trial, only nine men from Prince Edward County had been charged with murder, and only two—Joseph Thomsett and George Lowder—had been convicted.[14] Business interests reinforced Pictonians' historical pride in their civility: by the turn of the century, when the town began to pin its hopes for economic development on tourism, an execution in the county jail courtyard would have undone years of promotional work.

Refusing to convict an outsider who had killed another foreigner profoundly defined and reasserted these moral and economic bonds of community. As both circus workers and Blacks, the men involved were itinerant "others" who fell outside of the conservative, white norm. [...] The death of one was startling, but more easily dismissed than the other's execution, with the publicity it would inevitably have garnered.[15] Yellow Johnson was nobody's neighbour, employee, or father, and, in that sense, his murder was more a curiosity for Pictonians than a rupture in town life. As the trial proceeded, Young's spirited defence would frame these decidedly "unlegal" sentiments in terms that townsfolk understood—in appeals to British-Canadian loyalism. [...]

Local Memory, Local Justice

In the course of tracing how the crown's case had derailed, the local crown attorney, a man attuned to the tenor of life in Picton, concluded that the jury had cloaked prejudices beneath the flag of British justice. Brown judged that three factors—antipathy towards Clute, Pictonians' painful memory of the last executions, and the town's concern over its reputation—had prompted the jury to acquit. Clute himself took the "vociferous cheering" at the announcement of the verdict to mean that Pictonians had been squarely behind the local defence lawyer from the beginning. What he failed to mention to his superiors was that his successful prosecution of Lowder and Thomsett almost twenty years earlier was still fresh in the minds of those who recalled their convictions as a miscarriage of justice. Jurymen in that trial had, like most laymen, naively assumed that their recommendation to mercy would prompt the executive to spare the pair from the gallows. Petitions for mercy were circulated throughout the community, and the men maintained their innocence to the end. Their poignant letters condemning the injustice of their convictions were published in local newspapers on the same day that their "horribly bungled" hangings were reported. Although the Belleville *Intelligencer* dutifully noted that "the general sentiment of the community is that the condemned met justice," doubt about the *character* of justice simmered long after they were buried in unmarked graves in the jail yard.[16]

Brown was less coy than Clute about the legacy of the Lowder-Thomsett hanging and its significance in turning Pictonians against the death penalty. "There has always been a suspicion in the minds of a number of people in this county that one of the last two men who were executed here in Picton might have been innocent," he explained to Cartwright. In Brown's opinion, the crown's case had been hamstrung once Clute took it on, and the jurymen in this murder case stoutly resisted Clute's call to put another man to death. "I think there is in this county at all events a growing sentiment against capital punishment," Brown generously offered. [...]

*****

The Most Favoured Spot on Earth

The trial of Side Show Shorty occurred at a pivotal moment in Picton's history, as it underwent a transition from an agricultural and manufacturing centre to a sleepy, tourist haven. Its cultural homogeneity was a comfort to anyone anxious about the growing number of "foreign" immigrants in big cities; over 86 per cent of the townspeople claimed British ancestry; the combined total of Aboriginals, Blacks, and Asians barely topped fifty.[17] Turn-of-the-century Picton appeared, in many respects, to be a place that time had passed by. The old loyalist town could still boast a handful of small-scale capitalist enterprises, such as fruit and vegetable canning, furniture, and wire-fencing factories. However, shrewd locals realized that Picton would never become a hub of industrialization after they saw the national railroad bypass their town. Faced with irregular service on the Central Ontario Railroad (Picton's branch line) and a dwindling number of Lake Ontario freight steamers and barges, the town could no longer compete with burgeoning

cities along the trunk lines that spanned the continent.

Picton might have spiralled into economic decline had enterprising locals not devised a novel way to sell their town.[18] In addition to exporting produce and grain, Picton would import tourists. In the hands of local promoters, economic stagnation could spell rustic charm; the undeveloped waterside could stand out as unspoilt beauty; and, above all, the marketing of Picton depended upon its image as a town snuggled in a bucolic setting, unblighted by evils of industrial urbanization.

This work of imaginative reinvention preoccupied the town council as it actively promoted tourism. In 1903 it commissioned Helen Merrill, daughter of Edwards [*sic*] Merrill, the long-serving county court judge, to write a news article "with a view to enlightening the Tourist public of Canada and the United States." As Boulter announced, the aim was to "set forth the numerous advantages of Picton as a place for summer tourists and holiday seekers to congregate and spend their summer vacations."[19] This was to be the first time that Picton actively reached out to big-city audiences by painting its simple virtues. Merrill's article was published in the Toronto *Mail and Empire*, ironically just one month before the murder.

*****

The mid to late nineteenth century marked the emergence of the tourism industry in Ontario, and Picton was one of many small towns to recast itself as a tourist destination.[20] Capitalizing on its location at the narrows of Lake Ontario, the town promoted itself, particularly to wealthy Torontonians and Rochesterians, as the gateway to the Thousand Islands, where tourists could take advantage of "delightful opportunities" for relaxation and pleasure. In 1874, for instance, steamship excursions from Picton to Kingston featured the added opportunity to visit the buildings and grounds of the Rockwood Asylum and the Kingston Penitentiary—price 50 cents or 75 cents for a gentleman and lady.[21] But even visitors with more time than money could afford to sojourn in Picton's environs. Local entrepreneurs exploited the county's natural wonder, Sandbanks Park, for commercial gain. By the century's end, several lakeside entertainments and resort hotels had sprung up, featuring lawn tennis, croquet, and pavilions for shoreline dances. Every summer, the "wildly beautiful" beach, graced by large dunes, lured casual picnickers and well-heeled holidayers by the thousands from upstate New York and southern Ontario.[22] These urban tourists indulged their passion for Ontario's wilderness at a time when cities were swallowing it up at a frightening pace. In this romanticized world of sun and surf, the disagreeable side effects of industrial progress—dirt, noise, and crime—could be forgotten.[23]

Picton became a service centre and stopover point for travellers whose destinations were Sandbanks and the Thousand Islands. Six hotels lined Main Street, including the Quinte, where Shorty claimed he had sung and danced on the night of the murder. Regular summer festivities included strawberry socials, church picnics, and brass band concerts, but the most popular event was the annual agricultural fair, shepherded by prominent locals.[24] To offset the costs of maintaining the grounds and running the annual fair, the County Prince Edward Agricultural Society regularly ran horse races on its track and rented its facilities for social or political gatherings. Travelling shows were also permitted to rent the grounds, and in the spring of 1903 the society contracted with the Pan-American Circus to let its lot, including the grandstand and crystal palace, for 22 July—the height of the tourist season.[25] As was customary in the circus business, advertisements were placed in the local papers, huge posters were plastered onto city buildings and rural barns, and local businessmen were given complimentary tickets in exchange for placing the bold, brightly coloured advertisements in their windows.[26] The summer of 1903 promised to be eventful, although hardly in a manner that Miss Merrill or the town council had anticipated.

Others in the Circus

Because both the accused and the victim in the Negro Murder were not only outsiders but troupers, the circus's history and its place in the imagination of small-town Ontarians offers further insight into Side Show Shorty's acquittal. By the time the Pan-American came to Picton, such "cyclones of refined merriment" had been blowing across the continent for generations.[27] Until the late nineteenth century, most circuses travelled over land either by wagon or by truck, but in the 1870s the larger "mud shows," as they were called, began to move from town to town by rail.[28] The majority were small—usually only three cars; nevertheless, according to one circus historian, "back then, a railroad circus, whatever its size, was synonymous with all that was mighty, magnificent, and ultra-modern."[29]

With its twenty-four cars, two hundred employees, and appointments that "were up to date in every particular," the Pan-American Circus was, by the standard of the times, a big-league show.[30] Their 1903 season began in Missouri (their wintering grounds) on 9 May and, by the end of the month, they were in Canada. Canadian audiences, like American ones, were captivated by Zelleno the Mystic's "acts of prestidigitation," Signor Frank Cereno's troupe of dancing dogs, and by the circus's headline act—the Cook Sisters, equestriennes extraordinaires. In 1903 the Pan-American also offered its audiences something never seen before: "the wondrous new woman of the wild west"—the Cowgirl Riding a Steer. "No one," the newspapers insisted, "should miss seeing her."[31]

*****

[...] Though circuses may have appeared chaotic, they were actually highly structured operations. The military efficiency of their acts was only the most obvious expression of a very orderly world of wonders. Circuses were big businesses that operated according to a strict time-work discipline. Indeed, as impressive as the Pan-American's offerings were, "greater wonder by far," according to the journalist Whiting Allen, " ... is the really marvellous system which governs every element of its organization and makes possible its smooth and certain operation on such a stupendous scale."[32] From selecting the route that the show travelled, to familiarizing themselves with the various regulations that governed travelling shows in each place on the itinerary, contracting for the sites and provisions, and arranging for proper advance advertising, successful circus proprietors' business acumen rivalled their headliners' performance skills. [...]

Far behind the footlights, men like Yellow and Shorty stood at the lowest rung of the circus hierarchy. Their status is crucial to understanding why troupers and towners alike responded to the murder with relative equanimity. In all the big circuses, a strict division of labour both reflected and reproduced the hierarchical social relations that existed in the wider world of which it was a part. Owners and managers stood at the top of the circus hierarchy; beneath them, the chief division was between labourers and performers. Though wages divided circus employees into two broad classes, the distinction between labourers and performers was reinforced and certainly complicated by gender and race—and by species as well, for animals like Rajah, the Pan-American's celebrated elephant, commanded a degree of respect that was limited to only the circus's brightest stars.

Aside from the women who worked at wardrobing, circus labour was exclusively male. The circus's labour aristocracy consisted of the "bosses": the Boss Hostler, in charge of the animals; the Canvas Boss, in charge of putting up and taking down the tents; and the Boss Razor-back, who commanded the general labourers (to "raise your back"). Workingmen's time books and the pictorial evidence show that much of the labour power, particularly of the less skilled variety, was provided by Blacks, whose colour consigned them, in the eyes of the white owners, to subservience.[33]

*****

[...] Men like Johnson and Clarke were not just others, but were paid and portrayed as the lowest of the low: unskilled and casual labourers who joined the show for anywhere from a few days, weeks, or months.[34] These were the circus's lumpen class: "unemployed men who wanted to work, plus the tramps and other transients who had reasons of their own for wishing to keep moving." These men could easily be the targets of violence perpetrated by those who were supposed to be their compatriots.[35] As one trouper recalled, after a day of hard physical labour circus labourers returned to the railcars, where "they were crammed two to a bunk and in tiers three high. Terrible, unimagined things happened in those cars. We knew there were fights and sometimes killings. When that happened, they would just toss the corpse onto the tracks, where it would probably be run over by a freight train or two before it would ever be found. Nobody knew the names of those men anyhow."[36] Nor did anyone care. Zelleno's matter-of-fact response to Yellow's death, then, typified white bosses' impression that the men who made the circus run were dispensable.

*****

The Circus as Other

As important as Shorty's and Yellow's status is to understanding Pictonians' reactions to the murder, we cannot overlook the otherness of the circus itself as a factor that contributed to the verdict. For townspeople who rarely encountered people unlike themselves, the circus embodied what Mary Douglas termed "radical strangeness."[37] The mere presence of circus folk, whether they were from Missouri or the Middle Kingdom, symbolically ruptured town life, then moved on quickly, leaving the rupture a tangy memory. Whether it was Picton, Gananoque, Parry Sound, Saint John, or any of the other places on their 1903 route, the Pan-American's complement of personnel—animal, vegetable, and mineral—contrasted with the homogeneity of town society. Simply in terms of race and ethnicity, circus folk were different; under the big top and shunted to the sideshow, those differences were transformed into entertainment.

*****

Shorty's acquittal was a hierarchical inversion that matched anything the Pan-American had ever offered its audiences. Here was something that, if "Never Before Seen," certainly was a rarity: a lowly Black American—an other in another world—who escaped the noose in white, rural, loyalist Ontario, aided only by the county solicitor, who himself overcame the odds and trumped the crown's ringer brought in especially to prosecute. The verdict in *R. v. Clarke* did not simply set Shorty free: it signified, however briefly, the triumph of Black over white, and of local justice (both literally and figuratively) over state law.

Shorty's escape from death was due in part to his and Yellow's status as others. But if the fact that *R. v. Clarke* was considered the Negro Murder by townsfolk was important in understanding its disposition, so too was the fact it was a *circus* murder. Circuses had long been associated with disorder, but in modern circuses like the Pan-American, that chaos was constructed and commodified by the demands of the market and the clock, and, most importantly, it was contained within the boundaries of the big top and the sideshow. Unlike the pre-modern carnival that engulfed entire communities, the modern circus was an invited, licensed spectacle that established boundaries between the audience and the performers. As a controlled spectacle of the other, the circus affirmed the cohesion and normalcy of the communities that hosted it. Even though the circus's disorder sometimes spilled out of its rings into the towns, the problem left when the circus did; its disorder, however distasteful, was not endemic to the community. As Picton's grand jury told Judge Teetzel at the opening of the 1903 fall assizes, "While we regret the unfortunate occurrence which has for a time cast a shadow over the fair name of our county, we console ourselves with the thought so ably expressed by you that all the parties concerned being foreigners our reputation is not in any way affected."[38]

Conclusion

Yellow Johnson's death at the hands of a person or persons unknown one summer night in Picton, Ontario, led to the unlikely juxtaposition of what, on the surface, appeared to be two very different institutions: the circus and the trial. For historians, and particularly for social historians, the unique and exceptional can be problematic in the search for larger patterns and meaning in the past. Yet, for us, the value of this unusual episode actually lies in its singularity. The encounter between the circus and the trial suggested a reading of the trial in light of the circus; in the process, we made several observations regarding the modern circus, the trial of Shorty Side Show, trials in general, and the relationship between law and community.

Modern circuses, unlike their medieval antecedents, did not supplant existing social orders with radical alternatives. Over the course of the eighteenth and nineteenth centuries, carnivalesque outbursts and rough amusements were contained, cleansed of their bawdiness, broken up, and repackaged into a variety of popular entertainments. […] One could argue that far from unleashing a moment of radical play, the modern circus was emblematic of the status quo. Though performances teased spectators with the promise of chaos and subversion, they delivered highly orchestrated events in which little was left to chance. Disorder in the modern circus had been domesticated; it was fixed to particular spaces and times, and performed according to the demands of strict time-work discipline. Like the trains that conveyed them, circuses ran on time, for big businesses required predictability to ensure their profits.

*****

Just as the circus held out the promise of disrupting the status quo while actually reaffirming it, so too the verdict in *R. v. Clarke* reinforced inequality. Courts were spaces where the high and the low purportedly met as equals. Rich or poor, black or white, male or female, all were ostensibly equal before the law. Trials like

Shorty's were public performances that affirmed equality and proved that justice was blind. [...] The verdict was painful for those who considered it a travesty of justice, but the law and the social order it upheld was in no danger of being subverted. Shorty's acquittal was counter-hegemonic only insofar as it reversed the usual hierarchy of the circus's division of labour. A man who laboured unseen, in the shadow of the big tents where white performers dazzled audiences, suddenly made headlines by appearing in the centre ring of the court. Instead of barking out orders and hurling abuse, the white bosses in his case spoke feelingly of his right to a fair trial.

*****

Shorty's acquittal inspired a bout of self-congratulation, for in Prince Edward County the jury had proved that even the lowest of the low benefited from His Majesty's justice. On a grander scale, as the defence argued, it showed that Canadians, unlike their former slave-holding neighbours, were thankfully free of racist prejudice. The verdict not only spoke well for British law, but also for the rural white, conservative, and loyalist community that stood as an emblem of all that was best in Canada. [...]

*****

Notes

1. According to the jail register, Edward Clarke was a "circusman," thirty years of age, a U.S. citizen (with residence in Missouri), professing "no religion," unable to read or write, married, and intemperate. He was committed on 22 July 1903 by G.C. Curry, police magistrate. Prince Edward County Jail Register, 1877–1907, Archives of Ontario (AO), RG 20, F-33, vol. IC.

2. The only mention of the case in Picton's and Prince Edward County's many histories appears in *Pioneer Life on the Bay of Quinte, Including Genealogies of Old Families and Biographical Sketches of Representative Citizens* (1904; Belleville: Mika Publishing 1983). Local historian David Taylor confirms that Pictonians had virtually forgotten the trial prior to the authors' inquiries.

3. Aside from the coroner's report and several letters written by crown prosecutors and the attorney general, no further legal records, including a transcript of the trial, have survived.

4. Picton *Gazette*, 24 and 28 July 1903. "The Negro Murder" was the title of the article that appeared on 28 July.

5   In Picton, ten practising lawyers were listed in 1903, *Canada Law List (Hardy's)* (Toronto: Canadian Legal Publishing Company 1903). Edward M. Young was a prominent local who traced his ancestry back to Oliver Cromwell.

6. Roger Clute (1848–1931) practised law in Belleville. He was appointed a QC in 1890. In 1903, shortly before the Clarke trial, he moved to Toronto to become the senior partner in Clute, Macdonald, Macintosh, and Hay. He was appointed to the High Court of Justice in 1905, and, in 1913, was elevated to the Exchequer division, where he served until his death. He was the commissioner on the Royal Commission on Chinese and Japanese Immigration in 1900, and vice-president of the Toronto Bar Association. Law Society of Upper Canada Archives, biographical files.

7. *Gazette*, 23 Oct. 1903; *Times*, 22 Oct. 1903. Both local papers published on a semi-weekly basis.

8. *Gazette*, 23 Oct. 1903.

9. On the importance of architecture, space, and dress codes in courtrooms, see John N. Hazard, "Furniture Arrangement as a Symbol of Judicial Roles," in Alison Dundes Renteln and Alan Dundes, eds., *Folk Law: Essays in the Theory and Practice of Lex non Scripta* (New York: Garland 1994), and W.N. Hargreaves-Mawdsley, *A History of Legal Dress in Europe until the End of the Eighteenth Century* (Oxford: Clarendon 1963).

10. Paul Bouissac, "Clown Performances as Metacultural Texts," in his *Circus and Culture: A Semiotic Approach* (Bloomington: Indiana University Press 1976), 164–9. Bouissac, who once managed a circus, notes that clowns often insert local references into set jokes to engage the audience.

11. On the ceremonies attached to the holding of assizes in early modern England, see John Beattie, *Crime and the Courts in England, 1660–1800*

(Princeton: Princeton University Press 1986), chap. 7. On its associations with majesty and the grandeur of the law, see Douglas Hay, "Property, Authority, and the Criminal Law," in Hay et al., eds., *Albion's Fatal Tree: Crime and Society in Eighteenth-Century England* (London: Allen Lane 1975), 17–63.

12. Bouissac notes that accidents resulting in death are rare, yet their publicity serves to heighten anxiety that anything, at any moment, might go drastically wrong. *Circus and Culture*, 124. In capital trials, the possibility of conviction on a lesser charge, such as manslaughter in place of murder, is a kind of safety net.

13. Peter Stallybrass and Allon White, *The Politics and Poetics of Transgression* (London: Methuen 1986), 176–7.

14. The breakdown of murder charges is as follows: two in 1880, three (including Thornsett and Lowder) in 1883, and four in 1888. The first murder trial after Shorty's (the defendant was a local man, and the victim, a local woman) occurred in 1906, but it resulted in a manslaughter conviction. Prince Edward County Jail Register.

15. Several Toronto papers covered both the murder and the trial.

16. Belleville *Weekly Intelligencer*, 12 June 1884. Extensive coverage of the trial also appeared in the Belleville *Daily Ontarian*, the *Trent Valley Advocate*, the *Trenton Courier*, and the Toronto *Globe*. The *Intelligencer* published the full text of each man's pitiful letters. A letter written by Thomsett to his "Dear kind and loving mother" was never mailed but was kept by the governor of the jail. It has been reprinted numerous times, most recently in Richard and Janet Lunn, *The County: The First Hundred Years in Loyalist Prince Edward* (Picton: Prince Edward County Council 1967).

17. Picton's population was listed at 3698 in the 1901 census. Of that number, 3161 listed England, Ireland, and Scotland as their "origin." The largest non-Anglo ethnic group were the Germans at 225. There were six "Negros" and four Chinese in town. In Hallowell, still technically a separate jurisdiction but essentially a less wealthy part of the town, twenty-five "half breeds" and eighteen "Indians" were listed. Canada, *Census*, 1901, table xi, "Origins of the People," 340–1.

18. After a boom period, from 1860 to 1890, when Prince Edward County barley fetched high prices from upstate makers, the county never again enjoyed the same level of agricultural prosperity. David R. Taylor, "Historical Background," in Roger C. Greig, *The Splendour of Prince Edward County* (Belleville: Mika Publishing 1991), 6–12. On the development of tourism in the period, see Roy I. Wolfe, "The Summer Resorts of Ontario in the Nineteenth Century," *Ontario History* 54, 3 (1962): 149–61.

19. Mayor Wellington Boulter, Address to Council, 1 June 1903, Town of Picton, Council Minutes, AO, MS-754, reel 3 (1889–1904).

20. Most tourist spots, such as the Muskokas, were reached by steamers, and many offered musical entertainment and refreshments on board. Wealthier travellers favoured steamers as well. When the Prince Edward County Old Boys' Association paid a return visit to Picton in 1904, members also enjoyed an outing to the Thousand Islands—a round trip journey of 120 miles for a fare of $1.00. Prince Edward County Archives, A 74 13 D.

21. Reprinted in Lunn and Lunn, *The County*, 348.

22. Ibid., 355–8. The sand advanced at a rate of 15 feet per year until reforestation efforts halted its progress in the 1890s. The Wellman House, the Alexandra, and an unnamed hotel at Massassaga Point were popular spots for company picnics, family holidays, and romantic getaways. Bookings at the Alexandra, which operated from 1908 to 1917 when it burned down, had to be made one year in advance. Brenda M. Hudson, *Pride of Place: A Story of the Settlement of Prince Edward County* (Belleville: Mika Publishing 1982), 63–4.

23. Patricia Jasen, *Wild Things: Nature, Culture, and Tourism in Ontario, 1790–1914* (Toronto: University of Toronto Press 1995).

24. Reflecting on the town's hotels in the late nineteenth century, the Lunns wrote: "Picton had gracious hotels decorated in high Victorian elegance, their bars (to which no man took his family) gracefully curved and highly polished," Lunn and Lunn, *The County*, 355.

25. The town council did not issue a licence, as was generally the practice in larger cities. Unfortunately, the business accounts of the Agricultural Society have not survived.

26. Advancemen secured advertising space in towns and along circus routes. Because of the fierce competition among circuses, local property owners were made to sign agreements that they would not permit rivals' posters to be placed on their property. In exchange, these people were granted a certain number of free passes in accordance with the number and size of the advertisements posted. Circus World Museum and Archives (Baraboo, Wisconsin) (CWMA), Gollmar Brothers, Ledger Book (1904).

27. The turn of the century is usually identified as the "golden age" of the American circus, "a brief, sunny period when there could never be too many circuses." See John Culhane, *The American Circus: An Illustrated History* (New York: Henry Holt 1990), 163.

28. Dean Jensen, *The Biggest, the Smallest, the Longest, the Shortest: A Chronicle of the American Circus from Its Heartland* (Madison: Wisconsin Book Publishers 1975), 57, 194. Also see Joe McKennon, *Circus Lingo Written by a Man Who Was There* (Sarasota, Fla: Carnival Publishers 1980), 63. For a contemporary view of American circus life, see Don B. Wilmeth and Edwin Martin, *Mud Show: American Tent Circus Life* (Albuquerque: University of New Mexico Press 1988).

29. George Chindahl, *A History of the Circus in America* (Caldwell, Idaho: Caxton 1959), 124; and Jensen, *The Biggest*, 101.

30. Aug. 1903, and from the Arcadia, Wisconsin, *Leader* in 1902, CWMA, Lemen Brothers/Pan-American Circus, Clippings File.

31. Under the headline "Cowgirl Riding a Steer," a local newspaper reported that "She is surely ahead of her time, and anyone who doubts it and wishes to be convinced can have proof-positive when the Great Pan-American Shows, Roman Hippodrome, Monster Museum, Oceanic Aquarium and Congress of Living Phenomena will exhibit." CWMA, Pan-American Circus File, Le Clair Zelleno, "The Mystic," ed., "Route Book, Great Pan-American Shows, Season of 1903," 22.

32. Whiting Allen, "The Organization of the Modern Circus," *Cosmopolitan Magazine*, 1902, 374. CWMA, Adam Forepaugh-Sells Floto Vertical File.

33. See the pay scale for the Walter L. Main circus, dated 11 May 1902, which notes that "salaries for inexperienced and cheaper class of labour" are $3 per week, but if the circus "should go south and use Darkies," the wages would be $2 per week. "The above," it is noted, "will average with the Salaries paid with all the large American shows." CWMA, "African Americans in the Circus," vertical file.

34. Loomis Dean and Ernie Anderson, "Hot Rails!" *White Tops* Nov.–Dec. 1992: 38–43.

35. George L. Chindahl to Mr. Sloat, 11 Sept. 1956. Chindahl Papers, Wis. Miss. 310, box I, Correspondence, March–Nov. 1956.

36. Dean and Anderson, "Hot Rails!" 43.

37. Mary Douglas, "My Circus Fieldwork," *Semiotica* 85 (1985): 201–4.

38. Grand Jurors' Presentment, Fall Assizes, Picton; foreman, G. Nelson Rose, *Gazette*, 23 Oct. 1903.

CHAPTER 13

"Gentlemen, This Is No Ordinary Trial": Sexual Narratives in the Trial of the Reverend Corbett, Red River, 1863

Erica Smith

• • • • • • • • • • • • • • • • • • • •

For nine days in February of 1863, often late into the night, a melodrama of chaste and fallen womanhood unfolded in the modest courthouse in Red River Settlement (present-day Winnipeg). The Reverend Griffith Owen Corbett, an Anglican minister in the parish of Headingley, stood accused by Simon and Catherine Thomas of having seduced their daughter Maria, a sixteen-year-old girl of mixed descent and a servant in the Corbett household.[1] According to Maria Thomas's testimony, her employer had repeatedly forced himself upon her. When she became pregnant, Corbett, who had some medical knowledge acquired by attending lectures at King's Hospital in London, subjected her to several attempted abortions. He failed to interrupt the pregnancy and she gave birth to a child shortly before the trial. Corbett was arrested and, on the basis of Thomas's testimony and that of about 100 witnesses, found guilty of the crime of attempting to procure an abortion. The court sentenced him to six months' imprisonment, in spite of the eloquent rhetoric of his counsel, James Ross, who had hoped to acquit his client by persuading the jury that Maria Thomas was a "common prostitute" in the parish.

Among the attentive spectators sat Ross's colleague, William Coldwell, a journalist from Canada and now resident in the colony.

Coldwell took shorthand notes (unfortunately lost) which he and Ross later reworked into a journalistic tour de force in their newspaper, *The Nor'Wester*. Grandly entitled "The Trial of the Century," the story was serialized as a front-page, three-month sensation.

Taking advantage of the inherent theatricality of nineteenth-century court proceedings, *The Nor'Wester*'s opening editorial on the subject dramatized the trial as a "tragedy" headed for an inexorable "denouement," a "deplorable finale," and a "final curtain,"[2] with the participants in the proceedings as *dramatis personae*. James Ross, the son of an Okanagan woman and a prominent retired Scottish fur trader, stage-managed the courtroom drama[3] as well as its literary reconstruction, and cast himself simultaneously as author, director, and lead. Several Headingley residents, witnesses called to testify about the plaintiff's character, appeared briefly in minor roles. The Reverend Corbett's appearance was exceedingly brief; Ross was likely reluctant to highlight an English man of the cloth as the villain of the piece.

The two major female actors, Maria Thomas and the English wife of the accused, Abigail Corbett, played opposing roles. They were cast as one of the nineteenth century's most powerful and pervasive dualities of womanhood: the fallen woman and the chaste wife, or "angel in the house."[4] As paired metaphors, the women had a symbolic import that far outweighed their actual roles in the legal proceedings. Abigail Corbett was never called to the witness box and remained a shadowy presence, but as an Englishwoman and wife, she enacted the pivotal role of Thomas's counterpart by opposition.

The Nor'Wester's staging of this event is a prime example of how the construction of a narrative gave new meaning to real persons and events. In a deconstructive vein, this paper mines James Ross's journalistic elaboration of key social and literary themes for answers to the questions: why did this particular discourse of sexuality emerge in Red River in 1863? Where did Ross acquire it and why did he give it so much attention? What practical impact did the polarization of women have on Red River?

The Corbett trial has been interpreted as reflecting a social and political conflict which was indigenous, and in some senses unique, to Red River.[5] But a closer examination of *The Nor'Wester*'s consciously literary techniques and strategies reveals that its writers saw Red River's identity and destiny as tied to a larger story whose plot was dominated by British social structures, institutions, and modes of thought. The leading gentlemen of the trial proceedings were primarily British-born or British-oriented middle-class Victorians whose ideas, attitudes, dreams, and fantasies informed Red River's official sexual code. This is not to imply that their attitudes were uniform or fixed within a stable and homogeneous "Victorian frame of mind." They did, however, share the collective sexual anxieties of their day, as well as its common-sense thinking about women, which naturalized the perceived gulf between respectable women and prostitutes.

Labelled the "great social evil,"[6] the "problem" of prostitution permeated every sector of British society, and generated masses of printed material penned by purity campaigners, politicians, philanthropists, novelists, and journalists. By the 1860s, "the prostitute" was imprinted on middle-class consciousness as a cultural archetype of moral depravity and

physical contagion.[7] James Ross was aware of and attuned to this mode of thinking, as his speeches and cross-examinations indicate. It is worthwhile to examine how the son of an old fur trader acquired and applied that discourse.

With the encouragement of his teacher and mentor David Anderson, the Bishop of Rupert's Land, Ross had won a scholarship to the University of Toronto's Knox College in 1853, graduating with distinction five years later. As a student, he inhabited a landscape of knowledge marked by the intellectual currents and gender assumptions of the educated classes of Britain. Thus it was to Britain that he turned for his iconography when he constructed, for the benefit of the court, a portrait of Maria Thomas, which transformed a mixed-blood daughter of Red River into a typical Victorian prostitute who traded sexual favours for money and dress, articulated inappropriate sexual knowledge, and gadded about in public, destroying the domestic happiness of respectable families and the reputations of respectable neighbourhoods.

Ross proceeded first to discredit Thomas's credibility by questioning her virtue:

> Maria says ... that she had now for the first time known a man. From the evidence you will hear—I think you will easily draw the inference that she must have had sexual intercourse before this time ... her high principle succumbed before a bribe and ... she willingly bartered her character and her chastity for gain.[8]

Ross's further "evidence" revealed that Thomas had accepted money and a dress from Corbett. The significance of the monetary gift paled momentarily, however, as the dress aroused a flurry of interest in the courtroom. The women of the parish who testified about Maria's character perceived the dress as a social marker with which she inappropriately adorned her body. To them, its stylishness ("black French merino" with a "fine black silk fringe") indicated its expensive quality and, implicitly, Maria Thomas's social pretensions. Ross, however, also perceived the dress to have been a temptation to this suggestible and corrupted young woman and invested it with moral significance.

The tendency to judge character from dress, the inner state from the outer, flourished in nineteenth-century discourse and was, in the 1860s, particularized in the image of the prostitute. Searching for the origins of the great social evil, the influential English surgeon and social reformer William Acton, for example, wrote that woman's vanity and love of dress sounded the first alarm bell of a predilection for a life of prostitution. Acton's concern reverberated widely, as when a New England doctor opined: "As a medical man, I will give my opinion as to what encourages prostitution; idleness and the love of finery."[9] In Rupert's Land, the theme echoed in the frequent refrain of fur traders who made pejorative associations between Indians' love of fine clothing and their low moral development.[10]

Thomas's apparently difficult confinement left marks on her body which were interpreted as further evidence of moral failure in addition to physical decline. As she stood in the witness box "with her babe in her arms,"[11] the presiding judicial officer, recorder John Black, noted the pathos of her "wistful, withered, haggard" countenance. Although Black sympathized with Thomas's plight, he was also convinced of the inevitability of the standard denouement of illicit sexual encounters: lost virtue, banishment from respectable society, broken health, a sad death.

> To the unfortunate woman herself, the consequences of this prosecution cannot alas! ... affect her very much. By some one or other, she has already been deprived of all that makes female character valuable—her virtue; and probably there is now nothing on earth that concerns her but preparation for death.[12]

No doubt the clergymen in the courtroom, shaken by the disclosures and anxiously awaiting the verdict, were reminded of Genesis and Eve's punishment for her ill-conceived curiosity, as Ross went on to draw a connection between Maria Thomas's prurience and her perusul of Corbett's medical books:

> Maria ... was a girl of lewd tendencies, and of a reckless, licentious disposition, who seized every opportunity to revel in those improper delights which an inspection and perusal of medical works would offer her! ... who more likely than she to pry into these books, examine the woodcuts, and read eagerly the details and explanations given.[13]

Thomas's exposure to "obscene pictures" swept away whatever remnant of innocence she might still have possessed. Illustrations of sexual matters were in themselves indecent, and potent stimuli to misbehaviour. As a later Canadian clergyman warned: "No man can look upon obscene pictures without the danger of photographing upon his mind that which he might subsequently be willing to give thousands of dollars to obliterate."[14] Ross reflected this widespread perception when he declared that the medical illustrations would "leave a vivid and lasting impression" on a susceptible mind.[15]

Turning to the prostitute's celebrated opposite, the chaste wife, Ross introduced the absent Abigail Corbett in a domestic vocabulary which drew attention to her exemplary relationship to her husband. As a faithful wife, "the dear partner of his bosom," she was "in continual tears—plunged in hopeless grief over her husband's tribulations.[16] Notions of the stability of the respectable monogamous family as a domestic sanctum permeated his opening address to the jury:

> I implore you [to find Corbett innocent] by all that is valuable in life, by all that is precious in domestic happiness, by all that is dear in an unsullied name.[17]

In contrast to his detailed portrait of Maria Thomas, Ross sketched Abigail Corbett in brief, broad strokes, confident that the audience to which he spoke would fill in the details themselves. The judge, the medical men, his fellow journalists, and legal colleagues had British cultural ties; they knew and shared his terms of reference:

> I need not speak of Mrs Corbett's character, or paint her noble, pure feelings. We see it in her very face, we notice it in her conversations, in her manner, her every movement: she is a refined, honest, pure-hearted noble Englishwoman.[18]

As Ross constructed her, Abigail Corbett epitomized that quintessential symbol of respectable Victorian womanhood, universally admired in the 1860s and beyond: the angel in the house. Ross moulded her to fit the particulars most frequently applied to this paragon: sterling character, noble sentiments, refined emotion, genteel deportment, and most importantly, sexual purity.

Victorian discourse about woman's sexual purity turned frequently on discussions of her natural passivity. Countless pamphlets, treatises, sermons, and books were devoted to the invention of a passive, asexual feminine ideal. In 1850, the writer of one influential article in the *Westminster Review* noted approvingly, if impressionistically: "Women whose position and education have protected them from exciting causes, constantly pass through life without ever being cognizant of the promptings of the senses."[19] The reformer William Acton was more direct, although no less impressionistic: "Many of the best mothers, wives and managers of households, know little of or are careless about sexual indulgence. Love of home, children, and of domestic dunes are the only passions they feel."[20]

By the 1860s, women's sexual passivity was a matter for debate.[21] When Maria Thomas claimed that she had been drugged and was therefore unable to resist Corbett's advances, she provoked an outburst from Ross in which he revealed his own assumptions. Women were by nature passive, he argued, but for a pure woman, apathy and supineness posed no danger, as he put it, to "her most sacred parts." As a protection

against predatory males, nature had provided woman with an innate involuntary response that sprang immediately to her defence the instant her chastity was threatened.[22] She was thus rendered "sacred from the rude touch of impure hands."[23] As he believed that no sleeping draught had the potency to overcome nature, Ross's subsequent question was rhetorical:

> What kind of medicine could put her into such a profound sleep as to make her unconscious while a man lay with her! ... the thing is preposterous. In such circumstances the girl would involuntarily shrink from the ravisher, even in her profoundest sleep. She would become cognisant of her impending shame and dishonor—innocent nature would recoil and revolt and she *must* awake.[24]

The angel in the house, by definition physically weak and vulnerable to the storms and stresses of life, spent most of her life confined to the home. Thomas's robustness and "romping" behaviour, in contrast, proved that she did not belong to that frail sisterhood, for in spite of her ordeal, Ross said,

> she was vigorous and healthy, walked briskly, foolishly gossiped, as usual, and jested with great glee on impure topics .... Instead of finding this sick girl in bed or passively reclining on some couch or sofa—she was from home romping about the neighborhood doubtless pursuing her vocation of impure gossip and wretched scandal.[25]

Ross's words call to mind William Acton's report of the general medical opinion that "as a rule" prostitutes were endowed with "iron bodies" and resilient constitutions.[26] The passage also highlights the extent of the inconsistencies and confusions in Victorian conceptualizations of female sexuality: Maria Thomas was at once "withered" (according to Black) and "vigorous," a contradiction that both counsel and judge overlooked.

In summing up his case, Ross drew conclusions from his own construct of Maria

Thomas as a fallen woman. It was for the most part a decontextualized abstraction, largely uninfluenced by the evidence at hand. What accounted for Ross's exaggerated construction of Maria Thomas as a prostitute?

On one level, given Ross's financial interest in the fledgling newspaper, a trial involving illicit sex was simply good copy: *The Nor'Wester* was pandering to the public's fascination with scandalous exposés. It was also a form of self-advertisement for the editors, who proudly proclaimed that their reportage of the "trial of the century ... no doubt rivals some of the *causes la plus celebres* of other lands."[27]

But *The Nor'Wester*'s higher purpose was to be a conveyor of moral truths, and Ross's dichotomizing of womanhood sprang from wider concerns. By 1863 Red River was a substantial community of considerable interest to outsiders observing its moral condition. *The Nor'Wester*'s coverage attracted critical comment in the *Montreal Witness*,[28] but Red River was also drawing positive attention from a variety of easterners who were converging on Red River in the 1860s.[29] Acutely aware of an opportunity to advance the reputation of his mixed race, Ross was determined to demonstrate his and Red River's devotion to and defence of British values.

In this project, he drew support from the racial ideas of Daniel Wilson, the Scottish-born professor who held the chair in history at the University of Toronto when Ross was a student there, and whose best-known work, *Prehistoric Man*, was published in 1863. Addressing the question of intermarriage between Indians and whites, Wilson wrote that the offspring of such unions constituted an important "ethnical element" which could only benefit the development of the Canadian nation.[30] Worried about the role of people of biracial ancestry in the new order, Ross seized on the professor's appealing thesis, optimistically predicting in *The Nor'Wester* that Red River's "fusion of races ... would do no discredit to any community," and that mixed-bloods "can claim equality with pure whites in all those qualities which go to constitute merit."[31]

In fact, most visitors to Red River appeared impressed by its moral progress. Travellers frequently praised the colony as an oasis in a desert, an example of the triumph of civilization over brute nature. Sir John Henry Lefroy's sigh of relief on reaching Red River after his western subarctic travels ("Here again one encounters civilization"[32]) was a typical refrain among such gentleman adventurers returning from the wilderness and encounters with "primitive" Indians. The colony's schoolchildren were commended in these accounts for their "decorum," and high-achieving men such as James Ross were singled out as "improved" and a "credit" to their race.[33] Such improvement narratives by influential outsiders helped to foster pride in the emergence of a civilized society at Red River. By mid century the leading families of the settlement were also fashioning their own image of a community devoted to British definitions and requirements of respectability.[34]

At first glance, then, Ross's public construction of his countrywoman as a prostitute—condemning Maria Thomas in order to achieve the elevation of the mixed-blood community to which they both belonged—would appear to be a major paradox. It is important to recall, however, that being defined as "prostitute" placed Maria Thomas beyond the pale of respectable society and its discourses. Moreover, the prostitute metaphor was remarkably flexible and could be expanded to draw attention to all kinds of social problems. Ross found it a useful vehicle to highlight his most pressing concerns: community respectability and the purification of Red River's sexual mores.

The first requisite of respectability was to exorcise the ghost of a fur-trade past haunted by images of illicit sexual congress. In the censorious Christian discourse of the clergymen of Red River, Native women living with men in unions not sanctioned by the church were little better than prostitutes, regardless of the stability and longevity of their marriages "according to the custom of the country." Seizing on the rhetoric of shame as a way out of burdensome relationships, and the notorious example of Hudson's Bay Company Governor George Simpson, several fur trade officers abandoned their country wives. They frequently spoke of their past relationships in a vocabulary of sexual disgust.[35]

As mid century Red River distanced itself from old fur-trade ways, the polarization of women as either promiscuous or pure was made absolute. Within the prevailing racial discourse, Indian women were agents of men's ruin and white women agents of men's salvation. On this theme, the views of the Red River elite were in tune with those of the Aborigines Protection Society, a humanitarian organization founded in London, England, in 1837. The report of its rescue mission, published in 1856, represented a wave of protest, a kind of backlash against the sexual licence of the British colonial social order in western North America and elsewhere. Viewing the social landscape of Rupert's Land through a filter of popular ethnological and gender assumptions, the society concluded that Native women's promiscuity was responsible for the "low morals" of Hudson's Bay Company men. Like Britain's social reformers exhorting middle-class women to reclaim prostitutes, they also expressed a deep commitment to the notion that British women should effect "the mental and moral improvement" of the Company's servants. Marriage to respectable white women was the fur traders' best hope of reclamation and deliverance from their deplorable liaisons.[36] However, commentators for the Society admitted that their solutions were more idealistic than practical since white wives were in short supply in Rupert's Land. They were also silent about the question of whether the majority of HBC servants found such preachings to have any real meaning in their lives. Indeed, many of these men had neither the means nor the inclination to adorn their lives with the graces of a white angel, a "lovely, tender exotic."[37]

Yet traders, too, were men of their time. Ambitious and conscientious veterans of the fur trade were, like Alexander Ross, father of

James, concerned about their families' standing within the shifting social patterns of their ever-widening world. Instead of acquiring white wives, however, most officers with families in Red River focused intense attention upon elevating their daughters. They were to serve as bridges from a cloudy past to a respectable present and bright future. The fathers' concern to train the girls for British-style middle-class domesticity and marriage to white men has been well documented.[38] But the paternal anxiety to cultivate and protect their sexual purity went beyond a wish to see them advantageously established. In her study of nineteenth-century girlhood, Deborah Gorham has noted the pervasiveness of the "daughter-as-redeemer" theme in the novels of the time. In these books, daughters as agents of salvation rescue fathers from the consequences of past moral transgressions.[39] This insight is worth exploring with reference to Red River's racially mixed families. The purity of half-British daughters, if carefully cultivated, could in effect wipe familial slates clean of the immoral past and elevate the respectability of the paterfamilias, his country wife, and the community in the process.

Red River fathers such as Alexander Ross spared neither effort nor expense to nurture their daughters' moral development and safeguard their chastity.[40] Their project was both reanimated and legitimized after 1860 by Darwin's buoyant discoveries about the developmental potential of the human race as it progressed towards perfection. One of their tenets was that if mixed-blood daughters were to mature properly, it was necessary to minimize maternal influences. Thus Red River reversed the British trend of mothers inculcating moral values in young children, as well-intentioned fathers with Native wives involved themselves in the early religious education of their daughters.[41] British-style schools took over where the fathers left off.

Significantly, calls for such schools came both from the gentlemen of the HBC's Northern Council as well as the governor of Assiniboia, Eden Colvile, for whom the education of "the young women of this Country" was "a matter of great importance."[42] The schools aimed to provide the enabling conditions and fertile ground for the flourishing of sexual purity[43] and were thus usually under the charge of governesses from Britain. One of these "excellent importations" was Harriet Milk, who arrived in Red River in 1851, "on the invitation of the Bishop of Rupert's Land, to establish a school for young ladies."[44] The school flourished and was tellingly described by the young Peter Jacobs, a student at the boys' school, as "swarming with angelic beings."

But the most powerful moulding force in the elevation of girls in Red River was Matilda Davis, herself a daughter of the country. Like James Ross, she arose as a shining example of what exposure to a civilized British milieu could accomplish. Her HBC officer father, John Davis, sent her to England to be educated. When she returned to establish a school in the Red River parish of St. Andrew's in about 1840, she brought with her solid British middle-class values and a trunk full of books and pamphlets with such titles as "Home Life," "The Excellent Woman," and "A Mother's Mission."[46] According to the celebratory written and oral testimony of several Red River descendants, Davis not only taught a solidly academic curriculum, but also stressed "all the feminine accomplishments of the day" and the graceful deportment she had learned during a stint as governess in the homes of some of Britain's "prominent families."[47] One former pupil later told her daughter of being taught by Miss Davis "how to sit, how to walk," during her stay at what she referred to as "finishing school."[48]

Davis also imported the high-minded doctrine of duty upheld by educated British women of her generation. Intent on raising the level of her countrywomen,[49] she joined the crusade popularized by the influential English philanthropist and social reformer Hannah More, who exhorted her middle-class female readers to elevate the moral tone of society by educating their less fortunate sisters. More's writings, an enduring staple of British girls'

school literature, also guided the education of Red River's young women.[50]

School records, James Ross's newspaper, and reports of church sermons all help to document Red River's pursuit of middle-class British ideals in this period. The columns of *The Nor'Wester* provided guidance to families aspiring to gentility through prescriptive homilies with such titles as "The Happy Woman," "Comfort at Home," and "The Gentlemen at Home." Similarly, Red River's Presbyterian minister, John Black, a brother-in-law of James Ross, preached domestic propriety in texts such as that which one parishioner glossed simply as "husbands love your wives [and] wives love your homes."[51] Other preachers warned about the dangers of female vanity and emphasized standard proper comportment of the body, modest dress, and sedate behaviour.[52]

The new sexual code was reflected in the shift from the HBC's earlier stress on the teaching of basic literacy and Christian morality to a more explicit directive in 1851. Its educational goal was now "to weaken the mischievous and destructive energy of those violent and untamed qualities of human nature which so frequently manifest themselves in society in a half-civilized state."[53] The discreetly worded reference to unregulated sexuality was not lost on Red River's teachers, who applied themselves assiduously to their mission. In the memoirs of former pupils, the governesses emerge as strict guardians of reputations, ever vigilant "for signs of promiscuous behaviour."[54]

Maria Thomas probably escaped such surveillance, for the project of bringing daughters up to a suitable standard was anchored in class values, and reserved for those who could afford the costs. Elite colony residents showed little interest in educating the "abandoned" daughters of country marriages, who were assumed to lack the budding virtues of chastity and piety which, with careful cultivation, could be brought to flower.[55] An education based on "the social etiquette of the day" would be a wasted effort on them.[56] Maria Thomas, described as a "poor girl," and the daughter of "poor folk," was raised by a Cree-speaking mother who testified in the Cree language at the trial. Thus the Thomas family inhabited the lower rungs of Red River's social ladder, and their circumstances prohibited Maria from receiving an education in refinement.

Maria Thomas was no passive victim, however. Her responses to Ross's cross-examinations countered his claims with certainties of her own. Unlike Ross's theatrical narrative, Thomas's formulation of her story appeared as straight chronicle, stripped of imaginative glosses.[57] Its coherence was diffused, however, because it was printed in several scattered fragment, comprising her "answers" to questions which *The Nor'Wester* did not specify. In contrast, the speeches of Ross and Judge Black were given dozens of uninterrupted column inches. Thomas's story was thus framed within their narrative and meaning system, or so it would seem at first glance.

A closer scrutiny reveals, however, that the papers on which Ross and *The Nor'Wester* inscribed their drama were not blank pages. They were palimpsests, scored and criss-crossed with traces of older stories—both Native and European—that proved difficult to erase even as late as 1863. These stubborn scripts of sexuality and sex-related practices (enduring country marriages and Cree courtship patterns, for example) interrogate *The Nor'Wester*'s dichotomous metaphors. As layered texts, heavily written over in the Corbett trial, they also offer counter-readings for understanding how Red River responded to new ideas and made sense of a changing and tension-ridden social order. But that is, indeed, another script and another story. What is of note here is that the scaffolding for the staging of the trial, its forms of dramatic and textual representation—the metaphors, allusions, and vocabulary—are themselves sources of historical knowledge.

Notes

1. The daughter of Simon Thomas and Catherine Linklater, and a pupil in Rev. James Hunter's Sunday school, Maria's family connections were British, Anglican, and Cree. A brother, born in 1844, was named Thomas, a fact suggesting a link with Governor Thomas Thomas, although it may merely reflect the tendency in Red River to name children after influential persons. Of note is the fact that only Maria Thomas's Cree connections were stressed in the trial. James Hunter Journal, NAC mfm, A91; Anglican Parish Registers, Provincial Archives of Manitoba (PAM), MG-7.

2. *The Nor'Wester*, 3 March 1863.

3. Joseph James Hargrave, *Red River* (Montreal: John Lovell, 1871), p. 171.

4. Coventry Patmore, *The Angel in the House* (London: George Bell and Son, 1896). *The Angel in the House* was a poetic construct which captured the imaginations of several generations of writers and social commentators. Patmore wrote the poem, he said, as a celebration of married love. But modern historians, analyzing its gender politics, found that his Angel operated as an influential prescription for flesh-and-blood women. Edmund Gosse, *Coventry Patmore* (London: Hodder and Stoughton, 1905); Carol Christ, "Victorian Masculinity and the Angel

in the Home," in Martha Vicinus, ed., *A Widening Sphere: Changing Roles of Victorian Women* (Bloomington: Indiana University Press, 1977).

5. Frits Pannekoek, "The Rev. Griffith Owen Corbett and the Red River Civil War of 1869–70," *Canadian Historical Review* 57 (1976), pp. 133–50.

6. Barbara Kanner, *Women in English Social History 1800–1914*, vol. 2 (New York: Garland, 19S8), p. 483. E.M. Sigsworth and T.J. Wyke, "A Study of Victorian Prostitution and Venereal Disease," in Martha Vicinus, ed., *Suffer and Be Still: Women in the Victorian Age* (Bloomington: Indian University Press, 1973), p. 80. Leonore Davidoff and Catherine Hall, *Family Fortunes: Men and Women of the English Middle Class, 1789–1950* (Chicago: University of Chicago Press, 1987), p. 89.

7. A major study of Victorian prostitution is Judith R. Walkowitz, *Prostitution and Victorian Society: Women, Class and the State* (New York: Cambridge University Press, 1980).

8. *Nor'Wester*, 30 March 1863.

9. Sigsworth and Wyke, 82. For the connection between finery and prostitutes, see Mariana Valverde, "The Love of Finery: Fashion and the

Fallen Woman in Nineteenth-Century Social Discourse," *Victorian Studies* 32 (Winter 1989) 169–188. Valverde uncovered a veritable "debate on finery" in the official documents on prostitution.

10. Erica Smith, "Something More Than Mere Ornament: Cloth and Indian-European Relationships in the Eighteenth Century," master's thesis, University of Winnipeg, 1991.

11. NAC, James Hunter Journal, mfm, A91. James Hunter to Henry Venn, 7 January 1863.

12. *The Nor'Wester*, 12 May 1863.

13. *The Nor'Wester*, 30 March 1863.

14. Rev. Sylvanus Stall, *What a Man Ought to Know* (Philadelphia, 1901), p. 241. Cited in Michael Bliss, "'Pure Books on Avoided Subjects': Pre-Freudian Sexual Ideas in Canada," J. Atherton, J.P. Heisler, and Fernand Ouellet, eds., Canadian Historical Association, *Historical Papers* (1968–70), p. 95.

15. *The Nor'Wester*, 30 March 1863.

16. *The Nor'Wester*, 13 March 1863.

17. *The Nor'Water*, 13 March 1863. A number of Ross's private letters also upheld the sanctity of the woman-home-family triad. "Ah yes!—It has been well remarked that 'mother,' 'home,' and 'heaven' seem to sound the sweetest words in our language, and when, papa, the last two become synonimous [*sic*] terms, they become a hundredfold sweeter," he wrote to his father. PAM, Alexander Ross Collection, James Ross to Alexander Ross, 13 July 1854.

18. *The Nor'Wester*, 30 March 1863.

19. William Greg's article, "Prostitution," published in the *Westminster Review* in 1850, is reprinted in *Prostitution in the Victorian Age: Debates on the Issue from 19ᵗʰ Century Critical Journals* (Westmead, England: Gregg International, 1973).

20. By 1860, the passionless wife had her masculine counterpart in the domesticated, sexually restrained, middle-class husband. Sexual control, or the mastery of passion, was one of the great moral imperatives aimed at men during this time. Too complex to flesh out here, the masculine gendering of sexuality awaits fuller treatment, but it may be briefly noted that the consequences of his sexual transgression were far-reaching and disastrous for Corbett. Disgraced and labelled "an awful blackguard" by his clerical colleagues in Red River, he returned to England shortly after the trial. When be begged the Archbishop of London, A.C. Tait, for a position, he did so on the basis of this "blameless life for some twenty years ... prior to the storm which burst out abroad." Tait had been alerted to the scandal by David Anderson, Bishop of Rupert's Land, and delayed giving Corbett his answer until, he said, he was "satisfied respecting the past." PAM, M627, Lambeth Palace Library, Tait Papers.

21. Acton's passionless stereotype was being vigorously challenged by the 1860s, mostly by medical men, who argued that women as well as men were capable of sexual arousal. See Carl Degler, *At Odds: Women and the Family in America from the Revolution to the Present* (New York: Oxford University Press, 1980), especially chapter 11.

22. See Peter T. Cominos, "Innocent Femina Sensualis in Unconscious Conflict," in Martha Vicinus, ed., *Suffer and Be Still: Women in the Victorian Age* (Bloomington, Indiana University Press, 1973), p. 157.

23. *The Nor'Wester*, 30 March 1863.

24. *The Nor'Wester*, 30 March 1863.

25. *The Nor'Wester*, 30 April 1803.

26. Stephen Marcus, *The Other Victorians: A Study of Sexuality and Pornography in Mid Nineteenth-Century England* (Toronto: Bantam Books, 1967), p. 5.

27. *The Nor'Wester*, 3 March 1863.

28. They condemned the two editors for printing such "disagreeable records" in a "family magazine," a judgment perhaps not unmixed with professional envy. Hargrave, *Red River*, p. 271.

29. William Coldwell, the journalist who took shorthand notes of the trial, had professional as well as attitudinal ties to Canada. Like Ross, he was concerned to present Red River in the best possible light to reassure Canadian expansionists, whose ambitions they shared. Doug Owram, *Promise of Eden: The Canadian Expansionist Movement and the Idea of the West 1856–1900* (Toronto: University of Toronto Press, 1980).

30. Suzanne Zeller, *Inventing Canada: Early Victorian Science and the Idea of a Transcontinental Nation* (Toronto: University of Toronto Press, 1987), p. 261.

31. The *Nor'Wester*, 14 October 1863. See also Red River Bishop David Anderson's exegesis of Hebrews 1, 1–12, a synthesis of Christianity, ethnology, and history, in which the sons (the Native and mixed-blood catechists of the youthful and vigorous colonial church) surpass the stately father (the Church of England). Anderson, *Children Instead of Fathers: A Christmas Ordination Sermon, Preached at St. John's Church, Red River, on Sunday, December 25, 1854* (London, 1854).

32. NAC, MG 24 H25, Sir John Henry Lefroy Journal, 1843–44.

33. Robert Courts, "Anglican Missionaries as Agents of Acculturation: The Church Missionary Society

at St. Andrews, Red River, 1830–1870," in Barry Ferguson, *The Anglican Church and World of Western Canada 1820–1970* (Regina: Canadian Plains Research Center, 1991), p. 56. Adam Thorn, a former resident, reporting on the progress of the mission to an Aberdeen audience, held James Ross up as an "example of the progress of Red River" in particular and of "civilization in general." PAM, Alexander Ross Collection, Adam Thorn to Alexander Ross, 27 March 1855.

34. The 1860s saw the establishment of a cricket club, a public library, a reading club, a temperance society, and a scientific institute in Red River.

35. Sylvia Van Kirk, *"Many Tender Ties": Women in Fur-Trade Society, 1670–1870* (Winnipeg: Watson and Dwyer, 1980), especially chapter 7. The language of George Simpson is the most obvious example of a fur trade officer's distaste for Indian women's sexuality and his own sexual past. See also the letters of his friend and colleague, James Hargrave, discussed in Jennifer S.H. Brown, "Changing Views of Fur Trade Marriage and Domesticity: James Hargrave, His Colleagues, and The Sex," *Western Canadian Journal of Anthropology* 6 (1976), p. 3. Hargrave's comments echo the obsession with "the woman question" that plagued British male discourses at the time; in them the term "the Sex" (signifying women) was a common phrase.

36. Aborigines Protection Society, *Canada West and the Hudson's Bay Company* (London; William Tweedie, 1856), pp. 6, 16. William Acton expressed precisely the same sentiments in *Functions and Disorders of the Reproductive System* (1857). See Marcus, *The Other Victorians*, p. 32.

37. The word "exotic," applied by Chief Factor James Douglas to white women in the Northwest and vaguely assumed to be a term of admiration, could mean quite the reverse. Douglas, married to a woman of mixed descent, was possibly using the term ironically to undercut the prevailing discourse. To William Acton, for example, it meant an unusual freakish person (Marcus, 16). Similarly, it is difficult to ignore the satirical implications of such descriptions of the ideal (white) wife immortalized by Chief Factor Donald McKenzie in his epigram: "[N]othing can give greater comfort to a husband than the satisfaction of having a wife who is nearly mute," or the parodic elements in John Stuart's impression of Frances Simpson disembarking at Red River: "Grace was in all her steps—heaven in her Eye—In all her gestures Dignity & love." Quoted in Brown, "James Hargrave," p. 103, and G.P. de T. Glazebrook, *The Hargrave Correspondence* (Toronto: Champlain Society. 1938), p. 57, respectively.

38. Van Kirk, "Many Tender Ties," especially chapter 7; Thomas F. Bredin, "The Red River Academy," *The Beaver* (Winter 1974), p. 14.

39. Deborah Gorham, *The Victorian Girl and the Feminine Ideal* (Bloomington: Indiana University Press, 1982), pp. 42–43.

40. Van Kirk, *"Many Tender Ties,"* p. 148.

41. W.J. Healy, *Women of Red River* (Winnipeg: Russell, Lang & Co., Ltd, 1923), pp. 80–81.

42. E.E. Rich and A.M. Johnson, eds., *London Correspondence Inward from Eden Colvile, 1849–1851* (London: Hudson's Bay Record Society, 1956), p. 156.

43. Two examples are the St. Cross school and Miss Davis's Academy.

44. Rich and Johnson, pp. 156, 160.

45. PAM, MG 1C14, Alexander Ross Collection, Peter Jacobs to James Ross, 19 December 1853.

46. PAM, MG 2 C24, Matilda Davis School Collection.

47. Mrs. George Bryce, *Early Red River Culture*, Historical and Scientific Society of Manitoba, Transaction no. 57 (Winnipeg: Manitoba Free Press), p. 15.

48. Winnipeg, Museum of Man and Nature Library. Flora Smith Oral History Tape 106.

49. Bryce, *Early Red River Culture*, p. 15.

50. Healy, *Women of Red River*, p. 260.

51. PAM, Alexander Ross Collection, Jemima Ron to James Ron, 28 June 1854.

52. Healy, *Women of Red River*, p. 34.

53. E.H. Oliver, *The Canadian North-West: Its Early Development and Legislative Development*, vol. I (Ottawa: Government Printing Bureau, 1914), p. 365.

54. Healy, *Women of Red River*, p. 82.

55. Bredin, "The Red River Academy," p. 11.

56. Bredin, "The Red River Academy," p. 11; Bryce, *Early Red River Culture*, p. 14.

57. The content of Thomas's version was, I suspect, left more or less intact because it was not considered worthy of notice, let alone editorial reworking. The known facts about her life are scanty. She died in 1867 and the child, Anne Elizabeth, was raised by the Thomas family. Hargrave, *Red River*, p. 387.

CHAPTER 14

The Relocation Phenomenon
and the Africville Study

Donald H. Clairmont and Dennis William Magill

· ·

To seek social change, without due recognition of the manifest and latent functions performed by the social organization undergoing change, is to indulge in social ritual rather than social engineering.[1]

—Robert K. Merton

Halifax, the foundation city of English-speaking Canada, experienced much change during its first two hundred years of existence. Yet the facelift and redevelopment it has undergone since the late 1950s have effected a change as dramatic as the 1917 explosion that levelled much of the city. Stimulated by the Stephenson Report of 1957,[2] urban renewal and redevelopment have resulted in the relocation of thousands of people, the demolition of hundreds of buildings, and the construction of impressive business and governmental complexes. The Africville relocation was part of the larger redevelopment pattern; Africville residents constituted some eight to ten percent of the people affected by approved urban renewal schemes in the city of Halifax during the relocation years.

Africville was a black community within the city of Halifax, inhabited by approximately four hundred people, comprising eighty families, many of whom were descended from settlers who had moved there over a century ago. Tucked away in a corner of the city, relatively invisible, and thought of as a "shack town," Africville was a depressed community both in physical and in socio-economic terms. Its dwellings were located beside the city dump, and railroad tracks cut across the one dirt road leading into the area. Sewerage, lighting, and other public services were conspicuously absent. The people had little education, very low incomes, and many were underemployed. Property claims were in chaos. Only a handful of families could establish legal title; others claimed squatter rights; and still others rented. Africville, long a black mark against society, had been designated for future industrial and harbour development. Many observers reported that despite these liabilities there was a strong sense of community and that some residents expressed satisfaction with living in Africville.

In 1964 the small black ghetto of Africville began to be phased out of existence. By that time most residents of Halifax, black and white, had come to think of Africville as "the slum by the dump." Most Haligonians, including some Africville residents, did not regard the community as viable and recognized a need for planned social change. The relocation plan announced by the city of Halifax, which purported to be more than simply a real estate operation, appeared to be a response to this need. The plan emphasized humanitarian concern, included employment and education programs, and referred to the creation of new opportunities for the people of Africville. To the general public, the proposed relocation was a progressive step.

In addition to official pronouncements, there were other indications that the Africville program would be more humane and progressive than the typical North American urban relocation. Halifax city council had adopted recommendations contained in a report submitted by a noted Canadian welfare specialist experienced in urban renewal. There was much preliminary discussion of the relocation by city officials among themselves, with Africville residents, and with a "caretaker" group of black and white progressionals associated with the Halifax Human Rights Advisory Committee. Relocation plans were not ad hoc and haphazard. City officials were required to articulate their policies well and in detail; many implications and alternatives were considered.

There were also indications in the relocation decision-making structure that the Africville program might realize its official rhetoric. A social worker was appointed by the city to take front-line responsibility for the varied aspects of the relocation and to act as liaison between the city administration and the relocatees. The social worker, who was on loan from the Nova Scotia Department of Public Welfare, had a measure of autonomy vis-à-vis the city and an independent contingency fund to meet day-to-day emergencies and opportunities with a minimum of bureaucratic delay. In negotiating the real estate aspects of relocation, the social worker brought proposed agreements before a special advisory committee consisting of aldermen and several members of the Halifax Human Rights Advisory Committee.

In terms of its rationale, public rhetoric, and organizational structure, the Africville relocation seemed worthy of study. The plan was liberal-oriented (that is, aimed at ending segregation and providing improved opportunities for the disadvantaged), welfare-oriented (that is, it hoped to coordinate employment, educational,

and rehabilitative programs with the rehousing of people), and run by experts (that is, the planning, execution, and advice were provided by professionals). An examination of the Africville relocation could be expected to yield greater fundamental insight into planned social change than would a study of typical relocation programs that were accomplished by administrative fiat and stressed primarily the physical removal of persons. It seemed important to study and evaluate the Africville relocation both in its particularity and against the background of general relocation issues.

There were additional reasons for studying the Africville relocation. First, Africville was part of a trend in the 1960s for governmental initiative in relocation programs, and there was reason to expect that other tentative relocations in Nova Scotia and elsewhere would be patterned after the Africville experience. Second, Africville had attracted national and even international notice, and there was broad public interest in the relocation. Third, accounts of pre-relocation social conditions and attitudes were available. Two surveys had been conducted,[3] and other material was available in city records. Finally, in 1968 the Africville relocation had already been acclaimed locally as a success. One city alderman noted:

> The social significance of the Africville program is already beginning to show positive results as far as individual families are concerned. The children are performing more satisfactorily in school and they seem to take more of an interest in their new surroundings. This report is not intended to indicate that the program has been 100 percent successful; however I believe it can be said that it has been at least 75 percent, judging by the comments of the relocated families.[4]

Private communication with city officials and relocation officials in the United States and Canada brought forth praise for the organization and rhetoric of the Africville relocation.

Was the Africville relocation a success? If so, from whose perspective? To what extent?

What accounted for the success or lack of it? It is hoped that answers to these and related questions will contribute to an appreciation of the Africville relocation and of relocation generally.

The Relocation Phenomenon

Relocation must be seen in the context of a general North American mobility pattern, and certain distinctive features should be noted. The most important distinction is that relocation is part of planned social change carried out, or at least approved, by public agency. The initiation of relocation, as seen by the relocatees, is usually involuntary and an immediate function of the political process. Our present concern is with relocation as it pertains to private residences, involves neighbourhoods or communities, and is a function of comprehensive programs of social change. This kind of relocation accounts for but a small measure of the mobility noted in Canada and the United States, but it was significant because it was distinctive. It was noted earlier that the Africville relocation was itself part of a much larger redevelopment project in the city of Halifax. In terms of the sweep of lifestyle change, even such large urban projects have been dwarfed by post-Second World War Canadian relocation projects in the Arctic and in Newfoundland. In 1953, Newfoundland, with 6000 miles of coastline and approximately 1150 settlements, undertook a program to move people from the small outposts to larger viable communities which could be serviced efficiently. Between 1965 and 1970 over 3250 households were moved.[5]

As many low-income Americans and Canadians can testify, urban renewal is a prime example of forced relocation. Urban renewal legislation began in the 1940s in both countries. By 1968 approximately forty-five Canadian urban redevelopments had been initiated at a cost of 270 million dollars for 1500 cleared acres.[6] While the scope of urban renewal in Canada was quite small in the light of American experience, the Canadian program was significant enough that one can complain that there were too few Canadian studies looking into the politics, issues, and human consequences of renewal programs. To overcome this lack of knowledge and to place the Africville relocation in perspective, more comprehensive themes will be discussed in this introduction.

From a political-administrative perspective there are four relocation models: the traditional, development, liberal-welfare, and political. The Africville project is the best Canadian example of the liberal-welfare type of relocation. [...] These models vary along six dimensions: (1) ideological premises; (2) formulation of policy; (3) implementation of policy; (4) intended beneficiaries; (5) central actors and organizational units; and (6) key problems. These models are ideal types to which actual relocation programs correspond to a greater or lesser degree.

The Development Model

The development model was the most prevalent political-administrative approach to relocation in North America. This type of relocation was usually justified in terms of supposed benefits for the system as a whole, whether the system is society, the city, etc. It was usually initiated by order of political authorities and administered by bureaucrats; it was not anticipated that relocatees would benefit other than indirectly. The underlying ideology of the development model was system-oriented and neo-capitalist; an accurate statement of its premise in urban renewal has been offered by Wallace: "[it considers] renewal, as a public activity, to be intervention in a market and competitive system and to be justified by the need to make up for imperfections in the market mechanism that impede the adjustment process, to eliminate conditions which are economic or social liabilities."[7] In the context of contemporary urban renewal, the development model incorporated the usual city-design approach, focusing on questions of beautification, zoning, and structure,[8] and was usually intended to increase the city tax base and achieve civic pride or attract industry.

The development model can be illustrated by past urban renewal programs in Toronto. Ignoring relocatees as viable interest groups the programs operated implicitly on the basis of certain ideological premises: to correct imperfections in the social system (removal of so-called slums) and overall system development (economic growth), or both. As is the case in many Canadian cities, Toronto's past development policy was closely linked to the businesses and commercial-property industry which provided homes, apartment buildings, shopping centres, and industrial complexes. Thus the elimination of "blight areas" and construction of highrise apartment and office buildings generated an important source of urban revenue. Referring to this policy of "dollar planning," Fraser observed:

As long as Toronto, [in 1972] like all other municipalities in Canada has to depend upon property taxes as its sole source of income, the overwhelming power of development interests in determining the direction and quality of Toronto's growth will remain unchallenged.
[...] [T]he key to a municipality's prosperity remains its rate of growth; Toronto planners have been consistently ignored by city councils that have been over the years almost exclusively uninterested in any discussions about the quality of that development.[9]

A non-urban example of the development model of relocation has been described by John Matthiasson, in his study of the forced relocation of a band of Cree Indians in Northern Manitoba. The Cree were relocated to make way for a gigantic power project; they were not involved in the project planning and despite their displeasure "they accepted in a fatalistic manner the announcement of the relocation. They believed that the decision had been made by higher authorities, and that they had neither the right nor power to question it."[10]

The development model of relocation had its limitations. In particular, its econocentric and "undemocratic" features were criticized. The assumption that relocatees benefit indirectly

from relocation was challenged, as was the premise that the system as a whole somehow redistributed fairly the benefits accruing from forcing people to move and facilitating the development of private industry. Some critics argued that if one included social-psychological factors in one's conception of costs, the relocatees could be seen as subsidizing the rest of the system. The criticism had some effect, and the liberal-welfare model became increasingly common.[11] One official explained:

In the fifteen years since [urban renewal's] inception, we have seen a progressive broadening of the concept and a strengthening of tools. We have seen, increasingly, both the need for, and realization of, rapprochement between physical and social planning, between renewal and social action. But the fully effective liaison of the two approaches has almost everywhere been frustrated by the absence of the tools to deal as effectively with the problems of human beings as with the problems of physical decay and blight.[12]

Another writer has observed

social welfare can no longer be treated as the responsibility of private and more or less bountiful ladies and gentlemen or as the less respected branch of the social welfare community and the city government. Tied as it is to the concerns as dear to the heart of the country as economic prosperity it merits a place in the inner sanctum, particularly of planning commissions.[13]

The Liberal-Welfare Model

The "rediscovery" of poverty,[14] the war on poverty, the increasing pressure "from below" upon the development model, and the broadening definition of urban renewal led to the widespread emergence of the liberal-welfare-oriented approach. The liberal-welfare model, like the development model, emphasized expertise and technical knowledge in its operation and administration, and invariably was initiated by public authority. The principal difference is that the liberal-welfare model purported to benefit the relocatees primarily and directly. Under this model, welfare officials often saw themselves as "caretakers" for the relocatees; one relocation official has said, "the department of relocation is the tenants' advocate."[15] The liberal-welfare model of relocation was characterized by a host of social welfare programs supplemental to housing policies and was regarded as an opportunity for a multifaceted attack on poverty and other problems. It was this liberal-welfare model and its assumptions that shaped the rhetoric underlying the 1963–64 decision to relocate Africville.

Ideologically, the liberal-welfare model was much like the development model in that it tended to operate with a consensus model of society and posited a basic congruency between the interests of relocatees and those of society as a whole. It was "undemocratic" in the same sense as the development model; the low-status relocatees were accorded little attention, either as participants in the implicit political process or as contributors to specific policies or plans of action. There was an effort, however, to persuade rather than to ignore the relocatees. Criticism of the liberal-welfare model of relocation was related primarily to the ideological level. Some writers noted that liberal welfarism had become part of the establishment of contemporary North American society.[16] Its proponents were presumed to be handmaidens of strong vested interests, reconciling the disadvantaged and patching up the symptoms of social malaise. Critics pointed out that the special programs associated with the liberal-welfare model of relocation tended to be short-term and unsuccessful. The welfare rhetoric often diverted attention from the gains and benefits accruing to the middle-income and elite groups in society. The critics attacked the liberal-welfare model on the premise that the social problems to which it is ostensibly directed could be solved only through profound structural change effecting a redistribution of resources, and by providing relocatees with the consciousness and resources to restructure their own lives.

The liberal-welfare model is best illustrated by the Africville relocation, discussed at length in this book. The community of Africville was defined as a social problem, and relocation was regarded as an intervention strategy designed to help solve the "social and economic problems of Africville residents." The central actors in the formation and implementation of relocation policy were politicians, bureaucrats, experts, and middle-class caretakers; there was no meaningful collective participation by Africville residents. The relocatees were to be major beneficiaries through compensation, welfare payments, and rehabilitative retraining programs. The major problem with the relocation was that, although rooted in liberal-welfare rhetoric, it failed to achieve its manifest goals.

The Political Model

The liberal-welfare model of relocation was revised and developed both as a response to criticism at the ideological level and in reaction to its lack of operational success. There was a growing interest in citizen participation in all phases of relocation; in the firmer acceptance, structurally and culturally, of the advocacy function of relocation officials; in the co-ordination of relocation services; and in the provision of resources. It is difficult to assess how far this interest has been translated into fact. There appeared to be a shift in the 1970s, at least conceptually, to the political model of relocation and a frank recognition that relocation usually entailed a conflict of interest, for example, between the relocatees and the city. There was an attempt to structure the conflict by providing relocatees with resources to develop a parallel structure to that of the government. Although society and the relocatee were considered to benefit equally, this political perspective assumed that relocatees benefited both directly and indirectly; directly in terms of, say, housing and other welfare services, and indirectly by participating in the basic decision-making and the determination of their life situation. The political model of relocation was based on the premise that social problems were political problems and emphasized solutions through political action; relocation was approached primarily as a situation in which problems were solved not by the application of expertise but by the resolution of conflicting interests.

Beyond the considerable costs (the dollar cost is less hidden than in the other relocation model) and administrative difficulties entailed, there were other grounds for criticism of the political model. There was a tendency to overemphasize the solidarity and common interests of relocatees, to exaggerate the multiplying effects of political participation in relocation,[17] and to raise serious questions about how far government could proceed or would proceed in fostering extra-parliamentary political action.

Citizen participation, a core element in the political model, was institutionalized in the United States by the community action programs of the 1964 Economic Opportunity Act. Numerous books and articles, far too many to cite, have discussed the reasons, operations, and failures of "maximum feasible participation" of the poor in the war on poverty.[18] Citizen participation was also part of the United States model city programs, which required that local residents be involved in the planning process and implementation of changes in their neighbourhoods. Contrasted with the United States, Canada has relatively few examples of related social-animation projects. The rise of "militant" citizen groups was a phenomenon which developed later in Canada. The public outcry against the community work of the Company of Young Canadians and the subsequent governmental intervention to close this organization may be an indication of the limits of this perspective. The only Canadian publication illustrating the political model of a relocation is Fraser's study of Toronto's Trefann Court. Trefann Court residents successfully fought off a development-type relocation project; subsequently, the conflict arising from different interests was recognized as an integral part of the city's social organization. Despite internal community conflict between homeowners and tenants, a number of community residents, leaning heavily on outside "resource people," developed a cohesive organization and set up

a working committee (a parallel structure) to establish a conceptual scheme for community change in conjunction with the existing city bureaucracy. The Trefann Court case also pointed to a key problem in the political model, that of assessing the representativeness of any one group of citizens to speak, argue, or vote for an entire community. With the establishment of "parallel structures," many citizens grow frustrated with the tedious detail involved in committee work. In Fraser's words:

> The fact that the Working Committee operated under formal rules of order, dominated by minutes, reports, rules of procedure and legislative decorum widened the gap between the committee and the community. As debates became more lengthy, detailed and technical, the meetings became harder to follow for the ordinary Trefann resident who might drop in.[19]

The Traditional Model

Finally, there is the traditional model of relocation in North American society. This is a limiting type of relocation carried out under governmental auspices, for it is a form of planned social change characterized by self-help and self-direction. It is the neighbourhood or community leaders, often indigenous minority-group leaders working through indigenous social organizations, who plan and carry out the relocation, generally with official support and some resource commitment by government agencies. The traditional model entails a largely laissez-faire strategy whereby the relocatees benefit directly and technical expertise is used to advise rather than to direct. Criticism of this approach contends that, without political action, neither the available resources nor the generation of initiative can be effective in the case of low-status groups.

There are numerous examples of the traditional model of relocation. Group settlement and resettlement in various parts of Canada have been common. The relocation of Beechville, a black community on the outskirts of Halifax, is an example within the Halifax metropolitan area. Community leaders, anticipating a government attempt to relocate the residents, organized themselves into a co-operative housing association, received funds from Central Mortgage and Housing Corporation, and reorganized their community partly on their own terms. The scope available for traditional relocation models lessens as society becomes more technocratic and centralized.

Conceptual Framework

Throughout this book our emphasis will be on the liberal-welfare model of planned social change and its implementation during the Africville relocation. During the analysis we focus on questions of power and exchange among the various participants of the relocation. Thus, from the perspective of power and exchange,[20] we can examine the power resources and relationships among the individual persons and groups involved in the relocation, the historical evolution of these social facts, the goals held by the different parties, and the strategies and tactics employed in establishing the terms of the relocation "contract." We can also analyse the role of outsiders, experts, and community "leaders" and focus on questions such as the mobilization of advocacy, relocation resistances and alternatives, and the relation of rhetoric to action. It is vital in the Africville case to have a larger historical view, observing the historical exchange patterns between the city and the Africville people and tracing the implications of these patterns in making Africville "ripe for relocation" and in influencing the relocation decision-making and mechanics.

An aspect of this perspective concerns the context of negotiations and the bargaining strategies developed by the parties involved. Accordingly, attention was devoted to probing the relocatees' knowledge about the relocation; their strategies (use of lawyers, co-operation with fellow relocatees, and development of special arguments in dealing with city officials), and their perceptions of the city's goals, strategies, and resources. The relocation social worker completed a questionnaire concerning each relocated family which paid

considerable attention to his negotiations with relocatees and his perception of their goals, strategies, and resources. This perspective included the concepts of rewards, costs, profits, and distributive justice. It would appear, for instance, that relocatees would have been satisfied with the relocation if rewards exceeded costs and if they thought that the city and other relocatees would not "get a better deal." Information concerning rewards, costs, sense of distributive justice, and satisfaction was obtained through the questionnaires, the interviews, and the case studies.

Despite problems in measuring each relocatee's perception of the relative profit accruing to himself or herself, other relocatees, and the city of Halifax, and problems occasioned by differences between long-term and short-term effects, this power and exchange approach is significant for the relocation literature which often appears to keep aloof from the "blood and guts" of relocation transaction. Equally important, by placing the Africville relocation within a typology of relocation models, it is possible to explore the domain consensus (that is, the basic terms of reference held in common and prerequisite to any exchange) associated with the liberal-welfare approach, and especially how such domain consensus (for example, "disadvantaged communities or people have few intrinsically valuable resources and need to be guided by sympathetic experts") develops and how it sets the limits and context of bargaining and reciprocity.

Research Strategies

The methods employed in this study were varied: questionnaires, in-depth interviews, historical documents, newspapers, case studies, and "bull sessions" with relocatees. A useful baseline source of data was the survey of Halifax blacks, including Africville, conducted in 1959 by the Institute of Public Affairs, Dalhousie University. The original questionnaires were available for re-analysis, an important consideration since many of the data were not published and the published material contained several significant inaccuracies.[21] The 1959 survey questionnaire provided basic demographic data as well as information concerning mobility aspirations, employment, education, and social life.

The collection of data for this study began in 1968. The researchers arranged for two students from the Maritime School of Social Work to prepare twenty case studies.[22] A review of the students' case studies and field notes, guided by the perspective developed by the researchers, aided the drafting of a questionnaire. In 1968 current addresses of the relocatees were also traced and brief acquaintance interviews were conducted.

The most intensive data collection period was June to December 1969. One of the researchers (D.W.M.) conducted in-depth, tape-recorded interviews with individual people associated with the relocation decision-making and implementation: politicians, city officials, middle-class caretakers, the relocation social worker, consultants, and Africville relocatees involved in the decision-making. During these interviews an open-ended interview guide[23] was used to explore knowledge of Africville and awareness of pre-1964 relocation attempts and also the actual relocation decision-making and mechanics. Each of the approximately two-hour interviews was transcribed and analysed for patterns. Many quotations used in this book are taken from these tape-recorded interviews.

Concurrently, the other researcher (D.H.C.), with two assistants, was meeting informally with the relocatees, individually and in "bull sessions." On the basis of these experiences and the case studies, we drafted and pre-tested an extensive questionnaire. From September to December, 1969, the questionnaire was employed by interviewers hired and trained by the researchers. The lengthy questionnaire[24] asked about the relocatee's background characteristics: life in Africville, personal knowledge of relocation decision-making processes, relocation strategies, negotiations, costs, rewards, and post-relocation conditions. The questionnaire was given to all household heads and spouses who had lived in Africville and had received a relocation settlement of any kind. Approximately 140 persons were

interviewed, several in places as far distant as Winnipeg and Toronto.

In June, 1969, the relocation social worker spent eight days answering a questionnaire[25] on the relocatees' background characteristics, his relocation bargaining with each relocatee, and his perception of the latter's rewards, costs, and strategies. Such data enabled us to analyse more precisely the relationships among parties to the relocation, for similar data from the relocatees and their perception of the relocation social worker were obtained from the relocatee questionnaire.

Two other research tactics were employed at the same time as the interviews were conducted. One of our assistants was conducting in-depth, tape-recorded interviews with black leaders in the Halifax area concerning their assessment of Africville and the implications of relocation. Another assistant was gathering historical data and interviewing selected Africville relocatees concerning the historical development of the community. Important sources of historical data were the minutes of Halifax City Council (read from 1852 to 1969), reports of the Board of Halifax School Commissioners, the Nova Scotia Public Archives, files in the Registry of Deeds, the Halifax Mail-Star library, and the minutes of the Halifax Human Rights Advisory Committee. In all phases of research, the Africville files in the Social Planning Department, City of Halifax were of especial value.

Phases of the Africville Study

The Africville Relocation Report, in addition to being an examination of relocation and planned social change and a contribution to the sparse literature on blacks in Nova Scotia, represents a fusion of research and action. The researchers did not begin the study until virtually all the Africville people had been relocated, and the research strategy resulted in the study being more than an evaluation.[26] The process of obtaining collective as well as individual responses, and of establishing a meaningful exchange with relocatees, fostered collective action from former Africville residents. Some local government officials objected to what they have referred to as the researchers' "activist" bias. The researchers maintain, however, that exchanges had to be worked out with the subjects of research as well as with the funding agencies. The liberal ethic posits informed voluntary consent as fundamental to adult social interaction; informed voluntary consent requires, in turn, meaningful exchange among the participants.

The study began in October, 1968 with a meeting of relocated Africville people. This was the first time since relocation that former residents of Africville had met collectively. This stormy meeting, called by the researchers, was a public airing of relocatee grievances and led to relocatee support of the proposed study. Subsequent talk of forming committees to press grievances with the city of Halifax was an important result of the meeting. The researchers encouraged this tendency, for the expressed grievances appeared legitimate, and the researchers considered that it would be both possible and important to tap a collective or group dimension in the relocation process as well as to study the usual social-psychological considerations.

Later in the same week, at a meeting that the researchers had arranged with city officials, relocation caretakers, and civic leaders, the researchers related the expressed grievances of the relocatees and urged remedial action. General support for the proposed study was obtained at this second meeting, and the pending reconsideration of relocation by the city's newly created Social Planning Department was crystallized.

During the winter and spring of 1969, as the present study was being planned in detail, the action-stimulus of the researchers' early efforts was bearing fruit. Social Planning Department officials were meeting with the relocatees and, as it were, planning the second phase (not initially called for) of the Africville relocation. With provincial and municipal grants totalling seventy thousand dollars, the Seaview Credit Union was organized to assist relocatees experiencing financial crises; in addition, plans were formulated to meet housing and employment needs, and special consideration was to be given to former Africville residents whose needs could be met within the city's existing welfare system. A relocatee was hired to manage the credit union and to assist with other anticipated programs.

During the main data-gathering period, the summer of 1969, and in line with a decision to obtain collective as well as individual responses, the researchers met with informed groups of Africville relocatees to discuss current and future remedial action. It became apparent that the so-called second phase of the relocation would be inadequate to meet the people's needs. There was little identification with the credit union and it was floundering, for many relocatees who became members were either unable or unwilling to repay loans. Other anticipated programs and action promised by the city were delayed or forgotten due to bureaucratic entanglements and to lack of organization and pressure on the part of the relocatees.

The relocatees still had legitimate grievances related to unkept promises made at the time of relocation and later. With the formation of the Africville Action Committee, a third phase of the relocation began in the fall of 1969 and winter of 1970. The task of this new committee, developed from group discussions held between the researchers and relocatees, was to effect governmental redress through organized pressure. Several position papers were developed by the Africville Action Committee and negotiations were reopened with the city of Halifax. Although numerous meetings of relocatees were held during the first half of 1970, problems within the Africville Action Committee and the absence of resource people until the fall of 1970 hindered progress. With the committee stumbling along, and the credit union and other city-sponsored projects either ineffectual or nonexistent, the relocation process appeared to have petered out. The action committee was reactivated when one of the authors (D.H.C.) returned to Halifax permanently in the fall of 1970 and groups of relocatees were subsequently reinvolved in reading and criticizing a draft of the present study and in evaluating the relocation and the remedial action taken. Since the fall of 1970, the Africville Action Committee was active. Widespread support for its claims was obtained from community organizations, subcommittees were established to deal with questions of employment, housing, and financial compensation; and city council authorized the establishment of a city negotiating team to meet with representatives of the action committee.

In 1974, at the time of publication of the first edition of this book, the Africville Action Committee, to all intents and purposes, had ceased to function. Although it could claim some credit for a special employment training program through which a number of unemployed Africville relocatees had found jobs, the action committee fell far short of its goals. The city's lack of a positive imaginative response and the internal organizational problems of the action committee hindered other proposals. What remained in 1974 was a reorganized credit union, a modest base for further redress and group action. However, by 1999 the Seaview Credit Union was no longer in existence; it had collapsed over two decades ago. However, the community is not dead. As noted in the preface of this revised [1999] edition, Africville still thrives in the hearts and minds of many of the relocatees. In addition, Africville still has rich symbolic value for fostering black consciousness in Nova Scotia.

Postscript

Throughout the study, we consciously and deliberately attempted to achieve a viable fusion of research and social responsibility. The research focussed on the collective responses of the group as well as on individual responses. At each stage in the study (conception, data gathering, data analysis, and preparation for publication) the collective and individual inputs that gave the study an action potential were obtained from relocatees. Drafts of appropriate chapters were sent for critical comment to officials and others involved in the relocation. The study became a stimulus to action because the normal researcher-subject exchanges could be worked out in concrete, actual terms. This was preferable to the usual research situation where, in effecting exchanges with the people being studied, the researcher typically makes vague references to the possible benefit of the study and does little or nothing to follow up implied promises of action.[27] But, of course, our research strategy has its weakness too. It is difficult to feel satisfied that the kind of exchange relations that we established had productive consequences. Despite our involvement (in the early 1970s) with petitions, committee work, and attempts at rational problem solving, little redress of the inadequacies of the relocation program was achieved and the manifest goals of the liberal-welfare rhetoric of the relocation remain, in large measure, unrealized.

Notes

1. *Social Theory and Social Structure* (Glencoe, Ill.: The Free Press, 1949), p. 80.

2. Gordon Stephenson, *A Redevelopment Study of Halifax, Nova Scotia* (Halifax, N.S.: City of Halifax, 1957).

3. *The Condition of the Negroes of Halifax City, Nova Scotia* (Halifax: Institute of Public Affairs, Dalhousie University, 1962); and G. Brand, Interdepartmental Committee on Human Rights: Survey Reports (Halifax: Nova Scotia Department of Welfare, Social Development Division, 1963).

4. Minutes of the Halifax City Council, Halifax, September 14, 1967.

5. The Government of Newfoundland initiated the program in 1953. In 1965 a joint federal-provincial program was initiated under a resettlement act. In 1970 the program was placed under the direction of the Federal Department of Regional Economic Expansion. For an overview of the resettlement program, see Noel Iverson and D. Ralph Matthews, *Communities in Decline: An Examination of Household Resettlement in Newfoundland,* Newfoundland Social and

Economic Studies, No. 6 (St. John's, Nfld.: Memorial University of Newfoundland, Institute of Social and Economic Research, 1968). For a critical assessment of studies of the resettlement program, see Jim Lotz, "Resettlement and Social Change in Newfoundland," *The Canadian Review of Sociology and Anthropology* 8 (February, 1971): 48–59.

6. See Table 4, "Completed Redevelopment Projects" in Urban Renewal (Toronto: Centre for Urban and Community Studies, University of Toronto, 1968). Reprinted from *University of Toronto Law Journal*, 18, No. 3 (1968): 243.

7. David A. Wallace, "The Conceptualizing of Urban Renewal," *Urban Renewal* (Toronto: Centre for Urban and Community Studies, University of Toronto, 1968), 251.

8. An example of such a project is one reported by Thurz in southwest Washington, D.C. Little was done for the relocatees, but the relocation was widely acclaimed for its futuristic redevelopment design. For a critique of this approach, see Daniel Thurz, *Where Are They Now?* (Washington, D.C: Health and Welfare Council of the National Capital Area, 1966). See also, Jane Jacobs, *The Death and Life of Great American Cities* (New York: Random House, 1961).

9. Graham Fraser, *Fighting Back: Urban Renewal in Trefann Court* (Toronto: Hakkert, 1972), p. 55.

10. John Matthiasson, "Forced Relocation: An Evaluative Case Study," paper presented at the annual meeting of the Canadian Sociology and Anthropology Association, Winnipeg, 1970.

11. In recent years some minor progressive modifications have been introduced with reference to the development model; these deal with advance notice and public hearings, relocation compensation, and the availability of housing stock. See, Robert P. Groberg, *Centralized Relocation* (Washington, D.C: National Association of Housing and Redevelopment Officials, 1969).

12. William L. Slayton, "Poverty and Urban Renewal," quoted in Hans B.C. Spiegal, "Human Considerations in Urban Renewal," *Urban Renewal*, op. cit., 311.

13. Elizabeth Wood, "Social Welfare Planning," quoted in Spiegel, op. cit., 315.

14. For a discussion of this, see Kenneth Craig, "Sociologists and Motivating Strategies," M.A. Thesis, University of Guelph, Department of Sociology, 1971.

15. Groberg, op. cit., p. 172.

16. See Alvin W. Gouldner, *The Coming Crisis of Western Sociology* (New York: Basic Books, 1970), pp. 500–502.

17. Relocation is a short-term consideration, for most services brought to bear on relocatee problems rarely extend beyond rehousing. A more general critique of the multiplying effect of citizens' involvement in relocation is given by S.M. Miller and Frank Riessman, *Social Class and Social Policy* (New York: Basic Books, 1968).

18. The historical antecedents and reasons for the legislation are discussed in Daniel Moynihan, *Maximum Feasible Misunderstanding* (New York: Free Press, 1970). For an alternative interpretation, see Francis Fox Piven and Richard A. Cloward, *Regulating the Poor: The Functions of Public Welfare* (New York: Random Vintage Books, 1972), pp. 248–284. The operation of the program is discussed by Ralph M. Kramer, *Participation of the Poor: Comparative Community Case Studies in the War on Poverty* (Englewood Cliffs, N.J.: Prentice Hall, 1969).

19. Fraser, op. cit., p. 262.

20. For a discussion of this theoretical perspective, see Peter M. Blau, *Exchange and Power in Social Life* (New York: Wiley, 1964); and George Caspar Homans, *Social Behavior: Its Elementary Forms* (New York: Harcourt, Brace and World, 1961).

21. *The Condition of the Negroes of Halifax City,* Nova Scotia, op. cit.

22. Sarah M. Beaton, "Effects of Relocation: A Study of Ten Families Relocated from Africville, Halifax, Nova Scotia," Master of Social Work Thesis, Maritime School of Social Work, Halifax, N.S., 1969; and Bernard MacDougall, "Urban Relocation of Africville Residents," Master of Social Work Thesis, Maritime School of Social Work, Halifax, N.S., 1969.

23. The interview guide is published in Donald H. Clairmont and Dennis W. Magill, *Africville Relocation Report* (Halifax: Institute of Public Affairs, Dalhousie University, 1971), pp. A131–A135.

24. Ibid., pp. A97–A128.

25. Ibid., pp. A83–A96.

26. Some relocation studies have been carried out as part of the relocation decision-making, see William H. Key, *When People Are Forced to Move* (Topeka, Kansas: Menninger Foundation, 1967), mimeographed; others have been concurrent with the relocating of people, see Herbert J. Gans, *The Urban Villagers: Group and Class in the Life of Italian Americans* (New York: The Free Press, 1962). The present study is unique in that it fostered collective action carried out after the relocation.

27. See Craig, op. cit.

References

Beaton, Sarah M. "Effects of Relocation: A Study of Ten Families Relocated from Africville, Halifax, Nova Scotia," Master of Social Work Thesis, Maritime School of Social Work, Halifax, N.S., 1969.

Blau, Peter M. *Exchange and Power in Social Life.* New York: Wiley, 1964.

Brand, G. *Interdepartmental Committee on Human Rights: Survey Reports.* Halifax, N.S.: Nova Scotia Department of Welfare, Social Development Division, 1963.

Clairmont, Donald H., and Dennis William Magill. *Africville Relocation Report.* Halifax,

N.S.: Institute of Public Affairs, Dalhousie University, 1971.

Craig, Kenneth. "Sociologists and Motivating Strategies." Unpublished M.S. Thesis, University of Guelph, Department of Sociology, Guelph, Ontario, 1971.

Fraser, Graham. *Fighting Back: Urban Renewal in Trefann Court.* Toronto: Hakkent, 1972.

Gans, Herbert J. *The Urban Villagers: Group and Class in the Life of Italian Americans.* New York: The Free Press, 1962.

Gouldner, Alvin W. *The Coming Crisis of Western Sociology.* New York: Basic Books, 1970.

Groberg, Robert P. *Centralized Relocation.* Washington, D.C.: National Association of Housing and Redevelopment Officials, 1969.

Homans, George Casper. *Social Behavior: Its Elementary Forms.* New York: Harcourt, Brace and World, 1961.

Iverson, Noel. *Communities in Transition: An Examination of Planned Resettlement in Newfoundland.* St. John's, Nfld.: Institute of Social and Economic Research, Memorial University of Newfoundland, 1967.

Jacobs, Jane. *The Death and Life of Great American Cities.* New York: Random House, 1961.

Key, William H. *When People Are Forced to Move.* Topeka, Kansas: Menninger Foundation, 1967. Mimeographed.

Kramer, Ralph M. *Participation of the Poor: Comparative Community Case Studies in the War on Poverty.* Englewood Cliffs, N.J.: Prentice Hall, 1969.

Lotz, Jim. "Resettlement and Social Change in Newfoundland," *The Canadian Review of Sociology and Anthropology,* VIII (1971) pp. 48–59.

MacDougall, Bernard. "Urban Relocation of Africville Residents." Master of Social Work Thesis, Maritime School of Social Work, Halifax, N.S., 1969.

Matthiasson, John. "Forced Relocation: An Evaluative Case Study." A paper presented at the annual meeting of the Canadian Sociology and Anthropology Association, Winnipeg, 1970.

Merton, Robert K. *Social Theory and Social Structure.* Glencoe, Ill.: The Free Press, 1949.

Pivin, Francis Fox, and Richard A. Cloward. *Regulating the Poor: The Functions of Public Welfare.* New York: Random Vintage Books, 1972.

Spiegel, Hans B. "Human Considerations in Urban Renewal," *Urban Renewal.* Toronto: Centre for Urban and Community Studies, University of Toronto, 1968. Reprinted from *University of Toronto Law Journal,* XVIII, 3 (1968).

Stephenson, Gordon. *A Redevelopment Study of Halifax, Nova Scotia.* Halifax, N.S.: City of Halifax, 1957.

Thurz, Daniel. *Where Are They Now?* Washington, D.C.: Health and Welfare Council of the National Capitol Area, 1966.

Wallace, David A. "The Conceptualizing of Urban Renewal," *Urban Renewal.* Toronto: Centre for Urban and Community Studies, University of Toronto, 1968. Reprinted from *University of Toronto Law Journal,* XVIII, 3, (1968).

City of Halifax (Chronological)

Halifax, City of. *Minutes of the Halifax City Council, 1852–1970,* passim.

_____. *Report of the Halifax School Commissioners,* 1883.

_____. *The Master Plan for the City of Halifax as Prepared by the Civic Planning Commission,* Ira P. MacNab, Chairman. Halifax, N.S., November 16, 1945.

_____. *Report by the City Manager to the Mayor and City Council,* August 19, 1954.

_____. *Report of the Housing Policy Review Committee,* Alderman Abbie Lane, Chairman. Halifax, N.S., August 8, 1961.

_____. Memorandum from D.A. Baker, Assistant Planner, to K.M. Munnich, Director of Planning, City of Halifax, January 2, 1962. Industrial Mile File, Development Department.

_____. Memorandum from the City Manager to the Mayor and Members of the Town Planning Board, February 20, 1962. Industrial Mile File, Development Department.

_____. Planning Office. Map P500/46, Industrial Mile-Africville Area: Land Ownership and Buildings, July 26, 1962.

_____. Letter from Dr. Allan R. Morton to the Mayor of Halifax and Members of the City's Health Committee, August 9, 1962. Africville File, Social Planning Office.

_____. Report by Dr. A.R. Morton, Commissioner of Health and Welfare, August 28, 1962, Mimeographed.

_____. Report by G.F. West, Commissioner of Works, September 6, 1962, Mimeographed.

_____. Report by J.F. Thompson, City Assessor, September 7, 1962, Mimeographed.

_____. *Minutes of City Council's Africville Sub-committee*, 1966–1967, passim.

_____. *City of Halifax: Prison Land Development Proposals, Report No. 1, Survey and Analysis, Volume 2, Social Factors,* June 23, 1969.

_____. *City of Halifax: Prison Land Development Proposals, Report No. 2, Area Conceptual Plan,* October 14, 1969.

Other Government Sources

Halifax, County of. Registry of Deeds, Books 10 to 1654, passim.

Nova Scotia Legislative Assembly. *Journal and Proceedings of the House of Assembly,* 1849–1855, passim.

Nova Scotia. Public Archives of Nova Scotia, Vols. 77 and 451.

_____. Public Archives of Nova Scotia, Assembly Petitions (Education, 1860) File on Africville.

_____. Public Archives of Nova Scotia, Census, City of Halifax, 1851.

_____. Public Archives of Nova Scotia. Census of 1871.

CHAPTER 15

Criminalizing the Colonized: Ontario Native Women Confront the Criminal Justice System, 1920–60

Joan Sangster

• • • • • • • • • • • • • • • • • • • •

Over the past decade, Aboriginal women's conflicts with the law and their plight within the penal and child welfare systems have received increasing media and government attention. Framed by the political demands of Native communities for self-government, and fuelled by disillusionment with a criminal justice system that has resolutely failed Native peoples—both as victims of violence and as defendants in the courts—government studies and royal commissions have documented the shocking overincarceration of Native women.[1] At once marginalized, yet simultaneously the focus of intense government interest, Native women have struggled to make their own voices heard in these inquiries. Their testimony often speaks to their profound alienation from Canadian society and its justice system, an estrangement so intense that it is couched in despair. "How can we be healed by those who symbolize the worst experiences of our past?" asked one inmate before the 1990 Task Force on federally sentenced women.[2] Her query invokes current Native exhortations for a reinvention of Aboriginal traditions of justice and healing; it also speaks directly to the injuries of colonialism experienced by Aboriginal peoples.

Although we lack statistics on Native imprisonment before the 1970s, overincarceration may well be a "tragedy of recent vintage."[3] This article explores the roots of this tragedy, asking when and why overincarceration emerged in twentieth-century Ontario; how legal and penal authorities interpreted Aboriginal women's conflicts with the law; and in what ways Native women and their communities reacted to women's incarceration. Drawing primarily on case files from the Mercer Reformatory for Women, the only such provincial institution at the time,[4] I investigate the process of legal and moral regulation that led to Native women's incarceration from 1920 to 1960. Admittedly, such sources are skewed towards the views of those in authority: inmate case files are incomplete and partisan, strongly shaped by the recorder's reactions to the woman's narrative. Arrest and incarceration statistics are also problematic: they homogenize all Native and Métis nations under the designation "Indian,"[5] and they predominantly reflect the policing of Aboriginal peoples and the changing definitions of crime. However partial, these sources reveal patterns of, and explanations for, increas[ed] incarceration; women's own voices, however fragmented, are also apparent in these records, offering some clues to [the] women's reactions [...][6]

Native women's criminalization bore important similarities to that of other women, who were also arrested primarily for crimes of public order and morality, who often came from impoverished and insecure backgrounds, and whose sexual morality was a key concern for the courts. The convictions of Aboriginal women are thus part of a broader web of gendered moral regulation articulated through the law—the disciplining of women whose behaviour was considered unfeminine, unacceptable, abnormal, or threatening to society. This "censuring" process of distinguishing the immoral from the moral woman was also sustained by the medical and social work discourses used within the penal system; these attitudes constituted and reproduced relations of power based on gender, race, and economic marginality.[7] Granted, the law was one of many forms of regulation—accomplished also through the church, the school, and the family—but it remained an important one. As the "cutting edge of colonialism,"[8] the law could enact the "final lesson" and perhaps the most alienating one for Aboriginal women: incarceration.

The experiences of Native women were also profoundly different from those of other women: they were shaped by racist state policies of "overregulation" linked to the federal Indian Act, by the racialized constructions of Native women by court and prison personnel, and by the cultural chasm separating Native from non-Native in this time period. In short, the legal regulation of these women was an integral component of the material, social, and cultural dimensions of colonialism.[9]

*****

As the only provincial reformatory for women, the Mercer, located in Toronto, took in women from across the province who received sentences varying from three months to two years.[10] Although extreme caution should be exercised in using the Mercer numbers, they do suggest patterns of emerging overincarceration.[11] The most striking fact of Native women's imprisonment [...] was its increase over time. In the 1920s, few Native women were listed on virtually every page. Of overall "intakes" (women admitted, repeaters or not) in the 1920s,

only thirty-nine were Native women, or about 2 per cent of the prison population. Every decade thereafter, the number of Native women taken in not only doubled but increased as a proportion of admissions—from 4 per cent in the 1930s to 7 per cent in the 1940s to just over 10 per cent in the 1950s. Yet over these years, the native population remained constant at about 1 per cent of the general population.[12] [...]

*****

[...] By the 1950s, [...] Native women were overrepresented in liquor charges. Overall, alcohol offences represented about 50 per cent of the admissions, but for Native women they were as high as 70 per cent.[13]

For Native women, crimes of public poverty and moral transgression always dominated over crimes against private property or the person. Vagrancy, an elastic offence that included everything from prostitution to drunkenness to wandering the streets, dominated as the most significant charge for Native women in the 1920s (50%) and 1930s (31%). In both these decades, prostitution and bawdy house charges came second, and, by the 1930s, breach of the Liquor Control Act (BLCA), especially the clause prohibiting drunkenness in a public place, was assuming equal importance. In the next two decades, alcohol-related charges came to dominate as the reason for incarceration (32% in the 1940s, and 72% in the 1950s), with vagrancy and prostitution convictions ranking second. Theft, receiving stolen goods, and break and enters comprised only 6 per cent of the convictions in the 1940s and 1950s, while violence against the person represented only 2 per cent of the charges in these years. That issues of sexual morality and public propriety were central to native incarceration can be seen in the increasing use of the Female Refuges Act (FRA), which sanctioned the incarceration of women aged sixteen to thirty-five, sentenced, or even "liable to be sentenced," under any Criminal Code or bylaw infractions for "idle and dissolute" behaviour. While this draconian law was used most in Ontario the 1930s and 1940s, for Native women it was increasingly applied in the 1940s and 1950s.[14]

*****

[...] Even if the official charge was not alcohol related, the crime was often attributed to alcohol consumption. [...] Women often lost custody of their children when both alcohol problems and poverty indicated neglect to the authorities; sometimes the children were deserted, sometimes they were left in the hands of relatives who, poor themselves, could not cope easily. One poverty-stricken woman left her children aged three to nine in a tent, and they were later found looking for food in garbage cans. Incarcerated for intoxication, she immediately lost her children to the Children's Aid Society (CAS).

*****

[...] By the 1950s, at least 50 per cent of all the Native women admitted had already been in the Mercer before. A few women, often homeless and sometimes with alcohol problems, were being admitted twenty or thirty times.[15] One recidivist case was typical: in the late 1930s, Susan, a seventeen year old, was brought up before a small-town magistrate on a charge of "corrupting children." An orphaned foster child now working as a domestic, she was arrested for engaging in sex with a local man at his family home in front of children. The initial report also claimed she had no occupation, "has been mixed up in other immorality and was correspondent in a divorce case."[16] After serving her term, and giving birth to a child in prison, Susan stayed in Toronto, but she had few skills and little education. Two years later, she was incarcerated under the Venereal Disease Act, perhaps a sign that she has turned to prostitution to support herself. Struggling with alcohol problems, she went back and forth between her home town and Toronto, trying with little success to collect enough relief to survive. When relief officials tried to force her into the local refuge, she went to live in her brothers' abandoned hen house. Eventually she was sent back to Mercer for two

years, convicted under the FRA as an "idle and dissolute" woman. She remained in Toronto, and, over the next fifteen years, was jailed repeatedly under BLCA charges: by 1959 she had thirty-six admissions. Often convicted on the standard thirty days or a $25 fine penalty, she—like many Native women—could not afford the fine, so spent time in the Mercer.

*****

[...] Family dissolution, domestic violence, intense poverty, low levels of education, the likelihood of foster care, or CAS intervention in the family were [...] evident in many women's backgrounds. [...] Women struggled, sometimes against great odds, to sustain family ties even when illness, transience, or removal of children made it difficult. "She never knew her parents but she has five younger siblings [spread over residential schools and CAS care] ... whom she writes to try and keep the family together," noted the reformatory psychiatrist in one instance.[17]

Women's geographical origins and the location of their convictions are significant, indicating one of the major causes of overincarceration: the spiraling effects of economic deprivations and social dislocation. In the interwar period, the majority of women were convicted in southern Ontario, especially Toronto and Hamilton, or in Sarnia, Sault Ste Marie, or Sudbury—cities close to many reserves.[18] Following the Second World War, more Native women originally came from more remote areas further north. By the 1950s, even though the majority of convictions were in southern Ontario, the place of origin, in over a third of these cases, was Manitoulin, North Bay, Thunder Bay, or other northern places.[19] This moving "frontier of incarceration" suggests the importance of urbanization and/or deteriorating economic and social circumstances as the stimulus for women's conflicts with the law.[20]

[...] Natives living on many reserves were finding themselves in difficult economic [straits]. No efforts were made to encourage new economic development, a reform desperately needed because many reserves had a fixed resource base and a growing population. The Depression accentuated subsistence problems, reducing some Aboriginal communities to relief far below the already pitiful levels in the cities.[21] Similar dilemmas [...] plagued more isolated reserves after the war, when corporate resource development, the decline of fur prices, and new transportation routes began to have a dramatic impact on northern communities. As the effect of colonization permeated further north, the consequences were increased social dislocation and conflict, and more intervention by Euro-Canadian police forces, especially when Aboriginal peoples were off their reserves.[22] Indeed, women who fled to cities in search of jobs and social services found little material aid, but faced the complicating, intensifying pressure of racism.[23] One of the most dramatic examples of the colonial "penetration" of the North was that of Grassy Narrows. When this isolated community was relocated closer to Kenora, the community's sense of spatial organization, family structure, and productive relations were all undermined. Proximity to the city brought increased access to alcohol and the malignancy of racism; "the final nail in the coffin" was mercury poisoning of their water and their fish supply.[24]

[...] Official federal policies of acculturation, though increasingly viewed as unsuccessful, persisted in projects such as residential schools, which were experienced by as many as one-third of Native youth in the early decades of the twentieth century. [...] The isolation of children from their communities, the denigration of their culture and language, and the emotional and physical abuse left many women scarred for life.[25] [...] Aboriginal leaders now argue that violence, alcoholism, and alienation were actually the direct results of such schooling.[26]

[...] Despite evidence that prison was no solution to "alcoholism"[27] and may have worsened the problem, penal punishment continued to be the response of the authorities. [...]

*****

[...] By the late 1960s, critics of existing theories of alcoholism among Native peoples argued that there was no direct evidence that "Indians were more susceptible" to alcoholism and that the precise forms that "out-of-control" behaviour took had more to do with culture than biology,[28] [...] some even seeing it as a muted form of "protest."[29] [...]

[...] Magistrates failed to see it as an outcome of systemic social problems. [...] Court pronouncements [...] divulged a fatalistic equation of Natives and alcohol: "She is an Indian girl and probably will never stay away from the drink," quoted one magistrate in 1945. A decade later the same complaint was advanced: "They spend up to 8 months in jail and are the biggest problem I have ... I do not know any remedy for this type of person."[30]

*****

[...] By the late nineteenth century, political and media controversies had created an image of Native women in the public mind: supposedly "bought and sold" by their own people as "commodities, they were easily "demoralized" sexually, and a threat to both public "morality and health."[31] [...]

Incarceration was also justified for paternalistic motives: magistrates claimed that, by incarcerating Native women, they were protecting them from becoming an "easy target for the avaricious" or the "victim of unprincipled Indian and white men." [...] This [...] was evident in the trial of a young Aboriginal woman from southern Ontario who was sent to the Mercer for two years on FRA charges of being "idle and dissolute." The arresting RCMP officer insisted she was "transient, with no work and has been convicted on many alcohol charges over the past few years." She had been caught "brawling with white men," he continued, "and has been found wandering, her mind blank after drinking." Moreover, it was believed that she was a "bad influence on a fifteen year old who has also been led astray." The magistrate lectured the woman: "My girl, I hope that by removing you from unscrupulous white men and Indian soldiers and alcohol that you will start a new life. It is too bad that such a good-looking Indian like you should throw your life away. Other men buy the liquor for you, then you suffer, and they escape."

*****

The complaint that women who drank heavily would easily corrupt others was also common. In some cases, it was Native families who feared this prospect: "She should serve her whole term; she is better in there," wrote one father, fearing his daughter, if released, would be influenced by her mother, who also drank. [...] Women whose children had been removed [...] [became] a candidate for incarceration. "She has had four children with the CAS," noted one magistrate, "she has chosen the wrong path, now her children are a public charge." Such women were also portrayed as poor material for rehabilitation. As one magistrate noted of a deaf woman charged under the Indian Act: "There is no doubt that children will continue to the end of her reproductive age, or until a pathological process renders her sterile. She is also likely to drink steadily. The prospect of improvement is remote. Institutionalization, if available, is suitable."[32]

[...] Declarations of "protection," [...] were clearly inscribed with both gender and race paternalism, for they presumed an image of proper feminine behaviour, stressing sexual purity and passivity within the private nuclear family, and the need for Native women to absorb these "higher" Euro-Canadian standards. Similarly, teachers in the residential schools often claimed that Native girls were easily sexually exploited, prone to returning "to the blanket."[33] Aboriginal women were thus both infantilized as vulnerable and weak, and also feared as more overtly and actually sexual.

[...] Even after incarceration, these attitudes were significant because they shaped possibilities of parole, alcohol treatment, and rehabilitation; convinced that Native women would be recidivists, little was done to discern their needs. Not surprisingly, many

women became even more alienated within the reformatory.

[...] First Nations women were separated from prison personnel by [race], class, and cultural differences. Inmates encountered revulsion, antipathy, resignation, and sometimes sympathy from the experts whose "scientific" language of clinical analysis and case work often masked subjective, moral judgments. [...] The very word *reserve* had a different meaning from words like *poor* or *bad neighbourhood* used between the 1930s and 1950s to describe the backgrounds of white women: reserves were associated with degeneracy, backwardness, and filth. One "progressive" social worker, writing about Indian juveniles in the 1940s, decried racial prejudice and the poverty on reserves, but at the same time reiterated many racist images, describing Indians as "savage, childish, primitive and ignorant."[34]

[...] The image of the reserve as a place of hopelessness was especially evident in probation reports. Native families sometimes offered probationers accommodations, even when houses were crowded, yet officials equated such offers with a lack of awareness about the need for basic moral and social standards. They were especially critical of congested conditions, likely seeing proximity of the sexes as encouraging immorality. They were also suspicious of those living a transient life, "in the Indian mode,"[35] who might easily succumb to alcohol use, unemployment, and poverty. "Home conditions primitive ... the home is a disreputable filthy shack on the reserve," were typical observations. Aboriginal people who did not fit this stereotype were then portrayed as unusual: "Above average Indian home which is adequately furnished, clean and tidy," noted one probation report, while another officer claimed a father was "one of few Indians in the area who does not drink."[36]

*****

Probation reports also revealed a Catch-22 that Native women faced in terms of rehabilitation. Social workers debated whether reserve or city life would be more corrupting for released women, but they often recommended removing women from their original home or reserve. However well intentioned the effort to isolate her from past problems, this strategy left women in foreign surroundings, alienated by language and cultural differences, often directly faced with racism. This situation was well captured in a parole report that claimed one woman was now "an outlaw on the Reserve" because of her promiscuity, and her parents there were heavy drinkers who lived in a "small, filthy home." It was unwise to return her there, the officer noted, but added: "We realize the extreme difficulty in placing an Indian girl in some other centre, where society is loath in accepting her." [...]

[...] [Indian] agents were endowed with the powers of justices of the peace under the Indian Act, thus creating an extra layer of oppressive legal regulation for Native women. The level of surveillance of the economic, social, and moral lives of Native families by the agent was astounding. When called on to assess parole, his report might comment on the family's church attendance, the marital status, education, employment, and social lives of siblings and parents, his judgment of their moral standards, and intimate details of the woman's life. The agent could initiate the proceedings sending a woman to the Mercer, or assist police efforts to incarcerate her. [...] Moreover, the evidence presented by the agent could be little more than heresay. "There are complaints that she is hanging around the hotel, going into rooms with men ... we hear that she is in the family way," testified the police chief in one case. The Indian agent supported him, claiming he had spoken with her doctor and discovered she was pregnant.[37]

*****

[...] Psychiatrists who examined women's suitability for "clinic" (alcohol) treatment were seldom [...] supportive. Repeatedly, a woman's silence, a means of coping with alien surroundings (and, in some cases, related to language differences) was read negatively as evidence of a passive personality. [...]

There is no evidence that these experts read any of the contemporary anthropological literature, especially on the Ojibwa women who dominated at the Mercer. Irving Hallowell, for instance, argued in the 1940s that culture shaped personality structure and that the Ojibwa were highly reserved emotionally, avoiding direct confrontation or anger with others; this restraint, he argued, was a product of their hunting and gathering way of life, their spiritual beliefs, and social organization.[38] [...]

Medical and social work experts at the Mercer had a different measuring stick. What was crucial in their world view, especially by the 1950s, was an embrace of the "confessional" mode, introspection, a critical understanding of one's family background as the "cause" of addiction, and a professed desire to change one's inner self. Native women in the Mercer almost invariably refused to embrace this therapeutic model. [...]

[...] Displaying a level of realism, honesty, acceptance, and stoicism that the authorities interpreted as passive fatalism, Native women often openly admitted to the charge against them, making no excuses. "She freely admits neglect of [her children] and does not make any further comment," a psychiatrist mused; he was even more baffled by a woman's "extraordinary honesty about her unwillingness to work."[39] Several contemporary legal workers noted that honesty about the "crime" and guilty pleas, rather than any demand for the system to *prove* one guilty, distinguished the Ojibwa value system.

*****

[...] In contrast to the authorities, many Native families rejected the idea that behaviour caused by alcohol was a crime, a perception that remains strong in many Aboriginal communities today.[40] "I do not believe that my wife should be punished for drinking," wrote one distressed husband; "some soldiers bought the whiskey to our reserve and I thought they were our friends." A father and daughter from southern Ontario appeared one day at the Mercer office, asking for the release of the mother. They appealed to the authorities by saying she could get employment in the tobacco fields, and added that there was no reason to keep someone just because of occasional disturbances while drunk: "She is fine unless under the influence of alcohol," they implored, to no effect. [...]

Most Native families [...] also had difficulty understanding why incarceration was the punishment. In more isolated Ojibwa communities, the chief and council, or sometimes elders, had imposed different sanctions for wrongdoing than those imposed by the Euro-Canadian justice system. Social control was effected through elders' lectures about good behaviour, connected to spiritual instruction, or through fear of gossip or of the "bad medicine" of supernatural retribution. If a person broke communal codes, shaming and confession were crucial to rehabilitation; indeed, when the confession was public, the "transgression" was washed away.[41] Only in extreme cases was banishment of the individual considered the answer.[42] Similarly, in Iroquois societies, ostracism, ridicule, or prohibitions on becoming a future leader were all used to control behaviour, admittedly an easier prospect in smaller, tightly knit communities in which the clan system also discouraged conflicts.[43]

*****

On some occasions, local attempts by the families or communities to alter women's behaviour were combined with the strategies of the Euro-Canadian justice system. Maria's case is a good example. Charged repeatedly with intoxication and with neglect of her children, Maria lost them to various institutions: three children were sent to a residential school, one was in CAS care, and one was in the sanatorium. The Indian agent complained to the crown attorney that she resumed drinking as soon as she was released. The chief on the reserve wanted to help her and tried to work out a plan for her rehabilitation, promising the return of her children and a house on the reserve if she could refrain from drinking for two months. Her

failure to meet his conditions may speak not only to her addiction but to the desolation she still felt about losing her children.[44]

*****

Families sometimes felt a sense of shame at a woman's conflicts with the law—this was all the more difficult on reserves where each family's history was well known—and thus encouraged her removal. One Ojibwa woman on a reserve told the CAS that "she did not want anything to do with her sister, as she [engages in prostitution] and sends men to her sister who does not want this kind of life." "She has been refused care by the people of her own community, so we had to take the children," a social worker's report concluded. Some relatives indicated to probation officers that they would not take the women back into the family after incarceration. One trapper from the North wrote a letter to the Mercer, relaying similar sentiments: he "did not want his [wife] to return," as he could not deal with her drinking and would rather "support his children on his own."[45]

Reserve communities sometimes discussed these problems together, with or without the Indian agent, then asked for legal intervention. More than one community signed letters or petitions about moral problems they perceived in their midst. One petition included signatures from the woman's grandparents, cousins, aunts, and uncles who said "in the interests of morality on the Reserve and of the accused, she should be sent to the Mercer Reformatory." The fact that an uncle stood with her in court "as a Friend," as well as the wording of the petition, suggests that the Indian agent had a role in the petition, and that her relatives had been persuaded that this "banishment" would help her and restore peace on the Reserve.[46]

In cases like this one, customary community controls and Euro-Canadian law are intertwined,[47] though the latter clearly assumed more power. Why, then, was Euro-Canadian legal regulation accepted, perhaps increasingly so, during this time period?[48] First, not all these women were reserve and/or treaty Indians.

Many had become urban dwellers; some were of mixed-race descent. Moreover, not all women came from reserves where traditional forms of justice were fully preserved; the continuance of customary controls depended on the power of the Indian agent and local police, the geographical isolation and economic and social equilibrium of the reserve, and the political will of its occupants to vigorously defend their right to rule themselves.[49] [...] As communities were increasingly influenced by the Euro-Canadian justice system and by attempts to acculturate them, they may have acquiesced to some of the premises of this governing system.[50] However disassociating the influence of the Euro-Canadian criminal justice system was, it came to exert some ideological sway over communities, a process of hegemony that was unavoidable given the colonial imbalance of power and the ongoing assault on Native societies by those claiming cultural superiority.

*****

In many cases of internal condemnation and control, crimes of sexual immorality occasioned the most concerted opposition from the community. Historians and anthropologists agree that, at first contact, there was more sexual autonomy for Native women, more egalitarian practices of marriage and divorce, and more acceptance of illegitimate children within many aboriginal cultures.[51] But these traditions were challenged by European values, and, by the early twentieth century, observers in both Iroquois and Ojibwa communities stressed the great importance placed on lifelong marriage, as well as disapproval of some kinds of sexual behaviour.[52] Ethnographic texts written from the 1930s to the 1950s pointed to the "mixture of conflicting beliefs,"[53] both European and Native, in Aboriginal cultures, especially in relation to marital and sexual norms [...]. One highly controversial text claimed that northern Ojibwa women were increasingly subject to violence as their social importance and sexual autonomy were undermined within the community.[54]

Anthropological reports and oral traditions in the mid twentieth century also indicate that chiefs acted as custodians of morality, discouraging women from leaving their husbands for new partners, and deterring the practice of serial monogamy if they felt it undermined the stability of the community. "Yes, the Indian Agent on the reserve did try to make people stick to their marriages, [but] so did the chief and council," remembers one Northern Ojibwa woman.[55] Although her observation referred to the sexual regulation of men and women, other evidence suggests that sexual/social control was likely to focus more stringently on women: the political and social effects of colonialism on gender relations had provided male leaders with access to such power and furnished ideological encouragement for the patriarchal control of women's sexuality.

*****

[...] The majority of First Nations women sent to the Mercer were criminalized on the premise of moral and public order infractions linked to alcohol, or for prostitution, venereal disease, or child neglect charges, [...] framed by economic marginality, family dissolution, violence, and sometimes previous institutionalization. [...] Three crucial, interconnected factors shaped the emerging process of overincarceration: the material and social dislocation precipitated by colonialism, the gender and race paternalism of court and penal personnel, and the related cultural gap between Native and Euro-Canadian value systems, articulating very different notions of crime and punishment.

*****

The experiences of these women, [...] which the moral regulation of First Nations women through incarceration was, first and foremost, a "legitimated practice of moral-political control, linked to conflicts and power relations, based on class, gender and race."[56]

While women's actual voices, feelings, and responses are difficult to locate within this regulatory process, the general pattern of Aboriginal alienation from Euro-Canadian justice—particularly for more isolated communities unused to Canadian policing—is a repeated theme in women's stories. However, customary Aboriginal practices could be refashioned and used by Canadian authorities, so much so that Native communities and families might also use the legal system to discipline their own. Native acceptance of Canadian law was one consequence of ongoing attempts to assimilate Aboriginal people, but it was not a simple reflection of European dominance. It also revealed attempts to cope with the negative effects of social change that were devastating [to] individuals and families: in the process of struggling to adjust to the dislocations of colonialism, communities sometimes abetted the incarceration of Native women.

Native women seldom found solace or aid in the reformatory and, tragically, many returned to prison repeatedly. First Nations women often responded to their estrangement from the law and the reformatory with silence and stoicism—perhaps in itself a subtle form of noncompliance—though a very few, along with their families, voiced unequivocal renunciations of this system, their voices a preview to the current sustained critique of the inadequacy of Euro-Canadian "justice" for Aboriginal peoples.

Notes

1. Native women are disproportionately represented in federal prisons—an area *not* dealt with in this article. There are also considerable regional variations in overincarceration. In Ontario, 1980s statistics showed Native people to be about 2 per cent of the population, while Native women comprised 16 per cent of provincial admission to correctional institutions; in the North, local arrest rates were far higher. See Ontario, Ontario Advisory Council on Women's Issues, *Native Women and the Law* (Toronto 1989); Carol Laprairie, "Selected Criminal Justice and Socio-Economic Data on Native Women," *Canadian Journal of Criminology* 26, 4 (1984): 161–9; Canada, Royal Commission on Aboriginal Peoples, *Aboriginal Peoples and the Justice System: Report of the National Round Table on Aboriginal Justice* (Ottawa 1993); Canada, Law Reform Commission, *Report on Aboriginal Peoples and Criminal Justice* (Ottawa 1991); Manitoba, *Report of the Aboriginal Justice Inquiry of Manitoba* (Winnipeg 1991).

2. Anonymous, quoted in Canada, Correctional Services, *Creating Choices: The Report of the Task Force on Federally Sentenced Women* (April 1990), 9.

3. Bradford Morse, "Aboriginal Peoples, the Law and Justice." In R. Silverman and M. Nielsen, eds., *Aboriginal Peoples and Canadian Criminal Justice* (Toronto: Butterworths 1992), 56. In Manitoba it is surmised that Native inmates began to predominate after the Second World War. Manitoba, *Report of the Aboriginal Justice Inquiry*, I: 87; and John Milloy, "A Partnership of Races: Indian, White, Cross-Cultural Relations in Criminal Justice in Manitoba, 1670–1949," paper for the Public Inquiry into the Administration of Justice for Native Peoples of Manitoba.

4. The Mercer Reformatory for Women was used because it drew inmates from across the province for a variety of common "female" crimes. Few women at this time were sent to the federal penitentiary. City and county jail registers sometimes noted race, but a statistical study of all Ontario's city and county registers has yet to be undertaken.

5. Under "complexion," the Mercer register noted if an inmate was "Indian" or "negress." The designation Indian included Indian and Métis, treaty and non-treaty women. Statistics taken from the Mercer register are also problematic because women might be charged with one crime, but incarcerated for other reasons as well. Women sometimes gave different names and altered their ages. Because of the various problems with statistics, the registers are used primarily to suggest some overall trends.

6. The problems and possibilities of using such case files are explored in Linda Gordon, *Heroes of Their Own Lives: The Politics and History of Family Violence* (Boston: Viking 1988), 13–17; Steven Noll, "Patient Records as Historical Stories: The Case of the Caswell Training School," *Bulletin of the History of Medicine* 69 (1994): 411–28; Regina Kunzel, *Fallen Women, Problem Girls: Unmarried Mothers and the Professionalization of Social Work, 1890–1945* (New Haven: Yale University Press 1993), 5–6.

7. Colin Sumner, "Re-thinking Deviance: Towards a Sociology of Censure," in Lorraine Gelsthorpe and Allison Morris, eds., *Feminist Perspectives in Criminology* (Philadelphia: Milton Keynes 1990) and "Foucault, Gender and the Censure of Deviance," in Sumner's edited collection, *Censure, Politics and Criminal Justice* (Philadelphia: Milton Keynes 1990).

8. Martin Chanock, *Law, Custom and Social Order: The Colonial Experience in Malawi and Zambia* (Cambridge: Cambridge University Press 1985), 4.

9. Many studies of colonialism have focused on the eighteenth and nineteenth centuries, especially on kin and productive relations; fewer carry the story into the twentieth century. Karen Anderson, *Chain Her by One Foot: The Subjugation of Women in Seventeenth-Century New France* (New York: Routledge 1991); Sylvia Van Kirk, *Many Tender Ties: Women in Fur Trade Society* (Winnipeg: Watson and Dwyer 1979); Jennifer Brown, *Strangers in Blood: Fur Trade Company Families in Indian Country* (Vancouver: University of British Columbia Press 1980); Carol Devens, *Countering Colonization: Native American Women and Great Lakes Missions, 1630–1900* (Berkeley: University of California Press 1992); Eleanor Leacock, "Montagnais Women and the Jesuit Program for Colonization," in her edited collection, *Myths of Male Dominance* (New York: Monthly Review Press 1981), 43–62; Carol Cooper, "Native Women of the Northern Pacific Coast: An Historical Perspective, 1830–1900," *Journal of Canadian Studies* 27, 4 (1992–3): 44–75; Joanne Fiske, "Colonization and the Decline of Women's Status: The Tsimshian Case," *Feminist Studies* 17, 3 (1991): 509–36. On Iroquois women, see Judith Brown, "Economic Organization and the Position of Women among the Iroquois," *Ethnohistory* 17 (1970): 151–67; Sally Roesch Wagner, "The Iroquois Confederacy: A Native American Model for Non-sexist Men," in William Spittal, ed., *Iroquois Women: An Anthology* (Ohsweken: Irocrafts 1990), 217–22; Elizabeth Tooker, "Women in Iroquois Society," in Spittal, ed., *Iroquois Women*, 199–216. On Ojibwa women, see Patricia Buffalohead, "Farmers, Warriors, Traders: A Fresh Look at Ojibwa Women," *Minnesota History* 48 (1983): 236–44. For interrogation of the dominant emphasis on the decline of women's status, see Joanne Fiske, "Fishing Is Women's Business: Changing Economic Roles of Carrier Women and Men," in Bruce Cox, ed., *Native Peoples, Native Lands: Canadian Inuit, Indians and Métis* (Ottawa:

Carleton University Press 1987), 186–98; Nancy Shoemaker, "The Rise or Fall of Iroquois Women," *Journal of Women's History* 2 (1991): 39–57.

10. Some women came in with sentences of less than three months.

11. I examined 598 files for basic information on the charge, conviction, age, and place of birth, but many files were incomplete beyond this point, so I concentrated on a core of 300 files as the basis of my analysis.

12. The numbers for the decades are as follows: 39 in the 1920s, 80 in the 1930s, 109 in the 1940s, and 370 in the 1950s. Population statistics taken from Census of Canada, 1931, vol. 2, table 31, show Ontario Indians as 0.9 per cent of the total population; Census of Canada, 1941, vol. I, table II, lists Indians as 0.8 per cent of the total; Census of Canada, 1951, vol. 2, table 32, also shows 0.8 per cent.

13. Ontario, *Annual Report of the Inspector of Prisons and Public Charities*, 1920–60.

14. Although FRA convictions for Native women remained a small proportion (about 5%) of overall incarcerations from 1920 to 1960, the act was used more in the later period. On the FRA, see Joan Sangster, "Incarcerating 'Bad' Girls: Sexual Regulation through the Ontario Female Refuges Act," *Journal of the History of Sexuality* 7, 2 (1996): 239–75.

15. Changes to the Indian Act in 1951 allowed provinces to legalize the sale and possession of intoxicants (previously illegal) to Indians off the reserve. Sharon Venne, ed., *Indian Acts and Amendments, 1865–75* (Saskatoon: University of Saskatchewan Native Law Centre 1981), 344–5. However, this change made little difference to Native women in the Mercer, who were usually charged, throughout this whole period, under the provincial liquor laws. Local law enforcement may have used the Indian Act more. See note 13.

16. OA Mercer case file 12128, 1940s (the first charge was in the late 1930s). For the initial charge, the man was convicted of selling liquor and received a jail sentence.

17. OA Mercer case file 15510, 1950s; case file 16665, 1950s.

18. I recognize that these women came from different First Nations, but the records do not reveal their specific Aboriginal identity. Authorities claimed that women from Ojibwa groups dominated, though there were clearly some Iroquois and Cree women as well.

19. In other cases, the conviction takes place in a northern city—for example, Kenora or Thunder

Bay—but the place of origin is a more isolated reserve or town.

20. Some scholars argue that "economic marginalization" was most noticeable in the twentieth century, especially after 1945. See Vic Satzewich and Terry Wotherspoon, *First Nations: Race, Class and Gender Relations* (Toronto: Nelson 1993), 49–50. On the (contrasting) case of the late nineteenth century, see R.C. Macleod and Heather Rollason, "'Restrain the Lawless Savage': Native Defendants in the Criminal Court of the North West Territories," *Journal of Historical Sociology* 10, 2 (1997), 157–83.

21. Robin Brownlie, "A Fatherly Eye: Two Indian Agents in Georgian Bay, 1918–39" (PhD dissertation, University of Toronto 1996), 52, 418.

22. R.W. Dunning, *Social and Economic Change among the Northern Ojibwa* (Toronto: University of Toronto Press 1959), chap. 7.

23. David Stymeist, *Ethnics and Indians: Social Relations in a Northwestern Ontario Town* (Toronto: Peter Martin 1971).

24. A. Shkilnyk, *A Poison Stronger Than Love: The Destruction of an Ojibwa Community* (New Haven: Yale University Press 1985).

25. "It seems unlikely that before 1950 more than one-third of Inuit and status Indian children were in residential school." J.R. Miller, *Shingwauk's Vision: A History of Native Residential Schools* (Toronto: University of Toronto Press 1996), 411. On gender, see *Shingwauk's Vision*, chap. 8, and Joanne Fiske, "Gender and the Paradox of Residential Education in Carrier Society," in Jane Gaskell and Arlene Tigar McLaren, eds., *Women and Education* (Calgary: Deslig 1991), 131–46.

26. Assembly of First Nations, *Breaking the Silence: An Interpretive Study of Residential School Impact and Healing as Illustrated by the Stories of First Nations Individuals* (Ottawa 1994).

27. The term *alcoholism* was used at the time in connection with these women, but we don't really know if they were alcoholics, or simply being policed for alcohol use.

28. Craig MacAndrew and Robert Edgerton, *Drunken Comportment: A Social Explanation* (Chicago: Aldine 1969).

29. Nancy Oestreich Lurie, "The World's Oldest Ongoing Protest Demonstration: North American Indian Drinking Patterns," *Pacific Historical Review* 40 (1971): 311–33.

30. OA Mercer case file 9955, 1940s; and case file 13139, 1950s.

31. Sarah Carter, "Categories and Terrains of Exclusion: Constructing the 'Indian Woman' in the Early Settlement Era in Western Canada," in Joy Parr and Mark Rosenfeld, eds., *Gender and History in Canada* (Toronto: Copp Clark 1996), 40–1. See also Daniel Francis, *The Imaginary Indian: The Image of the Indian in Canadian Culture* (Vancouver: Arsenal Press 1992), 122. On an earlier period on the Eastern seaboard, see David Smits, "The 'Squaw Drudge': A Prime Index of Savagism," *Ethnohistory* 29, 4 (1982): 281–306.

32. OA Mercer case file 7644, 1930s; case file 11419, 1950s; case file 8646, 1940s; case file 16461, 1950s.

33. That is, Native unions unsanctified by the church. Miller, *Shingwauk's Vision*, 227.

34. Mary T. Woodward, "Juvenile Delinquency among Indian Girls" (MA thesis, University of British Columbia 1949), 2, 21. Similar images of the reserve which stressed a "culture of poverty" can also be seen in the Hawthorn report as late as the 1960s. See H. Hawthorn, *A Survey of Indians of Canada* (Ottawa 1966), I: 56–7.

35. For example, those living in a tent in the summer when the family was trapping. OA, Mercer case file 15034, 1950s.

36. OA Mercer case file 14305, 1950s; case file 14768, 1950s; case file 12984, 1950s.

37. OA Mercer case file 9332, 1940s. In this case the magistrate corrected police for offering heresay evidence, but this criticism was rare.

38. Irving Hallowell, *Culture and Experience* (Philadelphia: University of Pennsylvania Press 1955). This collection included earlier articles, published in major psychiatric, sociological, and anthropological journals in the 1940s, such as "Some Psychological Characteristics of the Northeastern Indians" (1946), "Aggression in Saulteaux Society" (1940), and "The Social Function of Anxiety in a Primitive Society" (1941).

39. OA Mercer case file 16664, 1950s.

40. Shkilnyk, *A Poison Stronger Than Love*, 25.

41. Hallowell, *Culture and Experience*, 272. Sickness could be interpreted as a form of punishment for sexual or moral transgressions; private confession could be the cure. Irving Hallowell, "Sin, Sex and Sickness in Saulteaux Belief," *British Journal of Medical Psychology* 18 (1939): 191–7. Contemporary accounts also suggest that the public confession, not incarceration, is considered the "disciplinary end" in some Aboriginal cultures. See Patricia Monture-Angus, *Thunder in My Soul: A Mohawk Woman Speaks* (Halifax: Fernwood Books 1995), 238–40; Rupert Ross, *Dancing with a Ghost: Exploring Indian Reality* (Markham: Octopus Books 1992); Kjikeptin Alex Denny,

"Beyond the Marshall Inquiry: An Alternative Mi'kmaq Worldview and Justice System," in Joy Mannett, ed., *Elusive Justice: Beyond the Marshall Inquiry* (Halifax: Fernwood 1992), 103–8.

42. Hallowell, *Culture and Experience*; Shkilnyk, *A Poison Stronger Than Love*; Edward Rogers, *The Round Lake Ojibwa* (Toronto: University of Toronto Press 1962).

43. Michael Coyle, "Traditional Indian Justice in Ontario: A Role for the Present?" *Osgoode Hall Law Journal* 24, 2 (1986): 605–33.

44. OA Mercer case file 11232, 1950s.

45. OA Mercer case file 9318, 1940s; case file 7609, 1930s.

46. It was clear they did not accept her behaviour, which was claimed to be "promiscuous," OA Mercer case file 7057, 1930s.

47. The relationship between customary law and Euro-Canadian law with regard to sexuality is discussed in Joan Sangster, "Regulation and Resistance: Native Women, Sexuality and the Law, 1920–60," paper presented to the International Development Institute, Dalhousie University, April 1997.

48. Given the paucity of historical studies, it is difficult to ascertain if this practice was increasing, decreasing, or stable. A period characterized by intense social dislocation and/or increased federal regulation might have led to increased use of the Euro-Canadian laws.

49. Some communities, even less isolated ones in the south, had a stronger history of rejecting Euro-Canadian "rule" and maintaining their own sovereignty. A case in point is that of the Six Nations Reserve.

50. This was true of some elected chiefs who came to ally themselves politically and ideologically with the Indian agent.

51. Many studies examined Iroquois and Huron nations, and fewer looked at Ojibwa nations. Studies of plains and northern peoples indicate different gender roles and possibly asymmetry. See John Milloy, *The Plains Cree: Trade, Diplomacy and War 1790–1870* (Winnipeg: University of Manitoba Press 1988); Laura Peers, *The Ojibwa of Western Canada, 1780–1870* (Winnipeg: University of Manitoba Press 1994); Joan Ryan, *Doing Things the Right Way: Dene Traditional Justice in Lac La Martre, NWT* (Calgary: University of Calgary Press 1995).

52. Hallowell, *Culture and Experience*, chap. 13, and his "Sex and Sickness in Saulteaux Belief," in Rogers, ed., *The Round Lake Ojibwa*; Sally Weaver, "The Iroquois: The Consolidation of the Grand River Reserve in the mid Nineteenth Century, 1847–1875," in Edward Rogers and Donald Smith, eds., *Aboriginal Ontario: Historical Perspectives on the First Nations* (Toronto: Dundurn 1994): R.W. Dunning, *Social and Economic Change among the Northern Ojibwa* (Toronto: University of Toronto Press 1959).

53. Rogers, ed., *The Round Lake Ojibwa*, B47.

54. Ruth Landes, *Ojibwa Women* (New York: AMS Press 1938). Landes described a culture affected by colonization, rather than earlier, "traditional" Ojibwa culture. Devens, *Countering Colonization*, 124–5.

55. Informant quoted in Shkilnyk, *A Poison Stronger Than Love*, 89.

56. Colin Sumner, "Crime, Justice and Under-development: Beyond Modernisation Theory," in Colin Sumner, ed., *Crime, Justice and Underdevelopment* (London: Heinemann 1982), 10.

CHAPTER 16

Creating "Slaves of Satan" or "New Canadians"? The Law, Education, and the Socialization of Doukhobor Children, 1911–1935

John McLaren

• •

It is not difficult to find in the historiography of Canadian education instances of the invocation of law to support policies that have had as their objective the compliance of deviant populations or ethnic or religious minorities with mainline "Canadian values." The deployment of law to produce social or cultural homogeneity is evident in the establishment of Upper Canada's public school system in the 1840s,[1] progressive denial or erosion of French-language education in Manitoba, Ontario, and New Brunswick,[2] the Indian residential school system,[3] attempts to force public education on communalist Christians, such as the Strict Mennonites and Hutterites,[4] and coercion of Jehovah's Witness children into religious and patriotic exercises.[5] It is also clear that the targets of such strategies have not been reticent about resisting them, whether it be through legal challenge, civil disobedience, non-cooperation, or in rarer instances, violence.[6] Of all of these records of conflict, none matches that of the Doukhobors with the government and the "British" population of British Columbia in terms of both durability and visceral quality.

Fundamental differences existed between many Doukhobors and the non-Doukhobor community over the value and utility of education as a formal, institutional process. To the majority of the Doukhobor community

in British Columbia, in the first twenty-five years of their settlement in the province, formal education under the control of the state was both unnecessary and dangerous. The knowledge and skills of life, as well as religious precept, were learnt within the family and village community:

> To us education means being a good Doukhobor. That is, to love all living things and to do no evil, not to shoot, not to eat meat, not to smoke, not to drink liquor. We teach these things to our children. And more, too. The mothers teach their daughters to bake and cook and to spin and embroider, and the fathers teach their sons to be handy with the axe, a carving knife, a team of horses.[7]

State-run education was threatening because of its capacity to subvert community beliefs, values, and practices, to undermine the respect of young members of the community for their elders, and ultimately to lure them away from family and village into the temptations and hazards of the world outside. As Doukhobor representatives observed in their response to William Blakemore's 1912 Royal Commission inquiry into the community, state education prepared children for war and led inexorably to the exploitation of others.[8] Not even the prospect of higher education impressed them. University graduates were described as "crack brained people" who "swallow down all the national people's power and the capital" while others are left to starve.[9]

Within the non-Doukhobor community formal education lay at the heart of attempts by both state and community to engender pride in Anglo-Canadian achievement, and to build a nation with the capacity to meet the challenges of an increasingly complex society and dynamic economy.[10] [...]

Two general comments are in order on the history of Doukhobor education between 1911 and 1935 and its legal resonances, which help to explain the tensions between the community and the state. First, periods of conflict were interspersed with periods of calm. These cycles reflected on the one hand disturbance and anxiety within the Doukhobor community over external pressures for its conformity in matters of education, and, on the other, accommodation between the group and the state, where a degree of compromise was possible, or seemed strategically advisable. Both the theory and practice of leadership among the Doukhobors ascribed great, even semi-divine, authority to the leader. However, because the leader had to rely on charisma to impress the faithful and so to maintain credibility and power, community sentiment had in certain circumstances to be respected and taken into account.[11] When the leader and community were at one, or he had been able to use his persuasive powers to good effect, concerted community action was possible. At other times, however, when the community was split or he had failed to get his way, then there was a tendency on the part of the leadership to steer clear of decisive action, and sometimes to backtrack. If incautious decisions that offended the community or part of it were made, then factionalism could easily take hold. [...]

Second, the application of the law in the matter of school attendance and truancy during this period was marked by the progressive turning of the legal ratchet by the government

to induce compliance. At times this was to involve individually or in combination the Department of Education, the Premier's Office, the Attorney General's Department, the Office of the Provincial Secretary, and the British Columbia Provincial Police. The legal strategies attempted moved quickly from the imposition of individual to that of collective responsibility, and ultimately to the more dramatic and invasive expedient of using child custody procedures to resocialize some Doukhobor children.

The conflict over education in British Columbia was originally secondary to a dispute relating to vital statistics legislation. At the encouragement of Peter Verigin the Lordly, the first Doukhobor leader in Canada, community Doukhobor families had enrolled their children in a government-built school at Grand Forks, and another had been built by the community at Brilliant.[12] Community members were far less compliant, however, in the matter of registering births and deaths. When resistance to the Births, Deaths and Marriages Registration Act[13] came to light in 1912, the deputy attorney general, J.P. McLeod, ordered the provincial police to prosecute vigorously any lawbreakers.[14] Four Doukhobor men in Grand Forks were subsequently arrested for failure to register a death. The community's reaction, encouraged by Verigin, was to withdraw their children from school.[15]

The result was a stand-off between the community and Victoria on both vital statistics and school attendance laws, which induced the Conservative government of Sir Richard McBride to appoint William Blakemore as a Royal Commission to investigate the Doukhobors and their relations with state and community. In his 1912 report the commissioner recommended that accommodation be made with the community as a means of securing their observance of both vital statistics and school attendance laws.[16] On education Blakemore advocated the establishment of a working relationship between the Department of Education and the community that would allow for the appointment of Russian-speaking teachers to work in conjunction with the Canadian teachers in Doukhobor schools, and a modification of the curriculum so that it included only the elementary subjects.[17] However, neither the Doukhobors nor the government proved responsive to the report.

The community objected to an ill-advised recommendation by the commissioner advocating that the group's military exemption be cancelled. This coloured the Doukhobors' general feelings about Blakemore's conclusions, including the recommendations on education. In reacting to the report Verigin was moved to register his first recorded objection to schooling in principle since his arrival in Canada, describing the practices of "boy scouting, military drill etc." as "the most pernicious and malicious of this age."[18] In British Columbia, through the initiative of the Lord Srathcona Trust, money had been set aside for military drilling and exercises within the school system.[19] The connection between what Blakemore had advocated on the military exemption and the schools' commitment to military training was all too clear to the suspicious Doukhobors. Verigin's objection to schooling under these conditions had the effect of solidifying the community's resistance to both the school attendance and vital statistics laws.

For its part Victoria proved to be more interested in listening to non-Doukhobor criticism of the community in the Kootenays and calls for more vigorous enforcement of the law. The government was only too aware of the political significance of this issue in that region of the province. […]

*****

Non-Doukhobors were not willing to have truck with a different ethnic group that did not play by the "rules." By May 1913, as the Doukhobors showed no inclination to comply with either the vital statistics or school attendance laws and the authorities had lost patience, the attorney general, William Bowser, was directed by the premier to "take whatever

proceedings are necessary to enforce our *Vital Statistics Act* [*sic*] against these people.[20]

Taking legal action against the Doukhobors proved to be easier said than done, because members of the community refused to speak to anyone in authority or anyone suspected of aiding the police in their inquiries. The Attorney General's Department was advised by one of its solicitors, A.V. Pineo, who visited the Kootenays on a fact-finding mission, that the difficulties associated with enforcing vital statistics, schools, and public health legislation stemmed not only from refusal of members of the community to cooperate, but also from the problem of applying notions of individual responsibility to a group practising communalism.[21] Pinpointing the "occupier," "parent or guardian," or "owner or occupant"—the individuals who were the stated targets of prosecution or action under the Births, Deaths and Marriages Registration Act,[22] the Public Schools Act,[23] and the Health Act[24] respectively—in multi-family dwelling houses was proving to be an exercise in frustration. Pineo counselled a new strategy that would concentrate on imposing fiscal penalties rather than imprisonment for breaches of the law and place the onus in terms of enforcement and execution on the community and its leadership.[25] […]

Pineo's sentiments were converted into legislative form in the Community Regulation Act of 1914.[26] Although the long title of the statute gave the impression that it was designed to protect women and children living in communes, the wording of the sections left no doubt that it was designed to force compliance of the whole Doukhobor community with provincial registration, schools, and public health legislation. The act applied to any person living, sojourning or found in, upon or about a settlement or community under communal or tribal conditions, as distinguished from the ordinary and usual conditions of family life and residence.[27] Although the Doukhobors were not named specifically, exemptions were provided for military or naval establishments and Indians, the only other "communities" that might have fallen within the provisions of the legislation.

Under the terms of the act it was the responsibility of each member of the community to register births and deaths, to carry out statutory obligations in respect of schooling of children between the ages of seven and fourteen, and to abide by the duties imposed by the Health Act.[28] Membership in the community was shown if one witness had seen the person targeted in, upon, or about the lands occupied in a communal manner.[29] Failure to comply with the responsibilities under the act was an offence punishable on summary conviction by a fine of not less than $25.[30] Recovery of any penalty imposed under the act could be realized by the distress and sale of any goods and chattels in, upon, or about the lands or premises of the community.[31]

*****

Ironically, the resolve of the government to get tough was to achieve little in the short run. The reaction of the Doukhobor community was predictably negative. It was not community resistance, however, that threatened to subvert Victoria's legal strategy, but the legislation itself. When the government came to enforce the new law, it worried about whether it had made a fatal error in one of the assumptions that supported it, the ownership and legal control of the land on which the community had settled. Far from being community property, it was registered in the name of Peter Verigin as an individual. Accordingly, there were doubts that the act would pass scrutiny if challenged.[32] A further complication had been raised by the regional school inspector, A.E. Miller of Revelstoke. In a report to the Department of Education, Miller noted that school attendance was only compulsory if a child's home was within three miles of a public school by a "passable public road." As the roads in most Doukhobor settlements were privately owned, he doubted whether, strictly speaking, the parents were caught by the act.[33]

Before the legislation could be tested, the attorney general and Peter Verigin reached a compromise on the education issue. By this accord Doukhobor children would attend school, but would be exempt from religious observance and the military drill in place at many schools with the support of the Strathcona Trusts.[34] Both men, it seems, saw benefits in mutual resolution of the truancy problem while the country was at war.[35]

During the period from 1915 to 1922 tension between the Doukhobors and Victoria over education diminished as enrolments increased and new schools were built and occupied.[36] Although school attendance from the community was not universal, it steadily grew under the benign coaxing of A.E. Miller, the school inspector with responsibility for the Kootenays. Miller rejected coercion of Doukhobor parents because, he felt, it would encourage resistance to the law.[37]

By 1922, however, trouble on the education front was brewing again. The problems flowed in large part from the resolve of John Oliver's Liberal government to enforce school attendance in Doukhobor villages.[38] Amendments to the Public Schools Act in 1920 made provision for the establishment of "community rural districts" to incorporate Doukhobor schools. These operated under the control of the newly established Council of Public Instruction (the cabinet), and provision was made for communal assessment to cover the costs of education in the districts.[39] In the event of a community's refusal to pay, the Department of Education was empowered to seize its property to offset the expenditures. The day-to-day affairs of these districts were put in the hands of official trustees.[40]

The approach of the department was clear. Where the problems of attendance were generic, as school enrolments fell below what the authorities considered a reasonable level, the strategy was to reduce or remove grants to school boards and charge the educational costs directly against the local community. Under the amendments to the Public Schools Act, the Council of Public Instruction was empowered to increase the financial assessment of a local community, "where in the opinion of the Superintendent of Education the attendance of pupils [at the school] is less than a reasonable percentage of the children in the community rural school district available for attendance at that school, or where by reason of the non-attendance of pupils without the consent of the Superintendent the school is closed."[41]

The truancy of individual students was to be cured by charging the parents under the Public Schools Act, and, if necessary, executing judgment against community property under the Community Regulation Act.[42] This was no longer an idle threat, for the latter enactment was now operative. Verigin had transferred the land from his own name to that of an incorporated body, the Christian Community of Universal Brotherhood (CCUB), in 1917. Pressure on the Doukhobor community to comply with the school attendance provisions was further intensified by the raising of the compulsory school age to fifteen years in 1921.[43]

The legislative initiatives and subsequent actions of the Oliver government were part of a conscious policy of "Canadianization" that was being argued by educationalists at this time. One of the leading proponents of this view was James T.M. Anderson, who, as school inspector for the Yorkton area of Saskatchewan, had authored an influential book on the subject in 1918.[44] This work strongly advocated the public education of the young of non-English-speaking immigrants as the way to achieve a virtuous, monolingual, homogeneous Canadian society and polity.[45] Anderson decried the experiments with bilingual education tried in Manitoba, and was less than flattering about the work and training of "foreign-speaking" teachers.[46] He was particularly critical of the resistance of the community Doukhobors to public education, under the baleful influence of Verigin.[47] The answer to the Doukhobor education "problem," he asserted, lay in state intervention.

*****

It was a disciple of Anderson, E.G. Daniels, who replaced A.E. Miller in 1922 as the school inspector for the Kootenay region. Daniels possessed a strong commitment to "Canadianizing" the Doukhobors, and he had no compunction about using the law to achieve that end.[48] His arrival coincided with a general growth of dissatisfaction within the Doukhobor community over its apparently tenuous economic position and the perceived hostility of both the government and its non-Doukhobor neighbours toward it.[49] In the educational context this was manifest in increasing truancy and refusal by the community to countenance new school building.[50]

None of this was to deter Daniels. With gusto and a firm belief in the rectitude of what he was doing, he had two new schools approved for the Brilliant district to accommodate Doukhobor children.[51] When the Doukhobors refused to erect them, arguing that there were not enough children to justify the expense, the Department of Education undertook the work. A levy of $6,000 covering the cost of construction was assessed against the community. Verigin, moreover, was warned that unless parents sent their children to these schools, the department would be forced to charge against community property to meet operational costs, in particular teachers' salaries.[52]

Meanwhile trouble was brewing in the Grand Forks school district. In the school at Outlook, which had both Doukhobor and non-Doukhobor students, the enrolment had fallen below what the Department of Education considered to be a reasonable level. Parents were, it seems, withdrawing their children from school on Verigin's instructions.[53] Victoria, prompted by Daniels, notified the trustees that unless the school was better attended, it would be closed.[54] As this meant the loss of a grant of $1,100, the local school board suddenly became active. They advised Doukhobor parents to send their children to school, and when they refused, summonses were issued and Magistrate McCallum fined eight parents $25 each under the compulsory attendance provision of the Public Schools Act.[55] He also warned them that if they continued in their resistance, the next punishment would be more severe. Furthermore, he said, if their fines were not paid by 26 December 1922, their goods would be liable to seizure.

Police attempts to persuade John Zeburoff, an executive member of the community, that the fines must be paid proved fruitless. The community's position, Zeburoff announced, was that while an education might be desirable, it could not be forced on any of its members. It was for the mothers of the children to decide.[56] Meanwhile Verigin wrote to the premier protesting the province's action and indicating parents were content to have their children attend school, but only to the age of ten.[57]

Unwilling to wait any longer for compliance, the attorney general, Alexander Manson, directed on 23 January 1933 that steps be taken to execute the distress warrants.[58] This was done without incident by police under the command of Inspector Dunwoody of Fernie on 29 January. They seized a truck belonging to the community.[59] Shortly afterward the fines were paid by a solicitor for the Christian Community of Universal Brotherhood and the truck was restored.

Any belief that the truancy issue had been resolved once and for all was soon dashed. Despite assurances by Michael Cazakoff, the vice-president of the CCUB, that parents would send their children to school, attendance remained low.[60] It seems the community expected that in return for agreeing to send their children to school, the fines paid by the parents in early February would be remitted. The Grand Forks school board firmly rejected any such proposal.[61]

When Daniels, at the behest of the board, successfully prosecuted six more parents in April and proceedings were taken to enforce the penalties by distress, zealots among the Doukhobors began to take matters in hand. The secretary of the Grand Forks School board reported to the attorney general on 14 April advising of an attempt to burn down the Outlook school, a nude protest close to Central Public School in the city, and an incursion by another group of Doukhobors into the same school in which they sang and spoke to the children in one of the junior grades.[62] As the protesters seemed to the board members to be insane, they requested that their mental condition be investigated and the local community protected from them.[63] Manson responded by ordering the police to arrest anyone found parading in the nude and, following the suggestion of the school board, to have those arrested examined for their sanity.[64]

*****

The use of incendiarism as a form of protest was something for which the Doukhobor leadership was unprepared. Verigin the Lordly, who had supported the withdrawal of children from school in the first place, condemned the firing of schools in communications with the government, but felt powerless to deal with the perpetrators within the community. In a letter in April 1924 he made his feelings known to Premier Oliver and sought the cooperation of the government and police in calling the anarchistic "Nudes," as he described the zealots, to account. Their crimes were, he suggested, directed against him for supporting the education of Doukhobor children. Because no school had escaped the arsonists' torch, he feared that if education were rendered in households, the houses would be the next buildings to go up in flames. He could, he claimed, provide the names of the culprits.[65]

For its part Victoria was disinclined to pursue the incendiarists. Despite the fact that the campaign of resistance was now directed against the institutions of the state, the advice and offer of cooperation by Verigin was ignored.[66] Only one person was brought to book for incendiarism, although the government continued to enforce the compulsory attendance provisions of the Public Schools Act.[67]

After Verigin's death in the early morning of 29 October 1924 in an explosion on a train in the Kettle Valley between Brilliant and Grand Forks, Victoria turned up the heat on school attendance, supposing the community to be in a demoralized state and thus especially vulnerable and malleable.[68] Events came to a head in April 1925. Inspector Dunwoody of the British Columbia Provincial Police and School Inspector P.H. Sheffield received a resounding "Nyet!" at a mass meeting of 2,500 Doukhobors at Brilliant on 5 April 1925 to their request that the community obey the school laws. Thereupon the police conducted a major raid in order to seize community property in lieu of unpaid fines of $4,500 imposed on thirty-five Doukhobor parents for breaches of the Public Schools Act.[69] Inspector Dunwoody and a squad of ten constables and one hundred road-gang navvies forced their way into a community warehouse, seizing office equipment, supplies, and cut lumber. The goods, appraised at $5,400, were sold for a total of $3,360.[70]

At this juncture the climate on Doukhobor education suddenly changed. The children returned to classrooms, and plans to rebuild the destroyed schools went ahead.[71] It is not clear whether the government's "mailed fist" approach had prevailed for the moment, or the community had relented pending the arrival of their new leader from the Soviet Union—Peter Petrovich Verigin, the "Purger" as he described himself. The latter had let it be known by letter to the community that he favoured compliance with the education laws.[72] Victoria entertained no doubts that a combination of resolve to enforce the law and a significant show of force in applying the principle of communal responsibility had brought the Doukhobors to their senses and the recalcitrant to heel.[73] [...]

On his arrival in North America in September 1927 the younger Verigin indicated that he was interested in an accommodation with the state on schooling. In a judicious response to a reporter's question he stated:

Yes we will take everything of value which Canada has to offer, but we will not give up our Doukhobor souls. We will educate our children in the English schools, and we will also set up our own Russian schools and libraries.[74]

These views, when they were repeated in the Kootenays and began to permeate the consciousness of the Doukhobor community in British Columbia, were to lead to dissension in the ranks. The zealots, now clearly recognizable as the Sons of Freedom, began engaging in a new round of civil disobedience. Convinced that they were the true conscience of Doukhoborism, and increasingly inclined to give an inverted meaning to what the leader proclaimed as community policy, they had persuaded themselves that Verigin's calls for accommodation with the state on education were in fact an invitation to resistance.[75] During 1928 and early 1929 the Freedomites began marching, stripping, and on occasion, disrupting schools.[76] This was all in the cause of condemning what one of their leaders, Peter Maloff, described as a system that was turning Doukhobor children into "slaves of Satan."[77] School enrolments declined dramatically as both zealot and sympathetic or anxious community parents removed their children from school.

Meanwhile the government in Victoria had done nothing to accommodate the desire of community Doukhobors to exercise some control over how and what their children were taught. A proposal in November 1927 from the younger Verigin that Russian be introduced into their schools was rejected out of hand.[78] As the new Liberal premier, John MacLean, who had previously served as education minister, put it in characteristically ethnocentric terms:

The government ... will not tolerate, and I am sure the legislature would not approve, the use of any foreign language in the public schools of this province. Should we grant a concession to the Doukhobors, peoples of many nationalities here would be entitled to ask for the use of their language in the schools and we should have a real dual language question on our hands.[79]

During 1929, school burnings broke out again. In mid August a group of 109 protestors sought to march on Nelson. They stripped when the police and Verigin sought to dissuade them.[80]

All were arrested, charged with public nudity, and sentenced to six months in jail.

At this point a change occurred in the government's strategy on Doukhobor education. In dealing with the eight children arrested along with their parents outside Nelson, Victoria decided to invoke the Infants Act in order to make them wards of the province.[81] Under that statute the superintendent of neglected children was empowered "to apprehend, without warrant, any child apparently under the age of eighteen years ... [with] no parent capable and willing to exercise proper parental control over the child."[82] Superintendent Thomas Menzies, in a statement to the hearing on wardship conducted by Magistrate J. Cartmel in Nelson, indicated that the purpose of invoking this provision was "for the purpose of seeing that they are properly cared for *until they are a certain age*" [emphasis added].[83] He interpreted the latter term as meaning until the age of eighteen, or such time as the parents proved capable of caring for them "in a fit and proper manner." A primary objective would be to ensure that they were educated in the public school system. Clearly Menzies saw the exercise as allowing him to hold the children beyond the expiry of their parents' sentences, a position expressly accepted by Judge Cartmel.[84]

It was no coincidence that R.H. "Harry" Pooley, the attorney general in the recently elected Tory government of Simon Fraser Tolmie, announced contemporaneously that the Tolmie government intended to get tough with the Doukhobors. It proposed, he said, "to sequestrate a number of their younger children by proper court action under the Neglected Children's Act and place them under such bodies as Children's Aid societies for education." If the Doukhobors behaved themselves, Pooley stated, they would get their children back; if not, "they will lose more children until we have them all under training in institutions."[85]

This limited experiment was not a success. Some of the children turned out to be above school age and, in the mind of the attorney general, not ripe for resocialization. The target

of any future initiatives of this type, Pooley asserted, should be "young children; and those whose education can be attended to."[86] Furthermore, the children refused to cooperate and twice ran away during mid September 1929 while in the care of the Vancouver Children's Aid Society. [...]

The resentment of both parents and children easily fed into the Freedomite martyr myth, and together with action by Verigin to disavow their conduct and move them off community land as criminals, was to lead to further acts of defiance. Victoria, for its part, saw no connection between unrest among the Sons of Freedom and its policies. From the viewpoint of the Tolmie government, the "Doukhobor problem" stemmed from the group's adherence to autocratic and irresponsible leadership, and their communal mode of living. The conclusion was that action was required to rid the country of Verigin, who was believed to be both the *Eminence grise* behind the zealots and a dangerous Bolshevik, and at the same time to bring the Sons of Freedom to heel.

The abortive attempts to deport Peter Verigin II have been chronicled elsewhere.[87] The plan, for that is what it was, to deal with the Sons of Freedom was worked out in Victoria and facilitated by Ottawa.[88] The Dominion government of R.B. Bennett, elected in 1930, bowed to pressure from the British Columbian authorities and amended the Criminal Code in 1931 to provide for the detention of Freedomite protesters for longer periods. Public nudity was converted from a summary conviction offence with a maximum penalty of six months in jail to one carrying a maximum sentence of three years.[89] [...]

It was not long before the amended *Criminal Code* provision was invoked. The opportunity to test the plan to neutralize the Sons of Freedom presented itself during May and June 1932. A series of nude protests took place in the Kootenays, first in protest at Verigin's continued rejection of the radicals' conduct and then in reaction to their treatment by the authorities and the law.[90] By mid June close to 600 men and women had been arrested, charged with and convicted of public nudity, and uniformly sentenced to three years in jail. They were taken off to a special penal facility established by the federal authorities on Piers Island off the north end of the Saanich peninsula.[91]

It fell to the province to deal with the children of parents sent to Piers Island. As whole families were involved in all but the first protest in May, the children had been placed in temporary quarters in Nelson along with their parents while the logistics of finding a prison for the adults were worked out.[92] The number of children in custody ultimately swelled to 365. The children were divided up in due course between orphanages, foster homes in the lower mainland and Vancouver Island, and the Provincial Industrial Home and Industrial School in the Vancouver area to be cared for and educated for the three years their parents were expected to be inside.[93] Unlike the earlier experiment, however, the children were not adjudged wards of the province under the Infants Act. Through agreement between William Manson, the superintendent of welfare, his deputy Laura Holland, and Attorney General Pooley it was decided to treat the children as "destitutes."[94] Under the law and child welfare practice, this classification, which was typically appealed to "when a parent or guardian, though competent, was unable to provide for the child over a temporary period, often as a result of illness or during confinement of the mother," could be made without a court appearance or order.[95] However, the status, unlike that of wardship, preserved the rights of parents to custody and guardianship and required parental consent to decisions on the child's welfare.

The motives of the authorities in adopting this strategy almost certainly reflected a concern to avoid public scrutiny, which a court application would have engendered, and possible political challenge in the broader community, as well as a calculation that any dispensing with legal scruple would escape attention. The Department of Child Welfare did indeed ignore legal requirements by placing some of the children

in care over the objections of their parents. The advice of the attorney general was that parental refusal could be safely ignored.[96] To the extent that legal and welfare authorities proceeded without parental consent, Victoria was acting beyond its powers and in a thoroughly illegal manner. Fortunately for it, the gamble paid off as there were no legal challenges to its actions by the Freedomites, who did not have access to the community's legal representatives and were suspicious of lawyers in any event.

*****

Whether or not this experiment might have worked, changes with at least the younger children over the long haul became academic early in 1933. Exhibiting just how shallow and ill-conceived its policy on the Freedomites was, and how fickle it could be in the face of non-Doukhobor sentiment, the Tolmie government decided that the resocialization plan must terminate in mid-stream. Facing pressure within the conservative business establishment for drastic cuts in existing social welfare expenditures as a way of navigating the Depression, and criticisms from radical and progressive MLAs that it was spending significantly more on the Doukhobor children in care than on families forced onto welfare, the provincial government lost its nerve and determined that it could no longer support the children within the child welfare system.[97]

As luck would have it, a solution to the governments problem was suggested by members of the Doukhobor community in the Kootenays. At a meeting with Doukhobor representatives in December 1932 the deputy attorney general, Oscar Bass, was advised of the interest of both independent and orthodox families in having Freedomite children whose parents were on Piers Island committed to their care.[98] The matter was referred to William Manson, the superintendent of welfare, who indicated that the placement of children in approved Doukhobor families on the understanding that the government could not pay for care provided a convenient and acceptable way of relieving the cost burden on the province and its taxpayers. Although he believed that the children were doing well in conventional care locations, that "a favourable impression was being made on them and that, if they remained for the full three years of their parents' sentences, might well become good Canadian citizens," he agreed that these positive signs did not justify "the heavy expenditure."[99]

By the beginning of March 1933 the decision had been made by Victoria to move all the children back to the Kootenays or to Doukhobor families elsewhere.[100] As in the case of the original decision to consign the children to care at the coast, lack of parental consent was blithely ignored.[101] […]

*****

The result of being moved from pillar to post in this way was to create further confusion in the minds of the children.[102] Some were placed in families with different values and beliefs from those of their parents. Some were used primarily as an additional source of labour by people struggling through the Depression. The bruised psyches that resulted from the insensitive treatment the children had received at the hands of the authorities while their parents were incarcerated were compounded by the early release of the adult Freedomites late in 1934 and early in 1935.[103] Predictably, these people, who had been forced to while away the better part of three years without anything to show for it than the disruption of their lives and rejection by other segments of their own community and by non-Doukhobor society, were extremely embittered. This was a state of mind that all too easily rubbed off on their children. In the case of some of these young people, the mental scars of those years forcibly separated from their parents were not to heal, with the result that they grew into a new generation dedicated to violent resistance to materialism and further attempts by the state to assimilate them.[104]

The coercive experiments in enforcing school attendance laws between 1911 and 1935 achieved only partial success. Although by the latter date most community Doukhobor children were attending school, the Freedomites continued their resistance.[105] Burnings of schools were to break out again between 1936 and 1938. Then a lull occurred, as first the financial ruination and breakup of the CCUB took a devastating economic toll on the orthodox community, and then the outbreak of war produced a sense of solidarity between the factions in resisting any attempt to conscript Doukhobor men into the Armed Forces.[106] However, an extended pattern of Freedomite resistance began again in 1944, fuelled by concerns about the prosperity enjoyed by many members of the community during and after the war, disputations about the leadership of the Doukhobors, and renewed pressures by Victoria to force compliance with vital statistics and schools legislation.[107] This period was to last until the mid 1960s and was marked by a spiralling record of firings and bombings of Doukhobor property and public facilities—the work of the most fanatical Freedomites— and draconian government action. The latter included the removal of several waves of Sons of Freedom children from their parents under child welfare legislation starting in 1954, and their detention and attempted resocialization in a special facility in New Denver in the Slocan Valley under the administration of the Department of Education.[108] Most of the children were released on an undertaking by their mothers to the magistrate who had committed them, Judge William Evans of Nelson, that they would ensure their attendance at school. While some of these children were absorbed with little ostensible resistance into the educational and socio-economic life of the larger community, others reacted by denying their heritage, or by joining in new acts of depredation by the zealots.[109]

At the core of this long-running dispute were two diametrically opposed views of the state and its meaning. Both of these interpretations flowed from belief systems that claimed a monopoly on virtue. The Doukhobors, especially the orthodox and the Freedomites, rejected the state as evil—an entity in the name of which countless acts of warfare, violence, rapine, theft, and deceit had been practised with tragic consequences to humankind. Both it and its agents were to be ignored, or, if necessary, resisted. These feelings were accentuated by a conviction that the Doukhobors had found the "true way" both in terms of their faith and way of life. They recognized the divine spark working in each and every member of the group that made them equal in the sight of God, and as equals, they accepted the value of working together in harmony for the good of the community. All that was necessary to their spiritual and material welfare, they believed, existed in the community. For many orthodox Doukhobors and the Sons of Freedom (but not the independents), these gifts were exclusive and not to be shared with others. For a minority they were to be protected at all costs, even by the use of depredation and violence, if necessary.

On the non-Doukhobor side the rhetoric held that the highest form of duty was that of patriotism—that the individual's first obligation was to the state, which in turn was the guarantor of his or her liberty, property rights, and opportunities for self-fulfilment. To the extent that there was a religious dimension to this rhetoric, it assumed a God who recognized the value of political communities and patriotism and was discerning enough to know the virtuous and villainous among the nations. The idealization of the state was buttressed by strong nativist feeling among the predominantly British population of British Columbia, which drew on a long tradition of racial and ethnic stereotyping and discrimination.[110] These people preached that British government and law represented the zenith of human achievement and British stock the purist and intellectually most sophisticated in the world. They were also propelled by a nagging feeling that British power and influence were on the wane, and that British people and institutions needed to close ranks against foreigners and their inferior customs and traditions in order to preserve their ascendancy. In its more extreme forms this mind-set produced a set of fears about "race

suicide." In the case of the dominant community in the Kootenays, racist consciousness manifest itself in the practice of many people to describe themselves as "white" in order to differentiate themselves from the Doukhobor residents.[111] By the early 1930s the Doukhobors were clearly targeted by most members of the dominant community as an insolent and uncivilized group who should be denied their communal heritage and assimilated, forcibly if necessary.

*****

The government of British Columbia was to learn a lesson from the fiasco of this early attempt at enforced resocialization. When the Social Credit government of W.A.C. Bennett determined in 1954 to solve the Sons of Freedom problem once and for all by removing children from Freedomite families, it was careful to establish a special facility at New Denver exclusive to the children, and to treat the initiative as an educational one using the experience and skills of teachers, rather than those of child welfare professionals, and to keep the charges in custody for an extended period of years.[112] There is general agreement in the literature that this later experiment had greater success than its predecessors in turning the hearts and minds of many of the children, even though most writers have also argued that it was unnecessary and involved a massive denial of civil liberties.[113]

*****

In British Columbia neither those in politics nor in the bureaucracy were willing to stand up to racist and nativist sentiment in the non-Doukhobor community. Nor do they seem to have been enthusiastic in learning about Doukhobor history and understanding the political and social dynamics at work in the community. The very few voices of reason, like that of A.E. Miller, were effectively voices crying in the wilderness. Only as the effects of later dispersal and assimilation were felt and the non-Doukhobor population began to develop greater sensitivity to civil liberties and became more accepting of cultural and ethnic diversity were serious accommodations made with the Doukhobors over education and other bones of contention with the state.

The result of this sad story has not been the crushing of the culture, but a great deal of social dysfunction and individual and group unhappiness. As with other oppressed ethnic groups, there has developed a resolve to recapture and share the values and traditions that were formerly so despised on the outside and obsessively shielded on the inside. However, as the most recent dispute between Victoria and a segment of the Freedomites in the Kootenays over land occupancy and taxation shows, the ghosts of past intransigence and misunderstanding live on.[114]

Notes

1. N. McDonald and A. Chaiton, eds., *Egerton Ryerson and His Times* (Toronto: Macmillan 1977); H. Graff, "'Pauperism, Misery and Vice': Illiteracy and Criminality in the Nineteenth Century," 11 *Journal of Social History* (1977), 245; Susan Houston, "Victorian Origins of Juvenile Delinquency: A Canadian Experience," 12 *History of Education Quarterly* (1972), 254; "Politics, Schools and Social Change in Upper Canada," 53 *Canadian Historical Review* (1972), 249.

2. Douglas Schmeiser, *Civil Liberties in Canada* (Oxford: Oxford University Press 1964), 125–95.

3. J.R. Miller, *Skyscrapers Hide the Heavens: A History of Indian-White Relations in Canada* (Toronto: University of Toronto Press 1989), 97–115, 130–2, 189–207; C. Haig-Brown, *Resistance and Renewal: Surviving the Indian Residential School* (Vancouver: Tillacum Library 1988).

4. William Janzen, *Limits on Liberty: The Experience of Mennonite, Hutterite and Doukhobor Communities in Canada* (Toronto: University of Toronto Press 1990), 88–115, 142–61.

5. William Kaplan, *The State and Salvation: The Jehovah's Witnesses and Their Fights for Civil Rights* (Toronto: University of Toronto Press 1990), 88–115, 142–61.

6. See Michael Cross, "'The Laws are Like Cobwebs': Popular Resistance to Authority in mid Nineteenth Century British North America," in Peter Waite, Sandra Oxner, and Thomas Barnes, eds., *Law in a Colonial Society* (Toronto: Carswell 1984), 103–4; Schmeiser, *supra* note 2; Haig-Brown, *supra* note 3; P. Tennant, *Aboriginal Peoples and Politics: The Indian Land Question in British Columbia, 1849–1989* (Vancouver: UBC Press 1990), 79–81; Janzen, *supra* note 4; Kaplan, *supra* note 5.

7. Maurice Hindus, "Bookless Philosophers," *The Century Magazine*, January 1923, 105, quoted in Janzen, *supra* note 4, 116–17.

8. William Blakemore, *Report of the Royal Commission on Matters Relating to the Doukhobor Sect in the Province of British Columbia*, British Columbia, *Sessional Papers*, 1913, T58.

9. Ibid. It is important to recognize that some Canadian Doukhobors chose early on to depart from communal modes of living and working the land. The "independents" who farmed individually, while still adhering to many of the religious and cultural traditions of the group, favoured education for their children, even within the public school system. The independents by and large remained in Saskatchewan when the exodus to British Columbia took place between 1908 and 1913. On the much quieter history of Doukhobor education in the prairie province, see John Lyons, "The (Almost) Quiet Evolution: Doukhobor Schooling in Saskatchewan," *Canadian Journal of Ethnic Studies* (1976), 23.

10. Neil Sutherland, *Children in English Canadian Society: Framing the Twentieth Century Consensus* (Toronto: University of Toronto Press 1976), 155–241; Timothy A. Dunn, "The Rise of Mass Schooling in British Columbia, 1900–1929," and Jean Mann, "C.M. Weir and H.B. King: Progressive Education or Education for the Progressive State," in J.D. Wilson and D.C. Jones, eds., *Schooling and Society in Twentieth Century British Columbia* (Calgary: Detselig 1980), chs. 1 and 4.

11. Max Weber, *Economy and Society: An Outline of Interpretive Sociology*, Vol. 1 (New York: Bedminster Press 1968), 215–6.

12. George Woodcock and Ivan Avakumovic, *The Doukhobors* (Toronto: McClelland & Stewart 1977), 245.

13. Births, Deaths, and Marriages Registration Act, RSBC 1911, c. 22.

14. British Columbia Archives and Record Service (BCARS), GR1323, Attorney General Correspondence, reel B2086, File 4488-16-12,14, letter J.P. McLeod to Chief Constable J.A. Dinsmore, Grand Forks, British Columbia Provincial Police (BCPP), 28 May 1912.

15. Ibid., letter Dinsmore, BCPP, Grand Forks, to McLeod, 13 July 1912.

16. Blakemore, *supra* note 8, at T66.

17. Ibid.

18. Koozma Tarasoff, *Plakun Trava—The Doukhobors* (Grand Forks, BC: Mir Publishing Society 1982), 122.

19. British Columbia, *Sessional Papers*, 1911, "Public Schools Report for 1909–1910, No. 39," 1911, A58.

20. BCARS, GR 1323, Reel B2077, File 7021-1-12, 98, letter McBride to Bowser, 26 May 1913.

21. BCARS, GR1323, reel B2094, File 7547-7-13, 59-60, report by A.V. Pineo to Bowser, 8 Nov. 1913, 63–4.

22. Births, Deaths, and Marriages Registration Act, RSBC 1911, c. 22, s. 23.

23. Public Schools Act, RSBC 1911, c. 206, s. 140.

24. Health Act, RSBC 1911, c. 98, s. 140.

25. Ibid., 68.

26. Act to make Provision for the Welfare and Protection of Women and Children Living under Communal Conditions, SBC 1914, c. 11.

27. Ibid., s. 2.

28. Ibid., s. 5.

29. Ibid., s. 3. Membership was also extended by s. 6 to every registered owner of land "used by or for or in connection with a settlement or community by any persons living or sojourning or being found in, on or about a settlement or community" as defined by ss. 2 and 3. By s. 10 where the name of a member of the community was unknown, that person could be assigned a name or number by a justice for purposes of the act.

30. Ibid., s. 7.

31. Ibid., s. 9.

32. Woodcock and Avakumovic, *supra* note 12, at 251.

33. University of British Columbia Special Collection Library, D. Ms. 13 (iv), report Miller to Alexander Robinson, Superintendent of Schools, 31 March 1915, 8–9.

34. Ewart Reid, *The Doukhobors in Canada* (MA thesis, McGill University, 1932), 118. On the Strathcona Trust and its funding of military exercises at schools in British Columbia, see *supra* note 19.

35. Reid, *supra* note 34, at 118, suggests that Verigin was anxious not to provide an excuse for the government of Canada to conscript Doukhobors. Bowser seems to have been motivated by a desire to resolve this irritant while the First World War was being waged.

36. Woodcock and Avakumovic, *supra* note 12, at 251.

37. Janzen, *supra* note 4, at 129.

38. On the government's purpose, see report of speech by J.D. MacLean, Minister of Education, *Victoria Daily Colonist*, 26 March, 1920, 6, 9.

39. Public Schools Act Amendment Act, SBC 1920, c. 82, s. 22 (inserting s. 115A into the existing act), further amended and consolidated, SBC 1922, c. 64, s. 129.

40. Ibid., s. 22 [s. 115A(10); s. 129(10)]. The trustee in each district was to be assisted by an advisory committee of three members of the community. The school inspectors for the region seem to have acted as the official trustees.

41. Ibid., s. 22 [s. 1115A(9); s. 129(9)].

42. The process of using both pieces of legislation to enforce the provisions of the Public Schools Act on truancy is set out in a memorandum from Attorney General Alexander Manson to Premier Oliver, 12 March 1925. BCARS, GR441, Premier Oliver Papers, Vol. 246, File 13.

43. Public Schools Act Amendment Act, SBC 1921, c. 56, s. 17.

44. J.T.M Anderson, *The Education of the New Canadian: A Treatise on Canada's Greatest Education Problem* (London: J.M. Dent 1918).

45. Ibid., 7–10.

46. Ibid., 93–115, 153–70.

47. Ibid., 32–4, 96.

48. L. Barton, "'Canadianizing' the Doukhobors: Government Attempts to Enforce Compulsory Education in British Columbia, 1911–1925" (Honours Paper, History 404, Okanagan University College 1993), 10–11. The author quotes from a letter sent by Daniels to the Board of School Trustees in Grand Forks, 18 Nov. 1922, expressing gratitude for the board's cooperation in the "Canadianization" process.

49. Woodcock and Avakumovic, *supra* note 12, at 254–5.

50. BCARS, GR441, Premier Oliver Papers, Vol. 246, File 13, Resume of File re Doukhobors, 8. This file seems to have been put together in late 1924 or early 1925 for purposes of advising the premier of the history of conflict with the Doukhobors on educational policy.

51. Ibid.

52. Ibid.

53. Woodcock and Avakumovic, *supra* note 12, at 255.

54. BCARS, GR441, Vol. 231, File 13, Hon. Dr MacLean's File, "Doukhobors and Grand Forks School Board," 1.

55. Ibid.
56. Ibid., 1–2. Zeburoff also used the opportunity to criticize the teacher at the Outlook school, Josephine Spence, for what he claimed was her testimony against the Doukhobors in court. He demanded that she be dismissed and replaced with a "Christian woman."
57. Ibid, letter from Verigin to Oliver, 31 Dec. 1922. Oliver replied on 3 January 1923, indicating that the government had no desire to persecute or embarrass Verigin, but the law was the law as far as school attendance was concerned, and applied to the Doukhobors like everyone else.
58. Ibid., 2.
59. Ibid.
60. BCARS, GR441, Vol. 246, File 13, Resume of File on the Doukhobors, 4, makes reference to a meeting between Cazakoff and the minister of education and attorney general at which Cazakoff had assured the government representatives that the community would substantially abide by the law on school attendance. This was reported by Attorney General Manson to the secretary of the Grand Forks School Board by letter on 6 February, ibid.
61. The Department of Education was favourably disposed. However, when inquiries were made by the attorney general about the Grand Forks board's position in his letter of 6 February, the board reported that it had decided to withhold the fines, on its solicitor's advice, to cover costs. The minister of education rejected Cazakoff's attempt to link the undertaking on attendance and repayment of the fines, stressing that the government had no discretion when it came to enforcement of the law (letter MacLean to Cazakoff, 15 Feb. 1923).
62. BCARS, GR441, Vol. 246, File 13, letter from John Hutton, Secretary, Grand Forks School Board, to Attorney General Manson, 14 April 1923.
63. BCARS, GR441, Vol. 231, File 13, letter from Mayor George Hull to Premier Oliver. See also resolution of the Board of Trade of the same date communicated on 20 April.
64. BCARS, GR441, Vol. 246, File 13, letter from Manson to Mayor Hull, 25 April 1923.
65. BCARS, GR441, Vol. 239, letter Peter Verigin to Premier John Oliver, 25 April 1924.
66. Verigin wrote to A. McQueen, the provincial assessor at Kaslo, on 7 September expressing his desire to seek accommodation with the government, and asking McQueen to try to persuade Premier Oliver, "himself a farmer," to visit Brilliant. McQueen sought to oblige by a memo to the premier, dated 8 September, but the latter declined

the invitation, saying that he had been over these matters before. BCARS, GR441, Vol. 239, File 13, 67.
67. Koozma Tarasoff, *In Search of Brotherhood: The History of the Doukhobors*, Vol. 2 (Vancouver: mimeograph, 1963), at 471–2.
68. Woodcock and Avakumovic, *supra* note 12, at 256. There is evidence too that the government was under continuing local pressure in the Kootenays to get tough with the Doukhobors. See BCARS, GR441, Oliver Papers, Vol. 239, File 13, letter from Secretary-Treasurer, Creston Liberal Association, to Oliver, 27 Oct. 1924. This communication described the Doukhobors as "a detriment to this country, similar to the Japanese in California" who need "a strong hand" as the only thing they are capable of appreciating. As the former MLA for Grand Forks, the Tory John McKie had also been killed in the explosion on the CPR. The minority Oliver government also had its more general image in the Kootenays to worry about, as a by-election approached.
69. Woodcock and Avakumovic, *supra* note 12, at 256–7.
70. Ibid.
71. Tarasoff, *Plakun Tram*, *supra* note 18, at 257.
72. Tarasoff, *In Search of Brotherhood*, *supra* note 67, at 527, quoting from a letter from Vereshagin and Plotnikoff, emissaries from the Christian Community of Universal Brotherhood, to Verigin in the Soviet Union, in P. Maloff, *Dukhobortsy: Ikh Istoria, Zihn i Bonba*, 33.
73. Mary Ashworth, *The Forces Which Shaped Them* (Vancouver: New Star Books 1979), 147. See also British Columbia, *Sessional Papers*, 1925, Department of the Attorney General, Report of the Provincial Police (J.H. McMulin), Y16.
74. Quoted in Ashworth, *supra* note 73, at 146–7.
75. Shortly after his arrival in Brilliant, Verigin had flattered the Sons of Freedom, describing them as the "ringing bells of Doukhoborism." The mental process of inversion of meaning is what Woodcock and Avakumovic, *supra* note 12, at 12 and 291, have described as the "upside-down" theory of discipleship. On the emergence of this radical wing of Doukhoborism, see J. Colin Yerbury, "The 'Sons of Freedom' Doukhobors and the Canadian State," 16 *Canadian Ethnic Studies* (1984), 45.
76. Ashworth, *supra* note 73, at 147.
77. *Vancouver Daily Province*, 3 May 1928, at 1, 26.
78. BCARS, GR441, Premier Oliver/MacLean Papers, Vol. 264, File 5, 11 Nov. 1927, letter Verigin to Hon. J.D. MacLean, Minister of Education. Verigin emphasized the need for Doukhobor education

to take account of the group's cultural needs and stressed the importance of autonomy in selection of Russian teachers. That the new leader had much to learn about political and social realities in Canada is evident in his expressed hope "that the Canadian Government will agree with me that the National Minority, represented by the Doukhobor population has their full right to its cultural self-determination."

79. *Victoria Times*, 28 Nov. 1927, 1.

80. Ashworth, *supra* note 73, at 147–8.

81. Infants Act, RSBC 1924, c. 112.

82. Ibid., s.56(j).

83. BCARS, GR2817, Provincial Secretary's Papers, Box 1, File 1, transcript of hearing under the Infants Act before J. Cartmel, Magistrate, County of Kootenay, Nelson, 6 Sept. 1929, 4. The story of this experiment is related in some detail in Ronald Hooper, *Custodial Care of Doukhobor Children in British Columbia, 1929 to 1933* (MA thesis, social work, UBC 1947), 23–31.

84. This presumably explains why Menzies did not proceed under s. 56(1), which provided for the apprehension of children of parents undergoing imprisonment on criminal charges. For Cartmel's position, see *supra* note 83, BCARS, GR28I7, transcript, 8.

85. *Victoria Times*, 31 Aug. 1929, at 15. The Conservatives had won the provincial election of July 1928. Pooley's remarkable announcement generated some protest from non-Doukhobors. A.W.D. Calvert, MD, wrote to the *Victoria Times*, 10 Sept. 1929, at 4, referring to the proposal as savouring of "barbarism" and pleading with the attorney general, "Recall your inquisitor before he perpetrates his ugly task of selecting and abducting these children."

86. BCARS, GR2817, Box 1, File 1, memorandum Pooley to Menzies, 24 Sept. 1929.

87. On this part of the strategy, see John McLaren, "Wrestling Spirits: The Strange Case of Peter Verigin II," *Canadian Ethnic Studies* 27 (October 1995), 95–130.

88. As early as September 1929 Attorney General Pooley had been advocating that "the ringleaders" should be convicted of "rioting charges" and sent to D'Arcy Island off Victoria. See BCARS, GR441, Premier Tolmie Papers, Vol. 283, File 4, telegram Pooley to Premier Simon Fraser Tolmie (in Toronto), 8 Sept. 1929.

89. Criminal Code Amendment Act, SC1931, c. 28, s. 2.

90. Woodcock and Avakumovic, *supra* note 12, at 298.

91. Records relating to the planning and implementation of this carceral experiment are in National Archives of Canada (NAC), RG73, Penitentiary Service Files, Vols. 43–5, 131.

92. Hooper, *supra* note 83, at 36–7.

93. Ibid., 40–2.

94. Ibid., 37.

95. Ibid., 37–8.

96. Ibid., 38. The issue of consent also arose in the context of medical treatment since, given the legal status of the children, no surgical operations could be conducted on them without parental consent. Hooper notes that a majority of the parents would not give this permission. Although a solution was effected after prolonged negotiations, trouble could have developed if the need for emergency surgery had occurred.

97. Hooper, *supra* note 83, at 99. The charge was raised that the government was spending $17.50 a month on each Doukhobor child in care, while the allowance for one child in a family receiving social assistance was only $2.50. No reference was made to the cost of non-Doukhobor children in care.

98. Hooper, *supra* note 83, at 99.

99. BCARS, GR2817, Box 1, File 5, memo Manson to Bass, 19 Dec. 1932.

100. This was the result of a letter from Superintendent of Welfare William Manson to his deputy, Laura Holland, 1 March 1933. Ibid.

101. Hooper, *supra* note 83, at 101–2.

102. Ashworth, *supra* note 73, at 153.

103. Hooper, *supra* note 83, at 105–6.

104. Woodcock and Avakumovic, *supra* note 12, at 318–19.

105. The view of the local school inspector was that, despite their attendance, it was not evident that the orthodox Doukhobor population really attached any great importance to formal education. Community identity was as strong as ever, the children left school at the earliest possible opportunity, and absenteeism was still a problem. See British Columbia, *Sessional Papers*, 65th Annual Report of the Public Schools, 1935–6, H47-8 (Inspector Jewett, Nelson School District).

106. Woodcock and Avakumovic, *supra* note 12, at 319–20.

107. Ibid., 321–31; Yerbury, *supra* note 75, at 58–61.

108. Margaret Hill, "The Detention of Freedomite Children, 1953–59," 18 *Canadian Ethnic Studies* (1986), 46.

109. Ashworth, *supra* note 73, at 167.

110. On racism in British Columbia that was directed against Asians, see Patricia Roy, *A Whiteman's Province: British Columbia's Politicians and Chinese and Japanese Immigrants, 1854–1914*

(Vancouver: UBC Press 1989); Peter Ward, *White Canada Forever: Popular Attitudes and Public Policy Toward Orientals in British Columbia*, 2nd ed. (Montreal and Kingston: McGill-Queen's University Press 1990); Hugh Johnston, *The Voyage of the Komagatu Maru: The Sikh Challenge to Canada's Colour Bar* (Vancouver: UBC Press 1989).

111. Woodcock and Avakumovic, *supra* note 12, at 244.
112. Hill, *supra* note 108, at 50–4.
113. Ibid., 57–9; Ashworth, *supra* note 73, at 161–70; Woodcock and Avakumovic, *supra* note 12, at 340–4; Janzen, *supra* note 4, at 137–40.
114. *Castlegar Sun*, 24 Aug. 1994, at 1.

Critical Thinking Questions

· ·

Chapter 12: Spectacular Justice: The Circus on Trial, and the Trial as Circus Picton, 1903, *Carolyn Strange and Tina Loo*

1. According to Strange and Loo, "the acquittal of a poor Black man powerfully affirmed the myth of equality before the law." How does Clarke's acquittal reinforce this notion? What do the authors mean by the "myth" of equality before the law?
2. Why did the jury return a verdict of not guilty? Were they trying to send a message to the courts? If Clarke had been charged today, do you think a similar verdict would have been entered?
3. From the evidence in the article, did the jury appear to have reached a proper verdict? How was that verdict related to the political economy of the area?

Chapter 13: "Gentlemen, This is no Ordinary Trial": Sexual Narratives in the Trial of the Reverend Corbett, Red River, 1863, *Erica Smith*

1. The author observes that "the scaffolding for the staging of the trial, its forms of dramatic and textual representation—the metaphors, allusions, and vocabulary— are themselves sources of historical knowledge." What does she mean?
2. How is the character of the victim portrayed by the defendant's counsel? Is the defence's attempt to portray her as a prostitute successful? What impact does this have on the jury verdict?
3. What problems are there in using a case like this to draw broader conclusions about Red River Society? Is the verdict an anomaly, or does it present the sentiments of the day? Is it appropriate to read between the lines to draw conclusions about the verdict?

Chapter 14: The Relocation Phenomenon and the Africville Study, *Donald H. Clairmont and Dennis William Magill*

1. Was the Africville relocation an example of liberal-welfare relocation as claimed by the City of Halifax? Using evidence from the text, what other model could this relocation also fit under?

2. Would the Africville relocatees have benefited further from relocation if they had followed the example of the Beechville relocation. Why or why not?

3. In a larger context of social regulation and control, how does this particular event demonstrate the attempt by the state and local authorities to use municipal bylaws to impose uniform standards on its residents?

Chapter 15: Criminalizing the Colonized: Ontario Native Women Confront the Criminal Justice, 1920–1960, *Joan Sangster*

1. What impact did Native status appear to play in the decision to incarcerate Native women? Does the evidence suggest that Native women were overincarcerated compared to other women?

2. According to the author, "most Native families and communities failed to see drinking as a crime, and they also had difficulty understanding why incarceration was the punishment." What other problems were unique in the way reserves were policed? What impact did this have on the overinvolvement of Native women with the criminal justice system?

3. What role did the Native community play in the incarceration of their wives, daughters, and mothers? How did they sometimes use the criminal justice system to address problems on the reserve?

Chapter 16: Creating "Slaves of Satan" or "New Canadians"? The Law, Education, and the Socialization of Doukhobor Children, 1911–1935, *John McLaren*

1. From the government's perspective, what was the primary threat? According to the Doukhobors, what was the major problem?

2. How did the government use education to undermine the Doukhobors, and what impact did this have on communities where there were a large number of Doukhobors? Why did the Doukhobors refuse to send their children to government-run schools?

3. McLaren questions whether the government could have resolved the dilemma in a less confrontational manner, rather than attempting to force the education issue. Why did Victoria appear to be so adamant about the need to educate Doukhobor children, especially given their greater willingness to accommodate Roman Catholics and the establishment of separate schools for Asian students?

Further Readings

. . . .

Pioneer Policing in Southern Alberta: Deane of the Mounties, 1880–1914 by William M. Baker (Calgary: Historical Society of Alberta, 1993).

This book is about Richard Burton Deane, and is a collection of reports written during his years as a Mounted police officer from 1883 to 1914. This was a significant period prior to the establishment of the RCMP and in the opening of the West. Deane was instrumental in supervisory positions in quelling unrest by insurgents, and the portrait drawn here gives an insight into the past. With stories ranging from booze to murder, the book provides revealing insights into social history and administration of justice in pioneer Alberta.

Colour Coded: A Legal History of Racism in Canada, 1900–1950 by Constance Backhouse (Toronto: Osgoode Society for Canadian Legal History, University of Toronto Press, 1999).

The author is a professor of law at the University of Western Ontario, and in this important text, illustrates the effects of White supremacy on the legal system. Using narratives of six court cases involving Aboriginal, Inuit, Chinese-Canadian, and African-Canadian individuals, we are shown the criminal prosecution of traditional Aboriginal dance to the trial of members of the Ku Klux Klan of Canada. These cases appear in a wide range of legal forums, including administrative rulings by municipal councils, trials before police magistrates, criminal and civil cases heard by the highest provincial courts, and by the Supreme Court of Canada.

Out of the Depths: The Experiences of Mi'kmaw Children at the Indian Residential School in Shubenacadie, Nova Scotia by Isabelle Knockwood (with Gillian Thomas) (Lockeport: Roseway, 1992).

This is one of the first books to describe life for Aboriginal children in residential schools in Canada. These residential or mission schools were used for the assimilation of Natives into White customs and language, and are now subject to large lawsuits. Based on personal recollections, this book is a moving read and an important contribution to the growing literature on Native experience.

We Were Not the Savages: A Mi'kmaq Perspective on the Collision between European and Native American Civilizations by Daniel N. Paul (Halifax: Fernwood, 2002).

Written by a Native elder, this book provides shocking information about the confrontations between Amerindian and European civilizations. It documents how a democratic Mi'kmaq people were brought to the edge of extinction, and the abuses suffered under the Canada's Indian Act. The author argues that Native peoples were peaceful, and subsequently suffered under colonization despite treaties designed to protect their rights.

The Courts and the Colonies: The Litigation of Hutterite Church Disputes by Alvin J. Esau (Vancouver: UBC Press, 2004).

Alvin J. Esau is professor in the Faculty of Law at the University of Manitoba. *The Courts and the Colonies* details a dispute within a Hutterite colony in Manitoba when the leaders attempted to force the departure of a group that had been excommunicated. This resulted in about a dozen lawsuits in Canada and the U.S., and placed the issues of shunning, excommunication, legitimacy of leadership, and communal property rights before the secular courts. He looks at the story behind this development, how the courts responded, and conflicts between outside (state) law and the traditional inside law of the Hutterites. Utilizing court records, he shows how what is at stake is the nature of freedom of religion in Canada and the extent to which our pluralistic society will accommodate groups that have a different legal system.

"Enough to Keep Them Alive": Indian Social Welfare in Canada, 1873–1965 by Hugh E.Q. Shewell (Toronto: University of Toronto Press, 2004).

Hugh Q. Shewell is an associate professor in the School of Social Work at York University. Indian welfare policy in Canada was used to marginalize First Nations peoples, and to foster their assimilation into dominant society in conjunction with more formal criminal justice system policies. The author explores the administration of social assistance policies on Indian reserves in Canada, showing how its roots lie in the pre-Confederation practices of fur trading companies. Using archival evidence from the National Archives of Canada supplemented by interviews, the book presents a critical analysis with a clear theoretical focus for looking at the oppression of Aboriginal peoples.

PART IV

Regulating Gender and Sexuality

• •

The criminal justice system is oriented to the regulation of the relations of class, age, ethnicity, gender, and sexuality. In this section we look at how developments in the criminal justice system centre around dominant versions of how men and women should act. The criminal justice system thus reflects and reproduces existing inequalities. Subjects' actions are not passive, and we can find resistance, but, as in the previous section, the power of the state is asymmetrically balanced against the individual.

In the first reading, Valverde recounts the role the social purity movement played in the moral reformation of Canada at the turn of the twentieth century. Alarmed with the depredations they found lurking in the city, a professional class of social workers, in concert with individuals associated with charitable organizations, began to focus on the spiritual and psychological morass they found so prevalent in Canadian society. These included sexual promiscuity, slothfulness, intemperate behaviour, and a general lack of industriousness. The principles of social reform helped to shape the working class, but in more subtle ways also altered the role of the middle class. In their attempts to curb the unchecked passions of the lower class, the bourgeoisie were recast as progenitors of civic pride and virtue.

In the next reading, Sangster's article nicely complements that on criminalizing the colonized in Part III. The Female Refugees Act was, from the point of view of the twenty-first century, a particularly insidious piece of legislation that regulated women's sexuality and controlled their reproduction. Targeted against women who were perceived to have weak morals, it reflected prevailing assumptions about sexual promiscuity and racial inequality. The author offers several examples to illustrate how the FRA's prosecutions and convictions were based on categories of social class, gender, and race. During this period the concern about White women engaging in interracial relationships was on the decline, but the incarceration rates for Native women started to increase. Women could be brought before a magistrate on the basis of a sworn statement, held without charge, and committed to the reformatory without trial. Again, the agents of surveillance were various, from police, parents, psychiatrists, social workers, Children's Aid Society workers, Indian agents, and magistrates.

In the third reading, which uses case files of prosecutions for sexual relations between boys and men in urban Ontario from 1890–1935, Maynard recounts sexual relations between boys and men. The case files present two problems. First, the age of the boys are not always specified. Second, the motivations for prosecution are not always known. Thus, at a time when the very act of homosexuality was subject to criminal prosecution, it is sometimes difficult to distinguish between cases of consensual same-sex relations and coercive attacks between male defendants and working-class male youth. What he shows us, however, is that same-sex encounters involved both coercion and consent, and the willingness of parents and professionals to intervene.

In the fourth reading, author Kelley Hannah-Moffat uses women's imprisonment to theorize the complexity of penal power, and to show how penal reform strategies evolve into complex patterns of governing and how governance is always gendered and racialized.

In the final reading, Kinsman documents the federal government's official policy on homosexuality in the civil service. Classified as a "character weakness," homosexuality was considered a threat to national security, and individuals who were identified as homosexual were subject to dismissal from the civil service. The Royal Canadian Mounted Police were charged with the responsibility of filtering out homosexuals from the civil service. Early attempts resulted in the designation of homosexuals into a number of categories, including alleged, suspected, and confirmed homosexuals. Alleged homosexuals were those who were named as homosexual by an informant or informants who were considered to be reliable. Suspected informants were those who were believed to be homosexual by a source or sources considered reliable by the RCMP. Finally, confirmed homosexuals were individuals who had either admitted to the RCMP that they were homosexual, or who had been convicted in court of a homosexual offence. Attempts at a more scientific classification schema resulted in the development of a mechanism for conclusively identifying individuals as homosexual. However, attempts to "recruit" members of the RCMP to serve as the normal basis against which a proclivity toward homosexuality could be adequately compared proved difficult. Apparently, police volunteers were reluctant to serve as models, lest homosexual tendencies be interpreted in their own responses. In addition, researchers concluded that there was no one type of homosexual; consequently, there could be no single test to determine homosexuality.

CHAPTER 17

Moral Reform in English Canada, 1885–1925: Introduction

Mariana Valverde

● ● ● ● ● ● ● ● ● ● ● ● ● ● ● ● ● ● ● ●

[...] The decades from the 1880s to World War One saw major changes in Canadian society, many of which have had a lasting influence. It can also be claimed with some plausibility that these were in fact transitional decades: in the 1870s Canada was a very sparsely populated, barely post-colonial state where farming and staples production predominated; by the 1920s the Native populations had been firmly marginalized, the weight of the economy had shifted toward industry and finance, and urban living had become the rule rather than the exception. By the 1920s the Canadian state had developed, at least in embryonic form, most of the institutions it has today and in English Canada a certain cultural consensus, based to a large extent on American and British influence but incorporating a new nationalism, had emerged and was being consolidated.

*****

As historians have pointed out, one important aspect of the growth of modern Canada was the development of an urban-industrial working class.[1] The correlate of that was the development of an urban bourgeoisie, certain sectors of which initiated a philanthropic project to reform or "regenerate" Canadian society. [...] The social reform movement of the turn of the century helped to shape the bourgeoisie, which led the

movements, as well as the working class, toward which they were generally aimed. [...]

*****

The economic and cultural developments that form the background to the reform movement analysed here were not unique to Canada. [...] The ideas and practices of class formation that were popular [...] were to a large extent adapted from English and American sources. The development of both unions and employers' associations, the workings of private charity and public relief, and the cultural practices of the various classes were all heavily influenced by the overall fact of Canadian dependence. In some cases, reformers imported certain ideas from abroad without reflecting on the extent to which Canadian realities made these ideas suitable. At other times, however, the uniqueness of Canada was highlighted by patriots who insisted that Toronto or Hamilton most definitely lacked the social evils plaguing Chicago or London.

It is very difficult, if not impossible, to make any general statements about the specificity of Canadian social reform movements; all that can be said is that the well-educated urban English Canadians who led these movements were definitely learning from English and, increasingly, American sources. [...] Canadians then (as now) tended to define themselves not so much positively but by way of a differentiation—from the Mother Country, first, and, in the twentieth century, from the United States. [...] Their self-image as healthy citizens of a new country of prairies and snowy peaks contributed both to twentieth-century nationalist ideas and to the success of the purity movement, one of whose symbols was pure white snow.

As Ramsay Cook has pointed out, at the turn of the century a large number of educated Canadians were interested in reforming their society and their state and building the foundations for what they thought could be a future of prosperity and relative equality. They envisaged this reform not as a series of small isolated measures but as a grand project to "regenerate" both society and the human soul.[2] [...] They called their project "moral reform," usually linked to social concerns in the common phrase "moral and social reform."

To study moral reform at the turn of the century, it is appropriate to focus primarily on the self-styled "social purity movement," which, along with temperance and Sunday observance, helped to constitute a powerful if informal coalition for the moral regeneration of the state, civil society, the family, and the individual. The social purity movement was a loose network of organizations and individuals, mostly church people, educators, doctors, and those we would now describe as community or social workers, who engaged in a sporadic but vigorous campaign to "raise the moral tone" of Canadian society, and in particular of urban working-class communities. In 1895, a Canadian clergyman speaking at an important Purity Congress in Baltimore described "social purity work in Canada" as including the following issues: prostitution, divorce, illegitimacy, "Indians and Chinese," public education, suppression of obscene literature, prevention (of prostitution) and rescue of fallen women, and shelters for women and children.[3] These same issues were addressed from an American perspective by other speakers,[4] who all agreed that purity work was not simply a question of banning obscene

books or suppressing prostitution but was rather a campaign to educate the next generation in the purity ideals fitting to "this age of light and water and soap."[5]

The image of reform as illuminating society while purifying or cleansing it was already an integral part of the temperance movement, which developed in the mid nineteenth century in the U.S. and Britain and was taken up in Canada by such organizations as the Woman's Christian Temperance Union and the Dominion Alliance for the Total Suppression of the Liquor Traffic.[6] Many of the organizations involved in both temperance education and lobbying for prohibition took up social purity work as part of their task. In some respects, temperance and social purity acted as a single movement. However, some people involved in social purity work (notably doctors and lay sex educators) did not necessarily support prohibition—even though they usually advocated voluntary abstinence from alcohol—and undoubtedly there were many prohibitionists who were rather single-minded and did not share some of the concerns grouped under the label of "social purity." It is thus appropriate to undertake the more limited task of describing and analyzing social purity work and ideas, remembering always its close connection to temperance—and to the other great single issue of moral reformers, Sunday observance—but without seeking to assimilate one cause into another.

Social purity was advocated by many of the same people responsible for spreading the "social gospel" in Canada; and since social gospel has been the subject of various studies[7] while social purity has been almost totally ignored by historians, a word about the relation between these two projects is in order. As defined by Allen, Cook, and others, "social gospel" refers to the attempts to humanize and/or Christianize the political economy of urban-industrial capitalism. Its prophets were generally moderately left of centre, but included such mainstream figures as W.L. Mackenzie King, who collaborated with the Presbyterian Board of Social Service and Evangelism in his youth and was influenced by social gospel ideas in his popular 1919 book, *Industry and Humanity*.

There was an overlap in both personnel and ideas between social gospel and social purity, and therefore one can only offer a tentative clarification: while the focus of social gospel activity was the economy and the social relations arising from production, social purity focused on the sexual and moral aspects of social life. Prostitution in all its forms was the only "social problem" guaranteed to unify the diverse constituencies—feminists, right-wing evangelicals, doctors, social reformers—of the social purity coalition; and "sex hygiene," or purity education, was one of the main positive remedies promoted. While sexual concerns were important or even central, one must guard against seeking analytical clarity at the expense of historical accuracy: for many of the people who lived it, social purity was intertwined with socio-economic reform. Thus, the term "social purity movement" will be used sparingly; it would be misleading to imagine it as a distinct movement with its own headquarters and publications, when in fact it was in one sense an aspect of a wider movement that also included critical studies of industrial conditions and other issues not generally regarded as "moral."

Philanthropy and "The Social"

Sexual morality was the main target of the social purity movement, but the purity campaign has to be understood in the context of a larger project to solve the problems of poverty, crime, and vice. This larger project was primarily the task of philanthropy, with state activity often being confined to supplementing private initiatives or acting like a philanthropy.

There are various ways of characterizing philanthropy, and perhaps it is easiest to define it by contrast with what came before, namely charity. Charity, the traditional means of relieving poverty, was largely individual and impulsive, and its purpose was to relieve the immediate need of the recipient while earning virtue points for the giver. Organized charity or philanthropy sought to eliminate both the impulsive and the individual elements of giving. The London philanthropists of the 1860s who pioneered modern methods of philanthropy and social work constantly denounced the "indiscriminate aims-giving" of charity as unscientific and backward.[8] They believed that the problem with charity was not that it was never enough, but, on the contrary, that there was too much of it and that the poor were becoming "pauperized" by dependence on abundant charity. [...]

Philanthropists hence sought to rationalize and often curtail the material aid, focusing instead on training the poor in habits of thrift, punctuality, and hygiene—an economic subjectivity suited to a capitalist society. They also sought to eliminate pity from giving while maximizing rational calculation, so that, for instance, rather than give to old people, who were favoured by traditional charity, there was a new emphasis on children and, indirectly, on women, for with them one was making an investment in the future of the nation.[9]

Another way of contrasting charity and philanthropy is to differentiate poverty—the problem addressed by charity—and pauperism. In England, there was a strict legal definition of pauperism in the Poor Law: however, there was also a broader meaning of the term, indicating a larger social process specific to capitalism and affecting the working class in general, not just legal paupers. The vicar of London's parish of Stepney put it as follows in 1904: "it is not so much poverty that is increasing in the East [end] as pauperism, the want of industry, of thrift or self-reliance."[10] The term "pauperization" indicated a loss of initiative and dignity, not just physical want or legal dependence on the parish. That pauperism was moral as well as economic is evident from the fact that drinking, irregular work habits, sexual laxity, and infrequent bathing were discussed as often if not more often than low wages and poor housing.

If pauperism was more than economic, philanthropy was not merely an economic project to soften the hard edges of industrial capitalism. Its work took place in and largely shaped what Jacques Donzelot has called "the social."[11] Characteristic of this new social philosophy was an unabashed interventionism. In a liberal state, economic policy at least has to try to respect the individual autonomy of capital owners, but social policy is characterized by the opposite movement, i.e., one of expansionism even into the private sphere of family and sexual life. There is no question of letting social forces play themselves out—in modern societies there is no invisible social hand, and so some degree of engineering by visible hands in or out of the state is necessary. David Garland describes the main British social programs of the period under study (social work, eugenics, social security, and criminology) as "extending the power of government over life."[12]

While Donzelot and Garland see "the social" as a distinct realm with fairly clear if shifting boundaries separating it from both politics and economics, I would argue that "the social" is not so much a separate sphere but a new way of conceptualizing any and all problems of the collectivity. Municipal politics and industrial policy, to give two examples, were in our period seen increasingly under the aspect of the social.[13] Industry was seen as needing some form of regulation (maximum hours and minimum wages, for instance) not because of any contradictions within the economic system itself, but rather because extreme exploitation was defined as a *social* problem, involving the creation of paupers, the breakdown of the family, and a general crisis in the cohesion of the social formation.[14] Political questions, from war to immigration, also came to be regarded as more than political. [...] Hence, economics and politics were increasingly socialized, while social problems were persistently seen as "moral" even by modern scientific experts outside of the social purity movement.

The term "social" was usually an adjective, and the relevant noun that came to mind most readily was "problem." In the 1820s and 1830s, both French and English sources had used the term "the social question"; after mid-century,

however, "the social" became fragmented into a multitude of "problems," among other reasons because the growth of specialized professions encouraged a fragmentation of jurisdictions within the social. Whether unitary or fragmented, however, the social domain was born problematic, as Donzelot's study indicates; and throughout the nineteenth century and into the first two decades of the twentieth, the answers to social problems were usually elaborated in the idiom of philanthropy. It thus followed that the first task of philanthropy was to enumerate and study, i.e., to know, "the social." [...] The work of knowing the poor became a great deal more than a means to the end of remedying poverty: it became a science for its own sake—social science, a term that in the late nineteenth century included the present-day fields of sociology and social work.[15] This thirst for knowledge led social researchers to leave the library and enter into the neighbourhoods and homes of the poor (home visiting was a central practice in nineteenth-century philanthropy). This investigation began with the kitchens, clothes, and cupboards of the poor, but it did not end there: the prying gaze of philanthropy sought to penetrate the innermost selves of the poor, including their sexual desires, which were uniformly conceptualized as vices (incest, illegitimacy, prostitution).

Sexual desire was probed not only from the standpoint of morality but also from the standpoint, and in the context, of the new field of public health. Unlike other health matters, however, sex was difficult to quantify. This was a great disappointment to reformers like English public health pioneer James Kay, who said: "Criminal acts may be statistically classed ... but the number of those affected with the moral leprosy of vice cannot be exhibited with mathematical precision. Sensuality has no record."[16] [...] An important wing of the purity movement devoted itself to the production of books, pamphlets, and lectures with which people could probe both their own and other people's sexual habits in order to remoralize the individual and the nation. The title of what was probably the most popular sex education book in turn-of-the-century Canada, *Light on Dark Corners: Searchlight on Health*,[17] captures the distinctive emphasis on probing and rooting out vice with the powerful light of quasi-medical knowledge.

Although there was general agreement on the need to study the poor, preferably in their own homes, there were endless arguments (especially in Britain) about whether the state or the private sector should be the main organizer of philanthropy. Amidst these debates, the status of philanthropy (whether private of public) as the main answer to the problem of the social was not questioned until the development of professional social work and systems of state welfare in the 1920s and 1930s—and even then, the legacy of philanthropy weighed so heavily on the new systems of relief that one could, with some justice, claim that philanthropy merely disguised itself as state-funded welfare and social work.[18]

*****

Nation, State, and Morality

*****

[…] Organizations [such] as the Lord's Day Alliance, were primarily concerned with preventing certain activities on Sundays, and it was only with the passage of time that reformers began to be more concerned about providing "suitable" Sunday activities such as picnics, supervised playgrounds for children, discussion groups for young people, and other activities classified as "rational recreation" (as opposed to commercialized amusements). […] The Lord's Day Alliance, and even the temperance movement, did not intend simply to stamp out one or more vices. They had a larger vision of how people ought to pass their time, how they ought to act, speak, think, and even feel. This vision—which I will here call "positive" not because it was necessarily good but to distinguish it from negativity, from mere prohibition—was often kept in the background

as they pursued their efforts to prevent or negate evil, but it was always present and it became increasingly prominent after the turn of the century.

*****

Pure foods and drinks, most commonly embodied in milk and water, were simultaneously physically and symbolically pure. Pure milk—white like the ribbons worn by the WCTU women—and clean, clear water represented moral health, truth, and beauty, in contrast not only to alcohol but to the deceitful adulterated milk and impure water of the unsanitary cities.[19] The whiteness of milk was also sometimes linked to the snow central to Canadian mythology: Havergal principal Ellen Knox typically told her schoolgirls that Canada had "a glistening line of the future, pure and free as her own ice-clad peaks of the Rockies."[20] The combination of whiteness and coldness made snow an appropriate symbol not only of Canada but also of purity.

If even the self-described prohibition movement (which nevertheless preferred the less negative name "temperance") is at least partially an example of what theorists since Foucault are calling "the positivity of power," the social purity movement must also be interpreted as a great deal more than simply a campaign against prostitution, immoral amusements, and other public manifestations of vice. Social purity was a campaign to regulate morality, in particular sexual morality, in order to preserve and enhance a certain type of human life. It was not merely a campaign to punish and repress. […]

The Great War caused a quantum leap in the concern about conserving human life. As Toronto's public health chief, Dr. Charles Hastings, put it in October of 1914,

National Conservation Commissions that have been engaged in the conservation of natural resources, such as forests, fisheries, mines etc., have in recent years embraced the conservation of human life and human efficiency.[21]

But as Hastings himself notes, even before the Great War caused a tangible crisis in human resources, men and women engage[d] in "nation-building" had stressed the need to conserve, preserve, and shape human life: to conserve its physical health, to preserve its moral purity, and to shape it according to the optimistic vision shared by all political parties of what Canada would be in the twentieth century. [...]

This is not to say [...] that the social purity movement was a stooge or puppet of the state; on the contrary, the various levels of government often lagged behind the initiatives of churches and professional groups. Dangerous as it always is to assume that the state is the only real agent of history, in the case of Canada at the turn of the century it would be ludicrous to assume that politicians or civil servants conspired to manipulate the powerful voluntary organizations. [...] State officials and agencies did often work with or fund private agencies, and the phenomenon of co-optation was not unknown. One cannot assume, however, that the state was—or is at present—always the dominant partner. Indeed, there are very good reasons why liberal-democratic states, far from desiring to absorb all social policy activity, have a vested interest in fostering non-state organizations that will co-operate in certain aspects of social policy, particularly in areas such as regulating morality and gender and family relations. Except in situations such as war or internal rebellion, explicitly moral campaigns are difficult for liberal democratic states to undertake with any degree of success, since such states portray themselves as neutral arbiters of opinions circulating in civil society. Such states also have a structural commitment to non-interference in private beliefs and activities of a moral and/or cultural nature. It is far easier for the state to respond to popular outcries than it is to orchestrate such a campaign on its own—although the Canadian state at its various levels has been known to sow the seeds of popular panics in order to then cast itself in the apparently neutral role of responding to popular demands.[22]

Another related reason why the state was not, and in fact could not have been, the main protagonist in the social purity campaign is that social purity was only partially concerned with restricting behaviour. States may have a monopoly over the legitimate use of force and may therefore be in a privileged position to enforce rules about behaviour, but the state can only make its citizens *internalize* certain values if it has the full and active co-operation of the family and of voluntary organizations.[23] [...] Many voluntary organizations were far more concerned about nation-building and even about strengthening the state than the state itself; they often chastised it for not exercising enough power, particularly in the areas of social welfare, health, and immigration.

[...] By the 1880s both the federal and provincial states seem to have acquired an almost unshakeable legitimacy in the eyes of the educated Anglophone middle classes. Municipal government was often denounced as corrupt, but the higher levels were remarkably free from criticism, and even as citizens agitated for changes in the personnel of the state, the structures themselves went largely unquestioned.

One reason for this trust is that civil society was very sharply divided: the Methodists would far rather see the state take control of education than risk giving more power to their Catholic rivals, and mainstream Protestants preferred to have the provinces take over social work rather than see the Salvation Army flourish. Ethnic, religious, and class divisions were highly visible and conflictive, and in the face of this obvious disunity the state had little difficulty in portraying itself as neutral.

Furthermore, Canadian state formation (with the important exception of Quebec) has as one of its ideological pillars the establishment of Protestantism as a kind of joint-stock state religion. Bruce Curtis's perceptive analysis of the successful construction of a sense of citizenship suffused with Protestantism through Rev. Egerton Ryerson's 1840s reforms helps to explain why churches and other quasi-evangelical bodies regarded the state as a friend rather than a competitor.[24]

*****

The building of a nation was rightly equated with the organization of assent, not just outward conformity to legal and administrative rules. This is one reason why the outright punishment of political or moral deviants came to be seen as a last resort and as an admission of failure. David Garland points out that the turn of the century witnessed a marked decline of eye-for-eye discourses on crime and their replacement by therapeutic and reformatory strategies.[25] While the criminal, the fallen, and the destitute were being increasingly seen as subjects of treatment through the medicalization of crime, sexuality, and poverty,[26] non-criminal populations and in particular youth were being seen as requiring a process of character-building, the individual equivalent of the nation-building just cited. [...]

*****

That the relentless scouring of the soul and shaping of individual character would have an immediate impact on public and national affairs, nobody doubted. The housecleaning metaphors utilized by maternal feminists such as Nellie McClung did not only seek to legitimize women's entry into the public sphere by comparing politics to a house in need of spring cleaning; they also established a parallel between what was known as "political purity" and personal hygiene. Physical and sexual hygiene—which were to a large extent in women's sphere—were the microcosmic foundation of the larger project of building a "clean" nation. [...]

*****

On his part, MP John Charlton, who in the 1880s and 1890s spearheaded many efforts to raise the age of consent, criminalize seduction, and promote sexual purity, introduced one of his many legislative efforts as follows: "No

vice will more speedily sap the foundations of public morality and of national strength than licentiousness ....[27]

*****

[...] The specific sexual activities targeted for control changed over the years: in the mid nineteenth century, masturbation, especially among boys, was the most talked about vice, while at the turn of the century prostitution would take the spotlight, to be replaced in the 1920s by fears about non-commoditized consensual sexual encounters among young people. But regardless of the specific sexual activity targeted, the loss of individual self-control over sexuality was perceived to have far-reaching consequences *even if nobody ever knew about it.* Again, it was not so much a matter of outward behaviour but a question of inner identity, of the subjectivity of citizens.

[...] The attempt to make young boys and girls learn self-control and develop character involved very specific ideas about the use to which such highly controlled units ought to be put, and about the class, gender, and racial composition of the nation being built.

The class basis of social purity is not a simplistic matter of middle-class reformers imposing their values on working-class communities. [...]

The doctors, clergymen, and women employers of servants did not [...] expect immigrants and prostitutes to live and think exactly like upper-class Anglo-Saxon Canadians. They did want both immigrants and social deviants to embrace the culture and values of Anglo-Saxon, Protestant, middle-class urban Canadians, but this was to ensure that the power of the WASP bourgeoisie would appear as legitimate. [...] Both social purity and philanthropy sought to establish a non-antagonistic capitalist class structure, not to erase class differences.[28]

The gender organization of social purity is also a complex question that cannot be summarized by saying the movement was male-dominated. The movement sought to reform and organize gender, not merely utilize it. This gender reform meant that some women were given the possibility of acquiring a relatively powerful identity as rescuers, reformers, and even experts, while other women were reduced to being objects of philanthropic concern. Men were equally divided by the social construction of masculinity of the social purity movement: if many men, particularly "foreigners," were seen as the epitome of impurity, other men were provided with a potential new identity as reformed, moralized, and domesticated males.

Women were often marginalized, especially in church organizations (expecting perhaps the Salvation Army). The vision of Canadian womanhood promoted by the movement was one stressing maternal selflessness and passive purity, a vision clearly reinforcing patriarchal privilege.[29] Nevertheless, large numbers of women were active in this movement, and they cannot be dismissed by seeing them as victims of false consciousness. The "search for sexual order"[30] central to the movement was seen by women to be in the women's best interests: males were viewed as the main culprits in sexual disorder (although some women blamed fallen women's wiles). Hence the protection of women against male harassment, sexual violence, and everyday disrespect was a legitimate feminist goal. Furthermore, the movement's upholding of a single standard of sexual morality ("the white life for two") did give a voice to married women's protest against philandering husbands.

The great paradox about femininity formation in/through moral reform campaigns was that certain middle-class women made careers out of studying "the problem" of the immigrant woman or the urban girl. These women doctors, social workers, deaconesses, and Salvation Army officers travelled freely around the city, protected by their uniform and their profession, and perhaps did not realize that their unprecedented freedom was built on the prior assumption that ordinary women were helpless objects in need of study and reform. The pure woman did not gain her purity exclusively through silence, chastity, and seclusion: she was partially public.

*****

Ann Douglas's insightful study of changes in American Protestantism in the nineteenth century traces the development of a sentimental Christianity in the 1830s and 1840s that softened and feminized the face of Protestantism. Harsh Calvinist theology was displaced by an alliance between sentimental women writers (Harriet Beecher Stowe is only the best known of these) and ministers who, after church disestablishment, had to win over influential ladies to maintain their position. In the Gilded Age, mid-Victorian sentimentality began to be in turn displaced by what was known as "muscular" Christianity, a new perspective connected to social Darwinism. The scientific/ muscular perspectives of the 1890s, however, supplemented rather than replaced the feminized religion constructed decades earlier.[31]

*****

[…] As nurturing and other domestic virtues increased in value, allowing women to serve in public roles through maternal feminism, social purity helped to reconcile the apparently passive virtue of purity with active masculinity. An effort was made by a section of the urban middle class to redefine masculinity as well as femininity as actively domestic. The challenge was to purge the new male bourgeoisie of the drinking and wenching habits of the aristocracy, while avoiding effete or ascetic disengagement from the claims of masculinity.

*****

[…] Purity was not simply the absence of lust: it was an active, aggressive process of self-mastery that could be likened to a military campaign. It was furthermore connected to the unambiguously masculine pursuit of worldly success. Sylvanus Stall explained that purity was good not only for one's family but for one's business: he admits that some irreligious men are wealthy, but on the whole, pure thoughts are positively correlated with large bank accounts. Walking through the better part of any town, is it not obvious, he asks, that "the wealth of the nation" is "largely in the hands of Christian men and Christian women? These are the people who have the best credit, who can draw checks for the largest amounts."[32] The Canadian Salvation Army often published stories about former male drunkards who, once saved from drink and sin, were able to impress bank managers enough to obtain loans with their new-found "character" as security.

Despite the obvious exaggeration in these stories, there was a grain of truth in the suggestion that male purity might reinforce the capitalist ethic, even in its apparently impure social Darwinist variety (as Paul Johnson's study of the differential fortunes of saved and non-saved male citizens of Rochester shows).[33] The discourse about the new reconstituted family, with a partially public mother and a partially domesticated father, was thus a discourse about class as much as about gender.

Finally, social purity had a clear racial and ethnic organization. The "whiteness" favoured by the movement was not merely spiritual but also designated (consciously or unconsciously) a skin colour. The racist fears about "the yellow peril" and about Anglo-Saxons being overrun by more fertile "races" (as they designated what are now called ethnic groups) pervaded Canadian politics and society throughout the period under study. [...] The specific contribution of the social purity movement to this general climate of racism is what needs to be highlighted here. This can be summarized by stating that the darker and hence lower races were assumed to be not in control of their sexual desires.[34] Lacking proper Christian and Anglo-Saxon training, they had not produced the right kind of self. "Racial

purity" is a phrase that appears but seldom in the tests studied, but the concept underlies common phrases such as "national purity" or "national health." Moral reformers had a significant impact on immigration policies, both directly by lobbying for such innovations as the medical/moral inspection of all immigrants and indirectly by creating a climate of opinion in which certain groups were perceived as morally undesirable. [...]

To conclude, then, the social purity movement was indeed concerned about urban vices, but its real aim was not so much to suppress as to re-create and re-moralize not only deviants from its norms but, increasingly, the population of Canada as a whole. This was a project the state could not possibly have carried out; voluntary organizations played a starring role in the campaign to reconstruct the inner selves, and in particular the sexual/moral identity, of Canadians. This movement is by no means explained by being labelled as an agency of social control or a Puritan effort at censorship and repression: the movement was held together not only by its attacks on vice but by a common vision of the pure life that individuals, families, and the nation would lead in the near future. Therefore, despite the obviously repressive features of this movement, it is more appropriate to see its coercion as regulation and not as suppression or censorship: the term "regulation," which connotes preserving and shaping something and not merely suppressing it, more adequately captures the aims and the modes of operation of this movement.[35]

Notes

1. G. Kealey, *Toronto Workers Respond to Industrial Capitalism* (Toronto, 1980); G. Kealey and B. Palmer, *Dreaming of What Might Be: The Knights of Labor in Ontario 1880–1900* (Toronto, 1987); B. Palmer, ed., *The Character of Class Struggle* (Toronto, 1986); Michael Piva, *The Condition of the Working Class in Toronto* (Ottawa, 1979).

2. Ramsay Cook, *The Regenerators: Social Criticism in Late Victorian English Canada* (Toronto, 1985).

3. Rev. C.W. Watch, "Social Purity Work in Canada," in A. Powell, ed., *National Purity Congress* (Baltimore, 1895), pp. 272–77.

4. These included Dr. Elizabeth Blackwell, Anthony Comstock, and Frances Willard (president of the U.S. Woman's Christian Temperance Union and one of the foremost reformers of her time).

5. Rev. Flint, in Powell, ed., *National Purity Congress*, p. 140.

6. See, for instance F.S. Spence, *The Facts of the Case: A Summary of the Most Important Evidence and Argument Presented in the Report of the Royal Commission on the Liquor Traffic* (Toronto, 1896). Spence claims that the first temperance convention in Canada was held in Halifax in 1834, but the movement only began in earnest in the late 1870s, and the Dominion WCTU was not founded until 1885.

7. The main source is Richard Allen, *The Social Passion: Religion and Social Reform in Canada 1914–1928* (Toronto, 1971). See also Dennis Guest, *The Emergence of Social Security in Canada* (Vancouver, 1985), pp. 31–34; Cook, *The Regenerators*, ch. 7.

8. See Gareth Stedman Jones, *Outcast London* (London, 1971), esp. pp. 244ff. See also Christine Stansell, *City of Women: Sex and Class in New York City 1789–1860* (New York, 1986), ch. 4; and C. Smith-Rosenberg, *Religion and the Rise of the American City: The New York City Mission Movement 1812–1870* (Ithaca, NY., 1971).

9. Jacques Donzelot summarizes this shift as follows: "In general, philanthropy differed from charity in the choice of its objects, based on this concern for pragmatism: advice instead of gifts, because it cost nothing; assistance to children rather than to old people, and to women rather than to men." *The Policing of Families* (New York, 1979), p. 66. Donzelot's analysis, based on the work of Foucault, has had a strong influence on many current analyses of nineteenth-century philanthropy.

10. Quoted in Stedman Jones, *Outcast London*, p. 244. See also Mariana Valverde, "French Romantic Socialism and the Critique of Political Economy" (Ph.D. thesis, York University, 1982), esp. ch. II, "The Debate on Misery and the Critique of Political Economy."

11. See Donzelot, *The Policing of Families*, for a lengthy analysis of the constitution of the social.

12. David Garland, *Punishment and Welfare: A History of Penal Strategies* (London, 1985), p. 153.

13. A well-known Canadian example of the treatment of economic questions as social questions is W.L. Mackenzie King, *Industry and Humanity* (1919). See also J.S. Woodsworth, *My Neighbor: A Study of City Conditions, A Plea for Social Service* (1911; reprinted 1972).

14. Donzelot, *The Policing of Families*, argues that poverty, the family, and population are the main three "problems" that made up the social in the early nineteenth century.

15. Bryan S. Green, *Knowing the Poor: A Case-Study in Textual Reality Construction* (London, 1983).

16. James Kay, *The Moral and Physical Condition of the Working Classes* (1832), quoted in Frank Mort, *Dangerous Sexualities: Medico-Moral Politics in England Since 1830* (London, 1987), p. 22.

17. B.G. Jefferis and J.L. Nichols, *Light in Dark Corners: Searchlight on Health* (Naperville, Ill., various editions from 1880s on). The 1922 edition was given the more modern title of *Safe Counsel or Practical Eugenics*.

18. Dennis Guest, in *The Emergence of Social Security in Canada* (Vancouver, 1985 [2nd ed.]), has a liberal framework that presupposes that whenever state benefits were organized on a philanthropic basis, this was either a mistake or a leftover of the past. The essays in A. Moscovitch and J. Alpert's edited collection *The "Benevolent" State*, however, demonstrate that many of the great new programs of the welfare state, such as mothers' allowances, were introduced for what one could only call philanthropic reasons such as concern for the eugenic future of the Canadian "race."

19. On the campaigns to clean up the city's water supply and ensure safe milk, see Paul A. Bator, "Saving Lives on the Wholesale Plan: Public Health Reform in the City of Toronto, 1900–1930" (Ph.D. thesis, University of Toronto, 1979). The protagonist of Bator's thesis, Dr. Charles Hastings, believed in the moralizing effects of pure milk and water.

20. E.M. Knox, *The Girl of the New Day* (Toronto, 1919), p. 5.

21. CTA, RG-11, Box 167, Monthly Report of the Medical Officer of Health for October 1914, p. 235.

22. For an elaboration of this argument, see M. Valverde and L. Weir, "The Struggles of the Immoral: More Preliminary Remarks on Moral Regulation," *Resources for Feminist Research*, 17, 3 (September, 1988), pp. 31–34.

23. This point is made, from a somewhat different perspective, in an important article by Nikolas Rose, "Beyond the Public/Private Division: Law, Power and the Family," *Journal of Law and Society*, 14, 1 (Spring, 1987), pp. 61–75. In Philip Corrigan and Derek Sayer, *The Great Arch: English State Formation as Cultural Revolution* (Oxford, 1985), the role of the state in moral regulation is highlighted, and their theorization has been influential here, but the agencies of regulation internal to civil society are obscured.

24. Bruce Curtis, "Preconditions of the Canadian State: Educational Reform and Construction of a Public in Upper Canada, 1837–1846," in A. Moscovitch and J. Alpert, eds., *The "Benevolent" State*

(Toronto, 1987), pp. 47–67. Curtis's insistence that educational reform was not merely social control or suppression of the working classes parallels the claim made above that social purity was more geared to moulding the subjectivity of citizens than simply controlling their behaviour. If the public education system was assigned the task of creating rationality and political subjectivity, the social purity movement sought to create an ethical/moral subjectivity.

25. David Garland, *Punishment and Welfare: A History of Penal Strategies* (London, 1985). Garland links "modern" penal strategies centred on treatment to social work and eugenics in an analysis that is extremely relevant to social purity even though he neglects to analyse the modernization of sexual and gender regulation. He also stresses that the liberal state, though obviously in charge of the prison system, had to leave the moral reformation of prisoners in the hands of private agencies such as the John Howard and Elizabeth Fry Societies and the Salvation Army.

26. On the medicalization of poverty in nineteenth-century philanthropy, see Christine Stansell, *City of Women: Sex and Class in New York 1789–1860* (New York, 1986); this idea is explored in Mariana Valverde, review-essay on Stansell's book, *Labour/ Le Travail*, 22 (Fall, 1988), pp. 247–57. On the medicalization of crime, see Garland, *Punishment and Welfare*, and Michel Foucault, *Discipline and Punish* (New York, 1979). For the medicalization of sexuality, see Lorna Weir, "Sexual Rule, Sexual Politics: Studies in the Medicalization of Sexual Danger 1820–1920" (Ph.D. thesis, York University, 1986); Frank Mort, *Dangerous Sexualities: Medico-Moral Politics in England Since 1830* (London, 1987).

27. John Charlton, MP, April 10, 1899, quoted in T. Chapman, "Sex Crimes in Western Canada 1890–1920" (Ph.D. thesis, University of Alberta, 1984), p. 44.

28. The American feminist, urban reformer, and social theorist Jane Addams did seek to homogenize American urban society through cultural means, but even she, who was more radical in class, gender, and racial terms than the leading social

purity activists in Canada, did not envision abolishing the economic basis of bourgeois class formation.

29. The goals of the social purity in terms of gender organization are captured in the statement made by the Methodist Board of Temperance and Social Reform in the context of the white slavery panic; the clergymen vowed not to cease in their struggle against white slavery until "[we can] restore the victim to her home and to a life of honor, purity, and helpfulness." UCA, Methodist DESS, Annual Report, 1911, p. 33.

30. Carolyn Strange, "The Toronto Social Survey Commission of 1915 and the Search for Sexual Order in the City," in Roger Hall et al., eds., *Patterns of the Past: Interpreting Ontario's History* (Toronto, 1988).

31. Ann Douglas, *The Feminization of American Culture* (New York, 1977). See also Carroll Smith-Rosenberg, *Religion and the Rise of the American City* (Ithaca, N.Y., 1971); Paul Johnson, *Shopkeepers' Millennium: Society and Revivals in Rochester, N.Y., 1815–1837* (New York, 1978); Nancy Hewitt, *Women's Activism and Social Change: Rochester, N.Y., 1822–1872* (Ithaca, N.Y., 1984); Mary P. Ryan, *Cradle of the Middle Class* (London, 1981).

32. Sylvanus Stall, *What a Young Husband Ought to Know* (Philadelphia, 1907 [1988]), pp. 68–71.

33. Johnson, *Shopkeepers' Millennium*, shows that men who were born again in the revivals of the 1830s and 1840s fared quite a bit better in business than their unconverted counterparts, partly because of the formal and informal credit and business links forged among members of the same congregation.

34. See Sander Gilman, *Difference and Pathology: Stereotypes of Race, Sexuality, and Madness* (Ithaca, N.Y., 1985).

35. I have adopted the term "moral regulation" from Philip Corrigan and Derek Sayer, *The Great Arch: English State Formation as Cultural Revolution* (Oxford, 1985). However, they do not differentiate between moral and other modes of social regulation; by contrast, I restrict the term to mean the formation of *ethical* subjectivity.

CHAPTER 18

Defining Sexual Promiscuity: "Race," Gender, and Class in the Operation of Ontario's Female Refuges Act, 1930–1960

Joan Sangster

• •

In 1942 an 18-year-old dishwasher, Anna, from Kenora, was put on a train to Toronto by the police to be transported to the Andrew Mercer Reformatory for Females for a period of one to two years. Removal from this northern community came after charges had been laid against her under the Female Refuges Act (FRA) because of her "idle and dissolute" life. Drunkenness and sexual promiscuity were supposedly the crimes that led to her incarceration. After receiving complaints that she was wandering the streets intoxicated, the local police had followed her from cafe to hotel to boarding house, at first removing her to the police station when she became ill after drinking, later collecting information on her liaisons with various men (Archives of Ontario [AO], 9332).

Like other young women, Anna was the focus of legal regulation under the FRA because her public alcohol consumption and sexual behaviour offended "community standards" and, in the view of police and court authorities, required drastic alteration. Yet, Anna's trial before a magistrate also took on a distinct character because she was of Native origin. The police chief claimed that she "had been seen in cafes with white boys ... coming in and out ... going into men's rooms .... [and that] she was a regular at the train station with white boys" (AO,

9332). His racial designation of her partners was significant: miscegenation implied her sexual debasement and was intended to spur the court into offering her "protection" (in the form of incarceration) from White men likely to take advantage of her. Also, one of those testifying against Anna was the local Indian agent, whose immense power of surveillance provided the court with ample information to be used against her. The agent testified that he had already charged her three times with liquor offences under the Indian Act, and he complained that she had been "fined and warned," to no avail (AO, 9332). He also claimed that a doctor had informed him of Anna's pregnancy, and on the stand he offered information on her family and background, which helped to persuade the magistrate to convict her. Hearing that Anna had been in an Anglican residential school confirmed the magistrate's view that she was incorrigible and in need of incarceration. "You went to Indian school for ten years," he said to her, "so you should know right from wrong" (AO, 9332). Anna's one-word answer in the affirmative probably had little effect on the magistrate, who sentenced her to an indefinite term in the Reformatory.

Anna's case also bears some strong similarities to those of other young women, from all racial and ethnic backgrounds, who were convicted under the FRA. Most of these women came from impoverished or working-class backgrounds and were perceived to be part of an "underclass" with weak or non-existent sexual morality and in dire need of character transformation and social (and reproductive) control. At first glance, masculinist definitions appear to be the defining character of all the FRA convictions. This law proscribed women's sexuality within a gender order based on hegemonic masculinity, the rejection of women's sexual activity outside of marriage, and the sanctification of the nuclear, father-headed family. However, the law was also applied in a class-specific manner. Women's material impoverishment always encouraged the likelihood of their arrest and was intertwined with expert discourses on what constituted "dissolute" sexual behaviour. Psychiatric and social work definitions of "sex delinquency," throughout this period, for example, were usually fused with images of working-class and poor women, and the criteria used by penal workers to assess women's rehabilitation were permeated with class biases. As Michel Foucault (1980:121) argued, sexual control is often most "intense and meticulous when it is directed at the lower classes."

While class and gender were crucial elements shaping the use of the FRA, race, too, was important. Indeed, the "simultaneity" of these factors in shaping women's experience of sexual regulation through the law should be the focus of our inquiry (Brewer, 1993; Roediger, 1993). As many Black feminists have argued, interrogating these categories alone may be unproductive, but in interplay, and in historical motion, the "paradigm becomes richer" (Brewer, 1993:27; see also Bannerji, 1993, 1995; Agnew, 1996). At the same time, capturing the complexity of "interlocking systems of domination" and the ways in which they "constitute each other," Sharene Razack (1998) has argued, remains an extremely difficult task. Some systems of domination may remain less visible, and ironically, our very use of a "language of colour" contradicts our attempts to deconstruct race.[1]

While the vast majority of women convicted under this particular draconian statute were White, and often of Anglo-Celtic origin, the legal and social understandings of "promiscuity"—so central to the FRA—were racialized, reflecting a dominant ideological construction of women (and men) of colour as licentious and weak in moral conviction, and, in contrast, White women as more moral and sexually pure.[2] It is the intention of this paper to outline, using two examples relating to the FRA, how the legal regulation of women's sexuality through this law was racialized and racist. On the one hand, convictions of White women who were sexually involved with Asian, Afro-Canadian, and Native men indicated fears that these women were especially debased and in need of carceral supervision because they had violated an important colour line. On the other hand, the increasing numbers of First Nations women convicted under the FRA, and the rationale for their incarceration, indicate that colonialism and racism made Native women more sexually suspect in the eyes of the law and more liable to legal prosecution.

As historians and legal scholars have repeatedly documented (for example, Backhouse, 1999; Tarnopolsky, 1982; Walker, 1997), Canadian law, through public policy, statute law, and judicial interpretation, played a significant role in constituting and reproducing racist ideologies, sanctioning discrimination, exclusion, and segregation based on race. Racial differentiation might be openly stated in legal statute, but also unfolds as the effect of legal and judicial practices, in laws and policy relating to everything from the franchise to employment to recreation to morality to immigration. Because the law both constitutes society and reproduces prevailing cultural assumptions, "common sense" notions of race were firmly embedded in the operation of Canadian law from colonial times through the twentieth century.[3] Although ideological constructions of race did alter over time, a persisting theme in legal discourse and practice was the assumption of White superiority and imperialist right.

Attempting to uncover the racial meanings created by law, and the power relations they reflect and reproduce, has been a central aim of critical race theory. A fundamental premise of this theory is that "race is socially constructed, and the law is central to that construction" (Haney Lopez, 1996:9). Racial meaning systems are grounded in both "the world of ideas and in the material geography of social life" (17) and they are sustained by both subtle ideological consent—clothed in rationales ranging from "necessity" to "protection," to "fairness"—as well as by repressive coercion.[4] The construction of race is also interconnected with class, gender, and sexuality (Anthias, 1990; Anthias and Yuval-Davis, 1992; Raczack, 1998). In the latter case, for instance, many Canadian laws ostensibly about employment (such as those barring White women from working for Chinese men) emerged because of fears of the sexual corruption of White women by Asian men.[5] Similarly, though the letter of the FRA statute never mentioned race, it was one factor shaping how the law was implemented, and in the process it, too, "created" race and racism.

What Was the Female Refuges Act?

The Female Refuges Act was enacted in 1897 to regulate the Industrial Houses of Refuge, which held women sentenced or "liable to be sentenced" by magistrates under local bylaw or Criminal Code infractions.[6] Specifically aimed at women between the ages of 16 and 35, presumably because these were women's more active sexual and reproductive years, the FRA designated refuges or correctional institutions as places where women were offered shelter, work, and reform as a means of counteracting their "unmanageability and incorrigibility." The initial FRA allowed a sentence of up to five years; this was amended to two years less a day in 1919, following a coroner's inquest into an inmate's death, after she tried to escape by jumping from a window of Toronto's Belmont Refuge (*Globe and Mail,* 12 April 1919).

In 1919, the Act was also broadened with a clause giving magistrates and judges new

wide-ranging powers. Any person could bring before a magistrate "any female under the age of 35 ... who is a habitual drunkard or by reasons of other vices is leading an idle and dissolute life." All that was needed was a sworn statement about the woman's behaviour, or in the case of parents and guardians, a claim that their daughter was "unmanageable and incorrigible."[7] No formal charge and trial were needed, and hearings were in private, although written evidence was supposedly required. Faced with criticisms about the Act, a 1942 amendment allowed sentences to be appealed before the Court of Appeal—though this appears to have been seldom used. In 1958, these sections were finally deleted after persistent lobbying of the government by the Elizabeth Fry Society, though in public, the government simply claimed that the issues involved were adequately covered by other Criminal Code and provincial statutes (Ontario Legislative Assembly Debates, March 1958).

The FRA allowed parents, police, welfare authorities, and the Children's Aid Society (CAS) to incarcerate women perceived to be out of sexual control. Although some women were also targeted when they were destitute, alcoholic, or had resorted to petty theft, the Act was used primarily to police women's sexual behaviour. For teenage girls already serving time in industrial or, later, training schools, the Act could increase their punishment by sending them to the Mercer Reformatory for up to two more years. Indeed, rather than sending convicted women to "low security" refuges where the indigent also lived, such as Belmont House or the Catholic Good Shepherd, some magistrates sent women straight to the Mercer Reformatory.

Although the total number of women convicted under the Act was small in comparison to other charges, such as public order and petty theft, the operation of the FRA provides important insight into the dominant definitions of sexual "promiscuity," or non-conformity, employed by the courts, social workers, and the medical profession at this time. These definitions not only punished "bad" girls, but were part of a broader web of moral regulation, setting out the ideal of "good" feminine sexuality against which all women, even those untouched by the criminal justice system, were judged.

The peak of FRA prosecutions came during the 1930s and World War II, though Native women increased as a percentage of the overall convictions in the post-World War II period.[8] Youth was the most distinguishing feature of all the women involved; indeed, the vast majority of those convicted were under 21. Most were Canadian-born and of Anglo-Celtic background, including first-generation British immigrants, though the presence of the latter group was not surprising given the influx of such immigrants to Ontario just before World War I and the tendency of immigrants to face economic and social dislocation.[9] Almost all the women came from either working-class or poverty-stricken backgrounds, with parents crossing the spectrum from the criminal classes to the skilled artisan. These young women usually had little education, having left school by 15, and their occupations, if they had one (and they often did not), were listed as domestic or, less often, waitress or factory worker.

The vast majority of FRA incarcerations resulted from three, often intertwined, factors: sexual promiscuity (termed here, non-conformity), illegitimate pregnancies, and venereal disease. Some of the women incarcerated were simply destitute runaways or street women, but for the overwhelming majority, dissolute was equated with errant sexuality. For Native women, charges of alcohol abuse and sexual promiscuity were often linked together by the authorities. Many FRA women either had an illegitimate child or were pregnant when they entered the Reformatory, and a significant number were treated for venereal disease. Their sentences were also stiff, as both the Mercer authorities and judges and magistrates claimed women needed a long period of time to effect real change in their character. On average, they received from one to two years, and women did not secure release easily, often serving the majority of their sentences.

Defining Promiscuity: Interracial Liaisons

A number of recurring patterns were evident in FRA convictions. In general, they reflected deep-seated anxieties that poor and working-class women were unruly and oversexual, either led astray or leading men astray. To this end, women who engaged in sexual activity in "public" spaces, did not exhibit the appropriate remorse about their sexual liaisons, or even boasted about them were especially suspect. The sexual activity of young women was threatening to worried parents when daughters disobeyed their parents, stayed out all night, ran away, consorted with "criminal" men and women, or contracted venereal disease. Pregnancy might also be a problem, particularly if the woman did not know the father well, or even who he was. Women with "too many" illegitimate children were a special focus of concern, and even though the files rarely mention sterilization, eugenic concerns undoubtedly percolated beneath the surface of some convictions, especially in the 1930s and early 1940s. Women perceived to have too many partners, or the wrong kind of partner (such as older, married men) were also targeted, though even one man could be one too many if parents objected to someone they felt was a bad influence on their daughter.

The wrong kind of partner was also defined by race.[10] Indeed, the way in which the courts interpreted promiscuity and prostitution rested on racist assumptions about the "instinctual" sexual behaviour of different races and the dangers of miscegenation, even if these were not openly stated. By the 1930s, strictly biological explanations of race, so popular at the turn of the century, were being replaced by theories that claimed both culture and biology created racial difference. Because those differences were also equated with a hierarchy, and a somewhat inevitable one, discrimination against people of colour, as well as Jews, was often condoned in the courts and in society (Walker, 1997).[11] It was not until the aftermath of World War II that a discernible shift in attitude occurred, characterized by increasing antipathy to the concept of racial discrimination, though "cultural racism" remained well entrenched in Canadian society (Razack, 1998).

During the 1930s and the early 1940s, however, interracial sex was seen as unacceptable and dangerous. This was made evident in an appeal before the Ontario upper court in 1930, in which a young woman challenged her two-year sentence for vagrancy handed out by Toronto Magistrate Margaret Patterson. The woman's nighttime socializing with "coloured" and White men and the fact that she lived with a "coloured railway porter" were central in the court's reassessment of the verdict. Debate centred especially on whether she had any "means of subsistence" and whether she was a prostitute. As the judge noted, to confirm the latter, she "has to do with more than one man," yet he could only find evidence of the relationship with the porter. However, the definition of "subsistence" gave the judge the loophole he was searching for: subsistence had to be not just legal, but "reputable," not contradicting "the moral standards of the community." Being supported by a coloured man, he concluded, is "not the kind of subsistence that the Criminal Code" had in mind! One can be excused for concluding that the judge was determined to follow any tortuous "logic" to find a way of upholding Patterson's conviction, based more fundamentally on his aversion to mixed-race couples than anything else (*Rex v. Davis*, 1930).

If the higher court was happy to set such standards, the lower courts were happy to follow, not only in official judgements but in the more general investigation, interviewing, and counselling of women by probation officers, doctors, and social workers. In another case presided over by Magistrate Margaret Patterson in the 1930s, a 17-year-old, who was described by her foster mother as "boy crazy" and untruthful, was found in a "bawdy house with a Chinaman" (AO, 6972). Patterson immediately remanded her into psychiatric care, a decision that underscored how women's sexual non-conformity was literally equated with their insanity. A young Toronto woman, who was arrested in 1940 on a charge of incorrigibility, was declared mentally slow by the court doctor. The court also heard that she was "not working" and refused to follow her stepfather's rules about a curfew, but her major crime seemed to be that she was living with "a coloured man." Sent first to the Salvation Army hostel, she ran away; when re-arrested, she was sent to the Mercer (AO, 8398).

White police, court workers, and some working-class families perceived men and women of colour, particularly Afro-Canadians, to be more sexually promiscuous, and feared Whites would become tainted or seduced by these lax morals; in cases involving Chinese men, fears also centred on their supposed roles as pimps and drug pushers (Murphy, 1923; Pon, 1996). It was often parents who called the police concerning their daughters' interracial liaisons, hoping to pressure their daughters into abandoning the relationship. Once the case was in motion, however, incarceration under the FRA became a distinct possibility. One father swore out a statement against his 19-year-old, who had left school at 14 and was employed as a mail clerk. Despite the apparent respectability of her wage labour, he noted she was "keeping bad company ... she is now with a coloured man and pregnant by him." The case was originally brought to the police by a Catholic welfare agency that the girl contacted, hoping for assistance so she could keep her baby. They alerted the police and parents, and urged the woman to give up her baby, facilitating her return home to her parents after her sentence was served (AO, 8700).

Women could also be the focus of legal concern if they were sexually involved with Native men, though this was a less common scenario in large urban centres. One young woman from northern Ontario was incarcerated in the 1940s after her sexual relationship with a Native man became an issue. The court deemed her mother a bad example as she was living common law, but the mother also participated in the complaint against her daughter, who she charged was "running around with an Indian boy and would not get a job." Mabel claimed that her boyfriend "wanted to marry her" but became abusive "and threatened to kill her if she saw anyone else." The magistrate, despite his disbelief in her charges of violence, agreed that Mabel's conduct was satisfactory until she "started seeing a young Indian boy ... We will put this girl in a home. We can't have her running around with Indian boys like that" (AO, 9404).

In responding to their sentences, White women involved with men of colour sometimes claimed they did not understand why they were being punished, but in other cases they clearly understood that they should either profess shame or coercion if they were to escape the Reformatory. One 22-year-old British immigrant nursemaid, Elise, for example, was convicted under the FRA based on police information that she was "going around with H and other Chinamen and is now pregnant." Although the Attorney General later admitted that the evidence against her was "flimsy," Elise served three months before being released into the care of the Salvation Army. She had originally come to the attention of the police as a "public charge" sent to a hospital after taking quinine to try to induce an abortion. Trying to secure sympathy, she told the court that she came to Canada to join her sister, who was "living a bad life" and "forced" her to sleep with Chinese and Italian men (AO, 8634).[12] Whether this was true or not (and given her later, clever attempts to feign labour to escape from the police, it may not have been) mattered little: she clearly knew this was the expedient thing to declare.

Yet, another young woman, who later told her story to the Elizabeth Fry Society, claimed little understanding of the rationale for her arrest. Her recollections highlight how quickly decisions were made, with little regard for the due process of law. She was arrested when living with her Chinese boyfriend, after her father, who was actually from another province, came to town and sought out the help of the police. The police

arrived one morning as she sat in her dressing gown, and she remembers being whisked away and kept very much in the dark during the whole process. Without counsel, she misjudged the best strategy for securing her release:

> I was taken into a room and asked by a woman if I had ever slept with anyone else. I felt I would have to damage my character to save my boyfriend from blame. I said, "Yes" ... [and] I told her I was pregnant hoping that would help. Almost immediately I was taken to a courtroom .... [In court] I didn't see anyone else until the policeman [who arrested me] spoke from behind me.

After a few curt questions from the judge about her pregnancy, she offered to "get married" to her Chinese boyfriend if they would just let her out. It was the wrong tactic. She was remanded for a week in jail, then returned to court to be quickly sentenced to one year in the Belmont Refuge; after it closed, she was transferred to the Mercer Reformatory (Elizabeth Fry Society of Toronto, Copeland).

Magistrates and court and penal workers all displayed paternalism, horror, or revulsion towards the sexual behaviour of White and non-White women; nonetheless, specifically racist suppositions about women and men of colour were apparent. For example, if the parents of a girl were non-White, or had sexual relations with a person of colour, this was seen by court professionals as a rationale for the "lax" morals of the daughter. A disposition to immorality, they believed, could be passed on through familial contact. This "culture of immorality theory" worked against a young woman accused under the FRA, since the risk involved in not incarcerating her was so often determined by how "immoral" her family was. One Toronto teen, who was not working or attending school, was suspected of immorality; she was sent first to Belmont and later transferred to the Mercer so that she could learn some "self discipline." The court clearly believed that, left at home, she would be unduly influenced by her Native mother. "The father seems decent," reported a CAS worker, "but the mother is Indian and easy going in the home ... apparently the family can do anything it pleases. Mother is inefficient and unintelligent" (AO, 7223).

Although it was invariably the woman incarcerated, these cases also indicate how the sexuality of non-White men was supervised and censured more stringently than that of White men (Dubinsky, 1993:88–89; Odem, 1995:80–81; Strange, 1996:155–56). As other authors have documented, men of colour could become "villainized," the focus of intense suspicion concerning sexual crimes, as the image of their volatile, potentially lascivious sexuality was widely embraced across lines of class and gender (for example, Dubinsky, 1993; Dubinsky and Givertz, 1999; Murphy, 1923). The perceptions of men from "White ethnic" backgrounds who were not Anglo-Celtic sometimes played a role in the courts' perceptions of women's sexual morality, though in far more complex ways in these years. It was not simply ethnicity per se that determined the courts' views, but rather that of their overall assessment of the family's morality. White European immigrants who were employed, hard-working, and appeared to have embraced the "proper" moral values were not necessarily looked on with suspicion. However, if they did become involved in sexual "immorality," the fact of their ethnicity could be made an issue, their immorality blamed on their lack of "Canadian" values (Sangster, 1996).

First Nations Women and the FRA

Although relatively small numbers of women of colour were arrested for dissolute behaviour, their sexual behaviour was still perceived to be a threat, both to themselves and to the larger community (Sangster, 1999).[13] Native women and women of colour were almost always seen to be more prone to promiscuity, and Native women were believed to need paternalist protection. "She is a loose character, highly sexed, and particularly so when she

is drunk" (AO, 11089), noted a fairly typical magistrate's report for an Aboriginal woman. By the 1950s, the FRA cases do not indicate White women singled out especially because of their liaisons with men of colour, reflecting marginally different attitudes towards interracial relationships in Canadian society. On the other hand, after the late 1940s, the number of Native women incarcerated under the FRA multiplied, contradicting the overall trend for FRA arrests and reflecting the increasing over-incarceration of Native women in general (LaPrairie, 1984; Canada, 1993; Sangster, 1999).

This escalating pattern of incarceration was related directly to the intensifying effects of colonialism on Native communities. It is true that colonialism was hardly new: the denigration of Native cultures and missionary and government attempts to supplant traditional social structures and practices had existed for over a century. However, the post-World War II period saw new threats to patterns of traditional subsistence practised by many communities, the opening up of northern, previously isolated communities to hostile White populations, and the increased presence of Aboriginal peoples in urban areas, where they faced unemployment and racism. Social tensions and economic impoverishment resulted in ill health, alcoholism, and conflicts with the law, and Aboriginal families found few sources of aid other than "outside" legal and welfare authorities, which they sometimes avoided, fearing loss of their children or imprisonment.

Most Native women arrested under the FRA were brought before the court by the RCMP, local police, or the Indian agent for alcohol-related infractions; these were linked to charges of sexual immorality and illegitimate births, perceived to be inevitable, corollary crimes. Many already had convictions or run-ins with policing authorities, and some were literally destitute. As a sentencing report noted, one woman literally had no place of residence and no employment, nor any immediate family to help her. Under the circumstances, she had few alternatives, save for occasional prostitution, to sustain herself and deal with her alcoholism. Another sentencing report that noted a theft charge for "stealing clothes off a clothesline" (AO, 14355) underlined how economically marginal these women were.

If women did not have immediate family members with the resources to take them in, as many did not, then they were more likely to face incarceration. Moreover, First Nations women could be caught in the no-win situation caused by their lack of "official" Indian status on some reserves. Women who married Whites, of course, could not return to their home reserve, but even those who married into another reserve could be left without aid—depending on the whim of the local Indian agent. One woman in these circumstances was initially deserted by her husband and had to send her two children to live with her parents. The agent had little interest in helping her, in part because she "did not have status" on her husband's reserve, in part because she had a number of intoxication charges against her. Her decision to live with a White man nearby who had a criminal record was the last straw: faced with her refusal to testify against this "bootlegger," she was arrested under the FRA and sentenced to the Reformatory (AO, 8982).

Indian agents, as the opening story indicated, could also be a factor in a woman's incarceration, testifying against her before a magistrate or judge. Women living on reserves were subject to the agent's ongoing surveillance of their own and their families' lives, and most agents were not hesitant to make judgements about Native morality. Agents could be called on to judge women's possibility of parole as well, and their long list of comments on the family's churchgoing, education, drinking, and sexual habits reflected their immense powers of surveillance. While the agents exercised power because of their moral and political stature, in contrast, Native women were disadvantaged by language barriers (some needed translators in court) and their cultural alienation from the adversarial court processes in which they were involved.

It was not simply that First Nations women were surveyed—for women on welfare were, too—but that they were also surveyed using racist assumptions. Native women were seen as weaker in moral outlook, prone to alcoholism, easily corrupted by White men offering them alcohol, and likely to barter with their sexuality (Carter, 1996; Kline, 1995; Monture-Angus, 1995; Tiffany and Adams, 1985). "It is just another case of a girl coming here and going wild after the soldiers" (AO, 9337) commented one police report of a young First Nations woman. Another young woman was told by the magistrate:

> It is too bad that such a good looking Indian like you should throw yourself away. Other men buy the liquor for you, then you suffer and they escape .... I hope if you are removed from unscrupulous white men and Indian soldiers you might start a new life. (AO, 9004)

Once incarcerated, Native women still encountered assumptions, shared by male and female medical and penal experts, that they lacked the moral introspection necessary to "reform" themselves.

Removing women who drank alcohol was often seen as a means of "saving" younger, impressionable women from the likelihood of corruption. In his testimony urging incarceration, one RCMP officer noted that a woman from the reserve "is a bad influence ... she has led a fifteen year old astray" (AO, 9004; AO, 14212). In a similar manner, the authorities in a small city wanted a married woman, separated from her husband and two children, incarcerated, not simply because of her sexual activity but because she had let a minor share her apartment and engage in sexual activity with men (AO, 9900).

Many of the sentencing reports of Native women indicate experiences similar to those of non-Native women, shaped by impoverishment, addiction or ill health, violence, family dissolution, and experience with some form of state care, such as the Children's Aid Society, foster homes, or very occasionally, residential schools. Many Native women were "damned" by reports that their families had alcoholic or "immoral" members, who were offered up as explanations for the (inevitable) decline of these women, just as they were for other FRA women. "Her family history is a bad one," noted one sentencing report. "Her father is living with a woman not his wife ... and her mother is possibly worse than her, and certainly partly at fault for her behaviour" (AO, 9434). Moreover, there was a strong concern that both Native and non-Native women convicted under the FRA would likely produce illegitimate children who would become a burden on the state. After repeated alcohol charges, a woman with five children was sent to Mercer from the north. Since illness at four years had left her deaf, the Reformatory psychologist was unable to test her IQ, but this did not stop him from concluding she was mentally "slow." "No doubt children will continue until the end of her productive age, or until a pathological process renders her sterile," he commented, adding that "improvement is remote ... so to prevent future progeny institutionalization recommended" (AO, 16461).

Native families were less likely than White families to implicate their own daughters and wives to the authorities, but some certainly did. They were troubled, as White families were, with what they perceived to be women "out of control" and in desperate need of aid, so they turned to the Indian agent or local police for help. Communities and families did not always feel that they could help women who appeared to be suffering from addiction and were sexually "promiscuous," were destitute, and needed their children cared for as well. One single father from the north brought his daughter to Juvenile Court twice because he considered her a "bad influence on her sister and other girls." She had run away, had a baby, and according to the police "was picked up at drinking parties and was involved in a break and

enter" (AO, 10637). Another mother swore out a warrant when her 21-year-old daughter was "found intoxicated in hotel with an Indian" (AO, 8432). Occasionally, family members wrote to the Mercer asking that the woman not receive parole (AO, 9161). Certainly, some families, no matter how meagre their resources, offered unconditional aid to released women. In one case, a mother found that the penal authorities placed less faith in the healing powers of family if the family happened to be Native. She wrote to the Mercer Superintendent, asking to have her grandchild sent to her, but her wishes were disregarded and the child was put up for adoption (AO, 15166).

Families and communities were probably led to believe that the Reformatory was going to provide care and education. Judges and magistrates, when rendering their verdicts, constantly claimed that women would "learn a trade and ... be released ... to re-establish [themselves]" (AO, 14305) and that the Mercer was the place to send women who were "badly in need of care and treatment for alcoholism" (AO, 14176). Yet, these were precisely the things the Elizabeth Fry Society argued most women were not getting at the Mercer Reformatory. By the late 1950s, their political lobbying not only included attempts to abolish the FRA, but also requests for education, training, and addiction aid for women incarcerated in the Mercer. As well, they wanted both the federal and provincial governments to pay attention to the poverty in northern Native communities that was leading to over-incarceration (AO, RG 20, 13–185). The fact that Native women's over-incarceration increased in the years after this study indicates all too well that the Society's concerns were ignored, as well as the way in which incarceration only accentuated Native women's alienation (Sangster, 1999). Indeed, the final verdict on the FRA was summed up by the experiences of a Native woman, Alice, from a small Ontario town who was convicted under the FRA in the early 1940s. This was not her first sentence on a morality charge, and she had been destitute for some time, but the purpose of a lengthy FRA sentence was to "reform" her for good. Yet, after her release, Alice's name appeared repeatedly in the Mercer registers over the next decades, on vagrancy and alcohol charges (AO), 12128). For her, the FRA had done little to help, and perhaps more to intensify her problems with poverty, ill health, addiction, and racism.

Conclusion

These FRA convictions offer examples of the way in which the definitions of promiscuity employed by the courts, circulating also within the wider social context, were shaped within the interconnected categories of race, class, and gender. Trying to disentangle these as separate strands to assign one absolute pre-eminence is difficult because they were usually interwoven, hinged together "symbiotically," though not without some hierarchy (Razack, 1998).

Convictions of both White and Native women revealed high levels of impoverishment and ill health in women's backgrounds, with the courts unable to recognize, on a structural level, the material and social dislocations shaping women's conflicts with the law: the damaging results of poverty, their problems with addiction, and their experience of violence and institutional care. While there was some attempt by court and penal workers to pinpoint the "environmental" causes of their immorality, these were more likely to focus on women's "feeble-mindedness" or "immorality,"[14] not the material and social conditions of their lives.

At the same time, the FRA was a gender-specific piece of legislation, reflecting a double standard of sexuality that portrayed women's sexual activity as dangerous if it was expressed outside of heterosexual marriage; the protection of what were deemed "proper" familial roles was inextricably linked to the regulation of women's sexuality. The use of the FRA bolstered notions of inherent differences between male and female sexuality, linking natural female sexuality to passivity and premarital purity, and sanctifying an ideal family type in which the wife was constrained within monogamous domesticity and the daughter was a dutiful and chaste apprentice for this role.

Yet, the FRA convictions also reflected change over time; there was a declining concern with White women's interracial liaisons and intensified policing of Native women in the post- World War II period. The interaction of social knowledge about "race" with the law may have altered somewhat, but a general theme persisted: the very notion of which women were likely to be promiscuous, which women needed "protection," which women had a weaker moral constitution, was shaped by the equation of Whiteness with the protection of purity, and Aboriginal and women of colour with potential moral laxity. Indeed, Aboriginal women were subject to extra surveillance and control in part for this reason, lending credence to Kimberle Crenshaw's observation that, even if "consent and coercion" are both at work in the reproduction of racism through the law, coercion was often more salient for people of colour (Crenshaw, 1988). Although FRA convictions were clothed in protectionist language, in medical rationales, or even in reform rhetoric, they also worked, ideologically, to construct race and racism through the practice of the law.

Notes

1. In this paper, I have not explored sexual orientation and disability, which were less salient forces in the criminalization of women under the FRA.

2. Because this paper focuses on the Female Refuges Act, my discussion centres on the regulation of women's sexuality, though it is clear that male sexuality also was regulated according to race.

3. As James Walker and others emphasize, the legal construction of "race" in Canada was part of a broader historical and global process of European imperialism.

4. There is some debate about the relative importance of consent and coercion in this process. For one excellent exploration of this, see Crenshaw (1988).

5. There is also an argument that this had to do with Whites opposing the economic competition posed by Chinese businesses. For different statements on anti-Chinese laws and sentiment, see Backhouse (1994, 1996) and Walker (1998). Sexuality and race also converged in eugenic discourse and legislation. See McLaren (1990).

6. Royal Statutes of Ontario (RSO), 1897, c. 311, An Act Respecting Houses of Refuge for Females; RSO 1919, c. 84, An Act Respecting Industrial Refuges for Females (The Female Refuges Act), see especially section 15; RSO, 1927, c. 347, sections, 15–17. Emphasis added. Also see Dymond (1923: ch. 9). Women could be put in a Refuge for "bad habits" like drunkenness, if they were unable "to protect themselves" (p. 84). In this paper, I draw on case files of women sent to the Mercer Reformatory under the FRA.

7. This applied to daughters who were under 21. Using other laws, parents had essentially been able to do this before 1919.

8. About 60 per cent of all incarcerations took place during these years. However, Native women were seldom arrested under the FRA in the 1930s, more often in the 1940s (10 per cent) and 1950s (13 per cent). The number of Native women sent to the Mercer under the FRA therefore, was a small percentage of the overall numbers of Native women sent there: in the 1940s about 6 per cent, and in the 1950s, about 4 per cent. The overall number of intakes (repeaters or not) listed as Native in the Mercer went from 169 in the 1940s to 370 in the 1950s. Most Native women were convicted under alcohol and vagrancy laws. In a previous article (Sangster, 1999) detailing these numbers, a typographical error mistakenly rendered 169 into 109.

9. Many of the case files are incomplete in terms of such information. An immigrant was often noted as such if there was a possibility of deportation.

10. It is important to note, however, that these cases were a small minority of FRA cases.

11. Note that the Ontario government, even into the 1950s, kept statistics on training schools, which noted the "nationalities" of inmates, with Whites separated from three other "races: Hebrews, Negroes and Indians." See also AO, Dept. of Reform Institutions, RG 20-16-2, Container J9, letter to Supervisor of Training School for Boys, 24 Feb. 1953: "children born in Canada are Canadian unless they are Indian, Hebrew or Negro, when they are shown as the appropriate race."

12. In this explanation, she appears somewhat deferential, yet in other dealings with authorities, she was far less so, denouncing the CAS as "a bunch of bullies who just want me in jail."

13. It is important to note that the Ontario government did not keep statistics on the "race" of women sent to the Mercer Reformatory (though they did of girls sentenced to training schools). However, the prison registers usually noted, under complexion, "Indian," and it is clear from this designation that there were steady increases in First Nations women over lime, increasingly so in the post World War II period.

14. The fear of unregulated reproduction of "unsuitable" women (predominately framed by class, though also influenced by race) by middle-class professionals shaped some FRA prosecutions in the early years, though this probably persisted as an underlying concern in the 1940s and 1950s.

References

Agnew, V. 1996. *Resisting Discrimination: Women from Asia, Africa and the Caribbean and the Women's Movement in Canada*. Toronto: University of Toronto Press.

Anthias, F. 1990. "Race and class revisited," *Sociological Review* 28,1:19–42.

Anthias, F., and N. Yuval-Davis, eds. 1992. *Racialized Boundaries: Race, Nation, Gender and Colour and Class and the Anti-Racist Struggle*. London: Routledge.

Backhouse, C. 1994. "White female help and Chinese Canadian employers: Race, class, gender and law in the case of Yee Clun, 1924," *Canadian Ethnic Studies* 26, 3:34–52.

_____. 1996. "White women's labour laws: Anti-Chinese racism and early twentieth century Canada," *Law and History Review* 14:315–68.

_____. 1999. *Colour Coded: A Legal history of Racism in Canada, 1900–1950*. Toronto: University of Toronto Press.

Bannerji, H., ed. 1993. *Returning the Gaze: Essays on Racism, Feminism and Politics*. Toronto: Sister Vision Press.

_____. 1995. *Thinking It Through: Essays on Feminism, Marxism and Anti-Racism*. Toronto: Women's Press.

Brewer, R. 1993. "Theorizing race, class and gender: The new scholarship of black feminist intellectuals," in S. James and A. Busia, eds., *Theorizing Black Feminism: The Visionary Pragmatism of Black Women*. New York: Routledge.

Canada, Royal Commission on Aboriginal Peoples. 1993. *Aboriginal Peoples and the Justice System: Report of the National Round Table on Aboriginal Justice*. Ottawa.

Carter, S. 1996. "Categories and terrains of exclusion: Constructing the 'Indian Woman' in the early settlement era in western Canada," in J. Parr and M. Rosenfeld, eds., *Gender and Canadian History*. Toronto: Copp Clark, 40–61.

Copeland, J. "The Female Refuges Act," unpublished manuscript, Elizabeth Fry Society of Toronto Library.

Crenshaw, K.W. 1988. "Race, reform and retrenchment: Transformation and legitimation in antidiscrimination law," *Harvard Law Review* 101:1331–87.

Dubinsky, K. 1993. *Improper Advances: Rape and Heterosexual Conflict in Ontario, 1880–1929*. Chicago: University of Chicago Press.

Dubinsky, K., and A. Givertz. 1999. "'It was only a matter of passion': Masculinity and sexual danger," in K. McPherson, C. Morgan, and N. Forestall, eds., *Gendered Pasts: Historical Essays in Femininity and Masculinity in Canada*. Toronto: Oxford University Press, 65–79.

Dymond, A. 1923. *The Laws of Ontario Relating to Women and Children*. Toronto.

Foucault, M. 1980. *History of Sexuality*. New York: Vintage.

Haney Lopez, I. 1996. *White by Law: The Legal Construction of Race*. New York: New York University Press.

Kline, M. 1995. "Complicating the ideology of motherhood: Child welfare law and first nations women," in M. Finernan and I. Karpin, eds., *Mothers in Law: Feminist Theory and the Legal Regulation of Motherhood*. New York: Columbia University Press, 118–42.

LaPrairie, C. 1984. "Selected criminal justice and socio-economic data on native women," *Canadian Journal of Criminology* 26, 4:161–69.

McLaren, A. 1990. *Our Own Master Race: Eugenics in Canada, 1884–1945*. Toronto: McClelland & Stewart.

Monture-Angus, P. 1995. *Thunder in My Soul: A Mohawk Woman Speaks*. Halifax: Fernwood Press.

Murphy, E. 1923 [1973]. *The Black Candle*. Toronto: Coles Publishing.

Odem, M. 1995. *Delinquent Daughters: Protecting and Policing Adolescent Female Sexuality in the United States, 1885–1920*. Chapel Hill: University of North Carolina Press.

Ontario. 1897. *Royal Statutes*, c. 311.

_____. 1919. An Act Respecting Houses of Refuge for Females. Royal Statutes, c. 84.

_____. 1927. An Act Respecting Industrial Refuges for Females (The Female Refuges Act). Royal Statutes, c. 347, s. 15–17.

_____. 1953. Department of Reform Institutions. Report.

_____. 1958. *Legislative Assembly Debates*.

_____. Ministry of Correctional Services 1930–1960. Andrew Mercer Reformatory for Females Case Files.

Pon, M. 1996. "Like a Chinese puzzle: The construction of Chinese masculinity in Jack Canuck," In J. Parr and M. Rosenfeld, eds., *Gender and History in Canada*. Toronto: Copp Clark, 88–100.

Rafter, N.H. 1985. "Chastising the unchaste: Social control functions of a women's reformatory, 1894–1931," in S. Cohen and A. Scull, eds., *Social Control and the State: Historical and Comparative Essays*. Oxford: Basil Blackwell, 288–311.

Razack, S. 1998. *Looking White People in the Eye: Gender, Race and Culture in Courtrooms and Classrooms*. Toronto: University of Toronto Press.

Rex v. Davis, 1930.

Roediger, D. 1993. "Race and the working-class past in the United States: Multiple identities and the future of labor history," *International Review of Social History* 38:127–43.

Sangster, J. 1996. "Incarcerating 'bad girls': The regulation of sexuality through the female refuges act in Ontario, 1920–1945," *Journal of the History of Sexuality* 7:2.

_____. 1999. "Criminalizing the colonized: Ontario native women confront the criminal justice system, 1920–1960," *Canadian Historical Review* 80, 1:32–60.

Stephen, J. 1995. "The incorrigible, the bad and the immoral: Toronto's factory girls and the work of the Toronto Psychiatric Clinic," in L. Knafla and S. Binnie, eds., *Law, Society and the State: Essays in Modern Legal History*. Toronto: University of Toronto Press, 405–39.

Strange, C. 1996. *Toronto's Girl Problem: The Perils and Pleasures of the City, 1880–1930*. Toronto: University of Toronto Press.

Tarnopolsky, W. 1982. *Discrimination and the Law in Canada*. Toronto: Richard De Boo.

Tiffany, S., and K. Adams. 1985. *The Wild Woman: An Inquiry into the Anthropology of an Idea*. Cambridge: Schenkman.

Walker, J.W. St. G. 1997. *"Race" Rights and the Law in the Supreme Court of Canada*. Toronto: University of Toronto Press.

Walker, J.W. St. G. 1998. "The Quong Wing Files," in F. Iacovetta and W. Mitchinson, eds., *On the Case: Explorations in Social History*. Toronto: University of Toronto Press, 204–23.

CHAPTER 19

"Horrible Temptations":
Sex, Men, and Working-Class Male Youth
in Urban Ontario, 1890–1935

Steven Maynard

• •

As one man with a keen interest in boys observed about Toronto in 1898: "You can scarcely walk a block without your attention being drawn to one or more of the class called street boys." C.S. Clark went on to describe Toronto's street boys: "Some of the boys live at home, but the majority are wanderers in the streets, selling papers generally, and sometimes forced to beg. In the summer time they can live out all night, but in the winter they are obliged to patronize the cheap lodging houses …. Their ages run from ten to sixteen years …. They are generally sharp, shrewd lads with any number of bad habits and little or no principles …. Some of the larger boys spend a considerable portion of their earnings for tobacco and drink, and they patronize all the theatres."

Selling papers, begging, smoking, drinking, and theatre-going were only some of the vocations and vices of the street boy. "When a newsboy gets to be seventeen years of age he finds that his avocation is at an end, it does not produce money enough and he has acquired lazy, listless habits … He becomes a vagrant and perhaps worse. […] Consult some of the bell boys of the large hotels in Canada's leading cities, as I did, and find out what they can tell from their own experiences."[1]

*****

Generally speaking, […] the history of sexual relations between boys and men remains unwritten. This is surprising given the prominent place the subject occupies on the contemporary political scene. One thinks immediately of the physical and sexual mistreatment of boys by men in state- and church-run orphanages, training schools, and residential schools. Beginning with the 1989 Newfoundland Royal Commission on Mount Cashel (an orphanage for boys run by the Christian Brothers, a lay order of the Catholic Church), government inquiries and police investigations have documented the widespread abuse of boys in custodial institutions in nearly every province. […]

Intended as a contribution to the emerging field Canadian lesbian and gay social history, the aim of this article is to begin to think through the historical meanings and experience of sexual relations between boys and men.[2] It is based on the case files of criminal prosecutions involving sexual relations between boys and men in urban Ontario from 1890 to 1935.[3] An analysis of the case files reveals that boys' sexual relations with men were marked by both sexual dangers and sexual possibilities.[4] This contradictory mix of danger and desire can be introduced through the stories of two boys.

Arnold and Garfield

In 1917, fifteen-year-old Arnold lived in Toronto. One day early in August, as Arnold explained to the police, "I was coming out of the Star theatre. I met Thomas C. on Temperance Street." According to his case file, Thomas was a single, twenty-six-year-old "sausage-casing expert." "I walked to the corner of Temperance and Yonge street. I said it is nice weather. He asked me if I would go to His Majesty's Theatre. I went with him. He got 2 seats at the wall. I was sitting next to him. He drew his hand up my leg. I then went with him to Bowles Lunch. After supper we went to the Hippodrome and after the show I went home." On the day after Arnold first met Thomas, Arnold sought him out again. "On Aug. 5 I went to his room at 329 Jarvis and we went out and then I went home. Aug. 6 I met him again ... and we went to the Crown Theatre at Gerrard and Broadview and nothing happened. I went to his room on Aug. 8. He opened my pants and handled my privates and I pulled his private person until there was discharge and he did the same with me. He done this to me 8 times before Aug. 31st." In September, Arnold and Thomas left Toronto for western Canada, not returning until the end of the month. Asked by the court why he made the trip with Thomas, Arnold responded: "He paid my way to the West and fed and clothed me all this time." After their return to Toronto, Arnold and Thomas continued to see each other. As Arnold told the police, "I slept with him on Dec. 17th ... this was the last time." It is unclear from the case file how their relationship was discovered, but Thomas was charged and arrested by an inspector of the Morality Department and shortly thereafter Arnold was picked up and compelled to testify against his friend.[5]

In 1904, Garfield was seven years old and lived with his family in London, Ontario. One Saturday, while passing by the hospital, Garfield encountered a stranger who, as he told the judge, "asked me to go down the Hospital Hill and I wouldn't go." The man, a teamster employed by the City of London, "caught hold of me and

dragged me down the hill and I caught hold of the hospital boulevard post and he said if I wouldn't let go he would cut my hands off. He took me down the hill then he undone the back of my pants which were fastened up with braces. He took my pants down. He undone the front of his pants ... He took out a great big thing from the front of his trousers and he put in right behind me and I screamed it hurt. I could feel it. I screamed when he was taking me down the hill." As William E. explained to the London Police Court Magistrate, "I am in the post office service. The boy Garfield is my son. I first heard of this trouble when I came home about a little after five o'clock ... Garfield spoke to me about it. He told me what had occurred." The next day, Garfield's father laid a charge against the man for indecently assaulting his son.[6]

Arnold and Garfield told very different stories about their sexual relations with a man. Arnold sought out his sexual encounter, boldly striking up a conversation with Thomas on the street. Their dates and gradual build-up to sex resembled something akin to a courtship, and Arnold used a matter-of-fact language to describe their reciprocal sexual relations. Arnold's relationship with Thomas appears to have been based on a mixture of economic need and an insatiable desire for the theatre. For Arnold, as for many other poor boys, sexual relations were rooted in a distinct moral economy in which working-class boys traded sex in exchange for food, shelter, amusement, money, and companionship. Garfield did not seek out his sexual encounter—he was forcibly taken by a man who used him for his own sexual purposes—and Garfield described his experience in the language of assault and harm. The locations of sexual danger for boys (along with more mutual relations) were embedded in the social relations of working-class boy life in household, neighbourhood, and a variety of institutional settings.[7] For the historian accustomed to dealing with power based on gender, race, and class, the case files of sexual relations between boys and men are a forceful reminder that age was also a significant axis of power. [...] Sexual danger for boys was grounded in men's greater age and physical strength, as well as in their positions of power over boys within a number of different organizational settings. Second, there were age differences between boys. Older boys such as Arnold were able to turn men's interest to their own advantage, while younger boys like Garfield were more vulnerable to men's unsolicited and sometimes violent sexual advances.

*****

Bowles Lunch and Burlesque

Some of the boys who appeared before Ontario courts involved in sexual relations with men were among those who lived on the street. As sixteen-year-old Henry explained to the Ottawa police court magistrate in 1922, "I do not know where my father is and my mother is dead six years ago ... I have no home." Other boys moved back and forth between the street and various institutional homes. In Toronto and vicinity, boys moved in and out of the Newsboys' Lodging and Industrial Home, the Working Boys' Home, St. Nicholas Home (the Roman Catholic newsboys' home), the Victoria Industrial School for Boys, and a number of training schools. [...] Key to survival was the distinctive culture boys developed in the streets. [...]

Boys drew on the resources of street and homosexual subcultures for food and shelter. In October 1929, seventeen-year-old John M. left the Bowmanville Training School for boys just outside Toronto. He traveled to Ottawa "to see what it was like." John arrived in the city at two o'clock in the morning with no place to sleep. He headed for one of the few places open at such a late hour, the Bowles Lunch Counter. Cheap, all-night cafeterias and lunch counters were important social centres within homosexual subcultures. [...] It is unclear whether John knew in advance that Bowles was a popular homosexual haunt, but it was not long before he met someone. As John explained, "I went into Bowles Lunch near the Station on

Rideau Street." There he met Moise B., a single, twenty-nine-year-old labourer. Sitting next to each other in their booth at Bowles, they talked until six o'clock in the morning and then left for Moise's room "above his father's shoemaking shop." It was, according to John, "an ordinary room" with "a bed in one corner." "We got undressed and went to bed ... we were laying there a while and after a while" they had sex. It was to be the beginning of a brief relationship. John moved in with Moise. According to John, they slept with each other every night and for the next month or so and they had sex "about four times a week." John got a job at the Rideau Bowling Alley. Eventually, however, the police caught up with John, who apparently had left Bowmanville without permission and was sent back to the training school.[8]

Gossip about men circulated in the subaltern world of boys. As John said about Moise having sex with boys, "all the kids in the bowling alley were telling me about it." Or, as C.S. Clark noted about Toronto, "men and their acts of indecency are the talk of boys all over the city." For boys who were interested, such talk alerted them to the existence of men who had sex with boys and where those men could be found. [...]

As the stories of Arnold and John suggest, boys were crazy for "the Show." Rapidly expanding commercial amusement scenes in early twentieth-century Ontario cities were a magnet for boys. [...] Much like working girls who sometimes traded sexual favours with men to gain access to the city's amusements, boys with little or no money used sex as their ticket into the theatre. Sometimes boys were treated to the theatre after having sex with a man; other times sex took place in the theatre. [...] Given the way theatres attracted boys and men, and because they were one of the few public spaces that offered a degree of privacy, the dark recesses of galleries and balconies provided the necessary cover to have sex, theatres became important meeting places for homosexual encounters. [...] Also very popular were the many vaudeville and burlesque theatres centred around Queen and Bay streets, one of Toronto's principal working-class entertainment districts. Here one found Shea's Hippodrome, one of the city's largest vaudeville and moving-picture-show theatres, and the site of one of Arnold and Thomas's dates. [...]

Not all encounters between boys and men were furtive sexual acts that took place in the public world of boys' street culture. Boys often went on to form elaborate, long-lasting relationships with the men they met. It was in 1924, at a friend's house, when fifteen-year-old Thomas H. first met Edward B., an Ottawa doctor. Details of their relationship—they were together for over a year—came out during the trial that followed charges laid against the doctor by police. As in other cases in which boys were forced to testify against the men with whom they had sex or shared a relationship, Thomas was reluctant to incriminate his friend. [...]

*****

[Their] relationship bears a close resemblance to a common pattern of homosexual relationship in the early twentieth century, in which working-class boys were kept by wealthier men in the context of often long-lasting, mutually rewarding partnerships.[9]

Prostitutes and Perverts

Boys traded sex with men for food, shelter, and admission to the theatre, but most often, in what is best described as a form of casual prostitution, boys exchanged sex for money. David K.'s experience was typical. In 1914, David met a man on Yonge Street outside Simpson's Hall who asked him to go to the theatre. David claimed that the man, Edward W., a single, twenty-eight-year-old driver, said "it would be easy money for me to make 25 cents." David and Edward went to the theatre where, according to David, "I pulled his dickie up and down in the theatre ... it was dark ... he had his coat on and my hand worked under it." [...]

Given their importance as homosexual meeting places, theatres and their surrounding streets and lanes, especially those centred in the commercial amusement district around Queen

and Bay, were a central site of prostitution in Toronto. Boys hung out in and around movie houses looking for men. About 8:30 pm on a summer evening in 1922, Morris approached a man "outside the Reo Picture Show on Queen Street West near McCaul." "Let's go up the lane and do some dirty work," Morris suggested, "I want to make some money to go to the show." [...]

Boys who worked at hotels were particularly well placed to capitalize on their occupations. Sixteen-year-old William described one such encounter for the court: "He led me to the room and closed the door ... [He] took his pants off and proceeded to open up his B.V.D.'s ... He laid me on the bed and then laid on top of me." Asked by the court why he had done so, William explained that the man "asked me if I had any money and I told him no. He said I will give you some and also a job in the morning driving a truck .... He handed me a dollar when he was finished and said to take it and keep quiet." William, however, did not keep quiet; he reported the man to the police, who was then charged and found guilty of an indecent assault. It is not clear why William turned the man in; it may have been that although he was paid his one dollar—it was entered into the trial as an exhibit—he did not get a job driving a truck the morning after sex.[10]

Cases such as William's in which charges against men were laid by boys, not by the police, parents, or others, pose the question of why a boy would report to the police that he had been involved sexually with a man. Interestingly, almost all such cases involve scenarios in which boys were promised or expected something in return for sex, but the men failed to deliver. [...]

How boys regarded their sexual relations with men—how, if at all, it shaped their self-perceptions—is an intriguing question. It would appear that for some boys, sex with men was an outgrowth of or gave rise to a sense of sexual difference or identity. Seventeen-year-old William C., for example, had sex with men for money. William's, however, was more than the occasional act of prostitution; he regularly provided sexual services to men in a male brothel on Toronto's Young Street. William presented himself in court as a "self-confessed pervert." Many other boys resisted the identity of prostitute and pervert. [...] While refusing to admit involvement in homosexual prostitution is not surprising in the context of a court examination, such a denial must have been at times simply an indication that many boys who occasionally traded sex for money did not regard themselves as perverts or prostitutes.[11]

Bootblacks and Boarders

In addition to street boys, occasional prostitutes, and confirmed perverts, many boys were the sons of working-class families and their sexual relations were embedded in the conditions of working-class life. As labour and social historians have demonstrated, working-class boys were expected to contribute to the family economy, including by going out to work. Many boys went to work in the street trades, where they found jobs as newsboys, messenger boys, and shoeshine boys. Going out to work was one way in which a boy might become involved in sexual relations with men. [...] Work in the street trades was unstable and poorly paid, so boys devised ways—from "scrounging" to stealing—to supplement their modest wages. Some boys discovered that providing sexual favours to men was a way to earn pocket money. Alan, a ten-year-old newsboy from Sault Ste. Marie, told the court that, in the summer of 1918, "I was going to get my *Sault Star* to sell. This man was standing at the corner of Albert & Elgin Streets and asked me if I wanted to earn a nickel .... He took me to Hiawatha Hotel where he took me to a room, and he took down his pants, then he took my hand and made me rub his [thing] and he gave me 7C. [...]"

Many working-class families supplemented the household economy by taking in boarders and, perhaps not surprisingly, sex between a boy and male lodger was a common scenario. Consider the case of thirteen-year-old Sidney. In 1927, Sidney shared a bed with Joseph B.,

who had boarded in his family's household for about a year. During that time, as Sidney explained, "he always fooled with my privates." Displaying little knowledge of working-class life, the lawyer asked, "Why did you go back to sleep with him on occasions after the first time this happened—you knew what he was doing to you—why didn't you go to sleep some place else?" "I could not," replied Sidney, "all the beds were occupied in the house—there was only that bed." In often-crowded households, people had to double up. Significantly, the charge against the lodger was laid not by Sidney's parents but by a truancy officer who had made it his business to investigate Sidney's sleeping arrangements. Whether Sidney's parents were aware of his sexual liaisons with the lodger is unclear. They did know that they slept in the same bed. As Sidney's father told the court, "Yes, they both occupied the same room with the one bed." When Sidney was asked whether he ever told anyone about having sex with the lodger, he replied, "I did not say anything about it." "Why not?" asked the cross-examining lawyer. "He used to give me things—cigarettes and things."[12]

*****

Ravines and Railway Yards

Boys, especially young boys, encountered men looking for sex in the spaces boys carved out of the city in which to play, including on the streets of their own neighbourhoods. [...] Parks and ravines were another place boys could be found playing. Twelve-year-old Ben B. testified that "I was coming from Riverdale Park .... [The accused] asked me to go with him. He asked me to take my pants down and ... and he put his private in my backside. He was moving up and down. He gave me a one dollar bill after he had done it." [...] Other sexual encounters took place in school yards, vacant lots, fields, and on the Don River Flats. Boys who ventured away from their neighbourhoods to go exploring might also encounter a man. Alleine W. met a man when he "was down near the docks." Henry

B. encountered a labourer who "works on the railway" when he was playing "near the Gas Works." According to Henry, "he dragged me into a box car and did some dirty things."[13]

Because most of these boys did not seek out their sexual encounters but were discovered by men while at play, men had to devise ways to interest boys in sex. Ice cream and candy were two popular treats. As Sidney L. said about the man with whom he had sex, "he treated me to Ice Cream." With the fourteen cents he received from a man, eight-year-old Albert M. "bought two cones, I gave one cone to my brother and bought candy with the remaining four cents." [...]

When men's various methods to entice boys failed or once a boy began to resist, men could resort to physical coercion. As one young boy put it, "he got me in the house. He hurt me down there. It is still sore." The doctor who examined Tom backed up his story: "I found the anus dilated and very red." [...]

Boys Scouts and Big Brothers

[...] Reform work, or "boys' work" as it was often called, provided another social setting for sexual relations between boys and men. As historians have demonstrated, reform groups such as the Boy's Brigade, the YMCA, and the Boy Scouts, springing out of middle-class fears about the physical degeneration of the male working class and the effeminizing influence on boys of the domestic sphere, sought to restore boys to a proper state of manliness. [...] The objective of the east Toronto branch of the YMCA, known as the "Railroad Branch—a home for Railwaymen away from home," was "to make better men and boys ... to create and develop a more wholesome atmosphere in which men and boys may spend their leisure time." [...] Placing boys in the "more wholesome atmosphere" of all-male groups nourished homosocial relations between boys and men. [...]

*****

The case of Boy Scoutmaster Frederick T. provides [...] detail on the tensions between the

homosocial and homoerotic within boys' groups. Born in Scotland, Frederick was a single, thirty-seven-year-old chartered accountant. Referring to Frederick's life in Scotland, his brother stated that "he was always greatly interested in Church and Missions, and Boys Brigade Work, and when the Boy Scouts Movement became prominent he was one of the first to give the matter great impetus." When Frederick immigrated to Canada in 1911, he came to Toronto, took up residence at the Toronto Amateur Athletic Club, and resumed his work with the Boy Scouts. By 1916, Fred faced "serious charges preferred against him by boys under his command." [...]

Rather than physical force, men who worked in reform groups relied on other forms of power to extract sexual compliance from boys. In 1932, Harvey B. was a single, thirty-year-old curate and Sunday school teacher at a Toronto church. The local chapter of the Boy Scouts met at Harvey's church and, as one boy explained, "Mr. [B.] was around with the scouts a great deal." His usual routine involved offering boys rides in his automobile after Sunday School or a Scouts meeting. As Lloyd C. told police, "He took me to his garage. He took off my clothes, loosened down my underwear and he started feeling my privates." Another time, "He asked me who my body belonged to. I said: 'God, My Mother and Father.' He said: 'Is it none of mine?' I said nothing, then he kissed me and asked me if I loved him. I said: 'Yes sir.'" Harvey managed to maintain the boys' silence for as long as he did by playing on his position of authority, both his position as assistant to the parish priest and as a scoutmaster. [...]

*****

Not all sexual relations between boys and men within organizational settings were of a coercive character. In 1922, Harold was fourteen years old. He lived in Pickering with his foster parents. Harold had a long relationship with Edward, a forty-year-old scoutmaster. Edward lived in nearby Oshawa. They saw each other frequently, Edward making trips to Harold's home and becoming friends with Harold's foster family. Letters between Harold and Edward reveal an intense emotional and caring relationship. [...]

It is unclear from the case file how the sexual component of their relationship was discovered, but Edward was charged with several offences against Harold. [...]

Moral Reformers and Mothers

*****

Much of the impetus to regulate sexual relations between boys and men was rooted in the more general middle-class apprehension about the working-class boy. This is what Toronto Chief of Police H.J. Grasett meant when he referred in 1891 to "the boy question in Toronto" or, as he sometimes called it, the "boy nuisance." At the heart of the boy nuisance was the widely shared belief that working-class boys were responsible for a good deal of crime and vice in the city.[14] [...] Testifying before the 1889 Royal Commission on the Relations of Labor and Capital, former Toronto mayor and moral reformer W.H. Howland related his conversations with "respectable working people" who "told me that their boys were all right until they began to sell newspapers on the street at eleven and twelve o'clock at night, but then they got demoralized .... I am satisfied that in every city a large portion of the petty crime is done by these boys." For Howland, one of the chief sites of boys' demoralization was the street. In 1891, testifying this time before the Ontario Commission on Prisons and Reformatories investigating "all matters appertaining to juvenile criminality and vice," he warned that "the streets are full of temptation to children .... There are hundreds of things in street life that attract children." Howland was responsible for a number of solutions to the boy nuisance. He was the principal force behind the establishment in 1887 of the Victoria Industrial School for Boys. In the previous year, during his term as mayor, Howland appointed David Archibald staff inspector of the newly

established Morality Department of the Toronto police force.[15]

Like Howland, Archibald viewed the streets as one of the main threats to boys. Testifying before the Prison Commission, Archibald asserted that boys' criminal propensities were "developed through the associations that they form in the streets .... They learn gambling, tossing coppers, and they get into all sorts of vice." Much of the regulation of street boys emanated from the Morality Department. Archibald's wide mandate included the supervision of Toronto's "decency and morality, newsboys and boot-blacks." Much has been written about how the Morality Department implemented the 1890 city bylaw that forced newsboys and other street vendors under the age of sixteen to obtain licences, licences that were given if boys agreed to stay off the streets by attending school and taking up residence in suitable lodging homes. Beginning in 1893, constables from the Morality Department were appointed as truancy officers, and we have already seen the role they could play in regulating boys' sleeping arrangements. But Archibald also zeroed in more directly on boys' sexual relations with men. As early as 1886, Archibald noted in a report of his activities "several cases" of sexual relations between boys and men. [...]

Working alongside the police, sometimes prodding them into action, were moral reformers active in the social purity movement. While most social purity activists focused their energies on women, prostitution, and the "white slave trade," sex between men and boys did not go unnoticed. W. L. Clark, hired by the Methodist Church's Department of Temperance and Moral Reform in 1910 to give lectures to boys on sex hygiene and the "secret vice," repeated the story of a boy who said he was taught to masturbate by "a man in my home town." Clark warned that boys were often "taught that act by an older companion." [...]

The Toronto Vigilance Committee, formed in 1911, included in its work "efforts to aid in preventing boys being led astray by moral perverts." Reflecting the middle-class distrust of working-class children, the committee pinned responsibility for being led astray as much on boys as on "moral perverts." The Vigilance Committee encouraged its members to report all "frivolous young girls and boys likely to be easily enticed into wrong doing." [...]

In addition to the Morality Department and moral reformers, working-class parents, especially mothers, played a key role in regulating sexual relations between their sons and men. Boys' sexual relations with men sometimes came to mothers' attention not because their sons told them about the encounter but because mothers discovered something amiss in the course of child care. In 1915, nine-year-old William had been doing "dirty tricks" with a man in the neighbourhood. "I have been there often," William testified, "he gave me money to do dirty tricks .... He told me not to tell my mother, that's why I did not." Mrs H. explained to the court that while bathing William, she noticed "his person was swollen ... when I examined him it was sore." [...]

Not all mothers went to the police. As feminist historians have demonstrated, while working-class women made use of the police and other social services when needed, at other times they resented the intrusion of police constables, truancy officers, rent collectors, and moral reformers into their neighbourhoods, preferring to supervise their own streets.[16] Rather than go to the police, some mothers confronted men themselves. [...]

Mothers' different responses reflected the fact that working-class mothers had a range of understandings of sexual relations between boys and men. Certainly some mothers believed a wrong, an "evil thing," had been done which required punishment. [...] Other parents, however, did not react with shock or alarm. Harold B. told his father that on his way to school he sometimes stopped at Randal S.'s second-hand furniture shop, where Randal "took my pants down ... put his hands there [and] rubbed it lots of times .... He gave me three cents and five cents." According to Harold, "I told my father only once .... Father thought it was alright." [...]

Mothers too could take a rather pragmatic approach to their sons' sexual relations with men. For two months in 1921, Dominick lived with an Ottawa man in his house on Wilbrod Street. As Dominick told the court, "I was to mind his house and take the dogs out .... I took the dogs out in the morning 2 or 3 times." Dominick's duties extended beyond domestic labour. "I slept with him and three dogs in a bed in a room .... The first night I slept with him he started to touch my private parts. On another night he put my privates in his mouth and wanted me to put his privates in my mouth." Asked by the court how such an arrangement had been arrived at, Dominick said that, "he went to where I lived to hire me. He spoke to my mother." Asked if he ever told his mother about the sex, he replied that "I did not tell my mother about it. My mother told me I had to work." [...]

*****

London, Ontario—Then and Now

[...] In February 1994, two London men appeared in court on charges relating to sexual activity with boys. They were only two of dozens of men caught up in a police sweep that began in November of the previous year when London police announced they had uncovered a "child pornography ring." The London "kiddie porn ring," as it came to be known, had all the elements of a classic moral panic.[17] Given that the events in London unfolded while I was writing this article, it was perhaps inevitable that I found myself thinking about the relationship between past and present. [...]

One of the principle mechanisms of a moral panic is the construction of a threat—in the case of London, the so-called child pornography ring. [...] What the London police had discovered was a subculture in which "boys"—many of whom were street youth from London's poor east end—traded sex with men for money, cigarettes, drugs, and shelter. [...] The first and perhaps most obvious "lessons of history" is that far from being a recent phenomenon, Ontario boys have traded sex with men in exchange for money and gifts from at least the early twentieth century. In the face of the often-harsh economic fundamentals of life for poor and working-class boys, boys devised a range of survival strategies. Just as they learned to sell their physical labour in exchange for wages, they also learned to sell their bodies in return for food, shelter, money, or a night on the town, perhaps dinner at Bowles and a show at the Hippodrome. In pursuing men, boys engaged in a range of relations, including many brief, casual encounters and, like Thomas and his doctor friend or Harold and his scoutmaster, longer-lasting, sustaining relationships.

[...] Sexual danger existed primarily for younger boys, and it might be encountered while playing in a park or working in a shoeshine shop. Sexual danger was rooted in men's power, power that rested on men's greater age and physical strength. Other times, the very places designed to shelter, protect, and assist boys—Sunday School, the Boy Scouts, Big Brothers—were the places where sexual danger was best concealed. Then as now, cases of sexual coercion within organizational settings occasionally came to public attention. But the law's limited gaze on an individual culprit and on legal technicalities [...] obscured the broader context, particularly the way sexual coercion was rooted in institutional relations of unequal power between boys and men within such settings. A boy probably stood a better chance of escaping an unwanted sexual advance on the streets of his own neighbourhood, perhaps through the intervention of his mother, than he did in a Children's Aid Society shelter. Indeed, in some cases, rather than a form of danger or abuse itself, a boy's relationship with a man might be a way to escape physical abuse by parents in the home or by foremen in a factory.

[...] While the London panic undoubtedly uncovered some real cases of exploitation, its broader cultural implications and meanings had less to do with boys' exploitation and more with linking gay men to the sexual abuse of boys. Despite the frequency with which it has been hauled out over time, the homosexual as a molester of boys is in fact a relatively recent historical invention. As other historians have demonstrated, these links were forged, beginning in the 1930s, with the rising influence of psychiatry and the elaboration of what it termed the "criminal sexual psychopath." The link between homosexuality and child molestation became further entrenched in the culture during the postwar sex crime panics. [...] What is striking about the history of sexual relations between boys and men in early twentieth-century Ontario is the absence of the homosexual psychopath. Police constables, moral reformers, truancy officers, and sex advice givers made little attempt to construct the men with whom boys had sex as a particular sexual villain, nor did they describe their sexual relations between boys and men not to protect innocent victims from abuse and exploitation by homosexual psychopaths but to prevent "frivolous boys" from being "led astray" by "fallen men." [...]

In our own time, marked by widespread cultural anxieties over shifting gender and sexual relations spurred on by the feminist and lesbian/gay liberation movements, the complex and multiple meanings of sexual relations between boys and men are invariably constructed as cases of "child abuse" involving only boy victims and adult homosexual predators.[18] In the early twentieth century, the moral economy of many working-class boys and their families sustained a more expansive, nuanced understanding of both the dangers and the possibilities of sexual relations between boys and men. Whole communities might rise up when boys suffered at the hands of a man who used his position of trust and authority to wield sexual power over boys. At the same time, some working-class boys and their families recognized that, in a variety of ways, boys' sexual relations with men might provide a temporary escape from or way to alleviate their impoverishment. All of this suggests that early twentieth-century understandings of sexual relations between boys and men were markedly different from our own, highlighting the ways sexual meanings are subject to historical pressures and change.

Notes

For their helpful comments, I thank Veronica Strong-Boag, George Chauncey, Bryan Palmer, Neil Sutherland, and especially Henry Abelove. Thanks as well to the *CHR*'s anonymous readers. Earlier versions of this article were presented to Out of the Archives: A Conference on the History of Bisexuals, Lesbians and Gay Men in Canada, York University, January 1994, and The Second Carleton Conference on the History of the Family, Carleton University, May 1994.

1. C.S. Clark, *Of Toronto the Good* (Montreal 1898), 81–3, 90.
2. For historiographical background, see my article "In Search of 'Sodom North': The Writing of Lesbian and Gay History in English Canada, 1970–1990," *Canadian Review of Comparative Literature/Revue Canadienne de Litterature Comparée* 21 (March/June 1994): 117–32.
3. This article is drawn from my PhD dissertation, tentatively entitled "Toronto the Gay: Sex, Men, and the Police in Urban Ontario, 1890–1940" (Queen's University, in progress). My search through court records housed at the Archives of Ontario turned up 313 cases involving "homosexual" offences in Ontario for the period 1890–1935. It is not possible to pin down exactly how many or what percentage of these cases involved boys, as some cases did not specify the ages of (or provide other age-related information about) the parties involved. I have been able to identify seventy cases involving sexual relations between men and boys/male youth to examine for this article. These cases were processed under the criminal code categories of buggery, indecent assault upon a male, and gross indecency, the latter being by far the most frequent charge. On the legal history of these criminal code provisions, see Terry Chapman, "'An Oscar Wilde Type': 'The Abominable Crime of Buggery' in Western Canada, 1890–1920," *Criminal Justice History* 4 (1983): 97–118 and Chapman, "Male Homosexuality: Legal Restraints and Social Attitudes in Western Canada, 1890–1920," in Louis Knafla, ed., *Law and Justice in a New Land: Essays in Western Canadian Legal History* (Toronto 1986), 277–92. The cases employed here come from two different sets of court records: Archives of Ontario, Criminal Court Records, RG 22, Criminal Assize Indictment Case Files, Series 392 (hereafter AO, Criminal Assize Indictments, county/district, date, case number), and Archives of Ontario, Criminal Court Records, RG 22,

Crown Attorney Prosecution Case Files, various series (hereafter AO, Crown Attorney Prosecution Case Files, county/district, date, case number). As the crown attorney prosecution case files remain largely unprocessed and stored in temporary boxes, I will not cite box numbers. In order to be granted research access to the crown attorney's files, I was required to enter into a research agreement with the archives. In accordance with that agreement, all names have been anonymized and all case file numbers used here refer to my own numbering scheme and do not correspond to any numbers that may appear on the original case files.

4. There are some parallels here with the history of working-class girls and their sexual relations with men. As Christine Stansell has argued for nineteenth-century New York City, young girls learned "early about their vulnerability to sexual harm from grown men ... [but] also learned some ways to turn men's interest to their own purposes. Casual prostitution was one," Stansell locates the way "girls gambled with prostitution" firmly within the economic necessities dictated by life on the street, as well as within girls' desire for independence and amusement. By virtue of their gender, boys, especially older boys, stood a better chance than most girls in the luck of sexual draw with men. But the dialectic between vulnerability to sexual harm and turning that vulnerability around to one's own purposes also characterizes much about boys' sexual relations with men in early twentieth-century urban Ontario. Stansell, *City of Women: Sex and Class in New York, 1789–1860* (New York 1986), 182.
5. AO, Crown Attorney Prosecution Case Files, York County, 1918, case 35.
6. AO, Criminal Assize Indictments, Middlesex County, 1904, case 191.
7. I want to underscore that in arguing that sexual danger and desire were rooted in boys' street culture and working-class life, I am not suggesting that sex between boys and men was somehow unique to working-class existence. My concentration on working-class male youth stems from my own interest in working-class history and from the nature of my sources (working-class and immigrant boys turn up in the court records more often than middle-class boys because the former were subject to greater police and legal surveillance). Middle-class boys also had sex with men, but the social organization of their sexual relations was

different. For instance, rather than on the street, middle-class boys developed sexual relations with men in private boarding schools. On romantic friendships and sexual dangers in boys' boarding schools, see, for example, Jean Barman, *Growing Up British in British Columbia: Boys in Private School* (Vancouver 1984), and James Fitzgerald, *Old Boys: The Powerful Legacy of Upper Canada College* (Toronto 1994). See also E. Anthony Rotundo, "Romantic Friendship: Male Intimacy and Middle-Class Youth in The Northern United States, 1800–1900," *Journal of Social History* 23 (Fall 1989): 1–25.

8. AO, Crown Attorney Prosecution Case Files, Carleton County, 1929, case 171. I discuss Bowles Lunch and other late-night diners as homosexual sites in more detail elsewhere in my dissertation. The importance of these spaces was first drawn out by George Chauncey in *Gay New York: Gender, Urban Culture, and the Making of the Gay Male World, 1890–1940* (New York 1994), 163–77.

9. AO, Crown Attorney Prosecution Case Files, Carleton County, 1925, case 155. On the pattern of homosexual relationships in the early twentieth century in which working-class male youths were kept by wealthier men, see Kevin Porter and Jeffrey Weeks, eds., *Between the Acts: Lives of Homosexual Men, 1885–1967* (London 1991). See also the wonderful photographic evidence of the long relationship between architect Montague Glover and Ralph Hall, his young, working-class chauffeur and lover, in James Gardiner, *A Class Apart: The Private Pictures of Montague Glover* (London 1992).

10. AO, Criminal Assize Indictments, Lambton County, 1925, case 192

11. AO, Crown Attorney Prosecution Case Files, York County, 1917, case 23. […]

12. AO, Crown Attorney Prosecution Case Files, Carleton County, 1927, case 164. On boarding as a working-class survival strategy, see Bettina Bradbury, "Pigs, Cows, and Boarders: Non-Wage Forms of Survival among Montreal Families, 1861–1891," *Labour/Le Travail* 14 (1984): 9–46.

13. AO, Crown Attorney Prosecution Case Files, York County 1913, case 96; 1920, case 106; 1909, case 92; 1916, case 22.

14. *Report of the Commissioners Appointed to Enquire into the Prison and Reformatory System of Ontario, 1891* (Toronto 1891), 700. Toronto Police Department, "Annual Report of the Chief Constable, 1890," Toronto City Council, *Minutes*, 1891, app. C. 27. For more on the turn-of-the-century "boy problem," see Neil Sutherland, *Children in English Canadian Society: Framing the Twentieth Century Consensus* (Toronto 1976), and Harry Hendrick, *Images of Youth: Age, Class, and the Male Youth Problem, 1880–1920* (London 1990).

15. Howland's testimony before the Royal Commission on the Relations of Labor and Capital, cited in Michael Cross, ed., *The Workingman in the Nineteenth Century* (Toronto 1974), 106–7. *Report of the Commissioners Appointed to Enquire into the Prison and Reformatory System in Ontario, 1891*, 689.

16. See Ellen Ross, *Love and Toil: Motherhood in Outcast London, 1870–1918* (New York 1993).

17. On the mechanisms of moral panics, I am following Jeffrey Weeks, *Sexuality and Its Discontents: Meanings, Myths, and Modern Sexualities* (London 1985), 45.

18. It scarcely needs pointing out that the historical shifts in the meaning of sexual relations between boys and men towards the current hegemonic and homophobic understanding of such relations as the product of homosexual predation has done nothing to help those boys who have experienced sexual abuse at the hands of men. The identification of the sexual abuse of boys as a social problem is a very recent phenomenon. It has come about not through the efforts of those who obfuscate the issue of men's power of homosexualizing the abuse of boys but through the work of women and men, including lesbians and gay men, to confront child sexual abuse. See, for example, *Loving in Fear: Lesbian and Gay Survivors of Childhood Sexual Abuse* (Toronto 1992).

CHAPTER 20

Mother Knows Best:
The Development of Separate Institutions
for Women

Kelly Hannah-Moffat

• •

> The sentimental cult of domestic virtues is the cheapest method
> at society's disposal of keeping women quiet without seriously
> considering their grievances or improving their position.
> —Myrda and Klien 1993

*****

Most revisionist studies of the functional and instrumental aspects of penality, although instructive, offer little insight into how penal logics operate and how they affect and are affected by wider logics of reform. David Garland's analysis (1990) of modern punishment offers an alternative approach to understanding some recent changes in penality and can aid in the analysis of women's imprisonment Garland's project—to understand theoretical developments in the sociology of punishment—makes a significant contribution to this field of inquiry. He notes that penal policy is "a rich and flexible tradition which has always contained within itself a number of competing themes and elements, principles and counter-principles … its key terms have been developing a fluid rather man fixed, producing a series of descriptions—*moral reform, training, treatment, correction, rehabilitation, deterrence, incapacitation*—for what it is penal sanctions do" (7; emphasis added). He asserts that these "competing and flexible themes" have played a critical role in establishing and legitimating technical

apparatuses designed to punish and control deviants while simultaneously furthering the social engineering of a "good" society. For example, Garland (6) suggests:

> In normal circumstances the administrators and employees of a penal system understand and justify their own actions within the established ideological framework—a working ideology. This official ideology is a set of categories, signs, and symbols through which punishment represents itself to itself and others. Usually this ideology provides a highly developed rhetorical resource which can be used to give names, justifications, and a measure of coherence to a vast jumble of things that are done in the name of penal policy. Not the least of its uses is to supply the means to explain (or explain away) failures and to indicate the strategies which will, it is hoped, prevent their reoccurrence.

Garland's argument can be expanded to help us understand and theorize developments in women's penality. For example, maternalism— one prominent working ideology of modern punishment—was employed by both reformers and administrators to challenge the failures of the penitentiary (custodial) model and to justify the creation of separate institutions for women prisoners. The operation of these institutions relied on a maternal logic that was combined with other ideologies informing penal administrations, such as labour, religious, moral, and domestic training. A maternal logic, as an example of Garland's working ideology, provides a "coherence to a vast jumble of things" that are done to and for women prisoners by well-intentioned reformers and administrators. Besides legitimating the things done to improve conditions in women's prisons, maternal logic can be used to understand some of the failures to change certain repressive elements of custodial regimes, and some of the overtly punitive technologies that were used when women failed to conform to maternal notions of reformability. Maternalism is a versatile concept, one easily linked to a wide variety of disciplinary practices.

The image of motherhood that underpins maternal logic is difficult to contest Maternal ideals are flexible enough to be combined with a wide variety of penal techniques that also rely on a versatile range of ideologies. Implicit in the concept of motherhood is an almost universally accepted productive or positive discipline. To varying degrees, certain forms of maternalism have been accepted or rejected by institutions at different historical moments. [...]

The Creation of Separate Institutions for Women Prisoners

Impact of the American Women's Prison Reform Movement in Canada

Penal theorists and reformers had a profound influence on nineteenth-century penal policy. However, as Zedner notes (1991b:130), "the most coherent sources of penal policy for women lay mainly outside government policy making circles and arose from publicized but largely voluntary efforts." Secular and evangelical penal philosophies were combined with maternal logics to devise a separate strategy of maternal reform for women prisoners. Penal reformers and administrators used maternal logics to forge improbable coalitions that led to women governing female prisoners under the authority of maternal benevolence (cf. Koven and Michel 1993).

By the late 1840s, female prisoners were usually supervised by women officials in makeshift women's wings of mixed prisons. The conditions in these units prompted changes that fundamentally altered the face of women's penality. Throughout the nineteenth and early twentieth centuries, American maternalists, inspired by the work of Elizabeth Fry, spearheaded a reform movement that ultimately affected Canada, Britain, and the United States. The construction of separate prisons for women, based on the principle of maternal guidance, was a result of this wave of reform. The movement affected more than simply women's prisons; it fundamentally changed the governance of women more generally. In the sphere of penality, it led to the hiring of many women matrons—an accomplishment that had several unanticipated consequences. Underpinning these strategies was a reformative maternal logic that incorporated some elements of evangelical maternalism, but was largely reliant on moral definitions of criminality and on secular interpretations of women's natural expertise as mothers. In this, it differed from the evangelical maternalism advocated by Elizabeth Fry and her Ladies' Committee.

In order to institute a women-centred program of governance, maternal reformers had to do three things: reconstruct the tarnished image of women convicts; "sell" the importance of proper maternal guidance; and convince the authorities to build separate prisons for women. These objectives were partially based on a critique of failed custodial models. The establishment of Ontario's Andrew Mercer Reformatory for Women in 1874 was an example of the mobilization of a maternal logic. Once it was built, a women-centred form of governing, envisioned and administered by women, was able to emerge.

Custodial Catastrophes and Maternal Interventions

The American women's reform movement began in 1840, when several individuals and small groups of women, concentrated in New York, Massachusetts, and Indiana, took up the cause of women prisoners as their special mission (Freedman 1981:22). This movement peaked between 1870 and 1920 with the building of several reformatories for women (Rafter 1992; Freedman 1981, 1996). As Freedman (1981) notes, this movement evolved from a critique of state responses to women's deviance and from the perceived inability of the state to sufficiently care for "fallen sisters." While insisting that the state had a moral obligation and duty to appropriately care for and reform female convicts, women reformers attempted to accomplish this task themselves through their own good will and charity. Women reformers' calls for state accountability with respect to the care of female convicts and for an endorsement of their own strategies significantly altered women's penality. [...]

The early activities of these women were similar to those of Elizabeth Fry: reformers visited the women in custody, advocated improved conditions, and eventually developed associations to help women prisoners reintegrate into their communities. In an effort to improve conditions in American women's prisons, women reformers donated their time and money (used to hire matrons and acquire basic amenities, such as soap and food). [...] The first separate custodial institution for women was Mount Pleasant Female Prison at Ossining, New York, which opened in 1835. According to Rafter (1992:16), the founding of this institution was a milestone in women's corrections because it was the first women's prison in the United States that was deliberately established; before then, women's units had been haphazardly developed as appendages to men's prisons. Mount Pleasant Prison was governed by two innovative women, Eliza Farnham and Georgiana Bruce, who experimented with reformational techniques. These foreshadowed the "great reformatory movement" just ahead (Rafter 1992:16–17).

Prior to the development of a semi-organized reform movement, a few dedicated American reformers worked, often in isolation, within the system and with administrators to improve the conditions of women prisoners, most of whom were held in men's prisons. It was the interest of charitable women such as Dorthea Dix, Abigail Hopper Gibbons. Mary Wister, and Sarah Doremus that inspired changes in penal practice and policy and encouraged a new generation of reformers, who eventually succeeded in designing specific programs for normalizing women prisoners. When early American reformers encountered resistance to their ideas about specialized institutions for female criminals, they established private institutions (Pollock-Byrne 1990:42). Before the emergence of separate prison facilities and institutional programs for women, these reformers opened homes and designed private reformative programs for prostitutes, pregnant women, wayward girls, and orphans.[1] These early manifestations of maternal concern helped generate a strong current of reform that eventually swept most women out of men's prisons and into institutions run entirely for and by women (Rafter 1992:16; Freedman 1981).

*****

The Importance of Maternal Guidance

[...] In an effort to feminize justice for women, maternal reformers embarked on a campaign of institution building that emphasized the attributes of a loving, moral mother. The architectural ideal for the reformatory differed from that for the penitentiary. Reformatories for women were to be based on a cottage plan rather than a congregate model. This artificial "home" was to be an embodiment of domestic and maternal ideals. This female ethos created a distinct disciplinary rationality that promoted the matriarchal role of a mother (or older sister) in a traditional white, middle-class familial setting.

[...] By the late 1800s, several states (as well as certain parts of Britain and Canada) were beginning to construct reformatories for the rehabilitation of female convicts.[2] This emphasis on the separation of female convicts was consistent with the emerging philosophies of new penologists, who underscored the importance of classifying inmates by age, sex, and offence history. These projects were part of a much broader shift in social expectations vis-à-vis the role of punishment and the obligation of the state—a shift characterized as "welfare penality" (Garland 1985) or "socialized justice" (Chunn 1992). While these institutions continued to segregate and incapacitate, punishment under the reformatory model had a new purpose: to rehabilitate the inmate. For women, "rehabilitation" had specific meanings. Rafter (1992:159) argues that the reformatory regime served two important reformative purposes: to train women to accept a standard of propriety that dictated chastity before marriage and fidelity afterwards; and to instruct women in homemaking, a competency they would use upon release as either a dutiful wife and mother or as a domestic servant in someone else's home. [...]

This regime was based on faith in women's innate capacities to reform. The expectation was that a mother's love and power could become a model for regulating, correcting, and normalizing deviant women. [...] The reformatory model exemplified several of the themes expressed decades earlier by Elizabeth Fry: religious and moral regulation of women; the employment of an all-female staff; vocational training (particularly in domestic services); and the classification and separation of different types of offenders. [...]

The hiring of virtuous female role models was deemed essential to the effective operation of a women-centred maternal strategy. The employment of women was predicated on the belief that the female prisoner by nature required special treatment that could only be provided by other women. Reformers argued that women's natural capacities and moral force

qualified them for employment in women's prisons. Many well-intentioned reformers moved beyond philanthropic advocacy to secure employment and status in the new reformatories. Female administrators, influenced by maternal ideals and new secular technologies of reform, complemented the diminished but nonetheless crucial role of evangelical maternalists, who continued to strive for the salvation of fallen women. Some men supported the view that women were innately qualified to work in and administer women's prisons; however, many were unwilling to grant women authority over these new institutions (Freedman 1981:61).

In the second half of the nineteenth century, matrons were qualitatively different from their earlier counterparts (Rafter 1992). The newer matrons were more carefully selected and trained than their predecessors. Ironically, the new matron was expected to exhibit the characteristics of a middle-class homemaker and to inspire prisoners to become respectable, in spite of her own role outside of the home.[3] The use of prison matrons became commonplace in most penal institutions, when the number of female convicts permitted. The hiring of matrons seems to have been more closely regulated and scrutinized after the mid-1800s. Lists of criteria for matrons begin to appear in Prison Association records and reports around that time.[4] While it was preferable to have virtuous women working in prisons, it was difficult to attract them to this stigmatized and low-paying work.

By 1867, some prison associations had established a set of criteria for hiring matrons. For example, a report on prisons in the United States and Canada assembled by the Prison Association of New York (PANY) noted that while in many respects the qualifications for female officers were the same as those for male officers,[5] it was especially important that female officers be "distinguished for modesty and demeanour, and the exercise of domestic virtues, and that they possess an intimate knowledge of household employment, which will enable them to teach the ignorant and neglected female prisoner how to economize her means, so as to guard her from the temptations caused by waste and extravagance" (PANY 1867:125). [...]

Creating a "Reformable Subject"

Central to the maternal penal strategy was the existence of a dutiful and daughterly subject who would be amenable to, or at least tolerant of, this new penal environment. The public image of convicts as first redeemable and later treatable was critical to the legitimacy of reformers. Accordingly, new conceptions of the female criminal, women's expertise, and the reformatory model evolved together (Rafter 1992). Drawing on their experiences working with women prisoners and their children, leaders of the movement began by challenging existing impressions of criminal women as wretched, depraved, and unreformable savages. They challenged the "archetype of the Dark Lady, a woman of uncommon strength, seductive power, and evil inclination" and instead promoted a "new concept of the female offender as childlike, wayward and redeemable, a fallen woman that [sic] was more sinned against than a sinner herself" (Rafter 1992:49). Enthusiastic reformers suggested that the female criminal was a "fragile vessel," neglected and ill advised in her choices, a woman who could be redeemed through proper instruction and guidance. [...] In 1844 Margaret Fuller, a prominent maternalist, argued that women prisoners were victims who needed help to overcome the circumstances that led them to crime: "Born of unfortunate marriages, inheriting dangerous inclinations, neglected in childhood, with bad habits and associates, as certainly must be the case of some of you, how terrible will be the struggle when you leave this shelter" (Chevigny 1976; cited in Freedman 1981:30). [...]

*****

While many institutions set out initially to reform all women who came through their doors, these regimes were quickly modified to reflect the material reality that all women were not equally suitable for or willing to participate in reformatory regimes. This realization prompted the development of a complex classification schema that used clearly defined selection criteria to screen admissions and handpick the "most appropriate" candidates. Reformers and administrators attempted to recruit young white women who were, by and large, first offenders convicted of relatively minor offences. Women perceived as "unreformable" were given less attention and were more likely to remain in local jails or be sent to penitentiaries if their sentence permitted. This led to a bifurcated system of corrections: over time, a residual category of female convicts classified by reformers as beyond hope became a necessary evil. Rather than admitting that maternal strategies failed with some convicts, reformers defined certain "experienced" women as unwilling and unable to reform. Thus, limitations and barriers to reform were blamed on the individual rather than on maternal strategies. [...]

The Andrew Mercer Reformatory and the Reformatory Ideal

*****

In Canada, separate reformatories for women were not developed through feminist lobbying; rather, they were a state-generated project. State reformers influenced by American penality, such as J.W. Langmuir (J.W. Langmuir, Ontario Prison Inspector, 1868) encouraged the state to adopt a maternal penal reform strategy predicated on the belief that virtuous women could uplift their fallen sisters.[6] Langmuir was disturbed by the lack of classification[7] and idleness of inmates in local jails. Based on evidence of American experts, he concluded that women were "able to exercise great power and influence, in practical ways towards reclaiming the criminal and fallen of their sex" (Oliver 1994:524). Langmuir advocated the construction of a distinct and potentially less expensive women's reformatory, wherein women could receive "the great moral benefits of the separate principle" (Strange 1983:10). [...]

Langmuir's successful use of a maternal logic secured support for the construction of the

Mercer Reformatory. In 1874, the Mercer opened its doors under the supervision of Mrs. O'Reilly. The Mercer[8] signified the institutionalization of this new form of women's governance, which drew on a variety of rationalities and technologies to justify and promote a specific women-centred strategy. [...] Institutional rhetoric stressed a language of domesticity and informality, as Berkovits notes: the building itself was not referred to as a prison, but as a "house," the all-female corps of guards were called "attendants," and the prisoners themselves, "residents." Superintendent O'Sullivan [who succeeded O'Reilly] often quite overtly referred to the prisoners as her "daughters" and herself as their "mother." Staff members were referred to by first name (Mr. John, or Miss Margaret, for example), and were collectively described as "the family." O'Sullivan's own relatives mixed freely with the inmates, and they were well known to each other (1995:3–4).

*****

In many respects, the construction of the prison as a home ignored material and legal realities that reflected the ultimately repressive aspects of a court-imposed custodial sentence. Women's behaviour in the Mercer was constantly monitored, and mobility was severely limited. Most of the women sent to the Mercer were unwilling participants. As such, they were not always receptive to maternal reform strategies. [...]

Maternally Based Programs of Prisoner Reform

Specialized programming for women prisoners was one innovation of the Mercer regime. Part of the Mercer's public appeal lay in its claim to reform fallen women through a strict gender-specific regime of hard labour, moral and religious training, and after-care. Norms of domesticity and the ideal of true womanhood were central to the Mercer's programming strategy; however, administrators also relied on the same technologies promoted in early

penitentiaries. The programs offered combined basic education with religious, moral, and domestic training. They also taught obedience, servility, and the importance of knowing one's place in society (Ruemper 1994:372). These programs included the Clean Speech Society (a modified Swearer's Anonymous), hard labour to instil discipline, and vocational training to prepare women for careers in domestic service.

Industrial training played a significant role in offender reform. According to Oliver (1994:540–1), Inspector Langmuir "habitually referred to the Mercer as an Industrial Reformatory." Similarly, Superintendent O'Reilly regarded the work program as central to the institutional maternal regime. Her acceptance of the conventional Protestant wisdom about the relationship between idleness and crime is illustrated in the following passage: "Of all wretched women the idle are the most wretched. We try to impress upon them the importance of labour, and we look upon this as one of the great means of their reformation" (Ontario Prison Inspector, Annual Reports 1881; cited in Oliver 1994:541).

This commitment to labour was extended to sentencing practices. Langmuir tried hard to convince Premier Mowat to educate sentencing authorities about the importance of industrial training at the Mercer, and the need for sentences long enough to ensure an appropriate training regime (Oliver 1994:541). While the training received by women was gender specific (laundering, sewing, knitting, and domestic service), the Mercer's emphasis on labour was not unique: the ideal of productive labour was central to most Canadian penitentiary and reformatory regimes. While Langmuir and O'Reilly were campaigning for industrial training in the 1880s, concerns were repeatedly being raised about the absence of productive training for women inmates at Kingston Penitentiary, where women had been incarcerated since 1835. These concerns about idleness and productive training for women prisoners continued to be voiced throughout the late nineteenth century and into the twentieth.

The normative regulation of women prisoners continued after they were released from the Mercer. For instance, the scheme for parole was designed to reinforce the importance of proper womanly conduct, which, when exhibited, allowed prisoners to earn marks toward the rebate of their sentences (Strange 1983). Mercer officials arranged employment for women on release; on some occasions, members of Superintendent O'Sullivan's own family hired prisoners as domestics to satisfy their parole. This seemingly well-intentioned practice served to regulate women's compliance with parole regulations; it also ensured continued surveillance of female prisoners after release. The regulation of women through the parole process began with ensuring that female prisoners were "appropriately employed upon release." Most women were employed as domestic servants. Factory jobs and other types of employment in the city were dismissed as inappropriate because of the temptations of city life. This was consistent with early beliefs that women's crime was a result of exposure to negative influences and, in particular, the absence of "good" maternal and domestic influences. Community strategies of surveillance and regulation were an integral component of newly emerging after-care services. In the twentieth century, well-intentioned women became involved in the policing and normalization of ex-convicts by hiring them as domestic servants and befriending them upon release.[9] Once the Mercer opened, more and more Canadian reformers found another outlet for their talents. Consistent with the objectives of evangelical maternal logic, reformers from the Upper Canadian Bible Society sent female prisoners bibles; at the same time, the Tract Society, the YMCA, and the Committee of the Hospital for Side Children supplied religious literature (Ruemper 1994:361). Representatives from local churches, the Prisoners' Aid Society, the Salvation Army, and the Women's Christian Temperance Union visited the women and provided a variety of religious services, such as preaching, bible reading, praying, and counselling. Organizations such as the Salvation Army and the Prisoners' Aid Society also aided the women's reintegration into the community by providing them with monetary, spiritual, and emotional support.[10]

[...] Reformers ensured that once individuals were released from the Mercer they continued to conform to the ideals of domesticity and "true womanhood" taught at the reformatory. Their main objective was to ensure that these women did not fall back into their old habits. For example, reformers often met women at the door of the prison on the morning of their discharge to ensure they had appropriate clothing, lodgings, and employment (generally in domestic service). If a woman was not prepared for release, she could choose to go to a home of refuge, such as a Magdalene Asylum, a Salvation Army Prison Gate Home, or a Rescue Home. These homes were often extensions of institutional regimes.

The women released from the Mercer were encouraged to keep in touch and reassured that they would always be welcome "home." Letter writing was a common way of continuing to regulate [...] women after their release. Oliver (1994) and Berkovits (1995) suggest that the correspondence between superintendent and ex-prisoners was a testament to the maternal success of the Mercer; in contrast, Strange (1983) shows that maternalism had marked regulatory effects. O'Sullivan's diligent correspondence with some inmates revealed to her certain details of their private lives that she might not have learned otherwise. [...]

*****

Maternally minded reformers joined forces with prison officials to continue to govern women even when the reformatory had no legal authority to regulate their behaviour (Wetherell, 1979). Images of a mother raising her child to observe the proper manners and habits of bourgeois society dominate the narratives of the Mercer. The propensity of the staff to check up on and maintain contact with released inmates extends this metaphor by suggesting that children require constant supervision, support, and guidance—even throughout their adult lives. The task of "post-adolescent mothering" was bureaucratized through the development of formal release mechanisms, the hiring of social workers, and the development of state-sponsored after-care services. At the same time, initiatives similar to those of the Mercer staff illustrate an extension of the state's obligation to not only punish but also rehabilitate prisoners through techniques of maternal governance.

"Daughterly Subjects"

Consistent with the Mercer's familial emphasis, the reformatory selected matrons by stressing the importance of "loving but demanding mothers who forgave past errors but insisted on obedience"; to complement this role, penal administrators preferred to deal with "daughterly subjects" (Strange 1983:20). [...] There was a preference for young, single, white females who were Protestant, Canadian-born, literate, and temperate and who had some experience in domestic and personal service (Ruemper 1994:371). However, the women incarcerated at the Mercer did not conform to these ideals.

[...] Oliver (1994:542–3) notes that in the early years of the Mercer, while over half the prisoners were classified under the occupational category "domestic" (which included homemakers, maids, cooks, laundresses, and servants), over one-quarter of the remaining population was classified as "prostitutes." Although there appears to have been a sharp decline in the number of prostitutes who were sent to the Mercer between 1891 and 1900, and an increase in the number of domestics, Oliver (1994:543) suggests that these shifts were more likely a result of changes in policing strategies and classification procedures, and did not reflect a radical shift in inmate characteristics. Whether the changes in occupational classifications were made by institutional officials or by police, they are instructive for two reasons. First, they demonstrate the inconsistency between "ideal" and "real" subjects of maternal reform campaigns: in practice, Mercer officials were obligated to accept all prisoners sent to the

Mercer by sentencing authorities (Oliver 1994:537). Second, the stigmatization of women by labelling them as prostitutes is inconsistent with a benevolent maternal desire to redeem basically innocent women. Seen in this light, the overrepresentation of women prisoners in the category "domestic" provided a convenient rationale for domestic training programs and wider maternal reform strategies.

The antithesis of the maternal ideal is the unco-operative and recalcitrant woman. Some accounts of the Mercer's regime suggest that there were serious difficulties in managing certain prisoners through maternal strategies. Both Berkovits (1995) and Strange (1983) describe several occasions when maternal strategies failed to break the spirit of certain prisoners. Berkovits's (1995) analysis of women prisoners' resistance to maternal strategies is theoretically limited; even so, he does offer some interesting examples of the tensions that existed between prison officials and their charges. For example, he indicates that institutional officials observed the following behaviours: inmates quarrelling among themselves in nurseries, fighting, throwing dishes, stealing tools to make weapons, tearing their clothing, breaking furniture, assaulting staff members, and swearing and uttering threats (1995:5). [...] Clearly, some of the women at the Mercer defied conventional stereotypes of the "reformable woman" or "daughterly subject."

Attempts were made to segregate these women from the rest of the population so that criminally experienced women, such as a brothel keepers, could not corrupt apparently naïve women. These women's actions often led to some form of institutional discipline. These "unreformable" women tended to be subjected to punitive techniques designed to physically compel submission (such as cold baths or a "good spanking") or to be segregated and confined in "punishment rooms," in which they received few benefits of the "loving home" to which they were confined.[11] [...]

Mercer officials also used more invasive physical techniques of restraint and corporal punishment, such as whipping and the use of handcuffs. When one inmate serving an indefinite sentence went on a hunger strike after being placed in segregation for threatening to kill Attendant Mick, Superintendent O'Sullivan, on the advice of the surgeon, advocated the use of a "cold bath" to encourage her to behave.[12] When entire cell blocks disobeyed institutional rules and regulations, forms of mass punishment, such as deprivation of lighting and prolonged periods of being locked in a cell, were used to encourage conformity. However, some of the more severe corporal punishments used in the "maternal regime" at the Mercer to deal with recalcitrant inmates were formally discouraged by penitentiary officials. The rules and regulations of penitentiary discipline in the late 1800s formally discouraged corporal punishments, segregation on a diet of bread and water beyond six consecutive meals, and segregation beyond six nights.

The Mercer's male surgeon, Dr King, played an important paternal role in disciplining inmates, and the superintendent often deferred to Dr King in disciplinary matters. His "diagnosis" often resulted in cures that were not easily distinguishable from typical means of punishing inmates. Berkovits (1995:9) notes that some of Dr King's techniques bordered on cruelty and were consistent with the beliefs of the surgeon at the "more strict" central prison for men. For example, the "cold bath," which required "plunging a refractory inmate into a cold bath then briefly strangling her under water until she submitted" to the wishes of prison officials (Strange 1983:53), was a medically sanctioned treatment. The "cold water treatment, a similar procedure, was described by Superintendent O'Sullivan as follows: "Shutting a woman in an empty cell properly equipped for the purpose and ... as I have explained before to you, turning the hose not directly upon the woman but upon the walls of her cell; Dr King states that this has usually been found effective, and one three minute application is sufficient" (cited in Berkovits 1995:8).

[...] These descriptions of penal discipline seem inconsistent with the image of a loving mother, but they do conform to a particular image of familial relations of power in which the father figure plays the role of disciplinarian. Clearly, nonmaternal methods of prisoner management were often used, as were scientific technologies of reform, which became increasingly popular after the turn of the century. New scientific methods of discipline such as hypnosis, and older techniques such as the cold bath and segregation (legitimated with a medical logic), were combined with more maternal forms of discipline, such as eliciting promises to behave and minor suspensions of privileges.

*****

There is little evidence to support the contention that perception of a woman's potential for reform informed the placement of women in reformatories as opposed to prisons or the federal penitentiary. While the woman's history was likely considered at the time of sentencing, the decision whether to send a woman to a reformatory instead of the penitentiary was usually governed by the length of her sentence, not necessarily her character, notwithstanding that the two were related. After Confederation (1867), a woman who received a custodial sentence of less than two years was usually sent to a prison or reformatory. If her sentence was greater than two years, she was sent to one of the federal institutions that accepted female inmates. In general, the institution where a woman served her sentence was governed by her proximity to that institution at the time of sentencing. Women do not seem to have been uniformly classified and sent to the "most appropriate institution." Before the Mercer opened, little thought was given to the character of the offender and her potential for reform. While the degree of judicial concern about a woman's reformability is unclear, we do know that officials at the Mercer were becoming increasingly concerned about the reformability of their clientele (Strange 1983).

Although the limitations of the maternal logic were profound, maternal penal reformers continued to resort to domestic metaphors and to support the creation of separate institutions for female prisoners. Admittedly, the role and status of certain women was threatened by the perceived limitation of regimes predicated on the innate abilities of women, but at the same time, links between maternal logic and modern scientific logic created new opportunities. The integration of maternal and scientific ideals resulted in a new type of maternalism that advocated new rehabilitation programs administered by professionally "trained" women. Even though the main weakness of the Mercer and other reformatories was that it was impossible to turn a prison into a home, future generations of penal reformers would resurrect the metaphor of motherhood and the ideal of "a home." The absence of "good mothering" would continue to be perceived as a cause of crime, and a maternally tempered prison environment would continue to play an important role in attempts to resocialize and normalize women. The instruction and training of inmates advocated by reformers from the early twentieth century on would emphasize sociological, psychological, and medical interventions that retained many elements of the ideology of separate spheres. [...]

Conclusions: Maternal Success or Failure?

Was the Mercer a success? Feminist historians and Oliver (1994) make competing claims. They all agree that the Mercer provided an alternative to the neglect that women suffered in prisons and custodial regimes, but they differ in their evaluations of the regime's "administrative" success. Strange (1983) notes that after a concentrated attempt to institute a regime of kind discipline, it became evident that maternalistic efforts could not fulfil the lofty and unrealistic goal of reform. The common opinion among feminist historians is that despite the best intentions of maternal reformers, these icons of motherly discipline were undermined by the material realities of imprisonment. [...]

[...] Rafter (1992:41) and Strange (1983) both argue that reformatory in general, and specifically women's reformatory officials

and maternalists who advocated the use of indeterminate and indefinite sentences, did not adhere to the principle of proportionality. Rafter notes that "those who lobbied for reformatories maintained that it was quite proper to ignore the rule of proportionality because their aim was not to punish but to treat—to retrain and reform, processes that required time. But in light of the concept of proportionality the up-to-three (or however many) years was a high price to pay for minor offenses" (41).

******

The Mercer is an important page in both the history of Canadian imprisonment and the genealogy of maternal logics. When we place this experience in a "wider correctional context," it becomes apparent that the problems encountered in attempts to institute a maternal regime in many ways epitomize the contradictory nature of the correctional enterprise—a contradiction that Ekstedt and Griffiths (1988) and other Canadian correctional historians have characterized as "the split personality of corrections." Rather than a "split personality," it is perhaps more appropriate to think about the *multiple* personalities of women's penality. Prisons, penitentiaries, and reformatories have adopted two fundamentally contradictory objectives: to punish and to reform. At different historical junctures, these contradictions are evident in political and administrative reform discourse. The failures of the silent system, the rehabilitative model, and the maternal strategy had a common basis. While new technologies often emerge promising something new, better, and more humane, they are ultimately compromised by the existing institutional culture. Oliver seems to ignore this. While the Mercer may very well have differed from other institutions of the time by virtue of its feminine ethos, it is problematic, as Rothman suggests, to assume that this regime was an inevitable and sure step in the progress of humanity. Perhaps what is most interesting about these projects is how they contributed to a particular history of the governance of women by women under a rubric of motherhood that legitimated a variety of techniques. The Mercer was a historically specific attempt by women to govern women prisoners as women. Opinions remain divided on whether the maternal ideal of a caring but strict home was accomplished.

Notes

1. In Canada, a similar phenomenon occurred with the development of several rescue homes and homes for fallen or pregnant women. The Salvation Army and other Christian organizations played an active role in the development and operation of these homes.

2. For a comparison of the Mercer and other reform-oriented men's prisons, see Oliver (1994) and Wetherell (1979).

3. The hiring of matrons in women's prisons paralleled and was influenced by wider struggles to integrate women into the workforce. One movement that was particularly relevant in Canada and in the United States was the "police matrons" movement. This was spearheaded by a variety of reform organizations, such as the Prison Association of New York (PANY), the Women's Christian Temperance Union (WCTU), and the National Council of Women of Canada (NCWC). This struggle was premised on the belief that women had a legitimate and valuable role to play in regulating and policing women—specifically criminal women.

4. One example of such a list is found in PANY's report, written by E.C. Wines and Theodore W. Dwight, titled "Report on the Prisons and Reformatories of Canada and the United States." [...] During the 1840s, middle-class women in New York City formed a women's branch of PANY.

5. Like matrons, male keepers were morally regulated. The qualifications for male officers, as stipulated in the Prison Association of New York's 1867 report, indicated that male officers had to be men who were honest, sober, mild-tempered, quiet-mannered, "pure in their conversations," decisive, energetic, humane, benevolent, sincere, discreet, efficient, impartial, vigilant, religious, moral, distinguished in habits of industry, order, and cleanliness, and knowledgeable of human nature in its various aspects and relations (PANY, 1867:120–2). A detailed rationale for each of these qualifications can be located in PANY (1867:120–1).

6. Both Strange (1983) and Oliver (1994) provide evidence that confirms the cross-fertilization of ideas about women's punishment and its administration between Canada and various American states. Similarly, various Canadian historians and reports, such as Report on the Prisons and Reformatories of the United States and Canada (PANY 1867) and the proceedings of the Canadian Penal Congress [in 1949] illustrate that American reformers and penal administrators regularly visited Canada and shared their views on prison management with their Canadian counterparts.

7. The conditions that made the adequate classification of offenders in Ontario jails difficult are documented in Wetherell (1979).

8. For a more detailed history of the Andrew Mercer Reformatory for Women in Ontario, see Strange (1983), Oliver (1994), Ruemper (1994), and Berkovits (1995). These accounts focus on the reformatory as an institution, not on the wider social and political processes around it.

9. Specific examples of the activities of women associated with the Ottawa Elizabeth Fry Society (OEFS) can be located in Stewart (1993).

10. Both the Salvation Army and the Prisoners' Aid Association operated homes for released women. For additional details on the activities of some of these reformers, see Wetherell (1979) [and] Ruemper (1994). [....] Reformers such as the Prisoners' Aid Association (PAA) and the Salvation Army were involved in similar activities in men's facilities.

11. For a more complete discussion of the disciplinary regime at the Mercer, techniques of punishment, and concerns about the inculcation of unreformable women, see Strange (1983).

12. The surgeon, Dr John S. King, supervised and advocated the use of this technique during the reign of superintendents O'Reilly and O'Sullivan. This particular incident is cited in Berkovits (1995:7).

References

Berkovits, J.G. (1995). "Maternal Influence: Inmate Culture in the Andrew Mercer Reformatory for Women, 1880–1915." Unpublished discussion paper, Department of History, University of Toronto, Toronto, Ontario.

Chunn, D. 1992. *From Punishment to Doing Good: Family Courts and Socialized Justice in Ontario, 1880–1940*. Toronto: University of Toronto Press.

Ekstedt, J., and C. Griffiths. 1988. *Corrections in Canada: Policy and Practice*. Toronto: Butterworths.

Freedman, E. 1979. "Separation as a Strategy: Female Institution Building and American Feminism, 1870–1930." *Feminism Studies* 5(3): 512–29.

_____. 1981. *Their Sisters' Keepers: Women's Prison Reform in America, 1830–1930*. Ann Arbor: University of Michigan Press.

_____. 1996. "The Prison Lesbian: Race, Class, and the Construction of the Aggresive Female Homosexual, 1915–1965." *Feminist Studies* (Summer).

Garland, D. 1985. *Punishment and Welfare: A History of Penal Strategies*. Brookfield: Gower Publishing.

_____. 1990. *Punishment and Modern Society*. Oxford: Oxford University Press.

Koven, S., and S. Michel. 1993. *Mothers of a New World: Maternalist Politics and the Origins of the Welfare State*. London: Routledge and Kegan Paul.

Oliver, P. 1994. "To Govern by Kindness: The First Two Decades of the Mercer Reformatory for Women." In J. Phillips, T. Loo, and S. Lewthwaite, eds., *Essays in the History of Canadian Law: Crime and Criminal Justice* (vol. v). Toronto: The Osgoode Society for Canadian Legal History.

Pollock-Byrne, J. 1990. *Women, Prison and Crime*. Pacific Grove, CA: Brooks/Cole Publishing.

Prison Association of New York (PANY). 1867. *Report on the Prisons and Reformatories of the United States and Canada*. Albany: Van Benthuysen and Son's Steam Printing House.

Rafter, N.H. 1992. *Partial Justice: Women, Prison, and Social Control*, 2nd ed. New Brunswick: Transaction Publishers.

Ruemper, W. 1994. "Locking Them Up: Incarcerated Women in Ontario 1857–1931." In L. Knafla and S. Binnie, eds., *Law, Society, and the State: Essays in Modern Legal History*. Toronto: University of Toronto Press.

Strange, C. 1983. "The Velvet Glove: Maternalists Reform at the Andrew Mercer Reformatory, 1872–1927." Unpublished master's thesis, University of Ottawa.

Stewart, L. 1993. *Women Volunteer to Go to Prison: A History of the Elizabeth Fry Society of British Columbia, 1939–1989*. Victoria, BC: Orca Publishers.

Wetherell, D.G. 1979. "To Discipline and Train: Adult Rehabilitation Programmes in Ontario Prisons, 1874–1900." *Histoire Sociale/Social History* 12(23): 145–65.

Zedner, L. 1991. *Women Crime and Custody in Victorian England*. Oxford: Clarendon Press.

CHAPTER 21

"Character Weaknesses" and "Fruit Machines": Towards an Analysis of the Anti-Homosexual Security Campaign in the Canadian Civil Service, 1959–1964

Gary Kinsman

• •

Introduction

"Sexual abnormalities appear to be the favorite target of hostile intelligence agencies, and of these homosexuality is most often used," stated a 1959 Canadian Security Panel memorandum. The memo went on:

> The nature of homosexuality appears to adapt itself to this kind of exploitation. By exercising fairly simple precautions, homosexuals are usually able to keep their habits hidden from those who are not specifically seeking them out. Further, homosexuals often appear to believe that the accepted ethical code which governs normal human relationships does not apply to them. Their propensity is often accompanied by other specific weaknesses such as excessive drinking with its resultant instabilities, a defiant attitude towards the rest of society, and a concurrent urge to seek out the company of persons with similar characteristics, often in disreputable bars, night clubs or restaurants.[1]

The memo continues pointing out that

> From the small amount of information we have been able to obtain about homosexual behaviour generally, certain characteristics appear to stand out—instability, willing self-deceit, defiance towards society, a tendency to surround oneself with persons of similar propensities, regardless of other considerations—none of which inspire the confidence one would hope to have in persons required to fill positions of trust and responsibility.[2]

These quotes are from one of the previously secret government documents on the anti-gay/anti-lesbian security campaigns in the Canadian civil service that Canadian Press secured in 1992 through the Access to Information Act.[3] In the ways these texts were mobilized within state security regime relations, they could have been devastating for the lives of those identified as gay or lesbian. They were part of constructing gay men and lesbians as a particular type of social problem and were an integral part of the construction of heterosexual hegemony[4] within Canadian state formation.[5]

During the late 1950s and early 1960s these texts were used to organize problems for hundreds of lesbians and gay men who lost their jobs or were demoted to less "sensitive" positions in the federal civil service. The Royal Canadian Mounted Police (RCMP) collected the names of thousands of possible homosexuals, and the government funded and sponsored research into means to detect homosexuals. Homosexuals were designated a "national security threat" because of their "character weakness," which supposedly left gay men and lesbians open to blackmail by Soviet agents. [...]

*****

Homosexuals as a National Security Danger

The 1950s and the early 1960s were years of the social construction of homosexuality as a national, social, and sexual danger in Canada. This occurred in the context of the reconstruction and transformation of patriarchal and heterosexist hegemonic relations after the "disruptions" of the war mobilizations. There were at least three aspects of the construction [...]: the purge campaigns in the civil service, military, and the RCMP; the related immigration legislation changes of 1952, which prevented homosexuals from immigrating to Canada and were tied into "security" concerns; and the construction of homosexuals as a "sexual danger" (especially to young people) through the extension of criminal sexual legislation and through mass media coverage.[6] In this paper I focus on this first aspect.

In the context of the Cold War, McCarthyism, and "national security" scares, homosexuals were designated a "threat to national security." The anti-homosexual campaigns were linked to anti-communist and anti-Soviet campaigns in the US and Canada. One of the dominant political themes in much of the western world from the late 1940s through the 1960s and beyond was that of the Cold War and the construction of "communism" and the "Soviet empire" as a major threat.[7]

In Canada, the anti-communist campaigns were less public and extensive than in the US,[8] although they made the work of socialists and progressives in unions, the peace movement, and community groups extremely difficult and dangerous at times. Immigrants and artists were also targeted. In right-wing, conservative, and often liberal discourse, homosexuals were either associated directly with communism and spying for the USSR or were seen as an easy

target for blackmail. [...] Homosexuals were often constructed not only as violators of sexual and gender boundaries, but also as violators of class and political boundaries.[9] [...] Through a series of trials and spy scandals in England, homosexuality came to be associated with spying and treason affecting how homosexuality was portrayed in official circles in Canada.[10]

*****

The strategy of extending criminalization included the existing offenses of "gross indecency" and "buggery" and the new sentencing procedure of Criminal Sexual Psychopath. [...] This procedure, which was continued in Dangerous Sexual Offender legislation enacted in 1961, made consensual homosexual activity discovered by the police (or able to be "proven" by the police in court) into grounds for indefinite detention. This constructed homosexuality [...] as a criminal sexual danger.[11] These criminalization practices, oriented the work of the RCMP and other police forces. [...] It was crucially through the criminal code and the activities it mandated for the police that homosexuals were constructed as a criminal problem.[12]

[...] Homosexuality (especially between men) was officially viewed as a threat to discipline and bureaucratic hierarchy. This was especially the case in the military and in para-military forms of organization like the police where heterosexual masculinity was a major organizing ideology. Fighting men were identified with heterosexual masculinity, not with homosexuals who were visualized as "gender inverts" and not "real men."[13]

In the military lesbianism was seen as a threat to the "proper" femininity of female recruits and the policing of "lesbianism" was a way of regulating the activities of all women in these institutions. In the armed forces there were policies and procedures for excluding and "disposing" of "sex deviates."[14]

[...] Through NATO, Canadian and American officials shared common concerns over "internal security." Canadian and US security officials engaged in a common security language, and they shared similar organizing concepts and discourse as well as information.[15]

As part of this interaction the Security Panel sent D.F. Wall, secretary of the Security Panel, along with Professor Wake, who was studying detection strategies for homosexuality for the panel, to the US in 1961 to study "security" procedures there. This included [...] policies regarding homosexuals. Wall's report focused on some of the differences between Canadian and US security screening policies and procedures and became one of the texts leading up to the new Cabinet Memorandum on "Security in the Public Service" in 1963.

The Security Panel

In response to official security concerns, a Security Panel was established in Canada in 1946. The investigative powers of this new panel were officially authorized by a cabinet directive in 1948.[16] [...]

In 1948, the departments of national defence and external affairs were designated by security officials as vulnerable to subversion. Dismissals of homosexuals had started by 1952.[17] In the two decades that followed, every homosexual in the civil service had reason to fear discovery and dismissal as hundreds of people were fired or transferred. [...]

[...] The panel was chaired by the Secretary to the Cabinet and reported directly to the Cabinet. The panel was part of the ruling regime with important links with broader state relations. Permanent representatives on the panel included the Privy Council and the departments of National Defence, External Affairs, and the RCMP with others more occasionally represented.[18] The RCMP was the investigative agency for the panel and was mandated by cabinet to perform security investigations. The RCMP had the sole authority to make inquiries in all civilian departments (in the armed forces military intelligence was also involved) and the panel had to negotiate with the department involved if an employee was identified as a security risk by the RCMP. Deputy ministers often made the decisions about dismissals or transfers.

The emphasis in the workings of the panel was on secrecy and the proceedings in Canada were much less public and visible than in the US. Given this secrecy, there was no appeal from a denial of security clearance. There was no possibility for independent review. In what were seen to be serious cases, civil servants were asked to resign or were dismissed with no opportunity to defend themselves against the allegations that had been made. While initially the Security Panel's focus was on people with political "disloyalties," the RCMP soon began to uncover civil servants with "moral" or "character" failings which, it was argued, made them vulnerable because they had something to hide.

Thousands of lesbians and gay men and suspected homosexuals were affected by this security campaign. A 1961 memo reported that "During the course of these investigations, the R.C.M. Police have identified some 460 public servants as confirmed, alleged or suspected homosexuals. Of these about one-third have since left the service through resignation or dismissal."[19] In 1961–62 the RCMP reported having identified 850 suspected and proven homosexuals in the civil service.[20] [...]

*****

Usually the Security Panel [...] focused on men, given it was predominantly men who were in these "security" positions in the Canadian civil service during these years and given the more public construction of male homosexuals as a social threat. [...] The notion of "character weakness" did include lesbianism, but lesbianism was rarely distinctly written about in these texts. Usually the references to "homosexuals" referred to gay men. [...]

The Conceptual Organization of the Security Campaign

*****

This conceptualization of "character weaknesses" became a part of personnel selection and screening practices as new forms of administration and management of the civil service were put in place in the early 1960s. This was part of the continuing entry of psychiatric and psychological knowledge into social and state administration which had begun in the military and other sites and was intensified during the World War II mobilizations and post-war reconstruction.[21]

*****

Concepts are key to how ruling gets organized including for the security regime. The ideological concepts of "national security" and "character weaknesses" were crucial to how this "security" campaign against homosexuals was organized and how these practices were mobilized and held together.

First there was a concept of "national security," which was defined in opposition to "threats" from communists, socialists, peace activists, unionists, and "sex perverts," among others. The concept of "national security" rests on notions of the interests of the "nation,"[22] which in the Canadian context is defined by capitalist, racist, and patriarchal relations; the features of Canadian state formation which were historically based on the subordination of the indigenous peoples, the Québécois and the Acadians; and historically had been allied with the British empire and later with US imperialism.

*****

In the context of defence of "national security," homosexuals were then inscribed into an ideological collecting category of "character weaknesses," which supposedly made them vulnerable to blackmail. This collecting category also included drunkenness, adultery, and "promiscuity," although it became increasingly homosexualized in the discussions and practices of the security regime. [...]

Analysis of the Security Panel Texts— The Active Debate over How Wide the Campaigns Should Be

Possible limitations in previous security procedures[23] were raised in May 1959 in a memo by D.F. Wall [...] to other members

of the Panel.[24] This memo was in response to an apparent request from Prime Minister Diefenbaker for clarification. Wall wrote that "It is the Prime Minister's wish that the matter be examined to determine whether it might be possible to treat cases of character weaknesses differently from those involving ideological beliefs, without of course weakening present security safeguards."[25]

This constructed a clearer separation in the security discourse between political disloyalty and character weaknesses, [...] separate[ing] out "communists" from "homosexuals," who often had [...] been conflated together in right-wing and security discourse. The 1955 cabinet directive had not made such a clear distinction, although it did state in reference to character defects that "such defects of character may also make them unsuitable for employment on grounds other than security."[26]

[...] The title of the memo is "Security Cases Involving Character Weaknesses with special reference to the Problem of Homosexuality." Despite very little cited evidence, Wall established that homosexuality was the most frequently used "character weakness" and was the major route used by Soviet intelligence.[27] In investigating this, Wall referred to US and United Kingdom procedures and reports. [...]

*****

These were crucial terrains of debate in the Security Panel for the next few years. In 1959 the homosexual screening program had been initiated in the federal civil service. The RCMP struggled to defend and expand this campaign and engaged in an extension of the campaign to investigations outside the civil service where thousands of names were collected. Since all homosexual acts [were] then against the law, the RCMP approach was also shaped by the criminalization of homosexuality. [...]

*****

The early 1960s was the beginning of the period when different strategies in Canadian state agencies were taken up in response to the expansion of lesbian and gay networks and community formation. The 1957 British Wolfenden regulatory frame of the partial decriminalization of homosexual acts began to be used to contest the influence of the expanding criminalization strategy by the mid 1960s in Canada. At the same time in the early 1960s, the hegemonic regulatory strategy was still one that defined homosexuality as a national, social, sexual, and criminal danger.

*****

In October 1959 there was discussion of Wall's memo at the Security Panel where the basic debate was again over how narrow or wide the security campaign against homosexuals should be.[28] Robert Bryce, chair of the Panel, argued for a relatively wide-ranging approach, but he did not think that homosexuals should be dismissed from the public service but instead should be transferred to less "sensitive" positions. The RCMP and deputy ministers of Justice and National Defence argued for a wider interpretation with the deputy minister of National Defence, questioning "whether persons suspected of homosexuality should be permitted to enter the public service in any capacity."[29] As a result of these disagreements, they could not recommend any change to existing security policy.

*****

The RCMP—Extending the Campaign

In May 1960 the RCMP submitted its contribution "Homosexuality within the Federal Government Service" to the Security Panel discussion. They requested clearer terms of reference and argued that existing policy restrictions "which prohibit our interviewing homosexuals should be set aside from this type of investigation." They argued that "necessary provision be made for us to interview at our discretion any person who we may consider to be of assistance to our enquiry."[30]

*****

[...] Despite the ebb and flow of security scares, the RCMP, along with the military hierarchy, were consistent in their stance that homosexuals should not be in government service. The RCMP set up an investigative unit within the force, called A-3, to hunt down and purge homosexuals within its ranks and within the government more generally. Informants would watch bars and parks frequented by gays and they attempted to get homosexual men to inform on others. Reportedly this met with some initial success.[31]

*****

In June 1960 there was a Security Panel discussion on the RCMP memo, "Homosexuality within the Federal Government Service."[32] There was only a quorum of the Security Panel in attendance; as R.B. Bryce reported, they tried to keep the discussion "limited to the smallest circle possible."[33] In the discussion the Commissioner of the RCMP reiterated the RCMP request for more explicit guidance especially given how "recent investigations indicated that the problem [of homosexuality] was becoming increasingly widespread, and the accumulation of the names of persons against whom allegations had been made was growing with each new enquiry."[34]

This posed administrative difficulties for the RCMP about how to handle and use this information. There were some initial problems with the "ideological" construction of homosexuals as a tiny minority with certain identifiable characteristics (like marks of gender inversion) that didn't fully prepare them for the numbers they began to uncover. They were beginning to unearth gay and lesbian networks during a period in which these networks were expanding and becoming more visible.

In response to this extended campaign, the Under-secretary of State for External Affairs pointed to "the danger of this kind of investigation developing into a sociological survey in which the security aspects were lost sight of, and suggested that it did not serve our present purpose to make a determination of the probable proportion of homosexuals in the population."[35] He stressed that the RCMP should only be concerned with investigating homosexuals if it was a security matter.

Although clearly homosexuality was seen to be a problem by all participants, it was recorded that they felt "that the question of prosecutions for homosexual offenses would probably not arise through present investigations. ..."[36] In the clash between the broader criminalizing and more narrow security frames, the majority of the panel members at this meeting sided with the narrower security frame. The minutes stated "that where security was not a factor, there did not appear to be any reason for the RCMP to report allegations of homosexuality to the employing department."[37]

For the RCMP whose work was also shaped by the criminalization of homosexuality, or for the military with their policies against homosexuals in any position, their practices would also have been shaped by their institutional policies. But at the same time the minutes recorded "that there appeared to be some reduction in the risk to security if the RCMP and the employing department were aware that an employee had homosexual tendencies."[38] [...] This allowed the RCMP to continue its extended investigations without the Security Panel as a whole giving direct approval to what it was doing. [...]

This led to the memo for the Prime Minister and Minister of Justice by R.B. Bryce. In the initial December 1960 version of this memo, there was a fairly strong defence of the expanded character of RCMP security investigations, including moving beyond civil service.[39] This expanded role, however, still did not satisfy the RCMP. [...]

*****

They asked for Ministerial approval for "The following proposed courses of action." The first priority was "that the Security Panel ask those departments with missions abroad to classify according to risk those positions whose nature and location is such that their incumbents might be subjected to pressure for intelligence

purposes" and "that these departments, with whatever assistance the RCMP are able to provide, make a careful study of the incumbents of these positions to ensure, in so far as possible, that they are not susceptible to blackmail, either through homosexual activity or other indiscreet behaviour" and "that in cases where incumbent of a vulnerable position is found to be a homosexual, departments be asked to consult the Secretary of the Security Panel before any action is taken concerning the employee."[40]

The second priority included considering whether positions other than those abroad are vulnerable and that

consideration be given to setting up a program of research ... with a view to devising tests to identify persons with homosexual tendencies. It is hoped that such tests might aid in the identification of homosexuals already employed in the government service, and eventually might assist in the selection of persons who are not homosexuals for service in positions considered vulnerable to blackmail for intelligence purposes. (The Commissioner of the R.C.M. Police feels that these tests should be extended to prevent, where possible, the initial engagement of homosexuals in the government service on the grounds that they are usually practicing criminals under Sections 147 and 149 of the Criminal Code of Canada.)[41]

This was the proposal that would lead up to the development of the "fruit machine" research. The revised memo by Bryce was discussed by the cabinet on 26 January 1961.

A New Cabinet Directive

These meetings, memos, and the cabinet discussion led up to a new Cabinet Directive on "Security in the Public Services of Canada" in December 1963.[42] Public announcements were made by the new Prime Minister and Minister of Justice regarding this. This text referred to good personnel administration and distinguished between those who were politically disloyal and those who were unreliable. At the same time the language used in this text is somewhat different from that used in the Security Panel and RCMP documents. Rather than using homosexual, it refers to "illicit sexual behaviour."

*****

This directive laid out procedures and a mandated course of action. [...] A person applied for a position in the civil service where they would have access to what was designated to be "classified" information or was promoted into such a position. Either the Civil Service Commission or departments and agencies (where the employment is not under the Civil Services Act) would then initiate security investigations. The RCMP would be called in with the possible involvement of a deputy minister or head of the agency concerned.

If the person was discovered to be a homosexual or to have some other sort of "unreliability," they would then be transferred to a less "sensitive" position or they would be dismissed. There was now the possibility for review within the department or agency including review by the deputy minister or head of the agency or by a review board of members of the Security Panel.[43] At the same time there was also the research on detecting homosexuals that the Security Panel was simultaneously engaged in.

Attempting to Develop a "Fruit Machine"

The Security Panel also mandated research on the detection of homosexuals. In doing this there was an important reliance on psychiatric and psychological knowledge, which was premised on the assumption that gay men and lesbians were either psychologically "abnormal" or suffered from a "disorder." As in most other research, the "normality" of heterosexuality was assumed and homosexuality was defined as the problem.

Following up on the approval for such a study in the Security Panel memo to cabinet in early 1961, Professor F.R. Wake (who died in November 1993) of Carleton University was funded to go to the US by National Health and Welfare to research and study detection tests and technologies regarding homosexuality. Previously Wake had been the first chair of the Psychology Department at Carleton and a researcher for the Royal Commission on the Criminal Law Relating to Criminal Sexual Psychopaths in the 1950s.[44] He produced a report in 1962 which got the actual "fruit machine" research going. This research was funded by National Health and Welfare. [...]

The "fruit machine" research arose both from an apparent interest by Wake in doing research on homosexuality (usually articulated as an interest in "suitability" for employment) and also to establish a more effective and efficient mode of surveillance and investigation than that of costly and labour-intensive RCMP field investigations. [...]

The name "fruit machine" was given to this project, according to John Sawatsky, by members of the RCMP who did not want to be recruited to be among the "normals" to be tested on it.[45] The "fruit machine" project involved psychiatrists, psychologists, and the departments of National Defence and Health and Welfare for four years, but it never worked and the Defence Research Board eventually cut its funding. The research suffered from major technical problems as well as problems with getting the required numbers of "research subjects."

Dr. Wake, in his 1962 "Report on Special Project,"[46] focused on the "problem of suitability" in employment, and stressed from his review of the research in the US that there was no single method of tests that could detect homosexuality. Instead a battery of tests was needed. [...] He took up a general position that there was something wrong with homosexuals which makes them unsuitable for certain positions, that they can be identified, and their behaviour treated and controlled.

He argued that control of homosexuality is much more likely than cure, and he reported "encouraging trends" working with antidepressant drugs and reported reversal in direction of desire by means of aversion therapy.[47] He argued that "while a great deal of research needs to be done, much of it might be paid for by early moderate success reducing the current load on investigative staffs."[48]

*****

Since Wake argued there was no single, distinct homosexual personality type, there could be no single test. Under "Methods of Detecting Homosexuality," he surveyed the various detection tests and procedures that had been used to try to identify homosexuals. These ranged from psychiatric interviews, to medical examinations, to various tests for changes in emotional conditions. These included the Polygraph (lie-detector) test, which Wake argued had too many problems to be useful; the Plethysmograph, which measures blood volume in the finger by electronic or pneumatic means; the Palmer Sweat test, which responds to perspiration; the Projective Tests; Word Association Tests; the Pupillary Test; the Span of Attention Test, based on the time spent attending to various images (which Zamansky of Northeastern University had constructed as an apparatus to test for homosexuality in 1956); and Masculinity/Femininity Tests with all their gender and sexuality assumptions.[49]

*****

In his conclusions Wake argued that more research was needed. He proposed a research experiment that would combine

The Hess-Polt papillary test with suitable visual stimuli; a measure of skin perspiration ..., the plethysmograph with a modification to measure pulse rate. Subjects: Fifteen normal males; fifteen normal females; fifteen homosexual males; fifteen homosexual females. As the experiment progresses, additional normal and homosexual subjects in unspecified numbers. All subjects to be supplied by the RCMP... [50]

*****

Then Wake outlined the procedure to be used—

The experimental stimuli will be pictures designed to elicit the subject's interest in males and females .... The first sixty subjects will be processed to determine the reaction patterns of normals and homosexuals. Then, using these patterns as criteria, the experimenter will attempt to distinguish homosexuals presented by the RCMP, where nothing of the subject is known to the research team. Those methods proving successful will be retained for continuing research.[51]

This research was more psychologically oriented than earlier studies that sometimes focused on biological anomalies (like marks of gender inversion on the body).[52] It was directed at finding a "scientific" means to test "involuntary" responses that demonstrated sexual orientation. [...]

Predictably there were many problems in trying to get this experiment to work. [...]

*****

The 1965–66 Directorate of Security and Intelligence (DSI) Annual Report noted that "To date the tests have been inconclusive, the main obstacle to the Program being a lack of suitable subjects for testing purposes."[53] In the same report of 1966–67, they stated that, "Although the research group has made some progress, the objective has not, as yet been achieved."[54] A major problem in the operationalizing of the experiment was with perfecting the technology itself, which had to be adapted to deal with people of different heights, with different sized pupils, and different distances between eyeballs.[55] The "fruit machine" never worked and it was eventually abandoned in 1967.

*****

Some Conclusions—Heterosexual Hegemony and the Security Regime

This investigation [...] points us towards an analysis of the social organization of the anti-homosexual security campaign within Canadian state formation. We can begin to see the impact this campaign had on thousands of people's lives and [...] aspects of how it was organized through the textually mediated practices of the security regime. There were struggles within the security regime between a broader framework for the anti-homosexual campaign and a narrower security framework. While in general the narrower security frame won out by 1963, there was also an allowance for the wider campaign to take place through the practices of the RCMP. There was also the development of research on the detection of homosexuals as part of the security campaign. [...]

Despite significant changes as a result of social struggles, there remains today a continuing and deeply rooted heterosexism in Canadian state institutions shaped in part by the active legacies of these conceptions and policies. There continues to be major problems that lesbians and gay men encounter in job-related discrimination. The historical and social roots of these policies need to be exposed more clearly, and much more critical research remains to be done. Finally, this historical work [...] poses important questions of redress and compensation for those whose careers and lives were destroyed by these policies. Doing this research is thereby linked to current struggles to dismantle heterosexual hegemonic relations.

Notes

This article is dedicated to all those who resisted the security campaign.

Thanks to Cynthia Wright for prodding me into doing this work and also to Kevin Crombie, Svend Robinson's office, Steven Maynard, Lorna Weir, Patrizia Gentile, Heidi McDonnell, Chris Burr, and to the three reviewers for *Labour*. Thanks also to David Kimmel and Daniel Robinson for letting me read their important paper on the security campaign prior to its publication. It has been published as "The Queer Career of Homosexual Security Vetting in Cold-War Canada," *Canadian Historical Review*, 75 (1994), 319–45. Thanks to Patrick Barnholden for his love and support. This paper is also dedicated to the memory and work of George Smith (1935–1994) from whom I learned so much. At the same time none of these people bear any responsibility for what I have written here. Earlier versions were given as papers and presentations at the Canadian Sociology and Anthropology Association meetings at Carleton, 5 June 1993; for the Saint Mary's University Centre for Criminology, 20 October 1993; and for the Acadia University History Department, 24 November 1993. As general references for this article, see Gary Kinsman, *The Regulation of Desire* (Montreal 1987); "Official Discourse as Sexual Regulation: The Social Organization of the Sexual Policing of Gay Men," PhD thesis, University of Toronto, 1989; and "'Inverts,' 'Psychopaths,' and 'Normal' Men: Historical Sociological Perspectives on Gay and Heterosexual Masculinities," in Tony Haddad, ed., *Men and Masculinities: A Critical Anthology* (Toronto 1993), 3–35.

1. D.F. Wall, Memorandum to the Security Panel, "Security Cases Involving Character Weaknesses, with Special Reference to the Problem of Homosexuality," 12 May 1959, 12. This document was secured through a Canadian Security and Intelligence Service (CSIS), Access to Information Request (AIR).

2. Ibid., 13. In the language used in this excerpt, the author is building on earlier notions of homosexuals as psychopathic personalities. See Gary Kinsman, "Official Discourse as Sexual Regulation: The Social Organization of the Sexual Policing of Gay Men," PhD thesis, University of Toronto, 1989, 71–89.

3. See the Canadian press stories by Dean Beeby, which were based on these documents. They were printed in *The Globe and Mail*, 24 April 1992, 1–2 as "Mounties staged massive hunt for gay men in civil service" and "RCMP hoped 'fruit machine' would identify homosexuals." I will refer to the individual documents that the Canadian Press secured the release of through Access to Information requests throughout these notes.

4. On heterosexual hegemony, see Kinsman, *The Regulation of Desire* (Montreal 1987) and "Official Discourse as Sexual Regulation."

5. On state formation, see Philip Corrigan and Derek Sayer, *The Great Arch: English State Formation as Cultural Revolution* (Oxford 1985).

6. On this general social context, see *The Regulation of Desire*, 113–33; "Official Discourse as Sexual Regulation," and Kinsman, "'Inverts,'

'Psychopaths,' and 'Normal' Men: Historical Sociological Perspectives on Gay and Heterosexual Masculinities," in Tony Haddad, ed., *Men and Masculinities: A Critical Anthology* (Toronto 1993), 3–35. On the immigration law, see Philip Girard, "From Subversion to Liberation: Homosexuals and the Immigration Act, 1952–1977," *Canadian Journal of Law and Society*, 2 (1987), 1–27.

7. On the US experience, see US Congress Senate, Committee on Expenditure in Executive Departments, *Employment of Homosexuals and Other Sex Perverts in Government*, Washington, 15 December 1950, reprinted in Jonathan Katz, ed., *Government Versus Homosexuals* (Arno Reprint, New York 1975); Committee on Cooperation with Governmental (Federal) Agencies of the Group for the Advancement of Psychiatry, "Report on Homosexuality with Particular Emphasis on This Problem in Governmental Agencies," Report No. 30, January 1955; John D'Emilio, *Sexual Politics, Sexual Communities* (Chicago 1983), especially 40–53; John D'Emilio, "The Homosexual Menace: The Politics of Sexuality on Cold War America," in John D'Emilio, *Making Trouble* (New York 1992), 57–73; and Richard Cleaver, "Sexual Dissidents and the National Security State, 1942–1992," in Richard Cleaver and Patricia Myers, eds., *A Certain Terror, Heterosexism, Militarism, Violence and Change* (Chicago 1993), 171–208.

8. Philip Girard has argued that the anti-homosexual witch hunt in Canada was much stronger than the campaign against leftists, socialists, or communists. See Girard, "From Subversion to Liberation," 5. More research is needed to determine whether this claim is justified.

9. See *The Regulation of Desire*, 121.

10. See *The Regulation of Desire*, 121. On the English experience, also see Simon Shepherd, "Gay Sex Spy Orgy: The State's Need For Queers," in Simon Shepherd and Mick Wallis, *Coming on Strong: Gay Politics and Culture* (London 1989), 213–30 and L.J. Moran, "The Uses of Homosexuality: Homosexuality for National Security," *International Journal of the Sociology of Law* 19 (1991), 149–70.

11. See "Official Discourse as Sexual Regulation."

12. See George Smith, "Policing the Gay Community: An Inquiry into Textually-Mediated Social Relations," *International Journal of Sociology of the Law*, 16 (1988), 163–83.

13. On this, see *The Regulation of Desire*; "Official Discourse as Sexual Regulation," and "'Inverts,' 'Psychopaths,' and 'Normal' Men."

14. On lesbians and women in the military, see Cynthia Enloe, *Does Khaki Become You?* (London 1983) and the interview with Cynthia Enloe, "Heterosexist Masculinity in the Military," *Sojourner*, 18 (June 1993), 2–4; Alan Berube and John D'Emilio, "The Military and Lesbians During the McCarthy Years," *Signs*, 9 (1984), 759–75; and Leisa D. Meyer, "Creating G.I. Jane: The Regulation of Sexuality and Sexual Behaviour in the Women's Army Corps During World War II," *Feminist Studies*, 18 (1992), 581–601. More generally, see *The Regulation of Desire* and "Official Discourse as Sexual Regulation."

15. See Reginald Whitaker, "Origins of the Canadian Government's Internal Security System, 1946–52," *Canadian Historical Review*, LXV 2 (1984), 169–70, and Len Scher, *The Un-Canadians: True Stories of the Blacklist Era* (Toronto 1987), especially the interview with Reginald Whitaker, "The FBI and the RCMP," 238–9.

16. This section is generally based on Philip Girard, "From Subversion to Liberation," 6-8 and Reginald Whitaker, "Origins of the Canadian Government's Internal Security System."

17. John Sawatsky, *Men in the Shadows* (Don Mills 1983), 124.

18. Its composition at a meeting in 1959 was— Secretary to the Cabinet (the chair), Deputy Minister of Citizenship and Immigration, Deputy Minister of National Defence, Deputy Minister of Defence Production, Deputy Minister of Justice, Commissioner of RCMP, Under-secretary of State for External Affairs, member of Civil Service Commission, and a member of the Privy Council Office (who was the secretary). Minutes of the 68th meeting of the Security Panel, 6 October 1959 by D.F. Wall, Secretary of the Security Panel.

19. R.B. Bryce, Memorandum for the Prime Minister and the Minister of Justice, "Security Cases Involving Homosexuality," 26 January 1961, 2.

20. Directorate of Security and Intelligence Annual Report, 1961–1962, 22.

21. Nikolas Rose, *The Psychological Complex* (London 1985) and "Official Discourse as Sexual Regulation."

22. On some of this, see Cynthia Enloe, *Does Khaki Become You? Militarization and Women's Lives* (London 1983) and her *Bananas, Beaches and Bases, Making Feminist Sense of International Politics* (London 1989) and also some of the articles in Andrew Parker et al., *Nationalisms and Sexualities* (New York and London 1992). On the construction of the nation in the Canadian context,

see comments in Roxana Ng, "Sexism, Racism, Canadian Nationalism," in Himani Bannerji, ed., *Returning the Gaze: Essays on Racism, Feminism and Politics* (Toronto 1993), 182–96, and Annalee Golz, "Family Matters, the Canadian Family and the State in the Postwar Period," *Left History*, 1 (Fall 1993), 9–49.

23. This was rooted in Cabinet Directive 29, "Security Screening of Government Employees," 1955.

24. D.F. Wall, Memorandum to the Security Panel, "Security Cases Involving Character Weaknesses, with Special Reference to the Problem of Homosexuality," 12 May 1959.

25. Ibid., 1.

26. Ibid. This provided a broader opening for campaigns against homosexuals or others with "character weaknesses" in the civil service on other than security grounds.

27. Wall memo, 12 May 1959, 12. This was argued even though little evidence was ever put forward to defend this claim. For instance—"In only one of the cases investigated has there been evidence that an attempt has been made to blackmail any of these persons for intelligence purposes." (R.B. Bryce "Memorandum for the Prime Minister and the Minister of Justice, Security Cases Involving Homosexuality," 19 December 1960 version, 2). And "there is one case on file where an attempt was made to compromise a Canadian government employee" (Report of the Directorate, 1959–1960, Part II Security Branch "A," Appendix G, Appendix to Annual Report on Homosexuality among Federal Government Employees, 42).

28. D.F. Wall, Secretary of the Security Panel, Minutes of the 68th meeting of the Security Panel, 6 October 1959.

29. Ibid., 5.

30. Here they are referring to a general prohibition on directly interviewing alleged homosexuals presently in the civil service implied in Security Panel directives. They also wanted the decision over when departments should be provided with information about homosexuals in their ranks left to the RCMP's discretion and "we would also appreciate clarification on whether or not we should provide the department concerned with information on a homosexual who is not employed on duties having access to classified material." These quotes come from Appendix C "RCMP Request for Terms of Reference—May 1960, Brief for Discussion on Reports of Mr. Don Wall and Dr. F.R. Wake on Personnel Security Matters in the USA," 4 March 1963.

31. Ibid., 42–5 and John Sawatsky, *Men in the Shadows*, 125–7.

32. Security Panel minutes, a special meeting of a quorum of the Security Panel, 24 June 1960, taken by D.F. Wall, issued 26 July 1960.

33. Ibid., 1.

34. Ibid., 2.

35. Ibid., 2.

36. Ibid., 4.

37. Ibid., 4.

38. Ibid., 4.

39. R.B. Bryce, "Memorandum for the Prime Minister and the Minister of Justice, Security Cases Involving Homosexuality," 19 December 1960 version, 1.

40. R.B. Bryce, "Memorandum for the Prime Minister and the Minister of Justice, Security Cases Involving Homosexuality," 26 January 1961 version, 3–4.

41. Ibid., 4. Notice how the RCMP raises the criminalization of homosexuality course of action in their support for extending the campaign to encompass all government workers.

42. Cabinet Directive No. 35, "Security in the Public Service of Canada," 18 December 1963.

43. Cabinet Directive No. 35, "Security in the Public Service of Canada," 18 December 1963.

44. See Bill Walther and David Berndhart, Department of Psychology, "In Memoriam, Robert Wake and Russell Wendt," *This Week at Carleton* (20 January 1994), 3 and *The Report of the Royal Commission on the Criminal Law Relating to Criminal Sexual Psychopaths* (Ottawa 1958).

45. Sawatsky, *Men in the Shadows*, 133.

46. Dr. F.R. Wake, "Report on Special Project," 19 December 1962.

47. See Dr. F.R. Wake, "Report on Special Project," 16. The aversion therapy he referred to was conducted by B. James in 1962 (16). He also discussed a number of treatments to alter behaviour (14), and stated that "Mental health personnel these days prefer not to speak of a cure (a change from homosexuality to heterosexuality) but rather of a change to controlled sexual behaviour, which would be more comfortable for the subject, for he is now divested of anti-social activities" (15). Wake opted for homosexuality being caused in most cases by "a combination of environmental circumstances during the years of childhood or early youth" (1). He stated that it was "not a matter of heredity or of the individual's perverse choice" (1). He was quite aware of the "liberal" psychological and sexological work then going on in the US and mentioned the work of Evelyn Hooker,

who critiqued the notion of male homosexuals as "unstable" and the Kinsey reports (1–3). He even was aware of the distinction being made between overt and covert homosexuals Hooker used that was developed in the work of Maurice Leznoff on male homosexuals in Montréal. On Leznoff, see *The Regulation of Desire*, 117–9 and Maurice Leznoff, "The Homosexual in Urban Society," MA thesis, McGill University, Montreal, 1954. Although Wake knew about and used this more "liberal" work, he articulated it to a more "investigative" and "control"-oriented perspective. Later he stated that "The general run of opinion ... is that homosexuals almost always are maladjusted" (15) even though he referred to Hooker as holding a contrasting opinion.

48. Wake, "Abstract of the Report," for the "Report on Special Project."

49. On the development of masculinity/femininity tests, see Joseph H. Pleck, "The Theory of Male Sex Role Identity: Its Rise and Fall, 1936 to the Present," and Miriam Lewin, "Psychology Measures Femininity and Masculinity" in Miriam Lewin ed., *In the Shadows of the Past: Psychology Portrays the Sexes* (New York 1984).

50. Wake, "Report on Special Project," 17.

51. Ibid. Wake also urged that connections be maintained with the network of sex researchers in the US, including Evelyn Hooker, Wardell B. Pomeroy, William H. Masters, and John Money. He suggested that the Department of Health and Welfare assume this liaison role. It was clear that this liaison was not to take place on security grounds as Wake wrote that "anyone effecting this liaison probably will have to have a front to cover his interest in 'suitability'" (18). A critical reader can get a sense here that "suitability" was a term that could be coded with security concerns and also with more "liberal" research concerns. It seems that the sex researchers Wake had contact with in the US would have had little idea of who was supporting his research or of its direct security connections.

52. This can be contrasted with the research technologies and strategies examined in Jennifer Terry's [...] article, "Theorizing Deviant Historiography," in *differences*, 3 (Summer 1991), 60.

53. Directorate of Security and Intelligence Annual Report, 65–6, 33.

54. Directorate of Security and Intelligence Annual Report, 66–7, 27.

55. Sawatsky, *Men in the Shadows*, 135–7.

Critical Thinking Questions

. . . .

Chapter 17: Moral Reform in English Canada, 1885–1925: Introduction, *Mariana Valverde*

1. What was identified as being in major need of correction by the social reform movement? How does it represent a particular rather than a universal definition of deviance?
2. Who were the major players in the moral reform movement? How do they represent an ideological viewpoint in the definition of criminality, and the need to do something about it?
3. Valverde uses an interesting collection of sources to conduct her study. How does this broaden the scope of historical research?

Chapter 18: Redefining Sexual Promiscuity: "Race," Gender, and Class in the Operation of Ontario's Female Refuges Act, 1930–60, *Joan Sangster*

1. In 1919, the FRA adopted a new clause providing judges and magistrates with wide-ranging powers. What powers were these? What problems were created, and which society was responsible for abolishing these sections of the FRA?
2. Although the FRA was a gender-specific piece of legislation, responsible for monitoring the sexuality of both White and non-White women, non-White men were also subject to supervision. How were they treated differently than White men in this regard?
3. Prior to World War II, White women represented the majority of women incarcerated under the FRA. During the post-World War II period, incarceration rates of Native women increased significantly. What factor contributed to this escalating pattern of incarceration? Explain.

Chapter 19: "Horrible Temptations": Sex, Men, and Working-Class Male Youth in Urban Ontario, 1890–1935, *Steven Maynard*

1. What problems occur when historians use court records to interpret past events? Is it possible to separate current attitudes and emotions and to analyze records that were written for one purpose (to prosecute a defendant), and to use them for another (to gain a broader understanding of how homosexual relations were viewed)?

2. How did the police pressure victims to participate? What does it say about the status of "victim" if they had to be threatened to compel them to co-operate?
3. Maynard concludes the discussion with a comparison of London, Ontario, in 1904 and 1994. Were the offences at the end of the century the same as those that were prosecuted at the beginning? Were the cases at the beginning of the century evidence of a moral panic? If so, why did it occur?

Chapter 20: Mother Knows Best: The Development of Separate Institutions for Women, *Kelly Hannah-Moffat*

1. What does the author mean by "maternal logic"? How did this ideal inform the way female prisoners were handled within the reformatory? A lack of female criminals meant that a female offender was more likely to be placed in an institution closest to where she lived at the time of sentencing, rather than the one that might best suit her needs. What evidence is there to suggest that the reformation of female convicts was not considered as important to justice officials as by prison staff?
2. How did the social climate of the day create the opportunity to develop different ways to penalize women prisoners? Were women, as prisoners, receptive to this "modern method"? Did prison officials consider all women offenders susceptible to reformation?
3. The author indicates understandings of female criminality were informed by American and English models of governance. What problems might prison reformers encounter in attempting to adopt foreign models of justice?

Chapter 21: "Character Weaknesses" and "Fruit Machines": Towards an Analysis of the Anti-Homosexual Purge Campaign in the Canadian Civil Service, 1959–1964, *Gary Kinsman*

1. Throughout this period, homosexuals were dismissed from the civil service, they were not allowed to immigrate to Canada, and homosexuality was a criminal offence. Why were homosexuals, as a group, considered such a threat to national security?
2. In the 1950s, the government became increasingly concerned about the infiltration of communists. Focusing on "character weaknesses," attempts were made to establish a link between the communist problem and homosexuality. How did this focus broaden the anti-homosexual campaign?
3. What was the purpose of the "fruit machine"? What problems did researchers encounter in their attempts to find a more scientific way to identify homosexuals? According to Sawatsky, members of the RCMP who did not want to be the normals in the research named the project the "fruit machine." What does this say about attitudes within the RCMP toward homosexuals?

Further Readings

• •

Courted and Abandoned: Seduction in Canadian Law by Patrick Brode (Toronto: Osgoode Society for Canadian Legal History and University of Toronto Press, 2002).

Patrick Brode is an independent scholar and lawyer in Windsor, Ontario. Being pregnant outside marriage in frontier Canada had profound legal implications for the mother, her family, and the alleged father. Little known is that Overseers of the Poor often sued putative fathers for child support, so liability for damages for seduction, and breach of promise of marriage were a major feature of early Canadian law. Brode studies court cases across the country and the communities in which they arose. This book is a testament to how early Canadians tried to control sexuality and courtship, even consensual activity among adults.

Petticoats and Prejudice: Women and Law in Nineteenth-Century Canada by Constance Backhouse (Toronto: University of Toronto Press, 1991).

This book is an interesting read for those interested in the plight of women in nineteenth-century courts. She looks at various topics, including marriage, infanticide, prostitution, and divorce. A serious and prolific scholar, she looks at women in a way that will appeal to feminists and lawyers, using excerpts from court judgments, newspapers, and magazines.

Improper Advances: Rape and Heterosexual Conflict in Ontario, 1880–1929 by Karen Dubinsky (Toronto: The Chicago Series on Sexuality, History, and Society, 1993).

Improper Advances is one of the first books to explore the history of sexual violence. Based in rural and northern Ontario, Dubinsky uses criminal case files to tell individual stories of sexual danger: rape, abortion, seduction, murder, and infanticide. Her research supports the analysis that crimes are expressions of power, that courts are prejudiced by the victim's background, and that most assaults occur within the victims' homes and communities. Dubinsky refuses to see women as victims and sex as a tool of oppression. She says women took pleasure in sexuality, but attempted to punish coercive sex despite obstacles in the court system.

Uncertain Justice, Canadian Women and Capital Punishment 1754–1953 by F. Murray Greenwood and Beverley Boissery (Toronto: Dundurn Press, 2000).

Uncertain Justice is about women and the justice system, specifically murder and the issues that emerge when women are involved. There are stories of battered wives who kill their husbands, women wronged by serial adulterers, and victims of sexual abuse or poverty driven unwillingly into motherhood kill their children in moments of despair. On the one hand, women who murder their husbands are treated most harshly and with more disgust than husbands who murder their wives. However, on the other, women were also treated with chivalry and allowed clemency, such as in cases of sexual harassment, rape, or postpartum depression.

The Age of Light, Soap, and Water: Moral Reform in English Canada, 1885–1925
by Mariana Valverde (Toronto: McClelland & Stewart, 1991).

Mariane Valverde is a professor of criminology at the University of Toronto. This is one of those deceptively simple books that disguises a work of genius. She uses pamphlet literature from around the turn of the twentieth century to show the influence of the social reform movement on issues of deviance of the day: prostitution, homelessness, White slavery, and illiteracy. She shows how pamphlets were used to address an audience already receptive to issues of reform, particularly regarding issues of deviant sexuality.

PART V

Moral Regulation
of Personal Behaviour

• •

A common theme in the readings in this final section is the way the state is increasingly interested in defining permissible behaviour, and how the police were used to control immorality and deviance. One major problem is that the idea of deviance is highly subjective, and not all members of a society share either a common definition of what is deviant or how aberrant behaviour should best be controlled. As we shall see, however, the successful regulation of morality depends a great deal on how well advocates are able to convince the majority of the public that the problem at hand is a real one, is a pressing concern to the public, and poses a significant threat not only to individuals but to the very fabric of society. The issue is not a matter of personal conduct, but how individual choices—whether they involve monetary compensation for sexual services, the use of illegal narcotics, or the consumption of alcoholic beverages—affect the type of society in which citizens want to live.

In the first reading, McLaren explores the development of Canadian law on prostitution between 1867 and 1917 to consider how sexual activities between consenting adults could be viewed as a social threat. Initially, prostitution laws closely modelled those in effect in Great Britain. However, there were some differences in opinion in how to best respond to the problem of prostitution. In Great Britain, as long as streetwalkers kept a relatively low profile, the police tended to ignore them. In Canada, in contrast, the very act of being a prostitute was considered a crime, and the police could respond regardless of whether a formal complaint had been made. This is called a status crime, a criminal offence regardless of whether there was any illegal behaviour. Prostitutes who stayed off the streets did not fare much better in Canada. To use the somewhat quaint parlance that still exists in the Criminal Code, any person found in a "common bawdy-house" was subject to prosecution. Moreover, the law made no distinction between patrons and prostitutes; without lawful justification for being on the premises, either could be charged. In England, the law concerned itself with only the keeping of such an establishment.

In the second reading, the government's response to the non-medical use of opium is analyzed. What is little known is that the narcotics we define as illegal today were all criminalized in the 20th century. Initial attempts to control drugs and drug addiction were successful primarily because they focused on the use of opium among Chinese immigrants. The abuse of prescription drugs by middle-class White Canadians was not considered nearly as pressing. Until the early 1950s, the emphasis was on the prohibition of illegal narcotics, primarily through the incarceration of the offender. In an effort to determine the success of Canada's drug policy, the Senate Special Committee on the Traffic of Narcotic Drugs was given the mandate to determine the extent of the problem and the relationship between drugs and organized crime. With presentations from a number of police organizations, four main themes were evident: convicting the major traffickers was almost impossible; most addicts were criminals and complete social failures, and, as such, should be condemned rather than pitied; addicts were either unwilling or incapable of being rehabilitated, and any attempt to wean them off of drugs would be a complete failure; and the only way to get rid of the drug problem was to aggressively enforce charges for possession of illegal narcotics.

The final reading in this section looks at attempts to prohibit the sale and consumption of alcoholic beverages. One notable difference, however, is that Marquis looks at the issue from the perspective of those who had the primary responsibility of enforcing prohibition: the police. In contrast to the "war on drugs," the campaign against alcohol consumption was neither demanded by the police nor strengthened their position in the community. Indeed, enforcing prohibition was often difficult because some provinces and communities favoured prohibition more than others. And since the majority of convictions resulted in fines rather than jail, both wet and dry advocates shared the sentiment that municipalities were more interested in the generation of revenue than controlling the sale and consumption of alcoholic beverages.

CHAPTER 22

Chasing the Social Evil:
Moral Fervour and the Evolution of
Canada's Prostitution Laws, 1867–1917

John P.S. McLaren

● ● ● ● ● ● ● ● ● ● ● ● ● ● ● ● ● ● ● ●

*****

The relationship between criminal law and morality is one which has always evoked strong feelings. Moreover, the question of whether and how to use criminal law sanctions to curb sexual immorality has been particularly susceptible to both outbursts of moral fervour in the community at large and to the pressure exercised by crusaders and propagandists with moral missions.

*****

In this essay I use the development of Canadian law on prostitution between 1867 and 1917 as a paradigm of how moral concern, and the assumptions on which it proceeds, have influenced the development of the criminal law in the area of conduct branded as sexually aberrant. [...]

The Pattern of Change in the Prostitution Laws 1867 to 1917

Between 1867 and 1917 the body of criminal law in Canada on prostitution grew from a small group of provisions directed against both street and residential prostitution as forms of vagrancy, and the defilement of girls under twenty-one years of age secured by false pretences, to a more complex set of provisions which purported to protect females in general from the wiles of

the procurer, pimp, and brothel keeper, both within Canada and across international borders, and which gave the police wide powers to curb institutionalized prostitution. The growth in the range of conduct penalized by the laws was attended by the stiffening of the penalties stated and applied.

What explains this significant growth in the number and severity of the prostitution laws? The answer lies in the changes which took place in nineteenth- and early twentieth-century social attitudes towards the family and its female members, reflecting a growing concern about the moral dangers of the "modern world," and in the channelling of that concern into campaigns for social purity in general and sexual continence in particular. These changes in social values were not limited to Canada, but were felt in most Western countries. Given Canada's colonial past and geographical position, the process of social change and the legal response to it were influenced by events and policies in both Great Britain and the United States. [...]

The State of the Law on Prostitution in 1867

In 1867, British and Canadian law relating to prostitution and the protection of women and children from vice reflected the values of societies in which the desirability or efficacy of the state's intervention to condemn or control sexual errancy was not readily conceded. Where intervention was undertaken, the legal expedients served purely pragmatic ends. The law was also redolent of a social system in which women's virtue was valued predominantly in proprietary terms, to be protected only where their men's assets or lineage were in jeopardy. [...]

*****

Enforcement of the prostitution laws was both sporadic and capricious. In general, the police impulse was to practice toleration, with a level of intrusion sufficient to emphasize the fact that they were in control. If they felt control slipping, or they came under criticism or pressure from the community, the law could be and often was applied in the most repressive ways. Community attitudes, which invariably reflected middle-class values, varied depending on how far prostitution was seen as a direct threat to respectable members of the population, or necessary to local conditions. [...]

The law relating to the protection of women and children was even sparser than that on prostitution. The age of consent of a child to carnal knowledge, which had traditionally stood at ten years, was by 1867 twelve years in both Canada and Britain.[1] [...] Legislation had been passed grudgingly by the British Parliament in 1849 at the behest of the social reformer, Lord Ashley (later Shaftesbury), which limited protection to those under the age of twenty-one whose defilement had been secured by false pretenses.[2] The new offence was included in the English *Offences against the Person Act* of 1861, and subsequently adopted in the equivalent legislation in Canada in 1869.[3]

By 1850, especially in Britain, the realization was emerging that many of the social problems which were the consequence of industrialization, including those afflicting working-class women and children, could only be solved by state intervention and regulation. Nevertheless there was significant resistance to using legislation to protect women in the sexual sphere.[4] Widespread opposition existed, especially in Britain, among establishment and middle-class males, to the further criminalization of the sexual abuse or

exploitation of women and children, especially if it meant additional curbs on prostitution. This politically powerful group, which included many legislators, adhered to the view that prostitution was inevitable, if not necessary. Within that camp were politicians, law enforcement officers, and public health physicians whose experience pointed in that direction, those who viewed prostitutes as the protectors of middle-class female virtue, and those who felt that a more restrictive criminal law would cramp the style of themselves or their profligate offspring.[5] Despite a veneer of rectitude, some Victorian males found no moral problem in leading an ostensibly respectable family life, while at the same time seeking sexual excitement with prostitutes. Moreover, a proportion of those were attracted to juveniles. As establishment and middle-class girls were effectively "off limits" they felt no compunction about utilizing the services of working-class girls, who were often only too ready to oblige.[6]

*****

[...] By the middle of the nineteenth century an increasingly influential segment of the middle class in both countries was beginning to question the condition and values of the societies in which they lived. Industrialization and the prosperity that followed in its train had also brought untold suffering and evidence of a general decline in moral values, including attitudes towards sex. Those who felt like this pressed for reform of social values and the amendment of the law, including the criminal law. [...]

*****

The Early British Reformers and Their Impact

Not surprisingly, given the earlier pattern of industrialization and social dysfunction which it produced, the British reformers were earlier into the fray than their Canadian counterparts. [...]

[...] The abhorrence they felt for state-regulated prostitution in time drew their attention to its ubiquity on the Continent, and led to their collaboration with abolitionists in several other European countries. In the late 1870s, these contacts exposed something of a trade in young English women, spirited away from Britain by *placeurs* to serve in continental brothels, especially in Brussels and Paris.[7] When these revelations were confirmed by a Foreign Office investigator, pressure from the reformers and the more general public outcry persuaded Mr. Gladstone's government to refer the matter to a Select Committee of the House of Lords in 1881.

*****

The Lords' Select Committee was also asked to investigate the extent of child prostitution in Britain. The evidence satisfied their Lordships that a trade in English girls for European brothels had existed. Moreover, while the victims were not in all cases of impeachable moral character, they had clearly been misled as to the conditions in which they would be required to work.[8] Both police and social reformers attested to the large numbers of working-class children who were prostituting themselves in British cities, especially in London. [...] Although a number of witnesses pointed to social and economic factors which explained this errancy, greed and especially the desire for fashionable clothing were typically named as the prime motivations for the movement of young girls into prostitution.[9]

The members of the Committee felt that they had heard enough to warrant changing the law to make it a criminal offence to procure a woman to enter a brothel or to prostitute herself outside the United Kingdom, whether or not she knew of the purpose of the procurement. On the domestic front, they advocated raising the general age of consent to sixteen years and that for unlawful abduction to twenty-one. Moreover, it was recommended that brothel keepers be open to conviction for receiving into their establishments girls under the age of sixteen, and that the police be given the power to search such establishments where they had

reason to believe that juveniles were being harboured. They also advocated extending the powers of magistrates to remit delinquent children to industrial schools, reformative institutions established by legislation passed in the mid 1870s to provide both moral correction and work training to young people guilty of criminal offences, or in need of discipline.[10]

Early Canadian Attempts at Reform

In 1869, the existing vagrancy provisions in the criminal law were consolidated and expanded to embrace males found to be living on the avails of prostitution.[11] [...] The recommendations of the Lords' Committee were to induce some Canadian federal legislators to press for further reforms. As early as 1882, Mr. John Charlton, the M.P. for North Norfolk, introduced a private members' bill in the Commons for the punishment of seduction and other offences, including the inveigling or enticement of women into houses of prostitution. In doing so he made specific reference to the report of the United Kingdom Committee.[12] [...] In 1884, the revised bill was killed in the Senate, although the government did undertake to introduce its own legislation in due course.[13] *The Act Respecting Offences against the Person of 1885*,[14] a government measure, focused solely on procuring. The provision was more limited than that proposed by Charlton, in that the procuring of a woman for purposes of carnal knowledge or the inveigling or enticing of her into a house of ill fame or brothel was confined to cases of fraud. At a procedural level magistrates were given power to grant warrants to search premises where there was a reasonable belief that a woman who had been inveigled or enticed was being held.

*****

[...] The growing opinion that greater legal protection needed to be afforded to women and children is also evidenced by the establishment in Montreal of the Society for the Protection of Girls and Young Women. This organization [...] had developed its particular mandate at the behest of D.A. Watt, one of its founders, who was convinced that the procuring of girls and young women was widespread.[15] [...] During 1883, considerable regret was voiced by the Society over the Senate's blocking of Charlton's bill, and a petition was submitted to Parliament early in 1884 supporting the legislation.[16]

Greater success was achieved in this period in legislating for the reform and rehabilitation of prostitutes. The rescue impulse in Canada was as strong as it was in Britain. This concern was reflected by the establishment, primarily by female activists, of a number of refuges and shelters for reformed or potential prostitutes. These institutions were often given legislative sanction in the Provinces, and girls and women were referred to them by the courts.[17] When it became apparent that these institutions, with their rather grim combination of religious education and limited job training, were meeting with little success, the policy in Canada shifted to special women's prisons, to which prostitutes could be consigned for significant periods of time, during which correctional programs fitted to their needs would be able to take effect.[18] At the same time, the state began to address the problem of prevention. In 1879, the first legislative steps were taken in Ontario to remove delinquent children from their adverse surroundings and dissolute parents to industrial refuges in which proper values could be inculcated. Included were young girls deemed to be in need of protection from the lure of prostitution.[19]

Enter W.T. Stead!

[...] The British Parliament had proven singularly indifferent to the report of the Select Committee, and seemed disinclined to remedy gaps in the law which the Committee had identified. By 1885, some of the leading reformers had had enough of official prevarication and had enlisted the help of the crusading journalist, W.T. Stead, to force the hand of the politicians. Stead, who was not known for his caution, concluded that the best way to arouse public concern was to demonstrate how easy it was to buy a young English virgin for purposes of prostitution.

Following a lead supplied by Mrs. Butler, and with the help of Bramwell Booth, the son of the founder of the Salvation Army, he engineered the purchase of a fourteen-year-old girl whose mother was apparently ready to dispose of her for a price.[20] He also published a series of revelations in the *Pall Mall Gazette*, which he edited, of the investigations of a "secret commission" into the reality of vice in London. In the "Maiden Tribute of Modern Babylon," as the series was entitled, Stead condemned child prostitution as the most vicious form of "white slavery." Working-class children were, he claimed, being coerced into lives of depravity by all sorts of stratagems, from deceit to the use of force and drugs.[21] These "revelations," and Stead's subsequent imprisonment for the abduction of Eliza Armstrong, the fourteen-year-old subject of his stratagem, created a massive outburst of public indignation, as individuals throughout the social and political structure rallied to the cause of social purity.[22] In this emotion-charged climate, questions that might well have been raised about Stead's methods and the reliability of his information were ignored. For its part, Parliament, which was heavily influenced by this outpouring of public sentiment, passed the *Criminal Law Amendment Act* of 1885.[23]

The Act, which was to provide the inspiration and much of the form of subsequent Canadian legislation on procuring and bawdy houses, was aimed at the exploiters. It established a series of procuring offences designed to protect girls and women from those who would lead them into prostitution, either at home or abroad. Offences were to be punished with imprisonment up to two years "with or without hard labour."[24] The procuring of the defilement of a woman by threats, intimidation, fraud, or by the administration of a drug or other stupefying agent was also proscribed and a similar penalty attached.[25] The Act raised the age of consent to carnal knowledge to sixteen years and made it an offence for a householder to permit the defilement of a girl under sixteen years on his premises, or to abduct a girl under eighteen for purposes of carnal knowledge.[26] The detaining of any woman or girl against her will for purposes of carnal knowledge by any man or in a brothel was established as an offence, punishable with up to two years in prison.[27] Moreover, justices of the peace were empowered to issue search warrants for premises where there was reason to believe that a woman or girl was being held against her will, in order to effect her rescue.[28]

By way of stiffening the laws relating to brothels, the keeping, management, lease, or occupation of premises used as a brothel, and the permitting of the operation of a brothel by another on one's property, were established as summary conviction offences subject to a fine of twenty pounds or up to three months in prison, "with or without hard labour."[29]

The Criminal Law Amendment Act and Its Impact in Canada

The U.K. legislation did not escape the eagle eye of the indefatigable Mr. Charlton in Ottawa. He produced a further bill in 1886, which in addition to addressing his pet aversion, seduction, also contained several provisions taken from the imperial legislation. [...] On this occasion Charlton achieved greater success. His general provision on seduction and a more limited one on seduction under promise of marriage as well as that on inducing carnal knowledge were adopted.[30] [...]

The Campaign of D.A. Watt

Canada, largely as a result of parliamentary skepticism about the existence or extent of "white slavery," had opted for a pale shadow of the 1885 British legislation. D.A. Watt, of the Montreal Society for the Protection of Girls and Young Women, set out to change that. From the late 1880s to 1892, he waged a well coordinated and ultimately successful campaign to have the criminal law afford far greater protection to women and children.[31] [...] Working through the Society as the Chairman of its Legislation Committee, he drafted a series of bills, which were forwarded to the Department of Justice.[32] These various proposals for reform were collected and published in 1890 in a pamphlet,

Moral Legislation, a Statement Prepared for the Senate. Among the proposals contained in the document were an increase in the age of consent to carnal knowledge from twelve to sixteen years of age, the extension of the abduction law to protect poor girls as well as heiresses, the imposition of a precise legal obligation on parents and other guardians to take responsibility for protecting their children, the punishment of those procuring girls and women for prostitution and service in brothels both within and outside Canada, and the general protection of the young from vice.[33] [...]

*****

The Criminal Code and Morals Offences

[...] Watt was the only one of those responding to the draft Code who seems to have had any influence on its final substance.

In addition to provisions proscribing carnal knowledge of a girl under fourteen on any account, and the seduction of and illicit connection with previously chaste girls between fourteen and sixteen, women under twenty-one under promise of marriage, wards, servants, and female passengers on vessels, the Code also included detailed provisions on procuring.[34] Women under twenty-one who were not common prostitutes or "of known immoral character" were protected from procuring for the purposes of "unlawful carnal connection" within or outside Canada.[35] It was an offence to inveigle or entice any woman or girl into a house of ill fame or assignation, as it was to procure or attempt to procure any woman or girl to become a common prostitute in Canada or abroad.[36] Women and girls were protected from procurement to or from Canada for service in brothels, and from unlawful carnal connection procured by threat, intimidation, fraud, or the application of "any drug, intoxicating liquor, matter, or thing."[37] All of these offences were punished by up to two years imprisonment with hard labour. The procurement of a girl under sixteen by a parent, guardian, or householder for purposes of carnal knowledge, defilement, or prostitution drew stiffer penalties, up to fourteen years imprisonment depending on the age of the victim.[38] Like the *Criminal Law Amendment Act*, corroboration of the victim's story was required in the case of the procuring offences.[39]

In relation to the keeping of a bawdy house, which up until then had been dealt with under the vagrancy laws, an additional offence was included in the nuisance part of the Code prescribing up to one year's imprisonment for the operation of such an establishment.[40] Provision was also made for the securing of a search warrant where there was reason to suspect the harbouring of a woman or girl inveigled or enticed into a house of ill fame or assignation.[41] No special offence was included to cover the case of a landlord permitting his premises to be used as a bawdy house. In this the Code fell short of the protection afforded by the earlier British statute.

The Relevance and Efficacy of the British and Canadian Legislation

*****

There is nevertheless something of an air of unreality about the breadth and thrust of the legislative provisions. Both their form and rationale reflected the view that the most serious problem with prostitution was the external exploitation to which it was subject. The exploiters were seen as sinister, shadowy figures who were in the business of seducing or abducting girls and women to serve in establishments from which there was no easy means of escape. [...]

The legislation and its assumptions were deficient in a number of respects. In the first place, the reformers and legislators ignored the economic and social forces which led women and girls into prostitution. In their concern to apply middle-class morality to working-class problems, they failed to understand that if this was a moral problem it was one of the social immorality of consigning working-class families, and females in particular, to the type of living conditions and lack of economic opportunity in which prostitution was seen as an attractive option. [...]

*****

[...] By the age of twelve the surveillance of working-class children in the Victorian era by their parents was rare. They were expected by that age to earn their keep, which for girls often meant working outside the family as domestic servants. Within the crowded and squalid conditions in which they had lived with their families, sexual exploration and experience were by no means rare.[42] In addition to this they were not infrequently subjected to sexual abuse by their employers.[43]

A third problem relates to the identity of the exploiters. Granted that prostitution attracts its share of exploiters, the sensationalism surrounding the "white slavery" exposés seems to have deflected attention from the true character of the majority of those who lived in whole or in part on the profits of prostitution. [...] A proportion of those who ran bawdy houses in Upper Canada and Ontario were women of the same background and social circumstances as the prostitutes.[44] [...] Furthermore, it is not improbable that a proportion of the males involved in exploitation were from the same class, and the same socio-economic background as prostitutes. [...]

A fourth concern relates to the way in which the reformers seem to have ignored their own logic. Given their obsession to view the woman or girl who had succumbed to prostitution as a victim of male wiles, it is strange that this draconian body of law against exploiters was added to the existing law which penalized the prostitutes, rather than replacing it. [...] Even more puzzling is that, with the exception of Mr. Samuel Smith of Liverpool, a member of the British House of Commons, no one seems to have been willing to press publicity for the general criminalization of the customers of prostitutes.[45] [...] The answer to the first of these riddles has to be found in the schizophrenic Victorian middle-class view of prostitution.

Although the reformers were convinced that working-class girls and women were all too often being led into prostitution by rogues and bounders, they were still inclined to believe that some of the blame had to be attached to the lax moral values of that class.[46] [...] Viewed in this light it was necessary to show the female the error of her ways, by moral guidance and reproof where she had not yet gone astray, and by criminal law sanction where she had joined the ranks of the "fallen." The failure to extend the reach of the criminal law to the customer may be explained on more pragmatic grounds. Here the problem was not with the reformers but with the opposition. Despite the success of the social purity campaign, the idea that prostitution was inevitable, even necessary, was still strongly entrenched within male society. [...]

*****

The New White Slavery Scare and Its Legislative Impact

The dawn of the new century brought a decided increase in the concern surrounding prostitution and it exploitative elements, and a new wave of repression. A number of factors combined to produce further white slavery hysteria during the first decade which was international in its embrace. [...] During that period there was a significant trade over national borders and by steamship of females lured from disadvantaged locations in eastern Europe, the Levant, and the Orient to serve in brothels elsewhere.[47] Indeed, the traffic of girls and women from China was to reach as far as the west coast of Canada.[48] [...] Although there was little evidence to suggest that the tentacles of this trade extended to Britain, domestic precautions were taken involving the establishment of a special bureau at Scotland Yard and the extension of the activities of travellers' aid societies. Moreover, in 1905 the *Aliens Act* was enacted to give magistrates the discretionary power to repatriate foreign prostitutes from Britain.[49] [...]

*****

[...] The period before the First World War marks a period of high nationalism in which fears about the weakening of the racial integrity and strength of various peoples reached panic levels. In Britain it was seen as the moment of judgment for the imperial vision. In the United States and Canada it manifested itself in obsessions about the undermining of traditional Anglo-Saxon and Protestant values by the wave of new immigrants, many of whom were from non-English-speaking countries, and worse still, Roman Catholic or infidel in their faith.

*****

The paranoia [...] was also buttressed by prevailing views on sex and sexuality. As Michael Bliss has shown, in the first fifteen years of the century educated Canadians were exposed to popular books on human sexuality, typically produced in the United States and approved by orthodox physicians and clergymen, which were destined to add to their other worries about prostitution.[50] In these works the message was simple: sexual excess was at best the cause of declining health, and at worst of complete physical and mental decay. [...] A particular fear which was emphasized again and again in the white slavery literature was that of venereal disease.[51] This dreaded and, until 1910, incurable condition above all others was seen as striking at the physical and mental integrity of the family and thus the race. The disease seemingly spread from women of loose virtue to men, to their wives, and was inherited by their offspring. [...]

*****

By the turn of the century a national consciousness of prostitution and its ills were developing. Middle-class, protestant American was by then experiencing the sort of anxieties about industrialization and urbanization which had afflicted reformers in Britain in the 1850s and 1860s.[52] [...]

The major response to the "national" problem of prostitution in the United States was the *White Slave Traffic Act*, commonly known as the *Mann Act*, passed by Congress in 1910.[53] The Act not only sought to stop what was seen to be an extensive trade in procuring immigrant girls and women for service as prostitutes and in brothels, but also extended the prohibition to the transportation of females over state lines for prostitution or other immoral purposes.[54] [...]

*****

[...] By the early years of the present century the white slaver had made his way into the demonology of social reform groups in Canada. Increasingly, a loose alliance of women's groups, purity activists, and the major Protestant churches were calling for more significant political and social action to counteract prostitution in general and white slavery in particular. [...]

*****

Responding to the growing chorus of voices in the country advocating the expansion and stiffening of the criminal law to combat commercialized vice, the new Conservative Government in Ottawa was moved to act in 1913. The *Criminal Code Amendment Act* of that year contained a number of provisions relating to exploitation in prostitution.[55] Following the lead of the British Act of the previous year, although limiting it to a second or subsequent offence, whipping was added as a discretionary penalty for procuring.[56] The procuring provisions themselves were revised to drop the limitation of twenty-one years for the victims of the offence, and to exclude prostitutes from the protection of the inveigling offence. The Act also added the offences of concealment in a bawdy house, of spiriting new arrivals to Canada to bawdy houses and of exercising control, direction, or influence over a female for purposes of prostitution.[57] Procuring also became an offence subject to arrest without warrant.[58] A new exploitative offence of living wholly or in part on the avails of prostitution was added, supported by a presumption of guilt where the accused lived with or was habitually in the company of prostitutes with no visible

means of support, or residing in a house of prostitution.[59] The bawdy house provisions were tightened up by presuming a person who appeared to be a master or mistress to be one, treating the landlord as a keeper if he failed to eject a convicted tenant, and adding new offences of permitting the use of premises as a bawdy house, and of being a "found in."[60] A presumption that premises were a disorderly house was also established by the willful prevention or obstruction of a peace officer from entering.

*****

The Effects of Fifty Years of Moral Fervour

The legislative changes wrought in 1913 effectively rounded out the complex of moral provisions in the Canadian *Criminal Code*. Indeed, with the exception of the repeal of the streetwalker offence in the vagrancy section in 1972, and other changes made to reflect more clearly the reality that exploitation and prostitution can be practiced by either sex, the law in 1913 is basically that which applies today.[61]

The criminal statistics for the first seventeen years of the century, and especially for the years 1912 to 1917, might well have suggested to the social purists that there was some chance of their dreams being realized. The figures for convictions for seduction and abduction remained modest, although there was a discernible jump in the conviction rate in the second half of the period. During the first ten years the average annual conviction rate for seduction was 9.1.[62] For the years 1911–1917 the conviction rate increased to 34.14 per annum.[63] A similar, although more modest increase, was experienced in the conviction rate for abduction, from an average of 7.8 for the years 1901–1910 to a figure of 18.57 for the period of 1911–1917.[64] More encouraging perhaps was the fact that convictions for procuring became numerous enough to warrant reporting from 1911. Although the conviction rate vacillated between eleven and sixteen a year between 1911 and 1914 it then jumped to sixty-six in 1915, fell to thirty-four in 1916, and rose again to fifty-two in 1917.[65]

By far the most dramatic increases occurred in the figures for the vagrancy offences of keeping, frequenting, or being an inmate of a bawdy house. The average annual conviction rate for the years 1901–1910 was 1741.[66] For the later period it was 3868.[67] In the years 1914, 1915, and 1916 the figures were 4357, 4935, and 5469 respectively.

*****

Any cheer which these figures might have given the reformers was in all likelihood illusory. Despite the evidence of greater vigilance on the part of the police and greater success in prosecuting the "social evil," no significant dent was being made in the incidence of prostitution. Indeed, the record suggests that the "trade" and its practitioners and customers merely readjusted their habits to deal with more draconian enforcement patterns. [...] As in the United States and Britain the evidence in Canada suggests that vigorous enforcement directed against organized brothels in discrete areas merely led to a dispersal of the "trade," and an increase in street prostitution.[68] Moreover, the exploitation practiced by bawdy house keepers was replaced by the often more insidious influence and control of the pimp or "cadet" as he was often described.[69]

Perhaps the greatest shortcoming of the law was that the double standard was practiced consistently in its enforcement. A complex of legal provisions, which was designed primarily to attack the exploiters of prostitutes, was used predominately to harass and victimize the prostitutes themselves. True, for the first time prosecutions were brought in some numbers against the procurers and pimps, but their number pales into insignificance alongside the host of women charged with vagrancy and bawdy house offences. [...]

*****

It is a permissible, if tentative, conclusion that the Canadian prostitution laws did little or nothing to stop the exploitation of prostitutes, let alone reduce the incidence of prostitution itself. Indeed, the law and its enforcement may in some respects have contributed to exploitation by driving the prostitutes into the clutches of pimps. Moreover, despite the protestations of both reformers and legislators that the end of the double standard was their primary aim, it continued to flourish, especially at the level of enforcement. The prostitutes remained the deviants, to be harassed when and how the law enforcement authorities willed it.

The Faulty Assumptions of the Social Purists

This preliminary analysis of the development of the prostitution laws and the impact of social purity makes it all too easy to criticize those who were in the forefront of social reform in the late nineteenth and early twentieth centuries. It has to be remembered that for all their strange thinking and practical foibles, the cause of the social purists was one which did produce social benefits. Some women and children were "saved," and the basis was laid for that part of the welfare state which has the protection of the young as its focus. Moreover, one of the strains in this type of thinking was in time to lead to the translation of the social gospel into progressive political action. [...]

*****

The social purity movement was an activist crusade bent on both social and legal reform. As with all such crusades, the end tended to dictate the means. The rhetoric of the campaign was often substituted for rational debate and discussion. There was also a tendency to canonize the heroes of the movement and to attach the character of dogma to their writings and utterances without any attempt to assess the reliability of their data or conclusions. [...]

*****

The combining of social activism with pressure for the invocation of the criminal law is by no means a purely historical phenomenon. It exists in our society, and can lead to the same dangers of excessive moral fervour and unthinking espousal of simplistic legal expedients. We are certainly not immune to "purity" crusades. Furthermore, we tend to cling to the sort of middle-class stereotypes which prevented the social purists from appreciating the true nature of the problems with which they were dealing. Although there may be more skepticism now about the claims of moral zealots, we are not beyond being unduly influenced by experts, especially when we believe that they have answers which support our claims. While the use and reworking of fictional stories is perhaps

less prevalent today than it was in the days of social purity, the advocates of moral reform are still capable of using dubious but oft-repeated factual information as if its constant repetition put its validity beyond question. Moreover, rhetoric and its capacity for obfuscating the issues is as much a problem now as it was then. Finally, there are many people now as then who attach an unwarranted and almost magical significance to law, especially criminal law, as the solution to complex social problems. If there is a lesson in all of this, it is that those responsible for social policy formulation have to be continually vigilant against being influenced by these features of the crusading mentality.

Notes

1. See *Offences against the Person Act* (1861), 24 and 25 Vict., c. 100, ss. 50, 51 (England). See G. Parker, "The Legal Regulation of Sexual Activity," 211–214, for details of earlier provisions in the Maritime colonies, Lower and Upper Canada all of which had increased the age to twelve. The wording of the English statute was translated to the Canadian *Offences against the Person Act* (1869), 32 & 33 Vict., c. 20, ss. 51, 52.

2. See *An Act to Protect Women from Fraudulent Practices for Procuring Their Defilement* (1849), 12 & 13 Vict., c. 74 (England).

3. *Offences against the Person Act* (1861), 24 & 25 Vict., c. 100, s. 49 (England); *Offences against the Person Act* (1869), 32 & 33 Vict., c. 20, 50 (Canada).

4. E. Bristow, *Vice and Vigilantes: Purity Movements in Britain since 1700* (Dublin: Gill & MacMillan Ltd., 1977).

5. Ibid., 52–53. The leading proponent of regulation of prostitutes for public health reasons was Dr. William Acton. For a sample of his views, see J. Murray, *Strong Minded Women and Other Lost Voices from 19th Century England* (New York: Pantheon Books, 1982), 394–397, 427–428. The prostitute as saviour of virtuous womanhood was a theme of the historian and essayist, William Leckey, ibid., 411–412.

6. See K. Chesney, *The Victorian Underworld*, 386–388; R. Pearsall, *The Worm in the Bud: The World of Victorian Sexuality* (Harmondsworth: Penguin Books, 1971), 358–366. Although the

desire of some customers in Canada for young girls has not been so clearly demonstrated as in England, the work of C. Backhouse, "Nineteenth-Century Canadian Prostitution Law: Reflection of a Discriminatory Society," unpublished paper, April 1983, 15–16, demonstrates that girls from their early teenage years were active in the trade. See also *infra* for the concern of Canadian legislators and reformers in the 1880s and 1890s about child prostitution and its sponsors.

7. Bristow, ibid., 85–90.

8. British Parliamentary Papers, *Report of the Select Committee on the Protection of Young Girls*, 1882, iii.

9. Ibid., Minutes of Evidence, 92–93 (Dunlap); 88 (Morgan); 8 (Miss Ellice Hopkins); 33 (Rev. J.W. Horsley).

10. Ibid., *Report*, iv–v.

11. *An Act respecting Vagrants* (1869), 32 & 33 Vict., c. 28 (Canada). Section 1 introduced the new offence of having no profession or calling to maintain oneself by, but for the most part supporting oneself by the avails of prostitution. The prescribed penalty was a maximum of two months imprisonment, fifty dollars, or both. The maximum penalty was later increased to six months: (1874) 37 Vict., c. 43, s. 1 (Canada). By legislation in 1881 it was made clear that accused could be sentenced to six months with or without hard labour: (1881) 44 Vict., c. 31, s. 1 (Canada).

12. Parliamentary Debates, House of Commons, 1882, 327. Charlton was a devout Presbyterian and a

founding member of the Dominion Lord's Day Alliance.

13. Parliamentary Debates, Senate, 1884, 365–368.

14. (1885), 48 & 49 Vict., c. 82 (Canada). In the Commons Charlton criticized the bill because it made no attempt to get at the person having illicit connection. Both an amendment by him to remedy that gap and a motion to refer the bill back to Committee were defeated. See Parliamentary Debates, H.C., 1885, 2767–2768.

15. Montreal Society for Protection of Girls and Young Women, Minutes Book, 1882–1891, PAC MG 281 129.

16. Ibid.

17. Backhouse, "Nineteenth-Century Canadian Prostitution Law," 52–53. Backhouse reveals that legislative status had been accorded to such establishments from earlier in the century (see, e.g., *Montreal Institute for Female Penitents* (1832), 3 Wm. IV, c. 35 (Lower Canada); *Toronto Magdalen Asylum* (1858), 22 Vict., c. 73 (Province of Canada). This process continued and intensified through the 1860s and 1870s.

18. Ibid., 53–56. Backhouse notes that the maximum penalty for vagrancy was increased to six months in 1874 *An Act Respecting Vagrants*. Complementary provincial and federal legislation authorized the custody of women convicted of provincial and federal offences respectively in provincial reformatories (see, e.g., *An Act Respecting the Andrew Mercer Reformatory for Females* (1879), 42 Vict., c. 38, s. 2 (Ontario); *An Act Respecting the Andrew Mercer Reformatory for Females* (1879), 42 Vict., c. 43 (Canada)). Moreover, special federal legislation was enacted requiring women convicted of vagrancy in Quebec to serve their sentences in the Quebec female reformatory prison. The *minimum* penalty which could be exacted was five years! See *An Act to Make Provision for the Detention of Female Convicts in Reformatory Prisons in the Province of Quebec* (1871), 24 Vict., c. 30, s. 2 (Canada).

19. Ibid., 56–57. See, e.g., *An Act to Establish an Industrial Refuge for Girls* (1879), 42 Vict., c. 39 (Ontario).

20. R. Schults, *Crusader in Babylon: W.T. Stead and the Pall Mall Gazette* (Lincoln: University of Nebraska Press, 1972), 130–131.

21. Ibid., 128–168; D. Gorham, "The 'Maiden Tribute of Babylon' Re-examined: Child Prostitution and the Idea of Childhood in Late-Victorian England," *Victorian Studies* 21 (1978), 353.

22. Schults, *Crusader in Babylon*, 169–192.

23. *Criminal Law Amendment Act*, (1885), 48 & 49 Vict., c. 69 (U.K.).

24. Ibid., s. 2.

25. Ibid., s. 3.

26. Ibid., s. 4–7.

27. Ibid., s. 8.

28. Ibid., s. 10.

29. Ibid., s. 13.

30. *An Act Respecting Offences against the Public Morals and Convenience* (1886), 49 Vict., c. 157, ss. 2, 4, 5.

31. D.A. Watt, *Moral Legislation: A Statement Prepared for the Information of the Senate* (Montreal: Gazette Printing Co., 1890), Appendix A, 37–41.

32. For the development of this program of lobbying, see Montreal Society for the Protection of Girls and Young Women, Minute Book, 1882–1891, PAC MG 281 129. See also Parker, "The Legal Regulation of Sexual Activity," 217–226.

33. Watt, *Moral Legislation*, 27–30, 43–46.

34. *The Criminal Code of Canada*, (1892), 55–56 Vict., c. 29, ss. 269, 181–184.

35. Ibid., s. 185(a).

36. Ibid., s. 185(b), (c).

37. Ibid., s. 185(e), (f), (g), (h), (i).

38. Ibid., ss. 186, 187.

39. Ibid., s. 684.

40. Ibid., s. 198.

41. Ibid., s. 574.

42. *Report of Select Committee on the Protection of Young Girls*.

43. This was true of a substantial minority of former servants according to J. Walkowitz, *Prostitution and Victorian Society: Women, Class and the State* (Cambridge: Cambridge University Press, 1980), 18.

44. Backhouse, "Nineteenth-Century Canadian Prostitution Law," 14–26.

45. Parliamentary Debates, House of Commons 1885, Vol. 300, 1419–1421. Smith, who wished to add an offence of "habitual solicitation," was primarily concerned to protect women and girls from the insults to which they were subjected in public places from potential customers.

46. See *Report of Select Committee on the Protection of Young Girls*, 1882, iii; and Gorham, "The 'Maiden Tribute' Reexamined."

47. Bristow, *Vice and Vigilantes*, 177–181. See also E. Bristow, *Prostitution and Prejudice: The Jewish Fight against White Slavery, 1870–1939* (Oxford: Clarendon Press, 1982).

48. P. Roy, "The Oriental Menace in British Columbia," in M. Horn & R. Sabourin (eds.), *Studies in*

Canadian Social History (Toronto: McClelland & Stewart, 1974), 289.

49. *Aliens Act* (1905), 5 Edw. 7, c. 13 (U.K.).

50. M. Bliss, "'Pure Books on Avoided Subjects': Pre-Freudian Sexual Ideas in Canada," [1975] Can. Hist. Assoc. Papers 89.

51. M. Connelly, *The Response to Prostitution in the Progressive Era* (Chapel Hill: University of North Carolina Press, 1980), 67–90. For an example of the treatment of venereal disease in contemporary anti-white slavery literature, see E. Bell, *War on the White Slave Trade* (Toronto: Coles Publishing Co., 1980), 281–304 (originally published, Chicago: C. Thompson Publishing Co., 1909).

52. Connelly, *The Response to Prostitution*, 281–304.

53. *White Slave Traffick Act*, U.S., Statutes at Large, vol. 36 (1910), 825–827.

54. See *Hoke v. U.S.* 227 U.S. 308 (1913); *Athanasaw v. U.S.*, 227 U.S. 308 (1913); *U.S. v. Holte*, 236 U.S. 140 (1915); *Caminetti v. U.S.*, 242 U.S. 470 (1917).

55. *Criminal Code Amendment Act* (1913), 3 & 4 Geo. V, c. 13.

56. Ibid., s. 9.

57. Ibid.

58. Ibid., 23.

59. Ibid., s. 9.

60. Ibid., ss. 1. 11.

61. By *The Criminal Code Amendment Act* (1915), 5 Geo. V, c. 12, s. 5, being an inmate of a bawdy house was made an indictable offence. By s. 7 of the same Act the vagrancy offences of keeping and being an inmate or frequenter of a bawdy house were repealed. Amendments in 1917 extended the definition of bawdy house to embrace establishments kept for the practice of acts of indecency—(1917), 7 & 8 Geo. V, s. 3.

62. Session Papers, 1900–1910; no. 7 (1900), no. 17 (1901–1910).

63. Session Papers, 1911–1917; no. 17.

64. Session Papers, 1900–1917; no. 7 (1900), no. 17 (1901–1917).

65. Session Papers, 1911–1917; no. 17.

66. Session Papers, 1900–1910; no. 7 (1900), no. 17 (1901–1910).

67. Session Papers, 1911–1917; no. 17.

68. D. Nilson, "The 'Social Evil': Prostitution in Vancouver 1900–1920," in B. Latham & C. Less (eds.), *In Her Own Right* (Victoria, B.C.: Camosun College, 1980), 215.

69. J. Bedford, "Prostitution in Calgary 1900–1914," *Alberta History* 29 (1981), 1, 7; L. Rotenberg, "The Wayward Worker: Toronto's Prostitute at the Turn of the Century," in J. Acton, P. Goldsmith, & B. Shepard (eds.), *Women at Work* (Toronto: Canadian Women's Educational Press, 1974), 57.

CHAPTER 23

The First Century:
The History of Non-Medical Opiate Use
and Control Policies in Canada, 1870–1970

Robert R. Solomon and Melvyn Green

• • • • • • • • • • • • • • • • • • • •

An Introductory Review of the First Century

Prior to 1908, few restrictions were imposed on the distribution or consumption of opiates, whether for medical or pleasurable purposes. Canada annually imported tons of raw opium and large quantities of processed opiates. Various low-cost opium preparations were freely distributed by doctors, traveling medicine shows, patent medicine companies, pharmacies, general stores, and Chinese opium shops. Although viewed as an individual medical misfortune or personal vice, opiate dependence was free from serious moral stigma. Indeed, in many circles, cigarette smoking and alcohol consumption were considered graver threats to public health and morals.

The decision to prohibit non-medical opiate use stemmed not from concern about its addictive properties, but rather from a redefinition of its moral impact by some vocal reformers. They came to perceive opiates as a menace that destroyed Christian inhibitions, thus exposing man's natural tendency to depravity. While similar campaigns against alcohol, tobacco, and other vices had only minor temporary effects, the anti-opium crusade fundamentally altered both public attitudes and the criminal law. This crusade succeeded because it was directed against Chinese opium smokers and Chinese

opium factories, but at the same time posed no threat to the larger number of predominantly middle-class and middle-aged Caucasian users who were addicted to the products of the established pharmaceutical industry.

The events following the passage of the first criminal drug law in 1908 reinforced alarmist views of drug use and users. [...] Parliament and the public were presented with stereotypical drug villains, who were primarily non-Christian and non-white, and who more than deserved the progressively harsher laws that were passed. The federal police and government drug bureaucracies, which were established in the early 1920s, aligned themselves with the moral reformers and anti-Asiatic forces in calling for stricter laws. In a series of near-annual amendments, Canada's drug statute was transformed during the 1920s into one of the country's most stringent pieces of criminal legislation.

By the early 1930s, federal police and drug officials emerged as Canada's only drug experts. [...] As law enforcement efforts increased, distribution patterns, the drug of choice, and the manner of consumption changed. After World War II, intravenous use of heroin, the most potent opium derivative, began to replace intravenous use of morphine, which had previously replaced the smoking of opium.

It was not until the early 1950s that the concept of treating rather than punishing addicts was first forcefully proposed. Relying heavily on their American counterparts, Canadian enforcement officials attempted to discredit the suggested treatment programmes, and instead argued for heavier sentences, more vigorous enforcement, and custodial treatment. Parliament tried to accommodate these divergent views, but ultimately adopted the enforcement community's recommendations in the 1961 legislation. Nevertheless, at least some of the more Draconian features of the early drug law were repealed at this time.

Canada's addict population grew slowly after World War II, and there was even a sustained heroin shortage in the early 1960s. A restructuring of the illicit heroin trade in the mid 1960s soon provided abundant supplies for the domestic market and also for trans-shipment to the United States. By the end of the decade, heroin was more readily available in Canada than ever before, and the addict population, which already had exceeded previous levels, was still increasing sharply.

The Chinese Opium Question, 1870–1908

Chinese Immigration and British Columbia's Anti-Asiatic Campaign

The first Chinese immigrants came to British Columbia in the 1850s (40, p. 508). Both the Chinese arriving directly from the Orient and those escaping from mounting racial discrimination in California were welcomed as a source of cheap labour for the railroads, mines, and other expanding industries. The Caucasian population viewed the Chinese as conscientious, thrifty, and law-abiding. Their smoking of opium was not considered to be physically harmful or socially degenerate. Yet, the public strongly disapproved of opium smoking among whites, because it involved mixing of the races—a matter considered far more serious than the drug's effects (28; 40).

At the time, the various levels of government were concerned about opium smoking only

for financial reasons. When British Columbia joined Confederation in 1871, the colonial duty on opium was replaced by the federal import tax (39a, Schedule B). The Chinese opium factories established in Victoria and later in Vancouver and New Westminster were subject to an annual $500 municipal licensing fee (41, p. 275).

The tolerant attitude to both the Chinese and opium smoking prevailed until the 1880s, when the decline in railroad construction and the gold rush restricted job opportunities in British Columbia. [...] As economic conditions worsened, complaints against the Chinese increased. They were criticized as being clannish, heathen, unsanitary, immoral, and disloyal to Canada (7; 25; 28; 36; 40; 42).[1]

*****

[...] Shortly thereafter, Parliament passed the *Chinese Immigration Act, 1885* (39b, s. 14), which imposed a $50 tax on Chinese immigrants entering British Columbia. [...]

Continued public hostility prompted Parliament to double the tax [...] in 1901 (39c, s. 6) and to establish the 1902 Royal Commission on Chinese and Japanese Immigration. The Commission concluded that all Chinese immigration should be prohibited and that, in the interim, the tax should be increased to $500. [...] [N]o opium-treated proposals were made. Parliament raised the tax to $500 in 1904 (39d, s. 6), but did not prohibit Chinese immigration until 1923 (39l).

The 1904 tax, unlike the two previous measures, apparently contributed to a temporary reduction in Chinese immigration[2] (6). However, a sharp increase in Japanese immigration in the mid 1900s (21) stirred another wave of public hostility. As in the past, the anti-Asiatic crusade in California served as a model. In September 1907, a leader of the Exclusion League of San Francisco came to Vancouver for the express purpose of encouraging anti-Japanese sentiment. On September 7, a labour demonstration against the Japanese erupted into rioting (21). The federal government dispatched Mackenzie King, then Deputy Minister of Labour, to investigate the incident and to compensate Asians who had suffered losses (15). King was confronted during his investigation with claims from two Chinese opium merchants. Startled by the existence of an established Chinese opium industry, King strongly recommended in his official report that Parliament immediately eliminate the evil (11; 22; 40).

Canada's First Criminal Opium Prohibition

King pursued the opium issue during his visit to Vancouver and undertook a second unofficial investigation in his capacity as a concerned citizen (23). His private report contained four dominant themes. The first three related to the increasing popularity of opium smoking among white men and women, the size of and profits from the Chinese opium trade, and the fact that it operated in open violation of the provincial pharmacy legislation. The fourth and perhaps most important point was that Canada, as a Christian nation, had to set an example in the international campaign against opium (23).

*****

Less than three weeks after King submitted his private study, Parliament enacted the country's first criminal opium prohibition. The [...] bill moved through the House of Commons without discussion. [...] The 1908 *Opium Act* made it an indictable offence to import, manufacture, offer to sell, sell, or possess to sell opium for non-medical purposes, but prohibited neither simple possession nor use (62e). Violation of the statute was punishable by incarceration for up to three years and/or a $1,000 fine.

A comparison of the *Opium Act* with the other drug-related legislation introduced in the same year suggests that racial and economic factors were largely responsible for the success of the campaign against opium smoking. After prolonged discussions with industry representatives, the government enacted the *Proprietary or Patent Medicine Act* (11; 39f) of 1908. The legislation, which had been revised to take into account the Pharmaceutical Association's views, basically regulated, rather

than prohibited, the non-medical use of patent medicines. The Act banned the use of cocaine and excessive amounts of alcohol in patent medicines. It also required manufacturers to register with the government and to label products containing any scheduled drug. While heroin was included in the schedule, opium and morphine were not. [...] The accommodating attitude to the industry is noteworthy considering that far more people were probably addicted to opiates through the use of patent medicines than through the smoking of opium (7; 11; 16; 41).[3]

*****

[...] The 1908 drug reform legislation left Caucasian interests in the patent medicine and tobacco industries relatively unscathed, while it criminalized Chinese opium distributors and sacrificed Chinese business interests. The Chinese, a politically powerless and, at least in the west, a despised alien minority, were ideal targets for Canada's moral reformers and politicians.

The Expansion of the Criminal Prohibition, 1909–1929

The Opium and Drug Act of 1911

The passage of the 1908 *Opium Act* enhanced King's reputation as a social reformer and opium expert, furthered his political career, and led to his appointment to the 1909 Shanghai Opium Commission—the first international conference which was called for the purpose of suppressing the trade. King won a seat in the 1908 federal election and was appointed Labour Minister the next year (11). Following his return from Shanghai in 1909, he introduced a drug bill dealing exclusively with opium, only to withdraw it in favour of broader legislation after being warned of Montreal's growing "cocaine curse" (8; 11).

*****

[...] The 1911 *Opium and Drug Act* (39g) was discussed at length. King set the tone of the debate, quoting extensively from newspaper accounts of Montreal's cocaine wave (19a), and speaking of Canada's leadership role in the international drug suppression campaign.[4] [...] The 1908 statute was repealed; morphine, cocaine, and eucaine were added to the drug schedule; and new user-oriented offences were created. The importation, manufacture, sale, transportation, and possession of scheduled drugs were prohibited, except for medical or scientific purposes. The smoking of opium and merely being present in an opium "resort" without lawful excuse were also made offences. The Act placed restrictions on wholesale and retail distributors, physicians, and other health-care professionals. Police powers of search and seizure were expanded, and a special search warrant was created for drug cases (39g). The Act gave magistrates discretion to award half of an offender's fine to the person who had provided the information leading to conviction (39g).

Although the provincial and municipal police lacked an explicit enforcement mandate, there was an average of over 900 convictions a year between 1912 and 1920 (34b; 34c; 34d; 34e; 34f). The courts apparently did not view drug offenders as serious criminals—about 90 per cent of drug convictions resulted in fines, a trend consistent across Canada during this period. The conviction statistics suggest that the illicit trade was confined almost exclusively to the cities in Quebec, Ontario, and British Columbia. In the east, Caucasians controlled the traffic, dealing primarily in morphine and cocaine smuggled into Canada from Europe. In British Columbia, Chinese opium distributors with contacts in the Orient dominated the trade (34b, c, d, e, f).

International Drug Control Efforts

*****

The Shanghai Opium Commission was followed by a second international conference at which the 1912 Hague Opium Convention was formulated. The Convention was appended to the Versailles Treaty ending World War I and, as a result, did not come into general effect until the treaty was ratified in the 1920s (43). However, American complaints that opiates were being diverted from Canada's licit trade to the United States' black market (11) prompted Canada to adopt the Convention's import and export provisions in 1919 (39b). The Canadian government fulfilled the Convention's remaining requirements in the 1920 drug amendment and also strengthened record-keeping procedures, increased some penalties, and renamed the statute the *Opium and Narcotic Drug Act* (39i). [...]

[...] As law enforcement efforts increased the risks of arrest and financial loss, major traffickers switched from opium and morphine to heroin distribution. Heroin is several times more potent than morphine and is easier to dilute, thus providing traffickers with a greater profit potential. During the early 1920s, heroin began to replace morphine as the drug of choice in the United States and first appeared in eastern Canada (14; 18; 24; 26).

*****

The Resurgence of the Moral Reform Movement and Anti-Asiatic Sentiment

Many of the forces that prompted the enactment of the 1908 *Opium Act* re-emerged in 1920. That year saw the launching of a well-publicized moral crusade against drugs, the revival of anti-Asiatic hostility in British Columbia, and the establishment of a federal drug agency, which, like King, served as a political catalyst for the enactment of legislation.

In 1920, *Maclean's Magazine* initiated a series of articles for the express purpose of arousing public demands for stricter drug legislation. The articles provided the first detailed coverage of the issue in any popular Canadian magazine, and it later formed part of Canada's first drug book, *The Black Candle* (30). Mrs. Emily Murphy, a magistrate and a judge of the Edmonton Juvenile Court, authored both the book and the articles. She approached the drug problem with a combination of genuine concern and strict Protestant morality. Her writing contained social, medical, and statistical information drawn from Canada and abroad, but it was interwoven with anecdotes, popular racial biases, and moral fables.

[...] The reader was provided with two images of drug users—victim and villain. The victim was invariably white and usually young. The list of villains included: Chinese and black pushers who were motivated by greed and lust for white women; "aliens of colour" who were unwitting cogs in an international drug conspiracy designed "to injure the bright-browed races of the world" (30); "script doctors" who prescribed drugs for profit; and "the ring," a mysterious and ruthless drug syndicate (30). Two characteristics shared by victim and villain alike were their overwhelming desire to infect others, particularly the young, and their need to commit crime. [...] Even though the drug was virtually unknown in Canada, Murphy warned of the dangers of "marihuana" addicts. Quoting American police officials, she reported that these addicts were rendered raving maniacs capable of savage killings while under the drug's influence.

[...] Critical of the sentences imposed by her fellow judges, Murphy called for mandatory minimum sentences, whipping, deportation of convicted aliens, and the establishment of a drug treatment prison on a remote island.

*****

The renewal of the anti-Asiatic campaign in British Columbia during the early 1920s fuelled public demands for drastic action against drug offenders. Service clubs, church organizations, civic groups, and the Anti-Asiatic Exclusion League pressed for immediate legislative action. British Columbia's members of Parliament were the major force in the enactment of the 1923 *Chinese Immigration Act*, which in essence prohibited Chinese immigration (391).[5] [...] The Chinese were publicly identified as the primary villains in the drug trade; their prey was Canada's unsuspecting youth. One Vancouver Member of Parliament, quoting the secretary of the Anti-Asiatic Exclusion League, bluntly informed Parliament that:

Here we have a disease, one of many directly traceable to the Asiatic. Do away with the Asiatic and you have more than saved the souls and bodies of thousands of young men and women who are yearly being sent to a living hell and to the grave through their presence in Canada (19b).

*****

The Federal Drug Bureaucracy

*****

In 1920, the newly created federal Department of Health was given responsibility for supervising Canada's drug law and international treaty obligations. An agency, later named the Narcotic Division, was established within the department to discharge these duties (11; 34g). In the same year, the Royal Canadian Mounted Police (RCMP) force was founded and given a mandate to enforce all federal law. The new force was not uniformly welcomed, and it relied heavily on rigorous drug enforcement as one means of justifying its existence. [...]

*****

The RCMP became a staunch ally of the Narcotic Division, serving as its enforcement arm. When its officers encountered difficulties, the RCMP turned to the Division, which acted as its spokesman in proposing remedial legislation. In the early 1920s, the federal government began to employ special prosecutors to handle all drug cases and to provide advice to local drug enforcement units. The Division encouraged federal prosecutors to appeal unfavourable court decisions and, in turn, drafted legislation to assist these prosecutors in obtaining convictions and stiff sentences (17).

Given its statutory mandate, its allies in enforcement and prosecution, and its direct access to the responsible cabinet minister, the Narcotic Division usually secured quick passage of its legislative proposals. [...] In a near-annual series of amendments, the federal drug bureaucracy transformed Canada's drug statute into one of the country's most punitive pieces of criminal legislation. The six legislative revisions between 1921 and 1927 (39l, m, n, o, p) were consolidated in the *Opium and Narcotic Drug Act*, 1929 (62s), the major features of which are outlined below.

Health-care professionals were required by the Act to maintain detailed records of their drug transactions and were prohibited from prescribing or supplying drugs, except for medical purposes (39q). As a result of the Narcotic Division's interpretation of what constituted "medical purposes," doctors were prosecuted for providing maintenance doses to addicts. [...] Violations of these provisions were punishable by up to five years' imprisonment.

Cannabis was added to the drug schedule in 1923, presumably as a result of Mrs. Murphy's warning. Illicit importing, exporting, manufacturing, selling, or possession of any scheduled drug were made serious offences. Any person occupying a premise or vehicle in which drugs were found was deemed to be in possession, unless he could prove that the drugs were there without his authority, knowledge, or consent (39q). [...] Aliens convicted of the more serious offences were subject to mandatory deportation at the end of their prison sentence (39q). The right to appeal a drug conviction was severely curtailed (39e).

*****

Despite greater police powers, the annual number of drug conviction, which had peaked in the early 1920s, fell rapidly by the end of the decade to about 200 (27). Probably the most important factor in this decline was the dying out of older generations of Chinese opium smokers, which had provided the majority of offenders. The prohibition against Chinese immigration, the deportation of more than 500 convicted Chinese offenders during the 1920s (35), and reduced public interest also contributed to this trend.

*****

The Continuation of the Law Enforcement Approach, 1930–1952

*****

The drug law underwent only three substantive changes between 1930 and 1952: the offences of cultivating opium and cannabis were added in 1938 (39r); the deportation provisions were transferred to the new immigration legislation in 1952 (39s); and the Schedule was expanded to include new compounds and synthetic narcotics.

*****

Canada's illicit drug trade changed far more profoundly than did its drug policy. The war severed Pacific shipping lines, halted the flow of opium from the Orient, and crippled the Chinese opium distribution system (33a). North America's Chinese syndicates were unable to re-establish this system after the war because China, previously their largest source, was torn by civil war. When the Communist government finally came to power in 1949, they eliminated the traffic (38). The focus of the international trade shifted to the Middle East, where the export markets were controlled by French-Corsicans and other Europeans. North America's Chinese distributors had no contacts with these suppliers and, in any event, their traditional market within the Chinese community was rapidly disappearing (37). By 1945, offenders of Chinese origin accounted for only 10 per cent of Canada's drug convictions (20). [...]

Developments abroad also influenced Canada's east-coast traffic during this period. The repeal of alcohol prohibition in 1932 largely eliminated the illicit alcohol trade, prompting New York Mafia syndicates to expand their illicit drug activities. They obtained heroin from the French-Corsican laboratories of Paris and Marseilles and smuggled it into both American and Canadian east-coast ports abroad commercial ships (9; 14; 26). As in the west, the war disrupted smuggling operations and caused widespread shortages. Once the war ended, however, the east-coast distribution system was restored and strengthened. Several prominent French-Corsican racketeers, who had fled France to avoid prosecution for war crimes and for other offences, settled in Montreal. In conjunction with local and New York Mafia leaders, these expatriate French-Corsicans contributed to Montreal's emergence as a major trans-shipment centre for heroin en route to the United States. Mafia figures in Toronto and Hamilton established a parallel trans-shipment network, in some cases using unsuspecting Italian immigrants as drug couriers (9; 26). [...] Canada's east-coast Mafia soon completely dominated the domestic trade and played a major role in supplying the even more lucrative American market (5). There were sharp increases in American rates of heroin use after the war, whereas Canada's addict population apparently continued to fall.[6]

The Emergence of a Treatment Alternative, 1952–1961

It was not until the early 1950s that the policy of criminalizing, rather than treating, addicts was first seriously questioned. [...] Despite the lack of strong legislative support, some modest treatment programmes were initiated.

Discontent with the Law Enforcement Approach

Reports of spiralling rates of addiction among American ghetto youth and the televised American Senate hearings on organized crime sparked media accounts of similar issues in Canada (12). Even though official statistics indicated that Canada's addict population had been decreasing (40), these highly publicized events could not be ignored. Concern was expressed in Parliament, and by the Vancouver Community Chest, an association of social welfare agencies, which established a committee to study the local problem.

Relying on recent arrest and conviction statistics, the Committee concluded that heroin addiction was a growing problem in Canada,

particularly among the young (31; 40). [...] The [...] basic premise was that addiction should be regarded as a social and medical problem, not as a crime. With the support of the British Columbia Medical Association, the Committee called for the establishment of comprehensive drug education programmes, private experimental treatment centres, and narcotics clinics to dispense maintenance doses to registered addicts within a general rehabilitative programme. While favouring treatment for addicts, the Committee advocated more severe penalties for major traffickers (31). The Committee submitted its report to Mr. Martin, the federal Minister of Health and Welfare, in December 1952.

[...] Dr. Roberts, a senior official in the federal Department of Health and Welfare, basically rejected the Committee's treatment proposals in an article published in the February 1953 issue of the *Canadian Medical Association Journal*. Nevertheless, Dr. Roberts indicated that contrary to what was generally believed, the federal drug law did not prohibit physicians from treating addicts (32). Mr. Martin expressed the same view during the House of Commons debates on the 1954 drug amendments (19c).

Despite considerable support in the House of Commons for treating addicts (19c), the government only paid lip-service to this issue in the 1954 drug amendments. The 1954 statute (39t), like previous drug legislation, was largely shaped by the enforcement needs of the RCMP drug squads. The police had complained that usually they were only able to arrest traffickers for possession, because it was extremely difficult to apprehend them in the act of selling drugs. A new offence, possession for the purpose of trafficking, was created to alleviate this problem. Once the prosecutor established unlawful possession, the accused was required to prove that he had no intention of trafficking in the drug. If the accused failed to satisfy this onus of proof, he would be convicted of possession for the purpose of trafficking—an offence that carried the same penalties as trafficking. The maximum sentence for trafficking was doubled to fourteen years' imprisonment, the related fine provisions were deleted, but whipping was retained as a discretionary punishment (39t). Possession was made a separate offence, no longer subject to either fine or whipping (39t). The Minister of Health claimed that the six-month mandatory minimum sentence for possession had been retained to ensure that addicts could be adequately treated (19c). There were, however, no correctional drug treatment institutions, units, or even programmes in Canada at the time (19c).

The Vancouver Community Chest persisted in lobbying the federal and provincial governments (40). As a result of the Committee's efforts, British Columbia introduced the country's first correctional drug treatment programme and founded the province's Narcotic Addiction Foundation, a research, public education, and treatment facility centred in Vancouver. In conjunction with the University of British Columbia, the Community Chest obtained federal and provincial funding for a comprehensive scientific study of drug addiction in British Columbia (40).

*****

The 1955 Senate Special Committee

In 1955, the federal government established the Senate Special Committee on the Traffic in Narcotic Drugs in Canada under the chairmanship of a Vancouver senator. [...] The [...] Committee held hearings in the major Canadian cities, receiving testimony from physicians, drug researchers, the Vancouver Community Chest, social welfare agencies, private citizens, federal officials, police representatives, and H. Anslinger, the Commissioner of the American Bureau of narcotics (12).

*****

The testimony of the law enforcement officials was accepted almost without question. Ultimately, the Senate Special Committee advocated heavier trafficking penalties, and more aggressive enforcement of the possession

offence and drug-related crimes, such as prostitution and theft (12). Advocates of a social or medical approach to addiction were generally viewed as being well-meaning, but misguided. The Committee apparently considered drug treatment as simply another means of assisting the police in their fight against the illicit trade (12). [...]

[...] In 1956, Ontario opened its first custodial drug treatment programme at the Alex Brown Memorial Clinic in Toronto. In the late 1950s, the federal government started developing plans for Matsqui, a drug-treatment penitentiary at Abbotsford, British Columbia (29). Like their American predecessors [...], the Canadian correctional treatment programmes proved to have little positive impact on the prisoners' subsequent rates of addiction (4; 5).[7]

The Present Law: The 1961 Narcotic Control Act

The 1961 *Narcotic Control Act* clearly reflected the Senate Committee's enforcement priorities and preference for custodial treatment. The maximum penalty for trafficking, possession for the purpose of trafficking, importing, and exporting was raised from fourteen years to life. A mandatory minimum sentence of seven years' imprisonment was enacted for importing and exporting (39u). Except for murder and treason no criminal offence carries as great a minimum term. The option of proceeding by way of summary conviction in possession cases was repealed (39u). Nevertheless, the Act did eliminate some of the most severe features of the earlier legislation including: whipping, restrictions on appeals, the six-month minimum sentence for possession, and the provision deeming an occupant of a dwelling to be in possession of any drugs found therein. The restrictions on physicians' rights to prescribe drugs were removed from the Act and redefined in the regulations. The Minister of Health explained in the House that this change was intended to leave "to professional interpretation what is or is not a proper use of a narcotic. Actually, we hope to encourage doctors to take more responsibility for and interest in the health and well-being of an addict" (19d). Shortly thereafter, the Addiction Research Foundations of British Columbia and Ontario initiated methadone maintenance programmes, and the Canadian Medical Association established a committee to report on what constituted good medical practice in the care of narcotics addicts (12).

*****

The Decline and Subsequent Expansion of the Illicit Heroin Trade, 1961–1970

During the Senate Special Committee hearings, Canadian police officials had acknowledged their inability to stem heroin smuggling or to seriously disrupt the major syndicates. However, in the late 1950s the American Bureau of Narcotics and the RCMP initiated a series of conspiracy prosecutions against the senior figures in the North American heroin trade. These men had been largely immune to traditional enforcement techniques because they did not personally handle, possess, or sell the drugs. Expendable employees bore these risks. In a conspiracy prosecution, the police only had to establish that there was an agreement to commit an unlawful act between the accused and any of his partners, suppliers, purchasers, or underlings. [...]

The syndicates were caught off guard (37; 5). Within a six-year period, North America's largest heroin operations were rocked by over 100 arrests and convictions.[8] [...]

This unprecedented flurry of prosecutions contributed to a heroin shortage throughout North America. The scarcity was most apparent in Vancouver, the Canadian city with the largest addict population. The street price of a heroin capsule rose from five dollars in 1961 to fifteen dollars by the end of 1962. There were also corresponding increases in wholesale prices. According to the Vancouver RCMP, the purity of heroin decreased and the number of users fell sharply. [...] The heroin shortage in Canada

lasted until 1965, abating when the Mafia re-established its importing and distributing networks (37).

*****

There was little public interest in the drug issue until the mid-1960s, when media attention was focused on marijuana and LSD use. Grave concerns were expressed about the physiological and psychological effects of these drugs. Canadian police warned that the upsurge in hallucinogenic drug use was a prelude to a parallel rise in heroin addiction. The sordid details of life in Toronto's hippy community were given extensive media coverage, reinforcing public fears about the counterculture. Ominous statements were made about the future of Canada's youth. As in the past, Canadian perceptions were influenced by the American media and enforcement agencies (12).

[...] The *Narcotic Control Act*'s penalty provisions were criticized as being unduly severe given the cannabis offender's age and social background. Sweeping changes in federal cannabis law were discussed (see 12). Ultimately, the government enacted very modest legislation in 1969, which gave the prosecutor the option of proceeding by way of summary conviction in possession cases (39v)—a discretion that had only been withdrawn in 1961. Although this provision was intended for young, middle-class cannabis offenders, it was also invoked in some cases involving heroin users.

Public concern over the drug issue continued throughout the late 1960s, fuelled in large part by extensive media coverage. Academics, social welfare leaders, police officials, and prominent political figures all called for legislative action. The federal government responded to these diverse pressures by appointing a Royal Commission of Inquiry into the Non-Medical Use of Drugs, under the chairmanship of Gerald Le Dain, the Dean of Osgoode Hall Law School (12). The Commission issued its interim report in 1973 (2; 3; 4; 5). Despite these comprehensive reports, there has not been a significant change in the *Narcotic Control Act* since 1969.

Although there was a marked increase in the Canadian addict population during the late 1960s, the heroin trade changed far less dramatically than the hallucinogenic drug market. The epidemic increases in heroin use that swept the United States simply did not materialize in Canada. Nevertheless, there were significant developments in the domestic heroin traffic. In the early 1960s, heroin use was confined to Montreal, Toronto, Hamilton, Winnipeg, and Vancouver. During the late 1960s, small pockets of heroin trafficking and use developed, albeit temporarily in some cases, in Halifax, Kingston, London, Windsor, Calgary, Edmonton, Victoria, and a number of small cities and towns in British Columbia. Once prevalent only within the downtown core of the major cities, the trade spread outwards as additional suburban outlets opened. By the end of the 1960s, heroin was more readily available than it had ever been (37).

Conclusion

Canadian narcotics control policy has been shaped by various factors, the least significant of which have been the physiological effects of the opiates themselves. The early laws were the product of moral reformers, racism, and the political maneuvering of Mackenzie King and the federal drug bureaucracy. By 1930 the drug law had been transformed into an inordinately representative statute, characterized by sweeping police powers, punitive sanctions, and severe encroachments on civil liberties. The addicts' image, the law, and the drug bureaucracy's control over drug policy went unchallenged during the next two decades.

When the policy of criminalizing addicts was first questioned in the 1950s, Parliament deferred to the views of the drug bureaucracy and re-affirmed its commitment to stringent enforcement. Nevertheless, some of the severe features of the early law were repealed, doctors were again permitted to treat addicts, and health issues were discussed. The upsurge in cannabis and hallucinogenic drug use in the late 1960s generated renewed public interest and demands for reforms. Except for the creation of the Le Dain Commission, these events had little impact on policy. There was, however, a moderation in the general tone of the drug debate. Members of the academic, legal, and medical communities began to question perceptions about drug use and users, the breadth of police powers, the effectiveness of enforcement, and the law's impact on offenders. These latest developments are, of course, the most difficult to assess because there has been no comprehensive government response to these concerns or to the Le Dain Commission reports. Aside from the government's almost annual discussion of cannabis reform, the drug law and policies of the 1960s have evidenced little change.

Throughout this 100-year period, Canada's illicit trade has evolved in step with domestic enforcement and international market forces. Regardless of internal policies, the Canadian heroin trade will continue to be profoundly affected by developments abroad, particularly those in the United States. The relatively uninterrupted success of the illicit traffic, in the face of concerted enforcement efforts, attests to its economic vitality.

References

1. Canada. *Report of the Department of Health for the Fiscal Year Ended March 31, 1928*. Ottawa, 1929.

2. Canada. Commission of Inquiry into the Non-Medical Use of Drugs. *Interim Report*. Ottawa: Queen's Printer, 1970.

3. Canada. Commission of Inquiry into the Non-Medical Use of Drugs. *Cannabis*. Ottawa: Information Canada, 1972.

4. Canada. Commission of Inquiry into the Non-Medical Use of Drugs. *Treatment*. Ottawa: Information Canada, 1972.

5. Canada. Commission of Inquiry into the Non-Medical Use of Drugs. *Final Report*. Ottawa: Information Canada, 1973.

6. *Canada Year Book, 1915*, 1916.

7. Chapman, T. Drug usage and the *Victoria Daily Colonist*: The opium smokers of Western Canada.

In: Knafla, L. (ed.). *Canadian Society for Legal History. Proceedings 1977.* pp. 60–75, 1977.

8. Chapman, T. The anti-drug crusade in Western Canada, 1885–1925. In: Bercuson, D., and Knafla, L. (eds.). *Law and Society in Canada in Historical Perspective.* Calgary: University of Calgary, 1979.

9. Charbonneau, J. *The Canadian Connection.* Ottawa: Optimum, 1976.

10. Clark, C. *Tales of the British Columbia Provincial Police.* Sidney, B.C.: Gray's Publishing, 1971.

11. Cook, S. *Ideology and Canadian Narcotics Legislation, 1908–1923.* M.A. thesis, University of Toronto, 1964.

12. Cook, S. *Variations in Response to Illegal Drug Use.* Unpublished research study. Alcoholism and Drug Addiction Research Foundation, Toronto, 1970.

13. Curran, R.E. Some aspects of Canada's narcotic-drug problem. *Food Drug Cosmetic Law Journal,* 10:850–60 (December 1955).

14. Cusak, J.T. Response of the government of France to the international heroin problem. In: Simmons, L. and Said, A. (eds.) *Drugs, Politics, and Diplomacy: The International Connections.* Beverly Hills, Calif.: Sage, 1974.

15. Dawson, R.M. *William Lyon Mackenzie King: A Political Biography.* Toronto: University of Toronto Press, 1958.

16. Duster, T. *The Legislation of Morality: Law, Drugs and Moral Judgment.* New York: Free Press, 1970.

17. Green, M. A history of Canadian narcotics control: The formative years. *University of Toronto Faculty of Law Review,* 37:42–79 (1979).

18. Harvison, C. *The Horsemen.* Toronto: McClelland & Stewart, 1967.

19. House of Commons. Canada. *Debates.*
    a. January 26, 1911.
    b. May 8, 1922.
    c. June 1, 1954.
    d. June 7, 1961.

20. Josie, G. *A Report on Drug Addiction in Canada.* Ottawa: Department of National Health and Welfare, 1948.

21. Kawakami, K. *Asia at the Door: A Study of the Japanese Question in the Continental United States, Hawaii and Canada.* New York: Fleming H. Ravell Publishing Co., 1914.

22. King, W.L.M. Losses sustained by the Chinese population of Vancouver, B.C. on the occasion of the riots in that city in September, 1907. *Sessional papers 1907–8,* no. 74f.

23. King, W.L.M. The need for the suppression of the opium traffic in Canada. *Sessional papers 1908,* no. 36b.

24. Lyle, D. The logistics of junk. *Esquire,* March 1966.

25. Mark, G. Racial, economic and political factors in the development of America's first drug laws. *Issues in Criminology,* 10:49–72 (1975).

26. McCoy, A., Reid, C., and Adams II, L. *The Politics of Heroin in Southeast Asia.* New York: Harper & Row, 1972.

27. MacFarlane, B.A. *Drug Offences in Canada.* 2nd ed. Toronto: Canada Law Book, 1986.

28. Morgan, P.A. The legislation of drug law: Economic crises and social control. *Journal of Drug Issues,* 8:53–62 (1978).

29. Murphy, B. *A Quantitative Test of the Effectiveness of an Experimental Treatment Programme for Delinquent Opiate Addicts.* Ottawa: Department of the Solicitor General of Canada, 1972.

30. Murphy, E.F. *The Black Candle.* Toronto: Thomas Allen, 1922.

31. "Ranta Report." *Drug Addiction in Canada: The Problem and Its Solution.* Reprinted as "Here's program to fight drug menace," Vancouver *Province,* July 30, 1952.

32. Roberts, C.A. The problem of drug addiction. *Canadian Medical Association Journal,* 68:112–15 (1953).

33. Senate. Canada
    a. Special Committee on the Traffic in Narcotic Drugs in Canada. *Proceedings,* 1955.

34. *Sessional Papers.* Canada.
    a. 1912, no. 11, Report of the Department of Customs.
    b. Vol. 47, 1912–1913, no. 17, Criminal Statistics.
    c. Vol. 50, 1915, no. 17, Criminal Statistics.
    d. Vol. 52, 1917, no. 17, Criminal Statistics.
    e. Vol. 54, 1919, no. 10d, Criminal Statistics.
    f. Vol. 57, 1921, no. 10d, Criminal Statistics.
    g. 1921, no. 12, Report of the Department of Health for the fiscal year ending March 31, 1920.

35. Sharman, C.H.L. Narcotic control in Canada. *Police Journal,* 3:535–49 (1930).

36. Smith, R. Status politics and the image of the addict. *Issues in Criminology,* 2:157–75 (1966).

37. Solomon, R. the criminal prohibition of non-medical opiate use in Canada. Unpublished research study, Commission of Inquiry into the Non-medical Use of Drugs, 1972.

38. Solomon, R., and Versteeg, H. *A review of the development and present state of the illicit*

international heroin trade. Ottawa: Health and Welfare Canada. Non-medical Use of Drugs Directorate, 1978.

39.   *Statutes of Canada*.
  a.   *An Act Respecting the Customs*, s.c. 1867–8, c. 6.
  b.   *The Chinese Immigration Act, 1885*, s.c. 1885, c. 71.
  c.   *The Chinese Immigration Act, 1900*, s.c. 1900, c. 32.
  d.   *The Chinese Immigration Act, 1903*, s.c. 1903, c. 8.
  e.   *An Act to prohibit the importation, manufacture, and sale of Opium for other than medicinal purposes*, s.c. 1908, c. 50.
  f.   *The Proprietary or Patent Medicine Act*, s.c. 1908, c. 56.
  g.   *The Opium and Drug Act*, s.c. 1911, c. 17.
  h.   *An Act to amend the Opium and Drug Act*, s.c. 1919 (2nd sess.), c. 25.
  i.   *An Act to amend the Opium and Narcotic Drug Act*, s.c. 1920, c. 31.
  j.   *An Act to amend the Opium and Narcotic Drug Act*, s.c. 1921, c. 42.
  k.   *An Act to amend the Opium and Narcotic Drug Act*, s.c. 1922, c. 36.
  l.   *The Chinese Immigration Act, 1923*, s.c. 1923, c. 38.
  m.   *The Opium and Narcotic Drug Act, 1923*, s.c. 1923, c. 22.
  n.   *An Act to amend the Opium and Narcotic Drug Act, 1923*, s.c. 1925, c. 20.
  o.   *An Act to amend the Opium and Narcotic Drug Act, 1923*, s.c. 1926, c. 12.
  p.   *Opium and Narcotic Drug Act*, R.S.C. 1927, c. 144.
  q.   *The Opium and Narcotic Drug Act*, 1929, s.c. 1929, c. 49.
  r.   *An Act to amend the Opium and Narcotic Drug Act*, 1929, s.c. 1938, c. 9.
  s.   *The Immigration Act*, s.c. 1952, c. 42.
  t.   *An Act to amend the Opium and Narcotic Drug Act*, s.c. 1954, c. 38.
  u.   *Narcotic Control Act*, s.c. 1961, c. 35.
  v.   *An Act to amend the Food and Drugs Act and the Narcotic Control Act and to make a consequential amendment to the Criminal Code*, s.c. 1969, c. 41.

40.   Stevenson, G.H., Lingley, L.P.A., Trasov, G.E., and Stanfield, H. *Drug Addiction in British Columbia*. Vancouver: The University of British Columbia, 1956.

41.   Trasov, G.E. History of the opium and narcotic drug legislation in Canada. *Criminal Law Quarterly*, 4:274–82 (1962).

42.   Williams, D. *"The Man for a New Country": Sir Matthew Baillie Begby*. 1977.

43.   Willoughby, W. *Opium as an International Problem: The Geneva Conferences*. New York: Arnold Press, 1976.

Notes

1.   A parallel sequence of events occurred in California about a decade earlier, and this served as a model for the campaign in British Columbia (25; 28; 36).

2.   Chinese immigration fell from 4,847 in 1904 to 77 in 1905. It increased significantly after 1908, peaking in 1913 at 7,455 (6) and earning the federal government $3,500,000—about half of which was paid to British Columbia.

3.   There is no doubt that the opium-smoking trade in Canada was dwarfed by the patent medicine industry. In 1908, King reported that there were at least seven factories producing smoking opium, which together generated sales of between $600,000 and $650,000 (23). Not all of this smoking opium was consumed domestically. Large quantities of legally produced Canadian smoking opium were smuggled into the lucrative American market (10). […]

4.   King's public posturing about Canada's moral leadership in the international anti-opium movement is ironic. As a member of the British delegation to the Shanghai Commission, King was hardly in the vanguard of this movement. Britain had largely created and consciously fostered the opium smoking trade in China, in blatant defiance of Chinese law. Britain only reluctantly agreed to co-operate in international suppression efforts after its profits from the opium trade had declined, and domestic and foreign criticism of its opium policies became impossible to ignore (15). […]

5.   The Act limited immigration to members of the diplomatic corps, Chinese children born in Canada who had left temporarily for educational or other purposes, specified classes of Chinese merchants, and Chinese students attending Canadian universities or colleges. Even a lawful Chinese resident of Canada was required to register prior to

leaving the country temporarily, in order to ensure re-entry. The Act also provided for the deportation of any Chinese resident, except for a Canadian citizen, who fell within one of fifteen prohibited classes. These classes included persons who were likely to become a public charge; drug addicts; illiterates; persons of "constitutional psychopathic inferiority"; and persons who were mentally and physically defective to the extent that it affected their ability to earn a living.

6. Stevenson et al. (40) list the official Canadian estimates from 1924 to 1955, which suggest that there was a steady decline throughout this period. See, however, 33a, p. 61, for an RCMP estimate of the post-war addict population.

7. The Matsqui treatment programme was carefully designed, generously funded and staffed, and vigorously evaluated. Yet, despite these close-to-ideal conditions, the results were extremely disappointing. Matsqui's research officer reported that "the rate of recidivism approached 100%." It is curious that the addicts in the more intensive treatment programme did worse than those in the other programme. The research officer suggested that the intensive programme, rather than curing addiction, helped the addicts to become better adjusted, self-assured addicts who were capable of committing more offences and thereby purchasing more heroin (29).

8. In the late 1950s, Vito Genovese, then North America's most powerful Mafia leader, and fourteen of his associates were convicted of conspiracy to import heroin. Early in 1960, Giuseppe Cotroni, Robert Rene of Montreal, and twenty-nine high-ranking Mafiosi in New York were arrested and charged with conspiracy to traffic in heroin. Later in 1960, three Canadian Mafia distributors centred in Toronto and another twenty Mafia members in New York were arrested and charged with conspiracy to import heroin. Several years later, Lucien Rivard of Montreal was extradited to the United States to stand trial for conspiracy to import heroin. In the early 1960s, one of Vancouver's largest heroin distributors retired to avoid the risk of a conspiracy prosecution, while the other major distributor was arrested for conspiracy to traffic. North America's four largest importing and distributing operations were destroyed and the principal distributors in Canada's three largest cities were serving long prison terms (9).

CHAPTER 24

Regeneration Rejected: Policing Canada's War on Liquor, 1890–1930

Greg Marquis

• • • • • • • • • • • • • • • • • • • •

Alcohol use was a dominant public question in most parts of North America during the late nineteenth and early twentieth century.[1] In Canada, both academic and popular historians have examined the ideology and politics of early twentieth-century restrictions on beverage alcohol.[2] Less is known about the actual links between liquor and social conditions such as poverty and crime or about the enforcement side of Canada's dry laws, other than the sense that the latter was a failure that contributed to repeal.[3]

Both extremes in the debate on liquor made extensive use of moralizing, anecdote, and statistics to justify their causes. The exaggerated claims of dry activists met with equally subjective arguments from the "wets." The prohibition era produced a series of powerful "legends" that continue to influence our understanding of the "great Experiment." These include the belief that dry laws gave rise to modern organized crime, encouraged greater disrespect for the law, and actually increased the incidence of alcohol consumption.[4]

*****

This paper reviews prohibition from the point of view of [...] Canada's police. The period in question began with the hearings of the Royal Commission on the Liquor Traffic

and a ground swell of prohibitionist activity on the provincial and municipal levels leading to the 1898 national referendum, moved into a decade-long experiment with prohibition in most provinces, and ended with the adoption, in all but one jurisdiction, of government liquor sales. These years also coincided with the awakening, among municipal and provincial police, of professional consciousness on the national level. The two movements were not unconnected. The political defeat of prohibition helped smooth the way for the triumph of the crime-fighting police professional. In contrast to the late 20th-century "war on drugs," the "war on alcohol" was neither demanded by the police nor served to legitimize their position.[5]

The Police and the Liquor Question

*****

[...] The police reacted to public concern about drinking (expressed through the press, clergy, and temperance organizations) with increased prosecutions for license violations and drunkenness, but worried that their legitimacy, especially amongst the working class, would be endangered by an aggressive policy.[6] Indeed liquor enforcement, even in strong temperance towns, did not enjoy community consensus. The police often found it difficult to properly regulate legal taverns, hotel bars, and liquor shops, let alone suppress unlicensed establishments. By the late nineteenth-century temperance pressure in most jurisdictions had decreased the number of retail licenses, raised license fees, and shortened hours of business.[7] Despite this tightening cordon, liquor regulation was no more popular with the guardians. A number of 1890s police officials supported the view of Winnipeg's police chief, who opined that the enforcement of license provisions conflicted "with other duties in regard to the detection of crime."[8] [...]

The extensive hearings of the Royal Commission on the Liquor Traffic, 1892–93, are an invaluable source for understanding the response of Canada's police officials to alcohol regulation. Many of the officials who testified were of the generation which formed the Chief Constables's Association of Canada in 1905.[9] Much of the questioning centred on public drunkenness, the difficulties of liquor enforcement, and the respective merits of licensed sales versus partial prohibition under the Scott or Canada Temperance Act (CTA). [...] The Scott Act applied to one town or county, but not the next, and allowed brewers and distillers to continue manufacturing in dry zones. Its enforcement depended on the success of special inspectors hired by the municipality and the cooperation of police and public. By 1902 the CTA was in force in one city and twenty-six counties, all, with two exceptions, in the Maritimes. Some areas, such as Yarmouth, Nova Scotia and vicinity, were known to be more dry than others.[10]

Most of the criminal justice officials, including magistrates and court clerks, who testified in 1892–93 questioned the wisdom of prohibition and attributed improved public behaviour to provincial license laws. A New Brunswick police magistrate opined that the Scott Act in Fredericton and Saint John county (where Saint John was wet and adjacent Portland was dry) had been a fiction. A former police chief praised the CTA in principle, yet discussed difficulties in securing evidence and reliable

witnesses in liquor prosecutions. The town marshall responsible for enforcing the statute in Moncton admitted that at least a dozen illegal bars continued to operate. He agreed with the local stipendiary magistrate that "memory seems more defective in Scott Act cases than in ordinary cases," a reference to the challenge of finding prosecution witnesses.[11] [...]

Quebec police officials, according to the evidence of the Liquor Traffic inquiry, tended to favour the license system. Conditions in that province in the 1890s, in the opinion of temperance forces, were old-fashioned in the extreme. Grocery dealers, for example, were allowed to sell spirits by the bottle (and illegally sold it by the glass) and working-class neighbourhoods in Montreal were well supplied with bars and wet eateries. For the city's chief constable, general prohibition was not only "not desirable" but also contingent upon "an army of revenue officers." The license system afforded municipal and provincial police unlimited access to licensed premises, whereas the search of private dwellings necessitated a magistrate's warrant. Chief Leon Phillip Vohl and Recorder E.A. Dery of Quebec City doubted if a dry law could be enforced, as did Montreal's police magistrate, sessions judge, and license commissioner. According to Montreal's recorder, police officials believed that liquor enforcement "depreciates the force" as investigating officers were looked upon as informers. Both the superintendent of the provincial police liquor squad for greater Montreal and the municipal chief of detectives admitted to relying on "informers" or "specials," asserting that it was "impossible to bring the people to total abstinence." These officers favoured restrictions such as a reduction in the number of licenses, the disenfranchisement of liquor dealers and publicans and the imprisonment of license violators.[12] [...] In 1910 the premier "deprecated absolute Prohibition ... and expressed his hope that Quebec's License Law would become the model for the Dominion."[13]

In Ontario, where dry sentiment was a powerful force, the police varied in their opinions on the relative merits of saloons (traditional working-class haunts) versus hotel bars and open versus "high" licensing. A number believed that prohibition, under the right conditions, was enforceable. Yet Toronto Chief Constable Henry J. Grasett asserted that "you could not enforce it without increasing the number of officials and making it Russian." When asked about statistics on public drunkenness, Grasett suggested a direct relationship between the number of police on duty and the volume of arrests. His staff sergeant, David Archibald, was more in the moral reform camp and blamed the failure of past measures on the unwillingness of the temperance lobby to back up the police and inspectors. Similarly, Ottawa's chief advised that the "temperance people should have something to say" in the appointment of independent liquor inspectors. The police chiefs of Peterborough, Milton, Guelph, and Hamilton were all unflattering in their comments on the Scott Act. The latter testified that prohibition would be against public opinion and "would keep a large army busy." All agreed that liquor enforcement was a major problem in police-community relations.[14] [...]

Most of the western police officials (municipal, provincial and federal) who testified before royal commission doubted the wisdom of dry laws. The west had experienced partial prohibition, a permit system enforced by the North-West Mounted Police, until the introduction of a license law in the early 1890s. According to the standard academic account of the NWMP, the Mounties became "highly ambivalent" in their attitudes towards the liquor ordinance once white settlers began to make known their opposition.[15] In the 1892 testimony a NWMP inspector described the Canada Temperance Act back east as a failure and the territorial chief license inspector rejected total prohibition as impractical. The chair of the territorial assembly's executive committee opposed granting blanket power to search persons and residences. NWMP Commissioner Herchmer, recalling the permit decades, admitted that "we did not like to examine respectable peoples'

goods." Herchmer claimed that the temperance element did little but criticize the police in the newspapers.[16] [...] Police officials in British Columbia supported their Prairie counterparts. Sergeant John Langley of the provincial constabulary did not view prohibition as a workable measure; Victoria's chief constable, who supported legal sales, reported that his city was "one of the quietest places I have ever seen." His Vancouver counterpart concurred, as did Police Magistrate George A. Jordan. Although enforcement officials who testified in British Columbia, Manitoba, and the North-West Territories were sceptical of prohibition, the movement was already gaining ground locally by the 1890s.[17]

*****

By 1900 the liquor traffic, even in frontier resource regions, was an issue that would not go away. Police officials were forced to moderate their somewhat libertarian views as prohibitionists garnered more and more support. Pressure for enforcement was strongest in the Maritimes, Ontario, and the Prairies, but even British Columbia, where liquor had not been as culturally divisive, was influenced by a wave of social purity that swept up the West coast. Vancouver, in imitation of most North American urban police departments, soon had its dry squad, operating with part-time undercover spotters to punish illegal vendors and individuals "found in" disorderly houses.[18]

Despite periodic drives against illegal booze and gambling, prostitution, and other consensual crimes, the police often were "compromised missionaries"[19] or "reluctant partners" in the war on vice.[20] [...]

There are suggestions that the typical Canadian policeman was not firmly in the camp of the drys. Recruits were expected to be sober, but drinking was the most common dereliction of duty in the nineteenth and early twentieth century. In 1892 the Montreal recorder (police magistrate) testified that policemen investigating license violations "sometimes became drunkards themselves, because they go from one inn to the other taking drinks." There was a long tradition of publicans treating patrol officers. Halifax's city marshall revealed that he allowed constables to enter licensed premises only in the company of a sergeant. The early North-West Mounted Police, reflecting its military ethos, was troubled by heavy alcohol use and attempted to control its personnel, in true military fashion, through wet canteens.[21] [...] Toronto policemen and Montreal officers in uniform were ordered to stay away from taverns. Weaver notes that by the early 1900s the Hamilton police "had been moved toward outward compliance with standards of moral conduct.[22] Yet the image of the hard-drinking cop survived as part of urban folklore.[23]

The Police and Dry Criminology

Prohibitionist criminology, embraced by most moral and social reformers, alleged direct links between alcohol and social problems, as did a number of prominent international experts on criminality.[24] Mainstream society held that alcohol use was partly a cause, not simply a result, of poverty and deviancy. Yet most Canadians subscribed to conservative theories of criminality and believed that individuals, through sin, weakness, or greed, ultimately were responsible for their misdeeds. A host of "uplift" organizations, however, were committed, at least in part, to environmental explanations of social pathology. Crime was high on the list of ills supposedly generated by the liquor traffic. A prohibitionist handbook of 1881 attributed "70 per cent of the crime, 60 percent of the pauperism, 20 percent of the insanity" and a large proportion of "disease, waste, misery and death" to liquor.[25] [...]

Although prohibitionists supported education and moral suasion as instruments in reaching the public, the Canada Temperance Act, war-time prohibition, and provincial dry laws were all built around enforcement. The police, therefore, were of more than passing interest to dry crusaders. In the American case, speeches, posters, pamphlets, and cartoons suggested that the police were allies of the liquor traffic and

responsible for sustaining the very criminality they were charged with preventing. Canadian temperance workers, if somewhat more restrained, were attracted to this theory. The existence of citizen's committees to monitor town councils and magistrates courts and to gather evidence against Canada Temperance Act offenders, for example, suggests that prohibition enforcement through the normal channels was an unrealistic expectation.[26]

Arrest statistics were important in the liquor debate. Temperance enthusiasts tended to view individuals charged with drunken and disorderly behaviour not only as victims but also part of the local crime problem. [...] The Dominion Alliance for the Total Suppression of the Liquor Traffic, in an 1890s pamphlet, estimated that one-half of public expenditures on jails, alms houses, and asylums could be blamed on liquor. The minority report of the Royal Commission on the Liquor Traffic, penned by Reverend Joseph McLeod, a New Brunswick Free Will Baptist, was a classic Victorian temperance essay that blamed drink for "violations of family affections and the destruction of domestic peace.[27]

*****

Canada's official "criminal class," the inmates of federal penitentiaries, were, according to government reports, a surprisingly temperate lot. One would like to know more about the manner in which such statistics were recorded, but most convicts were described as either abstainers or moderate in their "social habits." The Dominion Superintendent of Penitentiaries reported in 1917 that 80 per cent of federal inmates were moderate drinkers. The Quebec Bureau of Statistics likewise reported a low incidence of "immoderate" liquor use among persons convicted from 1898 to 1917. In 1924, in an address to the Union of Nova Scotia Municipalities, prison reformer J.B. Fielding reflected on the alleged connections between alcohol and criminality: "We often casually refer to drink as the salient feature associated with crime, so it is a curious fact that when we refer to the Federal Reports, we find there are many more total abstainers incarcerated than drunkards, and I believe the same holds good in our local jails."[28] Earlier a Dominion Bureau of Statistics (DBS) official analysing the habits of persons convicted between 1887 and 1919 had concluded that "inebriety has little or no influence over criminality" and "that by far the greatest percentage of crime is committed by the moderate or non-drinking class." Similarly, the DBS in 1920 was unable to satisfactorily conclude whether prohibition had achieved its objective.[29]

Initiative arrests for drunkenness or drunk and disorderly behaviour constituted the largest component of nineteenth- and early twentieth-century urban police department and police court business. [...] But did the police view public drunkenness as "real" crime? Elsewhere it has been argued that the rounding up of drunks, an important police duty well past World War I, did little to build an image of professionalism.[30] Yet the man on the beat, in stages assisted by electric call box systems, patrol wagons, telephones, and automobiles, functioned as a combination bouncer and baby sitter. Constables were recruited not for their education or sensitivity to social issues, but for size and physical abilities. [...] Discretion toward the street offender was important in police-community relations.[31] The CCAC, in search of a professional image, did not stress the "street cleaning" tradition of the occupation. The association, with its crime control focus, was more interested in law amendments in connection with vagrancy, prostitution, drug dealers, juvenile delinquents, habitual criminals, and firearms. Its early conventions, covered in the *Canadian Municipal Journal,* reflect an abiding concern with crime control, not public order.[32]

Prohibition-Era Policing

Following the Laurier government's refusal to enact national prohibition in 1898, anti-liquor forces turned their attention back to the municipal and provincial levels. In 1901 Prince Edward Island became the first province to enact its own dry law.[33] Elsewhere provincial

governments were tightening up alcohol regulation. [...] Saskatchewan closed all bars, made liquor a government monopoly and raised the drinking age from sixteen to eighteen. In the period 1915–17, a combination of Social Gospel sentiment, political expediency, and war-time patriotism led every province except Quebec to restrict or ban the retail liquor trade. Even *la belle provence* was drier than its reputation: as of 1916 a majority of the municipalities in Quebec were under local option. In 1918 the federal government, as an emergency conservation measure, shut down Quebec's bars and outlawed the interprovincial transit of beverage alcohol. For prohibitionists, the millennium had arrived; a host of social problems, ranging from war to sweat shops, were expected to wither away under the weight of national and provincial dry laws.[34]

The legislation of the 1910s was, by Canada Temperance Act standards, harsh. [...] Under the amended Ontario Temperance Act (OTA), provincial police were authorized to arrest without a warrant and seize the automobiles of bootleggers. The original Ontario statute gave dry agents the right to search land and vehicles without a warrant and compelled convicted drunks to name the source of their alcohol on pain of imprisonment. The Nova Scotia Temperance Act (1911 amendments) carried a mandatory jail term for second offences and allowed search without warrants. Persons convicted under the New Brunswick Intoxicating Liquor Act (1916), like those under the PEI and Nova Scotia statutes, were refused the right of appeal.[35]

On the other hand the new dry laws, to win initial political support and public acceptance, were based on a degree of compromise In New Brunswick, for example, the sale of two per cent beer was licensed and "temperance" beer (less than two per cent) was sold without provincial license. Consumer demand, needless to say, encouraged breweries to manufacture and sell an over strength beverage, which appears to have been delivered to beer shops in broad daylight. Druggists and doctors were also allowed to prescribe liquor for medicinal purposes, industrial alcohol continued to be manufactured, and export warehouses remained legal.[36] Licensed vendors, who benefited from their political connections, were well placed to abuse the system. The Nova Scotia Temperance Act, prior to 1926, allowed vendors to sell twelve-ounce prescriptions of spirits to each patient daily.[37]

*****

[...] Prominent persons warned that banning the bar would necessitate a large and dangerous expansion of police powers. Other powerful wet arguments were that prohibition was not "British," would cause a net increase in crime and would discredit the administration of justice.[38] During the 1916 House of Commons debate, an Ontario MP warned that outlawing liquor would mean that "the policeman's club must be behind every man to make him good."[39] The Winnipeg Great War Veterans Association interpreted a total ban as "class legislation" that would only inspire fraud and deception. [...]

The war on liquor, in contrast to more recent anti-drug efforts, brought few operational advantages to the Canadian police, repressive legislation notwithstanding. There was little federal legislation outside of wartime prohibition, and no national body of enforcement officers. [...] Enforcement and prosecution fell to the provincial and municipal authorities. A number of chief constables invoked prohibition sentiment for special cases, such as additional vigilance and sanctions against "foreigners" engaged in bootlegging, but for the most part dry laws were an unwelcome innovation.[40]

Canada's police administrators believed themselves more hard-pressed and unappreciated than ever during the prohibition years, which coincided with burgeoning community demands on their departments. Judging by the proceedings of the Chief Constables Association, police managers were loathe to seek greater powers over the use of alcohol by the average citizen. Yet Canada's police chiefs actively pursued amendments to the Criminal Code and other federal statutes in the name of crime control. Significantly, the new national police statistical

system inaugurated by the Dominion Bureau of Statistics totally ignored liquor enforcement and public order arrests.[41] [...]

In the spring of 1918 Ottawa, as a war measure, outlawed the manufacture and sale of beverages containing more than 2.5 per cent alcohol.[42] The immediate effect of national prohibition seemed to vindicate the arguments of the moral reformers. The trend to increased order had begun under provincial prohibitory regimes, but most likely related to the complex circumstances of a society at war. Tens of thousands of young, single men, for example, were in the armed forces. Winnipeg's arrests for drunkenness for one quarter of 1916 fell by 80 per cent. In Ottawa's police court, summary convictions for 1916–25 (Ontario Temperance Act years) were 38 per cent less than for the period 1906–15. The chief constable of Moncton, New Brunswick, although cynical about local option, expressed optimism that provincial and national prohibition would diminish every level of crime so that "in three years time, every city and town in the Dominion could cut its police force in half." The extension of prohibition to the city of Halifax in 1916 was followed by a 50 per cent reduction in arrests for drunkenness. The chief of Saint John praised New Brunswick's dry law: "our jails are empty, our towns and cities are orderly and people are clothed and in their right mind for the first time in years."[43] [...] Partly because of these initial developments, a number of historians credit the movement with a degree of success in curbing drunkenness and general disorder.[44]

Despite these trends, [...] police officials continued to display little affection for the reform-inspired campaign to ban the bar. The police served largely an urban population and cities and towns, even in Ontario and the Maritimes, were split on prohibition. This inspired senior officers to make rare public pronouncements on the importance of ensuring the legitimacy of the criminal justice system. A standard professional complaint was that the police, undermanned, under-equipped, and underpaid, were being asked to enforce too many unpopular laws.[45] [...]

[...] With plebiscites endorsing prohibition in New Brunswick, Manitoba, Alberta, Saskatchewan, Ontario, and Nova Scotia in 1920–22, activists worked hard to keep all enforcement agencies "on their toes."[46] The involvement of groups such as the Woman's Christian Temperance Union and clergy in liquor enforcement probably generated little support among chief constables. Manitoba's chief enforcement officer in 1916 was Reverend J.N. McLaren. Chief Inspector J.A. Ayearst of the 1920s OPP had been a Methodist minister who lobbied the premier for stricter local option enforcement. Ayearst was appointed a provincial liquor inspector and served with the Ontario liquor license board before heading the Ontario Provincial Police OTA Branch. [...] In 1918 Baptist minister W.D. Wilson, New Brunswick's Chief Liquor Inspector, received a polite hearing before the Chief Constables' Association, but his suggestion that the organization admit as full members officials engaged in prohibition work fell on deaf ears.[47] [...]

In the early to mid 1920s, an age of at least partial prohibition and falling liquor consumption, many law enforcement officials spoke of a crime wave. In 1918 William Banks, editor of the CCAC's *Canadian Police Bulletin*, had warned chief constables to "not be carried away with the delusion that crime will decrease because of the temperance wave which is fortunately going to engulf this continent." Banks, an abstainer and prudish Toronto theatre censor, foresaw post-war moral decay because of a decline in religious authority. He also argued that saloons and other homosocial drinking establishments had at least kept men off the streets; modernity bred mobility, consumerism, and a culture of male-female sociability, with casual liquor use intruding on middle-class family life. Young men, including war veterans, Banks continued, now had "time for other sources of amusement and I am most regretfully compelled to confer that I do not think that they will go for a higher amusement ideal."[48] [...] The head of the Alberta Provincial Police, speaking to the Chief Constables' Association in 1924 on "The Rising Tide of

Lawlessness," argued that prohibition was the worst example of the failure of law to inculcate a law-abiding spirit.[49]

The Ontario Temperance Act, implemented in 1916 when three-quarters of the province was already under local option, had closed all public drinking establishments but allowed breweries and distilleries to operate for export. With convictions for drunk and disorderly behaviour in Ontario one third lower for the period 1916–20 than 1911–15, prohibitionists were convinced that the law was doing more good than harm.[50] The measure was discussed on several occasions at annual conventions of the CCAC, which was dominated by Ontarians. [...] In 1923 Toronto's chief constable noted that "it would appear that the police have a hopeless task as long as distillers and brewers are making and sending out larger quantities of liquor." In his next annual report the chief suggested that OTA violators be given automatic jail terms rather than fines, which amounted to "a license to carry on an illegal business."[51] [...]

Police officials, liquor inspectors, and customs officers from all regions reported on the time, difficulty, and expense in investigating and prosecuting moonshiners, bootleggers, and smugglers. The situation became more complex in 1920 when the United States, which shared a long largely unpatrolled border with Canada, where breweries and distillers continued to operate, enacted national prohibition. A declining regional economy made smuggling attractive to many Maritimers. [...] In 1927 the RCMP, as a result of a federal-provincial agreement, took over provincial policing in rural Saskatchewan, bringing the Mounties into direct conflict with violators of the Criminal Code and provincial statutes such as the liquor law. [...] The RCMP also reported the illegal production of sake in British Columbia. In 1922 the Regina *Leader*, commenting on the failure of law to root out the liquor traffic, noted that the Saskatchewan Provincial Police had been doubled in size and a considerable amount of public money expended in enforcing the provincial dry law.[52]

Despite tougher laws, the legal proof required to convict bootleggers continued to cause police a degree of discomfort. Spotters and undercover agents, essential for most successful prosecutions, were a potential Achille's heal because of the "buy and bust" approach and the fact that the use of informers clashed with the supposed traditions of "British justice." The Alberta Provincial Police, for example, employed dozens of part-time agents in its liquor enforcement branch. [...]

[...] Dry activists viewed local enforcement agents as underpaid, lacking sufficient powers, and too subservient to town and city councils. Wets and moderates often shared an alternative view of these officers, who in their eyes had politicized the machinery of justice. In the late nineteenth-century Ontario, the appointment of known prohibitionists as license commissioners, Canada Temperance Act inspectors, and even magistrates had given rise to non-cooperation, public hostility, and perjury on the part of witnesses, jurors, and even magistrates.[53]

Even when armed with warrants or writs of assistance, provincial and municipal prohibition inspectors in Nova Scotia were continually challenged by operational constraints such as fortified doors in premises suspected of bootlegging and the difficulty of proving the identity of the real owner. Statistics from Nova Scotia indicate that temperance inspectors in the late 1920s conducted nine or ten searches for every prosecution or seizure of contraband.[54] [...] Following their victory over the pro-government control Tories in 1927, PEI's Liberals introduced amendments to the prohibition statute. [...] The amendments included higher fines and longer jail sentences, the extension of criminal liability to landlords, and the right to search the premises of a recently-convicted offender without a warrant.[55]

*****

Prohibition, the great social issue of the 1910s and early 1920s, and scourge of provincial politics, was neither endorsed nor condemned by the Chief Constables' Association of Canada in the official sense. [...]

During the 1920s, CCAC conventions reflected a new prohibition-related concern, duplication and competition among enforcement agencies. [...] Liquor regulation was a major force behind the creation of the new provincial organizations, which were modelled on the federal agency and often staffed by former Mounties. Temperance forces in Alberta and Saskatchewan considered provincial constabularies more accountable than the Royal North-West Mounted Police, which, although officially under the provincial Attorney General, was a federal force insulated from local politics. [...]

At their 1922 Victoria convention Canada's police chiefs passed a resolution demanding greater cooperation among municipal, provincial, and federal agencies. The association, dominated by municipal chiefs, was uneasy about the 1919-20 reorganization of the Royal North West Mounted Police into the Royal Canadian Mounted Police. Chief Martin Bruton of Regina described friction between different police forces and complained about the Saskatchewan Provincial Police upstaging municipal forces in terms of newspaper publicity. Many of these investigations centred around liquor. [...]

The worst turf war was in Ontario, where the OPP, under political pressure to enforce the Ontario Temperance Act, in the words of one municipal chief, employed "a class of men that we, as police officers, cannot cooperate with."[56] By 1918 the OTA was monopolizing the resources of the provincial police. Yet the United Farmers' government, which took office in 1919, gave the provincial constabulary poor grades on liquor enforcement. [...] Under pressure for arrests, seizures, fines, and convictions, provincial officers became more aggressive in urban areas, with predictable results. The local police, although careful to point to their own success with the OTA, argued that provincial activity was discrediting policing in general.[57] These arguments mirrored those used by Citizens's Liberty League for Moderation and other enemies of prohibition.[58]

Bureaucratic Alliance: Government Control

During the 1920s, as the spirit of wartime sacrifice ebbed, Canada's ban on liquor gradually gave way to a policy of government control and sales, first in Quebec and British Columbia. Quebec voted overwhelmingly in 1919 for the sale of beer and light wines. Two years later the Taschereau government established a commission with a complete monopoly on spirits and wine. Brewers, distillers, war veterans, and organized labour were the chief lobby groups pushing for a relaxation of wartime restrictions. The Prairie provinces, where per capita consumption traditionally exceeded the national average, followed the British Columbia example in the mid 1920s, New Brunswick and Nova Scotia in 1927 and 1930. Practical problems of public finance also aided the wet cause. The profits from liquor sales, one-fifth of Quebec's provincial revenues, were used primarily in road construction and secondarily to support charity and education.[59] [...]

The alleged failure of enforcement was a leading argument in support of repeal of provincial dry laws. In Hamilton, Ontario, Rocco Perri, "King of the Bootleggers," publicly ridiculed the policing of the OTA. In 1925 the New Brunswick liquor control authorities admitted to defeat by estimating that three-quarters of the alcohol circulating in the province was contraband. Halifax's city council went on record as opposing prohibition for having "produced amongst our people a system of despicable spying, and perjury, deceit and a tendency to lower the moral tone of the community." [...]

During the 1920s the majority of Canada's provinces moved from being dry to "moist." [...] Enforcement of a less rigorous system promised greater public consensus, a message echoed south of the border by the Association Against the Prohibition Amendment. The government of Ontario, by the mid 1920s one of the remaining bastions of prohibition, appointed a respected former president and general manager of Canadian National Railways to head the provincial liquor control commission. New Brunswick, to assuage its drys, secured a United Church minister to chair its new liquor control board. [...] Proponents of moderation, recognizing that the prohibition movement was far from dead at the local level, accepted restrictions such as permits, rationing, advertising, and price controls, beer parlours with as few comforts as possible, and limits on hard liquor sales in government stores. [...] The results of this "temperance hangover" lingered for many years in provinces such as Ontario and New Brunswick, where by the 1950s liquor laws were viewed in many circles as restrictive.[60]

The new provincial commissions, supposedly above politics, were responsible for enforcing licensing regulations, eradicating bootleggers, and seizing illegal stocks. Liquor store managers were given discretion to limit or blacklist individual customers buying suspicious quantities of alcohol. When licensed beer parlours or taverns appeared, government inspectors and proprietors and staff enforced regulation.[61] But the policy of government sales did not remove the liquor issue from the purview of the police. Under the new regime the police and liquor commissions had a common enemy, the bootlegger, who continued to thrive because of superior marketing abilities and more convenient hours abilities if not lower prices.[62] [...]

*****

Government alcohol sales in New Brunswick and Nova Scotia accelerated the expansion of provincial policing in the rural districts, which had depended on part-time, amateur constables. Provincial prohibition inspectors and constables in the 1920s represented a transition towards provincial control of policing. The New Brunswick Provincial Police, founded in 1927, and the Nova Scotia Police, organized in 1930, were made responsible for new liquor control acts. In short order they, along with their counterpart in PEI, were absorbed by the RCMP as a result of the federal-provincial contracts of 1932.[63] [...]

The declining relative importance of public order arrests to policing in the decades after

World War I provides a clue as to the CCAC's relative lack of concern about the liquor question. Police bureaucracies were partially motivated by institutional imperatives. Departments depended upon statistics and reports to justify their budgets to political authorities, and municipal largesse was limited. Until the rise of the automobile, the urban police needed drunks. [...] By the late 1920s there were over one million registered automobiles in Canada and the careless driver, not the staggering drunk, was becoming, statistically, the stock in trade of the police.[64]

Conclusion

Prohibition was an intensely political issue. It achieved legislative recognition in the 1910s only through organization, publicity, lobbying, and campaigning. Significantly, none of this activity was carried out by Canada's police. The emerging crime-control doctrine of Canadian police scorned political "interference," the professional term for unwelcome demands for public accountability. [...]

*****

[...] Prohibition failed only partially; it contributed to lower per capita liquor consumption and removed many of the harmful aspects of saloon life. In 1930, most respectable wets still opposed the open bar. More importantly, Canada's drys struck back from "beyond the grave" through a system of government control and sales through which agents of the state, as Phyne suggests, were concerned primarily with revenue protection.[65] In wet areas, provincial legislation "established restrictive codes which to this day [1975] severely prescribe the conditions for the purchase of liquor in state-owned stores and for the consumption of liquor in public places."[66]

*****

The issue of alcohol regulation in early twentieth-century Canada, in contrast, provoked little consensus, which is precisely why the most extreme form of liquor control was repealed.

This despite the support of industrial capital and widespread evidence of alcohol's health and social costs.[67] [...] The legal edifice erected and dismantled between 1900 and 1930, in contrast with policy on narcotics, more or less exempted possession and consumption of liquor in private dwellings. By the 1920s, with improvements in housing and the proliferation of commercial amusements, this approach constituted less of a burden on the working class, which in the previous century had depended on the social space of taverns.

[...] For the enforcers, the half-hearted war on liquor was an externally-imposed mandate that inhibited the development of true professionalism. [...] In the period 1890 to 1930, the police accepted neither the social reform nor medical rationale for prohibition; much like the situation with prostitution enforcement, they tended to favour only public order arguments.[68]

After the dry era, the Canadian police entered a relative golden age in terms of relations with the community. Morality enforcement could still cause short-term embarrassments, yet gone was the intense regional and national press and interest group scrutiny of police that characterized the first three decades of the century. Prostitution, gambling, and corruption garnered more attention than liquor, although the four usually were related. Police officials projected a crime-fighting image, adapted to new roles, and were able to contain liquor enforcement as long as it remained a local public order issue. Temperance interests and middle-class voters demanded periodic crackdowns and a minimum level of enforcement. The police, provincial license inspectors, and liquor store managers worked out the details.[69] Police professionalism had been developed as a defensive reaction to the Social Gospel critique of the justice system; the partial decline and rechannelling of that critique, symbolized by the political defeat of prohibition, helped to ensure a freer hand for Canadian police agencies for years to come.

Notes

1. For a differing opinion, see Carolyn Strange, *Toronto's Girl Problem: The Perils and Pleasure of the City, 1880–1930* (Toronto: University of Toronto Press, 1995), p. 90, which suggests that prostitution was identified as the chief "social evil" of the era.

2. For temperance and prohibition, see: Richard Allen, *The Social Passion: Religion and Social Reform in Canada, 1914–28* (Toronto: University of Toronto Press, 1971); James Gray, *Booze: The Impact of Whiskey on the Prairies* (Toronto: MacMillan of Canada, 1972); B.J. Grant, *When Rum Was King: The Story of the Prohibition Era in New Brunswick* (Fredericton: Fiddlehead Books, 1984); C.W. Hunt, *Booze, Boats and Billions: Smuggling Liquid Gold* (Toronto: McClelland and Stewart, 1988); C.M. Davis, "I'll Drink to That: The Rise and Fall of Prohibition in the Maritime Provinces," (Ph.D. Thesis, McMaster University, 1990); Gerald A. Hallowell, *Prohibition in Ontario, 1919–1926* (Ottawa: Ontario Historical Society, 1972); E.R Forbes, "Prohibition and the Social Gospel in Nova Scotia," in Forbes, ed. *Challenging the Regional Stereotype: Essays on the 20th Century Maritimes* (Fredericton: Acadiensis Press, 1989), pp. 13–40; John Herd Thompson, *The Harvests of War: The Prairie West 1914–1918* (Toronto: McClelland and Stewart, 1978), pp. 95–114; Robert A. Campbell, "Liquor and Liberals: Patronage and Government Control in British Columbia, 1920–1928," *B.C. Studies,* 77 (Spring 1988), pp. 30–53; Jan Noel, *Canada Dry: Temperance Crusades in Pre-Confederation Canada* (Toronto: University of Toronto Press, 1995); Reginald Smart and Alan C. Ogborne, *Northern Spirits: A Social History of Alcohol in Canada* (Toronto: Addiction Research Foundation, 1996).

3. Mariana Valverde, in *The Age of Light Soap and Water: Moral Reform in English Canada, 1885–1925* (Toronto: McClelland and Stewart, 1991) devotes little attention to the issue. John C. Weaver's study of Hamilton, *Crimes, Constables and Courts: Order and Transgression in a Canadian City, 1816–1970* (Kingston: McGill-Queen's University Press, 1995), although not discussing liquor enforcement and temperance in detail, does examine how the police negotiated demands for moral order. A useful anthology is Cheryl Krasnick Warsh, ed., *Drink in Canada: Historical Essays* (Kingston: McGill-Queen's University Press, 1993). C. Mark Davis examined

the legal framework in "Rum and the Law," in James H. Morrison and James Moreira, eds., *Tempered by Rum: Rum in the History of the Maritime Provinces* (Porters Lake: Pottersfield Press, 1988), pp. 42–52.

4. Norman H. Clark, *Deliver Us from Evil: An Interpretation of American Prohibition* (New York: W.W. Norton and Company Inc., 1976), ch. 8; Richard Hamm, *Shaping the Eighteenth Amendment: Temperance Reform, Legal Culture and the Polity, 1880–1920* (Chapel Hill: University of North Carolina Press, 1995); Kenneth M. Murchison, *Federal Criminal Law Doctrines: The Forgotten Influence of National Prohibition* (Durham: Duke University Press, 1994). Michael Woodiwiss, in *Crime, Crusades and Corruption: Prohibitions in the United States 1900–1987* (London: Pinter Publishers, 1988), argues that American prohibitions on gambling, sex, drink and drugs have fostered "a level of crime and corruption far in excess of more tolerant societies," p. l.

5. For professionalism and Canada's police, see Greg Marquis, "Canadian Police Chiefs and Law Reform: The Historical Perspective," *Canadian Journal of Criminology*, XIV (July–Oct.1991), pp. 385–406. One of the few case studies of prohibition enforcement is Jacques Paul Couturier, "Prohibition or Regulation? The Enforcement of the Canada Temperance Act in Moncton, 1881–1896," in Warsh, ed., *Drink in Canada*, pp. 144–65.

6. For a similar trend in England, see Jennifer S. Davis, "Prosecutions and Their Context: The Use of the Criminal Law in Later Nineteenth-Century London," in Douglas Hay and Francis Snider, eds., *Policing and Prosecution in Britain, 1750–1850* (Oxford: Clarendon Press, 1989), p. 421.

7. Nova Scotia's 1886 license act (shop, hotel, wholesale) continued the 1874 stipulation that two-thirds of the ratepayers in an electoral district had to approve a new license by petition. This law, resisted in Halifax, outlawed taverns: Judith Fingard, "'A Great Big Rum Shop': The Liquor Trade in Victorian Halifax," in Morrison and Moreira, eds., *Tempered by Rum*, pp. 97–99.

8. Greg Marquis, "'A Machine of Oppression Under the Guise of the Law': The Saint John Police Establishment, 1860–1890," *Acadiensis*, XVI (Autumn 1986), pp. 58–77; "Enforcing the Law: The Charlottetown Police Force," in T. Spira and

Douglas Baldwin, eds., *Gaslights. Epidemics and Vagabond Cows: Charlottetown in the Victorian Era* (Charlottetown: Ragweed Press, 1988); pp. 86–102; Canada, Royal Commission on the Liquor Traffic (RCLT), Evidence, Manitoba, pp. 8–9; 169–70; 370–71.

9. Greg Marquis, *Policing Canada's Century: A History of the Canadian Association of Chiefs of Police* (Toronto: University of Toronto Press, 1993).

10. *Statistical Yearbook of Canada,* 1901, pp. 596–97. The CTA allowed liquor for private and family use to be shipped into dry towns or counties. In CTA prosecutions for transporting liquor, the onus was on the accused to prove that the alcohol was for personal use: "Report of the Inspector-in-Chief Under the Nova Scotia Temperance Act, 1913," Nova Scotia *Journals of the House of Assembly,* appendix 26.

11. RCLT, Evidence, Maritimes, pp. 24–25; 373–74; 401–02; 687–97; 788–90.

12. RCLT, Evidence, Quebec, pp. 8–10, 167–68; 179–91, 238; 488–90; 238–46; 654–59.

13. *Canadian Annual Review,* 1910 (Toronto 1911), p. 438. By the early 1890s, one-fifth of the province's municipalities were under the pre-Confederation "Dunkin Act," which authorized municipal units to enact prohibitory by-laws.

14. RCLT, Evidence, Ontario, pp. 115–19; 581–83; 641–50; 704–09; 724–27 1346–47.

15. R.C. Macleod, *The North-West Mounted Police and Law Enforcement, 1873–1905* (Toronto: University of Toronto Press, 1976), p. 133; "Annual Report of the Commissioner of the North-West Mounted Police 1887," in *Report of the Commissioner of the North-West Mounted Police 1887* (Toronto: MacLean, Roger and Co., 1888), p. 10.

16. RCLT, Evidence, Manitoba, p. 71; 232; 236–37; 289–98; 298; 370–71; 430; 534–35; 601–02; 614–16; 619–20. The North-West Territories had a form of partial prohibition prior to the enactment of the 1892 "high license" and local option law.

17. Ibid., pp. 478–79; 534–35; 617–18.

18. Greg Marquis, "Vancouver Vice: The Police and the Negotiation of Morality, 1904–35," in Hamar Foster and John McLaren, eds., *Essays in the History of Canadian Law V: British Columbia and the Yukon* (Toronto: Osgoode Society, 1993), pp. 242–73.

19. John Weaver, "Introduction: Trends and Questions in New Historical Accounts of Policing," *Urban History Review,* XIX (Oct. 1990), p. 81.

20. John McLaren, "White Slavers: The Reform of Canada's Prostitution Laws and Patterns of Enforcement, 1900–1920," *Criminal Justice History,* VIII (1987), p. 108.

21. Michael McCulloch, "Most Assuredly Perpetual Motion: Police and Policing in Québec City, 1838–58," *Urban History Review,* XIX (Oct. 1990), p. 107; Gray, *Booze,* p. 28; Toronto *Globe and Mail,* February 14, 1919; RCLT, Evidence, Maritimes, p. 21; Quebec, p. 182; Manitoba, p. 387.

22. RCLT, Evidence, Manitoba, p. 619; Richard G. Powers, *Secrecy and Power: The Life of J. Edgar Hoover* (New York: The Free Press, 1987), p. 152; John Weaver, "Social Control, Martial Conformity and Community Entanglement: The Varied Beats of the Hamilton Police, 1895–1920," *Urban History Review,* XIX (Oct. 1990), p. 113.

23. Chief Constables' Association of Canada, *Proceedings of the Annual Convention,* 1915, pp. 12–13. For years the CCAC maintained a "snake pit," stocked with liquor, at its conventions. Occasionally these events were held in police stations.

24. James J. Collins Jr., ed., *Drinking and Crime: Perspectives on the Relationships between Alcohol Consumption and Criminal Behaviour* (New York: The Guilford Press, 1981), pp. xv–xvi.

25. George E. Foster, *The Canada Temperance Act and Prohibitionist Handbook* (Toronto: Hunter, Rose and Company, 1881) p. 82; RCLT, Maritimes, Appendix 11, p. 982. See also, Clive Emsley, *Crime and Society in England, 1750–1900* (New York: Longman, 1982), pp. 41–42.

26. Couturier, "Prohibition or Regulation," pp. 147–48. See the illustrations in K. Austin Kerr, *Organized for Prohibition: A New History of the Anti-Saloon League* (New Haven: Yale University Press, 1985).

27. *What It Costs* (Toronto, c. 1897), 2; F.S. Spence, *The Facts of the Case* (Toronto 1896), p. 83. For the minority report see, *Report of the Royal Commission on the Liquor Traffic* (Ottawa: Queen's Printer, 1895), pp. 509–691.

28. *Statistical Yearbook of Québec 1921* (Quebec: L.A. Proulx, 1921), p. 151; *Proceedings of the 19th Annual Convention of the Union of Nova Scotia Municipalities* (Halifax: 1924), p. 104. Of 3,888 persons convicted of indictable offences in 1901, "moderate" drinkers outnumbered the "immoderate" by two to one. See, *Statistical Yearbook of Canada,* 1901, p. 621.

29. "Criminal Statistics, 1919," *Sessional Papers,* 1920,10D, pp. x, xviii.

30. Greg Marquis, "Practical Criminology: The Early Years of the Chief Constables' Association of Canada," unpublished paper, 1991.

31. CCAC, *Proceedings*, 1922, p. 68; RCLT, Evidence, Manitoba, p. 328; 481; Robert M. Fogelson, *Big City Police* (Cambridge: Harvard University Press, 1977), pp. 48, 51; Hairing, *Policing a Class Society*, pp. 180–81. Beginning in 1890, the Toronto police were allowed to release persons of "otherwise good character" who had been picked up and held overnight for intoxication.

32. See, for example, the review of Criminal Code amendments in CCAC, *Proceedings*, 1913, pp. 18–30.

33. Ch. 3, "An Act Prohibiting the Sale of Intoxicating Liquor," *Statutes of Prince Edward Island, 1901*. In 1898 PEI had voted 89 per cent in favour of prohibition: Davis, "Rum and the Law," p. 47.

34. *Canadian Annual Review*, 1910, p. 540; Hallowell, *Prohibition*, pp. 3–36; Thompson, *The Harvests of War*, pp. 98–106. From 1913 to 1919 prohibitionists in the United States won twenty-five out of thirty-five state referenda (a number of them aimed only at closing the saloon, not outlawing private importation or possession of liquor): Jack S. Blocker Jr., *Retreat from Reform: The Prohibition Movement in the United States, 1890–1913* (Westport: Greenwood Press, 1976), pp. 238–39.

35. Ch. 2, "Nova Scotia Temperance Act," *Statutes of Nova Scotia*, 1910; Ch. 50, "An Act Entitled the Ontario Temperance Act," *Statutes of Ontario*, 1916; "Report of the Commissioner, 1919," British Columbia, *Sessional Papers, 1920*, II; *Canadian Annual Review* 1910, p. 456; Grant, *When Rum Was King*, pp. 180–81; Leonard Harkness, *History of the Amherst Police* (Sackville: BH Publications, 1989); Halifax *Mail,* 23 Aug., 1926.

36. Grant, *When Rum Was King*, ch. 7; *Canadian Annual Review*, 1924–25, pp. 374–75. The Canadian definition of "intoxicating" was 2.5 per cent alcohol; the Volstead Act labelled beverages with greater than 0.5 per cent alcohol as intoxicating: Clark, *Deliver Us from Evil*, pp. 132, 138.

37. Associations Against the Prohibition Amendment [AAPA], *The Last Outposts of Prohibition in Canada: Nova Scotia and Prince Edward Island* (Washington, DC: AAPA, 1929), pp. 6–7.

38. *Prohibition: The Views of Eminent Statesmen. Prominent Public Men and Leading Men of Business on the Question of Prohibition* (Hamilton, 189?).

39. *Montréal Gazette*, March 7, 1916.

40. Toronto, *Annual Reports of the Chief Constable*, 1910 (Toronto, 1911), p. 6.

41. Marquis, "Practical Criminology."

42. Robert Craig Brown and Ramsay Cook, *Canada 1896–1921: A Nation Transformed* (Toronto: McClelland and Stewart, 1974), p. 301; Davis, "Rum and the Law," pp. 48–49. In 1916 the federal "Doherty Act" had forbidden the shipment of liquor into a dry province unless the package was clearly marked with the contents and the names of consignor and consignee: Ch. 1, "An Act in Aid of Provincial Legislation Prohibiting or Restructuring the Sale or Use of Intoxicating Liquors," *Statutes of Canada*, 1916.

43. *Canadian Annual Review*, 1916, p. 680; "Report of the Inspector-in-Chief under the Nova Scotia Temperance Act, 1916"; Cheryl Krasnick Warsh, "'Oh Lord, Pour a Cordial in Her Wounded Heart': The Drinking Woman in Victorian and Edwardian Canada," in Warsh, ed., *Drink in Canada,* Table 3; CCAC, *Proceedings*, 1916, p. 53; 1918; p. 37.

44. Thompson and Seager, p. 65, relying on secondary sources, argue that arrest statistics in dry provinces prove that prohibition achieved results. Gray, in *Booze*, indicates that in the three Prairie provinces total arrests for drunkenness fell from 17,746 in 1913 to less that 5,000 in 1920: pp. 90–91. Grant, in *When Rum Was King*, pp. 27–68, offers a dimmer view of the movement. Davis identifies enforcement as the major weakness of prohibition. See, "I'll Drink to That," pp. 273–77.

45. CCAC, Proceedings. 1923, p. 87; Fogelson, *Big City Police*, 114–15; *Toronto Star*, July 11, 1919.

46. E.R. Forbes, ed., Clifford Rose, *Four Years with the Demon Rum* (Fredericton: Acadiensis Press, 1980), p. ix.

47. CCAC, *Proceedings*, 1918: *Canadian Annual Review*, 1924–25, pp. 373–74; AAPA, *The Last Outpost*, p. 19; Forbes, "Prohibition and the Social Gospel," p. 35; Grant, *When Rum Was King*, p. 31. Wilson had served as field secretary for a regional temperance federation. The Halifax *Mail* reported (Aug. 4, 1926) that Rev. Grant was authorized to appoint deputy inspectors "without taking into consideration their political views," but did not exercise full control over hirings and firings.

48. CCAC, *Proceedings*, 1918. p. 25.

49. Ibid., 1924, pp. 54–55; 1922; pp. 90–91; *CAR*, 1922, pp. 423–24.

50. Warsh, "'Oh, Lord, Pour a Cordial in Her Wounded Heart,'" table 2.

51. CCAC, *Proceedings*, 1917, pp. 18–19; 1922, p. 92; Toronto, *Annual Report of the Chief Constable (ARCC)*, 1923–24, pp. 8–9. The AAPA approvingly pointed out that Quebec under government sales had an lower overall crime rate (based on convictions) than Ontario under prohibition:

AAPA, *The Québec System: A Study in Liquor Control* (Wasington, D.C.: AAPA, 1928), pp. 31–32.

52. *Report of the Commissioner of the Royal Canadian Mounted Police*, 1927, p. 9; 13; *Canadian Annual Review*, 1922, p. 795. Manufacture in the home was not unique to "foreign" immigrants, but part of the larger self-sufficiency of home production in rural society: Norman Okihiro, *Mounties, Moose and Moonshine: The Patterns and Context of Outport Crime* (Toronto: University of Toronto Press, 1997), ch. 7.

53. Fanshawe, *Liquor Legislation in the United States and Canada*, pp. 384–86.

54. "Report of Inspector in Chief under the Nova Scotia Temperance Act, 1928." Grant recommended that "stout and barricaded doors" be made illegal and that premises be padlocked upon a third conviction.

55. AAPA, *The Last Outpost*, pp. 8–10. The PEI amendments, in spirit if not detail, parallelled the punitive 1929 Jones Act in the United States, which lifted the maximum Volstead penalties to five years in prison or a $10,000 fine: Hamm, *Shaping the Eighteenth Amendment*, pp. 267–68.

56. CCAC, *Proceedings*, 1922, pp. 119–22.

57. Dahn D. Higley, *OPP: The History of the Ontario Provincial Police Force* (Toronto: Queen's Printer, 1984), pp. 111–13; 123–26; *Canadian Annual Review*, 1922, p. 590; Toronto *Globe and Mail*, December 1, 1924. See also, Gray, *Booze*, pp. 217–18.

58. AO, Linton Papers, MU 7276, file 12, Government Control.

59. AAPA, *The Québec System*, pp. 4–6; Toronto *Globe and Mail*, January 12, 1927; Campbell, "Liquor and Liberals," pp. 36–38; Thompson, *The Harvests of War*, pp. 105–06.

60. *Canadian Annual Review*, 1924–25, p. 448; 1928–29, pp. 389, 401; Toronto *Globe and Mail*, January 14, 1921. The re-introduction of government sales in Saskatchewan in 1924 prohibited private club licenses, a feature of the British Columbia and Alberta systems. Quebec's system was applauded by the Association against the Prohibition Amendment in the United States: Kyvig, *Repealing National Prohibition*, p. 109; AAPA, *The Québec System*.

61. Robert A. Campbell, "Managing the Marginal: Regulating and Negotiating Decency in Vancouver's Beer Parlours, 1925–54," *Labour/le Travail*, 44 (Fall 1999), pp. 109-27.

62. Robert E. Popham and Wolfgang Schmidt, *Statistics of Alcohol Use and Alcoholism in Canada, 1871–1956* (Toronto: University of Toronto Press, 1958), Table III-l.

63. AO, F-8, G.H. Ferguson Papers, MU 1028, "Liquor Control in Western Canada," 1927; John F. Phyne "Prohibition's Legacy: The Emergence of Provincial Policing in Nova Scotia, 1921–1932," *Canadian Journal of Law and Society*, VII (2) (Fall 1992), pp. 157–84; Gerald F. Wallace, William Higgins and Peter McGahan, *The Saint John Police Story: Volume 3: The Slader Years 1930–1941* (Fredericton: New Ireland Press, 1993), ch. 4.

64. Toronto, *ARCC*, 1910–1930; Popham and Schmidt, *Statistics*, Table III-1; *Statistical Yearbook of Québec 1929*, p. 368; CCAC, *Proceedings, 1927*; Weaver, *Crimes, Constables and Courts*, ch. 5. Nationally, there were seven per cent fewer convictions for drunkenness during the largely wet 1930s than during the partly dry 1920s. The rate of drunkenness arrests per 100,000, nonetheless, remained higher in the 1930s than in the 1880s and 1890s (see Table 2). Locally there were variations. See Gerald F. Wallace, William Higgins, and Peter McGahan, *The Saint John Police Story, Vol 3: The Slader Years* (Fredericton: New Ireland Press, 1993), p. 160, note 33.

65. Phyne, "Prohibition's Legacy." In contrast, Robert A. Campbell argues that government control in British Columbia was concerned primarily with maintaining a balance between the demands of prohibitionists and repealers: "'Profit was just a circumstance': The Evolution of Government Liquor Control in British Columbia, 1920–1988," in Warsh, ed., *Drink in Canada*, pp. 172–92.

66. Clark, *Deliver Us from Evil*, p. 138.

67. John J. Rumbarger, *Profits, Power and Prohibition: Alcohol Reform and the Industrialization of America, 1800–1930* (Albany: SUNY Press, 1989).

68. John McLaren and John Lowman, "Enforcing Canada's Prostitution Laws, 1892–1934," in Martin Friedland, ed., *Securing Compliance: Seven Case Studies* (Toronto: University of Toronto Press, 1990), pp. 21–87.

69. Marquis, "Vancouver Vice," pp. 242–73; William Weintraub, *City Unique: Montréal Days and Nights in the 1940s and 1950s* (Toronto: McClelland and Stewart, 1996), ch. 3

Critical Thinking Questions

• •

Chapter 22: Chasing the Social Evil: Moral Fervour and the Evolution of Canada's Prostitution Laws, 1867–1917, *John P.S. McLaren*

1. What changes led to the development of prostitution laws? Does there appear to have been an increase in prostitution-related offences prior to the passage of the new laws?
2. How was prostitution dealt with prior to 1867? How did the police respond to prostitution following Confederation?
3. Canada's prostitution laws were modelled after British and American statutes. What problems did legislators find in attempting to create similar laws in Canada? Did prostitution appear to be either as prevalent or as widespread a problem in Canada?

Chapter 23: The First Century: The History of Non-Medical Opiate Use and Control Policies in Canada, 1870–1970, *Robert R. Solomon and Melvyn Green*

1. Why did the federal government send Mackenzie King, then-deputy minister of Labour, to Vancouver to deal with the riots? Did opium appear to be a problem at that time? How did King shift the focus to opium?
2. How did American influence impact on Canada's drug-control policies? Was Canada trying to develop a strong drug policy, or responding to American concerns?
3. Beginning in the 1950s, there was an attempt to treat addicts rather than criminalizing them for possession. What role did the police play in pressing for strong drug laws? How did Parliament respond?

Chapter 23: Regeneration Rejected: Policing Canada's War on Liquor, 1890–1930, *Greg Marquis*

1. How was the problem of alcohol dealt with across the country? How does this compare to the American response? Does prohibition appear to have been a success?

2. Were temperance advocates and prohibitionists able to establish a link between drunkenness and crime? What problems might there be in determining whether such a link existed?

3. According to Marquis, why should we be careful about drawing parallels between the "war on drugs" and the "war on alcohol"?

Further Readings

. . . .

Regulating Lives: Historical Essays on the State, the Individual, and the Law, edited by John McLaren, Robert Menzies, and Dorothy E. Chunn (Vancouver: UBC Press, 2002).

John McLaren is professor of law, University of Victoria; Robert Menzies and Dorothy Chunn are both professors of criminology, Simon Fraser University. In this book, the authors examine social control, moral regulation, and governmentality during the late nineteenth and early twentieth centuries. This text exhibits the wealth of theoretical and historical writings that has emerged, with discussions of diverse ways in which the state is interested in regulating people's lives. Topics include: incest in the courts, public regulation of alcohol in relation to ethnicity, public health initiatives regarding venereal disease, and the seizure and indoctrination of Doukhobor children.

Undressing the Canadian State: The Politics of Pornography from Hicklin to Butler by Kirsten K. Johnson (Halifax: Fernwood Books, 1995).

Through a detailed historical analysis of Canada's obscenity legislation, Johnson argues that the state implicitly supports the ideology of pornography. A controversial book from an alternative perspective, it sets contemporary legislation in a wider social and historical perspective. The author sees the possibility of law as a mechanism of the state with incredible power to transform gender relations. She concludes that politicians and state bureaucrats responsible for legislation fail to comprehend the complexity of pornography from a sociological point of view.

Spying 101: The RCMP's Secret Activities at Canadian Universities, 1917–1997 by Steve Hewitt (Toronto: University of Toronto Press, 2002).

Steve Hewitt is a visiting scholar in the Department of History at Purdue University, and an adjunct instructor in the Department of History at the University of Indianapolis.

Canadian security agents surveyed students and professors for "subversive" tendencies and behaviour since the end of the First World War. The RCMP infiltrated the campuses of Canada's universities and colleges to spy, meet informants, and gather information on thousands of Canadians, including prominent individuals such as Pierre Berton, Peter Gzowski, and René Lévesque.

Making Good: Law and Moral Regulation in Canada, 1867–1939 by Carolyn Strange and Tina Loo (Toronto: University of Toronto Press, 1997).

This book looks at the changing relationship between law and morality in Canada from Confederation to the Second World War. Strange and Loo argue that the attempt to regulate people through the law did not always meet with success, as values deemed "good" by the state were often repudiated by those on whom they were imposed. The authors examine major institutions that patrolled morality—the Department of Indian Affairs, the Ministry of Justice, and the North-West Mounted Police—and agencies that worked at local levels, such as police forces, schools, correctional facilities, juvenile and family courts, and morality squads. Through topics as diverse as gambling, marriage and divorce, and sexual deviance, *Making Good* shows that character building was critical to the broader project of nation building.

The New Criminologies in Canada, edited by T. Fleming (Toronto: Oxford University Press, 1985).

This is one of those classics you can often find in second-hand bookstores. Reminiscent of the new and critical criminologies in Britain, this text contains radical analyses of crime and criminal justice policy such as Elizabeth Comack's "The Origins of Canadian Drug Legislation: Labelling Versus Class Analysis." Grouped here are some of the more radical theorists working in criminology—a must-read.

Copyright Acknowledgements

• • • • • • • • • • • • • • • • • • • •

Erica Smith, "'Gentlemen, This is No Ordinary Trial': Sexual Narratives in the Trial of the Reverend Corbett, Red River, 1863," from *Reading Beyond Words: Contexts for Native History*. Peterborough: Broadview Press, 1998. Reprinted by permission of Broadview Press.

Donald H. Clairmont and Dennis William Magill, "The Relocation Phenomenon and the Africville Study," from *Africville: The Life and Death of a Canadian Black Community, 3rd edition*. Toronto: Canadian Scholars' Press, 1999. Reprinted by permission of Canadian Scholars' Press.

Joan Sangster, "Criminalizing the Colonized: Ontario Native Women Confront the Criminal Justice System, 1920–1960," from *The Canadian Historical Review*, 80:1, March 1999. Reprinted by permission of University of Toronto Press.

John McLaren, "Creating 'Slaves of Satan' or 'New Canadians'? The Law, Education, and the Socialization of Doukhobor Children, 1911–1935," from *Children, Teachers and Schools in the History of British Columbia*. Calgary: Temeron Books, 1995. Reprinted by permission of Temeron Books.

Mariana Valverde, "Moral Reform in English Canada, 1885–1925: Introduction," from *The Age of Light, Soap, and Water: Moral Reform in English Canada, 1885–1935*. University of Toronto Press/Canadian Social History Series, 1991. Reprinted by permission of University of Toronto Press.

Joan Sangster, "Defining Sexual Promiscuity: 'Race', Gender and Class in the Operation of Ontario's Female Refuges Act, 1930–60," from *Crimes of Colour: Racialization and the Criminal Justice System in Canada*, edited by Wendy Chan and Kiran Mirchandani. Peterborough: Broadview Press, 2001. Reprinted by permission of Broadview Press.

Steven Maynard, "'Horrible Temptations': Sex, Men, and Working-Class Male Youth in Urban Ontario, 1890–1935," from *The Canadian Historical Review* 78:2, 1997. Reprinted by permission of University of Toronto Press.

Kelly Hannah-Moffatt, "Mother Knows Best: The Development of Separate Institutions for Women," from *Punishment in Disguise: Penal Governance and Federal Imprisonment of Women in Canada*. University of Toronto Press, 2001. Reprinted by permission of University of Toronto Press.

Gary Kinsman, "Character Weaknesses and Fruit Machines: Towards an Analysis of the Anti-Homosexual Security Campaign in the Canadian Civil Service, 1959–1964," from *Labour/Le Travail* 35, Spring 1995. Reprinted by permission of Labour/Le Travail Committee on Canadian Labour History.

John McLaren, "Chasing the Social Evil: Moral Fervour and the Evolution of Canada's Prostitution Laws, 1867–1917," from *Canadian Journal of Law and Society* 1:125, 1986. Reprinted by permission of *Canadian Journal of Law and Society/Revue Canadienne Droit et Société*.

Robert R. Solomon and Melvyn Green, "The First Century: The History of Non-Medical Opiate Use and Control Policies in Canada, 1870–1970," from *The University of Western Ontario Law Review*, 20:2, 1982. Reprinted by permission of the Faculty of Law, University of Western Ontario.

Greg Marquis, "Regeneration Rejected: Policing Canada's War on Liquor, 1890–1930." Reprinted by permission of the author.